Emerging Research on Swarm Intelligence and Algorithm Optimization

Yuhui Shi
Xi'an Jiaotong–Liverpool University, China

A volume in the Advances in Computational
Intelligence and Robotics (ACIR) Book Series

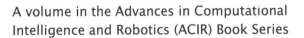

Managing Director:	Lindsay Johnston
Production Editor:	Christina Henning
Development Editor:	Erin O'Dea
Acquisitions Editor:	Kayla Wolfe
Typesetter:	John Crodian
Cover Design:	Jason Mull

Published in the United States of America by
Information Science Reference (an imprint of IGI Global)
701 E. Chocolate Avenue
Hershey PA, USA 17033
Tel: 717-533-8845
Fax: 717-533-8661
E-mail: cust@igi-global.com
Web site: http://www.igi-global.com

Library of Congress Cataloging-in-Publication Data

Emerging research on swarm intelligence and algorithm optimization / Yuhui
Shi, editor.
    pages cm
 Includes bibliographical references and index. ISBN 978-1-4666-6328-2 (hardcover) -- ISBN 978-1-4666-6329-9 (ebook) -- ISBN 978-1-4666-6331-2 (print & perpetual access) 1. Swarm intelligence. I. Shi, Yuhui, editor of compilation.
 Q337.3.E537 2014
 006.3'824--dc23
                                 2014019023

This book is published in the IGI Global book series Advances in Computational Intelligence and Robotics (ACIR) (ISSN: 2327-0411; eISSN: 2327-042X).

British Cataloguing in Publication Data
A Cataloguing in Publication record for this book is available from the British Library.

For electronic access to this publication, please contact: eresources@igi-global.com.

Advances in Computational Intelligence and Robotics (ACIR) Book Series

ISSN: 2327-0411
EISSN: 2327-042X

Mission

While intelligence is traditionally a term applied to humans and human cognition, technology has progressed in such a way to allow for the development of intelligent systems able to simulate many human traits. With this new era of simulated and artificial intelligence, much research is needed in order to continue to advance the field and also to evaluate the ethical and societal concerns of the existence of artificial life and machine learning.

The **Advances in Computational Intelligence and Robotics (ACIR) Book Series** encourages scholarly discourse on all topics pertaining to evolutionary computing, artificial life, computational intelligence, machine learning, and robotics. ACIR presents the latest research being conducted on diverse topics in intelligence technologies with the goal of advancing knowledge and applications in this rapidly evolving field.

Coverage

- Heuristics
- Cognitive Informatics
- Machine Learning
- Agent Technologies
- Natural Language Processing
- Computational Intelligence
- Artificial Life
- Evolutionary Computing
- Intelligent Control
- Algorithmic Learning

IGI Global is currently accepting manuscripts for publication within this series. To submit a proposal for a volume in this series, please contact our Acquisition Editors at Acquisitions@igi-global.com or visit: http://www.igi-global.com/publish/.

Titles in this Series

For a list of additional titles in this series, please visit: www.igi-global.com

Emerging Research on Swarm Intelligence and Algorithm Optimization
Yuhui Shi (Xi'an Jiaotong-Liverpool University, China)
Information Science Reference • copyright 2015 • 300pp • H/C (ISBN: 9781466663282) • US $225.00 (our price)

Face Recognition in Adverse Conditions
Maria De Marsico (Sapienza University of Rome, Italy) Michele Nappi (University of Salerno, Italy) and Massimo Tistarelli (University of Sassari, Italy)
Information Science Reference • copyright 2014 • 480pp • H/C (ISBN: 9781466659667) • US $235.00 (our price)

Computer Vision and Image Processing in Intelligent Systems and Multimedia Technologies
Muhammad Sarfraz (Kuwait University, Kuwait)
Information Science Reference • copyright 2014 • 312pp • H/C (ISBN: 9781466660304) • US $215.00 (our price)

Mathematics of Uncertainty Modeling in the Analysis of Engineering and Science Problems
S. Chakraverty (National Institute of Technology - Rourkela, India)
Information Science Reference • copyright 2014 • 441pp • H/C (ISBN: 9781466649910) • US $225.00 (our price)

Insight Through Hybrid Intelligence Fundamentals, Techniques, and Applications
Neil Y. Yen (The University of Aizu, Japan) Joseph C. Tsai (The University of Aizu, Japan) and Xiaokang Zhou (The University of Aizu, Japan)
Information Science Reference • copyright 2014 • 314pp • H/C (ISBN: 9781466648722) • US $195.00 (our price)

Global Trends in Intelligent Computing Research and Development
B.K. Tripathy (VIT University, India) and D. P. Acharjya (VIT University, India)
Information Science Reference • copyright 2014 • 601pp • H/C (ISBN: 9781466649361) • US $235.00 (our price)

Exploring Innovative and Successful Applications of Soft Computing
Antonio D. Masegosa (Universidad de Granada, Spain) Pablo J. Villacorta (Universidad de Granada, Spain) Carlos Cruz-Corona (Universidad de Granada, Spain) M. Socorro García-Cascales (Universidad Politécnica de Cartagena, Spain) María T. Lamata (Universidad de Granada, Spain) and José L. Verdegay (Universidad de Granada, Spain)
Information Science Reference • copyright 2014 • 375pp • H/C (ISBN: 9781466647855) • US $190.00 (our price)

Research Developments in Computer Vision and Image Processing Methodologies and Applications
Rajeev Srivastava (Indian Institute of Technology (BHU), India) S. K. Singh (Indian Institute of Technology (BHU), India) and K. K. Shukla (Indian Institute of Technology (BHU), India)
Information Science Reference • copyright 2014 • 451pp • H/C (ISBN: 9781466645585) • US $195.00 (our price)

DISSEMINATOR OF KNOWLEDGE

www.igi-global.com

701 E. Chocolate Ave., Hershey, PA 17033
Order online at www.igi-global.com or call 717-533-8845 x100
To place a standing order for titles released in this series, contact: cust@igi-global.com
Mon-Fri 8:00 am - 5:00 pm (est) or fax 24 hours a day 717-533-8661

Editorial Advisory Board

Table of Contents

Section 1
Swarm Intelligence Algorithms

Section 2
Swarm Intelligence Applications

Chapter 13
Andreas Janecek, University of Vienna, Austria
Ying Tan, Peking University, China

Detailed Table of Contents

Section 1
Swarm Intelligence Algorithms

Yuhui Shi, Xi'an Jiaotong-Liverpool University, China

In this chapter, the human brainstorming process is modeled, based on which two versions of a Brain Storm Optimization (BSO) algorithm are introduced. Simulation results show that both BSO algorithms perform reasonably well on ten benchmark functions, which validates the effectiveness and usefulness of the proposed BSO algorithms. Simulation results also show that one of the BSO algorithms, BSO-II, performs better than the other BSO algorithm, BSO-I, in general. Furthermore, average inter-cluster distance Dc and inter-cluster diversity De are defined, which can be used to measure and monitor the distribution of cluster centroids and information entropy of the population over iterations. Simulation results illustrate that further improvement could be achieved by taking advantage of information revealed by Dc, which points at one direction for future research on BSO algorithms.

Xin-She Yang, Middlesex University London, UK

Many metaheuristic algorithms are nature-inspired, and most are population-based. Particle swarm optimization is a good example as an efficient metaheuristic algorithm. Inspired by PSO, many new algorithms have been developed in recent years. For example, firefly algorithm was inspired by the flashing behaviour of fireflies. In this chapter, the authors analyze the standard firefly algorithm and study the chaos-enhanced firefly algorithm with automatic parameter tuning. They first compare the performance of these algorithms and then use them to solve a benchmark design problem in engineering. Results obtained by other methods are compared and analyzed. The authors also discuss some important topics for further research.

    Peng-Yeng Yin, National Chi Nan University, Taiwan
    Fred Glover, OptTek Systems, Inc., USA
    Manuel Laguna, University of Colorado, USA
    Jia-Xian Zhu, National Chi Nan University, Taiwan

A recent study (Yin, et al., 2010) showed that combining Particle Swarm Optimization (PSO) with the strategies of Scatter Search (SS) and Path Relinking (PR) produces a Cyber Swarm Algorithm that creates a more effective form of PSO than methods that do not incorporate such mechanisms. In this chapter, the authors propose a Complementary Cyber Swarm Algorithm (C/CyberSA) that performs in the same league as the original Cyber Swarm Algorithm but adopts different sets of ideas from the Tabu Search (TS) and the SS/PR template. The C/CyberSA exploits the guidance information and restriction information produced in the history of swarm search and the manipulation of adaptive memory. Responsive strategies using long-term memory and path relinking implementations are proposed that make use of critical events encountered in the search. Experimental results with a large set of challenging test functions show that the C/CyberSA outperforms two recently proposed swarm-based methods by finding more optimal solutions while simultaneously using a smaller number of function evaluations. The C/CyberSA approach further produces improvements comparable to those obtained by the original CyberSA in relation to the Standard PSO 2007 method (Clerc, 2008). These findings motivate future investigations of Cyber Swarm methods that combine features of both the original and complementary variants and incorporate additional strategic notions from the SS/PR template as a basis for creating a still more effective form of swarm optimization.

    Shi Cheng, University of Nottingham Ningbo, China
    Yuhui Shi, Xi'an Jiaotong-Liverpool University, China
    Quande Qin, Shenzhen University, China

Premature convergence occurs in swarm intelligence algorithms searching for optima. A swarm intelligence algorithm has two kinds of abilities: exploration of new possibilities and exploitation of old certainties. The exploration ability means that an algorithm can explore more search places to increase the possibility that the algorithm can find good enough solutions. In contrast, the exploitation ability means that an algorithm focuses on the refinement of found promising areas. An algorithm should have a balance between exploration and exploitation, that is, the allocation of computational resources should be optimized to ensure that an algorithm can find good enough solutions effectively. The diversity measures the distribution of individuals' information. From the observation of the distribution and diversity change, the degree of exploration and exploitation can be obtained. Another issue in multiobjective is the solution metric. Pareto domination is utilized to compare two solutions; however, solutions are almost Pareto non-dominated for multiobjective problems with more than ten objectives. In this chapter, the authors analyze the population diversity of a particle swarm optimizer for solving both single objective and multiobjective problems. The population diversity of solutions is used to measure the goodness of a set of solutions. This metric may guide the search in problems with numerous objectives. Adaptive optimization algorithms can be designed through controlling the balance between exploration and exploitation.

Premature convergence happens in Particle Swarm Optimization (PSO) for solving both multimodal problems and unimodal problems. With an improper boundary constraints handling method, particles may get "stuck in" the boundary. Premature convergence means that an algorithm has lost its ability of exploration. Population diversity is an effective way to monitor an algorithm's ability of exploration and exploitation. Through the population diversity measurement, useful search information can be obtained. PSO with a different topology structure and a different boundary constraints handling strategy will have a different impact on particles' exploration and exploitation ability. In this chapter, the phenomenon of particles getting "stuck in" the boundary in PSO is experimentally studied and reported. The authors observe the position diversity time-changing curves of PSOs with different topologies and different boundary constraints handling techniques, and analyze the impact of these settings on the algorithm's abilities of exploration and exploitation. From these experimental studies, an algorithm's abilities of exploration and exploitation can be observed and the search information obtained; therefore, more effective algorithms can be designed to solve problems.

Generally, constraint-handling techniques are designed for evolutionary algorithms to solve Constrained Multiobjective Optimization Problems (CMOPs). Most Multiojective Particle Swarm Optimization (MOPSO) designs adopt these existing constraint-handling techniques to deal with CMOPs. In this chapter, the authors present a constrained MOPSO in which the information related to particles' infeasibility and feasibility status is utilized effectively to guide the particles to search for feasible solutions and to improve the quality of the optimal solution found. The updating of personal best archive is based on the particles' Pareto ranks and their constraint violations. The infeasible global best archive is adopted to store infeasible nondominated solutions. The acceleration constants are adjusted depending on the personal bests' and selected global bests' infeasibility and feasibility statuses. The personal bests' feasibility statuses are integrated to estimate the mutation rate in the mutation procedure. The simulation results indicate that the proposed constrained MOPSO is highly competitive in solving selected benchmark problems.

Section 2
Swarm Intelligence Applications

Chapter 7

R. Rathipriya, Periyar University, India
K. Thangavel, Periyar University, India

This chapter focuses on recommender systems based on the coherent user's browsing patterns. Biclustering approach is used to discover the aggregate usage profiles from the preprocessed Web data. A combination of Discrete Artificial Bees Colony Optimization and Simulated Annealing technique is used for optimizing the aggregate usage profiles from the preprocessed clickstream data. Web page recommendation process is structured in to two components performed online and offline with respect to Web server activity. Offline component builds the usage profiles or usage models by analyzing historical data, such as server access log file or Web logs from the server using hybrid biclustering approach. Recommendation process is the online component. Current user's session is used in the online component for capturing the user's interest so as to recommend pages to the user for next navigation. The experiment was conducted on the benchmark clickstream data (i.e. MSNBC dataset and MSWEB dataset from UCI repository). The results signify the improved prediction accuracy of recommendations using biclustering approach.

Chapter 8

T. O. Ting, Xi'an Jiaotong-Liverpool University, China

In this chapter, the main objective of maximizing the Material Reduction Rate (MRR) in the drilling process is carried out. The model describing the drilling process is adopted from the authors' previous work. With the model in hand, a novel algorithm known as Weightless Swarm Algorithm is employed to solve the maximization of MRR due to some constraints. Results show that WSA can find solutions effectively. Constraints are handled effectively, and no violations occur; results obtained are feasible and valid. Results are then compared to previous results by Particle Swarm Optimization (PSO) algorithm. From this comparison, it is quite impossible to conclude which algorithm has a better performance. However, in general, WSA is more stable compared to PSO, from lower standard deviations in most of the cases tested. In addition, the simplicity of WSA offers abundant advantages as the presence of a sole parameter enables easy parameter tuning and thereby enables this algorithm to perform to its fullest.

Chapter 9

Li-Minn Ang, Edith Cowan University, Australia
Adamu Murtala Zungeru, Federal University of Oye-Ekiti, Nigeria
Kah Phooi Seng, Edith Cowan University, Australia
Daryoush Habibi, Edith Cowan University, Australia

Social insect communities are formed from simple, autonomous, and cooperative organisms that are interdependent for their survival. These communities are able to effectively coordinate themselves to achieve global objectives despite a lack of centralized planning. This chapter presents a study of artificial insect algorithms for routing in wireless sensor networks, with a specific focus on simulating termites and their behaviours in their colony. The simulating behaviour demonstrates how the termites make use of an autocatalytic behaviour in order to collectively find a solution for a posed problem in reasonable time. The derived algorithm termed Termite-Hill demonstrates the principle of the termite behavior for solving the routing problem in wireless sensor networks. The performance of the algorithm was tested on static and dynamic sink scenarios. The results were compared with other routing algorithms with varying network density and showed that the proposed algorithm is scalable and improved on network energy consumption with a control over best-effort service.

Chapter 10

The multi-robot coverage path-planning problem involves finding collision-free paths for a set of robots so that they can completely cover the surface of an environment. This problem is non-trivial as the geometry and location of obstacles in the environment is usually not known a priori by the robots, and they have to adapt their coverage path as they discover obstacles while moving in the environment. Additionally, the robots have to avoid repeated coverage of the same region by each other to reduce the coverage time and energy expended. This chapter discusses the research results in developing multi-robot coverage path planning techniques using mini-robots that are coordinated to move in formation. The authors present theoretical and experimental results of the proposed approach using e-puck mini-robots. Finally, they discuss some preliminary results to lay the foundation of future research for improved coverage path planning using coalition game-based, structured, robot team reconfiguration techniques.

Chapter 11

In this chapter, a path relinking method for the maximum cut problem is investigated. The authors consider an implementation of the path-relinking, where it is utilized as a subroutine for another meta-heuristic search procedure. Particularly, the authors focus on the global equilibrium search method to provide a set of high quality solutions, the set that is used within the path relinking method. The computational experiment on a set of standard benchmark problems is provided to study the proposed approach. The authors show that when the size of the solution set that is passed to the path relinking procedure is too large, the resulting running times follow the restart distribution, which guarantees that an underlying algorithm can be accelerated by removing all of the accumulated data (set P) and re-initiating its execution after a certain number of elite solutions is obtained.

Chapter 12

This chapter addresses the issue of image segmentation by clustering in the domain of image processing. Fuzzy C-Means is a widely adopted clustering algorithm. Bio-inspired optimization algorithms are optimal methods inspired by the principles or behaviors of biology. For the purpose of reinforcing the global search capability of FCM, five Bio-Inspired Optimization Algorithms (BIOA) including Biogeography-

Based Optimization (BBO), Artificial Fish School Algorithm (AFSA), Artificial Bees Colony (ABC), Particle Swarm Optimization (PSO), and Bacterial Foraging Algorithm (BFA) are used to optimize the objective criterion function, which is interrelated to centroids in FCM. The optimized FCMs by the five algorithms are used for image segmentation, respectively. They have different effects on the results.

Chapter 13

Andreas Janecek, University of Vienna, Austria
Ying Tan, Peking University, China

Low-rank approximations allow for compact representations of data with reduced storage and runtime requirements and reduced redundancy and noise. The Non-Negative Matrix Factorization (NMF) is a special low-rank approximation that allows for additive parts-based, interpretable representation of the data. Various properties of NMF are similar to Swarm Intelligence (SI) methods: indeed, most NMF objective functions and most SI fitness functions are non-convex, discontinuous, and may possess many local minima. This chapter summarizes efforts on improving convergence, approximation quality, and classification accuracy of NMF using five different meta-heuristics based on SI and evolutionary computation. The authors present (1) new initialization strategies for NMF, and (2) an iterative update strategy for NMF. The applicability of the approach is illustrated on data sets coming from the areas of spam filtering and email classification. Experimental results show that both optimization strategies are able to improve NMF in terms of faster convergence, lower approximation error, and/or better classification accuracy.

Preface

Swarm intelligence refers to a group of nature-inspired population-based heuristic optimization algorithms and is closely related to the evolutionary computation. A decade ago, there were four major population-based heuristic optimization algorithms under the evolutionary computation umbrella. They are evolutionary programming, evolution strategy, genetic algorithm, and genetic programming. In 1990s, other nature-inspired population-based heuristic optimization algorithms started to appear, such as particle swarm optimization algorithm, which was inspired by the collective behavior of a group of birds searching for food and originally developed by Dr. Russell Eberhart and Dr. James Kennedy in 1995. These nature-inspired algorithms were not noticed or at least not attractive to the majority of the evolutionary computation community at the beginning. With unremitting efforts of researches on them and consequently continuous improvement of their performance, these nature-inspired algorithms started to be noticed, and more and more researchers started to conduct researches on these algorithms and to develop new nature-inspired algorithms. For example, in 1998, the first two special sessions on particle swarm optimization algorithms were organized in the 1998 Conference on Evolutionary Programming and the 1998 IEEE International Conference on Evolutionary Computation, respectively, which were merged as one single annual international conference named as the IEEE Congress on Evolutionary Computation in 1999. In 2004, the first special issue on particle swarm optimization algorithm was published in *IEEE Transactions on Evolutionary Computation*, volume 8, number 3. These nature-inspired algorithms share the same characteristic that differentiates them from the major four evolutionary computation algorithms. There is no standard definition of swarm intelligence. Generally speaking, each of them is a population-based heuristic optimization algorithm that is inspired or motivated by the collective behavior of small and simple objects such as the ants in ant colony optimization algorithm and birds in particle swarm optimization algorithm. These nature-inspired algorithms gradually became more and more attractive and popular among the evolutionary computation research community, and together they were named swarm intelligence, which became a little brother of the major four evolutionary computation algorithms under the evolutionary computation umbrella. Now, it has become a major component of the evolutionary computation and even sometimes is considered as a research area in parallel with evolutionary computation. For the four evolutionary algorithms, two major operations involved in them are crossover and/or mutation operations, which differentiate them from other population-based heuristic optimization algorithms; therefore, they can be referred as evolution-inspired optimization algorithms instead of nature-inspired optimization algorithms. Publication on swarm intelligence has been increasing rapidly. According to scholar.google.com, on March 9, 2014 by searching "particle swarm," there are 113,000 items. By considering papers that are not included in Google Scholar, especially those published in non-English journals and conferences, the number of published papers on particle swarm optimization algorithms alone could, at least, be doubled. With the rapid growth of swarm intelligence, there have been new journals developed that are dedicated to swarm intelligence. For example, the *Journal of Swarm Intelligence* published by Springer with Dr. Marco Dorigo as its Editor-in-Chief; the *International Journal of Swarm Intelligence Research* published by IGI Global with Dr. Yuhui Shi as its Editor-in-Chief; the *Journal of Swarm and Evolutionary Computation* published by Elsevier with Dr. P. N. Suganthan and Dr. S. Das as its Editors-in-Chief; the *International Journal of Swarm Intelligence and Evolutionary Computation* published by OMICS Publishing Group with Dr. Qiangfu Zhao as its Editor-in-Chief; the *International Journal of Swarm Intelligence* published by the INDERSCIENCE Publishers with Dr. Jagdish Chand Bansal as its Editor-in-Chief. There are conferences organized that are dedicated to swarm intelligence. For example, in 2003, the first IEEE Symposium on Swarm Intelligence was organized and held in Indianapolis, Indiana, USA, April 24-26, which was chaired by Dr. Yuhui Shi and Dr. Russell Eberhart. It has been held since then, and the 2014 IEEE Symposium on Swarm Intelligence will be held in Orlando, Florida, USA, December 9-12, 2014, which will be chaired by Dr. Yuhui Shi and Dr. P. N. Suganthan. Other conferences dedicated to swarm intelligence (or at least with swarm intelligence as a big component) are the IEEE Congress on Evolutionary Computation, the Genetic and Evolutionary Computation Conference, the International Conference on Swarm Intelligence, ANTS International Conference (or Workshop) on Swarm Intelligence, the International Conference on Swarm Intelligence Based Optimization, to name just a few.

Swarm intelligence is a collection of nature-inspired population-based heuristic optimization algorithms. It includes ant colony optimization, artificial immune system, bacterial foraging optimization algorithm, bee colony optimization algorithm, brain storm optimization algorithm, firefly optimization algorithm, fireworks optimization algorithm, fish school search optimization algorithm, particle swarm optimization algorithm, shuffled frog-leaping algorithm, to name just a few. New swarm intelligence algorithms keep appearing. Every developed swarm intelligence algorithm has its own characteristic due to its source of inspiration. Therefore, the very first research direction on swarm intelligence is on its algorithm studies and developments. Each swarm intelligence algorithm has its strength and weakness. To further explore its uniqueness and its suitability for problem solving, it will be helpful and necessary to enlarge its strength and to reduce its weakness. Furthermore, it will be expected to combine beneficial component of each algorithm together to come out or design a better performed optimization algorithm in the sense that the algorithm can solve one kind of problem better than others. Certainly, it will be very difficult, if not impossible, to design one single swarm intelligence algorithm that is the best for solving all kinds of optimization problems by considering the no-free-lunch theorem. For example, for solving unimodal optimization problems, it will be more beneficial to have the algorithm to have fast convergence and fine tuning capability, while for solving multimodal, especially those complicated multimodal, optimization problems, an optimization algorithm needs not only to have the capability to converge but also the capability to diverge when the algorithm falls into local optimum which is not a satisfactory and good enough solution to the optimization problem being solved. For those complicated multimodal optimization problems, if it is critical to come out a good enough solution, it will be nice for the algorithm to have the capability of chaotic behavior, which means that the algorithm can find any potential solution if time is not limited due to its ergodicity. In literature, there have been reports on researches on embedding chaotic operations into a swarm intelligence algorithm. For a swarm intelligence algorithm with chaotic operations to be practical and/or meaningful, it needs to consider the following: First, the algorithm should not be chaotic all the time, otherwise the algorithm more likely will take too long to come close to a good enough solution which will not be practical for it to solve an optimization problem.

Second, the algorithm needs the capability to fine-tune the solution, that is, when the chaotic operation brings the solution close to a good enough solution, it should be able to switch to a fine-tuning capability to finally search for a good enough solution. The chaotic operation can be applied to one (randomly selected) element in an individual or to whole individual; it can be applied once in each generation or once in a while or when it is determined to be necessary. Chaotic operation is helpful in one sense but it is harmful when too many chaotic operations are involved because the algorithm will end up without convergence at all. In summary, the algorithm with chaotic operations embedded should have the chaotic search (or global search) capability and the fine-tuning (or local search) capability for the algorithm to find a good enough solution within a reasonable time. Generally speaking, chaotic operation can be considered as a divergent operation and fine-tuning can be considered as a convergent operation. For a swarm intelligence to solve complicated multimodal optimization problems, it is necessary for the algorithm to have both convergence capability and divergence capability and the capability to switch between them when it is necessary. In general, an optimization algorithm can be considered to be in one of four states, which are global search state, local search state, transition from global to local search state, and transition from local to global search state. When the algorithm is in the global search state, it is to find a good potential or initial solution; when a good potential solution is found, the algorithm should be in transition from global to local search under which the algorithm is in the transition from global to local search state; when the algorithm is in the local search state, it is to fine tune the solution so that a good enough solution can be found; the algorithm is in transition from local to global search state when the algorithm in the local search state cannot find a good enough solution for a reasonable time. The algorithm is more likely to have been trapped in local optimum and needs to jump out the local optimum by going through the process of transition from local search state to global search state. The researches on having better performed swarm intelligence algorithms should focus on designing operations for each single state, combination of states, or all four states. This is the second research direction along which it is also necessary and/or helpful to define metrics that can monitor which state the algorithm is in at any time. To design different components in a swarm intelligence algorithm to focus on different search capability is somehow similar to what the memetic algorithms are about. In a memetic algorithm, one component is designed to focus on global search while the other is to focus on local search. To go one-step further, it will be nice to design one component of a swarm intelligence algorithm to find or evolve better search capability while the other is to do the actual search job to come out with a good enough solution. This is another research direction. In general, even though the swarm intelligence has been researched for a decade, it still lacks a solid theoretical foundation. To build up solid theoretical foundation for each swarm intelligence algorithm or an unified framework is a very important but extremely challenging task. In addition to the generally studied convergent and/or searchable properties, it should be critical and/or necessary to study how to measure the status that a swarm intelligence algorithm is in and further to control or guide the swarm intelligence algorithm to move into the status we would like it to move in. The researches on the observability and controllability of a swarm intelligence algorithm is an important research direction with which it is expected that we could monitor the performance of the algorithm and further control or guide the algorithm moving into the performance status we would like it to move so that the algorithm can solve an optimization problem more efficiently and effectively.

Each swarm intelligence algorithm was initially designed for solving one kind of optimization problem. For example, particle swarm optimization algorithm was originally designed to solve continuous optimization problem, while the ant colony optimization algorithm was designed to solve combinatorial optimization problems. Each algorithm has been further extended to other areas. For example, there are

xviii

binary particle swarm optimization algorithms out there for solving combinatorial optimization problems. Swarm intelligence algorithms were originally designed to solve single-objective optimization problems, but they have been extended to solve multi-objective optimization problems. Certainly, the simple and straightforward approach for modifying a single-objective optimization algorithm to be a multi-objective optimization algorithm is to convert a multi-objective optimization problem into a single-objective optimization problem. There are other different approaches to handle multi-objective optimization algorithms by using swarm intelligence algorithms, but the most significant and popular approach is to utilize the Pareto concept. For example, there are several Pareto-based multi-objective particle swarm optimization algorithms out there. The most researched multi-objective swarm intelligence algorithms are Pareto-based, and they usually perform well on solving multi-objective optimization problems with number of objectives being two or three. When the number of objectives increases, these Pareto-based multi-objective swarm intelligence algorithms will lose their efficiency and effectiveness and eventually lose their capability to solve multi-objective optimization problems when the number of objectives exceeds ten. In general, when the number of objectives is more than ten, almost every solution will be a non-dominated solution among all available solutions; therefore, Pareto-based concepts will no longer provide any meaningful guidance on searching Pareto front. Therefore, developing swarm intelligence algorithms that can be applied to solve many-objective (>10) optimization algorithms is one big but challenging research direction. This belongs to one kind of big data analysis with "big" in the sense of number of objectives of the optimization problems to be solved. Big data analysis is one emergent research area. From the perspective of optimization problems, it is also called large-scale optimization problems. Because of Internet and sensor network, etc., a huge amount of data are generated every day. How to analyze them to extract useful information is very critical; otherwise, we are wasting the available information. This is "big" in the sense of time or large scale in number of data points available. Different from this, the data collected at any time instance may contain many physical quantities, that is, each data point can be considered as a point in a high-dimensional space. This is "big" in the sense of space or large scale in the problem dimension. Generally speaking, swarm intelligence algorithms are good at solving small-scale optimization problems; when problem scale increases, swarm intelligence algorithms will become inefficient and/or ineffective to solve them, and eventually lose the capability to solve them. Usually, we consider the problem dimension larger than or equal to 1000 as a large-scale optimization problem, which is popular but very challenging for swarm intelligence algorithms to solve.

Another research direction on swarm intelligence is on its applications. Swarm intelligence algorithms have been successfully applied to solve many real-world applications, but more and more successful real-world applications are required to secure swarm intelligence algorithms always to be considered as a good candidate to solve a real-world application. Generally speaking, the study and development of swarm intelligence is not the purpose but a means to solve actual problems. Without being able to solve real-world applications, swarm intelligence cannot survive for long. It is the vitality of swarm intelligence for it being able to solve real-world problems so that more and more researchers will be attracted and be interested to do their researches on swarm intelligence, and more and more research funding can be made available to move the swarm intelligence research forward.

WHAT IS THE BOOK ABOUT?

This collection includes selected and (more or less) enhanced papers published in the 2011 and 2012 volume years of the *International Journal of Swarm Intelligence Research*. It does not intend to cover all aspects of researches on swarm intelligence and its applications but provides a snapshot of recent researches on swarm intelligence algorithms and their applications and may reflect some portion of research tendency on swarm intelligence. This collection can be used as a reference book for researchers who have been conducting researches on swarm intelligence and/or evolutionary computation, and/or those who are at least interested in learning more about swarm intelligence, and/or those who have intention to conduct researches in the areas of swarm intelligence. It can also be used as a reference book for graduate students and senior undergraduate students who are interested in learning swarm intelligence.

ORGANIZATION OF THE BOOK

There are 13 chapters in this collection, which are organized into two sections. Section 1 consists of six chapters, which are about current research works on swarm intelligence algorithms. Section 2 consists of seven chapters, which are about the applications of swarm intelligence algorithms.

Section 1: Swarm Intelligence Algorithms

Swarm intelligence includes a set of nature-inspired population-based heuristic optimization algorithms. Most of these swarm intelligence algorithms were inspired by simple objects with a low level of intelligence as a single object, but collectively, these simple objects can behave intelligently, for example, birds in particle swarm optimization algorithm, ants in ant colony optimization algorithm, fishes in fish school search optimization algorithm, etc. These simple objects with a low level of intelligence inspired researchers to simulate the collective collaboration and competition among them in order to design and develop these swarm intelligence algorithms with good capabilities to solve (complicated or complex) optimization problems. It is intuitive and natural to believe that by simulating the collaborative and competitive behaviors among objects with a high level of intelligence, a better population-based heuristic optimization algorithm could be designed and developed. Human beings are the most intelligent animals in the world; it then can be expected that better population-based heuristic optimization algorithms should be able to be developed by simulating human beings' intelligent behavior. One of the most commonly used human being problem solving skills is the brainstorming process in which a group of persons are gathered together to solve a problem that a single (experienced and/or knowledgeable) person finds very difficult, if not impossible, to solve by himself or herself, but together, they can solve it through brainstorming with high possibility. In the chapter "An Optimization Algorithm Based on Brainstorming Process," a new population-based heuristic optimization algorithm was proposed by Shi. It is inspired by the human being brainstorming process; therefore, is called the brain storm optimization algorithm. In the chapter, first Shi introduced one type of brainstorming process. A brainstorming process involves a group of persons with diverse background knowledge and experience generating ideas for solving a problem, usually facilitated by a facilitator with less knowledge and experience about the problem to be solved so that an unbiased brainstorming process can be conducted. To avoid tiredness of persons involved in a brainstorming process to guarantee an efficient and effective idea generation process, a brainstorming process usually is conducted within a limited time, about 60 minutes, within which usually three rounds of idea generation will be conducted. No matter whether the problem could be solved or not, within the 60 minutes or three rounds of idea generation process, the brainstorming process will be stopped and another one will be conducted at another time if it is deemed to be necessary. The brainstorming process is then modeled, which is then further standardized and abstracted as a flow chart in which each round of idea generation is represented as one loop of operations. Because a computer will not be tired, the number of loops in the flow chart can be any number, that is, the simulated number of rounds of idea generation process usually is much larger than three. In addition, to be standardized and convenient, an idea is represented as a solution (an individual) with fixed length, but changeable length could be used if it is necessary to meet the requirements for problem solving purpose. Based on the flow chart, two versions of brain storm optimization algorithms were designed and implemented. In a brain storm optimization algorithm, two kinds of major operations are designed to simulate the steps involved in the brainstorming process. The two operations are convergent operations and divergent operations. The convergent operation was implemented by k-means clustering algorithm and the divergent operation was implemented by adding Gaussian noise to individuals. The convergent operation focuses on fine tuning solutions to create good enough solutions quickly, while the divergent operation focuses on global search so that the algorithm can jump from local optima if it has been trapped in local optima. Therefore, in a brain storm optimization algorithm, in each generation, it has exploration and exploitation capability. The two versions of brain storm optimization algorithms are further tested on ten benchmark functions. The experimental results validated and illustrated the effectiveness and efficiency of the proposed brain storm optimization algorithms. In addition, two performance metrics are defined in the chapter. They are average inter-cluster distance and the inter-cluster diversity. The average inter-cluster distance measures the distribution of cluster centers, while the inter-cluster diversity provides measurement similar to information entropy of the population of individuals in the brain storm optimization algorithm. By taking advantage of information provided by the two metrics, the search process of a brain storm optimization algorithm could be monitored and controlled to have a better performed and balanced brain storm optimization algorithm.

Since the introduction of the particle swarm optimization algorithm in 1995, many other nature-inspired population-based heuristic optimization algorithms were designed and developed. One of them is the firefly optimization algorithm, which is inspired by the flashing behavior of fireflies and was introduced by Dr. Yang in 2008. In general, any swarm intelligence algorithm cannot guarantee finding a global optimum with 100% possibility, but instead, it can guarantee finding a good enough solution with high possibility. Like other swarm intelligence algorithms, premature convergence may occur in firefly optimization algorithm, that is, it may be trapped in any local optimum which is not a good enough solution to the problem to be solved. Nonlinearity in an optimization problem may lead to multimodality, which may cause an optimization algorithm to fall into a local optimum that is not a good enough solution; therefore, an optimization algorithm should have the capability to escape from local optima, and as a consequence, to have the capability to search other solution spaces that may contain good enough solutions, if not the global optimum. Traditionally, an optimization algorithm is designed to have the ability to avoid instability or chaotic behavior, but the chaotic behavior could be utilized in an optimization algorithm to help it jump out local optima when it is necessary. In the chapter "Analysis of

Firefly Algorithms and Automatic Parameter Tuning," Yang reviewed and analyzed the recently developed firefly optimization algorithm. Then by simplifying the firefly algorithm's equation with a single agent (individual), chaotic map can be obtained for the simplified firefly algorithm; therefore, chaotic behavior can be observed by changing a parameter of the chaotic map. It is natural to believe that the more complicated original firefly optimization algorithm should be able to enter the status with chaotic behavior by changing its parameter and chaotic tunneling can be observed in the firefly optimization algorithm to enable the algorithm to jump from one mode to another when solving complicated multimodal optimization problems. Consequently, parameters of the firefly optimization algorithm can be utilized to guide it to enter either a convergent search process or a chaotic (or divergent) search process to achieve a better and balanced performance. In the chapter, the author further discussed the automatic parameter tuning for the proposed chaos-enhanced firefly optimization algorithm, which was further tested on a benchmark design problem.

There are a lot of optimization algorithms that exist and are reported in the literature. Each optimization algorithm, no matter if it is a single-point-based algorithm or a population-based algorithm, has its own strength. One strength is more suitable and/or helpful for handling one kind of situation that could exist in the process of searching solutions for an optimization problem, but may be harmful for handling other kinds of situations. To take advantage of strengths embedded in different optimization algorithms, one algorithm is combined with one or more other algorithms to form a hybrid algorithm. A cyber swarm algorithm, which is a combination of particle swarm optimization algorithm with scatter search algorithm embedded with path relinking process, is a more effective particle swarm optimization algorithm than those particle swarm optimization algorithms without combing scatter search with path relinking process, which can provide better balance between intensification and diversification. In the chapter "A Complementary Cyber Swarm Intelligence," Yin et al. proposed a complementary cyber swarm algorithm, which performs similarly as the original cyber swarm algorithm but utilizes the tabu search in addition to the scatter search with path relinking process. The history search information is further utilized to guide or restrict the search so that it achieves better exploitation of the search area and better manipulation of adaptive memory, which consists of the best solutions observed throughout search process derived from tabu search. The proposed complementary cyber swam algorithm was tested on a large set of challenging test functions and was compared with the original cyber swarm intelligence and the standard PSO proposed by Dr. Clerc. Experimental results demonstrated that the proposed algorithm has better performance at least with regards to the tested benchmark functions.

In general, a good swarm intelligence algorithm has balanced capability between exploration and exploitation. The exploration capability means an algorithm's ability to search in a wider solution space so that solution areas within which good enough solutions could be found with high possibility could be located while the exploitation capability is an algorithm's ability to fine tune around found solutions. Without balanced exploration and exploitation capability, the algorithm will either move into local optima or lack of the capability to converge to a good enough solution. An optimization algorithm could be in convergence state or divergent state depending on whether the optimization algorithm has more exploration capability or more exploitation capability. To monitor or understand what status the algorithm is in, performance metrics should be defined to measure the status the algorithm is in. One possible performance metric is the diversity. *The degree of exploration and exploitation can be obtained by observing the diversity distribution and change of diversity over generations.* In the chapter "Population Diversity of Particle Swarm Optimizer Solving Single and Multi-Objective Problems," Cheng et al. first reviewed the definitions of population diversity, which includes position diversity, velocity diversity, and cognitive diversity for a particle swarm optimization solving single-objective optimization problems. Then the change of position diversity and cognitive diversity and ratio of position diversity over cognitive diversity are defined and discussed. For example, the ratio of position diversity over cognitive diversity can be used for comparison between the "search space" and "cognitive space." The definition of diversity was further defined in Pareto set in addition to that in the population of particles for particle swarm optimization algorithms to solve multi-objective optimization problems.

Premature convergence occurs when a particle swarm optimization algorithm cannot move its population of individual further; therefore, it cannot obtain a better solution; further, the algorithm is said to be stuck in a local optimum, which is not a good enough solution to meet requirements of acceptable solutions to the optimization problem to be solved. Premature convergence occurs when a particle swarm optimization algorithm is applied to solve a multimodal optimization problem; it also occurs when it is applied to solve a umimodal optimization problem. For example, for a unimodal optimization problem with boundary constraints, if boundary constraints are handled improperly, premature convergence may occur. Premature convergence has to be taken into consideration when designing particles swarm optimization algorithms for solving optimization problems, especially multimodal optimization problems. Boundary constraint handling is very important in applying a particle swarm optimization algorithm to solve both unimodal optimization problems and multimodal optimization problems in order to avoid premature convergence. In the chapter "Experimental Study on Boundary Constraints Handling in Particle Swarm Optimization from a Population Diversity Perspective," Cheng et al. experimentally studied boundary constraints handling techniques in particle swarm optimization algorithms with different topology structures. Population diversity is one good way to observe and monitor the search status and whether the particle swarm intelligence algorithm is in premature convergence or not. In this chapter, population diversity is defined as a measurement to measure the distribution of particles in the search space, and is then utilized to monitor the search process of particle swarm optimization algorithms with different topology structures and different boundary handling techniques. A particle swarm optimization algorithm with a different topology structure has different information propagation method and speed; therefore, a different boundary handling technique may be required for a particle swarm optimization algorithm with a different topology structure. In the chapter, the topology structures studied includes star structure, ring structure, four cluster structure, and von Neumann structure. The boundary constraints handling techniques studied include classical strategy, deterministic strategy, stochastic strategy, and modified stochastic strategy. Experimental results and observations revealed the tendency of particles' exploration capability and exploitation capability during the search process. For example, a deterministic boundary handling technique may improve the search performance of the particle swarm optimization algorithm with ring, four clusters, or Von Neumann structure, but not the star structure. Stochastic boundary handling technique can have good exploration capability; therefore, by further including the method of resetting particles in a small or decreased region, the particle swarm optimization algorithm will also retain good exploitation ability so that better performance can be achieved by the particle swarm optimization algorithm. A good particle swarm optimization algorithm generally should possess a good balance between its exploration capability and exploitation capability over its entire search process. In general, from the search tendency revealed by the population diversity, a more effective and efficient particle swarm optimization algorithm could be designed for solving an optimization problem by considering boundary handling technique and topology structure together.

For optimization problems, solutions that satisfy all constraints are called feasible solutions, while other solutions that violate at least one of constraints are called infeasible solutions. An optimization algorithm is required to find out a good enough feasible solution to an optimization problem with constraints. For most real world optimization problems, they are usually optimization problems with multiple objectives and constraints; these optimization problems are called constrained multi-objective optimization problems. The multiple objectives have conflicts among themselves, and the constraints define the feasibility of potential solutions. For a constrained multi-objective optimization problem, feasible solutions are those that are acceptable while infeasible solutions are those that need to be avoided. There are several existing techniques to handle constraints such as these by giving constraints higher priority to enable feasible solution areas to be searched with higher possibility than infeasible solution areas, by designing operators to allow only feasible solutions surviving into next generation, by defining dominance principles that rank all individuals including both feasible and infeasible solutions so that higher rank solutions will be preferred over generations, etc. In literature, there are multi-objective particle swarm optimization algorithms that have adopted these existing constraints handling techniques to handle constrained multi-objective optimization problems. In the chapter "A Particle Swarm Optimizer for Constrained Multiobjective Optimization," Leong et al. proposed to convert constraints into one extra objective so that the constrained multi-objective optimization problem is converted as an unconstrained multi-objective optimization problem; therefore, Pareto-based approach can be applied directly to solve the multi-objective optimization problem. The purpose of converting constraints into objectives is to have zero constraint violation after going through an evolutionary process. For example, a constrained k-objective optimization problem can be converted into an unconstrained (k+1)-objective optimization problem with all constraints being converted as an extra objective. This extra objective is defined as the constraint violation. The essential goals of the proposed algorithm are to search for feasible solutions through guiding obtained infeasible solutions towards feasible solutions over generations, and to converge to feasible optimal solution or Pareto front eventually. In order to achieve the above goals, the proposed constrained multi-objective particle swarm optimization algorithm utilizes the information related to particles' infeasibility and feasibility status to guide the particles to search for feasible solutions and to improve the quality of the optimal solution found, updates the personal best archive based on the particles' Pareto ranks and their constraint violations, adopts the infeasible global best archive to store infeasible non-dominated solutions, adjusts the acceleration constants depending on the personal bests' and selected global best's infeasibility and feasibility statuses, and integrates the personal bests' feasibility status to estimate the mutation rate in the mutation procedure. Simulation results on the benchmark functions illustrated that the proposed constrained multi-objective particle swarm optimization algorithm is highly competitive in solving the tested benchmark problems by comparing with the other three existing multi-objective optimization algorithms.

Section 2: Swarm Intelligence Applications

Web page recommendation systems recommend to a user pages that the user may be interested to navigate based on the user's interests or the user's usage profile, which can be discovered by processing from the user's preprocessed usage and clickstream data, so that the user can enjoy more efficient and effective personalized Web browsing experience. Numerous Web mining techniques, such as clustering algorithms, have been developed and applied to detect usage profiles. Clustering algorithms can be used to cluster users with similar browsing behaviors into the same cluster while users with dissimilar browsing behaviors into different clusters. In reality, users may be only interested in a particular subset of pages, for which traditional clustering algorithms are not good at clustering users by considering subset of pages at the same time. To address this, biclustering methods are introduced and utilized. In the chapter "Hybrid Swarm Intelligence-Based Biclustering Approach for Recommendation of Web Pages," Rathipriya and Thangavel proposed a combination of discrete artificial bees colony optimization and simulated annealing technique as the biclustering algorithm for Web page recommendation.

Drilling is an extremely common process in the manufacturing industry. Optimization of the drilling process is to utilize an existing model to predict an unknown parameter aiming to assist in decision making in order to save cost, in which an optimization algorithm plays a critical role. In the chapter "Optimization of Drilling Process via Weightless Swarm Algorithm," Ting proposed a novel algorithm known as weightless swarm algorithm to solve the maximization of material reduction rate in drilling process with some constraints. Compared with previous utilized particle swarm optimization approach, the weightless swarm algorithm is simpler and more stable.

Termites are relatively simple, autonomous, and decentralized insects. Individually, they cannot fulfill any complex task, but together through collaboration and coordination, they can be seen as intelligent entities able to perform complex tasks. In the chapter "Artificial Insect Algorithms for Routing in Wireless Sensor Systems," Ang et al. proposed an optimization algorithm called termite-hill for solving routing problems in wireless sensor networks. The termite-hill optimization algorithm was inspired by termites' collective behaviours. The proposed algorithm was further tested on WSNs with static and dynamic sink scenarios to illustrate its scalability and improvement on network energy consumption with a control over best-effort service.

Coverage path planning is an integral part of robotic exploration, which finds applications in areas such as automated reconnaissance, surveillance operations, automated inspection of engineering structures, automated lawn mowing, and automated vacuum cleaning. Area coverage can be realized by using multiple robots to form a team so that an initially unknown environment can be covered or explored by following guidance provided by an area coverage algorithm. An area coverage algorithm should ensure that the entire environment be covered or explored by at least one robot. Numerous area coverage algorithms exist in which the coverage problem is considered independently, that is, with each robot performing its action individually. In reality, there are different scenarios in which robots may be equipped with different sensors to perform different functionalities and all sensors together to team up to perform one single task. Under this scenario, the coverage problem should be taken care of together with the multi-robot formation problem. In the chapter "Coverage Path Planning using Mobile Robot Team Formations," Dasgupta developed multi-robot coverage path planning techniques using mini-robots that are teamed up to be coordinated for their movements. Furthermore, the author theoretically analyzed the proposed approach and conducted extensive experiments using *e-puck* mini-robots.

The objective of a max-cut problem is to find a cut in an undirected graph, which has the maximum sum of the edge weights, which is a NP-hard optimization problem. Path relinking method facilitates a local search. Along the path formed by a pair of solutions, that is, an initiating solution and a guiding solution, the path relinking method can generate a set of solutions along the path between or beyond the pair of solutions. A global equilibrium search algorithm facilitates global search. It can be used to generate a set of solutions with high quality, which can be further used as initial solutions for a local search algorithm to fine tune to find good enough solutions. The path relinking method and the global equilibrium search algorithm compensate each other. In the chapter "Path Relinking Scheme for the Max-Cut Problem," Shylo and Shylo proposed a hybrid search algorithm that combines the path relinking method with the global equilibrium search algorithm to take advantage of the strengths of both approaches, that is, to use the global equilibrium search algorithm to generate and maintain solutions with high quality, which are then used as initial solutions for path relinking method to fine tune around to obtain good enough solutions. The proposed hybrid algorithm was applied to solve max-cut problems. Experimental results illustrated the effectiveness of the proposed algorithm for solving max-cut problems.

Image segmentation is a problem to assign a label to every pixel of an image so that pixels with the same labels form one segment of the image. Through the image segmentation, it will result in a set of segments with pixels within the same segment being similar while pixels between different segments being quite different from each other; therefore, the representation of the original image will be simplified or changed into a different image which is more meaningful and easier to understand. Commonly used image segmentation approaches are clustering algorithms; one of which is the fuzzy C-Means algorithm. In the chapter "Image Segmentation Based on Bio-Inspired Optimization Algorithms," Mo et al. proposed a hybrid algorithm that combines the fuzzy c-means algorithm with a swarm intelligence algorithm to take advantage of strengths of both algorithms. Image segmentation problem is first represented as an optimization problem. Then a swarm intelligence algorithm is utilized to provide global search capability while the fuzzy-c-means algorithm is used to provide local search capability for solving the optimization problem. Five swarm intelligence algorithms are selected as the swarm intelligence algorithm utilized in proposed hybrid algorithm, respectively. They are biogeography-based optimization, artificial fish school algorithm, artificial bees colony, particle swarm optimization, and bacterial foraging algorithm. The proposed hybrid algorithms were tested on several image segmentation problems. Experimental results illustrated the good performance of the proposed algorithms.

Low-rank approximation approaches are used to reduce redundancy and noise in the data representation while capturing the essential information of the original data. Most commonly used low rank approximation approaches are singular value decomposition and principal component analysis, which provide the best approximation in the sense of the smallest Frobenius norm. However, these approximations usually contain elements with both positive and negative values. For many applications, negative values are not meaningful; therefore, low rank approximation approaches with all non-negative elements are sought, which are called non-negative matrix factorization. In the chapter "Swarm Intelligence for Dimensionality Reduction: How to Improve the Non-Negative Matrix Factorization with Nature-Inspired Optimization Methods," Janecek and Tan formed the non-negative matrix factorization as an optimization problem and proposed to use five different population-based heuristic optimization algorithms, which are particle swarm optimization algorithm, genetic algorithm, fish school search algorithm, differential evolution, and firework algorithm, to solve the optimization problem. Furthermore, initialization and iterative update strategies were designed and implemented in the five population-based heuristic optimization algorithms to improve the convergence speed, lower approximation error, and classification accuracy of the non-negative matrix factorization.

Yuhui Shi
Xi'an Jiaotong-Liverpool University, China
March 9, 2014

Acknowledgment

I would like to thank all reviewers for their continued support and effort. They retained the quality of the book volume. I thank all chapters' authors for their contributions. They made the book a possibility. I would also like to take this opportunity to thank the National Natural Science Foundation of China for its support under Grant Numbers 60975080 and 61273367, respectively. Last but not the least, my thanks go to the team, Kayla Wolfe, Jan Travers, Allyson Gard, and Erin O'Dea, at IGI Global for their support and patience. They worked diligently with me throughout the process of editing and production. It has been a pleasure and a learning experience for me to work with them. They made the book a reality.

Yuhui Shi
Xi'an Jiaotong-Liverpool University, China
March 9, 2014

Section 1
Swarm Intelligence Algorithms

Chapter 1
An Optimization Algorithm Based on Brainstorming Process

Yuhui Shi
Xi'an Jiaotong-Liverpool University, China

ABSTRACT

In this chapter, the human brainstorming process is modeled, based on which two versions of a Brain Storm Optimization (BSO) algorithm are introduced. Simulation results show that both BSO algorithms perform reasonably well on ten benchmark functions, which validates the effectiveness and usefulness of the proposed BSO algorithms. Simulation results also show that one of the BSO algorithms, BSO-II, performs better than the other BSO algorithm, BSO-I, in general. Furthermore, average inter-cluster distance D_c and inter-cluster diversity D_e are defined, which can be used to measure and monitor the distribution of cluster centroids and information entropy of the population over iterations. Simulation results illustrate that further improvement could be achieved by taking advantage of information revealed by D_c which points at one direction for future research on BSO algorithms.

INTRODUCTION

Many real-world applications can be represented as optimization problems of which algorithms are required to have the capability to search for optimum. Originally, these optimization problems were mathematically represented by continuous and differentiable functions so that algorithms such as hill-climbing algorithms can be designed and/or utilized to solve them. Traditionally, these hill-climbing like algorithms are single-point based algorithms such as gradient decent algorithms which move from the current point along the direction pointed by the negative of the gradient of the function at the current point. These hill-climbing algorithms can find solutions quickly for unimodal problems, but they have the problems of being sensitive to initial search point and being easily trapped into local optimum for nonlinear multimodal problems. Furthermore, these mathematical functions need to be continuous and differentiable, which instead greatly narrows the range of real-world problems that can be solved by hill-climbing algorithms. Recently, evolutionary algorithms have been designed and utilized to solve optimization problems. Different from traditional single-point based algorithms such as gradient decent algorithms, each evolutionary algorithm is a population-based algorithm,

DOI: 10.4018/978-1-4666-6328-2.ch001

which consists of a set of points (population of individuals). The population of individuals is expected to have high tendency to move towards better and better solution areas iteration over iteration through cooperation and/or competition among themselves. There are a lot of evolutionary algorithms out there in literature. The most popular evolutionary algorithms are evolutionary programming (Fogel, 1962), genetic algorithm (Holland, 1975), evolution strategy (Rechenberg, 1973), and genetic programming (Koza, 1992), which were inspired by biological evolution. In evolutionary algorithms, population of individuals survives into the next iteration. Which individual has higher probability to survive is proportional to its fitness value obtained according to some evaluation function. The survived individuals are then updated by utilizing evolutionary operators such as mutation operator, crossover operator, *etc*. In evolutionary programming and evolution strategy, only the mutation operation is employed, while in genetic algorithms and genetic programming, both the mutation operation and crossover operation are employed. The optimization problems to be optimized by evolutionary algorithms do not need to be mathematically represented as continuous and differentiable functions. They can be represented in any form. Only requirement for representing optimization problems is that each individual can be evaluated as a value called fitness value. Therefore, evolutionary algorithms can be applied to solve more general optimization problems, especially those that are very difficult, if not impossible, for traditional hill-climbing algorithms to solve.

Recently, another kind of algorithms, called swarm intelligence algorithms, is attracting more and more attentions from researchers. Swarm intelligence algorithms are usually nature-inspired optimization algorithms instead of evolution-inspired optimization algorithms such as evolutionary algorithms. Similar to evolutionary algorithms, a swarm intelligence algorithm is also a population-based optimization algorithm. Different from the evolutionary algorithms, each individual in a swarm intelligence algorithm represents a simple object such as ant, bird, or fish, *etc*. So far, a lot of swarm intelligence algorithms have been proposed and studied. Among them are particle swarm optimization(PSO) (Eberhart & Shi, 2007; Shi & Eberhart, 1998), ant colony optimization algorithm(ACO) (Dorigo, 1996), bacterial forging optimization algorithm(BFO) (Passino, 2010), firefly optimization algorithm (FFO) (Yang, 2008), bee colony optimization algorithm (BCO) (Tovey, 2004), artificial immune system (AIS) (Castro, 1999), fish school search optimization algorithm(FSO) (Bastos-Filho, 2008), shuffled frog-leaping algorithm (SFL) (Enusuff, 2006), intelligent water drops algorithm (IWD) (Shah, 2009), to just name a few.

In a swarm intelligence algorithm, an individual represents a simple object such as birds in PSO, ants in ACO, bacteria in BFO, *etc*. These simple objects cooperate and compete among themselves to have a high tendency to move toward better and better search areas. As a consequence, it is the collective behavior of all individuals that makes a swarm intelligence algorithm to be effective and efficient in problem optimization.

For example, in PSO, each particle (individual) is associated with a velocity. The velocity of each particle is dynamically updated according to its own historical best performance and its companions' historical best performance. All the particles in the PSO population fly through the solution space in the hope that particles will fly towards better and better search areas with high probability.

Mathematically, the updating process of the population of individuals over iterations can be looked as a mapping process from one population of individuals to another population of individuals from one iteration to the next iteration, which can be represented as $P_{t+1} = f(P_t)$, where P_t is the population of individuals at the iteration t, $f()$ is the mapping function. Different evolutionary algorithm or swarm intelligence algorithm has a different mapping function. Through the mapping function, we expect the population of individuals will be updated to become better and better solutions over iterations. Therefore mapping functions should possess the property of convergence. For nonlinear and complicated problems, mapping functions will be more like to move population of individuals toward local minima, which may not be good enough solutions to the optimization problems to be solved. A good mapping function should have not only the capability to converge, but also the capability to diverge when it gets trapped into local minima. As for evolutionary algorithms and swarm intelligence algorithms, they should have the capability to be in convergence or divergence state accordingly. A lot of researches have been done and reported with regards to this in literature. For example, in particle swarm optimization algorithms, mechanisms have been designed and/or utilized to preserve diversity to keep the algorithm to have good search capability. Different diversity measurements have been defined and monitored (Shi, 2008; Shi, 2009). Generally speaking, a better designed population-based algorithm should have a good balance of convergence and divergence.

In this paper, we will introduce a new optimization algorithm that is based on the collective behavior of human being, that is, the brainstorming process. It is natural to expect that an optimization algorithm based on human collective behavior could be a better optimization algorithm than existing swarm intelligence algorithms which are based on collective behavior of simple insects, because human beings are social animal and are the most intelligent animals in the world. The designed optimization algorithm will naturally have the capability of convergence and divergence.

The remaining paper is organized as follows. In Brainstorming Process section, the human brainstorming process is reviewed. In Modeling Brainstorming Process section, the model of a brainstorming process is proposed and discussed. In Brain Storm Optimization Algorithm section, two versions of novel optimization algorithms

inspired by human brainstorming process are introduced and described, followed by experiments and result discussion on benchmark functions. Finally, future research directions conclusions are given.

BRAINSTORMING PROCESS

Brainstorming process has often been utilized for innovative problem solving. It can solve a lot of difficult problems which usually can't be solved by a single person. In a brainstorming process, a group of people with diverse background are gathered together to brainstorm. A facilitator will usually be involved to facilitate the brainstorming process but not directly involved in idea generation himself/herself. The facilitator usually should have enough facilitation experience but have less knowledge about the problem to be solved so that generated ideas will have less, if not none, biases from the facilitator. The brainstorming process is used to generate many ideas as diverse as possible so that good solutions to solve the problem can be obtained from these ideas. The brainstorming process usually consists of several rounds of idea generations. In each round of idea generation, the brainstorming group is asked to come out a lot of ideas. At the end of each round of idea generation process, better ideas among them will be picked up and will serve as clues to generate ideas in the next round of idea generation process. In the brainstorming process, there is another (small) group of persons that serve the purpose to pick up better ideas from the ideas generated in each round of idea generation process. Through the brainstorming process, hopefully great and unexpectable solutions can occur from collective intelligence of human being, and the problem can be solved with high probability.

To help generate more diverse ideas, the Osborn's original four rules of idea generation in a brainstorming process (Osborn, 1963; Smith, 2002) should be obeyed. The four rules are listed in Table 1. One major role of the facilitator is to

Table 1. Benchmark functions tested in this paper

Function	Expressions	Range
Sphere	$f_1 = \sum_{i=1}^{d} x_i^2$	$[-100, 100]^d$
Schwefel's P221	$f_2 = \max_i \{|x_i|\}$	$[-100, 100]^d$
Step	$f_3 = \sum_{i=1}^{d} (|x_i + 0.5|)^2$	$[-100, 100]^d$
Schwefel's P222	$f_4 = \sum_{i=1}^{d} |x_i| + \prod_{i=1}^{d} |x_i|$	$[-10, 10]^d$
Quartic Noise	$f_5 = \sum_{i=1}^{d} i x_i^4 + \text{random}[0, 1)$	$[-1.28, 1.28]^d$
Ackely	$f_6 = -20 \exp\left(-0.2\sqrt{\dfrac{1}{d}\sum_{i=1}^{d} x_i^2}\right) - \exp\left(\dfrac{1}{d}\sum_{i=1}^{d} \cos(2\pi x_i)\right) + 20 + e$	$[-32, 32]^d$
Rastrigin	$f_7 = \sum_{i=1}^{d} [x_i^2 - 10\cos(2\pi x_i) + 10]$	$[-5.12, 5.12]^d$
Rosenbrock	$f_8 = \sum_{i=1}^{d-1} [100(x_{i+1} - x_i^2)^2 + (x_i - 1)^2]$	$[-30, 30]^d$
Schwefel's P226	$f_9 = -\sum_{i=1}^{d} (x_i \sin(\sqrt{|x_i|})) + 418.9829d$	$[-500, 500]^d$
Griewank	$f_{10} = \dfrac{1}{4000}\sum_{i=1}^{d} x_i^2 - \prod_{i=1}^{d} \cos(\dfrac{x_i}{\sqrt{i}}) + 1$	$[-600, 600]^d$

facilitate the brainstorming group to obey the Osborn's four rules.

Osborn's original rules for idea generation in a brainstorming process:

1. Suspend Judgment
2. Anything Goes
3. Cross-fertilize (Piggyback)
4. Go for Quantity

The four rules in Table 1 guide the idea generation in each round of idea generation during a brainstorming process. In order to keep the brainstorming group to be open-minded, there is no idea as good idea or bad idea, any idea is welcomed. For any idea generated during each round of idea generation process, there should be no judgment and/or criticism whether it is a good idea or bad idea. Any judgment should be held back until the end of this round of idea generation process when better ideas are picked up by problem owners. This is what the Rule 1 "Suspend Judgment" means. The Rule 2 "Anything Goes" means that any thought comes to your mind should be raised and recorded. Don't let any idea or thought pass by without sharing with other brainstorming group members. The Rule 3 "Piggyback" says any generated idea could and should serve as a clue to inspire the brainstorming group to come out more ideas. Ideas are not independently generated. They are related. The late generated ideas are inspired by and dependent on previously generated ideas. The Rule 4 "Go for quantity" says that we focus on generating as many ideas as possible. Hopefully quality of ideas will come out of quantity of idea naturally. Without generating large quantity of ideas, it is naive to believe that good quality ideas will come out.

The purpose to generate ideas according to rules in Table 1 is to keep the brainstorming group to be open-minded as much as possible so that they will generate ideas as diverse as possible. A brainstorming process generally follows the steps listed in Table 2 (Shi, 2011). After some time of brainstorming, the brainstorming group will become tired and narrow-minded, therefore it becomes harder to come out new diverse ideas. The operation of picking up an object in Step 6 in Table 2 serves for the purpose of helping brainstorming group to diverge from previously generated ideas therefore to avoid being trapped by the previously generated ideas. Picking up several good ideas from ideas generated so far is to cause the brainstorming group to pay more attention to the better ideas which the brainstorming group believes to be. The ideas picking-up works like

point-attraction for the idea generation process while ideas generation works like point-expansion. Therefore, there are attraction and expansion embedded in the brainstorming process naturally.

Steps in a brainstorming process:

Step 1: Get together a brainstorming group of people with as diverse background as possible;

Step 2: Generate many ideas according to the rules in Table 1;

Step 3: Have several, say 3 or 5, clients act as the owners of the problem to pick up several, say one from each owner, ideas as better ideas for solving the problem;

Step 4: Use the ideas picked up in the Step 3 with higher probability than other ideas as clues, and generate more ideas according to the rules in Table 1;

Step 5: Have the owners to pick up several better ideas generated as did in Step 3;

Step 6: Randomly pick an object and use the functions and appearance of the object as clues, generate more ideas according to the rules in Table 1;

Step 7: Have the owners to pick up several better ideas;

Step 8: Hopefully a good enough solution can be obtained by considering the ideas generated.

MODELING BRAINSTORMING PROCESS

The procedure of a brainstorming process listed in Table 2 can be described by the flow chart shown in Figure 1. There are three rounds of idea genera-

Table 2. Set of parameters for BSO algorithm

n	m	p_{5a}	p_{6b}	p_{6biii}	p_{6c}	k	Max_iteration	μ	σ
100	5	0.2	0.8	0.4	0.5	20	2000	0	1

Figure 1. Flow chart of a brainstorming process

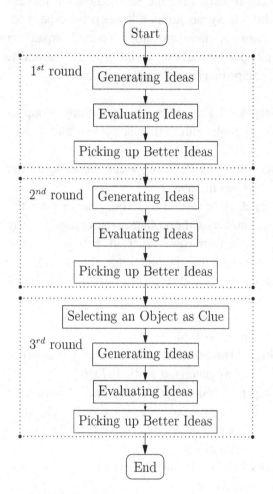

in Table 2. Each step in a brainstorming process therefore can be modeled (and/or simulated) and put together as a model for the brainstorming process as that shown in Figure 1, which will be further explained and modified in the following sub-sections.

Population

A solution to a problem with d variables to be optimized can be looked as a point in the d dimensional solution space. An idea can be considered as a potential solution, *i.e.* a point in the solution space. For the purpose of representing an idea as a potential solution to a problem, it is assumed that each idea can be represented by a vector with the same length as other vectors (ideas). Therefore to find a good solution is equivalent to find a point or a solution in the solution space. A group of ideas can therefore be considered as a population of solutions or individuals in the solution space. If for every round of idea generation in the brainstorming process, a fixed number of n ideas will be generated before the problem owners pick up good ideas, then these n ideas can be considered as a population of individuals (or solutions) with population size being n. Therefore, the human brainstorming process can be considered as generating a population of individuals iteratively three times as that shown in Figure 1. One round of idea generation can be considered as one iteration of individual generations in population-based optimization algorithms such as particle swarm optimization algorithm. The difference between them is the way how a new population of individuals is generated based on the current population of individuals.

Initialization

The Generating Ideas step in the very first round of idea generations can be considered as the population initialization in any population-based optimization algorithm. During the population initialization, to gather a group of people with as

tion involved in a brainstorming process in general. In each round of brainstorming process, there are several steps. For example, in the first round, there are idea generations, idea evaluations, and idea picking up. The idea evaluation step serves the purpose of finding out better ideas among ideas already generated. By idea evaluation, good ideas could be identified and picked up in the Picking up Better Ideas step, which simulates picking up good ideas by problem owners. The first round simulates Step 2 & 3 in Table 2. The second round is the same as the first round which simulates Step 4 & 5 in Table 2. The third round is the same as the first two rounds except that one additional step Selecting an Object as Clue is added to simulate randomly picking up an object as clues in Step 6

diverse background as possible can be considered as initializing the population of individuals randomly with uniform distribution over the dynamic range of the solution space. The whole population of individuals can be totally randomly generated or only portion of the population is randomly generated and the rest of the population of individuals will be generated by adding noise to the already randomly generated individuals. To preserve the initialized population to be diversified, usually *a priori* domain knowledge should not be utilized in the initialization process, unless when computation cost is the first priority, in which the domain knowledge should be utilized to initialize the population to find good solution quickly at the risk of premature convergence.

Clustering

Each round of idea generation generates enough ideas, but not necessary too many ideas because otherwise all the generated ideas will more like to diverge, and therefore will be far away from expected ideas which are close to expected solutions. To have diverse ideas is good to seek around all possible ideas to help find good potential solutions, but there should be a tradeoff between divergence and focus. We also need to pull the brainstorming group back to concentrate on generating ideas around some areas with high potential to speed up searching for good enough ideas. The problem owners in the brainstorming process serve this purpose. They are asked to pick good ideas from generated ideas. Because every problem owner has different expertise and knowledge, therefore the picked ideas will be different. They represent potential good ideas that have been generated so far. Next round of idea generation should better be conducted with focus on them. Certainly, it does not exclude idea generation by piggybacking other ideas, but with small probability. One way to simulate the idea picking up by problem owners is to use clustering algorithms. All the

individuals (ideas) in the population are clustered into several clusters. The number of clusters corresponds to the number of problem owners. The cluster center of each cluster corresponds to the idea(s) picked up by a problem owner. The cluster center for each cluster can be the best performed individual within this cluster. It can also be the centroid of the cluster.

One possible clustering algorithm is the k-means clustering algorithm (MacQueen, 1967), which requires to know the number of clusters k *a priori*. The number k corresponds to the number of problem owners, that is, the number of problem owners is fixed. The self-organizing feature map (Kohonen, 2007) is another kind of clustering algorithm, in which the number of clusters is unknown before running the algorithm. The number of clusters will be determined by the algorithm itself according to the distribution of individuals in the population. Other clustering algorithms (Xu, 2005) such as partitioning around medoids (Theodoridis, 2006), fuzzy c-means (FCM) (Nock, 2006), *etc.* can also be employed.

Individual Generation

For idea generations by piggyback, it is similar to randomly select one or several existing individuals (or ideas) and generate a new individual by adding noise to the selected individual(s). The purpose of doing this is to guarantee that new individuals (ideas) are generated by piggybacking existing individuals as diverse as possible. If a new idea (individual) x_{new} is generated by piggybacking one existing idea (individual) x_{old}, it can be written as

$$x_{new}^i = x_{old}^i + \xi(t) * random(t) \tag{1}$$

where x_{new}^i and x_{old}^i are the ith dimension of x_{new} and x_{old}, respectively; *random(t)* is a random function; $\xi(t)$ is a coefficient that weights the contribution of random value to the new individual. The above formula is similar to the mutation operation in evolutionary programming algorithm. The commonly utilized random function in mutation operation is the Gaussian function (Yao, 1997). Other random functions that can be used are Cauchy function (Yao, 1997), Lévy flights (Pavlyukevich, 2007), *etc.* Compared with Gaussian function, Cauchy function has a longer tail which makes it preferable if wider areas need to be explored (Yao, 1997).

If a new idea (individual) x_{new} is generated by piggybacking two existing ideas (individuals) x_{old1} and x_{old2}, it can be written as

$$x_{new}^i = x_{old}^i + \xi(t) * random(t) \qquad (2a)$$

$$x_{old}^i = w_1 * x_{old1}^i + w_2 * x_{old2}^i \qquad (2b)$$

where x_{old}^i is the weighted summation of the ith dimension of x_{old1} and x_{old2}; w_1 and w_2 are two coefficients to weight the contribution of two existing individuals. The above formula simulates generating new idea by piggybacking two existing ideas. Certainly, a new idea can also be generated by piggybacking more than two existing ideas.

No matter how many existing ideas (individuals) will be piggybacked to generate new ideas (individuals), the cluster centers will have high probability to be chosen to generate new ideas (individuals) compared with the other non-cluster-center ideas (individuals) which usually can be chosen with small probability.

The coefficient $\xi(t)$ weights the contribution of randomly generated value to the new individual. Generally, large $\xi(t)$ value facilitates exploration while small $\xi(t)$ values facilitates exploitation. When global search capability is preferred, for example, at the beginning of search process, $\xi(t)$ should give large value, while when local search capability is preferred, for example, at the end of search process, $\xi(t)$ should give small value. One possible function for $\xi(t)$ is

$$\xi(t) = logsig\left(\frac{\frac{T}{2} - t}{k}\right) * random(t) \qquad (3)$$

where $logsig()$ is a logarithmic sigmoid transfer function, T is the maximum number of iterations, and t is the current iteration number, k is for changing $logsig()$ function's slope, and $random()$ is a random value within $(0,1)$.

Disruption

After two rounds of idea generation, the mindset of the brainstorming group usually will be narrowed and therefore it becomes more difficult, if not impossible, for them to come out different and/or diverse ideas efficiently. To further explore whether there are potential good ideas out there somewhere, in the brainstorming process, an object will be randomly picked up, and the brainstorming group will be asked to generate new ideas which are more or less related to the functions and/or appearance of the object. The purpose of this is to help the brainstorming group disrupt from their current mindset, which is usually difficult to achieve. This disruption operation can be simulated by replacing selected ideas (individuals) with randomly generated individuals. Therefore, wider areas could be explored with higher probability by utilizing disruption operation.

As shown in Figure 1, there are three rounds of idea generation. The first two rounds are identical while the third round serves as the purpose of disruption with the step Selecting an Object as Clue. To further modulate the operations, this disruption operation could be distributed and shared among all three rounds of idea generation. Figure 2 shows the modified flow chart of the brainstorming process, which includes three identical rounds of idea generation. Each round of idea generation is shown in Figure 3 in which

Figure 2. Flow chart of a brainstorming process

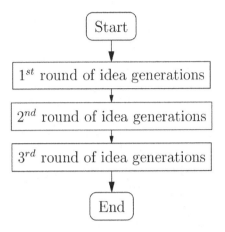

Figure 3. Flow chart of one round of idea generation

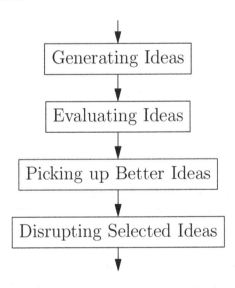

the step Selecting an Object as Clue is changed to be the step Disrupting Selected Ideas and it is put at the end of each round.

Selection

In a population-based optimization algorithm, generally speaking, if it is not because of specific requirements, the population size n is fixed and not changed during the algorithm running time.

During each iteration, number of new individuals will be generated, say p $(p \geq n)$, therefore there will exist $p+n$ number of individuals, among which only n will be copied into the next iteration due to the fixed population size. Similar to other population-based algorithms, how to select n from $p+n$ individuals is critical to the optimization algorithm inspired by the brainstorming process. One simple way is that for each existing individual in the population, a new individual is generated. This pair of individuals is compared. The better one will be kept as the individual into the next iteration. Another way could be to randomly pick up n pairs of individuals from the $n+p$ individuals, and the better one of each pair will be kept into the next iteration.

To further take advantage of information embedded in each pair of individuals, crossover operations could also be applied to each pair of individuals to generate two new offspring. The best of the four will then be copied into the next iteration.

In each round of idea generation shown in Figure 3, one more step Selecting Ideas is inserted right below the step Generating Ideas. Figure 4 shows the new flow chart of each round of idea generation.

In practice, limited time will be taken for a brainstorming process, otherwise, the brainstorming group will be tired to generate new meaningful ideas efficiently. Usually as a good practice, a brainstorming process takes approximately 60 minutes. As shown in the Figure 1, there are only three rounds of idea generation in a brainstorming process. But for a model to be executed by computers, the number of rounds of idea generation can be as large as that we want. Figure 5 shows the flow chart for a brainstorming process that can be simulated by computers. In Figure 5, the step 1ˢᵗ Round of Idea Generations is the same as the step One Round of Idea Generation shown in Figure 5. The purpose to have the extra step 1ˢᵗ Round of Idea Generations at the beginning is to be similar to the Initialization step in population-

Figure 4. Flow chart of one round of idea generation

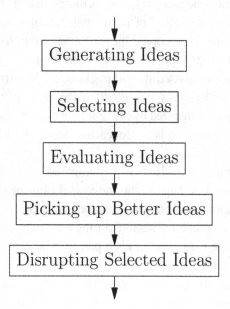

Figure 5. Flow chart of a brainstorming process

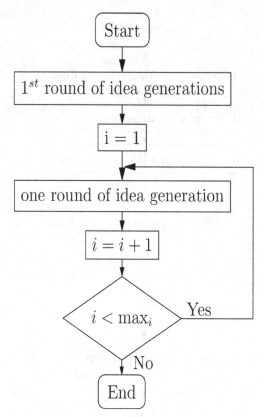

based algorithms. The *max_i* is the maximum number of rounds of idea generation we want to conduct. Therefore totally, *max_i* rounds of idea generation will be conducted in the brainstorming process shown in the Figure 5.

By implementing Figure 5, a model or algorithm to mimic the human being brainstorming process can be built.

BRAIN STORM OPTIMIZATION ALGORITHM

According to Figure 5, a brain storm optimization (BSO) algorithm can be designed by directly mapping the steps shown in Figure 5. By some straightforward rearrangement, one possible flow chart of the BSO algorithm is shown in Figure 6. In Figure 6, there are five main operations among which three operations are unique to the BSO algorithm and the other two operations are similar to those in other evolutionary algorithms.

In the procedure of the Brain Storm Optimization (BSO) algorithm shown in Figure 6, the first two steps are the initialization step and evaluation step which are the same as that in other swarm intelligence algorithms. In the initialization step, the population of individuals is usually uniformly and randomly initialized within the dynamic range of solution space. The population size *n* simulates the number of ideas generated in each round of idea generation in the brainstorming process. For the simplicity of the algorithm, the population size usually is set to be a constant number for all iterations in the BSO algorithm. In the evaluation step, each individual will be evaluated. An evaluation value (fitness) will be obtained to measure how good is an individual as a potential solution to the problem to be solved. The third step is to cluster the population of individuals into several clusters.

Figure 6. An Implementation of BSO algorithm

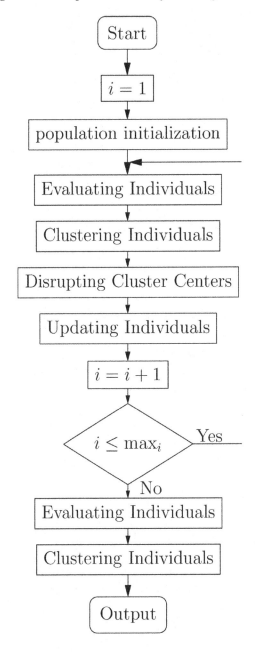

iteration, but will only be selected to execute with small probability.

The Updating Individuals step generally includes two sub-operations, i.e., Generating Individuals and Selecting Individuals, which is shown in Figure 7. As discussed in previous section, crossover operation could be utilized to further take advantage of existing search information. Figure 8 shows another possibility of the Updating Individuals operation which adds one additional sub-operation, i.e., crossover operation. One implementation of the BSO algorithm was introduced in (Shi, 2011) and is given in Table 3 here for convenience, in which the Updating Individuals operation shown in Figure 7 is

Figure 7. One implementation of updating individual operation

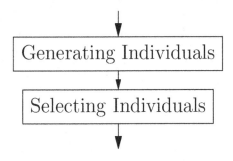

Figure 8. Another implementation of updating individual operation

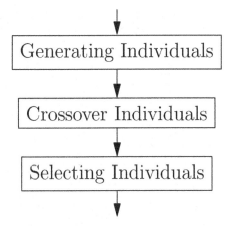

Different kind of clustering algorithms could be employed. In this paper, the k-means clustering algorithm will be used as the clustering algorithm. The disruption step randomly selects a cluster center and replaces it with a randomly generated individual. This step will not be executed in every

Table 3. Simulation results of BSO-I with different k

Function	k	Mean	Best	Worst	Variance
Sphere	10	1.20381E-11	2.55674E-86	5.27132E-10	5.61316E-21
	20	2.30827E-43	1.24079E-43	3.17853E-43	2.5931E-87
	25	9.4726E-35	5.55931E-35	1.33105E-34	3.78414E-70
	30	5.35092E-29	3.01328E-29	7.6509E-29	1.30974E-58
	40	7.70746E-22	4.18609E-22	1.10552E-21	2.74116E-44
	50	1.60782E-17	7.60191E-18	2.22015E-17	1.18045E-35
Rastrigin	10	17.11636	5.969754	29.84873	28.93288
	20	18.00875	8.954632	31.83866	20.98068
	25	17.17298	6.964713	23.879	13.24541
	30	17.15308	7.959667	29.84871	26.04389
	40	15.81984	6.964713	24.87396	17.95025
	50	16.21782	8.954632	25.8689	16.85928

implemented. By replacing the Step 6.d in Table 3 with two sub-steps shown in Table 4, another implementation of BSO algorithm can be achieved. To distinguish the two different implementations, the first one is noted as BSO-I and the second is noted as BSO-II for the purpose of description convenience. Intuitively, the BSO algorithms should be superior to other swarm intelligence algorithms, which are inspired by collective behaviors of inferior animals, because of the highest intelligence unique to human beings.

The procedure of the brain storm optimization algorithm in [SHI2011]:

1. Randomly generate n potential solutions (individuals);

Table 4. Simulation results of BSO-I on unimodal functions

Function	Dimension	Mean	Best	Worst	Variance
f_1	10	1.3989E-35	3.90855E-36	2.71203E-35	2.75801E-71
	20	9.77845E-35	6.11475E-35	1.37856E-34	3.55418E-70
	30	2.66069E-34	1.79135E-34	3.59892E-34	2.02141E-69
f_2	10	2.31285E-18	1.49658E-18	3.11619E-18	1.47169E-37
	20	5.05671E-18	3.69394E-18	6.40744E-18	4.41064E-37
	30	0.000235	3.18538E-08	0.001718355	1.55583E-07
f_3	10	0	0	0	0
	20	0	0	0	0
	30	0	0	0	0
f_4	10	9.28917E-18	5.51341E-18	1.21942E-17	1.81665E-36
	20	3.4224E-17	2.63097E-17	4.25525E-17	1.03733E-35
	30	1.9978E-06	5.84794E-17	9.94736E-05	1.97869E-10
f_5	10	0.000424	4.52215E-05	0.001140455	6.14016E-08
	20	0.002636	0.000613	0.008465	2.8024E-06
	30	0.00835095	0.001967	0.020706	1.33183E-05

2. Evaluate the n individuals;
3. Cluster n individuals into m clusters by k-means clustering algorithm;
4. Rank individuals in each cluster and record the best individual as cluster center in each cluster;
5. Randomly generate a value between 0 and 1;
   a. If the value is smaller than a pre-determined probability p_{5a},
      i. Randomly select a cluster center;
      ii. Randomly generate an individual to replace the selected cluster center;
   b. Otherwise, do nothing.
6. Generate new individuals
   a. Randomly generate a value between 0 and 1;
   b. If the value is less than a probability p_{6b},
      i. Randomly select a cluster with a probability p_{6bi};
      ii. Generate a random value between 0 and 1;
      iii. If the value is smaller than a pre-determined probability p_{6biii}, Select the cluster center and add random values to it to generate new individual.
      iv. Otherwise randomly select an individual from this cluster and add random value to the individual to generate new individual.
   c. Otherwise randomly select two clusters to generate new individual
      i. Generate a random value;
      ii. If it is less than a pre-determined probability p_{6c}, the two cluster centers are combined and then added with random values to generate new individual;

   iii. Otherwise, two individuals from each selected cluster are randomly selected to be combined and added with random values to generate new individual.
   d. The newly generated individual is compared with the existing individual with the same individual index, the better one is kept and recorded as the new individual;
7. If n new individuals have been generated, go to step 8; otherwise go to step 6;
8. Terminate if pre-determined maximum number of iterations has been reached; otherwise go to step 2.

Two sub-steps to replace Step 6.d:

d. The newly generated individual crossovers with the existing individual with the same individual index to generate two more individuals (offspring);
e. The four individuals are compared, the best one is kept and recorded as the new individual;

In the BSO algorithm, the number of cluster centers is usually set to be a small number, say $m=5$, and the number of generated individuals in each iteration is usually set to be a relatively large number, say $n=100$.

EXPERIMENTS AND DISCUSSIONS

Test Problems

To validate the brain storm optimization algorithms, ten benchmark functions listed in Table 1 are tested. Among them, the first five functions are unimodal functions and the remaining five functions are multimodal functions. They all are minimization problems with minimum zero. The third column in Table 1 is the dynamic ranges for the ten benchmark functions, which have been used to test population-based algorithms in literature. For each benchmark function, each of the tested BSO algorithms will be run *50* times to obtain reasonable statistical results.

Simulations on *k*

In (Shi, 2011), the BSO-I algorithm was tested on two benchmark functions, *i.e.*, the Sphere function and the Rastrigin function. The parameters are setup as that listed in Table 2. The purpose there is to validate the usefulness and effectiveness of the proposed BSO-I algorithm. Generally speaking, the parameter k determines the slope of the *logsig*() functions, therefore it determines the decreasing speed of the step-size $\xi(t)$ over iterations. Different k should have different impacts on the performance of BSO algorithms. In order to test the impact of k on BSO performance, we change the k value while all other parameter values are kept to be the same as that listed in Table 2. For this purpose, again only one unimodal function, Sphere function, and one multimodal function, Rastrigin function, are utilized. The dimension of the two functions is set to be *20*.

Table 3 shows the simulation results. The results given in Table 3 are mean, best, worst function values and their variance at the final iteration over *50* runs. From Table 3, it can be observed that generally there is no single parameter k value with which the BSO algorithm can have the best performance. From Table 3, relatively speaking, unimodal function (Sphere function) prefers to have relatively small k value while multimodal function (Rastrigin function) prefers to have relatively large k value. By considering the robustness of the BSO algorithm and from the results given in Table 3 itself, generally speaking, a good choice for the parameter k is 25 as a tradeoff between unimodal function and multimodal function. The obtained mean function values over *2000* iterations with parameter $k = 25$ are shown in Figure 9. From Figure 9, it can be observed that the BSO-I with $k = 25$ can converge fast when solving the Sphere function and Rstrigin function. In all simulations below, we will set the parameter k to be *25* with all other parameters are set as the same as that in Table 2.

Simulations on BSO-I Algorithm

The BSO-I algorithm is tested on the ten benchmark functions listed in Table 1 to illustrate the effectiveness and efficiency of the BSO-I

Figure 9. Obtained mean minimum values vs. iterations for BSO-I with k = 25

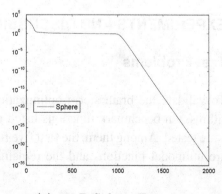

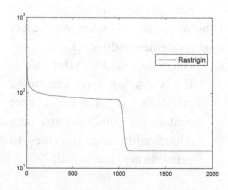

(a) 20-*D* Sphere Function   (b) 20-*D* Rastrigin Function

algorithm instead of only two benchmark functions in (Shi, 2011). Each function is tested with three different dimension setting, *10*, *20*, and *30*, respectively. The experimental results are given in Table 4 and 5 for unimodal functions and multimodal functions, respectively. From Table 4, it can be seen that good results can be achieved by BSO-I algorithm, and the results also show that the BSO-I is robust and reliable when it is applied to solve benchmark unimodal functions. From Table 5, it can be seen that good results can be obtained for function f_6, relatively good results can be obtained for functions f_7 and f_8, but not relatively good results are obtained for f_9 which is in general a difficult function to optimize, and for function f_{10}, good results can be obtained for it with dimension *20* and *30*, but not with dimension*10*, for which only relatively good results are obtained instead.

Simulation on BSO-II Algorithm

The BSO-II algorithm further exploits the search areas by generating two new offspring through utilizing crossover operation to crossover the newly generated individual with the existing individual with the same individual index. The BSO-II is applied to the ten benchmark functions with dimensions *10*, *20*, and *30*, respectively. The simulation results are given in Table 6 and 7 for unimodal functions and multimodal functions, respectively. From Table 6, we can observe that good results can be achieved by the BSO-II algorithm, and the results also show that the BSO-II is robust and reliable when it is applied to solve benchmark unimodal functions. From Table 7, it can be seen that good results can be obtained for function f_6, relatively good results can be obtained for functions f_7 with dimension 30 and f_8, but not relatively good results are obtained for f_9 which is in general a difficult function to optimize, and for function f_{10}, reasonable good results can be obtained. Compared with the observation from the BSO-I algorithm, very good results (the optimum) can be obtained for f_7 with dimension *10* and *20*. For f_7 with dimension *30*, the best results over *50* runs is *0* which is the optimum of the problem, but the worst and variance over *50* runs are *3.979836* and *1.010551*, which indicates that

Table 5. Simulation results of BSO-I on multimodal functions

Function	Dimension	Mean	Best	Worst	Variance
f_6	10	4.44089E-15	4.44089E-15	4.44089E-15	0
	20	4.44089E-15	4.44089E-15	4.44089E-15	0
	30	5.93303E-15	4.44089E-15	7.99361E-15	3.13741E-30
f_7	10	3.502256	0	5.969754	1.949178
	20	17.75005	8.954632	26.86387	15.12629
	30	34.56484	13.92943	51.7378	51.65143
f_8	10	6.330642	2.587793	29.36235	11.77892
	20	21.60337	15.83735	87.11474	255.4539
	30	42.02786	25.91331	296.7523	2073.832
f_9	10	1350.782	454.0165	2270.172	192322.2
	20	3012.657	1598.991	4501.054	570878.2
	30	4951.779	3652.088	6771.33	563448.4
f_{10}	10	1.35123	0.497182	2.21245	0.158512
	20	0.058446	0	0.9467	0.022289
	30	0.010777	0	0.056496	0.000163

Table 6. Simulation results of BSO-II on unimodal functions

Function	Dimension	Mean	Best	Worst	Variance
f_1	10	4.56E-36	2.61244E-36	7.53912E-36	1.13477E-72
	20	4.54E-35	2.98742E-35	6.19235E-35	7.00667E-71
	30	1.33E-34	9.34047E-35	1.65808E-34	2.53466E-70
f_2	10	1.52E-18	1.10811E-18	1.94476E-18	3.80565E-38
	20	3.86E-18	3.23175E-18	4.44916E-18	8.94695E-38
	30	5.85E-18	4.80866E-18	6.91767E-18	2.62081E-37
f_3	10	0	0	0	0
	20	0	0	0	0
	30	0	0	0	0
f_4	10	4.76E-18	3.30555E-18	6.17314E-18	5.02845E-37
	20	2.13E-17	1.54076E-17	2.52198E-17	5.11026E-36
	30	4.49E-17	3.56463E-17	5.22311E-17	1.57E-35
f_5	10	8.85E-05	3.18035E-05	0.000256579	1.69387E-09
	20	0.000319	0.000104	0.000853	2.24337E-08
	30	0.000766	0.000176	0.001733	1.00554E-07

Table 7. Simulation results of BSO-II on multimodal functions

Function	Dimension	Mean	Best	Worst	Variance
f_6	10	4.16E-15	8.88178E-16	4.44089E-15	9.47921E-31
	20	4.44E-15	4.44089E-15	4.44089E-15	0
	30	4.44E-15	4.44089E-15	4.44089E-15	0
f_7	10	0	0	0	0
	20	0	0	0	0
	30	0.855665	0	3.979836	1.010551
f_8	10	4.558798	2.019811	9.069095	0.862945
	20	28.514436	15.49093	83.89686	604.2519
	30	34.06948	25.85653	128.9086	505.6776
f_9	10	56.23811	0.000127	236.8768	5855.616
	20	499.023	118.4386	927.8028	48176.18
	30	1128.729	335.5784	1993.748	157231
f_{10}	10	0.150697	0.022151	0.531254	0.019883
	20	0.311937	0.017241	1.519837	0.110482
	30	0.090445	0	0.568672	0.011172

the BSO-II is better than the BSO-I, but it is still not robust when solving f_7 function.

To further compare the BSO-I and BSO-II algorithm, Figures 10 to 19 show curves which display the average evaluation function values over *50* runs vs. iterations for the ten benchmark functions tested. From the figures, it can be easily seen that the BSO-II algorithm performs better

Figure 10. Mean function evaluation values vs. iterations of sphere function

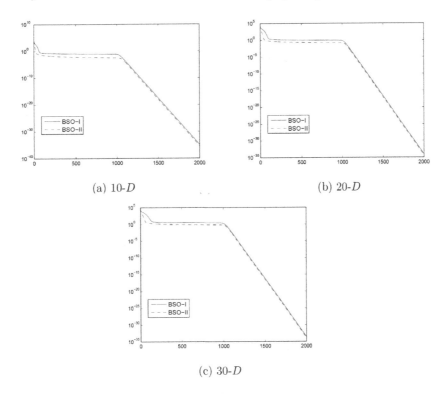

(a) 10-*D* (b) 20-*D*

(c) 30-*D*

Figure 11. Mean function evaluation values vs. iterations of Schwefel's P221

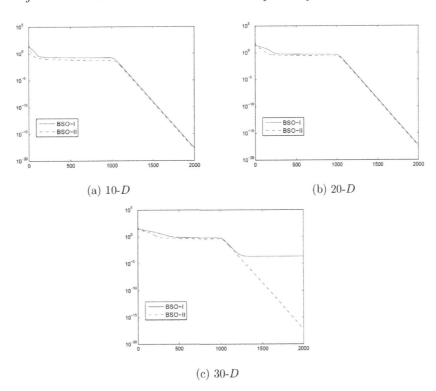

(a) 10-*D* (b) 20-*D*

(c) 30-*D*

Figure 12. Mean function evaluation values vs. iterations of step function

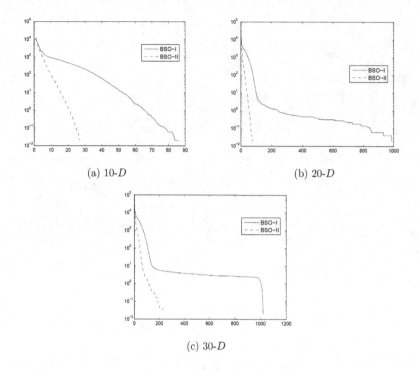

(a) 10-*D*　　　　　　　　(b) 20-*D*

(c) 30-*D*

Figure 13. Mean function evaluation values vs. iterations of Schwefel's P222

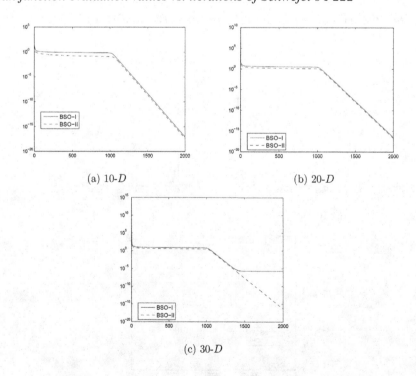

(a) 10-*D*　　　　　　　　(b) 20-*D*

(c) 30-*D*

Figure 14. Mean function evaluation values vs. iterations of quartic noise

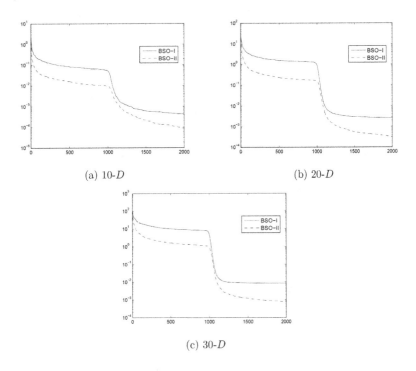

(a) 10-*D*   (b) 20-*D*

(c) 30-*D*

Figure 15. Mean function evaluation values vs. iterations of Ackely function

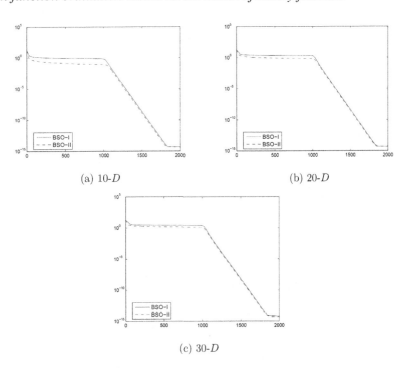

(a) 10-*D*   (b) 20-*D*

(c) 30-*D*

Figure 16. Mean function evaluation values vs. iterations of Rastrigin function

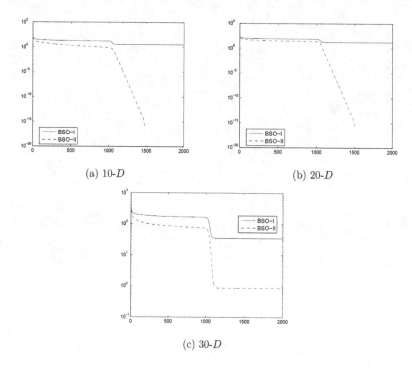

(a) 10-*D*   (b) 20-*D*

(c) 30-*D*

Figure 17. Mean function evaluation values vs. iterations of Rosenbrock function

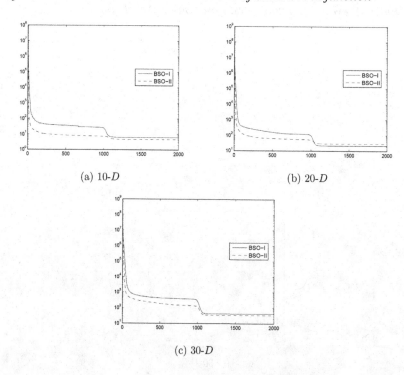

(a) 10-*D*   (b) 20-*D*

(c) 30-*D*

Figure 18. Mean function evaluation values vs. iterations of Schwefel's P226

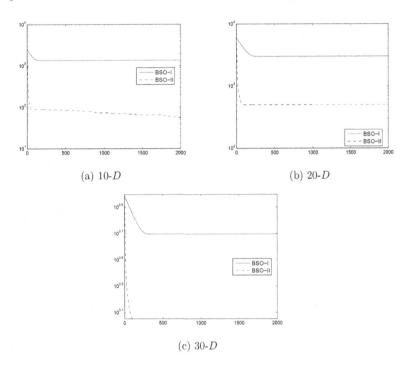

(a) 10-*D*   (b) 20-*D*

(c) 30-*D*

Figure 19. Mean function evaluation values vs. iterations of Griewank function

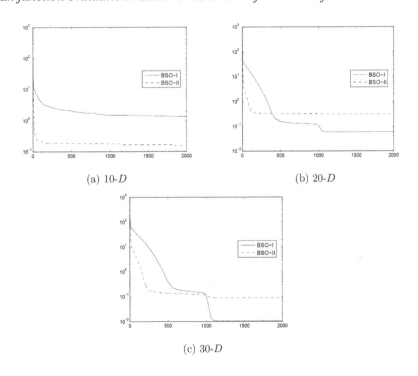

(a) 10-*D*   (b) 20-*D*

(c) 30-*D*

Table 8. Simulation results of D_c and D_e for BSO-I on unimodal functions

F	d	D_c				D_e			
		Mean	Short	Long	Variance	Mean	Small	Large	Variance
f_1	10	3.99E-20	3.02E-20	5.45E-20	2.87E-41	0.674	0.576	0.697	0.00056
	20	7.73E-20	5.84E-20	9.83-20	7.02E-41	0.658	0.566	0.697	0.000893
	30	9.92E-20	7.47E-20	1.16E-19	1.10E-40	0.645	0.473	0.695	0.001978
f_2	10	4.6E-20	3.31E-20	5.58E-20	2.71E-41	0.671	0.583	0.695	0.000528
	20	9.11E-20	6.98E-20	1.15E-19	1.17E-40	0.653	0.579	0.693	0.000653
	30	2.2E-19	1.40E-19	3.57E-19	2.36E-39	0.624	0.488	0.694	0.002807
f_3	10	0.006908	0.005538	0.008269	2.80E-07	0.685	0.666	0.697	7.604E-05
	20	0.007145	0.005921	0.007997	1.89E-07	0.666	0.572	0.695	0.000567
	30	0.006818	0.005485	0.007595	2.15E-07	0.653	0.499	0.693	0.001402
f_4	10	4.44E-19	3.24E-19	5.95E-19	3.44E-39	0.674	0.608	0.699	0.000481
	20	8.54E-19	6.73E-19	1.12E-18	1.01E-38	0.652	0.567	0.698	0.000925
	30	1.12E-18	8.86E-19	1.55E-18	1.83E-38	0.640	0.554	0.694	0.001363
f_5	10	0.06774	0.031242	0.107543	0.000272	0.609	0.484	0.681	0.002202
	20	0.041977	0.016624	0.071656	0.000163	0.604	0.394	0.686	0.003644
	30	0.029224	0.010858	0.04638	6.94E-05	0.591	0.389	0.682	0.004305

Table 9. Simulation results of D_c and D_e for BSO-I on multimodal functions

F	d	D_c				D_e			
		Mean	Short	Long	Variance	Mean	Small	Large	Variance
f_6	10	1.01E-16	7.83E-17	1.24E-16	6.71E-35	0.677	0.617	0.698	0.00023
	20	1.01E-16	7.28E-17	1.25E-16	1.30E-34	0.642	0.560	0.695	0.001086
	30	1.14E-16	1.01E-18	2.21E-16	5.69E-33	0.613	0.384	0.692	0.003186
f_7	10	2.57E-10	1.31E-16	4.39E-10	1.16E-10	0.607	0.450	0.692	0.002966
	20	1.90E-10	4.56E-17	7.13E-10	3.82E-20	0.604	0.448	0.690	0.002892
	30	1.22E-10	1.22E-17	7.10E-10	3.49E-20	0.589	0.378	0.695	0.004818
f_8	10	1.15E-17	6.43E-19	5.77E-17	1.06E-34	0.622	0.505	0.688	0.002294
	20	2.22E-17	1.17E-18	8.01E-17	3.61E-34	0.600	0.456	0.686	0.003408
	30	2.75E-17	1.49E-18	1.81E-16	1.05E-33	0.588	0.349	0.692	0.00625
f_9	10	1.91E-09	5.68E-17	3.89E-09	7.92E-19	0.618	0.115	0.685	0.007802
	20	2.32E-09	3.22E-16	4.14E-09	8.62E-19	0.603	0.378	0.692	0.004574
	30	2.16E-09	6.82E-17	4.30E-09	1.30E-18	0.593	0.097	0.683	0.00893
f_{10}	10	1.21E-11	7.22E-19	8.07E-11	3.72E-22	0.589	0.097	0.693	0.01162
	20	5.01E-11	5.05E-18	9.57E-11	6.74E-22	0.602	0.362	0.689	0.003937
	30	5.21E-11	3.854E-16	9.28E-11	5.74E-22	0.610	0.506	0.696	0.002307

Table 10. Simulation results of D_c and D_e for BSO-II on unimodal functions

F	d	D_c				D_e			
		Mean	Short	Long	Variance	Mean	Small	Large	Variance
f_1	10	2.35E-20	1.80E-20	3.00E-20	5.86E-42	0.674	0.609	0.696	0.000435
	20	5.3E-20	4.39E-20	6.41E-20	2.37E-41	0.676	0.568	0.696	0.000443
	30	7.5E-20	6.48E-20	8.77E-20	3.51E-41	0.674	0.612	0.695	0.000363
f_2	10	3.16E-20	2.50E-20	4.16E-20	1.36E-41	0.675	0.597	0.697	0.000592
	20	7.4E-20	5.56E-20	8.36E-20	3.47E-41	0.658	0.586	0.694	0.000782
	30	1.06E-19	9.13E-20	1.22E-19	5.64E-41	0.658	0.540	0.696	0.001079
f_3	10	0.007209	0.005138	0.008104	2.81E-07	0.685	0.652	0.698	8.749E-05
	20	0.007577	0.006727	0.008262	1.37E-07	0.685	0.610	0.697	0.000214
	30	0.00797	0.007136	0.008711	1.77E-07	0.677	0.622	0.695	0.000298
f_4	10	2.51E-19	1.77E-19	3.58E-19	1.42E-39	0.667	0.546	0.697	0.000904
	20	5.58E-19	4.59E-19	8.08E-19	5.04E-39	0.658	0.509	0.699	0.001228
	30	8.14E-19	5.89E-19	1.11E-18	9.52E-39	0.662	0.567	0.696	0.001039
f_5	10	0.073914	0.052208	0.104325	0.000129	0.649	0.509	0.695	0.00143
	20	0.066032	0.044808	0.095853	0.000149	0.638	0.515	0.692	0.001513
	30	0.062562	0.041369	0.102545	0.000142	0.624	0.326	0.688	0.003219

Table 11. Simulation results of D_c and D_e for BSO-II on multimodal functions

F	d	D_c				D_e			
		Mean	Short	Long	Variance	Mean	Small	Large	Variance
f_6	10	9.83E-17	1.13E-18	1.25E-16	8.10E-34	0.684	0.616	0.698	0.00025
	20	1.17E-16	7.84E-17	1.47E-16	1.68E-34	0.655	0.570	0.693	0.000735
	30	1.02E-16	5.82E-17	1.38E-16	3.12E-34	0.597	0.419	0.691	0.00392
f_7	10	4.63E-10	3.95E-10	5.28E-10	1.12E-21	0.688	0.665	0.698	5.111E-05
	20	4.9E-10	4.10E-10	5.46E-10	8.55E-22	0.681	0.615	0.698	0.000203
	30	4.85E-10	4.03E-10	5.68E-10	8.28E-22	0.663	0.590	0.698	0.000578
f_8	10	1.93E-13	3.12E-19	9.66E-12	1.87E-24	0.589	0.411	0.687	0.004572
	20	1.52E-16	7.17E-19	6.67E-16	1.98E-32	0.599	0.434	0.683	0.003304
	30	1.38E-16	8.33E-19	6.48E-16	2.28E-32	0.585	0.468	0.668	0.002776
f_9	10	2.13E-09	0	3.22E-09	6.53E-19	0.571	0.097	0.685	0.024857
	20	3.42E-09	0	4.95E-09	1.38E-18	0.595	0.097	0.693	0.024992
	30	5.79E-09	3.21E-09	7.72E-09	9.25E-19	0.634	0.443	0.697	0.003643
f_{10}	10	3.24E-11	1.51E-19	6.07E-11	5.18E-22	0.623	0.421	0.694	0.002855
	20	5.89E-11	1.35E-18	1.04E-10	1.04E-21	0.625	0.493	0.694	0.002619
	30	8.63E-11	2.99E-20	1.24E-10	1.40E-21	0.631	0.499	0.691	0.002384

Figure 20. Mean average inter-cluster distance vs. iterations of sphere function

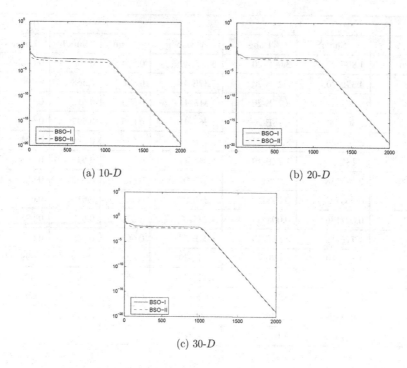

(a) 10-*D* (b) 20-*D*

(c) 30-*D*

Figure 21. Mean average inter-cluster distance vs. iterations of Schwefel's P221

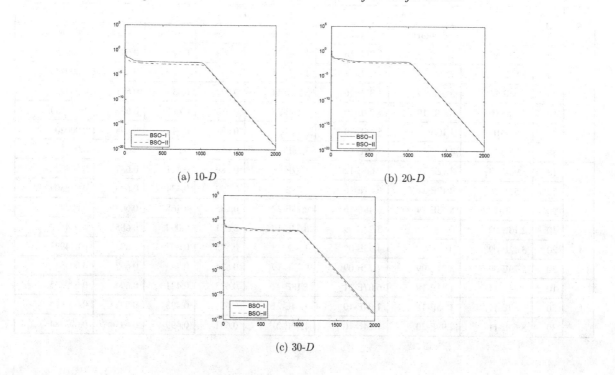

(a) 10-*D* (b) 20-*D*

(c) 30-*D*

than the BSO-I algorithm for all the benchmark functions with all three different dimensions except the Griewank function with dimension *20* and *30*. For Griewnak function with dimension *10*, the BSO-I can't obtain very good results but the BSO-II could. Therefore, even for the Griewank function, the BSO-II could be a better choice compared with the BSO-I algorithm. For function f_9, even though still not very good results are obtained by BSO-II, but BSO-II performs much better than BSO-I does.

Diversity

During each iteration, the population of individuals is clustered into *m* clusters. Individuals in each cluster are scattered with different distribution over iterations. To measure and monitor the distribution of individuals in each cluster, the following average intra-cluster distance is defined

$$d_c(x_i, x_j) = \left\| x_i - x_j \right\| \tag{4a}$$

$$\tilde{d}_c(x_i, x_j) = \frac{d_c(x_i, x_j)}{\left\| a - b \right\|} \tag{4b}$$

$$D_c = \frac{2}{q(q-1)} \sum_{i=1}^{q} \sum_{j=i+1}^{q} \tilde{d}(x_i, x_j) \tag{4c}$$

where *q* is the number of individuals in a cluster; $d(x_i, x_j)$ is the Euclidean distance between individual x_i and x_j; *a* and *b* are dynamic range; $\tilde{d}(x_i, x_j)$ is the normalized Euclidean distance between individual x_i and x_j; D_c is the normalized average intra-cluster distance for a cluster. For *m=5*, there will be *5* intra-cluster distances. In addition to *m* average intra-cluster distances, there will be one average inter-cluster distance to measure and/or monitor the distribution of cluster centers. The above formula for calculating average intra-cluster distance can also be utilized to calculate

the average inter-cluster distance except that here the x_i is the *i*th cluster center and number of individuals is *m*.

Over iterations, the number of individuals in each cluster will change. To measure and monitor the distribution of number of individuals in each cluster over whole population, the following inter-cluster diversity is defined

$$D_v = \sum_{i=1}^{m} \frac{(n_i - \bar{n})^2}{m} , \ \bar{n} = \frac{\sum_{i=1}^{m} n_i}{m} \tag{5}$$

where *m* is the number of clusters, n_i is the number of individuals in the *i*th cluster. D_v is similar to the definition of variance for distribution of number of individuals in each cluster among the population.

Another similar definition of the inter-cluster diversity can be defined as

$$D_e = -\sum_{i=1}^{m} p_i \log(p_i), \ \ p_i = \frac{n_i}{n} \tag{6}$$

where *m* is the number of clusters, n_i is the number individuals in the *i*th cluster. Therefore p_i is the percentage of individuals that the *i*th cluster has over the population. D_e is similar to the definition of information entropy. Therefore it can be looked as a measurement of information entropy for the population. When all the individuals are located in one cluster, the D_e has the smallest value, which is *0*; when all the individuals are equally distributed into each cluster, D_e has the largest value, which is *log(m)*. If *m =5*, D_e = *log(5) = 0.699*.

Table 8 and 9 give the results of average inter-cluster distance D_c and inter-cluster diversity D_e for ten tested benchmark functions at the end of BSO-I running. Table 10 and 11 give the results of average inter-cluster distance D_c and inter-cluster diversity D_e for ten tested benchmark functions at the end of BSO-II running. Figures 20-29 show mean average inter-cluster distance over *50* runs vs. iterations for the ten benchmark functions,

Figure 22. Mean average inter-cluster distance vs. iterations of step function

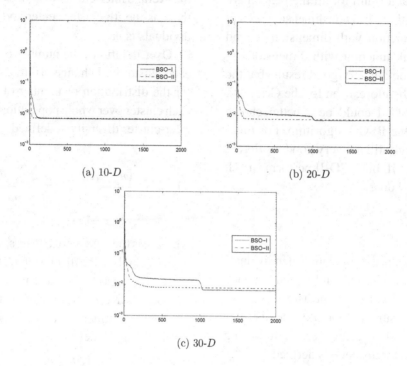

(a) 10-*D*

(b) 20-*D*

(c) 30-*D*

Figure 23. Mean average inter-cluster distance vs. iterations of Schwefel's P222

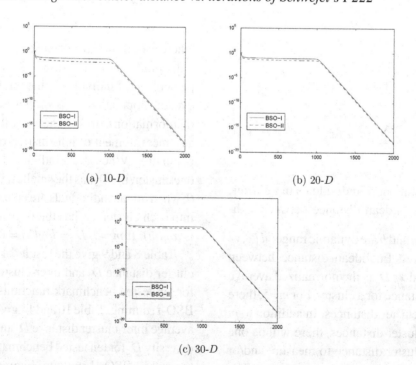

(a) 10-*D*

(b) 20-*D*

(c) 30-*D*

Figure 24. Mean average inter-cluster distance vs. iterations of quartic noise

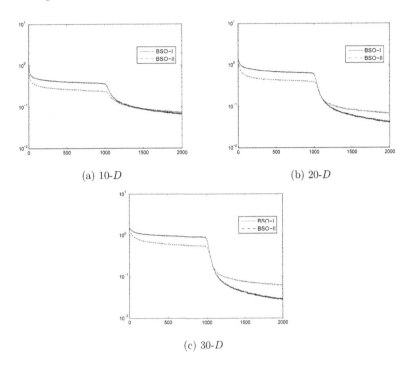

(a) 10-*D*   (b) 20-*D*

(c) 30-*D*

Figure 25. Mean average inter-cluster distance vs. iterations of Ackely function

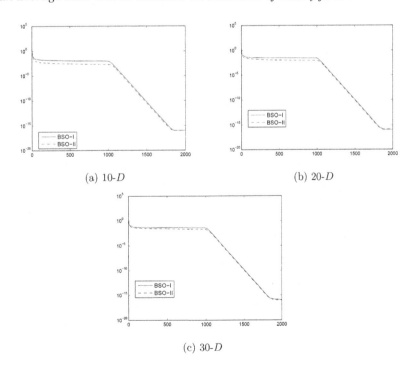

(a) 10-*D*   (b) 20-*D*

(c) 30-*D*

Figure 26. Mean average inter-cluster distance vs. iterations of Rastrigin function

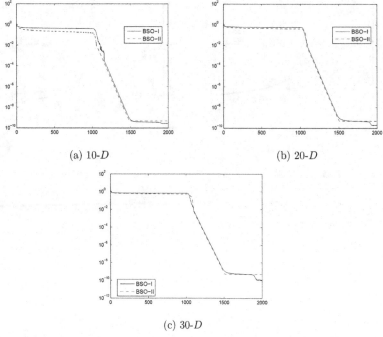

(a) 10-*D*   (b) 20-*D*

(c) 30-*D*

Figure 27. Mean average inter-cluster distance vs. iterations of Rosenbrock function

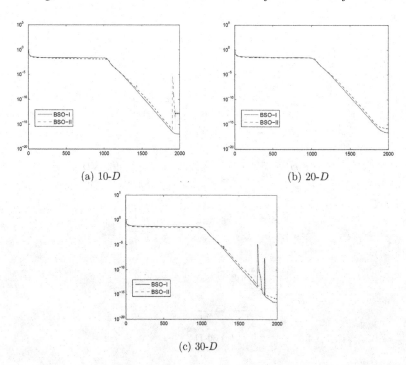

(a) 10-*D*   (b) 20-*D*

(c) 30-*D*

Figure 28. Mean average inter-cluster distance vs. iterations of Schwefel's P226

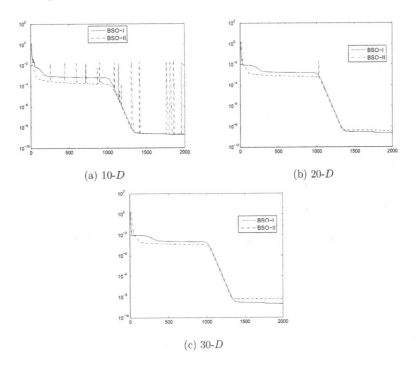

Figure 29. Mean average inter-cluster distance vs. iterations of Griewank function

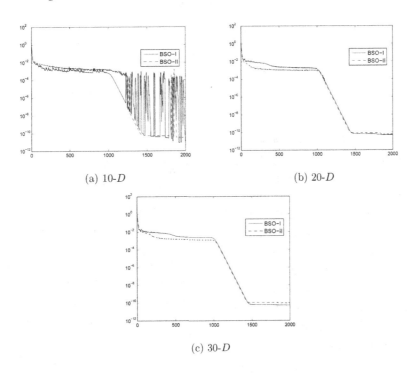

respectively. From both the Table 8-11 and Figure 20-29, it could be easily observed that the average inter-cluster distance quickly decreases over iterations and gets to very small values way before reaching the prefixed maximum iteration number for both BSO algorithms, which indicates that m clusters move close to each other very quickly, and therefore the algorithms may lose their search capabilities quickly, may converge quickly, or may be stuck in (local) optima quickly. By double checking the cluster centers over iterations, the same observation can be obtained. That tells us that when the above situation occurs, further improvement could be achieved by randomly move away from current cluster centers and at the same time increase the step-size to a relatively large value which then will be dynamically adjusted according to the formula (3).

The mean inter-cluster diversities of *50* runs over iterations for all benchmark functions seem to have similar behaviors except function f_9 with dimension *10* and *20*. Figure 30-31 display the curves of mean inter-cluster diversities over *50* runs vs. iterations for function f_1 as an example for unimodal functions and for function f_7 as an example for multimodal functions. Figure 32 displays the curves of mean inter-cluster diversities over *50* runs vs. iterations for function f_9 with dimension *20*. From Figure 30 and 31, the mean inter-cluster diversities tend to have relatively large values, which indicate that the population of individuals is generally well-uniformly divided into m clusters. This may be because the fixed number of clusters and the k-means clustering algorithm with randomly selecting k individuals as initial cluster centroid positions are used over iterations in the implementation of the BSO algorithms. If different initialization method for k-means clustering algorithm or a different clustering algorithm especially those with un-fixed number of clusters such as the self-organizing feature map is utilized, the mean inter-cluster diversity may behave quite different. From Figure 32 and Table 11, it can be seen that toward the end of BSO-II running for

function f_9, the number of individuals in each cluster is not uniformly distributed anymore, but clustered into one cluster with other *4* clusters with only *1* individual, in which the

$$D_e = -\left(4 * \frac{1}{100} * log_{10}\left(\frac{1}{100}\right) + \frac{96}{100} * log_{10}\left(\frac{96}{100}\right)\right) = 0.097.$$

FUTURE RESEARCH DIRECTIONS

There are two opposite operations in the BSO algorithm: convergent operation by utilizing clustering methods to converge to the m cluster centers and divergent operation by adding noise to generate new individuals. In one perspective, the future researches could/should be done alone the direction on designing different types of convergent operation and divergent operation. By design, both operations are conducted in the solution space, therefore, in another perspective, any and/or both operations could be designed to be conducted in other space, e.g. in objective space instead of solution space when solving multi-objective optimization problem. Furthermore, the original BSO was originally designed to solve real-valued optimization problems, but with some modifications, it should be able to solve discrete and binary optimization problems.

CONCLUSION

In this paper, we first modeled the human brainstorming process, then introduced two versions of Brain Storm Optimization algorithms. It is natural to believe that BSO algorithms should be superior to the optimization algorithms inspired by collective behavior of injects such as ants, birds, *etc.* because the BSO algorithms were inspired by the human brainstorming process. The proposed BSO algorithms were implemented and tested on ten benchmark functions, of which five are unimodal functions and the other five are multimodal

Figure 30. Mean D_e over 50 runs vs. iterations for sphere function with dimension d = 20

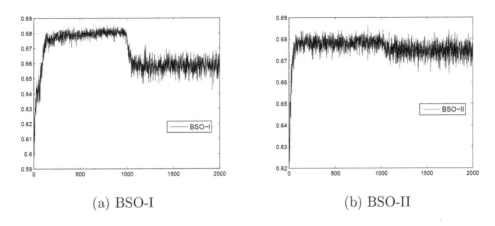

(a) BSO-I   (b) BSO-II

Figure 31. Mean D_e over 50 runs vs. iterations for Rastrigin function with dimension d = 20

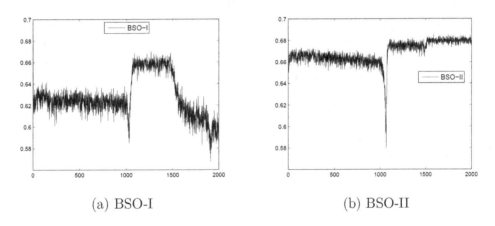

(a) BSO-I   (b) BSO-II

Figure 32. Mean D_e over 50 runs vs. iterations for Schwefel's P226 with dimension d = 20

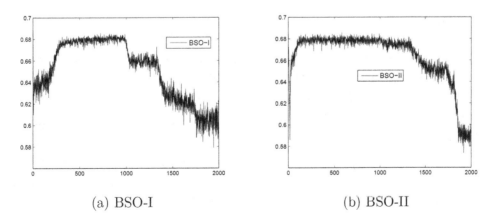

(a) BSO-I   (b) BSO-II

functions. Simulation results showed that both BSO algorithms performed reasonably well, and BSO-II performs better than BSO-I does in general. Furthermore, average inter-cluster distance D_c and inter-cluster diversity D_e were defined to measure and monitor the distribution of cluster centroids and the information entropy of the BSO population. Simulation results on D_c showed that further performance improvement for the BSO algorithms could be achieved by taking advantage of information revealed by the D_c, which is also one of future research directions.

Good optimization algorithms for solving complicated and nonlinear optimization problems should have the capability to converge in order to find better and better solutions, but at the same time, it should have the capability to diverge in order to escape from local optima which are not good enough solutions for the problem to be solved. The BSO algorithm during each iteration involves two opposite operations. One is the converge operation. Another is the diverge operation. Depending on the amplitude of noise, different scales of areas can be searched by the BSO algorithm. Therefore, the BSO algorithms naturally include contraction and expansion operations during each iteration by design. It should be a good choice for solving complicated and nonlinear optimization problems.

ACKNOWLEDGMENT

This paper is partially supported by National Natural Science Foundation of China under Grant Number 60975080 and 61273367, and by the Suzhou Science and Technology Project under Grant Number SYJG0919.

REFERENCES

Carmelo, J. A., Bastos-Filho, C.J.A., De Lima Neto, F.B., Anthony, J. C. C., Lins, A.J.C.C., Nascimento, A.I.S., & Lima, M.P. (2008). A novel search algorithm based on fish school behavior. In *Proceedings of IEEE International Conference on Systems, Man and Cybernetics* (pp. 2646-2651). IEEE.

de Castro, J. N., & Von Zuben, F. J. (1999). *Artificial immune systems: Part I -Basic theory and applications* (Tech. Rep. No. DCA-RT 01/99). Brazil, Campinas: School of Computing and Electrical Engineering, State University of Campinas.

Dorigo, M., Maniezzo, V., & Colorni, A. (1996). The ant system: Optimization by a colony of cooperating agents. *IEEE Transactions. Systems, Man. Cybernetics B, 26*(1), 29–41. doi:10.1109/3477.484436

Eberhart, R. C., & Shi, Y. (2007). *Computational intelligence, concepts to implementation*. San Francisco, CA: Morgan Kaufmann.

Eusuff, M., Lansey, K., & Pasha, F. (2006). Shuffled frog-leaping algorithm: A memetic meta-heuristic for discrete optimization. *Engineering Optimization, 38*(2), 129–154. doi:10.1080/03052150500384759

Fogel, L. J. (1962). Autonomous automata. *Industrial Research, 4,* 14–19.

Holland, J. H. (1975). *Adaptation in natural and artificial systems*. Ann Arbor, MI: University of Michigan Press.

Hosseini, H. (2009). The intelligent water drops algorithm: A nature-inspired swarm-based optimization algorithm. *International Journal of Bio-inspired Computation, 1*(1/2), 71–79. doi:10.1504/IJBIC.2009.022775

Kohonen, T., & Honkela, T. (2007). Kohonen network. *Scholarpedia*, 2(1), 1568. doi:10.4249/scholarpedia.1568

Koza, J. R. (1992). *Genetic programming: On the programming of computers by means of natural selection*. Cambridge, MA: MIT Press.

MacQueen, J. (1967). Some methods for classification and analysis of multivariate observations. In *Proceedings of the 5th Berkeley Symposium on Mathematical Statistics and Probability* (pp. 281-297). Academic Press.

Nock, R., & Nielsen, F. (2006). On weighting clustering. *IEEE Transactions on Pattern Analysis and Machine Intelligence*, 28(8), 1223–1235. doi:10.1109/TPAMI.2006.168 PMID:16886859

Osborn, A. F. (1963). *Applied imagination: Principles and procedures of creative problem solving* (3rd ed.). New York, NY: Charles Scribner's Son.

Passino, K. M. (2010). Bacterial foraging optimization. *International Journal of Swarm Intelligence Research*, 1(1), 1–16. doi:10.4018/jsir.2010010101

Pavlyukevich, I. (2007). Lévy flights, nonlocal search and simulated annealing. *Journal of Computational Physics*, 226(2), 1830–1844. doi:10.1016/j.jcp.2007.06.008

Rechenberg, I. (1973). *Evolutions strategie: Optimierung technischer Systeme nach Prinzipien der biologischen Evolution*. Stuttgart, Germany: Frommann-Holzboog.

Shi, Y. (2011, June 11-15). Brain storm optimization algorithm. In Y. Tan, Y. Shi, Y. Chai, & G. Wang (Eds.), *Proceedings of the Second International Conference on Advances in Swarm Intelligence* (LNCS) (vol. 6728, pp. 303-309). Berlin: Springer.

Shi, Y., & Eberhart, R. C. (1998). A modified particle swarm optimizer. In *Proceedings of the IEEE International Conference on Evolutionary Computation*. Anchorage, AK: IEEE.

Shi, Y., & Eberhart, R. C. (2008). Population diversity of particle swarm optimization. In *Proceedings of the Congress on Evolutionary Computation*. Hong Kong, China: Academic Press.

Shi, Y., & Eberhart, R. C. (2009). Monitoring of particle swarm optimization. *Frontiers of Computer Science in China*, 3(1), 31–37. doi:10.1007/s11704-009-0008-4

Smith, R. (2002). *The 7 levels of change* (2nd ed.). Arlington, VA: Tapeslry Press.

Theodoridis, S., & Koutroumbas, K. (2006). *Pattern recognition* (3rd ed.). New York, NY: Academic Press.

Tovey, C. (2004). The honey bee algorithm: A biological inspired approach to internet server optimization. *Engineering Enterprise, the Alumni Magazine for ISyE at Georgia Institute of Technology*, 13-15.

Xu, R., & Wunsch, D. II. (2005). Survey of clustering algorithms. *IEEE Transactions on Neural Networks*, 16(3), 645–678. doi:10.1109/TNN.2005.845141 PMID:15940994

Yang, X. (2008). *Nature-inspired metaheuristic algorithms*. Beckington, UK: Luniver Press.

Yao, X., Liu, Y., & Lin, G. (1997). Evolutionary programming made faster. *IEEE Transactions on Evolutionary Computation*, 3, 82–102.

ADDITIONAL READING

Cheng, S., Shi, Y., Qin, Q., & Gao, S. (2013, April). Solution clustering analysis in brain storm optimization algorithm. In *Proceedings of Swarm Intelligence (SIS), 2013 IEEE Symposium on* (pp. 111-118). IEEE.

Duan, H., Li, S., & Shi, Y. (2013). Predator-prey based brain storm optimization for DC brushless motor. *IEEE Transactions on Magnetics*, 49(10), 5336–5340. doi:10.1109/TMAG.2013.2262296

Jadhav, H. T., Sharma, U., Patel, J., & Roy, R. (2012, December). Brain storm optimization algorithm based economic dispatch considering wind power. In *Power and Energy (PECon), 2012 IEEE International Conference on* (pp. 588-593).

Krishnanand, K. R., Hasani, S. M. F., Panigrahi, B. K., & Panda, S. K. (2013). Optimal Power Flow Solution Using Self–Evolving Brain–Storming Inclusive Teaching–Learning–Based Algorithm. In *Advances in Swarm Intelligence* (pp. 338–345). Springer Berlin Heidelberg. doi:10.1007/978-3-642-38703-6_40

Radakrishnan, K. K. (2013, June). Optimal Power Flow Solution Using Self-Evolving Brain-Storming Inclusive Teaching-Learning-Based Algorithm. In *4th International Conference on Swarm Intelligence, Harbin, China, June 12-15, 2013*.

Ramanand, K. R., Krishnanand, K. R., Panigrahi, B. K., & Mallick, M. K. (2012). Brain Storming Incorporated Teaching–Learning–Based Algorithm with Application to Electric Power Dispatch. In Swarm, Evolutionary, and Memetic Computing (pp. 476-483). Springer Berlin Heidelberg.

Shi, Y., Xue, J., & Wu, Y. (2013). Multi-objective optimization based on brain storm optimization algorithm. *International Journal of Swarm Intelligence Research*, 4(3), 1–21. doi:10.4018/ijsir.2013070101

Sun, C., Duan, H., & Shi, Y. (2013). Optimal satellite formation reconfiguration based on closed-loop brain storm optimization. *Computational Intelligence Magazine, IEEE*, 8(4), 39–51. doi:10.1109/MCI.2013.2279560

Xue, J., Wu, Y., Shi, Y., & Cheng, S. (2012). Brain storm optimization algorithm for multi-objective optimization problems. In *Advances in Swarm Intelligence* (pp. 513–519). Springer Berlin Heidelberg. doi:10.1007/978-3-642-30976-2_62

Yang, Y. T., Shi, Y. H., & Xia, S. R. (2013). Discussion mechanism based brain storm optimization algorithm. *Journal of Zhejiang University*, 47(10), 1705–1711. doi: doi:10.3785/j.issn.1008-973X.2013.10.002

Zhan, Z. H., Chen, W. N., Lin, Y., Gong, Y. J., Li, Y. L., & Zhang, J. (2013, April). Parameter investigation in brain storm optimization. In *Swarm Intelligence (SIS), 2013 IEEE Symposium on* (pp. 103-110).

Zhan, Z. H., Zhang, J., Shi, Y. H., & Liu, H. L. (2012, June). A modified brain storm optimization. In *Evolutionary Computation (CEC), 2012 IEEE Congress on* (pp. 1-8).

Zhou, D., Shi, Y., & Cheng, S. (2012). Brain storm optimization algorithm with modified step-size and individual generation. In *Advances in Swarm Intelligence* (pp. 243–252). Springer Berlin Heidelberg. doi:10.1007/978-3-642-30976-2_29

KEY TERMS AND DEFINITIONS

Brain Storm Optimization (BSO) Algorithm: It is a population-based optimization algorithm and belongs to swarm intelligence algorithms. It was inspired by one of the human problem solving skills, i.e. brainstorming process. In each generation of BSO, it consists of two major operations, that is, a convergent operation through clustering approach, and a divergent operation through adding noise.

Brainstorming Process: A process that is facilitated by a facilitator and through which a group of people with diverse background gather together to generate diverse ideas to solve a problem that generally can't, or at least is very difficult to, be solved by a single person.

K-Means Clustering Algorithm: A clustering algorithm that partition n data points into k clusters so that each point belong to a cluster which the point is the nearest to.

Population-Based Optimization Algorithm: An optimization algorithm that is usually a heuristic algorithm and consists of a group of individuals (also called a population of individuals). Each individual represents a potential solution to the optimization problem to be solved. Through collaboration and/or competition among the population of individuals, a new population of individuals is obtained generation over generation in the hope that the population of individuals is moving towards better and better solution areas over generation.

Swarm Intelligence: A collection of heuristic optimization algorithms that are inspired by the collective behaviors of simple objects, such as birds in particle swarm optimization (PSO) algorithm, bacterial in bacterial foraging optimization (BFO) algorithm, *etc.* These simple objects cooperate and compete among themselves to have a high tendency to move toward better and better search areas. As a consequence, it is the collective behavior of all individuals that makes a swarm intelligence algorithm to be effective and efficient in problem optimization.

Chapter 2
Analysis of Firefly Algorithms and Automatic Parameter Tuning

Xin-She Yang
Middlesex University London, UK

ABSTRACT

Many metaheuristic algorithms are nature-inspired, and most are population-based. Particle swarm optimization is a good example as an efficient metaheuristic algorithm. Inspired by PSO, many new algorithms have been developed in recent years. For example, firefly algorithm was inspired by the flashing behaviour of fireflies. In this chapter, the authors analyze the standard firefly algorithm and study the chaos-enhanced firefly algorithm with automatic parameter tuning. They first compare the performance of these algorithms and then use them to solve a benchmark design problem in engineering. Results obtained by other methods are compared and analyzed. The authors also discuss some important topics for further research.

1. INTRODUCTION

Search for optimality in many optimization applications is a challenging task, and search efficiency is one of the most important measures for an optimization algorithm. In addition, an efficient algorithm does not necessarily guarantee the global optimality is reachable. In fact, many optimization algorithms are only efficient in finding local optima. For example, classic hill-climbing or steepest descent method is very efficient for local optimization. Global optimization typically involves objective functions which can be multi-modal and highly nonlinear. Thus, it is often very challenging to find global optimality, especially for large-scale optimization problems. Recent studies suggest that metaheuristic algorithms such as particle swarm optimization and firefly algorithm are promising in solving these tough optimization problems (Kennedy & Eberhart, 1995; Kennedy et al., 2001; Shi & Eberhart, 1998; Eberhart & Shi, 2000; Yang, 2008; Yang et al., 2013a) .

Most metaheuristic algorithms are nature-inspired, from simulated annealing (Kirkpatrick et al., 1983) to firefly algorithm (Yang, 2008; Yang, 2010a), and from particle swarm optimiza-

DOI: 10.4018/978-1-4666-6328-2.ch002

tion (Kennedy & Eberhart, 1995; Kennedy et al., 2001) to cuckoo search (Yang & Deb, 2010; Yang, 2014). These algorithms have been applied to almost all areas of optimization, design, scheduling and planning, data mining, machine intelligence, and many others (Gandomi et al., 2013a; Talbi, 2009; Yang, 2010a). On the other hand, chaotic tunneling is an important phenomenon in complex systems (Tomsovic, 1994; Podolskiy & Narmanov, 2003; Kohler et al., 1998; Delande & Zakrzewski, 2003; Shudo & Ikeda, 1998; Shudo et al., 2009). Traditional wisdom in optimization is to avoid numerical instability and chaos. Contemporary studies suggest that chaos can assist some algorithms such as genetic algorithms (Yang & Chen, 2002). For example, metaheuristic algorithms often use randomization techniques to increase the diversity of the solutions generated during search iterations (Talbi, 2009; Yang, 2010a). The most common randomization techniques are probably local random walks and Lévy flights (Gutowski, 2001; Pavlyukevich, 2007; Yang 2010b).

The key challenge for global optimization is that nonlinearity leads to multimodality, which in turns will cause problems to almost all optimization algorithms because the search process may be trapped in any local valley, and thus may cause tremendous difficulty to the search process towards global optimality. Even with most well-established stochastic search algorithms such as simulated annealing (Kirkpatrick et al., 1983), care must be taken to ensure it can escape the local modes/optimality. Premature convergence may occur in many algorithms including simulated annealing and genetic algorithms. The key ability of an efficient global search algorithm is to escape local optima, to visit all modes and to converge subsequently at the global optimality.

In this paper, we will first analyze the recently developed firefly algorithm (FA) (Yang, 2008; Yang, 2010b). Under the right conditions, FA can have chaotic behaviour, which can be used as an advantage to enhance the search efficiency, because chaos allow fireflies to sample search space more efficiently. In fact, a chaotic tunnelling feature can be observed in FA simulations when a firefly can tunnel through multimodes and jump from one mode to another modes. This enables the algorithm more versatile in escaping the local optima, and thus can guarantee to find the global optimality. Chaotic tunneling is an important phenomenon in complex systems, but this is the first time that a chaotic tunneling is observed in an optimization algorithm. Through analysis and numerical simulations, we will highlight that intrinsic chaotic characteristics in the FA can enhance the search efficiency. Then, we will introduce automatic parameter tuning to the chaotic firefly algorithm and compare its performance against a set of diverse test functions. Finally, we will apply the FA with automatic parameter tuning to solve a design benchmark whose solutions will be compared with other results in the literature.

2. FIREFLY ALGORITHM

Firefly Algorithm (FA) was developed by Xin-She Yang (Yang, 2008; Yang, 2010b), which was based on the flashing patterns and behaviour of fireflies. In essence, each firefly will be attracted to brighter ones, while at the same time, it explores and searches for prey randomly. In addition, the brightness of a firefly is determined by the landscape of the objective function.

The movement of a firefly i is attracted to another more attractive (brighter) firefly j is determined by

$$x_i^{t+1} = x_i^t + \beta e^{-\gamma r_{ij}^2}(x_j^t - x_i^t) + \alpha \, \varepsilon_i^t, \qquad (1)$$

where α, β and γ are parameters. Here, α controls the scale of randomization, β controls the attractiveness, while γ is a scaling factor. In addition, the second term is due to the attraction. The third term is randomization with α being the randomization parameter, and ε_i^t is a vector of random numbers drawn from a Gaussian distribution or other distributions such as Lévy flights. Obviously, for a given firefly, there are often many more attractive fireflies, and we can update its location in two ways: we can either go through all of them via a loop or use the most attractive one. For multiple modal problems, to use a loop while moving toward each brighter one is usually more effective, though this will lead to a slight increase of algorithm complexity.

Here $\beta \in [0,1]$ is the attractiveness at distance $r = 0$, and $r_{ij} = \| x_i - x_j \|_2$ is the 2-norm or Cartesian distance. For other problems such as scheduling, any measure that can effectively characterize the quantities of interest in the optimization problem can be used as the "distance" r. Furthermore, the randomization term can easily be extended to other distributions such as Lévy flights (Reynolds and Rhodes, 2009).

Firefly algorithm has received great attention in the literature, and there are about 1200 research publications between 2008 to 2014 (until the time of writing this chapter in Jan 2014). A comprehensive review of the firefly algorithm and its diverse variants was carried by Fister et al. (2013). Gandomi et al. (2013b) used various chaotic maps to extend FA with chaos, while Yang (2013) also extended FA to sovle multiobjective optimization problems.

As more studies have shown that FA is very efficient, a natural question is "why FA is so efficient?" To answer this question, let us briefly analyze the firefly algorithm. First, FA is swarm-intelligence-based, so it has the similar advantages that other swarim-intelligence-based algorithms have. In fact, from Equation (1), if we set γ=0 and α=0, FA becomes a simplified version of differential evolution (DE). If we replace x_j^t by the current best solution g*, Equation (1) becomes the accelerated particle swarm optimization (APSO). On the other hand, if we set β=0, FA becomes a variant of simulated annealing (SA). Therefore,

FA captures the characteristics of APSO, DE and SA in the same algorithm, and it is no surprise that FA can perform very efficiently.

Furthermore, FA has two major advantages over other algorithms: automatic subdivision and the ability of dealing with mulimodality. As the local attraction is stronger than the long-distance attraction, the population can automatically subdivide into subgroups, and each subgroup can potentially swarm around each mode. Therefore, FA can deal with multimodal problems naturally and can find multiple global optuma (if any) simultaneously.

3. CHAOS-ENHANCED FA

There are two ways to enhance FA with chaos. One way is to use various chaotic maps to replace some parameters in the standard FA so as to enhance the algorithm performance (Gandomi et al., 2013b). The other way is to use the intrinsic structure in the firefly algorithm by tuning its parameters on the edge of chaos. This latter approach will also show some chaotic tunneling ability, similar to the quantum tunneling in quantum mechanics.

In order to see the intrinsic tunneling ability, let us first carry out the convergence analysis for the firefly algorithm in a framework similar to Clerc and Kennedy's dynamical analysis (Clerc & Kennedy, 2002). For simplicity, we start from the equation for firefly motion without the randomness term

$$x_i^{t+1} = x_i^t + \beta e^{-\gamma r_{ij}^2} (x_j^t - x_i^t). \tag{2}$$

If we focus on a single agent, we can replace x_j^t by the global best g found so far, and we have

$$x_i^{t+1} = x_i^t + \beta e^{-\gamma r_i^2} (g - x_i^t), \tag{3}$$

where the distance r_i can be given by the ℓ_2-norm $r_i^2 = \| g - x_i^t \|_2^2$. In an even simpler 1-D case, we can set $y_t = g - x_i^t$, and we have

$$y_{t+1} = y_t - \beta e^{-\gamma y_t^2} y_t. \tag{4}$$

We can see that γ is a scaling parameter which only affects the scales/size of the firefly movement. In fact, we can let $u_t = \sqrt{\gamma} y_t$ and we have

$$u_{t+1} = u_t [1 - \beta e^{-u_t^2}]. \tag{5}$$

These equations can be analyzed easily using the same methodology for studying the well-known logistic map

$$u_{t+1} = \lambda u_t (1 - u_t). \tag{6}$$

The chaotic map of equation (5) is shown in Figure 1, and the focus on the transition from periodic multiple states to chaotic behaviour is shown in the same figure.

As we can see from Figure 1 that good convergence can be achieved for β<2. There is a transition from periodic to chaos at $\beta \approx 4$. This may be surprising, as the aim of designing a metaheuristic algorithm is to try to find the optimal solution efficiently and accurately. However, chaotic behaviour is not necessarily a nuisance; in fact, we can use it to the advantage of the firefly algorithm.

It is worth pointing out that no explicit form of a random variable distribution can be found for the chaotic map of (5). However, simple chaotic characteristics from (6) can often be used as an efficient mixing technique for generating diverse solutions. Statistically, the logistic mapping (6) with $\lambda = 4$ for the initial states in (0,1) corresponds a beta distribution. From the algorithm implementation point of view, we can use higher

attractiveness β during the early stage of iterations so that the fireflies can explore, even chaotically, the search space more effectively. As the search continues and convergence approaches, we can reduce the attractiveness β gradually, which may increase the overall efficiency of the algorithm. The simulations presented in the rest of this paper will confirm this.

4. AUTOMATIC PARAMETER TUNING

Apart from the population size n, there three parameters in the firefly algorithm. They are α, β and γ, which control the randomness, attractiveness and modal scales, respectively. For most implementations, we can take $\beta = O(1)$, $\alpha = O(1)$ and $\gamma = O(1)$. However, randomness reduction technique is often used as iterations continue, and this is often achieved by using an annealing-like exponential function

$$\alpha = \alpha_0 \eta^t, \tag{7}$$

or

$$\alpha \leftarrow \alpha \eta, \tag{8}$$

where $0 < \eta < 1$ is a cooling parameter. Typically, we can use $\alpha_0 = 1$ and $\eta = 0.9 \sim 0.99$. This equivalently introduces a cooling schedule to the firefly algorithm, as used in the traditional simulated annealing. Recently studies showed this works well (Yang, 2008). There may be better ways to tune this parameter and reduce randomness to be discussed later in this section.

It is worth pointing out that (1) is essentially a random walk biased towards the brighter fireflies. If $\beta_0 = 0$, it becomes a simple random walk.

As it is true for all metaheuristic algorithms, algorithm-dependent parameters can affect the performance of the algorithm of interest greatly, a

Figure 1. The chaotic map of the iteration Formula (5) in the firefly algorithm and the transition between from periodic/multiple states to chaos

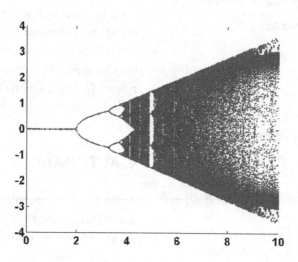

natural question is whether we can automatically tune these parameters? If so, what is the best way to fine-tune these parameters?

For randomness reduction, it should be linked with the diversity of the current solutions. One simple way to automatically tune α is to set α as proportional to the standard deviation of the current solutions. However, for multimodal problems, this standard deviation should be calculated for each local mode among local subgroups of fireflies. For example, for two modes A and B with current best solutions x_a^* and x_b^*, respectively, the population will gradually subdivide into two main subgroups with population sizes of n_1 and n_2, respectively, one around A and one around B. There are two standard deviations σ_A and σ_B which should be calculated among the solutions relative to x_a^* and x_b^*, respectively. Then the overall α should be a function of σ_A and σ_B. The simplest way is to combine them by weighted average

$$\sigma = \frac{\sigma_A n_1 + \sigma_B n_2}{n_1 + n_2}, \quad n_1 + n_2 = n. \quad (9)$$

As iterations continue, σ decreases in general. If we set

$$\alpha = \zeta\sigma, \quad 0 < \zeta < 1, \quad (10)$$

then α is automatically associated with the scale of the problem of interest. In practice, η may be affected by the dimensions d, so in our implementation we used $\zeta = \sqrt{d / (2d+1)}$. The parameter γ should be linked with the scale L of the modes. A simple rule is that the change of the attractiveness term should be O(1) through the search landscape, which provide a simple relationship $\gamma = 1 / \sqrt{L}$. Parameter β control the behavior of fireflies, however, its tuning is more subtle. From the above discussion of (5), when β is large, fireflies may experience chaotic behavior, and this can be used to enhance the search capability of the algorithm. In fact, from our intensive simulations, we have observed that fireflies can tunnel through all modes for multimodal function. This chaotic tunnelling effect of the algorithm can help to search the global optimality for highly nonlinear global optimization problems.

To demonstrate this, we now first use a non-linear multimodal function, namely, Ackley's function

$$f(x) = 20\exp[-0.2\sqrt{\frac{1}{d}\sum_{i=1}^{d}x_i^2}\,] + \exp[\frac{1}{d}\sum_{i=1}^{d}\cos(2\pi x_i)] - (20 + e), \tag{11}$$

which has the global maximum $f_* = 0$ at $x_* = (0, 0, ..., 0)$ in the range of $-32.768 \leq x_i \leq 32.768$ where $i = 1, 2, ..., d$ and d is the number of dimensions. In the 2D case, Ackley's function is shown in Figure 1. For 25 fireflies, a snapshot at $t = 15$ of search process using the firefly algorithm is shown in Figure 2. If we ignore the randomness by setting $\alpha = 0$ and $\beta = 4$ all the time, then we can trace any one particular firefly, say, firefly number 5, its

path of x-component displays a random-noise-like path. It is worth pointing out each firefly has the ability of tunneling through all modes, and distance of the tunnelling is controlled by the scaling factor γ and β.

During the iteration, if we reduce β gradually from a higher value, say, $\beta = 4$ to a lower value $\beta = 1$ by $\beta\eta^t + 1$ and also use equation (7), the algorithm can be expected to converge more quickly. So for the same firefly 5, if we reduce β gradually, as the iteration proceeds, this path will gradually settle down and converge to a global optimal point (Figure 3).

Now we have three version of FA: The standard version of FA with α as a cooling schedule, a chaos-enhanced FA with β reduced gradually, and the chaotic FA in combination with automatic parameter tuning (AutoFA). In the rest of the paper, we will carry out more testing and comparison of their performance.

Figure 2. Ackley's multimodal function

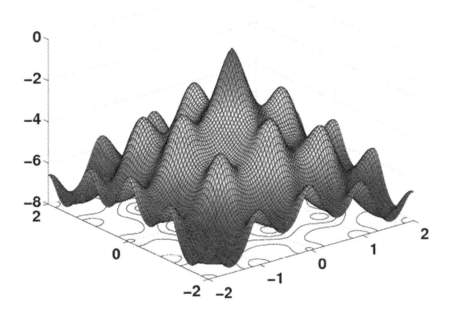

Figure 3. The snapshot of 25 fireflies during iteration $t = 15$

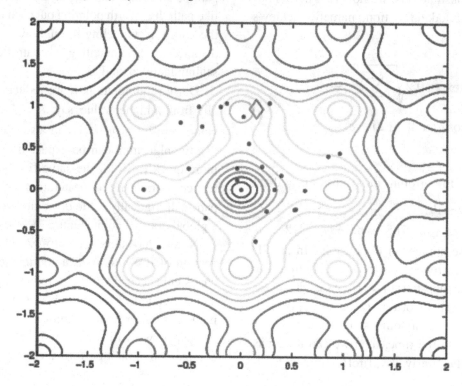

5. NUMERICAL EXPERIMENTS

Various test functions in the literature are designed to test the performance of optimization algorithms. Any new optimization algorithm should also be validated and tested against these benchmark functions. In our simulations, we have used the following test functions.

De Jong's first function is essentially a sphere function

$$f(x) = \sum_{i=1}^{d} x_i^2, \quad x_i \in [-5.12, 5.12], \quad (12)$$

whose global minimum $f_* = 0$ occurs at $x_* = (0, 0, ..., 0)$. Here d is the dimension.

The generalized Rosenbrock's function is given by

$$f(x) = \sum_{i=1}^{d-1} [(1 - x_i)^2 + 100(x_{i+1} - x_i^2)^2], \quad (13)$$

which has a unique global minimum $f(x_*) = 0$ at $x_* = (1, 1, ..., 1)$.

Schwefel's test function is multimodal

$$f(x) = \sum_{i=1}^{d} [-x_i \sin(\sqrt{|x_i|})], \quad -500 \le x_i \le 500, \quad (14)$$

whose global minimum $f_* = -418.9829d$ is at $x_i^* = 420.9687 (i = 1, 2, ..., d)$.

Rastrigin's test function

$$f(x) = 10d + \sum_{i=1}^{d} [x_i^2 - 10\cos(2\pi x_i)], \quad (15)$$

has a unique global minimum $f_* = 0$ at $(0, 0, ..., 0)$ in a hypercube $-5.12 \leq x_i \leq 5.12$ where $i = 1, 2, ..., d$.

Easom's test function has a sharp tip

$$f(x, y) = -\cos(x)\cos(y)\exp[-(x - \pi)^2 - (y - \pi)^2], \tag{16}$$

in the domain $(x, y) \in [-100, 100] \times [-100, 100]$. It has a global minimum of $f_* = -1$ at (π, π) in a very small region.

Rosenbrock's function

$$f(x) = \sum_{i=1}^{d-1} [(x_i - 1)^2 + 100(x_{i+1} - x_i^2)^2], \tag{17}$$

whose global minimum $f_* = 0$ occurs at $x_* = (1, 1, ..., 1)$ in the domain $-5 \leq x_i \leq 5$ where $i = 1, 2, ..., d$. In the 2D case, it is often written as

$$f(x, y) = (x - 1)^2 + 100(y - x^2)^2, \tag{18}$$

which is often referred to as the banana function.

The Michalewicz function

$$f(x) = -\sum_{i=1}^{d} \sin(x_i)[\sin(\frac{ix_i^2}{\pi})]^{2m}, \tag{19}$$

where $m = 10$ and $d = 1, 2, ...$. The global minimum $f_* \approx -1.801$ in 2-D occurs at $(2.20319, 1.57049)$, Griewangk's test function has many local minima

$$f(x) = \frac{1}{4000}\sum_{i=1}^{d} x_i^2 - \prod_{i=1}^{d} \cos(\frac{x_i}{\sqrt{i}}) + 1, \tag{20}$$

but a unique global mimimum $f_* = 0$ at $(0, 0, ..., 0)$ for all $-600 \leq x_i \leq 600$ where $i = 1, 2, ..., d$.

Yang's test function (Yang, 2010a)

$$f(x) = (\sum_{i=1}^{d} |x_i|)\exp[-\sum_{i=1}^{d} \sin(x_i^2)], \quad -2\pi \leq x_i \leq 2\pi, \tag{21}$$

which has a global minimum $f_* = 0$ at $(0, 0, ..., 0)$.

Rosenbrock's stochastic function was extended by Yang (Yang, 2010a)

$$f(x) = \sum_{i=1}^{d-1} [\varepsilon_i(x_i - 1)^2 + 100\varepsilon_{i+1}(x_{i+1} - x_i^2)^2], \tag{22}$$

whose global minimum $f_* = 0$ occurs at $x_* = (1, 1, ..., 1)$ in the domain $-5 \leq x_i \leq 5$ where $i = 1, 2, ..., d$.

The functions used in Table 1 are (1) Michaelwicz ($d = 16$), (2) Rosenrbrock ($d = 16$), (3) De Jong ($d = 16$), (4) Schwefel ($d = 8$), (5) Ackley ($d = 16$), (6) Rastrigin, (7) Easom, (8) Griewangk, (9) Yang $d = 16$, (10) Robsenbrock's stochastic function ($d = 8$).

We ran the simulations for 50 times for a given accuracy of $\delta = 10^{-5}$, and the search stops when the found best solution g_* is near the known solution x_*, that $\| x_* - g_* \| \leq \delta$. We then recorded the number of iterations for finding such best solutions. In this table, the second column corresponds to the average number of iterations and its standard deviation. The third column is the average ratio of the number of iterations of chaotic FA to the number of iterations for the standard FA when $\beta = 1$ (no chaos). The fourth column is the average ratio of the number of iterations of AutoFA to that of standard FA. These ratios reflect the computational effort saved. For example, if the average ratio is about 0.1, than about 90% of the computing effort is saved, that

Table 1. Comparison of standard FA, chaotic FA and AutoFA

Test Functions	FA	Chaotic FA (ratio)	AutoFA (ratio)
1	3752 ± 725	0.154 ± 0.022	0.108 ± 0.015
2	7792 ± 2923	0.175 ± 0.024	0.123 ± 0.017
3	2319 ± 337	0.069 ± 0.014	0.054 ± 0.012
4	7540 ± 125	0.097 ± 0.018	0.072 ± 0.014
5	3172 ± 723	0.071 ± 0.012	0.051 ± 0.010
6	11981 ± 970	0.093 ± 0.011	0.069 ± 0.009
7	7925 ± 1799	0.145 ± 0.027	0.127 ± 0.024
8	12592 ± 3715	0.112 ± 0.019	0.089 ± 0.012
9	7390 ± 2189	0.079 ± 0.011	0.057 ± 0.009
10	9125 ± 2149	0.037 ± 0.014	0.330 ± 0.049

is the efficiency has been increased by a factor of about 10.

We can see that the chaos-enhanced firefly algorithm indeed can improve its search efficiency significantly.

6. DESIGN OPTIMIZATION

There are many design benchmarks in the literature, however, the results are fragmental, as not all results are available and comparable. Here we select a well-known welded beam design, which has many results obtained by other methods in the literature (Ragsdell & Phillips, 1976; Cagnina et al, 2008; Gandomi et al, 2013a; Gandomi et al., 2011). The problem typically has four design variables: the width w and length L of the welded area, the depth h and thickness h of the main beam. The objective is to minimise the overall fabrication cost, under the appropriate constraints of shear stress τ, bending stress σ, buckling load P and maximum end deflection δ.

The problem can be written as

$$\text{Minimise } f(x) = 1.10471w^2 L + 0.04811dh(14.0 + L), \tag{23}$$

subject to

$$
\begin{aligned}
g_1(x) &= w - h \leq 0, \\
g_2(x) &= \delta(x) - 0.25 \leq 0, \\
g_3(x) &= \tau(x) - 13,600 \leq 0, \\
g_4(x) &= \sigma(x) - 30,000 \leq 0, \\
g_5(x) &= 0.10471w^2 + 0.04811hd(14 + L) - 5.0 \leq 0, \\
g_6(x) &= 0.125 - w \leq 0, \\
g_7(x) &= 6000 - P(x) \leq 0,
\end{aligned}
\tag{24}
$$

where

$$\sigma(x) = \frac{504,000}{hd^2},$$

$$Q = 6000(14 + \frac{L}{2}),$$

$$D = \frac{1}{2}\sqrt{L^2 + (w+d)^2},$$

$$J = \sqrt{2}\,wL[\frac{L^2}{6} + \frac{(w+d)^2}{2}],$$

$$\delta = \frac{65,856}{30,000hd^3},$$

$$\beta = \frac{QD}{J},$$

$$\alpha = \frac{6000}{\sqrt{2}wL},$$

$$\tau(x) = \sqrt{\alpha^2 + \frac{\alpha\beta L}{D} + \beta^2},$$

$$P = 0.61423 \times 10^6 \frac{dh^3}{6}(1 - \frac{d\sqrt{30/48}}{28}).$$

$$(25)$$

The simple limits or bounds are $0.1 \leq L, d \leq 10$ and $0.1 \leq w, h \leq 2.0$. This benchmark has been solved by many different methods, including simulated annealing (Hedar & Fukushima, 2006), genetic algorithms (Deb, 1991), particle swarm optimization (He et al., 2004; Cagnina et al., 2008), harmony search (Lee & Geem, 2004), differential evolution (Zhang et al., 2008) and firefly algorithm in this study.

It is worth pointing out that the constraints should be handled appropriately. In this case, we have used the penalty functions to incorporate the above nonlinear constraints (Yang, 2010a). Using our chaotic firefly algorithm with automatic parameter tuning, we have the following optimal solution

$$x_* = (w, L, d, h)$$
$$= (0.20573, 3.47049, 9.03662, 0.20573),$$
$$(26)$$

with

$$f(x^*)_{\min} = 1.72485. \qquad (27)$$

Our results are the same or better than the results obtained by other methods as summarized in Table 2.

From the above validation, comparison and benchmark design, we can see that chaotic FA with automatic parameter tuning is very efficient. Good convergence can be obtained by chaos-assisted tunnelling and automatic parameter adjustment. Effect and improvements become significant for multimodal problems.

7. FUTURE RESEARCH DIRECTIONS

Despite the success of the firefly algorithm and its diverse variants, there is still room for improvement. Firstly, theoretical analysis concerning the convergence and stability of the firefly algorithms

Table 2. Welded beam design

Refs	Method	w	L	d	h	cost	Evaluations
Deb	GA	0.2489	6.1730	8.1789	0.2533	2.4331	320,080
He et al.	PSO	0.2444	6.2175	8.2915	0.2444	2.3810	30,000
Cagnina et al.	PSO	0.2057	3.4705	9.0366	0.2057	1.7248	24,000
Hedar & Fukushima	SA	0.2444	6.2158	8.2939	0.2444	2.3811	56,243
Lee & Geem	HS	0.2442	6.2231	8.2915	0.2443	2.381	110,000
Zhang et al.	DE	0.2444	6.2175	8.2915	0.2444	2.3810	24,000
This study	AutoFA	0.2057	3.4705	9.0366	0.2057	1.7248	20,000

will be useful to gain insight into the working mechanisms of the algorithm. Secondly, it can be fruitful to use FA and also multiobjective FA to study large-scale, real-world applications. Thirdly, parameter tuning and control can be extended further so that parameters can be automatically tuned for a given problem (Yang et al., 2013b). Finally, hybridization with other algorithms may further improve the performance in many other ways.

8. CONCLUSION

Search for optimality in complex systems and global optimization problems requires efficient algorithms. Metaheuristic algorithms such as particle swarm optimization and firefly algorithm are becoming very powerful. We have used a dynamical system approach to study the convergence property of the firefly algorithm and discovered its intrinsic chaotic tunneling ability. This property can be used as an advantage to enhance search efficiency of the algorithm. For multimodal optimization problems, there is a risk for any algorithm to get trapped in local optima. Chaos-assisted tunneling in the firefly algorithm makes it particular suitable for dealing with nonlinear, multimodal optimization problems. Our analysis and numerical experiments indeed demonstrated that chaotic tunneling can increase the search efficiency significantly.

An important topic for further research is to vary the scheme of automatic parameter tuning. The present study presents just one of many ways for automatic tuning of algorithm-dependent parameters. Other methods may be more appropriate and more efficient for different types of problems. In addition, more studies are highly needed to investigate whether this approach can be directly applied to other algorithms for automatic parameter tuning.

Further research can focus on the theoretical framework and extensive numerical studies on how an algorithm can be enhanced by chaotic

tunneling, and thus may show insight into the working of an efficient algorithm. Such studies may help to design new generation truly intelligent optimization algorithms.

REFERENCES

Cagnina, L. C., Esquivel, S. C., & Coello, C. A. (2008). Solving engineering optimization problems with the simple constrained particle swarm optimizer. *Informatica*, *32*(2), 319–326.

Clerc, M., & Kennedy, J. (2002). The particle swarm - explosion, stability, and convergence in a multidimensional complex space. *IEEE Transactions on Evolutionary Computation*, *6*(1), 58–73. doi:10.1109/4235.985692

Deb, K. (1991). Optimal design of a welded beam via genetic algorithms. *AIAA Journal*, *29*(11), 2013–2015. doi:10.2514/3.10834

Delande, D., & Zakrzewski, J. (2003). Experimentally attainable example of chaotic tunneling: The hydrogen atom in parallel static electric and magnetic fields. *Physical Review A.*, *68*(6), 062110. doi:10.1103/PhysRevA.68.062110

Eberhart, E. C., & Shi, Y. (2000). Comparing inertia weights and constriction factors in particle swarm optimization. In *Proceedings of the Congress on Evolutionary Computation* (pp. 84–88). La Jolla, CA: IEEE Press.

Fister, J., Fister, I. Jr, Yang, X. S., & Brest, J. (2013). A comprehensive review of firefly algorithms. *Swarm and Evolutionary Computation*, *13*(1), 34–46. doi:10.1016/j.swevo.2013.06.001

Gandomi, A. H., Yang, X. S., & Alavi, A. H. (2011). Mixed variable structural optimization using firefly algorithm. *Computers & Structures*, *89*(23-24), 2325–2336. doi:10.1016/j.compstruc.2011.08.002

Gandomi, A. H., Yang, X. S., & Alavi, A. H. (2013a). Cuckoo search algorithm: A metaheuristic approach to solve structural optimization problems. *Engineering with Computers, 29*(1), 17–35. doi:10.1007/s00366-011-0241-y

Gandomi, A. H., Yang, X. S., Talatahari, S., & Alavi, A. H. (2013b). Firefly algorithm with chaos. *Communications in Nonlinear Science and Numerical Simulation, 18*(1), 89–98. doi:10.1016/j.cnsns.2012.06.009

Gutowski, M. (2001). Lévy flights as an underlying mechanism for global optimization algorithms. *ArXiv Mathematical Physics e-Prints*. Retrieved from http://arxiv.org/pdf/math-ph/0106003.pdf

He, S., Prempain, E., & Wu, Q. H. (2004). An improved particle swarm optimizer for mechanical design optimization problems. *Engineering Optimization, 36*(5), 585–605. doi:10.1080/03052150410001704854

Hedar, A. R., & Fukushima, M. (2006). Derivative-free simulated annealing method for constrained continuous global optimization. *Journal of Global Optimization, 35*(4), 521–549. doi:10.1007/s10898-005-3693-z

Kennedy, J., & Eberhart, R. C. (1995). Particle swarm optimization, In *Proc. of IEEE International Conference on Neural Networks* (pp. 1942-48). Piscataway, NJ: IEEE Press.

Kennedy, J., Eberhart, R. C., & Shi, Y. (2001). *Swarm intelligence*. San Francisco: Morgan Kaufmann Publishers.

Kirkpatrick, S., Gellat, C. D., & Vecchi, M. P. (1983). Optimization by simulated annealing. *Science, 220*(4598), 671–680. doi:10.1126/science.220.4598.671 PMID:17813860

Kohler, S., Utermann, R., Hagnni, R., & Dittrich, T. (1998). Coherent and incoherent chaotic tunneling near singlet-doublet crossings. *Physical Review E: Statistical Physics, Plasmas, Fluids, and Related Interdisciplinary Topics, 58*(6), 7219–7230. doi:10.1103/PhysRevE.58.7219

Lee, K. S., & Geem, Z. W. (2004). A new metaheuristic algorithm for continues engineering optimization: harmony search theory and practice. *Computer Methods in Applied Mechanics and Engineering, 194*(10), 3902–3933.

Pavlyukevich, I. (2007). Lévy flights, non-local search and simulated annealing. *Journal of Computational Physics, 226*(2), 1830–1844. doi:10.1016/j.jcp.2007.06.008

Podolskiy, V. A., & Narmanov, E. E. (2003). Semiclassical description of chaos-assisted tunneling. *Physical Review Letters, 91*(26), 263601. doi:10.1103/PhysRevLett.91.263601 PMID:14754050

Ragsdell, K., & Phillips, D. (1976). Optimal design of a class of welded structures using geometric programming. *Journal of Engineering for Industry, 98*(3), 1021–1025. doi:10.1115/1.3438995

Reynolds, A. M., & Rhodes, C. J. (2009). The Lévy fligth paradigm: Random search patterns and mechanisms. *Ecology, 90*(4), 877–887. doi:10.1890/08-0153.1 PMID:19449680

Shi, Y., & Eberhart, R. C. (1998). A modified particle swarm optimizer. In *Proceedings of IEEE International Conference on Evolutionary Computation* (pp. 69–73). Anchorage, AK: IEEE Press.

Shudo, A., & Ikeda, K. S. (1998). Chaotic tunneling: A remarkable manifestion of complex classical dynamics in non-integrable quatumn phenomena. *Physica D. Nonlinear Phenomena, 115*(3-4), 234–292. doi:10.1016/S0167-2789(97)00239-X

Shudo, A., Ishii, Y., & Ikeda, K. S. (2009). Julia sets and chaotic tunneling: II. *Journal of Physics A. Mathematical and Theoretical, 42*(26), 265102. doi:10.1088/1751-8113/42/26/265102

Talbi, E.-G. (2009). *Metaheuristics: From Design to Implementation*. New Jersey, NJ: John Wiley and Sons. doi:10.1002/9780470496916

Tomsovic, S., & Ullmo, D. (1994). Chao-assisted tunneling. *Physical Review E: Statistical Physics, Plasmas, Fluids, and Related Interdisciplinary Topics, 50*(1), 145–162. doi:10.1103/PhysRevE.50.145 PMID:9961952

Yang, L. J., & Chen, T. L. (2002). Applications of chaos in genetic algorithms. *Communications in Theoretical Physics, 38*(1), 168–192.

Yang, X. S. (2008). *Nature-Inspired Metaheuristic Algorithms*. Bristol, UK: Luniver Press.

Yang, X. S. (2010a). *Engineering Optimization: An Introduction with Metaheuristic Applications*. Hoboken, NJ: John Wiley & Sons. doi:10.1002/9780470640425

Yang, X. S. (2010b). Firefly algorithm, stochastic test functions and design optimisation. *International Journal of Bio-inspired Computation, 2*(2), 78–84. doi:10.1504/IJBIC.2010.032124

Yang, X. S. (2013). Multiobjective firefly algorithm for continuous optimization. *Engineering with Computers, 29*(2), 175–184. doi:10.1007/s00366-012-0254-1

Yang, X. S. (2014). Cuckoo Search and Firefly Algorithm: Theory and Applications. Heidelberg, Germany: Springer.

Yang, X. S., Cui, Z. H., Xiao, R. B., Gandomi, A. H., & Karamanoglu, M. (2013a). *Swarm Intelligence and Bio-Inspired Computation: Theory and Applications*. Waltham, UK: Elsevier. doi:10.1016/B978-0-12-405163-8.00001-6

Yang, X. S., & Deb, S. (2010). Engineering optimization by cuckoo search. *International Journal of Mathematical Modelling & Numerical Optimization, 1*(4), 330–343. doi:10.1504/IJMMNO.2010.035430

Yang, X. S., Deb, S., Loomes, M., & Karamanoglu, M. (2013b). A framework for self-tuning optimziaton algorithms. *Neural Computing & Applications, 23*(7-8), 2051–2057. doi:10.1007/s00521-013-1498-4

Zhang, M., Luo, W., & Wang, X. (2008). Differential evolution with dynamic stochastic selection for constrained optimization. *Information Science, 178*(15), 3043–3074. doi:10.1016/j.ins.2008.02.014

KEY TERMS AND DEFINITIONS

Algorithm: A precedure that provides step-by-step instructions for computation. In optimization, algorithms tend to be iterative.

Chaos: A deterministic map that can lead to large variations in the behaviour or states subject to small initial perturbations. Chaotic maps can be used to replace randomness due to their high mixing characteristics.

Firefly Algorithm: A swarm-intelligence-based optimization algorithm that mimics the flashing behaviour of fireflies. This algorithm can deal with multimodal optimization problems naturally and efficiently.

Metaheuristic: A class of algorithms that use a heuristic approach by producing solutions in a trial-and-error manner, but it also selects solutions based on their fitness. Such population-based algorithms can show emerging characteristics and can be efficient in solving optimization problems.

Optimization: A class of methods attempt to find the best solution to a given problem so that the objective function such as the energy efficiency (or costs) is maximum (or minimum).

Parameter Tuning: The variation of parameters used in an algorithm so that it can maximize the performance of the algorithm due to that fact that the parameter setting can affect the efficiency of an algorithm. Tuning of parameters is a higher level optimization problem.

Swarm Intelligence: A system of multiple agents can interact and may thus lead to some self-organized characteristics that are typical to some intelligence. Such collective behaviour is often referred to as collective intelligence or swarm intelligence.

Chapter 3
A Complementary Cyber Swarm Algorithm

Peng-Yeng Yin
National Chi Nan University, Taiwan

Fred Glover
OptTek Systems, Inc., USA

Manuel Laguna
University of Colorado, USA

Jia-Xian Zhu
National Chi Nan University, Taiwan

ABSTRACT

A recent study (Yin, et al., 2010) showed that combining Particle Swarm Optimization (PSO) with the strategies of Scatter Search (SS) and Path Relinking (PR) produces a Cyber Swarm Algorithm that creates a more effective form of PSO than methods that do not incorporate such mechanisms. In this chapter, the authors propose a Complementary Cyber Swarm Algorithm (C/CyberSA) that performs in the same league as the original Cyber Swarm Algorithm but adopts different sets of ideas from the Tabu Search (TS) and the SS/PR template. The C/CyberSA exploits the guidance information and restriction information produced in the history of swarm search and the manipulation of adaptive memory. Responsive strategies using long-term memory and path relinking implementations are proposed that make use of critical events encountered in the search. Experimental results with a large set of challenging test functions show that the C/CyberSA outperforms two recently proposed swarm-based methods by finding more optimal solutions while simultaneously using a smaller number of function evaluations. The C/CyberSA approach further produces improvements comparable to those obtained by the original CyberSA in relation to the Standard PSO 2007 method (Clerc, 2008). These findings motivate future investigations of Cyber Swarm methods that combine features of both the original and complementary variants and incorporate additional strategic notions from the SS/PR template as a basis for creating a still more effective form of swarm optimization.

DOI: 10.4018/978-1-4666-6328-2.ch003

1. INTRODUCTION

Metaheuristics are master strategies that guide and modify slave heuristics to produce solutions beyond those that are normally generated for local optimality. Effective metaheuristics make a search plan of *intensification* and *diversification* to reach a good trade-off between solution quality and computational effort. Intensification exploits information about elite solutions that were previously found as a basis for focusing the search in regions anticipated to harbor additional solutions of high quality. Diversification promotes the exploration of regions appreciably different from those previously examined in order to produce new solutions with characteristics that depart from those already seen. Intensification and diversification work together to identify new promising regions when the slave heuristics stagnate in the executed search courses. Many intelligent algorithms fall in the territory of metaheuristics. Some exemplary algorithms (Luke, 2009) are genetic algorithms (GA), simulated annealing (SA), ant colony optimization (ACO), tabu search (TS), particle swarm optimization (PSO), scatter search (SS), greedy randomized adaptive search procedure (GRASP), variable neighborhood search (VNS), to name a few. A recent survey and descriptive analysis of metaheuristic algorithms can be found in Sorensen and Glover (2010).

Slave heuristics embedded in metaheuristic methods often adopt *solution combination* or *neighborhood exploration* processes to generate new solutions based on the current state of search. Solution combination approaches produce new solutions by exchanging information between candidate solutions (for example, crossover operation executed in GA) or by using candidate solutions as *guiding points* for producing new solutions (for example, by reference to the best experiences in PSO or the path relinking (PR) process used in SS). Alternatively, neighborhood exploration employs incremental changes, called *moves*, which progress from one solution to another

within local regions called neighborhoods that are considered relevant to the search (as by changing one or a small number of elements within a current solution). Sophisticated neighborhood concepts like ejection chains (Glover, 1996b, Rego and Glover, 2009) have been proposed for tackling a variety of complex problems and various types of multiple neighborhood strategies (Glover, 1996a; Mladenovic & Hansen, 1997; Sörensen, Sevaux, & Schittekat, 2008; Lu, Hao & Glover, 2010) have been proposed for enriching the set of moves employed during the search. To avoid reversing the search course and prevent getting trapped in local optima, some solution attributes and move directions may be forbidden by means of *tabu restrictions* as proposed in tabu search, or *multi-start* mechanisms may be employed to initiate a new search thread in an uncharted region. There are other metaheuristic methods employing gradient-based or derivative-free supplementary procedures. The best of these methods are provided by Hedar and Fukushima (2006) and Duarte et al. (2007) for problems of moderate dimension, and by Hvattum and Glover (2009) and Vaz and Vicente (2007) for problems of large dimension. Duarte et al. (2011b) analyzes the performance of two path relinking variants: the static and the evolutionary path relinking. Both are based on the strategy of creating trajectories of moves passing through high quality solutions in order to incorporate their attributes to the explored solutions.

Methods that employ both solution combination and neighborhood exploration perform more effectively by carefully coordinating the slave heuristics with the master strategy employed. An illustration of this is provided, for example, by methods that integrate tabu search with classical direct search for global function optimization. Chelouah and Siarry (2005) proposed a continuous tabu simplex search (CTSS) method that uses the Nelder-Mead simplex algorithm to accelerate convergence towards a minimum within a detected promising region, while maintaining the tabu search (TS) restriction as a mechanism to search uncharted solution space. Hedar and Fukushima (2006) introduced a directed TS (DTS) method for non-linear global optimization which, instead of identifying promising regions before the application, immediately applies the Nelder-Mead method at every non-improving trial point obtained by the TS neighborhood search. A study of larger problems by Hvattum and Glover (2009) shows that the use of direct search methods different from the Nelder-Mead procedure can produce superior results.

Another approach (Nakano et al., 2007; Shen et al., 2008; Wang et al., 2007) akin to this research direction is the hybridization of PSO and TS. The TS processes for managing adaptive memory via responsive strategies enables PSO to implement intensification and diversification searches more effectively. On the one hand, the attribute values which produced high quality solutions in TS recency memory can be reserved for other particles in the future. On the other hand, less fit attribute values contained in the adaptive memory are designated as tabù-active and the particles are pulled away from these attribute values. The particle swarm and pattern search method (Vas & Vicente, 2007) referred to as PSwarm is a pattern search method incorporating particle swarm search as a step within its framework. In additional to the original mesh search, the particle swarm search can explore the nonconvexity of the objective function. More recently, Yin et al. (2010) introduced a Cyber Swarm Algorithm (CyberSA) as the marriage of PSO and the scatter search/path relinking (SS/PR) template that obtains improved outcomes. With the addition of an external memory, embodied in a reference set consisting of the best solutions observed throughout the evolution history, useful information is produced and maintained that is not attainable by relying on traditional PSO mechanisms involving particle experiences.

We propose a restricted variant of the CyberSA by strategically exploring special guidance and restriction information. The contributions of this work are: (1) the augmentation of the search capability of CyberSA by considering additional ideas from TS and SS/PR, (2) a multi-level (short term, middle term, and long term) memory manipulations designed to reinforce the search process, and (3) extensive performance evaluation of the proposed method with a large set of diverse benchmark functions.

The remainder of this paper is organized as follows. Section 2 presents a literature review of fundamental PSO methods relevant to our work. Section 3 proposes the Complementary Variant of the Cyber Swarm Algorithm and describes its salient features. Section 4 presents experimental results together with an analysis of their implications. Finally, concluding remarks and discussions are given in Section 5.

2. PSO LITERATURE REVIEW

The introduction of *particle swarm optimization* (PSO) has motivated many researchers to develop various swarm algorithms by drawing fruitful notions from other domains. These development efforts include two main types: the exploitation of guidance information and the hybridization with other intelligent search strategies.

2.1 Exploitation of Guidance Information

The PSO proposed by Kennedy and Eberhart (1995) has exhibited effectiveness and robustness in many applications, such as evolving artificial neural networks (Eberhart & Shi, 1998), reactive power and voltage control (Yoshida & Kawata, 1999), state estimation for electric power distribution systems (Shigenori et al., 2003), and image compression (Feng et al., 2007). PSO has drawn on a sociocognition model to gain recognition as a useful global optimizer. A swarm of particles is assumed to follow the social norm manifest of convergent behaviors. The social norm consists of quality experiences by comparing search trajectories of individual particles. This is an autocatalytic process that the social norm influences the individual behaviors which in turn collectively improve the social norm.

The original version of PSO is quite simple. A swarm of particles iteratively update their positional vectors by reference to previous positions and two forms of the best trajectory experience, namely, the personal best (*pbest*) and the global best (*gbest*). The personal best is the best position that a particle has experienced, while the global best is the best position ever experienced by the particles in the swarm. Let the optimization problem be formulated with R decision variables and a particle $P_i = (p_{i1}, p_{i2}, ..., p_{iR})$ representing a candidate solution whose search trajectory is iteratively determined by adding a velocity vector $V_i = (v_{i1}, v_{i2}, ..., v_{iR})$ to its previous position. According to Clerc's Stagnation Analysis (Clerc & Kennedy, 2002), the convergence of the particles' trajectories is mathematically guaranteed by the following equations.

$$v_{ij} \leftarrow K(v_{ij} + rand_1(pbest_{ij} - p_{ij}) + \phi_2 \, rand_2(gbest_j - p_{ij}))$$

$$K = \frac{2}{\left| 2 - (\phi_1 + \phi_2) - \sqrt{(\phi_1 + \phi_2)^2 - 4(\phi_1 + \phi_2)} \right|}$$

(with the constraint $\varphi_1 + \varphi_2 > 4$)

and

$$p_{ij} \leftarrow p_{ij} + v_{ij}$$

where φ_1 and φ_2 are the cognitive coefficients, *rand_1* and *rand_2* are random real numbers drawn from $U(0, 1)$, and K is the constriction coefficient. In essence, the particle explores a potential region defined by *pbest* and *gbest*, while the cognitive coefficients and the random multipliers change the weightings for the two best solutions in every iteration.

As indicated by the term "small world" in sociology, two people indirectly share information via the social network. The speed on which the information spreads depends upon the structure of the social network. Kennedy (1999) has studied the effects of neighborhood topologies on particle swarm performance. The local best leader (*lbest*), the best position visited by any member in the neighborhood of a designated given particle, is used as a substitute for *gbest*. He found that the best neighborhood topology depends on the problem context. The Star topology (the *gbest* version where each particle is connected to all particles in the swarm) spreads the individual information throughout the swarm most quickly and can expedite the convergence of explored solutions in unimodal function optimization problems. However, the Ring topology (each particle is connected to exactly two other particles) can usually produce better solutions on multimodal functions than the Star topology because the former structure postpones the information transmission between two arbitrary particles and is more effective in avoiding being trapped in local optimality. The performance of other topologies, such as Wheel or Pyramid, varies from problem to problem.

Miranda et al. (2007) proposed a *Stochastic Star* topology where a particle is informed by *gbest* with a predefined probability p. Their experimental results showed that the Stochastic Star topology leads in many cases to better results than the original Star topology. The standard PSO 2007 (Clerc, 2008) regenerates a random permutation of particles before each iteration. Hence, the resulting neighborhood structure is in essence a random topology.

While most of the PSO algorithm variants conduct the swarm evolution using two particle leaders, Clerc's Stagnation Analysis (Clerc & Kennedy, 2002) does not limit consideration to two cognitive coefficients, but only requires that the parts sum to a value that is appropriate for the constriction coefficient K. Mendes et al. (2004) have proposed to combine all neighbors' information instead of only using *lbest*. Let Ω_i be the set of neighbors' indices of particle i and let ω_k be an estimate of the relevance of particle k as being an informant of particle i. Then the velocity can be updated by

$$v_{ij} \leftarrow K(v_{ij} + \varphi \ (mbest_{ij} - p_{ij}))$$

and

$$mbest_{ij} = \frac{\sum_{k \in \Omega_i} \omega_k \phi_k \ pbest_{kj}}{\sum_{k \in \Omega_i} \omega_k \phi_k},$$

$$\phi = \sum_{k \in \Omega_i} \phi_k$$

and $\phi_k \in U\left[0, \dfrac{\phi_{\max}}{|\Omega_i|}\right]$

As all the neighbors contribute to the velocity update, the focal particle is fully informed.

The Cyber Swarm Algorithm (CyberSA), which has produced better results than the standard PSO 2007 method, uses three leaders in the velocity adjustment and extends the neighborhood topology by additionally including the reference set construction of the SS/PR template. The reference set is not restricted simply to neighbors, but consists of the best solutions observed throughout the evolution history. The CyberSA reinstates *pbest* and *gbest* in the group of leaders and systematically selects each member from the reference set as the third leader. Additional details of this method are discussed subsequently.

2.2 Hybridization with Outsource Strategies

Researchers have proposed that PSO may be extended by taking into account useful strategies from other methodologies. The obvious advantage

of hybridizing PSO is the potential for enhancing the intensification/diversification synergy and improving the regions selected to be explored in the course of the search. Often, hybrid algorithms exhibit better performance when solving complex problems, such as the optimization of difficult multimodal functions. These mechanisms are mainly found within the framework of evolutionary algorithms and adaptive memory programming concepts derived from tabu search.

In the hybrid algorithm proposed by Angeline (1999) particles with low fitness are replaced by those with high fitness using natural selection while these particles preserve their original best experience. This approach is reported to facilitate the exploration of highly promising regions while maintaining experience diversity. Lovbjerg et al. (2001) implement a hybrid approach by inserting a breeding (recombination) step after the movement of all particles. Particles are selected with equal probability to become parents and in turn are replaced by offspring that are generated using the arithmetic crossover operator. In order to keep diversity in the gene pool, particles are divided into subpopulations and the breeding is allowed both within a given subpopulation and between different subpopulations.

A hybridization of generalized pattern search (Audet & Dennis, 2003) with PSO is proposed by Vas and Vicente (2007) to produce the PSwarm algorithm that consists of alternating iterations of search and poll steps. The search enforces a step of particle swarm search (and expands the mesh size parameter) if such a step causes the individual bests of the particles to improve. Otherwise, the poll step is activated, consisting of applying one step of local pattern search (along the canonical mesh) on the best particle of the entire swarm. The mesh size parameter is either expanded or contracted according to whether the pattern search improves the best particle. PSwarm has been shown to outperform several optimizers on an experiment over a set of 122 benchmark functions.

A number of effective hybrids have been produced by incorporating various elements of tabu search. Nakano et al. (2007) divide the particles into two sub-swarms that play the roles of intensification and diversification, respectively. When an attribute value in the global best solution is not updated for a number of iterations, the attribute value is designated as tabu. The particles from the intensification sub-swarm fix the attribute values as specified by the tabu restrictions and contained in the global best solution, while the particles in the diversification sub-swarm are encouraged to pull away from solutions containing the tabu attributes. Shen et al. (2008) propose an approach called HPSOTS which enables the PSO to leap over local optima by restraining the particle movement based on the use of tabu conditions. Wang et al. (2007) enhances the diversification capability of PSO by setting the less fit attributes contained in the global best solution as tabu-active and repelling the particles from the tabu area.

The Cyber Swarm Algorithm (CyberSA) of Yin et al. (2010) creates an enhanced form of swarm algorithms by incorporating three features: (1) augmenting the information sharing among particles by learning from the reference set members, (2) systematically generating dynamic social networks in order to choose various solutions as the leaders such that the search can adapt to different functional landscape, and (3) executing diversification strategies based on path relinking approaches as a response to the status of the adaptive memory. Since the introduction of the CyberSA, it has been adopted in several applications including the keyboard character arrangement (Yin & Su, 2011) and the nurse rostering (Yin & Chiang, 2013). The method has also been extended to multi-objective optimization (Yin & Chiang, 2013) and estimation of distribution optimization (Yin & Wu, 2013). The success of the CyberSA has motivated us to examine another variant that draws on alternative ideas from the same sources.

3. COMPLEMENTARY VARIANT OF CYBER SWARM ALGORITHM

As disclosed in the literature discussed in Section 2, the performance of PSO can be improved by exploiting the guidance information and hybridizing the method with outsource strategies. Following this theme, the CyberSA creates an effective form of PSO by carefully selecting leading solutions and embedding scatter search/path relinking (SS/PR) strategies. The Complementary Cyber Swarm Algorithm (C/CyberSA) proposed here uses different sets of ideas from the adaptive memory programming perspective of tabu search and scatter search. As we show, the C/CyberSA can produce improvements comparable to those obtained by the original CyberSA in relation to those PSO methods that do not incorporate adaptive memory programming ideas.

3.1 Using Guidance Information

As previously noted, the choice of neighborhood topologies and leading solutions significantly affects the particle swarm performance. The literature discloses that the use of a dynamic neighborhood (Miranda et al., 2007; Clerc, 2008; Yin et al., 2010) and the local best solution *lbest* (Kennedy, 1999; Clerc, 2008) leads to a better performance. These notions create a form of multiple neighborhood search in which the neighboring particles (each maintaining a search trajectory) are selected at random or systematically and the local optimum corresponds to the best solution encountered by the multiple search trajectories.

Our proposed C/CyberSA method generates a random permutation of particles on a Ring topology before performing each iteration, so the neighboring particles are very likely different from those assigned at previous iterations. The three leaders, the local best solution (*lbest*) observed by the neighboring particles, the overall best solution (*gbest*) found by the entire swarm, and the individual best experience (*pbest*) for the operating particle, are used as the guiding solutions. More precisely, the C/CyberSA uses the following velocity updating formula for the *i*th particle,

$$
v_{ij} \leftarrow K \left(\begin{array}{c} v_{ij} + \left(\phi_1 + \phi_2 + \phi_3 \right) \\ \left(\dfrac{\omega_1 \phi_1 pbest_{ij} + \omega_2 \phi_2 lbest_{ij} + \omega_3 \phi_3 gbest_j}{\omega_1 \phi_1 + \omega_2 \phi_2 + \omega_3 \phi_3} - p_{ij} \right) \end{array} \right)
$$

(6)

The weight ω_i is selected to be the same for each of the three guiding solutions.

The advantage of using three guiding solutions has been empirically verified in several relevant studies. For example, Campos et al. (2001) found that in scatter search most of the high quality solutions come from combinations using at most 3 reference solutions. Mendes et al. (2004) have also more recently found that their FIPS algorithm (which treats the previous bests of all neighbors as guiding solutions) performs best when a neighborhood size of 2 to 4 neighbors is used, and increasing the neighborhood size causes the overall performance to deteriorate. The CyberSA method also achieves particularly good outcomes when using three strategically selected guiding solutions.

3.2 Using Restriction Information

The adaptive memory programming perspective of tabu search provides a fruitful basis for generating incentives and restrictions to guide the search towards more promising regions. The central idea is to compare previous states (e.g., selected solution attributes) stored in the adaptive memory to those states of new candidate solutions currently contemplated.

Our C/CyberSA approach uses multiple levels of adaptive memory to exploit the benefits of restriction information. Three categories of adaptive memory are employed: (1) a short-term memory (STM) that records the solutions visited by individual particles within a short span of recent history; (2) a middle-term memory (MTM) that tallies the solutions that pass a certain acceptance threshold dynamically changed according to the current state; and (3) a long-term memory (LTM) that tracks the frequency or duration of critical events and activates appropriate reactions. Immediately following, we present the implementation for STM and MTM, and the description for LTM is given in Subsection 3.3.

In PSO, a swarm of particles construct their individual search courses to accumulate rewarded experiences and there is no additional value in allowing particles to be transformed into recent previous solutions. We therefore use STM to prevent individual particles from reversing recent moves as they undergo the transformation to produce new particles. The notion of a "tabu ball" proposed by Chelouah and Siarry (2000) is adopted in our implementation. When a particle is replaced by a new solution based on Equation (6), the solution is designated as tabu-active with a tabu tenure. A tabu ball centered at this solution with radius r is created and prohibits the acceptance of new solutions produced inside this ball during its tabu tenure. Let the set of centers of currently STM active tabu balls be $\pi_{STM} = \{s_1, s_2, ..., s_T\}$, a new solution s' is rejected (tabu) if it is contained within any of the tabu balls, i.e., $\left\| s' - s_i \right\| \leq r, \ \forall s_i \in \pi_{STM}$, where $\left\| \cdot \right\|$ denotes the Euclidean norm. (Additional ways to generate "tabu regions" along with the possibility to use other distance norms are proposed in Glover, 1994.) However, the tabu restriction can be overruled if s' meets some aspiration criterion. The *Aspiration_by_objective* rule stipulates that a tabu solution s' can be accepted if its objective value is better than that of the overall best solution. To introduce a form of vigor into the search that accommodates varying widths of local minima, the tabu tenure of a tabu ball is determined dynamically and drawn randomly from a pre-specified range, motivated by the fact that a dynamic tabu tenure typically performs better than a constant tabu tenure in TS implementations. To finely tune the size of the tabu ball in accordance with different phases of the search, the ball radius r is reduced by a ratio β upon the detection of stagnation as noted in the next subsection.

For the implementation of tabu restrictions with MTM, we prevent a particle from updating its personal best (*pbest*) if the candidate solution is too close to the recent best of any particle. Again, a tabu ball is created for a newly produced *pbest* solution and the update of *pbest* is prohibited for any particle inside this tabu ball during its tabu tenure. Denote the set of centers of currently MTM active tabu balls by π_{MTM}. The MTM incorporates the same rules for the aspiration criterion, dynamic tabu tenure, and tabu ball radius reduction as enforced in the STM mechanism.

We do not impose a tabu restriction on the update of the overall best (*gbest*) because it is always beneficial to obtain a better overall best solution during the search (and such a solution automatically satisfies the aspiration criterion in any case).

3.3 Responsive Strategies

Longer term strategies responding to detections of critical changes in LTM are invoked when a short term strategy has lost its search efficacy. Successful applications of this principle have been seen in both static and dynamic optimization problems (James et al., 2009; Lepagnot et al., 2010), reinforcing the supposition that promising solutions having features differing from those previously seen are likely to be obtained by using longer term strategies.

One of the effective longer term strategies is path relinking (PR). (For recent surveys, see Ho & Gendreau, 2006; Rego and Glover, 2008.) PR is a search process which constructs a link between two or more strategically selected solutions. The construction starts with one solution (called the initiating solution) and moves to or beyond a second solution (referred to as the guiding solution). PR transforms the initiating solution into the guiding solution by generating moves that successively replace an attribute of the initiating solution that is contained in the guiding solution. The link can be constructed in both directions by interchanging the roles of the initiating and guiding solutions, or can proceed from both ends toward the middle.

PR can emphasize either intensification or diversification. For example, intensification strategies may choose reference solutions to be the best solutions encountered in a common region while diversification strategies can select reference solutions that lie within different regions. Reference solutions are selected according to their status in the LTM and the appropriate PR strategies are triggered upon the detections of critical events. We propose two responsive PR strategies and the corresponding triggering critical events in the following.

1. **Diversification PR strategy – Particle Restarting:** The C/CyberSA manages multiple particle search threads exploring promising regions in the solution space. The identified promising regions are located by using *pbest* which in turn is used to identify the particles to exploit these regions. A critical event arises when *pbest* has not improved for t_2 successive search iterations. This indicates the region has been over-exploited and the corresponding particle should be repositioned in an uncharted region to start a new round of search. In light of this, PR can focus on identifying new promising regions. We do this by selecting two reference solutions from two under-exploited regions, using the biased random approach proposed in the original CyberSA method. This approach generates a biased-random solution which is likely to be in a position at a maximal distance from all previous trial solutions. Let

the two reference solutions be $RandSol_1$ and $RandSol_2$, respectively. The diversification PR strategy is triggered by the critical event to construct a link $PR(RandSol_1, RandSol_2)$ between the two reference solutions. The best solution observed over the constructed link is designated as the initiating particle for restarting a new search thread. It is noted that although the particle has been repositioned, the content of the adaptive memory (such as *pbest*, *gbest*, tabu list, tabu tenure, and tabu ball radius) is retained.

The diversification PR strategy not only diversifies the search (by creating a new thread that has not been targeted before) but also tunnels through different regions that have contrasting features. This strategy is designed based on the anticipation that the solutions with fruitful information for the current search state are those contained in uncharted regions or near the boundaries between regions having contrasting features.

2. **Intensification PR Strategy – Swarm Shrinking:** The other critical event is the detection of swarm stagnation. This happens when the distributed particles have exhausted their search efficacy and the swarm overall best solution *gbest* has not improved for t_1 successive search iterations. We propose an intensification PR strategy named *swarm shrinking* which regenerates a new swarm within the neighborhood proximity of *gbest* to replace the original population of particles in order to intensify the search in the overall best region. Each particle in the new swarm is generated by applying a truncated PR process, Truncated_PR(*gbest*, $RandSol_1$), using *gbest* as the initiating solution and, again, employing a solution $RandSol_1$ produced by the biased random approach as the guiding solution. The truncated PR process starting with the initiating solution performs a few moves and only constructs a partial link. In

our implementation, we terminate the link construction when one tenth of the number of attributes in *gbest* have been replaced (at least one attribute has been replaced if *gbest* has less than 10 attributes). The best solution observed on the partial link is used to replace the original particle.

In the process of swarm shrinking, all the elements excluding the tabu ball radius in the adaptive memory hold their original values. The length of the tabu ball radius is halved to facilitate a finer search with the shrunken swarm.

3.4 C/CyberSA Pseudo Code

The C/CyberSA design is elaborated in the pseudo codes shown in Figure 1. The three important features (guidance information, restriction information, and responsive strategies) of the C/CyberSA are in boldface to emphasize these features within the algorithm. In the initialization phase (Step 1) the initial values for particle positions and velocities and the values for the elements (*pbest*, *gbest*, tabu ball radius, etc.) stored in the adaptive memory are given. In the main-loop iterations (Step 2), the swarm conducts its search using these three components. To generate a dynamic neighborhood, the particles are randomly arranged on a Ring topology. Each particle moves with the guidance information provided by $pbest_i$, $lbest_i$ and *gbest* (Step 2.2.1). However, any movement leading into a tabu ball stored in STM is prohibited (Step 2.2.3). The individual $pbest_i$ is updated if a better solution is produced by the movement which is not tabu by the MTM restriction (Step 2.2.4). Finally, as shown in Step 2.4, the intensification PR strategy is executed if *gbest* has not improved for a number of standing iterations. Otherwise, the diversification strategy is performed if a particular $pbest_i$ stagnates during the attempted improvement process.

Figure 1. Pseudo codes for the complementary cyber swarm algorithm (C/CyberSA)

1   Initialize.
 1.1 Generate N particle solutions, $P_i = (p_{i1}, p_{i2}, ..., p_{iR})$, $1 \leq i \leq N$, at random.
 1.2 Generate N velocity vectors, $V_i = (v_{i1}, v_{i2}, ..., v_{iR})$, $1 \leq i \leq N$, at random.
 1.3 Evaluate the fitness of each particle *fitness*(P_i), and set previous best solution *pbest$_i$* to P_i. Determine the overall best solution *gbest* as the best among all *pbest$_i$*.
 1.4 Set initial tabu ball radius r
2   Repeat until a stopping criterion is met.
 2.1 Generate a random permutation of particles on a Ring topology to determine local bests *lbest$_i$*, $\forall i = 1, ..., N$.
 2.2 For each particle P_i, $\forall i = 1, ..., N$, Do
 2.2.1 **Guidance:** Compute the velocity using the three strategically selected guiding solutions.

$$v_{ij} \leftarrow K\left(v_{ij} + \left(\varphi_1 + \varphi_2 + \varphi_3\right)\left(\frac{\omega_1\varphi_1 pbest_{ij} + \omega_2\varphi_2 lbest_{ij} + \omega_3\varphi_3 gbest_j}{\omega_1\varphi_1 + \omega_2\varphi_2 + \omega_3\varphi_3} - p_{ij} \right) \right)$$

 2.2.2 Compute the tentative movement $P_i' = P_i + V_i$.

 2.2.3 **STM restriction:** If $\left\| P_i' - s_i \right\| \leq r, \forall s_i \in \pi_{STM}$ and P_i' does not satisfy the aspiration criterion, goto Step 2.2.1.

 2.2.4 **MTM restriction:** If P_i' is better than *pbest$_i$* and $\left\| P_i' - s_i \right\| > r, \forall s_i \in \pi_{MTM}$, or P_i' satisfies the aspiration criterion,
     $pbest_i \leftarrow P_i'$

 2.3 Determine the overall best solution *gbest* as the best among all *pbest$_i$*, $\forall i = 1, ..., N$.
 2.4 **Intensification PR strategy (swarm shrinking):** If *gbest* has not improved for t_1 iterations, reinitiate all particles and halve the tabu ball radius by
     $P_i \leftarrow$ Truncated_PR$(gbest, RandSol_1)$, $\forall i = 1, ..., N$
     $r \leftarrow 0.5r$
  Diversification PR strategy (particle restarting): Else if a particular *pbest$_i$* has not improved for t_2 iterations, replace its particle by
     $P_i \leftarrow PR\left(RandSol_1, RandSol_2\right)$

4. EXPERIMENTAL RESULTS AND ANALYSIS

We have conducted extensive experiments to evaluate the performance of the C/CyberSA. The experimental results disclose several interesting outcomes in addition to establishing the effectiveness of the proposed method. The platform for conducting the experiments is a PC with a 1.8 GHz CPU and 1.0 GB RAM. All programs are coded in C++ language.

4.1 Performance Measures and Competing Algorithms

We measure the performance of competing algorithms in terms of effectiveness and efficiency. Effectiveness measures how close the quality of the obtained solution is to that of the optimal solution while efficiency assesses how fast a given algorithm can obtain a solution with a target quality.

The effectiveness measure is gauged by reference to the best objective value obtained by a competing algorithm that has been allowed to consume a maximum number of function evaluations equal to 160,000. (We selected this number because we observed the competing algorithms converge for most of the test functions after performing 160,000 evaluations.) When comparing the effectiveness of a target algorithm against a reference algorithm, a relative measure called merit is often used and defined as merit $= (f_p - f^* + \varepsilon)/(f_q - f^* + \varepsilon)$, where f_p and f_q are the mean best objective value obtained by the target algorithm and the reference algorithm, respectively, f^* is the known global optimum of the test function, and ε is a small constant equal to 5×10^{-7}. Without loss of generality, we consider all the test functions to involve minimization, and stipulate that the target algorithm outperforms the reference algorithm if the value of merit is less than 1.0 (where smaller values represent greater differences in favor of the target algorithm.)

We employ the policy widely adopted in the literature of representing the efficiency measure as the mean number of function evaluations required by a given algorithm in order to obtain an objective value that is sufficiently close to the known global optimum by reference to a specified gap.

Yin et al. (2010) have shown the advantages of the original CyberSA by comparing it with several other metaheuristics such as the Standard PSO 2007 (Clerc, 2008), C-GRASP (Hirsch et al., 2007), Direct Tabu Search, (Hedar & Fukushima, 2006), Scatter Search (Laguna & Marti, 2005), and Hybrid Scatter Tabu Search (Duarte et al., 2011a). In our present comparison we also include the PSwarm algorithm of Vaz and Vicente (2007), which embeds the swarm algorithm into the pattern search framework.

The parameter values used by the C/CyberSA have been determined based on preliminary experiments with a variety of test values, which led us to select the following settings. The size of the swarm is set to consist of 40 particles. At most five trial particles are produced by each "particle move" operation. The first non-tabu trial particle is accepted to be the next position of the focal particle, and the new position is marked as tabu with a dynamic tenure drawing a random value from the range [5, 15]. If all the five trial particles are tabu, the default aspiration chooses the one with the shortest tabu tenure to be released and accessed. The radius of the tabu ball is initialized to one percent of the mean range of variable values. The responsive longer term strategies (swarm shrinking and particle restarting) are executed when critical events are observed with the parameter settings of $t_1 = 100$ and $t_2 = 200$. As for the other competing algorithms, the parameter values are set to the suggested values according to their original papers.

4.2 Performance

4.2.1 Experiment 1

Our first experiment evaluates the effectiveness of the C/CyberSA with a set of 30 test functions that are widely used in the literature (Laguna & Marti, 2003; Hedar & Fukushima, 2006; Hirsch et al., 2007; Yin et al., 2010). All these functions are continuous and together they present a wide variety of different landscapes. A hundred repetitive runs are executed for each of the three methods compared: the Standard PSO 2007, CyberSA, and C/CyberSA. Each run of a given algorithm is terminated when 160,000 function evaluations have been exhausted and the best function value obtained is considered as the outcome of this run.

The mean best function value over the 100 independent runs and the merit value relative to the mean best result of the Standard PSO 2007 are shown in Table 1. The numerical values in the parentheses correspond to the standard deviation of the best function values over the 100 repetitions. We observe that, except for the simple functions where all competing algorithms can obtain the global optimum, CyberSA is more effective than the Standard PSO 2007 by being able to obtain a lower mean best function value for the test functions. The product of the merit values for the CyberSA is equal to 1.15E-36. The best function value reported by the CyberSA is significantly closer to the global optimum than that obtained by the Standard PSO 2007.

The C/CyberSA exhibits similar effectiveness as observed from its mean best function value and merit value. The product of the merit values for the C/CyberSA is 1.07E-40 which is even somewhat better than the corresponding product for the C/CyberSA. However, the C/CyberSA is less effective than CyberSA in finding the global optimum for the four functions Shekel(4, 5),

Table 1. Mean best function value with standard deviation and the merit value for the competing algorithms

R	Test Function	Standard PSO 2007	CyberSA	CyberSA Merit	C/CyberSA	C/CyberSA Merit
2	Easom	-0.9999 (0.0000)	-1.0000 (0.0000)	0.3333	-1.0000(0.0000)	0.33333
2	Shubert	-186.7202 (0.0071)	-186.7309 (0.0000)	4.67 E-5	-186.7309(0.0000)	4.67E-5
2	Branin	0.3979 (0.0000)	0.3979 (0.0000)	1.0000	0.3979 (0.0000)	1.0000
2	Goldstein-Price	3.0001 (0.0001)	3.0000 (0.0000)	0.0050	3.0000 (0.0000)	0.0050
2	Rosenbrock(2)	0.0000 (0.0000)	0.0000 (0.0000)	1.0000	0.0000(0.0000)	1.0000
2	Zakharov(2)	0.0000 (0.0000)	0.0000 (0.0000)	1.0000	0.0000(0.0000)	1.0000
3	De Jong	0.0000 (0.0000)	0.0000 (0.0000)	1.0000	0.0000(0.0000)	1.0000
3	Hartmann(3)	-3.8626 (0.0000)	-3.8628 (0.0000)	0.0025	-3.8628 (0.0000)	0.0025
4	Shekel(4, 5)	-10.1526 (0.0004)	-10.1532 (0.0000)	0.0008	-10.0038(0.7469)	248.8052
4	Shekel(4, 7)	-10.4019 (0.0008)	-10.4029 (0.0000)	0.0005	-10.3264(0.7612)	76.4323
4	Shekel(4, 10)	-10.5363 (0.0001)	-10.5364 (0.0000)	0.0050	-10.5364(0.0000)	0.0050
5	Rosenbrock(5)	0.4324 (1.2299)	0.0000 (0.0000)	1.16E-6	0.0000 (0.0000)	1.16E-6
5	Zakharov(5)	0.0000 (0.0000)	0.0000 (0.0000)	1.0000	0.0000 (0.0000)	1.0000
6	Hartmann(6)	-3.3150 (0.0283)	-3.3224 (0.0000)	6.76E-5	-3.3224 (0.0000)	6.76E-5
10	Sum-Squares(10)	0.0000 (0.0000)	0.0000 (0.0000)	1.0000	0.0000 (0.0000)	1.0000
10	Sphere(10)	0.0000 (0.0000)	0.0000 (0.0000)	1.0000	0.0000(0.0000)	1.0000
10	Rosenbrock(10)	0.9568 (1.7026)	0.1595 (0.7812)	0.1667	0.0000(0.0000)	5.23E-7
10	Rastrigin(10)	4.9748 (2.7066)	0.7464 (0.8367)	0.1500	0.3283(0.4667)	0.0660
10	Griewank(10)	0.0532 (0.0310)	0.0474 (0.0266)	0.8915	0.0426(0.0184)	0.8002
10	Zakharov(10)	0.0000 (0.0000)	0.0000 (0.0000)	1.0000	0.0000(0.0000)	1.0000
20	Sphere(20)	0.0000 (0.0000)	0.0000 (0.0000)	1.0000	0.0000(0.0000)	1.0000
20	Rosenbrock(20)	3.9481 (15.1928)	0.4788 (1.2955)	0.1213	0.0013(0.0078)	0.0003
20	Rastrigin(20)	24.9071 (6.7651)	6.8868 (3.0184)	0.2765	0.7960(1.2833)	0.0319
20	Griewank(20)	0.0129 (0.0137)	0.0128 (0.0130)	0.9910	0.0202(0.0195)	1.5682
20	Zakharov(20)	0.0000 (0.0000)	0.0000 (0.0000)	1.0000	0.0000(0.0000)	1.0000
30	Sphere(30)	0.0000 (0.0000)	0.0000 (0.0000)	1.0000	0.0000(0.0000)	1.0000
30	Rosenbrock(30)	8.6635 (6.7336)	0.3627 (1.1413)	0.0419	0.0632(0.0629)	0.0073
30	Rastrigin(30)	45.1711 (15.8998)	11.9425 (3.9591)	0.2644	1.4327(3.2848)	0.0317
30	Griewank(30)	0.0134 (0.0185)	0.0052 (0.0080)	0.3907	0.0187(0.0163)	1.3980
30	Zakharov(30)	0.9086 (4.8932)	0.0000 (0.0000)	5.5E-7	0.0000(0.0000)	5.5E-7

Shekel(4, 7), Griewank(20), and Griewank(30). This is compensated by the fact that the C/CyberSA demonstrates significantly greater effectiveness than the CyberSA in tackling the difficult functions like Rosenbrock and Rastrigin having ten or more variables. These findings motivate future investigations of Cyber Swarm methods that combine features of the original CyberSA and the C/CyberSA as a basis for creating a method that may embody the best features of both approaches. To get a rough indication of the promise of such an approach, we examined a "trivial combination" of the two methods as follows. Of the eleven functions that are not solved optimally by both CyberSA and C/CyberSA, we observe that CyberSA obtains better solutions on Shekel(4, 5), Shekel(4, 7), Griewank(20), and Griewank(30), while C/CyberSA obtains better solutions on Rosenbrock(10), Rastrigin(10), Griewank(10), Rosenbrock(20), Rastrigin(20), Rosenbrock(30) and Rastrigin(30). The maximum number of function evaluations required by CyberSA to find its best solution to any of the problems where it performs better is 104,416, while the maximum number of function evaluations required by C/CyberSA to find its best solution to any of the problems where it performs better is 137,504. Consequently, a "trivial combination" of the two methods that runs CyberSA for 104,416 function evaluations and C/CyberSA for 137,504 function evaluations would yield a method that provides the best solutions on all of these problems within a total number of 241,920 function evaluations. We have allotted a maximum of 250,000 function evaluations for the Standard PSO 2007 as a basis for fair comparison. The resulting version of Standard PSO 2007 does not perform much better than when the method is allotted 160,000 function evaluations, although it can solve Rosenbrock(5) and Zakharov(30) to optimality with 250,000 function evaluations. Consequently, the "trivial combination" of CyberSA and C/CyberSA likewise dominates the Standard PSO 2007 method when the latter is permitted to use 250,000 function evaluations, obtaining better solutions than the Standard PSO method on 16 test problems and matching the Standard PSO 2007 method on the remaining 14 problems. A more sophisticated way of combining the strategies employed by CyberSA and C/CyberSA would undoubtedly perform still better, thus reinforcing the motivation for future research to examine ways of integrating the TS and SS/PR strategies embodied in the CyberSA and C/CyberSA methods.

Finally, the value of the standard deviation listed in Table 1 also discloses that the computational results obtained by CyberSA and C/CyberSA from 100 independent runs are more consistent than those produced by the standard PSO 2007, recommending the use of the CyberSA and C/CyberSA from the worst-case analysis perspective.

4.2.2 Experiment 2

In the second experiment, we compare C/CyberSA with the Standard PSO 2007 and the PSwarn algorithm (Vaz & Vicente, 2007) with an extended set of test functions. The original set from Vaz and Vicente contains 122 test functions, although global optimum solutions were not identified for twelve of these to enable algorithmic performance to be evaluated in these cases. We thus solve the remaining 110 test functions by reference to the experimental setting used in Vaz and Vicente (2007). Thirty runs are executed for each competing algorithm, recording the number of function evaluations consumed when reaching the specified gap to the global optimum, with the limitation that the maximum number of function evaluations for each run is set to 10,000. For each test function, the best result (in terms of the number of function evaluations) obtained among the 30 runs is reported.

Table 2 lists the specified gap and the best result. The value in parentheses indicates the number of times among the 30 runs that the function value obtained by the algorithm reaches the specified gap. (The result for PSwarm does not include this success rate information because it was not provided in the original paper.) Overall, there are twelve test functions containing either 114, or 225, or 294 variables, which is extremely large by the usual standards for global function optimization. In these challenging cases all the competing algorithms fail to obtain a within-gap function value within 10,000 function evaluations. The function value finally obtained is marked with an asterisk (*) and is reported under the column of the corresponding algorithm. For these large and challenging test functions, the C/CyberSA method obtains the best function values with the same maximal number of function evaluations as the other methods. The Standard PSO 2007 ranks in second position while the PSwarm obtains the worst objective values for these functions. For the remaining 98 test functions which contain no more than 30 variables, we compare the number of test functions for each of the competing algorithms where the algorithm is unable to reach the specified gap within 10,000 function evaluations. Table 2 shows that the Standard PSO 2007 is less efficient than the other two methods and it fails to solve 17 test functions with satisfactory function values within the 10,000 function evaluation limit. PSwarm performs somewhat better by failing to reach the gap for only 13 test functions and the C/CyberSA method performs the best by solving all but 12 test functions.

Next we compare the efficiency for the test functions where the three competing methods can successfully solve to reaching the gap. We consider the number of function evaluations divided by 10,000 (excluding the cases where the algorithm fails to solve the test function) as the probability p_i that the corresponding algorithm fails to efficiently solve the test function i. Then the geometric mean of the efficiency probability $(1 - p_i)$ over the successfully solved cases can be derived by

$$\sqrt[|S|]{\prod_{i \in S} \left(1 - p_i\right)} \tag{7}$$

where S denotes the set of test functions where the corresponding algorithm successfully reaches the gap. We obtain the efficiency probability for the C/CyberSA, PSwarm, and Standard PSO 2007 as being 98.91%, 88.60%, and 83.23%, respectively, thus disclosing that the C/CyberSA is able to solve a wider range of test functions more efficiently than the other two algorithms. Moreover, the result also discloses that the PSwarm ranks as more efficient than the Standard PSO 2007 for this set of test functions.

Finally, we compare the success rate (the ratio of the 30 runs that the obtained function value reaches the specified gap) for the Standard PSO 2007 and the C/CyberSA. The success rate for the PSwarm is not available from its original paper. By excluding the failure cases where none of the 30 runs produces a solution that satisfies the gap, the overall success rate can be estimated by the geometric mean of individual rates. The over success rate for the Standard PSO 2007 and the C/CyberSA is derived according to the numbers listed in parentheses in Table 2, being 80.98% and 84.95%, respectively. In addition to solving five more test functions than the Standard PSO 2007, the C/CyberSA also manifests a higher success rate for the successfully solved cases. Consequently the C/CyberSA is more effective than the Standard PSO 2007 on all measures.

5. CONCLUDING REMARKS

Our Complementary Cyber Swarm Algorithm (C/CyberSA) draws on the basic principles underlying the original C/CyberSA method, but adopts different sets of ideas from tabu search (TS) and scatter search/path relinking (SS/PR). Extensive empirical tests with a set of 110 test functions shows that the C/CyberSA can produce improvements comparable to those provided by the CyberSA in relation to PSO methods that do not incorporate such ideas. The C/CyberSA exploits guidance and restriction information derived by applying adaptive memory strategies from TS to the history of swarm search and incorporates path relinking as an essential component to yield two long-term strategies as responses to the detection of critical events encountered in the search,

Our experimental results show that the C/CyberSA outperforms the PSwarm and the Standard PSO 2007 methods by finding more optimal solutions of the test problems and by simultaneously using a smaller number of function evaluations. In addition, we find that a "trivial combination" of C/

Table 2. Number of function evaluations to reach the specified gap to the global optimum by the competing algorithms

R	Test Function	Gap	Standard PSO 2007	PSwarm	C/CyberSA
10	ack	2.171640E-01	10000(0)	1797	84(27)
2	ap	8.600000E-05	440(30)	207	200(8)
2	bf1	0.000000E+00	2560(30)	204	86(30)
2	bf2	0.000000E+00	2240(30)	208	88(30)
2	bhs	1.384940E-01	80(30)	218	80(30)
2	bl	0.000000E+00	1000(30)	217	84(30)
2	bp	0.000000E+00	1440(30)	224	84(30)
2	cb3	0.000000E+00	1040(30)	190	84(30)
2	cb6	2.800000E-05	10000(0)	211	10000(0)
2	cm2	0.000000E+00	1160(30)	182	159(30)
4	cm4	0.000000E+00	2000(30)	385	84(30)
2	da	4.816600E-01	2720(30)	232	84(30)
10	em_10	1.384700E+00	10000(0)	4488	10000(0)
5	em_5	1.917650E-01	4480(2)	823	130(4)
2	ep	0.000000E+00	2320(30)	227	260(30)
10	exp	0.000000E+00	3240(30)	1434	84(30)
2	fls	3.000000E-06	10000(0)	227	10000(0)
2	fr	0.000000E+00	1160(29)	337	84(30)
10	fx_10	8.077291E+00	10000(0)	1773	10000(0)
5	fx_5	6.875980E+00	440(1)	799	10000(0)
2	gp	0.000000E+00	1840(30)	190	163(30)
3	grp	0.000000E+00	280(30)	1339	135(30)
10	gw	0.000000E+00	10000(0)	2296	10000(0)
3	h3	0.000000E+00	1280(30)	295	156(30)
6	h6	0.000000E+00	2680(14)	655	10000(0)
2	hm	0.000000E+00	1520(30)	195	84(30)
1	hm1	0.000000E+00	120(30)	96	84(30)
1	hm2	1.447000E-02	80(30)	141	80(30)
1	hm3	2.456000E-03	80(30)	110	80(30)
2	hm4	0.000000E+00	1480(30)	198	84(30)
3	hm5	0.000000E+00	960(30)	255	159(30)
2	hsk	1.200000E-05	120(30)	204	170(30)
3	hv	0.000000E+00	2560(30)	343	84(30)
4	ir0	0.000000E+00	5280(30)	671	114(27)
3	ir1	0.000000E+00	1480(30)	292	90(30)
2	ir2	1.000000E-06	1680(30)	522	144(30)
5	ir3	0.000000E+00	320(30)	342	172(30)
30	ir4	1.587200E-02	560(30)	8769	84(30)

continued on following page

Table 2. Continued

R	Test Function	Gap	Standard PSO 2007	PSwarm	C/CyberSA
4	kl	4.800000E-07	680(30)	1435	148(30)
1	ks	0.000000E+00	80(30)	92	80(30)
114	lj1_38	4.000000E-07	-65.83*	140.92*	-83.13*
225	lj1_75	4.000000E-07	18838.57*	35129.64*	5958.58*
294	lj1_98	4.000000E-07	134854.88*	193956.8*	35613.6*
114	lj2_38	4.000000E-07	146.48*	372.77*	161.2*
225	lj2_75	4.000000E-07	25227.97*	32450.09*	8302.73*
294	lj2_98	4.000000E-07	112291.68*	170045.2*	52087.07*
114	lj3_38	4.000000E-07	588.51*	1729.29*	283.24*
225	lj3_75	4.000000E-07	499130*	1036894*	118721*
294	lj3_98	4.000000E-07	7667493*	15188010*	2562334*
3	lm1	0.000000E+00	1760(30)	335	84(30)
10	lm2_10	0.000000E+00	4920(28)	1562	162(30)
5	lm2_5	0.000000E+00	2640(30)	625	84(30)
3	lv8	0.000000E+00	1560(30)	310	84(30)
2	mc	7.700000E-05	160(30)	211	84(30)
4	mcp	0.000000E+00	200(30)	248	164(30)
2	mgp	2.593904E+00	80(30)	193	80(30)
10	mgw_10	1.107800E-02	240(30)	10007	173(30)
2	mgw_2	0.000000E+00	80(30)	339	84(30)
20	mgw_20	5.390400E-02	560(27)	10005	133(28)
10	ma_10	0.000000E+00	10000(0)	2113	10000(0)
5	ml_5	0.000000E+00	2640(8)	603	135(15)
3	mr	1.860000E-03	560(27)	886	84(30)
2	mrp	0.000000E+00	1720(18)	217	185(24)
4	nf2	2.700000E-05	320(30)	2162	156(30)
10	nf3_10	0.000000E+00	10000(0)	4466	86(23)
15	nf3_15	7.000000E-06	10000(0)	10008	90(18)
20	nf3_20	2.131690E-01	10000(0)	10008	85(19)
25	nf3_25	5.490210E-01	10000(0)	10025	94(9)
30	nf3_30	6.108021E+01	10000(0)	10005	98(14)
10	osp_10	1.143724E+00	480(19)	1885	132(11)
20	osp_20	1.143833E+00	80(30)	5621	80(30)
114	plj_38	4.000000E-07	486.37*	774.64*	299.12*
225	plj_75	4.000000E-07	21733.21*	37284.11*	10953.88*
294	plj_98	4.000000E-07	111878.79*	179615.0*	39135.69*
10	pp	4.700000E-04	2320(30)	1578	84(30)
2	prd	0.000000E+00	1440(26)	400	126(30)
9	ptm	3.908401E+00	4280(2)	10009	10000(0)

continued on following page

Table 2. Continued

R	Test Function	Gap	Standard PSO 2007	PSwarm	C/CyberSA
4	pwq	0.000000E+00	2880(30)	439	84(30)
10	rb	1.114400E-02	10000(0)	10003	84(16)
10	rg_10	0.000000E+00	10000(0)	4364	170(9)
2	rg_2	0.000000E+00	1120(29)	210	84(30)
4	s10	4.510000E-03	1560(12)	431	84(30)
4	s5	3.300000E-03	1480(9)	395	10000(0)
4	s7	3.041000E-03	1400(17)	415	84(30)
10	sal_10	3.998730E-01	1400(30)	1356	84(30)
5	sal_5	1.998730E-01	800(30)	452	85(30)
2	sbt	9.000000E-06	1480(30)	305	129(30)
2	sf1	9.716000E-03	320(30)	210	84(30)
2	sf2	5.383000E-03	3280(30)	266	90(30)
1	shv1	1.000000E-03	80(30)	101	80(30)
2	shv2	0.000000E+00	640(30)	196	154(30)
10	sin_10	0.000000E+00	4560(29)	1872	85(30)
20	sin_20	0.000000E+00	8360(25)	5462	84(29)
17	st_17	3.081935E+06	4160(5)	10011	127(30)
9	st_9	7.516622E+00	10000(0)	10001	10000(0)
1	stg	0.000000E+00	80(30)	113	84(30)
10	swf	1.184385E+02	10000(0)	2311	10000(0)
1	sz	2.561249E+00	80(30)	125	80(29)
1	szzs	1.308000E-03	80(30)	112	80(30)
4	wf	2.500000E-05	10000(0)	10008	84(17)
10	zkv_10	1.393000E-03	3920(30)	10003	84(30)
2	zkv_2	0.000000E+00	1120(30)	212	84(30)
20	zkv_20	3.632018E+01	840(29)	10018	171(30)
5	zkv_5	0.000000E+00	3280(30)	1318	84(30)
1	zlk1	4.039000E-03	200(30)	119	126(30)
1	zlk2a	5.000000E-03	80(30)	130	80(30)
1	zlk2b	5.000000E-03	80(30)	113	80(30)
2	zlk4	2.112000E-03	240(30)	224	162(9)
3	zlk5	2.782000E-03	200(30)	294	166(5)
1	zzs	4.239000E-03	80(30)	120	80(23)

CyberSA and CyberSA that runs for 250,000 function evaluations strongly dominates the Standard PSO 2007 method when the latter method is allotted this number of function evaluations, obtaining better solutions on 16 out of 30 basic test cases and matching the quality of solutions obtained by the Standard PSO 2007 on the remaining 14 cases. These findings motivate future investigations of Cyber Swarm methods that combine features of both the original and complementary variants and incorporate additional strategic notions from SS and PR.

REFERENCES

Angeline, P. J. (1999). Using selection to improve particle swarm optimization. In *Proceedings of the IEEE International Joint Conference on Neural Networks* (pp. 84-89). IEEE.

Audet, C., & Dennis, J. E. Jr. (2002). Analysis of generalized pattern searches. *SIAM Journal on Optimization*, *13*(3), 889–903. doi:10.1137/S1052623400378742

Campos, V., Glover, F., Laguna, M., & Martí, R. (2001). An experimental evaluation of a scatter search for the linear ordering problem. *Journal of Global Optimization*, *21*(4), 397–414. doi:10.1023/A:1012793906010

Chelouah, R., & Siarry, P. (2000). Tabu search applied to global optimization. *European Journal of Operational Research*, *123*(2), 256–270. doi:10.1016/S0377-2217(99)00255-6

Chelouah, R., & Siarry, P. (2005). A hybrid method combining continuous tabu search and Nelder–Mead simplex algorithms for the global optimization of multiminima functions. *European Journal of Operational Research*, *161*(3), 636–654. doi:10.1016/j.ejor.2003.08.053

Clerc, M. (2008). Standard PSO 2007. Retrieved from http://www.particleswarm.info/Programs.html

Clerc, M., & Kennedy, J. (2002). The particle swarm explosion, stability, and convergence in a multidimensional complex space. *IEEE Transactions on Evolutionary Computation*, *6*(1), 58–73. doi:10.1109/4235.985692

Duarte, A., Marti, R., & Glover, F. (2007). *Adaptive memory programming for global optimization. Research Report*. Valencia, Spain: University of Valencia.

Duarte, A., Marti, R., Glover, F., & Gortazar, F. (2011a). Hybrid scatter-tabu search for unconstrained global optimization. *Annals of Operations Research*, *183*(1), 95–123. doi:10.1007/s10479-009-0596-2

Duarte, A., Marti, R., & Gortazar, F. (2011b). Path relinking for large scale global optimization. *Soft Computing*, 15.

Eberhart, R. C., & Shi, Y. (1998). Evolving artificial neural networks. In *Proceedings of International Conference on Neural Networks and Brain* (pp. 5-13). Academic Press.

Feng, H. M., Chen, C. Y., & Ye, F. (2007). Evolutionary fuzzy particle swarm optimization vector quantization learning scheme in image compression. *Expert Systems with Applications*, *32*(1), 213–222. doi:10.1016/j.eswa.2005.11.012

Glover, F. (1986). Future paths for integer programming and links to artificial intelligence. *Computers & Operations Research*, *13*(5), 533–549. doi:10.1016/0305-0548(86)90048-1

Glover, F. (1994). Tabu search for nonlinear and parametric optimization (with links to genetic algorithms). *Discrete Applied Mathematics*, *49*(1-3), 231–255. doi:10.1016/0166-218X(94)90211-9

Glover, F. (1996a). Tabu search and adaptive memory programming - Advances, applications and challenges. In Interfaces in Computer Science and Operations Research. Dordrecht, The Netherlands: Kluwer Academic Publishers.

Glover, F. (1996b). Ejection chains, reference structures and alternating path methods for traveling salesman problems. *Discrete Applied Mathematics*, *65*(1-3), 223–253. doi:10.1016/0166-218X(94)00037-E

Glover, F. (1998). A template for scatter search and path relinking. In J. Hao, E. Lutton, E. Ronald, M. Schoenauer, & D. Snyers (Eds.), *Artificial Evolution: Proceedings of Third European Conference (AE '97) (LNCS)* (vol. 1363, pp. 13-54). Berlin: Springer.

Glover, F., & Laguna, M. (1997). *Tabu Search*. Boston: Kluwer Academic Publishers. doi:10.1007/978-1-4615-6089-0

Hansen, N. (1997). Variable neighborhood search. *Computers & Operations Research*, *24*(11), 1097–1100. doi:10.1016/S0305-0548(97)00031-2

Hedar, A., & Fukushima, M. (2006). Tabu search directed by direct search methods for nonlinear global optimization. *European Journal of Operational Research*, *170*(2), 329–349. doi:10.1016/j.ejor.2004.05.033

Hirsch, M. J., Meneses, C. N., Pardalos, P. M., & Resende, M. G. C. (2007). Global optimization by continuous grasp. *Optimization Letters*, *1*(2), 201–212. doi:10.1007/s11590-006-0021-6

Ho, S. C., & Gendreau, M. (2006). Path relinking for the vehicle routing problem. *Journal of Heuristics*, *12*(1-2), 55–72. doi:10.1007/s10732-006-4192-1

Hvattum, L. M., & Glover, F. (2009). Finding local optima of high-dimensional functions using direct search methods. *European Journal of Operational Research*, *195*(1), 31–45. doi:10.1016/j.ejor.2008.01.039

James, T., Rego, C., & Glover, F. (2009). Multistart tabu search and diversification strategies for the quadratic assignment problem. *IEEE Transactions on Systems, Man, and Cybernetics. Part A, Systems and Humans*, *39*(3), 579–596. doi:10.1109/TSMCA.2009.2014556

Kennedy, J. (1999). Small world and megaminds: effects of neighbourhood topology on particle swarm performance. In *Proceedings of the Congress on Evolutionary Computation* (pp. 1931-1938). Washington, DC: Academic Press.

Kennedy, J., & Eberhart, R. C. (1995). Particle swarm optimization. In *Proceedings of IEEE International Conference on Neural Networks,* (vol. 4, pp. 1942-1948). IEEE.

Laguna, M., & Marti, R. (2003). *Scatter Search: Methodology and Implementation in C*. London: Kluwer Academic Publishers. doi:10.1007/978-1-4615-0337-8

Laguna, M., & Marti, R. (2005). Experimental testing of advanced scatter search designs for global optimization of multimodal functions. *Journal of Global Optimization*, *33*(2), 235–255. doi:10.1007/s10898-004-1936-z

Lepagnot, J., Nakib, A., Oulhadj, H., & Siarry, P. (2010). A new multiagent algorithm for dynamic continuous optimization. *International Journal of Applied Metaheuristic Computing*, *1*(1), 16–38. doi:10.4018/jamc.2010102602

Lovbjerg, M., Rasmussen, T. K., & Krink, T. (2001). Hybrid particle swarm optimizer with breeding and subpopulations. In *Proceedings of the Genetic and Evolutionary Computation Conference*. Academic Press.

Lu, Z., Hao, J.-K., & Glover, F. (2010). Neighborhood analysis: A case study on curriculum-based course timetabling. *Journal of Heuristics*. DOI10.1007/s10732-010-9128-0

Luke, S. (2009). *Essentials of Metaheuristics*, Retrieved from http://cs.gmu.edu/~sean/book/metaheuristics

Mendes, R., Kennedy, J., & Neves, J. (2004). The fully informed particle swarm: Simpler, maybe better. *IEEE Transactions on Evolutionary Computation*, *8*(3), 204–210. doi:10.1109/TEVC.2004.826074

Miranda, V., Keko, H., & Jaramillo, A. (2007). EPSO: evolutionary particle swarms. In L. C. Jain, V. Palade, & D. Srinivasan (Eds.), *Advances in Evolutionary Computing for System Design* (pp. 139–167). Springer-Verlag Berlin Heidelberg. doi:10.1007/978-3-540-72377-6_6

Nakano, S., Ishigame, A., & Yasuda, K. (2007). Particle swarm optimization based on the concept of tabu search. In *Proceedings of the IEEE Congress on Evolutionary Computation* (pp. 3258-3263). IEEE.

Rego, C., & Glover, F. (2009). Ejection chain and filter-and-fan methods in combinatorial optimization. In *Annals of Operations Research*. Springer Science+Business Media. DOI 10.1007/s10479-009-0656-7

Shen, Q., Shi, W. M., & Kong, W. (2008). Hybrid particle swarm optimization and tabu search approach for selecting genes for tumor classification using gene expression data. *Computational Biology and Chemistry*, *32*(1), 53–59. doi:10.1016/j.compbiolchem.2007.10.001 PMID:18093877

Sorensen, K., & Glover, F. (2010). Metaheuristics. In Encyclopedia of Operations Research (3rd ed.). Springer Science+Business Media.

Sörensen, K., Sevaux, M., & Schittekat, P. (2008). Multiple neighbourhood search. In commercial VRP packages: evolving towards self-adaptive methods. Lecture Notes in Economics and Mathematical Systems, 136, 239–253.

Takamu, S., Toshiku, G., & Yoshikazu, Y. (2003). A hybrid particle swarm optimization for distribution state estimation. *IEEE Transactions on Power Systems*, *18*(1), 60–68. doi:10.1109/TPWRS.2002.807051

Vaz, A. I. F., & Vicente, L. N. (2007). A particle swarm pattern search method for bound constrained global optimization. *Journal of Global Optimization*, *39*(2), 197–219. doi:10.1007/s10898-007-9133-5

Wang, Y. X., Zhao, Z. D., & Ren, R. (2007). Hybrid particle swarm optimizer with tabu strategy for global numerical optimization. In *Proceedings of IEEE Congress on Evolutionary Computation*, (pp. 2310-2316). IEEE.

Yin, P. Y., & Chiang, Y. (2013). Cyber swarm algorithms for multi-objective nurse rostering problem. *International Journal of Innovative Computing, Information, & Control*, *9*(5), 2043–2063.

Yin, P. Y., Glover, F., Laguna, M., & Zhu, J. X. (2010). Cyber swarm algorithms – improving particle swarm optimization using adaptive memory strategies. *European Journal of Operational Research*, *201*(2), 377–389. doi:10.1016/j.ejor.2009.03.035

Yin, P. Y., & Su, E. (2011). Cyber swarm optimization for general keyboard arrangement problem. *International Journal of Industrial Ergonomics*, *41*(1), 43–52. doi:10.1016/j.ergon.2010.11.007

Yin, P.Y., & Wu, H. (2013). Cyber-EDA: Estimation of Distribution Algorithms with Adaptive Memory Programming. In *Mathematical Problems in Engineering*. doi:10.1155/2013/132697

Yoshida, H., Kawata, K., Fukuyama, Y., & Nakanishi, Y. (1999). A particle swarm optimization for reactive power and voltage control considering voltage stability. In *Proceedings International Conference on Intelligent System Application to Power Systems* (pp. 117-121). Academic Press.

KEY TERMS AND DEFINITIONS

Metaheuristic: A generic computing framework that guides the course of an embedded heuristic(s) to search beyond the local optimality.

Multi-Start: A search strategy which guides the metaheuristic to restart a new search session in uncharted domain when the previous search session stagnates in improving the solution.

Particle Swarm Optimization: A metaheuristic which mimics the bird schooling behavior and is now broadly used as an optimizer.

Path Relinking: A scheme for solution combination method which promotes an initiating solution moving towards guiding solutions.

Responsive Strategy: A search strategy which responds to the status change of the adaptive memory.

Scatter Search: A metaheuristic which defines a search template containing five functional components, namely, the diversification generation method, the reference set update method, the subset generation method, the solution combination method, and the improvement method.

Tabu Search: A metaheuristic working with adaptive memory which avoids the reversal search to previously visited solutions.

Chapter 4
Population Diversity of Particle Swarm Optimizer Solving Single- and Multi-Objective Problems

Shi Cheng
University of Nottingham Ningbo, China

Yuhui Shi
Xi'an Jiaotong-Liverpool University, China

Quande Qin
Shenzhen University, China

ABSTRACT

Premature convergence occurs in swarm intelligence algorithms searching for optima. A swarm intelligence algorithm has two kinds of abilities: exploration of new possibilities and exploitation of old certainties. The exploration ability means that an algorithm can explore more search places to increase the possibility that the algorithm can find good enough solutions. In contrast, the exploitation ability means that an algorithm focuses on the refinement of found promising areas. An algorithm should have a balance between exploration and exploitation, that is, the allocation of computational resources should be optimized to ensure that an algorithm can find good enough solutions effectively. The diversity measures the distribution of individuals' information. From the observation of the distribution and diversity change, the degree of exploration and exploitation can be obtained. Another issue in multiobjective is the solution metric. Pareto domination is utilized to compare two solutions; however, solutions are almost Pareto non-dominated for multiobjective problems with more than ten objectives. In this chapter, the authors analyze the population diversity of a particle swarm optimizer for solving both single objective and multiobjective problems. The population diversity of solutions is used to measure the goodness of a set of solutions. This metric may guide the search in problems with numerous objectives. Adaptive optimization algorithms can be designed through controlling the balance between exploration and exploitation.

DOI: 10.4018/978-1-4666-6328-2.ch004

INTRODUCTION

Optimization, in general, is concerned with finding "best available" solution(s) for a given problem within allowable time. In mathematical terms, an optimization problem in $\mathcal{R}^n$, or simply an optimization problem, is a mapping $f : \mathcal{R}^n \to \mathcal{R}^k$, where $\mathcal{R}^n$ is termed as decision space (Adra, Dodd, & Griffin, *et al.*, 2009), parameter space (Jin & Sendhoff, 2009), or problem space (Weise, Zapf, & Chiong, *et al.*, 2009)), and $\mathcal{R}^k$ is termed as objective space (Sundaram, 1996). Optimization problems can be divided into two categories depending on the value of k. When $k = 1$, this kind of problems is called Single Objective Optimization (SOO), and when $k > 1$, this is called Multi-Objective Optimization (or Many Objective Optimization, MOO).

Particle Swarm Optimizer/Optimization (PSO), which is one of the evolutionary computation techniques, was invented by Eberhart and Kennedy in 1995 (Eberhart & Kennedy, 1995; Kennedy & Eberhart, 1995). It is a population-based stochastic algorithm modeled on the social behaviors observed in flocking birds. Each particle, which represents a solution, flies through the search space with a velocity that is dynamically adjusted according to its own and its companion's historical behaviors. The particles tend to fly toward better search areas over the course of the search process (Eberhart & Shi, 2001; Hu, Shi, & Eberhart, 2004).

Premature convergence occurs when all individuals in population-based algorithms are trapped in local optima. In this situation, the exploration of algorithm is greatly reduced, i.e., the algorithm is searching in a narrow space. For continuous optimization problems, there are infinite numbers of potential solutions. Even with consideration of computational precision, there still have great number of feasible solutions. The computational resources allocation should be optimized, i.e.,

maintaining an appropriate balance between exploration and exploitation is a primary factor.

Different problems have different properties. Single objective problem could be divided into unimodal problem and multi-modal problem. As the name indicated, a unimodal problem has only one optimum solution, on the contrary, a multi-modal problem has several or number of optimum solutions, of which many are local optimal solutions. Optimization algorithms are difficult to find the global optimum solutions because generally it is hard to balance between fast converge speed and the ability of "jumping out" of local optimum. In other words, we need to avoid premature in the search process.

Different computational resource allocation methods should be taken when dealing with different problems. A good algorithm should balance its exploration and exploitation ability during its search process. The concept of exploration and exploitation was firstly introduced in organization science (March, 1991; Gupta, Smith, & Shalley, 2006). The exploration ability means an algorithm can explore more search place, to increase the possibility that the algorithm can find "good enough" solution(s). In contrast, the exploitation ability means that an algorithm focuses on the refinement of found promising areas.

The population diversity (De Jong, 1975; Mauldin, 1984; Olorunda & Engelbrecht, 2008; Corriveau, Guilbault, & Tahan, *et al.*, 2012) is a measure of individuals' search information. From the distribution of individuals and change of this distribution information, we can obtain the algorithm's status of exploration or exploitation. An important issue in multiobjective is the fitness metric in solutions. The Pareto domination is frequently used in current research to compare between two solutions. The Pareto domination has many strengths, such as easy to understand, computational efficiency, however, it has some drawbacks:

1. It only can be used to compare between two single solutions, for several group of solutions, the Pareto domination is difficult to measure which group is better than others.
2. For multiobjective problems with large number of objectives, almost every solution is Pareto nondominated (Ishibuchi, Tsukamoto, & Nojima, 2008). The Pareto domination is not appropriate for the multiobjective problem with large number of objectives.

In this chapter, we will analyze and discuss the population diversity of particle swarm optimizer for solving single and multi-objective problems. For multiobjective problems, the population diversity is observed on both the particles and the solutions in the archive. The population of particles measures the distribution of the positions, while the population of solutions can be used to measure the goodness of a set of solutions. This metric may guide the search in multiobjective problems with numerous objectives. Adaptive optimization algorithms can be designed through controlling balance between exploration and exploitation.

The rest of the chapter is organized as follows: the basic PSO algorithm and the multiobjective optimization are reviewed in Section Preliminaries. In Section Population Diversity, several definitions of dimension-wise PSO diversities, which based on L_1 norm, are given on single objective optimization and multiobjective optimization. The Section Experimental Results gives the experiments on diversity monitoring for some single and multi-objective benchmark functions. The analysis and discussion of population diversities for single and multi-objective optimization are given in Section Analysis and Discussion. Finally, Section Conclusions concludes with some remarks and future research directions.

PRELIMINARIES

Particle Swarm Optimizer

Particle swarm optimization emulates the swarm behavior and the individuals represent points in the n-dimensional search space. A particle represents a potential solution. Each particle is associated with two vectors, i.e., the velocity vector and the position vector. The position x_{ij} and velocity v_{ij} represent the position and velocity of ith particle at jth dimension, respectively. For the purpose of generality and clarity, m represents the number of particles and n the number of dimensions. The i represents the ith particle, $i = 1, \cdots, m$, and j is the jth dimension, $j = 1, \cdots, n$ (Cheng, 2013).

The canonical PSO algorithm is simple in concept and easy in implementation. The velocity and position update equations are as follow (Shi & Eberhart, 1998; Kennedy, Eberhart, & Shi, 2001; Eberhart & Shi, 2007):

$$\mathbf{v}_i(t+1) \leftarrow w_i \mathbf{v}_i(t) + c_1 \text{rand}()$$
$$(\mathbf{p}_i - \mathbf{x}_i(t)) + c_2 \text{Rand}()(\mathbf{p}_g - \mathbf{x}_i(t)) \quad (1)$$

$$\mathbf{x}_i(t+1) \leftarrow \mathbf{x}_i(t) + \mathbf{v}_i(t+1) \quad (2)$$

where w denotes the inertia weight and usually is less than 1 (Shi & Eberhart, 1998; Shi & Eberhart, 2011; Cheng, Shi, & Qin, *et al.*, 2012), c_1 and c_2 are two positive acceleration constants, $\text{rand}()$ and $\text{Rand}()$ are two random functions to generate uniformly distributed random numbers in the range $[0, 1)$ and are different for each dimension and each particle, $\mathbf{x}_i = [x_{i1}, \cdots, x_{ij}, \cdots, x_{in}]$ represents the ith particle's position, $\mathbf{v}_i = [v_{i1}, \cdots, v_{ij}, \cdots, v_{in}]$ represents the ith particle's velocity, $\mathbf{p}_i = [p_{i1}, \cdots, p_{ij}, \cdots, p_{in}]$ is termed as personal best, which refers to the best position found by the ith particle, and $\mathbf{p}_g = [p_{g1}, \cdots, p_{gj}, \cdots, p_{gn}]$ is termed as local best, which refers to the position found by the members in the ith particle's neighborhood that has the best fitness value so far.

The basic procedure of PSO is given as Algorithm 1 below.

Multiobjective Optimization

Multiobjective Optimization refers to optimization problems that involve two or more objectives. Usually for multiobjective optimization problems, a set of solutions is sought instead of one. A general *multiobjective optimization problem* can be described as a vector function $\mathbf{f}$ that maps a tuple of n parameters (decision variables) to a tuple of k objectives. Without loss of generality, minimization is assumed throughout this chapter.

$$\text{minimize} \quad \mathbf{f}(\mathbf{x}) = (f_1(\mathbf{x}), f_2(\mathbf{x}), \cdots, f_k(\mathbf{x}))$$

$$\text{subject to} \quad \mathbf{x} = (x_1, \cdots, x_i, \cdots, x_n) \in \mathbf{X}$$

$$\mathbf{y} = (y_1, \cdots, y_j, \cdots, y_k) \in \mathbf{Y}$$

where x_i is a decision variable, $\mathbf{x}$ is called the *decision vector*, $\mathbf{X}$ is the *decision space*; y_j is

an objective, $\mathbf{y}$ is the *objective vector*, and $\mathbf{Y}$ is the *objective space*, and $\mathbf{f} : \mathbf{X} \rightarrow \mathbf{Y}$ consists of k real-valued objective functions.

Let $\mathbf{u} = (u_1, \cdots, u_k)$, $\mathbf{v} = (v_1, \cdots, v_k) \in \mathbf{Y}$, be two vectors, $\mathbf{u}$ is said to dominate $\mathbf{v}$ (denoted as $\mathbf{u} \preccurlyeq \mathbf{v}$), if $u_i \leq v_i, \forall i = 1, \cdots, k$, and $\mathbf{u} \neq \mathbf{v}$. A point $\mathbf{x}^* \in \mathbf{X}$ is called Pareto optimal if there is no $\mathbf{x} \in \mathbf{X}$ such that $\mathbf{f}(\mathbf{x})$ dominates $\mathbf{f}(\mathbf{x}^*)$. The set of all the Pareto optimal points is called the *Pareto set* (denoted as *PS*). The set of all the Pareto objective vectors, $PF = \{f(x) \in X \mid x \in PS\}$, is called the *Pareto front* (denoted as *PF*).

In a multiobjective optimization problem, we aim to find the set of optimal solutions known as the Pareto optimal set. Pareto optimality is defined with respect to the concept of nondominated points in the objective space.

POPULATION DIVERSITY

Premature convergence occurs in population-based algorithms. Holland has introduced a well-known phenomenon of "hitchhiking" in population genetics (Holland, 2000). In population-based algorithms, all individuals search for optima at the same time. If, compared with other individuals, some newly searched solution gives extremely good fitness value; all other individuals may converge rapidly toward it. It is difficult to

Algorithm 1. The basic procedure of particle swarm optimization

---

1: Initialize velocity and position randomly for each particle in every dimension.
2: While *not found the "good enough" solution or not reached the maximum number of iterations* do
3: Calculate each particle's fitness value
4: Compare fitness value between that of current position and that of the best position in history (personal best, termed as *pbest*). For each particle, if the fitness value of current position is better than *pbest*, then update *pbest* to be the current position.
5: Select the particle which has the best fitness value among current particle's neighborhood, this particle is called the neighborhood best (termed as *nbest*). If current particle's neighborhood includes all particles then this neighborhood best is the global best (termed as *gbest*), otherwise, it is local best (termed as *lbest*).
6: for each particle do
7: Update particle's velocity and position according to the equation (1) and (2), respectively.
8: end for
9: end while

---

handle premature convergence. Once individuals "get stuck" in local optima, the exploration of the algorithm is greatly reduced, i.e., solutions lose their diversity in decision space.

Another kind of premature convergence occurs due to improper setting of boundary constraints (Cheng, Shi, & Qin, 2011). A classic boundary constraint handling strategy resets a particle at boundary in one dimension when this particle's position is exceeding the boundary in that dimension. If the fitness value of the particle at boundary is better than that of other particles, all particles in its neighborhood in this dimension will move to the boundary. If particles could not find a position with better fitness value, all particles will "stick in" the boundary at this dimension. A particle is difficult to "jump out" of boundary even we increase the total number of fitness evaluations or the maximum number of iterations, and this phenomenon occurs with higher possibility for high-dimensional problems.

The most important factor affecting an optimization algorithm's performance is its ability of "exploration" or "exploitation". Exploration means the ability of a search algorithm to explore different areas of the decision space in order to have high probability of finding good optimum. Exploitation, on the other hand, means the ability to concentrate the search around a found promising region in order to refine a candidate solution. A good optimization algorithm optimally balances these conflicted objectives. Within the PSO, these objectives are addressed by the velocity update equation.

Many strategies have been proposed to adjust an algorithm's exploration and exploitation ability. Velocity clamp was firstly used to adjust the ability between exploration and exploitation (Eberhart, Dobbins, & Simpson, 1996). Like the equation (3), current velocity will be equal to maximum velocity or minus maximum velocity if velocity is greater than the maximum velocity or less than the minus maximum velocity, respectively. Adding an inertia weight is more effective than

velocity clamp because it not only increases the probability for an algorithm to converge, but have a way to control the whole searching process of an algorithm (Shi & Eberhart, 1998). There are many adaptive strategies to tune algorithms' parameters during the search (Cheng, Shi, & Qin, 2012a; Cheng, Shi, & Qin, *et al.*, 2012). The properties of population diversity in single objective optimization have been discussed in many papers (Cheng, Shi, & Qin, 2012c; Corriveau, Guilbault, & Tahan, *et al.*, 2012). The properties of population in multiobjective optimization and the difference between population diversity in SOP and MOP are still needed to be analyzed and discussed.

$$v_{ij} = \begin{cases} V_{max} & v_{ij} > V_{max} \\ v_{ij} & -V_{max} \le v_{ij} \le V_{max} \\ -V_{max} & v_{ij} < -V_{max} \end{cases} \quad (3)$$

Diversity in Single Objective Optimization

Population diversity of PSO is useful for measuring and dynamically adjusting an algorithm's ability of exploration or exploitation accordingly. Shi and Eberhart gave three definitions on population diversity, which are position diversity, velocity diversity, and cognitive diversity (Shi & Eberhart, 2008; Shi & Eberhart, 2009). Position, velocity, and cognitive diversity are used to measure the distribution of particles' current positions, current velocities, and *pbest*s (the best position found so far for each particles), respectively. Cheng and Shi introduced the modified definitions of the three diversity measures based on L_1 norm (Cheng & Shi, 2011a; Cheng & Shi, 2011b).

Position Diversity

Position diversity measures distribution of particles' current positions, therefore, can reflect particles' dynamics. Position diversity gives the current position distribution information of particles, whether the particles are going to diverge or converge could be reflected from this measurement. From diversity measurements, useful search information can be obtained. Definition of dimension-wise position diversity, which is based on the L_1 distance, is as follows

$$\bar{x}_j = \frac{1}{m} \sum_{i=1}^{m} x_{ij}$$

$$D_j^p = \frac{1}{m} \sum_{i=1}^{m} |x_{ij} - \bar{x}_j|$$

$$D^p = \sum_{j=1}^{n} w_j D_j^p$$

where $\bar{x}_j$ represents the pivot of particles' position in dimension j, and D_j^p measures particles position diversity based on L_1 norm for dimension j. $\mathbf{x} = [\bar{x}_1, \cdots, \bar{x}_j, \cdots, \bar{x}_n]$, represents the mean of particles' current positions for all dimensions, and $\mathbf{D}^p = [D_1^p, \cdots, D_j^p, \cdots, D_n^p]$, measures particles' position diversity based on L_1 norm for all dimensions. D^p measures the whole swarm's population diversity.

Velocity Diversity

Velocity diversity, which represents diversity of particles' "moving potential", measures the distribution of particles' current velocities. In other words, velocity diversity measures the "activity" information of particles. Based on the measurement of velocity diversity, particle's tendency of expansion or convergence could be revealed. The dimension-wise velocity diversity based on L_1 distance is defined as follows

$$\bar{v}_j = \frac{1}{m} \sum_{i=1}^{m} v_{ij}$$

$$D_j^v = \frac{1}{m} \sum_{i=1}^{m} |v_{ij} - \bar{v}_j|$$

$$D_j^v = \sum_{j=1}^{n} w_j D_j^v$$

where $\bar{v}_j$ represents the pivot of particles' velocity in dimension j, and D_j^v measures particles velocity diversity based on L_1 norm for dimension j. $\bar{\mathbf{v}} = [\bar{v}_1, \cdots, \bar{v}_j, \cdots, \bar{v}_n]$, represents the mean of particles' current velocities for all dimensions, and $\mathbf{D}^v = [D_1^v, \cdots, D_j^v, \cdots, D_n^v]$, measures velocity diversity of all particles for all dimensions. D^v represents the whole swarm velocity diversity based on L_1 norm.

Cognitive Diversity

Cognitive diversity, which represents distribution of particles' "moving target", measures the distribution of historical best positions for all particles. The measurement definition of cognitive diversity is the same as that of the position diversity except that it utilizes each particle's current personal best position instead of current position. The definition of dimension-wise PSO cognitive diversity is as follows

$$\bar{p}_j = \frac{1}{m} \sum_{i=1}^{m} p_{ij}$$

$$D_j^c = \frac{1}{m} \sum_{i=1}^{m} |p_{ij} - \bar{p}_j|$$

$$D^c = \sum_{j=1}^{n} w_j D_j^c$$

where $\bar{p}_j$ represents the pivot of particles' previous best position in dimension j, and D_j^v measures particles cognitive diversity based on L_1 norm for dimension j. $\mathbf{p} = [\bar{p}_1, \cdots, \bar{p}_j, \cdots, \bar{p}_n]$ represents the average of all particles' personal best position in history (*pbest*) for all dimensions; $\mathbf{D}^c = [D_1^p, \cdots, D_j^p, \cdots, D_n^p]$ represents the particles' cognitive diversity for all dimensions based on L_1 norm. D^c measures the whole swarm's cognitive diversity.

Without loss of generality, every dimension is considered equally in this chapter. Setting all weights $w_j = \dfrac{1}{n}$, then the position diversity, velocity diversity, and cognitive diversity of the whole swarm can be rewritten as:

$$D^p = \sum_{j=1}^{n} \frac{1}{n} D_j^p = \frac{1}{n} \sum_{j=1}^{n} D_j^p$$

$$D^v = \sum_{j=1}^{n} \frac{1}{n} D_j^v = \frac{1}{n} \sum_{j=1}^{n} D_j^v$$

$$D^c = \sum_{j=1}^{n} \frac{1}{n} D_j^c = \frac{1}{n} \sum_{j=1}^{n} D_j^c .$$

Change of Position Diversity and Cognitive Diversity

The position diversity and cognitive diversity measure the distribution of particles' current position and previous best position. From the change of position diversity and cognitive diversity, the algorithm's status of exploration and exploitation may be obtained. The change of position diversity and cognitive diversity are defined as follow:

$$C^p = D^p(t+1) - D^p(t)$$

$$C^c = D^c(t+1) - D^c(t)$$

where C^p is the change of position diversity, and C^c is the change of cognitive diversity.

From the changing of position diversity and cognitive diversity, the speed of swarm convergence or divergence can be observed. The changing of position diversity and cognitive diversity can be divided into four cases:

1. Position diversity increasing, cognitive diversity increasing, i.e., position diversity and cognitive diversity getting increased at the same time.
2. Position diversity decreasing, cognitive diversity decreasing, i.e., position diversity and cognitive diversity getting decreased at the same time.
3. Position diversity increasing, cognitive diversity decreasing.
4. Position diversity decreasing, cognitive diversity increasing.

For the first two cases, if the position diversity and cognitive diversity increase at the same time, the swarm is diverging, i.e., the algorithm is in the exploration status, and on the contrary, if the position diversity and cognitive diversity decrease at the same time, the swarm is converging, i.e., the algorithm is in the exploitation status. The last two cases reflect more complicated situations.

Ratio of Position Diversity to Cognitive Diversity

Cognitive diversity represents the distribution of all current moving targets found by particles. From the relationship of position diversity and cognitive diversity, particles' dynamical movement can be observed.

The ratio of position diversity to cognitive diversity is defined as follows:

$$R = \frac{\text{Position Diversity}}{\text{Cognitive Diversity}} = \frac{D^p}{D^c}$$

The ratio of position diversity to cognitive diversity indicates the movement of particles. If the value large than 1, the particles are searching in a relatively larger space, and the previous best solutions are in a relatively smaller space. On the contrast, if the value is less than 1, the particles' search is in a relatively smaller space. Different strategies should be utilized under these different situations to maintain an appropriate balance between exploration and exploitation.

Diversity in Multiobjective Optimization

Optimization has different meanings between single objective optimization and multiobjective optimization (Jin & Sendhoff, 2009). For MOO, optimization means to find not a single, but a lot, maybe infinite solutions. The population diversity is also important in multiobjective optimization (Zhang & Mühlenbein, 2004; Zhou, Zhang, & Jin, 2009). Unlike in single objective optimization, the diversity in multiobjective optimization not only concerns the convergence in decision space, but also the convergence in objective space. There are many discussions of population diversity in multiobjective optimization, such as convergence acceleration (Adra, Dodd, & Griffin, *et al.*, 2009), diversity management (Adra & Fleming 2011), and diversity improvement (Ishibuchi, Tsukamoto, & Nojima, 2010).

Population Diversity of Particles

For the single objective optimization, each individual represents a potential solution. The individual with the best fitness value is the best solution for the problem to be solved. For the multiobjective optimization, if an individual corresponds to a nondominated solution, this solution may be chosen to be put into an additional archive. All nondominated solutions are stored in the archive.

The population diversity should be measured on current solutions and the found nondominated solutions, i.e., the distribution of particles and distribution of solutions in the archive should both be observed. The measurement of distribution of particles is the same as that for PSO solving single objective problems. The position diversity, velocity diversity, and cognitive diversity should be measured. These diversity definitions and equations are the same as that for PSO for single objective optimization.

Population Diversity of Solutions

Unlike the single objective optimization, the multiobjective problems has many or infinite solutions (Bosman & Thierens, 2003). The optimization goal of an MOP consists of three objectives:

1. The distance of the resulting nondominated solutions to the true optimal Pareto front should be minimized;
2. A good (in most cases uniform) distribution of the obtained solutions is desirable;
3. The spread of the obtained nondominated solutions should be maximized, i.e., for each objective a wide range of values should be covered by the nondominated solutions.

The number of solutions in the archive may be different from that of particles. For the purpose of generality and clarity, h represents the number of solutions, n represents the number of problem dimensions, and k is the number of objectives. The u represents the u th solution, $u = 1, \cdots, h$, v is the v th objective, $v = 1, \cdots, k$, and j is the j th dimension, $j = 1, \cdots, n$. Two kinds of population diversity should be measured for solutions, diversity in solution space and diversity in objective space. Convergence in objective space is not preferred. All objectives should have a uniform distribution in the Pareto front.

Population Diversity of Pareto Set

Population diversity of Pareto set measures distribution of nondominated solutions in the search space, therefore, it can reflect solutions' dynamics. Definition of diversity of Pareto set, which is based on the L_1 norm, is as follows

$$\bar{s}_j = \frac{1}{h} \sum_{u=1}^{h} s_{uj}$$

$$D_j^s = \frac{1}{h} \sum_{u=1}^{h} |s_{uj} - \bar{s}_j|$$

$$D^s = \frac{1}{n} \sum_{j=1}^{n} D_j^s$$

where $\bar{s}_j$ is the center of solutions on dimension j, $\bar{\mathbf{s}} = [\bar{s}_1, \cdots, \bar{s}_j, \cdots, \bar{s}_n]$ represents the average of all solutions on each dimension. The parameter h is the number of solutions in the archive, h and number of particles m can be different. The vector $\mathbf{D}^s = [D_1^s, \cdots, D_j^s, \cdots, D_n^s]$ represents the diversity of Pareto set for all dimensions based on L_1 norm. D^s measures the diversity of solutions in Pareto set.

Population Diversity of Pareto Front

Population diversity of Pareto Front measures distribution of fitness value in the objective space, therefore, it can reflect goodness of solutions. Definition of diversity of Pareto front, which is based on the L_1 norm, is as follows

$$\bar{f}_v = \frac{1}{h} \sum_{u=1}^{h} f_{uv}$$

$$D_v^f = \frac{1}{h} \sum_{u=1}^{h} |f_{uv} - \bar{f}_v|$$

$$D^f = \frac{1}{k} \sum_{v=1}^{k} D_v^f$$

where $\bar{f}_v$ is the center of solutions on objective v, $\bar{\mathbf{f}} = [\bar{f}_1, \cdots, \bar{f}_v, \cdots, \bar{f}_k]$ represents the average of all fitness values for all objectives; $\mathbf{D}^f = [D_1^f, \cdots, D_v^f, \cdots, D_k^f]$ represents the diversity of Pareto front for each objective based on L_1 norm. D^f measures the diversity of fitness values in Pareto front.

The diversity measurement can be utilized to metrics the solutions of multiobjective optimization. One of the main differences between SOPs and MOPs is that MOPs constitute a multidimensional objective space. In addition, a set of solutions representing the tradeoff among the different objectives rather than an unique optimal solution is sought in Multiobjective optimization (MOO). How to measure the goodness of solutions and the performance of algorithms is important in MOO (Cheng, Shi, & Qin, 2012b). The defined diversity metrics have several properties: (Deb, & Jain, 2002)

1. **Comparability:** For the benchmark functions, the target (or desired) metric value (calculated for an ideally converged and diversified set of points) can be calculated. For the real world problems, the metric values can be compared.

2. **Monotonicity:** The metric should provide a monotonic increase or decrease in its value, as the solution gets improved or deteriorated slightly. This will also help in evaluating the extent of superiority of one approximation set over another.

3. **Scalability:** The metric should be scalable to any number of objectives. The Multiobjective optimization contains only two or three objectives, while the many objective optimization contains more than four objectives. The Pareto domination is utilized in these optimizations, however,

there has been reported that almost every solution is Pareto nondominated in the problems with more than ten objectives (Ishibuchi, Tsukamoto, & Nojima, 2010). For the large scale multiobjective problems, especially a problem with large number of objectives, the Pareto domination may not be appropriated to metric the goodness of solutions. In this situation, we need to consider the scalability of metrics. Although the scalability is not discuss a lot in current research, and it is not an absolutely necessary property, but if followed, it will certainly be convenient for evaluating scalability issues of Multi-Objective Evolutionary Algorithms (MOEAs) in terms of number of objectives.

4. **Computational Efficiency:** The metric should be computationally inexpensive, although this is not a stringent condition to be followed. In swarm intelligence algorithms, many iterations are taken to search the optima. Consider the number of iterations, a fast metric can accelerate the search speed.

EXPERIMENTAL STUDY

Benchmark Test Functions

Wolpert and Macerady have proved that under certain assumptions no algorithm is better than other one on average for all problems (Wolpert & Macready, 1997). Consider the generalization, eleven single objective and six multiobjective benchmark functions were used in our experimental studies (Yao, Liu, & Lin, 1999; Liang, Qin, & Suganthan, *et al.*, 2006; Zhang, Zhou, & Zhao, *et al.*, 2009). The aim of the experiment is not to compare the ability nor the efficacy of PSO algorithm with different parameter setting or structure, e.g., global star or local ring, but to measure the exploration and exploitation information when PSOs are running.

Single Objective Problems

The experiments have been conducted to test single objective benchmark functions listed in Table 1. Without loss of generality, five standard unimodal and six multimodal test functions are selected (Yao, Liu, & Lin, 1999; Liang, Qin, & Suganthan, *et al.*, 2006). All functions are run for 50 times to have statistical meaning for comparison among different approaches. Randomly shifting of the location of optimum is utilized in each dimension for each run.

Multiobjective Problems

There are six unconstrained (bound constrained) problem (Zhang, Zhou, & Zhao, *et al.*, 2009) in the experimental study, each problem has two objectives to be minimized. The unconstrained problem 1, 2, 3, 4, and 7 have a continuous Pareto front, the unconstrained problem 5 has a discrete Pareto front.

Unconstrained problem 1 (UCP1):

$$f_1 = x_1 + \frac{2}{|J_1|} \sum_{j \in J_1} \left[x_j - \sin(6\pi x_1 + \frac{j\pi}{n}) \right]^2$$

$$f_2 = 1 - \sqrt{x_1} + \frac{2}{|J_2|} \sum_{j \in J_2} \left[x_j - \sin(6\pi x_1 + \frac{j\pi}{n}) \right]^2$$

where $J_1 = \{j \mid j \text{ is odd and } 2 \leq j \leq n\}$ and $J_2 = \{j \mid j \text{ is even and } 2 \leq j \leq n\}$.

The search space is $[0,1] \times [-1,1]^{n-1}$. The Pareto front is

$$f_2 = 1 - \sqrt{f_1}, \qquad 0 \leq f_1 \leq 1.$$

Table 1. The benchmark functions used in our experimental study, where n is the dimension of each problem, $\mathbf{z} = (\mathbf{x} - \mathbf{o})$, $\mathbf{x} = [x_1, x_2, \cdots, x_n]$, o_i is an randomly generated number in problem's search space S and it is different in each dimension, global optimum $\mathbf{x}^* = \mathbf{o}$, $n = 100$, $f_{\min}$ is the minimum value of the function, and $S \subseteq \mathcal{R}^n$

Function	Test Function	S	$f_{\min}$
Parabolic	$f_0(\mathbf{x}) = \sum_{i=1}^{n} z_i^2 + \text{bias}_0$	$[-100, 100]^n$	-450.0
Schwefel's P2.22	$f_1(\mathbf{x}) = \sum_{i=1}^{n} |z_i| + \prod_{i-1}^{n} |z_i| + \text{bias}_1$	$[-10, 10]^n$	-330.0
Schwefel's P1.2	$f_2(\mathbf{x}) = \sum_{i=1}^{n} (\sum_{k=1}^{i} z_k)^2 + \text{bias}_2$	$[-100, 100]^n$	450.0
Step	$f_3(\mathbf{x}) = \sum_{i=1}^{n} (\lfloor z_i + 0.5 \rfloor)^2 + \text{bias}_3$	$[-100, 100]^n$	330.0
Quartic Noise	$f_4(\mathbf{x}) = \sum_{i=1}^{n} i z_i^4 + \text{random}[0,1) + \text{bias}_4$	$[-1.28, 1.28]^n$	-450.0
Rosenbrock	$f_5(\mathbf{x}) = \sum_{i=1}^{n-1} [100(z_{i+1} - z_i^2)^2 + (z_i - 1)^2] + \text{bias}_5$	$[-10, 10]^n$	180.0
Rastrigin	$f_6(\mathbf{x}) = \sum_{i=1}^{n} [z_i^2 - 10\cos(2\pi z_i) + 10] + \text{bias}_6$	$[-5.12, 5.12]^n$	-330.0
Noncontinuous Rastrigin	$f_7(\mathbf{x}) = \sum_{i=1}^{n} [y_i^2 - 10\cos(2\pi y_i) + 10] + \text{bias}_7$ $$y_i = \begin{cases} z_i & |z_i| < \dfrac{1}{2} \\ \dfrac{\text{round}(2z_i)}{2} & |z_i| \geq \dfrac{1}{2} \end{cases}$$	$[-5.12, 5.12]^n$	450.0
Ackley	$f_8(\mathbf{x}) = -20\exp\left(-0.2\sqrt{\dfrac{1}{n}\sum_{i=1}^{n} z_i^2}\right)$ $-\exp\left(\dfrac{1}{n}\sum_{i=1}^{n}\cos(2\pi z_i)\right) + 20 + e + \text{bias}_8$	$[-32, 32]^n$	180.0

continued on following page

Table 1. Continued

Function	Test Function	S	$f_{\min}$
Griewank	$$f_9(\mathbf{x}) = \frac{1}{4000} \sum_{i=1}^{n} z_i^2 - \prod_{i=1}^{n} \cos(\frac{z_i}{\sqrt{i}}) + 1 + \text{bias}_9$$	$[-600, 600]^n$	120.0
Generalized Penalized	$$f_{10}(\mathbf{x}) = \frac{\pi}{n} \{10 \sin^2(\pi y_1) + \sum_{i=1}^{n-1} (y_i - 1)^2$$ $$\times [1 + 10 \sin^2(\pi y_{i+1})] + (y_n - 1)^2\}$$ $$+ \sum_{i=1}^{n} u(z_i, 10, 100, 4) + \text{bias}_{10}$$ $$y_i = 1 + \frac{1}{4}(z_i + 1)$$ $$u(z_i, a, k, m) = \begin{cases} k(z_i - a)^m & z_i > a, \\ 0 & -a < z_i < a \\ k(-z_i - a)^m & z_i < -a \end{cases}$$	$[-50, 50]^n$	330.0

The Pareto set is

and

$$x_j = \sin(6\pi x_1 + \frac{j\pi}{n}), \quad j = 2, \cdots, n, \quad 0 \le x_1 \le 1.$$

$$y_i = x_j - x_1^{0.5(1.0 + \frac{3(j-2)}{n-2})}, \qquad j = 2, \cdots, n.$$

Unconstrained problem 2 (UCP2) (see Box 1)

The search space is $[0, 1]^n$. The Pareto front is

Unconstrained problem 3 (UCP3):

$$f_2 = 1 - \sqrt{f_1}, \qquad 0 \le f_1 \le 1.$$

$$f_1 = x_1 + \frac{2}{|J_1|} (4 \sum_{j \in J_1} y_j^2 - 2 \prod_{j \in J_1} \cos(\frac{20 y_j \pi}{\sqrt{j}}) + 2)$$

The Pareto set is

$$f_2 = 1 - \sqrt{x_1} + \frac{2}{|J_2|} (4 \sum_{j \in J_2} y_j^2 - 2 \prod_{j \in J_2} \cos(\frac{20 y_j \pi}{\sqrt{j}}) + 2)$$

$$x_j = x_1^{0.5(1.0 + \frac{3(j-2)}{n-2})}, \quad j = 2, \cdots, n. \quad 0 \le x_1 \le 1.$$

where

Unconstrained problem 4 (UCP4):

$$J_1 = \{j \mid j \text{ is odd and } 2 \le j \le n\},$$

$$f_1 = x_1 + \frac{2}{|J_1|} \sum_{j \in J_1} h(y_j)$$

$$J_2 = \{j \mid j \text{ is even and } 2 \le j \le n\},$$

Box 1.

$$f_1 = x_1 + \frac{2}{|J_1|}\sum_{j \in J_1} y_j^2$$

$$f_2 = 1 - \sqrt{x_1} + \frac{2}{|J_2|}\sum_{j \in J_2} y_j^2$$

where $J_1 = \{j \mid j \text{ is odd and } 2 \leq j \leq n\}$ and $J_2 = \{j \mid j \text{ is even and } 2 \leq j \leq n\}$, and

$$y_i = \begin{cases} x_j - [0.3x_1^2 \cos(24\pi x_1 + \frac{4j\pi}{n}) + 0.6x_1]\cos(6\pi x_1 + \frac{j\pi}{n}) & j \in J_1 \\ x_j - [0.3x_1^2 \cos(24\pi x_1 + \frac{4j\pi}{n}) + 0.6x_1]\sin(6\pi x_1 + \frac{j\pi}{n}) & j \in J_2 \end{cases}$$

The search space is $[0,1] \times [-1,1]^{n-1}$. The Pareto front is

$$f_2 = 1 - \sqrt{f_1}, \qquad 0 \leq f_1 \leq 1.$$

The Pareto set is

$$x_j = \begin{cases} \{0.3x_1^2 \cos(24\pi x_1 + \frac{4j\pi}{n}) + 0.6x_1\}\cos(6\pi x_1 + \frac{j\pi}{n}) & j \in J_1 \\ \{0.3x_1^2 \cos(24\pi x_1 + \frac{4j\pi}{n}) + 0.6x_1\}\sin(6\pi x_1 + \frac{j\pi}{n}) & j \in J_2 \end{cases}$$

$$0 \leq x_1 \leq 1$$

$$f_2 = 1 - x_1^2 + \frac{2}{|J_2|}\sum_{j \in J_2} h(y_j)$$

where $J_1 = \{j \mid j \text{ is odd and } 2 \leq j \leq n\}$ and $J_2 = \{j \mid j \text{ is even and } 2 \leq j \leq n\}$.

$$y_i = x_j - \sin(6\pi x_1 + \frac{j\pi}{n}), \qquad j = 2, \cdots, n.$$

and

$$h(t) = \frac{|t|}{1 + e^{2|t|}}.$$

The search space is $[0,1] \times [-2,2]^{n-1}$. The Pareto front is

$$f_2 = 1 - f_1^2, \qquad 0 \leq f_1 \leq 1.$$

The Pareto set is

$$x_j = \sin(6\pi x_1 + \frac{j\pi}{n}), \quad j = 2, \cdots, n, \quad 0 \leq x_1 \leq 1.$$

Unconstrained problem 5 (UCP5):

$$f_1 = x_1 + (\frac{1}{2N} + \varepsilon)\,|\sin(2N\pi x_1)| + \frac{2}{|J_1|}\sum_{j \in J_1} h(y_j)$$

$$f_2 = 1 - x_1 + (\frac{1}{2N} + \varepsilon)\,|\sin(2N\pi x_1)| + \frac{2}{|J_2|}\sum_{j \in J_2} h(y_j)$$

where $J_1 = \{j \mid j \text{ is odd and } 2 \le j \le n\}$,

$J_2 = \{j \mid j \text{ is even and } 2 \le j \le n\}$. N

is an integer, $\varepsilon > 0$, $N = 10$, $\varepsilon = 0.1$ in the parameter setting.

$$y_j = x_j - \sin(6\pi x_1 + \frac{j\pi}{n}), \qquad j = 2, \cdots, n.$$

and

$$h(t) = 2t^2 - \cos(4\pi t) + 1$$

The search space is $[0,1] \times [-1,1]^{n-1}$. The Pareto front has $2N + 1$ Pareto optimal solutions:

$$\left(\frac{i}{2N}, 1 - \frac{i}{2N} \right) \qquad \text{for } i = 0, 1, \cdots, 2N.$$

Unconstrained problem 7 (UCP7):

$$f_1 = \sqrt[5]{x_1} + \frac{2}{|J_1|} \sum_{j \in J_1} y_j^2$$

$$f_2 = 1 - \sqrt[5]{x_1} + \frac{2}{|J_2|} \sum_{j \in J_2} y_j^2$$

where

$J_1 = \{j \mid j \text{ is odd and } 2 \le j \le n\}$,

$J_2 = \{j \mid j \text{ is even and } 2 \le j \le n\}$

and

$$y_j = x_j - \sin(6\pi x_1 + \frac{j\pi}{n}), \qquad j = 2, \cdots, n.$$

The search space is $[0,1] \times [-1,1]^{n-1}$. The Pareto front is

$$f_2 = 1 - \sqrt{f_1}, \qquad 0 \le f_1 \le 1.$$

The Pareto set is

$$x_j = \sin(6\pi x_1 + \frac{j\pi}{n}), \quad j = 2, \cdots, n, \quad 0 \le x_1 \le 1.$$

Parameter Setting

Single Objective Optimization

In all experiments of PSO solving single objective problems, PSO has 50 particles. All functions are run 50 times to have statistical meaning for comparison among different approaches.

The parameter setting is the same as that of the standard PSO. In all experiments, PSO has 50 particles, $c_1 = c_2 = 1.496172$, and the inertia weight $w = 0.72984$ (Clerc & Kennedy, 2002; Bratton & Kennedy, 2007). For each algorithm, the maximum number of iterations is 5000 for 100 dimensional problems in every run. There is also a limitation in velocity to control the search step size. The setting could prevent particles from crossing the search boundary. The *maximum velocity* is set as follows:

$$\text{maximum velocity} =$$
$$0.2 \times \left(\begin{array}{l} \text{position upper bound} - \\ \text{position lower bound} \end{array} \right).$$

Multiobjective Optimization

In all experiments of PSO solving multiobjective problems, PSO has 250 particles. The maximum number h of solutions in archive is 100. The maximum number of iterations is 2000 for 10 dimensional problems in every run. Other parameters are the same as that of the standard PSO.

Boundary Constraints Handling

Many strategies have been proposed to handle the boundary constraints. However, with an improper boundary constraints handling method, particles may get "stuck in" the boundary (Cheng, Shi, & Qin, 2011). The classical boundary constraints handling method is as follows:

$$x_{i,j}(t+1) = \begin{cases} X_{\max,j} & \text{if } x_{i,j}(t+1) > X_{\max,j} \\ X_{\min,j} & \text{if } x_{i,j}(t+1) < X_{\min,j} \\ x_{i,j}(t+1) & \text{otherwise} \end{cases}$$

(4)

where t is the index number of the last iteration, and $t+1$ is the index number of current iteration. This strategy resets particles in a particular point-the boundary, which constrains particles to fly in the search space limited by boundary.

In the single objective optimization, for PSO with star structure, a stochastic boundary constraints handling method was utilized in this experiment. The equation (5) gives a method that particles are reset into a special area (Cheng, Shi, & Qin, 2011)

$$x_{i,j}(t+1) = \begin{cases} X_{\max,j} \times (\text{rand}() \times c + 1 - c) & \text{if } x_{i,j}(t+1) > X_{\max,j} \\ X_{\min,j} \times (\text{Rand}() \times c + 1 - c) & \text{if } x_{i,j}(t+1) < X_{\min,j} \\ x_{i,j}(t+1) & \text{otherwise} \end{cases}$$

(5)

where c is a parameter to control the resetting scope. When $c = 1$, particles are reset within a half search space. On the contrary, when $c = 0$, this strategy is the same as the equation (4), i.e., particles are reset to be on the boundary. The closer to 0 the c is, the more particles have a high possibility to be reset close to the boundary.

In our experiment, the c is set to 0.1. A particle will be close to the boundary when position is beyond the boundary. This will increase the exploitation ability of algorithm searching the solution close to the boundary.

A deterministic method, which resets a boundary-violating position to the middle between old position and the boundary (Zielinski, Weitkemper, & Laur, *et al.*, 2009), was utilized for PSO with local ring structure. The equation is as follows:

$$x_{i,j,G+1} = \begin{cases} \frac{1}{2}(x_{i,j,G} + X_{\max,j}) & \text{if } x_{i,j,G+1} > X\max,j \\ \frac{1}{2}(x_{i,j,G} + X_{\min,j}) & \text{if } x_{i,j,G+1} < X_{\min,j} \\ x_{i,j,G+1} & \text{otherwise} \end{cases}$$

(6)

The position in last iteration is used in this strategy. Both classic strategy and this strategy reset a particle to a deterministic position.

For the multiobjective particle swarm optimizer, the equation (4) is utilized to handle the boundary constraints.

Experimental Results

The result of PSO solving single objective problems is given in Table 2. The bold numbers indicate the better solutions. Five measures of performance are reported. The first is the best fitness value attained after a fixed number of iterations. In our case, we report the best result found after 5000 iterations. The following measures are the median value, worst value, mean value, and the standard deviation of the best fitness values for all runs. It is possible that an algorithm will rapidly reach a relatively good result while becoming trapped into a local optimum. These values reflect the algorithm's reliability and robustness.

From the result in Table 2, we can conduct that for seven functions f_0, f_1, f_3, f_4, f_8, f_9, and f_{10} good optimization results can be obtained, while for the other four functions f_2, f_5, f_6, and f_7, obtained results are not very good. This is because of the properties of the functions, some functions will become significantly difficult when the dimension increases.

Table 2. Results of PSO with global star and local ring structure for solving benchmark functions. All algorithms are run for 50 times, where "Best", "Median", "Worst", and "Mean" indicate the best, median, worst, and mean of the best fitness values for all runs, respectively.

Result		PSO with Global Star Structure				
	f_{min}	Best	Median	Worst	Mean	Std. Dev.
f_0	-450.0	-449.9999	-449.9045	-421.1076	-448.4784	5.01505
f_1	-330.0	-329.9999	-329.9993	328.3578	-316.8113	92.1670
f_2	450.0	4538.646	8024.012	23007.12	9129.964	3939.06
f_3	330.0	359	566	2220	635.6	314.235
f_4	-450.0	-449.9691	-449.9432	-449.1378	-449.9251	0.11416
f_5	180.0	272.4658	516.5409	1498.878	599.9292	246.224
f_6	-330.0	63.6766	320.3105	630.1263	312.8142	103.560
f_7	450.0	610.0011	802.0023	1059.000	803.5421	97.1025
f_8	180.0	182.4990	197.7353	199.8314	192.0871	7.48450
f_9	120.0	120.0809	120.2979	122.4966	120.3902	0.38224
f_{10}	330.0	330.0116	330.8841	333.4218	330.9681	0.67871
Result		PSO with Local Ring Structure				
	f_{min}	Best	Median	Worst	Mean	Std. Dev.
f_0	-450.0	-449.9999	-449.9999	-449.9999	-449.9999	3.62E-10
f_1	-330.0	-329.9999	-329.9999	-329.0500	-329.9771	0.13457
f_2	450.0	30211.37	40847.52	54352.03	41051.55	5739.44
f_3	330.0	330	331	337	331.3	1.5
f_4	-450.0	-449.9165	-449.8565	-449.8119	-449.8604	0.02441
f_5	180.0	269.4788	368.9582	442.3104	360.0133	41.4152

continued on following page

Table 2. Continued

Result		PSO with Global Star Structure				
f_6	-330.0	73.2817	325.6967	441.0884	*309.8727*	74.7981
f_7	450.0	836.0000	1034.000	1182.250	1022.319	86.6742
f_8	180.0	*180.0000*	181.9515	199.5519	*183.8464*	5.75737
f_9	120.0	*120.0000*	120.0000	120.5880	*120.0117*	0.08232
f_{10}	330.0	*330.0033*	330.7748	332.7372	*330.9090*	0.61122

Figure 1 shows a single-run results of PSO solving multiobjective problems. The multiobjective problems will become difficult with the increasing of objective's number and problem's dimension.

ANALYSIS AND DISCUSSION

Diversity in Single Objective Optimization

Different functions have different properties. Considered the number of local optima, the benchmark functions can be categorized as unimodal function and multimodal function. The benchmark functions also can be divided as separable function and non-separable function based on the interdependence among dimensions. Due to the limit of space, four representative benchmark functions in Table 3 are chosen to analysis different normalized population diversities.

Definition of Population Diversity

Figure 2 and 3 show the population diversities on particle swarm optimizer solving single objective problems. Figure 2 is PSO with star structure, and Figure 3 is PSO with ring structure. The diversity measures show the distribution of particles' positions, velocities, and cognitive positions. The PSO

with ring structure has more smooth curve than the PSO with star structure.

Change of Position Diversity and Cognitive Diversity

Figure 4 and 5 show the population diversity change on PSO solving the four single objective problems. The diversities measure the distribution of particles, and the convergence or divergence information can be obtained from the change of diversities. From the figures, some conclusions could be made that the diversity changes very quickly at the beginning of search which indicates that the particle swarm has a good global search ability. Particles then get clustered in a small region quickly. The convergence speed should be controlled during the search, the fast convergence may cause premature convergence.

Ratio of Position Diversity to Cognitive Diversity

Figure 6 shows the ratio of position diversity to cognitive diversity on PSO solving single objective problems. Particle swarm optimizer with star or ring structure has different properties. The particle swarm optimizer with star structure has a strong vibration in the ratio of position diversity to cognitive diversity. The particle swarm optimizer with

Figure 1. The solution of particle swarm optimizer solving multiobjective UCP problems

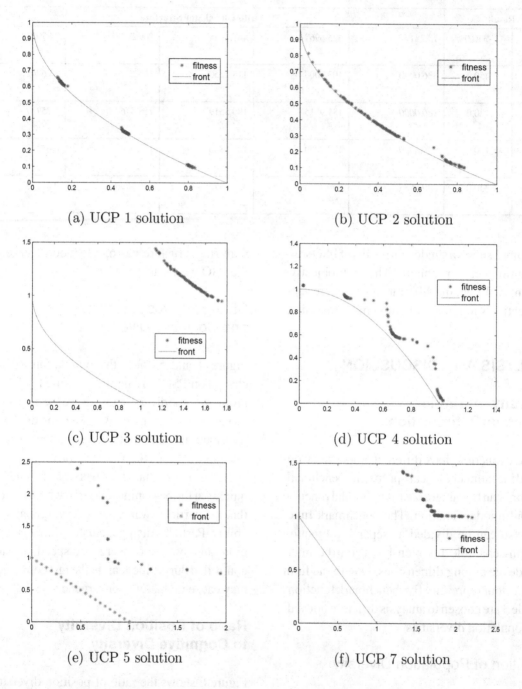

(a) UCP 1 solution

(b) UCP 2 solution

(c) UCP 3 solution

(d) UCP 4 solution

(e) UCP 5 solution

(f) UCP 7 solution

Table 3. Some representative benchmark functions

Parabolic	f_0	unimode	separable
Schwefel's P1.2	f_2	unimode	non-separable
Rosenbrock	f_5	multimode	non-separable
Ackley	f_8	multimode	separable

Figure 2. Population diversities observation on particle swarm optimizer with star structure solving single objective problems

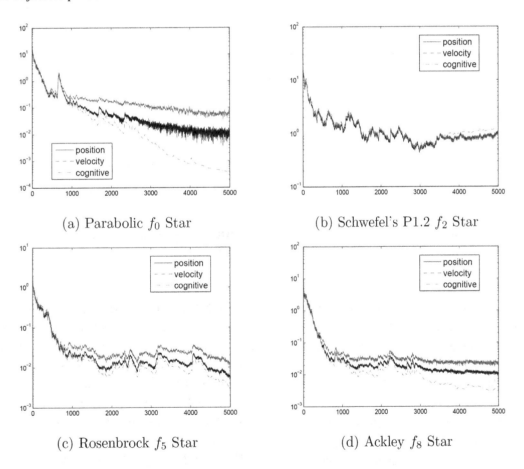

(a) Parabolic f_0 Star

(b) Schwefel's P1.2 f_2 Star

(c) Rosenbrock f_5 Star

(d) Ackley f_8 Star

Figure 3. Population diversities observation on particle swarm optimizer with ring structure solving single objective problems

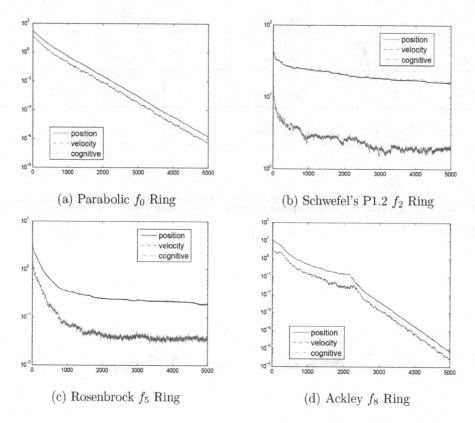

(a) Parabolic f_0 Ring

(b) Schwefel's P1.2 f_2 Ring

(c) Rosenbrock f_5 Ring

(d) Ackley f_8 Ring

ring structure has a smooth curve in the ratio of position diversity to cognitive diversity.

The ratio of position diversity and cognitive diversity show the comparison between the "search space" and "cognitive space." In PSO with star structure, a particle follows the global best, the position will change rapidly. In PSO with ring structure, the ratio is very stable. From Figure 3 and 6, the Parabolic f_0 and Ackley f_8 problems have good search results, and the diversities are decreased to a tiny value. We can conclude that in PSO with ring structure, the problems may get good results if its position diversity and cognitive diversity decrease to tiny value within a stable ratio.

Diversity in Multiobjective Optimization

Figure 7 displays the population diversities of PSO solving multiobjective problems. In Figure 7 (a), (c) and (e), the diversity curves in particles and solutions are very similar, on the contrast, diversity of positions and solutions have different changing curves in other figures.

The multiobjective particle swarm optimization algorithms (MOPSOs) have a fast convergence in solving MOPs (Domínguez & Pulido, 2011). The particles are very quickly converged to the solutions, corresponding to the population diversities; the diversities nearly have a straight line after few iterations.

Figure 4. Population diversity change observation on PSO with star structure solving single objective problems

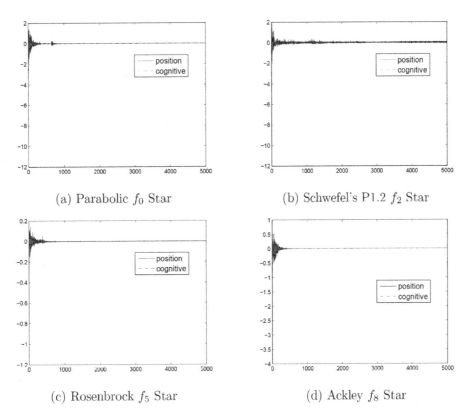

(a) Parabolic f_0 Star

(b) Schwefel's P1.2 f_2 Star

(c) Rosenbrock f_5 Star

(d) Ackley f_8 Star

DISCUSSIONS

Particle swarm has a different diversity changing in single and multiobjective problems. For single objective problems, we only consider the diversity in solution space, however, for multiobjective problems; the diversity in the objective space is also needed to be concerned.

For single objective problems, the diversity which decreases fast and may cause premature convergence, on the contrast, the diversity which decreases slowly may cause the algorithm searching ineffectively. The algorithm should have a proper decreasing diversity, and the diversity may also need to be enhanced during the search.

For multiobjective problems, a diversified target should be kept, i.e., the particles or solutions should not converge into a small region.

Maintaining the diversity in the search process is important for multiobjective optimization algorithms. More specifically, we want the searching results to be uniformly distributed, and the fitness of solutions to be close to the real Pareto front. This indicates that the diversity should be maintained on a proper level during the search. This is a problem-dependent setting for different problems having different shape of Pareto front and different number of solutions on Pareto front.

CONCLUSION

This chapter discussed an analysis of population diversity of particle swarm optimizer solving single and multi-objective problems. The performance of a search algorithm is determined

Figure 5. Population diversity change observation on PSO with ring structure solving single objective problems

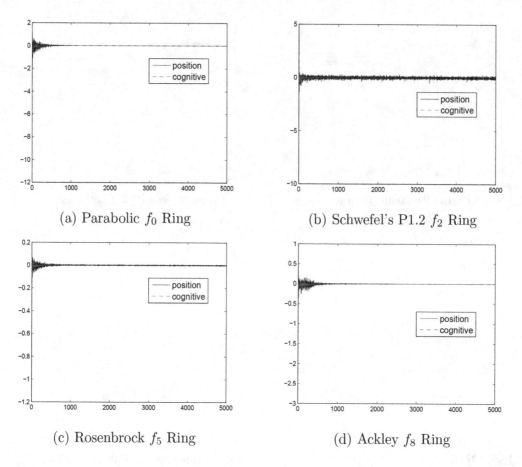

(a) Parabolic f_0 Ring

(b) Schwefel's P1.2 f_2 Ring

(c) Rosenbrock f_5 Ring

(d) Ackley f_8 Ring

by its two kinds of abilities: exploration of new possibilities and exploitation of old certainties. These two abilities should be balanced during the search process to obtain a good performance, i.e., the computational resources should be reallocated at algorithm running time.

For single objective optimization, the population diversity measures the distribution of particles, while for multiobjective optimization; the distribution of nondominated solutions also should be measured. From the observation of distribution and diversity change, the degree of exploration and exploitation can be obtained. In this chapter, we

have analyzed the population diversity of particle swarm optimizer solving single objective and multiobjective problems. Adaptive optimization algorithms can be designed through controlling balance between the exploration and exploitation.

For multiobjective optimization, different problems have different kinds of diversity changing curves. The properties of problem, such as "hardness", the number of local minima, continue or discrete Pareto front, all affects the performances of optimization algorithms. Through the information, the problems can be solved effectively.

Figure 6. The ratio of position diversity to cognitive diversity on PSO solving single objective problems

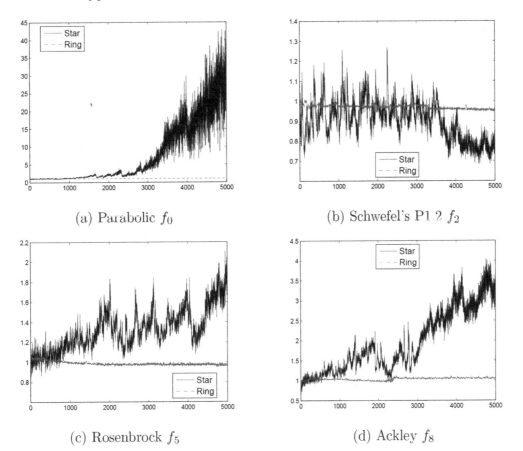

(a) Parabolic f_0

(b) Schwefel's P1.2 f_2

(c) Rosenbrock f_5

(d) Ackley f_8

Particles on the state of "expansion" or "converge" can be determined by the diversity measurement. From the population diversity, the diversity changing of PSO variants on different type of functions can be compared and analyzed. The particles' dynamical search state, the "hardness" of function, the number of local optima, and other information can be obtained. With the information, performance of an optimization algorithm can be improved by adjusting population diversity dynamically during PSO search process. The different topology structure of particles and the dimensional dependence of problems also affect the search process and performance of search algorithms. Seeking the influence of PSO topology structure and dimensional dependence on population diversity is the research need to be explored further.

The idea of population diversity measuring can also be applied to other evolutionary algorithms, e.g., genetic algorithm, differential evolution because evolutionary algorithms have the same concepts of current population solutions and search step. The performance of evolutionary algorithms

Figure7. Population diversities observation on PSO solving multiobjective UCP problems

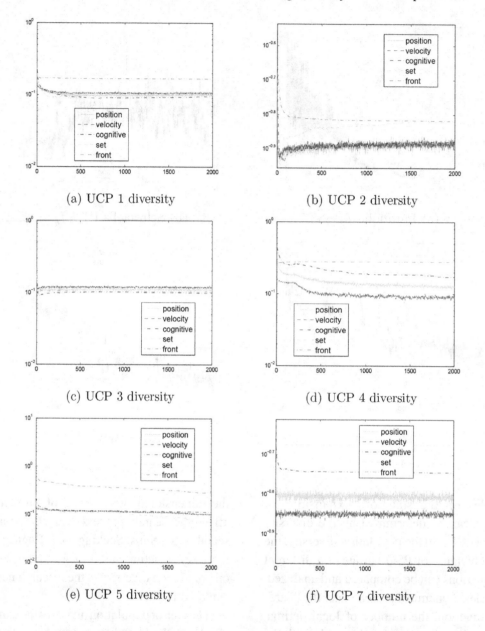

(a) UCP 1 diversity   (b) UCP 2 diversity

(c) UCP 3 diversity   (d) UCP 4 diversity

(e) UCP 5 diversity   (f) UCP 7 diversity

can be improved by taking advantage of the measurement of population diversity. Dynamically adjusting the population diversity controls an algorithm's ability of exploration or exploitation; hence, the algorithm could have higher possibility to reach optimum.

ACKNOWLEDGMENT

The authors' work is partially supported by National Natural Science Foundation of China under grant No.60975080, 61273367; and Ningbo Science & Technology Bureau (Science and Technology Project No.2012B10055).

REFERENCES

Adra, S. F., Dodd, T. J., Griffin, I. A., & Fleming, P. J. (2009). Convergence acceleration operator for multiobjective optimization. *IEEE Transactions on Evolutionary Computation*, 13(4), 825–847. doi:10.1109/TEVC.2008.2011743

Adra, S. F., & Fleming, P. J. (2011). Diversity management in evolutionary many-objective optimization. *IEEE Transactions on Evolutionary Computation*, 15(2), 183–195. doi:10.1109/TEVC.2010.2058117

Bosman, P. A. N., & Thierens, D. (2003). The balance between proximity and diversity in multiobjective evolutionary algorithms. *IEEE Transactions on Evolutionary Computation*, 7(2), 174–188. doi:10.1109/TEVC.2003.810761

Bratton, D., & Kennedy, J. (2007). Defining a standard for particle swarm optimization. In *Proceedings of the 2007 IEEE Swarm Intelligence Symposium (SIS 2007)* (pp. 120-127). IEEE.

Cheng, S. (2013). *Population diversity in particle swarm optimization: definition, observation, control, and application.* (Unpublished doctoral dissertation). University of Liverpool, Liverpool, UK.

Cheng, S., & Shi, Y. (2011a) Diversity control in particle swarm optimization. In *Proceedings of 2011 IEEE Symposium on Swarm Intelligence (SIS 2011)* (pp. 110-118). IEEE.

Cheng, S., & Shi, Y. (2011b) Normalized population diversity in particle swarm optimization. In Y. Tan, Y. Shi, Y. Chai, & G. Wang (Eds.), Advances in Swarm Intelligence (LNCS) (vol. 6728, pp. 38-45). Springer.

Cheng, S., Shi, Y., & Qin, Q. (2011). Experimental study on boundary constraints handling in particle swarm optimization: From population diversity perspective. *International Journal of Swarm Intelligence Research*, 2(3), 43–69. doi:10.4018/jsir.2011070104

Cheng, S., Shi, Y., & Qin, Q. (2012a) Dynamical exploitation space reduction in particle swarm optimization for solving large scale problems. In *Proceedings of 2012 IEEE Congress on Evolutionary Computation, (CEC 2012)*, (pp.3030-3037). Brisbane, Australia: IEEE.

Cheng, S., Shi, Y., & Qin, Q. (2012b). On the performance metrics of multiobjective optimization. In Y. Tan, Y. Shi, & Z. Ji (Eds.), Advances in Swarm Intelligence (LNCS) (vol. 7331, pp. 504-512). Berlin: Springer.

Cheng, S., Shi, Y., & Qin, Q. (2012c) Population diversity based study on search information propagation in particle swarm optimization. In *Proceedings of 2012 IEEE Congress on Evolutionary Computation, (CEC 2012)* (pp.1272-1279). Brisbane, Australia: IEEE.

Cheng, S., Shi, Y., Qin, Q., & Ting, T. O. (2012). Population diversity based inertia weight adaptation in particle swarm optimization. In *Proceedings of the Fifth International Conference on Advanced Computational Intelligence, (ICACI 2012)* (pp.395-403). ICACI.

Clerc, M., & Kennedy, J. (2002). The particle swarm—explosion, stability, and convergence in a multidimensional complex space. *IEEE Transactions on Evolutionary Computation*, 6(1), 58–73. doi:10.1109/4235.985692

Corriveau, G., Guilbault, R., Tahan, A., & Sabourin, R. (2012). Review and study of genotypic diversity measures for real-coded representations. *IEEE Transactions on Evolutionary Computation*, 16(5), 695–710. doi:10.1109/TEVC.2011.2170075

De Jong, K. A. (1975). *An analysis of the behavior of a class of genetic adaptive systems.* (Unpublished doctoral dissertation). Department of Computer and Communication Sciences, University of Michigan, Ann Arbor, MI.

Deb, K., & Jain, S. (2002). *Running performance metrics for evolutionary multi-objective optimization* (Technical Report 2002004). Kanpur Genetic Algorithms Laboratory (KanGAL), Indian Institute of Technology Kanpur.

Domínguez, J. S. H., & Pulido, G. T. (2011). A comparison on the search of particle swarm optimization and differential evolution on multi-objective optimization. In *Proceedings of the 2011 Congress on Evolutionary Computation (CEC2011)*, (pp. 1978-1985). Academic Press.

Eberhart, R., & Kennedy, J. (1995). A new optimizer using particle swarm theory. In *Proceedings of the Sixth International Symposium on Micro Machine and Human Science*, (pp. 39-43). Academic Press.

Eberhart, R., & Shi, Y. (2001). Particle swarm optimization: Developments, applications and resources. In *Proceedings of the 2001 Congress on Evolutionary Computation (CEC2001)*, (pp. 81-86). CEC.

Eberhart, R., & Shi, Y. (2007). *Computational Intelligence: Concepts to Implementations*. Morgan Kaufmann Publisher.

Eberhart, R. C., Dobbins, R. W., & Simpson, P. K. (1996). *Computational Intelligence PC Tools*. Academic Press Professional.

Gupta, A. K., Smith, K. G., & Shalley, C. E. (2006). The interplay between exploration and exploitation. *Academy of Management Journal*, *49*(4), 693–706. doi:10.5465/AMJ.2006.22083026

Holland, J. H. (2000). Building blocks, cohort genetic algorithms, and hyperplane-defined functions. *Evolutionary Computation*, *8*(4), 373–391. doi:10.1162/106365600568220 PMID:11130921

Hu, X., Shi, Y., & Eberhart, R. (2004) Recent advances in particle swarm. In *Proceedings of the 2004 Congress on Evolutionary Computation (CEC2004)*, (pp. 90-97). CEC.

Ishibuchi, H., Tsukamoto, N., & Nojima, Y. (2008). Evolutionary Many-Objective Optimization: A Short Review. In *Proceedings of the 2008 Congress on Evolutionary Computation (CEC2004)*, (pp. 2419-2426). CEC.

Ishibuchi, H., Tsukamoto, N., & Nojima, Y. (2010). Diversity improvement by non-geometric binary crossover in evolutionary multiobjective optimization. *IEEE Transactions on Evolutionary Computation*, *14*(6), 985–998. doi:10.1109/TEVC.2010.2043365

Jin, Y., & Sendhoff, B. (2009). A systems approach to evolutionary multiobjective structural optimization and beyond. *IEEE Computational Intelligence Magazine*, *4*(3), 62–76. doi:10.1109/MCI.2009.933094

Kennedy, J., & Eberhart, R. (1995) Particle swarm optimization. In *Proceedings of IEEE International Conference on Neural Networks*, (pp.1942-1948). IEEE.

Kennedy, J., Eberhart, R., & Shi, Y. (2001). Swarm Intelligence. Morgan Kaufmann Publisher.

Liang, J. J., Qin, A. K., Suganthan, P. N., & Baskar, S. (2006). Comprehensive learning particle swarm optimizer for global optimization of multimodal functions. *IEEE Transactions on Evolutionary Computation*, *10*(3), 281–295. doi:10.1109/TEVC.2005.857610

March, J. G. (1991). Exploration and exploitation in organizational learning. *Organization Science*, *2*(1), 71–87. doi:10.1287/orsc.2.1.71

Mauldin, M. L. (1984). Maintaining diversity in genetic search. In *Proceedings of the National Conference on Artificial Intelligence (AAAI 1984)* (pp. 247-250). AAAI.

Olorunda, O., & Engelbrecht, A. P. (2008). Measuring exploration/exploitation in particle swarms using swarm diversity. In *Proceedings of the 2008 Congress on Evolutionary Computation (CEC 2008)* (pp. 1128-1134). CEC.

Shi, Y., & Eberhart, R. (1998). A modified particle swarm optimizer. In *Proceedings of the 1998 Congress on Evolutionary Computation (CEC1998)* (pp. 69-73). CEC.

Shi, Y., & Eberhart, R. (1999). Empirical study of particle swarm optimization. In *Proceedings of the 1999 Congress on Evolutionary Computation (CEC 1999)* (pp. 1945-1950). CEC.

Shi, Y., & Eberhart, R. (2001) Fuzzy adaptive particle swarm optimization. In *Proceedings of the 2001 Congress on Evolutionary Computation (CEC2001),* (pp.101-106). CEC.

Shi, Y., & Eberhart, R. (2008). Population diversity of particle swarms. In *Proceedings of the 2008 Congress on Evolutionary Computation (CEC 2008)* (pp. 1063-1067). CEC.

Shi, Y., & Eberhart, R. (2009). Monitoring of particle swarm optimization. *Frontiers of Computer Science, 3*(1), 31–37. doi:10.1007/s11704-009-0008-4

Sundaram, R. K. (1996). *A First Course in Optimization Theory*. Cambridge University Press. doi:10.1017/CBO9780511804526

Weise, T., Zapf, M., Chiong, R., & Nebro, A. J. (2009). Why is optimization difficult? In Nature-Inspired Algorithms for Optimisation. Springer.

Wolpert, D., & Macready, W. (1997). No free lunch theorems for optimization. *IEEE Transactions on Evolutionary Computation, 1*(1), 67–82. doi:10.1109/4235.585893

Yao, X., Liu, Y., & Lin, G. (1999). Evolutionary programming made faster. *IEEE Transactions on Evolutionary Computation, 3*(2), 82–102. doi:10.1109/4235.771163

Zhang, Q., & Mühlenbein, H. (2004). On the convergence of a class of estimation of distribution algorithms. *IEEE Transactions on Evolutionary Computation, 8*(2), 127–136. doi:10.1109/TEVC.2003.820663

Zhang, Q., Zhou, A., Zhao, S., Suganthan, P. N., Liu, W., & Tiwari, S. (2009). *Multiobjective optimization Test Instances for the CEC 2009 Special Session and Competition* (Technical Report CES-487). Essex, UK: University of Essex.

Zhou, A., Zhang, Q., & Jin, Y. (2009). Approximating the set of Pareto-optimal solutions in both the decision and objective spaces by an estimation of distribution algorithm. *IEEE Transactions on Evolutionary Computation, 13*(5), 1167–1189. doi:10.1109/TEVC.2009.2021467

Zielinski, K., Weitkemper, P., Laur, R., & Kammeyer, K. D. (2009). Optimization of power allocation for interference cancellation with particle swarm optimization. *IEEE Transactions on Evolutionary Computation, 13*(1), 128–150. doi:10.1109/TEVC.2008.920672

KEY TERMS AND DEFINITIONS

Cognitive Diversity: Cognitive diversity, which represents distribution of particles' "moving target", measures the distribution of historical best positions for all particles. The measurement definition of cognitive diversity is the same as that of the position diversity except that it utilizes each particle's current personal best position instead of current position.

Exploitation: The exploitation ability means that an algorithm focuses on the refinement of found promising areas.

Exploration: The exploration ability means that an algorithm can explore more search place to increase the possibility that the algorithm can find good enough solutions.

Particle Swarm Optimizer/Optimization: Particle Swarm Optimizer/Optimization, which is one of the evolutionary computation techniques, was invented by Eberhart and Kennedy in 1995. It is a population-based stochastic algorithm modeled on the social behaviors observed in flocking birds. Each particle, which represents a solution, flies through the search space with a velocity that is dynamically adjusted according to its own and its companion's historical behaviors.

Population Diversity: Population diversity is a measure of individuals' search information in population-based algorithms. From the distribution of individuals and change of this distribution information, the algorithm's status of exploration or exploitation can be obtained.

Position Diversity: Position diversity measures distribution of particles' current positions, therefore, can reflect particles' dynamics. Position diversity gives the current position distribution information of particles, whether the particles are going to diverge or converge could be reflected from this measurement.

Premature Convergence: Premature convergence is a phenomenon that occurs in population-based algorithms. Premature convergence occurs when all individuals in population-based algorithms are trapped in local optima.

Velocity Diversity: Velocity diversity, which represents diversity of particles' "moving potential", measures the distribution of particles' current velocities. In other words, velocity diversity measures the "activity" information of particles.

Chapter 5
Experimental Study on Boundary Constraints Handling in Particle Swarm Optimization from a Population Diversity Perspective

Shi Cheng
University of Nottingham Ningbo, China

Yuhui Shi
Xi'an Jiaotong-Liverpool University, China

Quande Qin
Shenzhen University, China

ABSTRACT

Premature convergence happens in Particle Swarm Optimization (PSO) for solving both multimodal problems and unimodal problems. With an improper boundary constraints handling method, particles may get "stuck in" the boundary. Premature convergence means that an algorithm has lost its ability of exploration. Population diversity is an effective way to monitor an algorithm's ability of exploration and exploitation. Through the population diversity measurement, useful search information can be obtained. PSO with a different topology structure and a different boundary constraints handling strategy will have a different impact on particles' exploration and exploitation ability. In this chapter, the phenomenon of particles getting "stuck in" the boundary in PSO is experimentally studied and reported. The authors observe the position diversity time-changing curves of PSOs with different topologies and different boundary constraints handling techniques, and analyze the impact of these settings on the algorithm's abilities of exploration and exploitation. From these experimental studies, an algorithm's abilities of exploration and exploitation can be observed and the search information obtained; therefore, more effective algorithms can be designed to solve problems.

DOI: 10.4018/978-1-4666-6328-2.ch005

INTRODUCTION

Particle Swarm Optimization (PSO) was introduced by Eberhart and Kennedy in 1995 (Eberhart & Kennedy, 1995; Kennedy & Eberhart, 1995). It is a population-based stochastic algorithm modeled on social behaviors observed in flocking birds. A particle flies through the search space with a velocity that is dynamically adjusted according to its own and its companion's historical behaviors. Each particle's position represents a solution to the problem. Particles tend to fly toward better and better search areas over the course of the search process (Eberhart & Shi, 2001).

Optimization, in general, is concerned with finding the "best available" solution(s) for a given problem. Optimization problems can be simply divided into unimodal problems and multimodal problems. As indicated by the name, a unimodal problem has only one optimum solution; on the contrary, a multimodal problem has several or numerous optimum solutions, of which many are local optimal solutions. Evolutionary optimization algorithms are generally difficult to find the global optimum solutions for multimodal problems due to the possible occurrence of the premature convergence.

Most reported optimization methods are designed to avoid premature convergence in solving multimodal problems (Blackwell & Bentley, 2002). However, premature convergence also happens in solving unimodal problems when the algorithm has an improper boundary constraint handling method. For example, even for the most simplest benchmark function—Sphere, or termed as a Parabolic problem, which has a convex curve in each dimension, particles may "stick in" the boundary and the applied PSO algorithm therefore cannot find the global optimum at the end of its search process. With regards to this, premature convergence needs to be addressed in both unimodal and multimodal problems. Avoiding premature convergence is important in problem optimization, i.e., an algorithm should have a balance between fast convergence speed and the ability of "jumping out" of local optima.

Particles fly in the search space. If particles can easily get clustered together in a short time, particles will lose their "search potential." Premature convergence means particles have a low possibility to explore new search areas. Although many methods were reported to be designed to avoid premature convergence (Chen & Montgomery, 2011), these methods did not incorporate an effective way to measure the degree of premature convergence, in other words, the measurement of particles' exploration / exploitation is still needed to be investigated. Shi and Eberhart gave several definitions on diversity measurement based on particles' positions (Shi & Eberhart, 2008; Shi & Eberhart, 2009). Through diversity measurements, useful exploration and / or exploitation search information can be obtained.

PSO is simple in concept and easy in implementation, however, there are still many issues that need to be considered (Kennedy, 2007). Boundary constraint handling is one of them (Xu and Rahmat-Samii, 2007; Helwig, *et al.*, 2013). In this chapter, different boundary constraints handling methods and their impacts are discussed. Position diversity will be measured and analyzed for PSO with different boundary constraints handle strategies and different topology structures.

This chapter is organized as follows. Section Particle Swarm Optimization reviews the basic PSO algorithm, four different topology structures, and definitions of population diversities. Section Boundary Constraints Handling describes several boundary constraints handling techniques, which includes the classic strategy, deterministic strategy, and stochastic strategy. Experiments are conducted in Section Experimental Study followed by analysis and discussion on the population diversity changing curves of PSOs with different boundary constraints handling methods and four kinds of topology structures. Finally, Section Conclusions concludes with some remarks and future research directions.

PARTICLE SWARM OPTIMIZATION

For the purpose of generality and clarity, m represents the number of particles and n the number of dimensions. Each particle is represented as x_{ij}, i represents the ith particle, $i = 1, \cdots, m$, and j is the jth dimension, $j = 1, \cdots, n$. The basic Equations of the original PSO algorithm are as follow (Kennedy et al., 2001, Eberhart & Shi, 2007):

$$\mathbf{v}_i \leftarrow w\mathbf{v}_i + c_1 \mathrm{rand}() \times (\mathbf{p}_i - \mathbf{x}_i)$$
$$+ c_2 \mathrm{Rand}() \times (\mathbf{p}_g - \mathbf{x}_i) \qquad (1)$$

$$\mathbf{x}_i \leftarrow \mathbf{x}_i + \mathbf{v}_i \qquad (2)$$

where w denotes the inertia weight and usually is less than 1, c_1 and c_2 are two positive acceleration constants, $\mathrm{rand}()$ and $\mathrm{Rand}()$ are two random functions to generate uniformly distributed random numbers in the range $[0, 1]$, $x_i = (x_{i1}, x_{i2}, \cdots, x_{in})$ represents the ith particle's position, $v_i = (v_{i1}, v_{i2}, \cdots, v_{in})$ represents the ith particle's velocity, v_{ij} represents the velocity of the ith particle at the jth dimension, $\mathbf{p}_i$ refers to the best position found by the ith particle, and $\mathbf{p}_g$ refers to the position found by the member in its neighborhood that has the best fitness evaluation value so far.

Topology Structure

A particle updates its position in the search space at each iteration. The velocity update in Equation (1) consists of three parts, previous velocity, cognitive part and social part. The cognitive part means that a particle learns from its own search experience, and correspondingly, the social part means that a particle can learn from other particles, or learn from the best in its neighbors in particular. Topology defines the neighborhood of a particle.

Particle swarm optimization algorithm has different kinds of topology structures, e.g., star, ring, four clusters, or Von Neumann structure. A particle in a PSO with a different structure has different number of particles in its neighborhood with a different scope. Learning from a different neighbor means that a particle follows different neighborhood (or local) best, in other words, topology structure determines the connections among particles. Although it does not relate to the particle's cognitive part directly, topology can affect the algorithm's convergence speed and the ability of avoiding premature convergence, i.e., the PSO algorithm's ability of exploration and exploitation.

A topology structure can be seen as the environment for particles (Bentley, 1999). Particles live in the environment and each particle competes to be the global / local best. If a particle is chosen to be the global or local best, its (position) information will affect other particles' positions, and this particle is considered as a leader in its neighborhood. The structure of PSO determines the environment for particles, the process of a particle competing to be a leader is like an animal struggling in its population.

In this chapter, four most commonly used topology structures are considered. They are star, ring, four clusters and Von Neumann structure, which are shown in Figure 1.

- **Star:** The star topology is shown in Figure 1 (a). Because all particles or nodes are connected, search information is shared in a global scope, this topology is frequently termed as *global* or *all* topology. With this topology, the search information is shared in the whole swarm, and a particle with the best fitness value will be chosen to be the "leader." Other particles will follow this particle to find optimum. This topology can be seen as a completive competition pattern. In this pattern, each particle competes with all others in the population and

Figure 1. Four topologies used in this chapter: (a) Star topology, where all particles or nodes share the search information in the whole swarm; (b) Ring topology, where every particle is connected to two neighbors; (c) Four clusters topology, where four fully connected subgroups are inter-connected among themselves by linking particles; (d) Von Neumann topology, which is a lattice and where every particle has four neighbors that are wrapped on four sides.

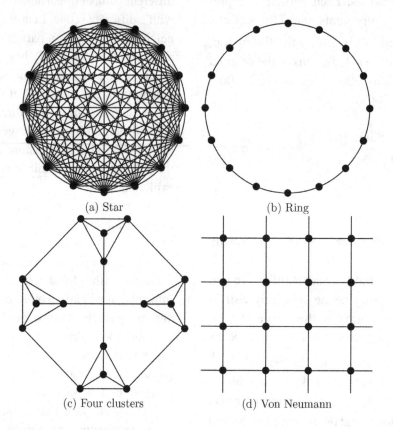

(a) Star   (b) Ring

(c) Four clusters   (d) Von Neumann

this requires $N-1$ total competitions for a single-species population of N particles.

- **Ring:** The ring topology is shown in Figure 1 (b). A particle is connected with two neighbors in this topology. A particle compares its fitness value with its left neighbor at first, and then the winner particle compares with the right neighbor. A particle with better fitness value in this small scope is determined by these two comparisons. This is like a small competition environment, each particle only competes with its two neighbors. This requires $2(N-1)$ to-

tal competitions for a population of N particles.

- **Four Clusters:** The four clusters topology is shown in Figure 1 (c). This topology can be seen as a species divided into four groups. Each group is a small star topology, which has a "leader" particle in this group, sharing its own search information. Besides that, each group has three link particles links to other three groups. The link particles are used to exchange search information with other three groups. For N particles, each group has $N/4$ particles, this needs $N-4$ competitions, plus with

12 times search information exchange. This requires $N + 8$ total competitions.

- **Von Neumann:** The Von Neumann topology is shown in Figure 1 (d). This topology is also named as *Square* (Mendes et al. 2004b) or **NWES** neighborhood (for North, East, West, and South) (Dorronsoro & Bouvry, 2011). In this topology, every particle has four neighbors that are wrapped on four sides, and the swarm is organized as a mesh. For N particles, this needs $4(N-1)$ total competitions.

Topology determines the structure of particles' connections and the transmission of search information in the swarm. Star and ring are the two most commonly used structures. A PSO with a star structure, where all particles are connected to each other, has the smallest average distance in swarm, and on the contrary, a PSO with a local ring structure, where every particle is connected to two near particles, has the biggest average distance in swarm (Mendes et al., 2003; Mendes 2004a; Mendes et al. 2004b).

Population Diversity

An algorithm's ability of "exploration" and "exploitation" is an important factor to impact its optimization performance (Olorunda & Engelbrecht, 2008). Exploration means the ability of an optimization algorithm to explore different areas of the search space in order to have high possibility to find good optimum. Exploitation, on the other hand, means the ability for particles to concentrate the search around a promising region in order to refine a candidate solution. A good optimization algorithm should optimally balance the two conflicted objectives.

Population diversity of PSO measures the distribution of particles, and the diversity's changing curve is a way to monitor the degree of convergence / divergence of PSO search process. In other words, the status of particles, whether it is in the state of exploration or exploitation, could be obtained from this measurement. Shi and Eberhart gave several definitions on diversity measurement based on particles' positions (Shi & Eberhart, 2008; Shi & Eberhart, 2009). Position diversity is used to measure the distribution of particles' current positions. Cheng and Shi introduced the modified definitions of the diversity measurement based on L_1 norm (Cheng & Shi, 2011a; Cheng & Shi, 2011b; Cheng, 2013).

From diversity measurements, useful search information can be obtained. Position diversity measures distribution of particles' current positions. One definition of position diversity, which is based on the L_1 norm, is as follows:

$$\bar{x}_j = \frac{1}{m} \sum_{i=1}^{m} x_{ij}$$

$$D_j^p = \frac{1}{m} \sum_{i=1}^{m} |x_{ij} - \bar{x}_j|$$

$$D^p = \sum_{j=1}^{n} w_j D_j^p$$

where $\bar{x}_j$ represents the pivot of particles' position in dimension j, and D_j^p measures particles position diversity based on L_1 norm for dimension j. Then we define $\bar{\mathbf{x}} = [\bar{x}_1, \cdots, \bar{x}_j, \cdots, \bar{x}_n]$, $\bar{\mathbf{x}}$ represents the mean of particles' current positions on each dimension, and $\mathbf{D}^p = [D_1^p, \cdots, D_j^p, \cdots, D_n^p]$, which measures particles' position diversity for each dimension. D^p measures the whole swarm's population diversity.

Without loss of generality, every dimension is considered equally in this chapter. Setting all $w_j = \frac{1}{n}$, then the position diversity of the whole swarm can be defined as:

$$D^p = \sum_{j=1}^{n} \frac{1}{n} D_j^p = \frac{1}{n} \sum_{j=1}^{n} D_j^p \qquad (3)$$

Position diversities, which are observed based on a dimension or on the whole swarm of particles, are experimented in Section 5 of the Chapter.

BOUNDARY CONSTRAINTS HANDLING

This section presents a brief survey on the main existing methods that deal with boundary constraints in the literature. Even PSO is simple and easy in implementation, there are still some issues need to be considered (Kennedy, 2007), and boundary constraints handling is one of the issues. There are different strategies to handle a particle's position when this particle exceeds its boundary limit.

"Stuck in" the Boundary

Algorithms are generally tested on the standard benchmark functions for the purpose of comparison. These functions have an optimum in the center of solution space (Yao et al., 1999). However, for real problems, we don't know the location of an optimum, and the optimum could be at any place in the solution space. With an improper boundary constraints handling strategy, a phenomenon of particles "stuck in" the boundary will occur.

A classic boundary constraint handling strategy resets a particle at boundary in one dimension when this particle's position is exceeding the boundary in that dimension. If the fitness value of the particle at boundary is better than that of other particles, all particles in its neighborhood in this dimension will move to the boundary. If particles could not find a position with better fitness value, all particles will "stick in" the boundary at this dimension.

A particle is difficult to "jump out" of boundary even we increase the total number of fitness evaluations or the maximum number of iterations,

and this phenomenon occurs more frequently for high-dimensional problems.

Classical Strategy

The conventional boundary handling methods try to keep the particles inside the feasible search space S. Search information is obtained when particles fly in the search space. However, if a particle's position exceeds the boundary limit in one dimension at one iteration, that search information will be abandoned. Instead, a new position will be reset to the particle in that dimension. The classic strategy is to set the particle at boundary when it exceeds the boundary (Zhang et al., 2004). The Equation of this strategy is as follows:

$$x_{i,j,G+1} = \begin{cases} X_{\max,j} & \text{if } x_{i,j,G+1} > X_{\max,j} \\ X_{\min,j} & \text{if } x_{i,j,G+1} < X_{\min,j} \\ x_{i,j,G+1} & \text{otherwise} \end{cases} \qquad (4)$$

where G is the number of the last iteration, and $G+1$ is the number of current iteration. This strategy resets particles in a particular point—the boundary, which constrains particles to fly in the search space limited by boundary.

Deterministic Strategy

A deterministic method was reported in (Zielinski et al., 2009), which resets a boundary-violating position to the middle between old position and the boundary. The Equation is as follows:

$$x_{i,j,G+1} =$$

$$\begin{cases} \frac{1}{2}(x_{i,j,G} + X_{\max,j}) & \text{if } x_{i,j,G+1} > X\max, j \\ \frac{1}{2}(x_{i,j,G} + X_{\min,j}) & \text{if } x_{i,j,G+1} < X_{\min,j} \\ x_{i,j,G+1} & \text{otherwise} \end{cases}$$

$$(5)$$

The position in last iteration is used in this strategy. Both classic strategy and this strategy reset a particle to a deterministic position.

Stochastic Strategy

Eberhart and Shi utilized a stochastic strategy to reset the particles when particles exceed the position boundary (Eberhart & Shi, 2007).

$$x_{i,j,G+1} =$$
$$\begin{cases} X_{\max,j} - (\frac{1}{2}\text{rand}()(X_{\max,j} - X_{\min,j})) & \text{if } x_{i,j,G+1} > X_{\max,j} \\ X_{\min,j} + (\frac{1}{2}\text{Rand}()(X_{\max,j} - X_{\min,j})) & \text{if } x_{i,j,G+1} < X_{\min,j} \\ x_{i,j,G+1} & \text{otherwise} \end{cases}$$
(6)

where rand() and Rand() are two random functions to generate uniformly distributed random numbers in the range [0, 1].

By this strategy, particles will be reset within the half search space when particles exceed the boundary limit. This will increases the algorithm's exploration, that is, particles have higher possibilities to explore new search areas. However, it decreases the algorithm's ability of exploitation at the same time. A particle exceeding the boundary means the global or local optimum may be close to the boundary region. An algorithm should spend more iterations in this region. With the consideration of keeping the ability of exploitation, the resetting scope should be taken into account. For most benchmark functions, particles "fly in" a symmetric search space. With regards to this,

$$X_{\max,j} = \frac{1}{2}(X^{top,j} - X^{bottom,j}) = \frac{1}{2}X^{scope,j}$$

and

$$X_{\min,j} = -X_{\max,j}.$$

The Equation of resetting particle into a special area is as follows:

$$x_{i,j,G+1} =$$
$$\begin{cases} X_{\max,j} \times (\text{rand}() \times c + 1 - c) & \text{if } x_{i,j,G+1} > X_{\max,j} \\ X_{\min,j} \times (\text{Rand}() \times c + 1 - c) & \text{if } x_{i,j,G+1} < X_{\min,j} \\ x_{i,j,G+1} & \text{otherwise} \end{cases}$$
(7)

where c is a parameter to control the resetting scope. When $c = 1$, this strategy is the same as the Equations (6), that is, particles reset within a half space. On the contrary, when $c = 0$, this strategy is the same as the Equation (4), i.e., it is the same as the classic strategy. The closer to 0 the c is, the more particles have a high possibility to be reset close to the boundary.

EXPERIMENTAL STUDY

Several performance measurements are utilized in the experiments below. The first is the best fitness value attained after a fixed number of iterations. In our case, we report the mean result found after the pre-determined maximum number of iterations. The second is the time t which indicates the times of particles stuck in the boundary. At the end of each run, we count the number of the particles, which has the best fitness value and which get stuck in boundary in at least one dimension. The number will be larger if a particle is stuck in boundary in more dimensions. All numbers will be summed after 50 runs. The summed number indicates the frequency of particles that may get stuck in boundary. Standard deviation values of the best fitness values are also utilized in this chapter, which gives the solution's distribution. These values give a measurement of goodness of the algorithm.

Benchmark Test Functions

The experiments have been conducted on testing the benchmark functions listed in Table 1. Without loss of generality, five standard unimodal and five multimodal test functions are selected (Liang et al., 2006; Yao et al., 1999).

All functions are run 50 times to ensure a reasonable statistical result necessary to compare the different approaches. Every tested function's optimal point in solution space S is shifted to a randomly generated point with different value in each dimension, and $S \subseteq \mathbb{R}^n$, $\mathbb{R}^n$ is a n-dimensional Euclidean space.

Velocity Constraints

In the experiments, all benchmark functions have $V_{min} = -V_{max}$, it means that V_{min} has the same magnitude but opposite direction. The velocity also has a constraint to limit particle's search step (Table 1).

if $v_{ij} > V_{max}$ then $v_{ij} = V_{max}$

else if $v_{ij} < -V_{max}$ then $v_{ij} = -V_{max}$

Parameter Setting

In all experiments, each PSO has 32 particles, and parameters are set as in the standard PSO, $w = 0.72984$, and $c_1 = c_2 = 1.496172$ (Bratton & Kennedy, 2007). Each algorithm runs 50 times.

Experimental Results

Observation of "Stuck in" Boundary

By applying the classic strategy of boundary handling method, the position will be reset on the boundary if the position value exceeds the boundary of the search space. Table 2 gives the experimental results of applying this strategy. Each benchmark function will be tested with dimension 25, 50, and 100 to see whether similar observation can be obtained. The maximum number of iterations will be set to be 1000, 2000, 4000 corresponding to dimension 25, 50, and 100, respectively.

From the results, we can conclude that each algorithm has different possibilities of "being stuck in" boundary when it is applied to different problems. Problem dimension does not have a significant impact on the possibility of particles "being stuck in" the boundary at least for the benchmark functions with dimensions 25, 50, and 100 that we tested. Furthermore, generally speaking, the PSO with star structure is more like to be attracted to and then to be "stuck in" the boundary, and the PSO with ring structure is less like to be "stuck in" boundary.

If particles are "stuck in" the boundary, it is difficult for them to "jump out" of the local optima even we increase the maximum number of fitness evaluations. The fitness evaluation number of each function with dimension 100 in Table 2 is $32 \times 4000 = 128\,000$, we then increase this number to $32 \times 10000 = 320\,000$. The experimental results are given in Table 3. From Table 3, we can see that there is no any significant improvement neither on the fitness value nor on the number of particles "stuck in" the boundary. This means that by only increasing the number of fitness evaluations cannot help particles "jump out" of boundary constraints. Some techniques should be utilized for particles to avoid converge to the boundary.

Table 4 gives the experimental results of the algorithm that ignores the boundary constraints. In the Table 4 and 5, only the PSO with star topology has the "t" column, while PSOs with other topologies do not have the "t" column because the "t" values are all zeros. For the same reason, other tables below do not have the "t" column. Particles take no strategy when particles meet the boundary. Some tested functions will get good

Table 1. The benchmark functions used in our experimental study, where n is the dimension of each problem, $\mathbf{z} = (\mathbf{x} - \mathbf{o})$, $\mathbf{x} = [x_1, x_2, \cdots, x_n]$. o_i is an randomly generated number in problem's search space S, it is the same for each function at different run, but different for different function in each dimension. Global optimum $\mathbf{x}^* = \mathbf{0}$, $f_{\min}$ is the minimum value of the function, and $S \subseteq \mathbb{R}^n$.

Function	Test Function	S	$f_{\min}$
Parabolic	$f_0(\mathbf{x}) = \sum_{i=1}^{n} z_i^2 + \text{bias}_0$	$[-100,100]^n$	-450.0
Schwefel's P2.22	$f_1(\mathbf{x}) = \sum_{i=1}^{n}\lvert z_i \rvert + \prod_{i=1}^{n}\lvert z_i \rvert + \text{bias}_1$	$[-10,10]^n$	-330.0
Schwefel's P1.2	$f_2(\mathbf{x}) = \sum_{i=1}^{n}(\sum_{k=1}^{i} z_k)^2 + \text{bias}_2$	$[-100,100]^n$	450.0
Step	$f_3(\mathbf{x}) = \sum_{i=1}^{n}(\lfloor z_i + 0.5 \rfloor)^2 + \text{bias}_3$	$[-100,100]^n$	330.0
Quadric Noise	$f_4(\mathbf{x}) = \sum_{i=1}^{n} i z_i^4 + \text{random}[0,1) + \text{bias}_4$	$[-1.28,1.28]^n$	-450.0
Griewank	$f_5(\mathbf{x}) = \dfrac{1}{4000}\sum_{i=1}^{n} z_i^2 - \prod_{i=1}^{n}\cos(\dfrac{z_i}{\sqrt{i}}) + 1 + \text{bias}_5$	$[-600,600]^n$	120.0
Rosenbrock	$f_6(\mathbf{x}) = \sum_{i=1}^{n-1}[100(z_{i+1} - z_i^2)^2 + (z_i - 1)^2] + \text{bias}_6$	$[-10,10]^n$	-330.0
Rastrigin	$f_7(\mathbf{x}) = \sum_{i=1}^{n}[z_i^2 - 10\cos(2\pi z_i) + 10] + \text{bias}_7$	$[-5.12,5.12]^n$	450.0
Ackley	$f_8(\mathbf{x}) = -20\exp\left(-0.2\sqrt{\dfrac{1}{n}\sum_{i=1}^{n} z_i^2}\right)$ $-\exp\left(\dfrac{1}{n}\sum_{i=1}^{n}\cos(2\pi z_i)\right) + 20 + e + \text{bias}_8$	$[-32,32]^n$	180.0
Generalized Penalized	$f_9(\mathbf{x}) = \dfrac{\pi}{n}\{10\sin^2(\pi y_1) + \sum_{i=1}^{n-1}(y_i - 1)^2$ $\times [1 + 10\sin^2(\pi y_{i+1})] + (y_n - 1)^2\}$ $+ \sum_{i=1}^{n} u(z_i,10,100,4) + \text{bias}_9$ $y_i = 1 + \dfrac{1}{4}(z_i + 1) \quad u(z_i,a,k,m) = \begin{cases} k(z_i - a)^m & z_i > a, \\ 0 & -a < z_i < a \\ k(-z_i - a)^m & z_i < -a \end{cases}$	$[-50,50]^n$	330.0

Table 2. Results of the strategy that a particle "sticks in" boundary when it exceeds the boundary constraints. All algorithms are run for 50 times, the maximum number of iterations is 1000, 2000, and 4000 when the dimensions are 25, 50, and 100, respectively. Where "mean" indicates the average of the best fitness values for each run, "times" t indicates the number of particle with the best fitness value "stuck in" the boundary at a dimension. The percentage shows the frequency of particles "stuck in" the boundary of the search space.

Fun.		Star		Ring		Four Clusters		Von Neumann	
	n	Mean	Times t	Mean	t	Mean	t	Mean	t
f_0	25	4950.914	301 (24.08%)	-441.0717	2 (0.16%)	347.1880	72 (5.76%)	-64.9233	36 (2.88%)
	50	18512.65	681 (27.24%)	-391.2514	29 (1.16%)	1284.592	249 (9.96%)	467.7678	178 (7.12%)
	100	66154.79	1552 (31.04%)	-269.469	48 (0.96%)	7744.016	615 (12.3%)	4053.870	421 (8.42%)
f_1	25	-312.9603	159 (12.72%)	-329.9257	2 (0.16%)	-328.008	38 (3.04%)	-328.354	30 (2.4%)
	50	-265.9373	575 (23%)	-326.8749	80 (3.2%)	-314.148	242 (9.68%)	-323.725	158 (6.32%)
	100	-170.1893	1212 (24.24%)	-299.1541	395 (7.9%)	-254.349	791 (15.82%)	-273.921	630 (12.6%)
f_2	25	6556.133	223 (17.84%)	1418.165	55 (4.4%)	1551.690	82 (6.56%)	1151.919	68 (5.44%)
	50	59401.84	838 (33.52%)	20755.67	286 (11.44%)	18687.75	411 (16.44%)	16730.74	327 (13.08%)
	100	149100.1	1614 (32.28%)	119188.2	762 (15.24%)	97555.70	1049 (20.98%)	93162.75	778 (15.56%)
f_3	25	6483.32	284 (22.72%)	439.7	8 (0.64%)	1105.8	86 (6.88%)	876.56	53 (4.24%)
	50	19175.24	724 (28.96%)	476.58	29 (1.16%)	2697.68	238 (9.52%)	1604.98	166 (6.64%)
	100	70026.22	1449 (28.98%)	859.12	36 (0.72%)	7688.02	396 (7.92%)	7021.66	311 (6.22%)
f_4	25	-446.843	245 (19.6%)	-449.9543	24 (1.92%)	-449.836	61 (4.88%)	-449.901	33 (2.64%)
	50	-386.667	696 (27.84%)	-449.8241	44 (1.76%)	-447.068	157 (6.28%)	-448.661	91 (3.64%)
	100	49.74071	1606 (32.12%)	-448.7530	67 (1.34%)	-418.627	359 (7.18%)	-433.289	282 (5.64%)
f_5	25	169.2253	319 (25.52%)	120.4066	7 (0.56%)	128.1231	88 (7.04%)	123.0943	36 (2.88%)
	50	308.2321	739 (29.56%)	121.6709	49 (1.96%)	141.3122	270 (10.8%)	128.9908	187 (7.48%)
	100	676.8980	1415 (28.3%)	122.7015	66 (1.32%)	194.1575	591 (11.82%)	156.2124	428 (8.56%)

continued on following page

Table 2. Continued

Fun.		Star		Ring		Four Clusters		Von Neumann	
f_6	25	102391.65	334 (26.72%)	-236.9387	25 (2%)	13681.40	107 (8.56%)	1472.597	76 (6.08%)
	50	1075433.7	870 (34.8%)	215.3156	118 (4.72%)	16784.12	368 (14.72%)	25350.40	287 (11.48%)
	100	3500148.0	1614 (32.28%)	*2311.019*	222 (4.44%)	167064.1	712 (14.24%)	123572.6	586 (11.72%)
f_7	25	529.9848	210 (16.8%)	503.0551	103 (8.24%)	500.5270	135 (10.8%)	497.6501	129 (10.32%)
	50	730.7713	445 (17.8%)	638.3773	196 (7.84%)	635.7780	281 (11.24%)	612.3373	253 (10.12%)
	100	1168.550	664 (13.28%)	968.5158	369 (7.38%)	957.5405	519 (10.38%)	*879.3672*	479 (9.58%)
f_8	25	192.2881	239 (19.12%)	181.1893	15 (1.2%)	186.4093	94 (7.52%)	184.0952	64 (5.12%)
	50	195.2231	420 (16.8%)	182.6727	69 (2.76%)	188.7666	267 (10.68%)	185.2521	183 (7.32%)
	100	199.0853	521 (10.42%)	191.6770	258 (5.16%)	191.9497	490 (9.8%)	*189.5658*	450 (9%)
f_9	25	7773207.1	250 (20%)	3567.791	15 (1.2%)	473424.72	76 (6.08%)	10931.296	54 (4.32%)
	50	163596583	749 (29.96%)	331.2763	172 (6.88%)	5365821.9	345 (13.8%)	2296129.5	291 (11.64%)
	100	1063146706	1765 (35.3%)	*5394.753*	394 (7.88%)	26421658	789 (15.78%)	6918596.1	646 (12.92%)

fitness value with most of the obtained solutions being out of the search space. This may be good for particles flying in a periodic search space (Zhang et al., 2004). However, most problems have strict boundary constraints which this strategy does not fit for.

Comparison of PSOs with Different Boundary Constraint Handling Techniques

Table 5 shows the results of PSOs with the deterministic strategy. A particle takes a middle value of the former position and the boundary limit value when the particle meets the boundary constraint. PSOs with ring, four clusters, and Von Neumann structure can obtain good fitness values by utilizing this strategy. However, "struck in" boundary will still happen for PSO with star structure for most problems. This is because particles with star structure will progressively move to boundary. With this tendency, particles will get clustered together at the boundary and be difficult to "jump out." Therefore, the exploration ability decreases over the iterations.

With a stochastic strategy, a particle will be reset to a random position when the particle meets the boundary. Table 6 gives the result of PSOs with the stochastic strategy, that is, a particle is reset to be within the upper half space when the particle meets the upper bound, and correspondingly, a particle is reset to be within the lower half space when the particle meets the lower bound. Compared with the classic strategy and the deterministic strategy, this strategy improves the result of PSO with the star structure, but it does not get better optimization performance for PSOs with other structures in this chapter.

In Table 6, particles are reset within half space when particles meet the boundary. This increases

Table 3. Results of the strategy that a particle stays at boundary when it exceeds the boundary constraints. Algorithms have a large maximum number of fitness evaluations, i.e. 10000. The dimension n is 100.

Fun.	Star		Ring		Four Clusters		Von Neumann	
	Mean	Times t	Mean	t	Mean	t	Mean	t
f_0	67822.60	1540 (30.8%)	-256.0704	70 (1.4%)	7843.960	604 (12.08%)	2944.748	410 (8.2%)
f_1	-176.428	1225 (24.5%)	-297.9756	475 (9.5%)	-237.3498	874 (17.48%)	-279.874	603 (12.06%)
f_2	126974.8	1675 (33.5%)	68200.22	845 (16.9%)	71934.29	1099 (21.98%)	68816.78	1002 (20.04%)
f_3	71393.22	1528 (30.56%)	931.7	45 (0.9%)	10083.18	529 (10.58%)	6138.18	371 (7.42%)
f_4	143.0742	1599 (31.98%)	-448.580	49 (0.98%)	-400.9793	425 (8.5%)	-439.6080	284 (5.68%)
f_5	723.8275	1556 (31.12%)	123.6233	106 (2.12%)	189.9494	589 (11.96%)	154.8893	454 (9.08%)
f_6	3963368.9	1881 (37.62%)	1690.535	299 (5.98%)	229710.9	810 (16.2%)	68857.72	640 (12.8%)
f_7	1201.7850	722 (14.44%)	965.6807	413 (8.26%)	971.4570	550 (11%)	912.0553	552 (11.04%)
f_8	199.5501	545 (10.9%)	193.9069	312 (6.24%)	194.2383	526 (10.52%)	190.3066	532 (10.64%)
f_9	969621012	1874 (37.48%)	73541.50	487 (9.74%)	42652667	979 (19.58%)	14202759	808 (16.16%)

an algorithm's the ability of exploration, and it decreases the ability of exploitation. A particle being close to the boundary may mean that the optimal area may be near the boundary, the resetting area should be restricted. Table 7 gives the result of resetting area limited to $[0.9V_{max}, V_{max}]$ when a particle meets the upper bound, and $[V_{min}, 0.9V_{min}]$ when a particle meets the lower bound. This strategy can obtain better results.

In both the Table 6 and 7, the resetting area does not change during the whole search process. Intuitively, at the beginning of search process, we want a large ability of exploration and small ability of exploitation to be able to search more areas of the search space (Shi & Eberhart, 1998; Shi & Eberhart, 1999). Correspondingly, at the end of search process, the exploitation ability should be more favored to find an optimum in "good" areas. With regards to this, the resetting search space should be dynamically changed in the search process. Table 8 gives the results of the

strategy that the resetting space linearly decreases in the search process.

By examining the experimental results, it is clear that different boundary constraints handling techniques have different impacts on particles' diversity changing and optimization performance. The deterministic strategy fits for PSOs with ring, four clusters and Von Neumann structure. Resetting particles randomly in a small area fits for all the four topologies utilized in this chapter. Using this strategy, the PSO with star structure will have a good balance between ability of exploration and exploitation, which get the best performance than other strategies.

Population Diversity Analysis and Discussion

Without loss of generality and for the purpose of simplicity and clarity, the results for one function from five unimodal benchmark functions and one

Table 4. Results of the strategy that a particles ignores the boundary when it exceeds the boundary constraints. All algorithms are run for 50 times, where "mean" and σ indicate the average and standard deviation of the best fitness values for each run. n is 100, and maximum iteration number is 4 000.

Fun.	Star			Ring		Four Clusters		Von Neumann	
	Mean	σ	t	Mean	σ	Mean	σ	Mean	σ
f_0	-449.6162	1.727025	0 (0%)	-449.9999	1.20E-06	*-449.9999*	6.47E-09	-449.9999	8.77E-07
f_1	-327.3012	6.104924	1 (0.02%)	-329.9900	0.025155	-329.9998	0.000425	*-329.9998*	0.000224
f_2	*35458.463*	9998.671	396 (7.92%)	116972.62	23299.66	66411.144	14308.29	71154.160	14523.52
f_3	3343.06	2330.047	39 (0.78%)	*334.28*	3.376625	353.92	39.25701	363.56	65.76508
f_4	-449.0495	2.311998	191 (3.82%)	*-449.6915*	0.055767	-449.8339	0.038184	*-449.8358*	0.039501
f_5	120.4391	0.890941	1 (0.02%)	*120.0007*	0.003132	120.0176	0.056479	120.0205	0.037423
f_6	-87.33991	69.15844	216 (4.32%)	-15.65356	67.65250	*-107.9635*	54.60742	-92.00367	58.01067
f_7	1058.2517	125.6292	412 (8.24%)	988.66426	63.58231	945.39263	74.93225	*892.9344*	65.63141
f_8	199.47550	1.349835	395 (7.9%)	199.26132	3.396034	194.99493	7.570846	*184.6948*	5.632849
f_9	*331.5831*	0.911304	117 (2.34%)	336.1132	2.149815	332.4632	1.849387	332.10723	1.336155

function from five multimodal functions will be displayed because others will be similar.

There are several definitions on the measurement of population diversities (Shi & Eberhart, 2008; Shi & Eberhart, 2009, Cheng & Shi, 2011b). The dimension-wised population diversity based on the L_1 norm is utilized in this chapter.

Position Diversity Monitoring

Figure 2, and 3 display the position diversity changing curves when PSO is applied to solve benchmark functions. Figure 2 displays the curves for the unimodal function f_0, and Figure 3 displays for multimodal function f_5. In both figures, (a) is for functions f_0 and f_5 with a classic boundary handling technique, (b) is for functions f_0 and f_5 with particles ignoring the boundary, (c) is

for functions f_0 and f_5 with particles close to boundary gradually, (d) is for functions f_0 and f_5 with particles resetting in half search space, (e) is for functions f_0 and f_5 with limited resetting space at a small range near boundary, (f) is for functions f_0 and f_5 with a linearly decreased resetting scope, respectively.

Figures 2, and 3, displayed the position diversity changing curves of particles with four kinds of topologies. Some conclusion can be made that PSO with star topology has the most rapid position diversity decreasing curve, and PSO with ring topology can keep its diversity in the large number of iterations, generally. PSO with four clusters and Von Neumann also keep their diversity well in the search process, and the curves of diversity changing are smooth in most times.

Table 5. Results of PSO with a deterministic boundary constraint strategy. Particles will be reset to the middle between old position and boundary when particle's position exceeds the boundary. n is 100, and iteration number is 4 000.

Fun.	Star			Ring		Four Clusters		Von Neumann	
	Mean	σ	t	Mean	σ	Mean	σ	Mean	σ
f_0	18125.68	12771.54	523 (10.46%)	-449.9999	3.15E-06	-409.4909	127.3536	-420.4673	155.7340
f_1	-267.2679	26.3105	368 (7.36%)	-324.0182	9.402653	-315.4557	15.36290	-324.0810	8.879355
f_2	63749.30	23677.19	11 (0.22%)	95768.66	21022.066	61791.362	17080.59	58886.36	14324.72
f_3	27628.66	14213.33	103 (2.06%)	343.04	25.91521	1378.16	1385.743	719.52	691.3372
f_4	-300.7705	173.088	0 (0%)	-449.7622	0.074653	-449.0363	1.945231	-449.3194	2.434300
f_5	271.0433	114.9603	508 (10.16%)	120.0399	0.192983	122.2650	5.086505	120.83178	1.275821
f_6	627095.6	1084062.7	657 (13.14%)	-46.8004	74.09709	360.9332	1304.484	66.08107	462.4078
f_7	1104.514	120.0267	20 (0.4%)	944.5443	70.81612	944.4611	87.02924	839.2663	68.15615
f_8	198.1596	2.591173	67 (1.34%)	183.1589	3.415466	185.4077	4.043386	183.4269	1.466134
f_9	88647933	232053019	333 (6.66%)	333.7982	1.770645	339.5574	51.57181	331.4686	1.385780

The impact of different boundary constraint handling strategy on the position diversity also can be seen from these two figures. The values of position diversity changing will be very small when we utilize classic or deterministic strategies, and on the contrary, the position diversity will be kept at a "large" value when we utilize a stochastic strategy. The different position diversity changing curves indicate that particles will get clustered to a small region when we utilize a classic or deterministic strategy, and particles will be distributed in the large region when we utilize a stochastic strategy.

The changing curves of position diversity reveal the algorithm's ability of exploration and/or exploitation. The position diversity of PSO with a stochastic strategy will keep a "large" value, which indicates that with this strategy, PSO will have a good exploration ability.

Position Diversity Comparison

Different topology structure and boundary constraint handling method will have different impact on PSO algorithms' convergence. Figure 4 and below give some comparison among PSOs with different structures. There are four curves in each figure, which are the minimum, middle, and maximum dimensional position diversity, and position diversity as a whole. It should be noted that the dimension which has the minimum, middle, or maximum value is not fixed and may change over iterations. In other words, if the dimension i has the minimum value at iteration k, and it may be the dimension j that has the minimum value at iteration $k+1$. The figures only display position diversity's minimum, middle and maximum values at each iteration.

Table 6. Results of the strategy that a particle is randomly re-initialized within the half search space when the particle meets the boundary constraints. n is 100, and maximum iteration number is 4 000

Fun.	Star		Ring		Four Clusters		Von Neumann	
	Mean	σ	Mean	σ	Mean	σ	Mean	σ
f_0	15106.480	5401.915	6395.5801	1164.004	6456.2857	1471.815	*5777.2014*	1252.942
f_1	-204.55407	27.57007	-283.72265	5.047291	-282.5310	7.374081	*-286.1511*	5.525085
f_2	90226.816	38529.56	128790.177	28617.91	*86885.81*	31845.28	89231.033	33283.20
f_3	16437.02	4735.015	7593.56	1181.772	6954.9	1147.187	*6874.76*	1237.944
f_4	-442.9050	5.455450	-447.7014	0.651993	-447.9193	0.610410	-448.1605	0.490777
f_5	266.77115	36.43274	186.8523	12.45620	180.9738	10.21838	*178.7420*	11.10882
f_6	68586.660	68055.93	16834.993	6821.930	13083.356	6063.868	*12442.671*	4804.749
f_7	903.1275	69.44400	928.1833	51.27520	870.4047	72.80328	*823.6537*	59.78453
f_8	193.9104	1.330059	190.0964	0.488740	190.1364	0.627680	189.6701	0.616846
f_9	1834.0033	8708.160	2073.1476	3587.605	489.12695	220.7106	*406.0229*	121.9164

Table 7. Results of strategy that a particle is randomly re-initialized within a limited search space when the particle meets the boundary constraints. n is 100, and the maximum iteration number is 4 000

Fun.	Star		Ring		Four Clusters		Von Neumann	
	Mean	σ	Mean	σ	Mean	σ	Mean	σ
f_0	-421.0384	106.7571	-446.7030	1.301631	*-448.6723*	0.544163	-448.2624	0.800959
f_1	-315.9906	14.73397	-329.2227	0.155278	-329.1543	2.610519	*-329.4232*	0.520195
f_2	*35799.38*	13401.02	99311.642	17424.32	56011.555	11425.04	56913.228	10526.66
f_3	2592.84	2381.520	*351.12*	6.556340	359.58	45.46123	368.96	77.62009
f_4	-449.5926	0.901977	-449.7613	0.055156	*-449.8691*	0.029105	-449.8604	0.034106
f_5	121.8713	3.279144	120.9374	0.090210	*120.5187*	0.120787	120.6400	0.102622
f_6	271.2483	757.2085	111.6548	176.7045	23.60728	144.9963	*1.658537*	120.5905
f_7	1059.5079	86.42771	971.4921	74.61998	930.1978	105.0998	*838.0115*	57.72716
f_8	197.5319	3.148760	183.0840	3.434429	182.9285	2.463089	*182.3226*	0.544321
f_9	331.9493	1.019762	334.1176	1.364879	332.1842	1.408311	*331.2558*	0.917983

Table 8. Results of the strategy that particles are randomly re-initialized in a linearly decreased search space when particles meet the boundary constraints. n is 100, and the maximum iteration number is 4000

Fun.	Star		Ring		Four Clusters		Von Neumann	
	Mean	σ	Mean	σ	Mean	σ	Mean	σ
f_0	1702.3219	2184.3429	*-408.3616*	10.80574	-399.17565	53.23343	-404.6038	49.48885
f_1	-264.9917	22.439393	-327.3860	0.269110	-326.7792	2.130535	*-327.5687*	0.721141
f_2	*53393.692*	19574.620	90638.595	19706.681	59016.266	16850.516	57652.796	17353.163
f_3	5143.02	3071.211	*420.66*	17.44890	495.92	152.5970	484.9	180.2659
f_4	-448.64071	1.947832	*-449.5890*	0.082450	-449.7233	0.075943	*-449.7304*	0.075108
f_5	143.2678	16.39704	*121.3696*	0.0904944	121.4365	0.420780	121.3901	0.284098
f_6	9488.6354	18895.481	695.27241	429.34077	461.98764	413.84524	*341.3105*	246.16785
f_7	932.30625	74.40180	929.71921	60.000384	894.04412	61.824412	*835.0238*	47.61768
f_8	193.20420	2.508372	*183.1691*	0.417221	184.14282	1.085659	183.6688	0.974338
f_9	335.42590	1.713722	338.85667	3.039058	335.04291	1.578953	*334.1127*	1.2826316

Figure 4 and 5 display the position diversity changing curves of a PSO with the classic boundary constraints handling method to solve unimodal function f_0 and multimodal function f_5, respectively. Four subfigures display the PSO with star, ring, four clusters, and Von Neumann topology, respectively. As can be seen from the figures, the dimensional minimum value of position diversity is quickly getting zero for PSO with star, four clusters, and Von Neumann topology, while the dimensional minimum value of position diversity will exist during the whole search process for the PSO with ring topology.

Compared with other topologies, the position diversity of PSO with star structure can get to the smallest value at the early iteration numbers, which means particles have clustered together in a small region, and any particle generally has the smallest distance to other particles. On the contrary, the position diversity of PSO with ring structure has the largest value, which means particles are distributed in a large region, and any particle generally has the largest distance to other particles.

Figure 6 and 7 display the position diversity curve of PSO with the strategy that a particle ignores the boundary constraints when the particle's position exceeds the limit. Figure 6 is for f_0, and Figure 7 is for f_5. Particles can keep their search "potential" with this strategy, the position diversity decreases in the whole search space, and not getting to zero at the end of each run.

Figure 2. Position diversity changing curves for PSO solving parabolic function f_0 with different strategies: (a) classic, (b) cross, (c) deterministic, (d) stochastic, (e) limit, (f) linear

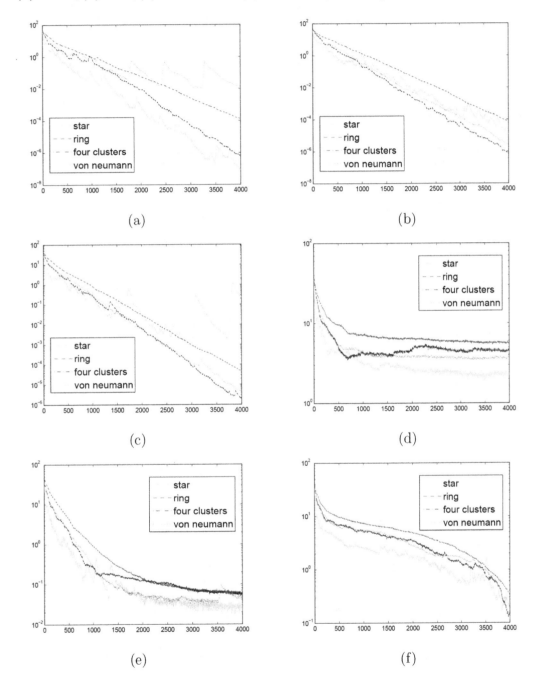

Figure 3. Position diversity changing curves for PSO solving multimodal function f_5 with different strategies: (a) classic, (b) cross, (c) deterministic, (d) stochastic, (e) limit, (f) linear

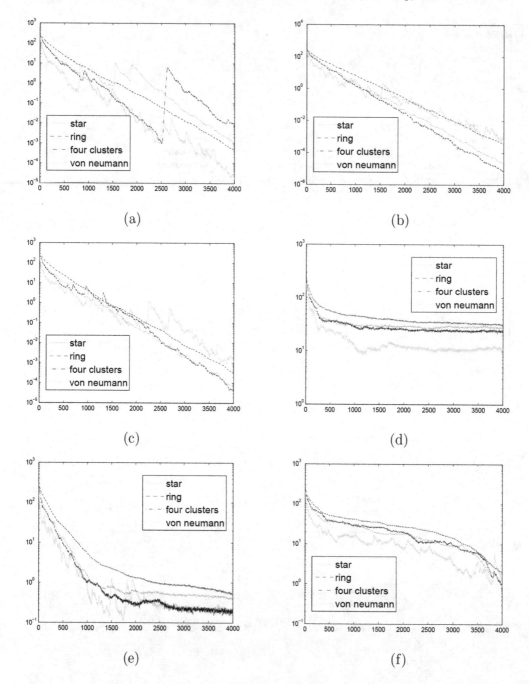

Figure 4. Comparison of PSO population diversities for solving unimodal function f_0 with classic boundary constraints handling techniques: (a) star, (b) ring, (c) four clusters, (d) Von Neumann

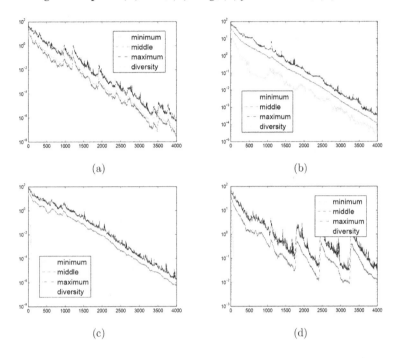

Figure 5. Comparison of PSO population diversities for solving multimodal function f_5 with classic boundary constraints handling techniques: (a) star, (b) ring, (c) four clusters, (d) Von Neumann

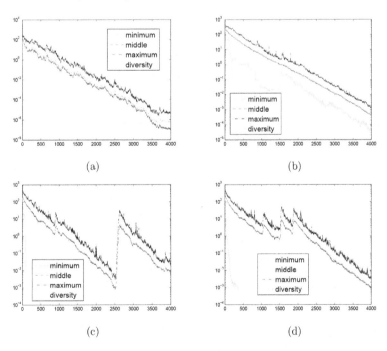

Figure 6. Comparison of PSO population diversities for solving unimodal function f_0 with exceeding boundary constraints handling techniques: (a) star, (b) ring, (c) four clusters, (d) Von Neumann

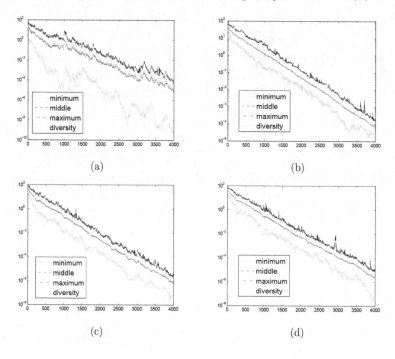

Figure 7. Comparison of PSO population diversities for solving multimodal function f_5 with exceeding boundary constraints handling techniques: (a) star, (b) ring, (c) four clusters, (d) Von Neumann

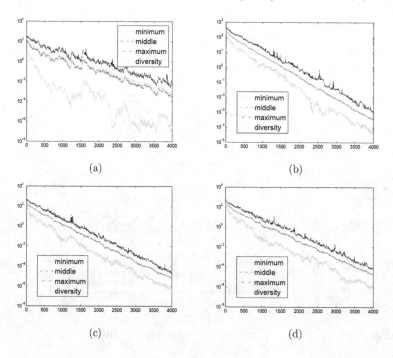

Figure 8. Comparison of PSO population diversities for solving unimodal function f_0 with deterministic boundary constraints handling techniques: (a) star, (b) ring, (c) four clusters, (d) Von Neumann

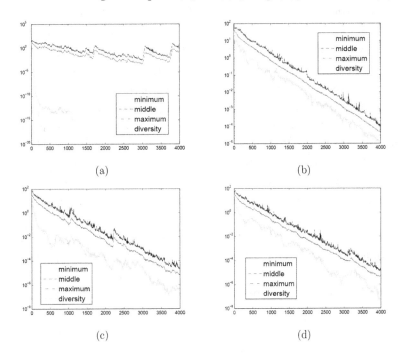

Figure 9. Comparison of PSO population diversities for solving multimodal function f_5 with deterministic boundary constraints handling techniques: (a) star, (b) ring, (c) four clusters, (d) Von Neumann

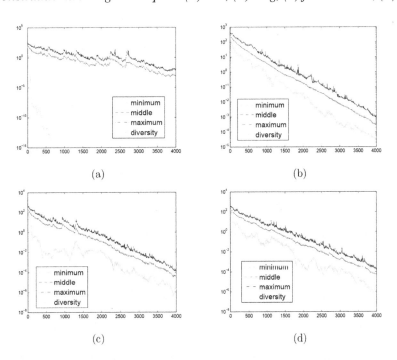

Figure 8 and 9 display the position diversity changing curves of PSO with a deterministic boundary handling strategy on unimodal function f_0 and multimodal function f_5. PSO with star topology is easily "stuck in" the boundary with this strategy, and the minimum of position diversity quickly became zero in Figure 8 (a) and Figure 9 (a). PSO with other three topologies have some ability to "jump out" of local optima. Figure 8 (c) and Figure 9 (c) display the diversity changing curves of PSO with four clusters structure. Figure 8 (d) and Figure 9 (d) display the diversity changing curves of PSO with Von Neumann structure. From Figure 8 (c), (d) and Fig 9 (c), (d), we can observe dramatically "up and down" changes of the position diversity curve, which may mean that as a whole, the search process is convergent but there are divergent process embedded in the convergent process.

Figure 10 and 11 display the position diversity changing curves of PSO with a stochastic boundary constraints handling technique to solve unimodal function f_0 and multimodal function f_5, respectively. By utilizing a half search space resetting technique, the values of position diversities are larger than that of PSOs with other strategies, which means that particles search in a larger region, i.e., the ability of exploration can be kept with this strategy. However, the ability of exploitation will be decreased when particles are getting close to the boundary. In general a distance between any pair of particles is larger than that in PSOs with other boundary constraint handling techniques at the same iterations.

Figure 12 and 13 display the position diversity changing curves of PSO with a linearly decreased resetting space to solve unimodal function f_0 and multimodal function f_5, respectively. Four subfigures are displayed for PSO with star,

Figure 10. Comparison of PSO population diversities for solving unimodal function f_0 with stochastic boundary constraints handling techniques that randomly reset particles in half search space: (a) star, (b) ring, (c) four clusters, (d) Von Neumann

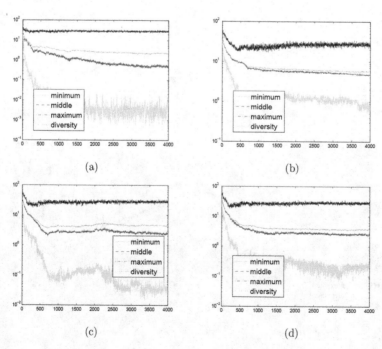

Figure 11. Comparison of PSO population diversities for solving multimodal function f_5 with stochastic boundary constraints handling techniques that randomly reset particles in half search space: (a) star, (b) ring, (c) four clusters, (d) Von Neumann

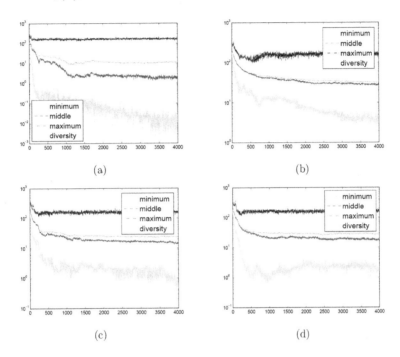

Figure 12. Comparison of PSO population diversities for solving unimodal function f_0 with stochastic boundary constraints handling techniques that randomly reset particles in a small and close to boundary search space: (a) star, (b) ring, (c) four clusters, (d) Von Neumann

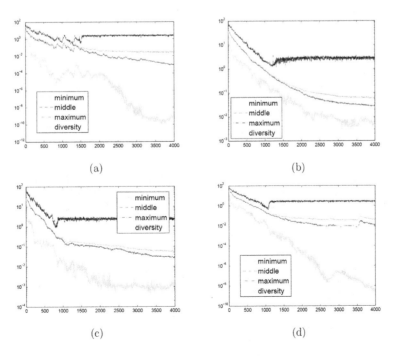

Figure 13. Comparison of PSO population diversities for solving multimodal function f_5 with stochastic boundary constraints handling techniques that randomly reset particles in a small and close to boundary search space: (a) star, (b) ring, (c) four clusters, (d) Von Neumann

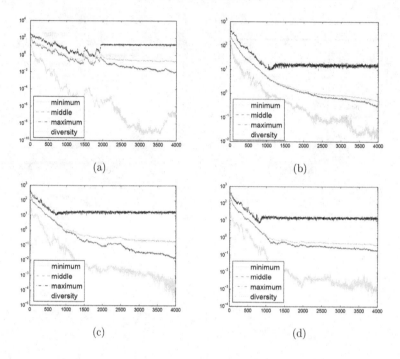

Figure 14. Comparison of PSO population diversities for solving unimodal function f_0 with stochastic boundary constraints handling techniques that randomly reset particles in a linearly decreased search space: (a) star, (b) ring, (c) four clusters, (d) Von Neumann

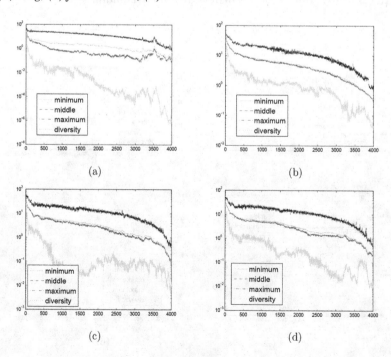

ring, four clusters, and Von Neumann topology, respectively. Like in other figures, the position diversities for PSO with star topology have the smallest value, and position diversities for PSO with ring topology have the largest value.

Figure 14 and 15 display the position diversity changing curves of PSO with a small resetting area to solve unimodal function f_0 and multimodal function f_5, respectively. PSO with this strategy can have a good balance between exploration and exploitation. From the figures we can see that the minimum position diversity is kept to a small value but not to zero in the whole search process. This means that particles can exploit some specific areas, and at the same time, particles will not be clustered together in this area. Particles can "jump out" of the local optima with this strategy, and the experimental results also show that PSO with this strategy can get a good performance.

From Figure 4 to 15 we can see that PSO with star topology can achieve the smallest value of position diversity, and PSO with ring topology has the largest value at the same iteration. PSO with four clusters and Von Neumann nearly have the same diversity curve in our experiments. In summary, the PSO with star topology has the greatest ability to exploit the small area at the same iteration, and on contrast, the PSO with ring topology has the greatest ability to explore new search areas.

The search "potential" of particles is important to an algorithm's performance. Particles "fly" in a limited area. To ensure the performance of algorithms, not only the center of search area, but also the areas close to the boundary should be searched carefully. Some strategy should be utilized for the reason that if we take no action, particles can easily cross the boundary limit, and not return to the "limited" search area. It is a frequently used

Figure 15. Comparison of PSO population diversities for solving multimodal function f_5 with stochastic boundary constraints handling techniques that randomly reset particles in a linearly decreased search space: (a) star, (b) ring, (c) four clusters, (d) Von Neumann

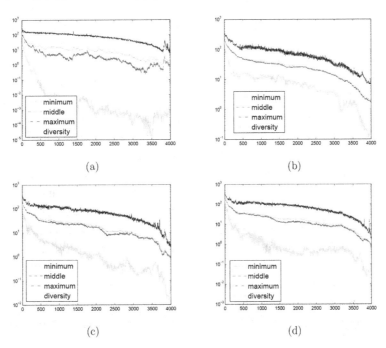

method that resets a particle's position when the particle meets the boundary. This method also has some drawbacks. Resetting a particle's position in a specific location will decrease the particle's search "potential", and the ability of exploration and exploitation will also be affected; on the other hand, resetting particles on a large area will decrease the algorithm's ability of exploitation, and particles will have difficulties to exploit the solution areas near the boundary.

From experimental results of applying a deterministic strategy and three variants of stochastic strategy, we can observe that the deterministic strategy usually can obtain better optimization performance for PSO with ring, four clusters, or Von Neumann structure than PSO with other strategies at least for the ten benchmark functions and three boundary constraints handling strategies we experimented in this chapter. A random re-initialization strategy fits for PSO with star, four clusters, and Von Neumann structures, and the space of re-initialization also should be considered. This conclusion is also verified on the population diversity observation.

Figure 8 and 9 display the position changing curves of PSO with deterministic strategy. It can be seen that particles in PSO with star topology are easily get clustered together. Some dimensional position diversities are quickly becoming zero, which may mean all particles stay in the same position and lose the search "potential" in these dimensions. All particles with four clusters and Von Neumann are also clustered together to the same position in some dimensions, i.e., the minimum position diversity becomes zero after several iterations.

PSO with random resetting strategy can avoid the above problem. Figure 10~15 displayed the position diversity curves of PSO with a stochastic strategy to handle boundary constraints. Particles can keep their position diversities with this strategy. Considering about algorithm's ability of exploitation, resetting particles in a small or decreased region can generally get better performance.

PSO with different topology will have different convergence speed. PSO with star structure has the fastest convergence speed, PSO with ring structure has the slowest speed, PSO with four clusters or Von Neumann structure is in the middle of them. Keeping particle's search "potential" and having a good balance of exploration and exploitation is important in the search process. Different boundary constraints handling strategy needs to be considered when we determine the PSO's topology because a proper strategy can give an improvement on algorithm's performance.

CONCLUSION

An algorithm's ability of exploration and exploitation is important in the optimization process. With good exploration ability, an algorithm can explore more areas in the search space, and find some potential regions that "good enough" solutions may exist. On the other hand, an algorithm with the ability of exploitation can finely search the potentially good regions, and find the optimum ultimately. An algorithm should have a good balance between exploration and exploitation during the search process.

In this chapter, we have reviewed the different strategies to handle particles exceeding the position boundary constraint. Position diversity changing curves were utilized to study variant of algorithm's ability of the exploration and/or exploitation. The position diversity changing curves of different variant of PSO were compared. From the position diversity measurement, the impacts of different boundary constraint handing strategies on the optimization performance were studied. Boundary constraints handling can affect particles' search "potential". The classic method resets particles on the boundary when particles exceed the boundary limit, which may mislead particles to the wrong search area, and cause particles "stuck in" the boundary.

The position diversities of PSO with star, ring, four clusters, and Von Neumann topology were experimented in this chapter. PSO with different topology will have different convergence. From the diversity measurement, the convergence speed and the ability of "jumping out" of local optima could be observed and/or analyzed. A deterministic boundary handling technique may improve the search results of PSO with ring, four clusters, or Von Neumann topology, but not star topology. Premature convergence still occurs in PSO with star topology. Stochastic method can avoid the premature convergence, and by resetting particles in a small or decreased region will keep PSO's ability of exploitation and therefore have a better performance.

Besides the boundary constraints handling techniques discussed in this chapter, there are many other methods, such as "invisible boundaries", "damping boundaries", etc. (Huang & Mohan, 2005; Xu & Rahmat-Samii, 2007). These methods will have a different impact on the optimization performance of PSO algorithms. As the same as the boundary constraints handling methods discussed in this chapter, these methods also can be analyzed by position diversity changing curves during the search process. The proper boundary constraint handling method should be considered together with the topology.

As indicated by the "no free lunch theory", there is no algorithm that is better than other one on average for all problems (Wolpert & Macready, 1997). Different variant of PSO fits for different kinds of problems. The comparison between different variants of PSOs and their population diversities should be studied when they are applied to solve different problems. The impact of parameters tuning on population diversity for solving different problems are also needed to be researched.

In addition to the position diversity, there are velocity diversity and cognitive diversity defined in PSO algorithms (Shi & Eberhart, 2008; Shi & Eberhart, 2009), which are unique to PSO algorithms. Experimental study on boundary constraints handling strategy based on velocity diversity and cognitive diversity should also be conducted to gain better understanding of PSO algorithms. The above are our future research work.

ACKNOWLEDGMENT

The authors' work is partially supported by National Natural Science Foundation of China under grant No.60975080, 61273367; and Ningbo Science & Technology Bureau (Science and Technology Project No.2012B10055).

REFERENCES

Bentley, P. J. (1999). *Evolutionary Design by Computers*. Morgan Kaufmann Publishers.

Blackwell, T. M., & Bentley, P. (2002). Don't push me! Collision-avoiding swarms. In *Proceedings of the Fourth Congress on Evolutionary Computation (CEC 2002)* (pp. 1691-1696). CEC.

Bratton, D., & Kennedy, J. (2007). Defining a standard for particle swarm optimization. In *Proceedings of the 2007 IEEE Swarm Intelligence Symposium* (pp. 120-127). IEEE.

Chen, S., & Montgomery, J. (2011). A simple strategy to maintain diversity and reduce crowding in particle swarm optimization. In *Proceedings of the 13th annual conference companion on Genetic and evolutionary computation (GECCO 2011)* (pp. 811-812). GECCO.

Cheng, S. (2013). *Population Diversity in Particle Swarm Optimization: Definition, Observation, Control, and Application.* (Unpublished doctoral dissertation). University of Liverpool, Liverpool, UK.

Cheng, S., & Shi, Y. (2011a). Diversity control in particle swarm optimization. In *Proceedings of the 2011 IEEE Swarm Intelligence Symposium* (pp. 110-118). IEEE.

Cheng, S., & Shi, Y. (2011b). Normalized population diversity in particle swarm optimization. In *Proceedings of the 2nd International Conference on Swarm Intelligence* (LNCS) (vol. 6728, pp. 38-45). Berlin: Springer.

Dorronsoro, B., & Bouvry, P. (2011). Improving classical and decentralized differential evolution with new mutation operator and population topologies. *IEEE Transactions on Evolutionary Computation, 15*(1), 67–98. doi:10.1109/TEVC.2010.2081369

Eberhart, R., & Kennedy, J. (1995). A new optimizer using particle swarm theory. In *Proceedings of the Sixth International Symposium on Micro Machine and Human Science* (pp. 39-43). Academic Press.

Eberhart, R., & Shi, Y. (2001). Particle swarm optimization: Developments, applications and resources. In *Proceedings of the 2001 Congress on Evolutionary Computation (CEC2001)* (pp. 81-86). CEC.

Eberhart, R., & Shi, Y. (2007). *Computational Intelligence: Concepts to Implementations*. Morgan Kaufmann Publisher.

Helwig, S., Branke, J., & Mostaghim, S. (2013). Experimental analysis of bound handling techniques in particle swarm optimization. *IEEE Transactions on Evolutionary Computation, 17*(2), 259–271. doi:10.1109/TEVC.2012.2189404

Huang, T., & Mohan, A. (2005). A hybrid boundary condition for robust particle swarm optimization. *IEEE Antennas and Wireless Propagation Letters, 4*(1), 112–117. doi:10.1109/LAWP.2005.846166

Kennedy, J. (2007). Some issues and practices for particle swarms. In *Proceedings of the 2007 IEEE Swarm Intelligence Symposium (SIS 2007)* (pp. 162-169). SIS.

Kennedy, J., & Eberhart, R. (1995). Particle swarm optimization. In *Proceedings of IEEE International Conference on Neural Networks* (pp. 1942-1948). IEEE.

Kennedy, J., Eberhart, R., & Shi, Y. (2001). *Swarm Intelligence*. Morgan Kaufmann Publisher.

Liang, J., Qin, A., Suganthan, P., & Baskar, S. (2006). Comprehensive learning particle swarm optimizer for global optimization of multimodal functions. *IEEE Transactions on Evolutionary Computation, 10*(3), 281–295. doi:10.1109/TEVC.2005.857610

Mendes, R. (2004a). *Population Topologies and Their Influence in Particle Swarm Performance.* (Unpublished doctoral dissertation). University of Minho, Minho, Portugal.

Mendes, R., Kennedy, J., & Neves, J. (2003). Avoiding the pitfalls of local optima: How topologies can save the day. In *Proceedings of the 12th Conference Intelligent Systems Application to Power Systems (ISAP 2003)*. IEEE Computer Society.

Mendes, R., Kennedy, J., & Neves, J. (2004b). The fully informed particle warm: Simpler, maybe better. *IEEE Transactions on Evolutionary Computation, 8*(3), 204–210. doi:10.1109/TEVC.2004.826074

Olorunda, O., & Engelbrecht, A. P. (2008) Measuring exploration/exploitation in particle swarms using swarm diversity. In *Proceedings of the 2008 Congress on Evolutionary Computation (CEC 2008)* (pp. 1128-1134). CEC.

Shi, Y., & Eberhart, R. (1998). Parameter selection in particle swarm optimization. In Evolutionary Programming VII (LNCS) (vol. 1447, pp. 591-600). Springer.

Shi, Y., & Eberhart, R. (1999). Empirical study of particle swarm optimization. In *Proceedings of the 1999 Congress on Evolutionary Computation (CEC 1999)* (pp. 1945-1950). CEC.

Shi, Y., & Eberhart, R. (2008). Population diversity of particle swarms. In *Proceedings of the 2008 Congress on Evolutionary Computation (CEC 2008)* (pp. 1063-1067). CEC.

Shi, Y., & Eberhart, R. (2009). Monitoring of particle swarm optimization. *Frontiers of Computer Science, 3*(1), 31–37. doi:10.1007/s11704-009-0008-4

Wolpert, D., & Macready, W. (1997). No free lunch theorems for optimization. *IEEE Transactions on Evolutionary Computation, 1*(1), 67–82. doi:10.1109/4235.585893

Xu, S., & Rahmat-Samii, Y. (2007). Boundary conditions in particle swarm optimization revisited. *IEEE Transactions on Antennas and Propagation, 55*(3), 760–765. doi:10.1109/TAP.2007.891562

Yao, X., Liu, Y., & Lin, G. (1999). Evolutionary programming made faster. *IEEE Transactions on Evolutionary Computation, 3*(2), 82–102. doi:10.1109/4235.771163

Zhang, W., Xie, X. F., & Bi, D. C. (2004). Handling boundary constraints for numerical optimization by particle swarm flying in periodic search space. In *Proceedings of the 2004 Congress on Evolutionary Computation (CEC 2004)* (pp. 2307-2311). CEC.

Zielinski, K., Weitkemper, P., Laur, R., & Kammeyer, K. D. (2009). Optimization of power allocation for interference cancellation with particle swarm optimization. *IEEE Transactions on Evolutionary Computation, 13*(1), 128–150. doi:10.1109/TEVC.2008.920672

KEY TERMS AND DEFINITIONS

Boundary Constraints Handling: In particle swarm optimization algorithm, particles may "stick in" the boundary. The boundary constraints handling strategies are some methods to handle the particles (or individuals) cross the search boundary, i.e., to handle the phenomenon that solutions out of the predefined search space.

Exploitation: The exploitation ability means that an algorithm focuses on the refinement of found promising areas.

Exploration: The exploration ability means that an algorithm can explore more search place to increase the possibility that the algorithm can find good enough solutions.

Particle Swarm Optimizer/Optimization: Particle Swarm Optimizer/Optimization, which is one of the evolutionary computation techniques, was invented by Eberhart and Kennedy in 1995. It is a population-based stochastic algorithm modeled on the social behaviors observed in flocking birds. Each particle, which represents a solution, flies through the search space with a velocity that is dynamically adjusted according to its own and its companion's historical behaviors.

Population Diversity: Population diversity is a measure of individuals' search information in population-based algorithms. From the distribution of individuals and change of this distribution information, the algorithm's status of exploration or exploitation can be obtained.

Position Diversity: Position diversity measures distribution of particles' current positions, therefore, can reflect particles' dynamics. Position diversity gives the current position distribution information of particles, whether the particles are going to diverge or converge could be reflected from this measurement.

Premature Convergence: Premature convergence is a phenomenon that occurs in population-based algorithms. Premature convergence occurs when all individuals in population-based algorithms are trapped in local optima.

Chapter 6
A Particle Swarm Optimizer for Constrained Multiobjective Optimization

Wen Fung Leong
Kansas State University, USA

Yali Wu
Xi'an University of Technology, China

Gary G. Yen
Oklahoma State University, USA

ABSTRACT

Generally, constraint-handling techniques are designed for evolutionary algorithms to solve Constrained Multiobjective Optimization Problems (CMOPs). Most Multiojective Particle Swarm Optimization (MOPSO) designs adopt these existing constraint-handling techniques to deal with CMOPs. In this chapter, the authors present a constrained MOPSO in which the information related to particles' infeasibility and feasibility status is utilized effectively to guide the particles to search for feasible solutions and to improve the quality of the optimal solution found. The updating of personal best archive is based on the particles' Pareto ranks and their constraint violations. The infeasible global best archive is adopted to store infeasible nondominated solutions. The acceleration constants are adjusted depending on the personal bests' and selected global bests' infeasibility and feasibility statuses. The personal bests' feasibility statuses are integrated to estimate the mutation rate in the mutation procedure. The simulation results indicate that the proposed constrained MOPSO is highly competitive in solving selected benchmark problems.

INTRODUCTION

In real-world applications, most optimization problems are subject to various types of constraints. These problems are known as the constrained optimization problems (COPs) or constrained multiobjective optimization problems (CMOPs) if more than one objective function is involved. Comprehensive surveys (Michalewicz & Schoenauer, 1996; Mezura-Montes & CoellCoello, 2006) show

DOI: 10.4018/978-1-4666-6328-2.ch006

a variety of constraint handling techniques have been developed to address the deficiencies of evolutionary algorithms (EAs), in which, their original design are unable to deal with constraints in an effective manner. These techniques are mainly targeted at EAs, particularly genetic algorithms (GAs), to solve COPs (Runarsson & Yao, 2005; Takahama & Sakai, 2006; Cai & Wang, 2006; Oyama *et al.*, 2007; Wang *et al.*, 2007, 2008; Tessema & Yen, 2009) and CMOPs (Binh & Korn, 1997; Fonseca & Fleming, 1998; CoelloCoello & Christiansen, 1999; Deb *et al.*, 2002; Jimenez *et al.*, 2002; Kurpati *et al.*, 2002; Chafekar *et al.*, 2003; Ray & Won, 2005; Hingston *et al.*, 2006; Geng *et al.*, 2006; Zhang *et al.*, 2006; Harada *et al.*, 2007; Woldesenbet *et al.*, 2009). During the past few years, due to the success of particle swarm optimization (PSO) in solving many unconstrained optimization problems, research on incorporating existing constraint handling techniques in PSO for solving COPs is steadily gaining attention (Parsopoulus & Vrahatis, 2002; Pulido & CoelloCoello, 2004; Zielinski & Laur, 2006; Lu & Chen, 2006; Liang & Suganthan, 2006; Wei & Wang, 2006; He & Wang, 2007; Cushman, 2007; Liu *et al.*, 2008; Li *et al.*, 2008;). Nevertheless, many real world problems are often multiobjective in nature. The ultimate goal is to develop multiobjective particle swarm optimization algorithms (MOPSOs) that effectively solve CMOPs. In addition to this perspective, the recent successes of MOPSOs in solving unconstrained MOPs have further motivated us to design a constrained MOPSO to solve CMOPs.

Considering a minimization problem, the general form of the CMOP with k objective functions is given as follows:

Minimize $\mathbf{f}\left(\mathbf{x}\right) = \left[f_1\left(\mathbf{x}\right), f_2\left(\mathbf{x}\right), \ldots, f_k\left(\mathbf{x}\right)\right],$

$\mathbf{x} = \left[x_1, x_2, \ldots, x_n\right] \in \Re^n$

subject to

$$g_j\left(\mathbf{x}\right) \leq 0, \qquad j = 1, 2, \ldots, m; \qquad (2a)$$

$$h_j\left(\mathbf{x}\right) = 0, \qquad j = m+1, \ldots, p; \qquad (2b)$$

$$x_i^{\min} \leq x_i \leq x_i^{\max}, \quad i = 1, 2, \ldots, n, \qquad (2c)$$

where $\mathbf{x}$ is the decision vector of n decision variables. Its upper ($x_i^{\max}$) and lower ($x_i^{\min}$) bounds in Equation (2c) define the search space, $S \subseteq \Re^n$. $g_j\left(\mathbf{x}\right)$ represents the jth inequality constraint, while $h_j\left(\mathbf{x}\right)$ represents the jth equality constraint. The inequality constraints that are equal to zero, i.e., $g_j\left(\mathbf{x}*\right) = 0$, at the global optimum ($\mathbf{x}*$) of a given problem are called *active constraints*. The feasible region ($F \subseteq S$) is defined by satisfying all constraints (Equations (2a)-(2b)). A solution in the feasible region ($\mathbf{x} \in F$) is called a feasible solution, otherwise it is considered an infeasible solution.

A general MOPSO algorithm consists of the five key procedures: 1) particles' flight (PSO equations), 2) particles' personal best (*pbest*) updating procedure, 3) particles' global best archive (*Gbest*) maintenance method, 4) particles' global best selection scheme, and 5) mutation operation. In the proposed design, we integrate the particles' dominance relationship, and their constraint violation information to each of these key procedures. The constraint violation information is formulated by two simple metrics that represent the particles' feasibility status individually and as a whole. The final goal is to solve the CMOPs by influencing the particles' search behavior in such that will lead them towards the feasible regions and the optimal Pareto front.

The remaining structure of this chapter is arranged as follows. A review of relevant works in this area is presented in *Literature Survey* section. The proposed constrained MOPSO (so called rank and constraint violation MOPSO or RCVMOPSO) is elaborated in *Proposed Approach* section. Comparative study and pertinent discussions are given in *Comparative Study* section. Concluding remarks of the study and the further research are provided in *Conclusion* section.

LITERATURE SURVEY

Publication literatures show majority of the novel constraint handling techniques to solve CMOPs are mainly designed for multiobjective evolutionary algorithms (MOEAs). This is partly due to their popularity and evolutionary algorithms were established earlier than other optimization algorithms such as particle swarm optimization, cultural algorithms, or artificial immune systems. Given the justifications, this section is dedicated to review various constraint handling techniques reported for MOEA designs.

In Fonseca and Fleming's framework (Fonseca & Fleming, 1998), the constraint handling is incorporated within a decision making framework based on goals and priority, in which the constraints are given higher priority than the objective functions during the evolutionary process. Hence, emphasis is given to searching for feasible solutions first then to searching for global solution next.

CoelloCoello and Christiansen (1999) developed two new MOEAs based on the notion of min-max optimum to solve CMOPs. These MOEAs only optimize feasible solutions since only feasible solutions will survive to the next generation and the crossover and mutation operators are designed in such only to produce feasible solutions. However, their algorithms may face difficulty in producing a set of feasible solutions at the initialization step and require large computational time if the feasible region is very small.

Binh and Korn (1997) proposed the Multiobjective Evolutionary Strategy (MOBES). This design includes dividing the infeasible individuals into different classes according to their "nearness" to the feasible region, ranking the infeasible individuals based on the class, computing fitness values according to proportion of feasible and/or infeasible individuals in the population, and incorporating a mechanism to maintain a set of feasible Pareto optimum solutions in every generation. Experimental results on some benchmark functions indicate MOBES is efficient in handling constraints in CMOPs.

Deb *et al.* (2002) introduced a constrained domination principle to handle constraint in their NSGA-II. An individual *i* is said to constrained-dominate an individual *j*, 1) if individual *i* is feasible and individual *j* is infeasible; 2) if both individuals *i* and *j* are infeasible and individual *i* has smaller constraint violations; and 3) if both individuals *i* and *j* are feasible and individual *i* dominates individual *j*. All feasible individuals are ranked via original Pareto dominance relationship while all infeasible individuals are ranked according to their degrees of constraint violations. This constraint handling technique is also adopted in micorgenetic algorithm (microGA) by (CoelloCoello & Pulido, 2001), and another MOPSO proposed by (CoelloCoello *et al.*, 2004).

Kurpati *et al.* (2002) incorporated the 'Constraint-First-Objective-Next' model into four proposed constraint handling techniques for multi-objective genetic algorithm (MOGA). In each of the first three techniques, each fitness assignment stage is based on one of the following guidelines: 1) feasible solutions are preferred over infeasible solutions; 2) the degree of constraint violation for the constraint functions should be used while handling constraints; and 3) the number of violated constraint functions should be taken into consideration while handling constraints. The fitness assignment stage in the fourth technique is based on the combination of the second and the third guidelines. The authors implemented their techniques to improve a constraint handling technique approach of CH-NA (Narayanan & Azarm, 1999). According to the experimental results, the authors concluded that their techniques outperformed CH-NA in terms of computational cost and the closeness of solutions to the true Pareto front; and also concluded that the fourth technique yielded more uniformly distributed Pareto front.

Hingston *et al.* (2006) investigated the differences between two multi-level ranking schemes for ranking the solutions (individuals). The first scheme is known as the objective-first ranking scheme in which the ranking procedure is based on objective values. The procedure is as follow: 1) solutions are first ranked via Pareto ranking scheme (Goldberg, 1989); 2) among those solutions with the same rank value, the most feasible one is considered better; and 3) for those solutions with the same rank value and feasibility, the one with larger crowding distance is better (Deb *et al.*, 2002). The second scheme is called the feasibility-first ranking scheme and the procedure is similar to objective-first ranking scheme except that the ranking is based on infeasibility function values. According to the simulation results, the authors concluded that the objective-first ranking scheme has the advantage of solving some difficult problems by allowing the infeasible solutions to remain in the search population longer and discover good solutions in the search space.

In the proposed MOEA by (Jimenéz *et al.*, 2002), Evolutionary Algorithm of Non-dominated Sorting with Radial Slots (ENORA), the constraint handling technique, allows feasible solutions to evolve towards optimality while infeasible solutions to evolve towards feasibility using the min-max formulation. The diversity mechanism divides the decision space into a set of radial slots along with the successive populations generated. Ray and Won (2005) also employ standard min-max formulation for constraint handling and divides the objective space into a predefined number of radial slots where the solutions will compete with members in the same slot for existence.

Harada *et al.* (2007) proposed Pareto Descent Repair (PDR) operator to repair the infeasible solution by searching for feasible solution closest to the infeasible solutions in the constraint func-

tion space. Their idea is to reduce all violated constraints simultaneously.

Geng *et al.* (2006) proposed a new constraint handling strategy to address the deficiency of Deb's constrained domination principle in NSGA-II (Deb *et al.*, 2002). In their proposal, infeasible elitists are kept to act as a bridge connecting any isolated feasible regions during the evolution process. In addition, they adopted the stochastic ranking (Runarsson & Yao, 2005) to obtain a balance in selecting between the feasible and infeasible elitists. Their idea is applied to NSGA-II and compared the performance with the original NSGA-II on six benchmark CMOPs. The proposed strategy shows significant improvement in terms of distributions and quality of the Pareto fronts on benchmark problems with disconnected feasible regions.

Two selection schemes are proposed for the hybrid of multi-objective differential evolution (MODE) and genetic algorithm (GA) with the ($N+N$) framework to solve CMOPs (Zhang *et al.*, 2006). The first selection scheme aims to preserve the population diversity and the current best solutions are generated by uniformly sampling the maximum objective value for each objective function in the nondominated set. For test problems with non-continuous true Pareto front, the first selection scheme may lead towards finding a portion of the Pareto optimal front. To solve the problem, the authors suggested selecting current best solutions from the current population that have the larger crowding distance and must be either feasible or infeasible with smaller constraint violation. The authors applied their schemes to a hybrid of MODE and NSGA-II with the ($N+N$) framework (DE-MOEA). Experiment results indicated that both schemes on DE-MOEA are superior in performance than CNSGA-II (Deb & Goel, 2001).

In (Chafekar *et al.*, 2003), the authors proposed two algorithms to solve CMOPs. For the first algorithm, Objective Exchange Genetic Algorithm for Design Optimization (OEGADO), each single-objective GA optimizes one objective or constraint function with independent population. Since there are many objectives and constraint functions, several GAs will run concurrently. At certain generations, the solutions found by all GAs will exchange information with each other. On the contrary, for the second algorithm, Objective Switching Genetic Algorithm for Design Optimization (OSGADO), a single-objective GA optimizes several objective functions in a sequential order, in which, one objective is optimized for a certain number of fitness evaluations, then switch to the next objective to optimize for a certain number of fitness evaluations, and this continues until the fitness evaluation for the last objective is completed. The process is repeated starting from the first objective to the last objective until the maximum number of fitness evaluations is reached. Based on the experimental study, OEGADO shows better and consistent performance.

Woldesenbet *et al.* (2009) proposed an adaptive penalty function that exploits the information of the solutions to guide the solutions towards the feasible region and search for optimum solution. They proposed a modified objective function value that consists of two key components: distance measure and adaptive penalty. Afterwards, the dominance relation of the solutions is checked using the modified objective function values. Their idea is incorporated into NSGA-II, but can be easily extended to any MOEAs. Simulation results show the superiority of their proposed algorithm in performance compared to the selected MOEAs.

Jan and Zhang (2010) designed the penalty function threshold to dynamically control the amount of penalty imposed upon infeasible solutions. The proposed penalty function encourages the algorithm to search for the feasible region and the infeasible region nearby the feasible region. The proposed algorithm modified the replacement and update scheme in MOEA/D-DE (Li & Zhang, 2009) for dealing with constraints in multiobjective

optimization problems. Experimental results have shown that this penalty approach is very promising.

Miyakawa and Sato (2012) introduced a parents selection based on two-stage non-dominated sorting of solutions and a directed mating in objective space into constrained MOEA. The algorithm classifies the entire population into several fronts by nondominated sorting based on constraint violation values first. Then, each obtained front by nondominated sorting based on objective function is re-classified to select the parent population from higher fronts. Genetic operators are applied between those solutions dominating the primary parent from the entire population and the secondary parent from the picked solutions to generate an offspring. This idea can give different priority to the same non-dominance level of constraint violation values by the non-dominance level of objective function values. The mating operation can utilize valuable genetic information of infeasible solutions to converge the primary parent towards its search direction in the objective space. The proposed algorithm achieves higher search performance than CNSGA-II (Deb & Goel, 2001) on the chosen benchmark function.

Hsieh *et al.* (2011) designed a hybrid constraint handling mechanism, which combines the ε-comparison method (Takahama & Sakai, 2006) and penalty approach to each constraint and control it by the amount of violation. The penalty method deals with the region where constraint violation exceeds the ε-value and guides the search toward the ε-feasible region. This constraint handling mechanism can provide more constraint information comparing with those methods that add all the constraints together. The algorithm is implemented by the well-known multiobjective evolutionary algorithm, NSGA-II, with the operators in differential evolution (DE). The simulation shows the competitive results on sixteen constrained multiobjective optimization problem instances.

Recently, Liu and Wang (2013) proposed a novel constrained multiobjective evolutionary algorithm based on decomposition and temporary register. They decompose the constrained multi-objective optimization problem into a number of subproblems and then optimize each subproblem in a collaborative manner. They introduced a novel constraint handling technique based on temporary register. Each subproblem has its own subpopulation and one temporary register. The subpopulation is composed of those individuals which has better objective values and lower constraint violations of this subproblem, while the temporary register is composed of those individuals that are found before. The crossover operator between each individual in the subpopulations and an individual which is randomly chosen from the corresponding temporary register are performed. The temporary register strategy ensures the individuals with better objective values and lower constraint violations have an opportunity to participate in the crossover and mutation, and do not get eliminated at once.

From the above reviews, the constraint handling techniques developed in these MOEAs can be categorized into several groups: adapt the techniques that are designed for single objective constraint optimization; make use of the original mechanism in an EA, for instance genetic operator in (CoelloCoello & Christiansen, 1999), to handle constraint as well as optimization of the objective functions; develop rules or principles to emphasize the priority of the feasible and infeasible solutions; and design new mechanisms, such as min-max formulation in (Jimenez *et al.*, 2002) or subpopulations approach in (Chafekar *et al.*, 2003), to evolve feasible solutions towards Pareto front while evolve the infeasible solutions towards feasibility boundary. Based on the state-of-the-art literature, the proposed constrained MOPSO involves adopting an existing constraint handling technique and modifies the mechanism of the original PSO to simultaneously handle constraints as well as optimization of the objective functions by using the feasibility ratio information in the swarm and rank-constraint violation indicator.

PROPOSED APPROACH

Multiobjective Constraint Handling Framework

Over the past decade, various constraint handling techniques were developed to solve COPs. These techniques were initially built for EAs, particularly genetic algorithm and recently, they were adopted into PSO designs. These techniques include penalty methods (Wang *et al.*, 2007), comparison criteria or feasibility tournament (Pulido & CoelloCoello, 2004; Zielinski & Laur, 2006; He & Wang, 2007), lexicographic ordering (Liu *et al.*, 2008), and multiobjective constraint handling techniques (Liang & Sugaanthan, 2006; Lu & Chen, 2006; Cushman, 2007; Li *et al.*, 2008), to name a few. The multiobjective constraint handling techniques, also called multiobjective optimization techniques for handling constraints, are based on multiobjective optimization concepts. The idea is to convert the constraints into one or more unconstrained objective functions and handle them via Pareto dominance relation. These techniques require neither penalty factors that need heuristic tuning nor balance the right proportion of selecting feasible and infeasible solutions in the population via selection criteria (Mezura-Montes & Coello-Coello, 2006; Cai & Wang, 2006). Due to these advantages, the proposed constrained MOPSO adopts the multiobjective optimization techniques.

Given a CMOP with k objective functions, as defined in Equation (1), the problem is transformed into an unconstrained $(k+1)$-objective optimization problem, with the p constraints ((i.e., Equations (2a) and (2b)) are treated as one objective. Equation (3) represents the formulation of the transformed objective functions described.

Minimize

$$\mathbf{f}\left(\mathbf{x}\right) = \left[f_1\left(\mathbf{x}\right), f_2\left(\mathbf{x}\right), \ldots, f_k\left(\mathbf{x}\right), cv\left(\mathbf{x}\right)\right],$$

where $cv(\mathbf{x})$ is the scalar constraint violation of a decision vector $\mathbf{x}$ (or particle) and it is mathematically formulated as below:

$$cv(\mathbf{x}) = \begin{cases} \dfrac{1}{p} \displaystyle\sum_{j=1}^{p} \dfrac{cv_j(\mathbf{x})}{cv^j_{max}}, & cv^j_{max} > 0 \\[2mm] 0, & cv^j_{max} = 0 \end{cases},$$

$$(4)$$

where

$$cv_j(\mathbf{x}) = \begin{cases} \max\left(0, g_j(\mathbf{x})\right), & j = 1,\ldots,m \\[2mm] \max\left(0, \left|h_j(\mathbf{x})\right| - \delta\right), & j = m+1,\ldots,p \end{cases},$$

$$(5a)$$

$$cv^j_{max} = \max_{\mathbf{x} \in CP} cv_j(\mathbf{x}). \tag{5b}$$

$cv_j(\mathbf{x})$ in Equation (5a) represents the jth constraint violation of a decision vector $\mathbf{x}$ and the problem-dependent parameter δ is the tolerance allowed for equality constraints, usually δ is set to 0.001 or 0.0001. If a particle or solution ($\mathbf{x}$) satisfies the jth constraints, then $cv_j(\mathbf{x})$ is zero, otherwise it is greater than zero. Each jth constraint violation ($cv_j(\mathbf{x})$) is normalized by dividing it by the largest violation of the jth constraint (cv^j_{max} in Equation 5(b)) in the *current* swarm population, CP. The constraint violations are normalized to treat each constraint equally. Then the normalized constraint violations are summed together to produce, $cv(\mathbf{x})$ that lies between 0 and 1 (Venkatraman & Yen, 2005).

In solving MOPs, our final goal is to find the Pareto optimum set. Although the Pareto dominance relation is used to solve the ($k+1$) optimization problem in Equation (3), in this case, we only need to find the Pareto front of k functions. This is because if the set of nondominated solutions found is infeasible (i.e., $cv(\mathbf{x}) > 0$), it is unacceptable no matter how high quality the Pareto front of the ($k+1$) objective functions is produced.

Only the set of nondominated solutions that are landed on the feasible regions (i.e., $cv(\mathbf{x}) = 0$) is considered potential Pareto front. Note that for the following discussions, we consider minimization for all objective functions unless specified otherwise.

General Framework

All of the existing constraint handling techniques involve two goals: 1) to search for feasible solutions and to guide infeasible solutions towards feasibility; and 2) to converge to the global optimal solution or Pareto front. In view of this fact, the proposed constrained MOPSO algorithm (in short called RCVMOPSO) encompasses the essential design elements to achieve these goals. Figure 1 presents the pseudocode of the proposed algorithm. The design elements are the key procedures (highlighted in boldface in Figure 1) and they are elaborated in the following subsections.

Update Particles' Personal Best Memory and Feasibility Ratio

Unlike solving for MOPs, the particles' personal best updating mechanism should take into consideration of dominance and the degree of constraint violation. Recently, Li *et al.* (2008) proposed two selection rules to update the particles' personal best: (Rule 1) a nondominated particle is better than dominated one; (Rule 2) a particle with lower constraint violation is better than a particle with higher constraint violation. Rule one is given higher priority. The drawback of these rules is to determine which rule should be prioritized first. If rule one is given higher priority, the progress of searching for feasible regions may slow down since personal best indirectly influence the particles' search behavior in the swarm population. On the contrary, if rule two is given a higher priority, all infeasible solutions will quickly land on the feasible regions but this will indirectly degrade the

Figure 1. Pseudocode of the proposed RCVMOPSO

```
Begin
/*Initialization
Initialize swarm population and velocity
Set Maximum iterations (tmax)
Set iteration t = 0
Update Particles' Personal Best Memory (Section III.C)
While t < tmax
     Calculate Fitness and Constraint violation for all particles
     Find particles' rank values via Pareto ranking
     Update Particles' Personal Best Memory (Section III.C)
     Calculate the Feasibility Ratio (rf) (Section III.C and Equation (7))
     Update Feasible and Infeasible Global Best Archive (Section III.D)
     Global Best Selection (Section III.E)
     Particle Update Mechanism (Section III.F)
     Mutation Operation (Section III.G)
     t = t + 1
EndWhile
Report optimal Pareto front in Feasible Global Best Archive
End
```

diversity in the swarm population and may results in premature convergence. Hence it is important to update personal best using both rules at the same time to maintain a balance between convergence to fitter particles and search for feasible regions.

In this study, we propose the following equation to incorporate the rank value and scalar constraint violation of a particle (with decision vector $\mathbf{x}$) to update the personal best if the latest recorded personal best of a particle is in infeasible region:

$$RC\left(\mathbf{x}\right) = \left(1 - \frac{1}{rank\left(\mathbf{x}\right)}\right) + cv\left(\mathbf{x}\right), \qquad (6)$$

where $RC\left(\mathbf{x}\right)$ is the rank-constraint violation indicator of a particle with decision vector $\mathbf{x}$, $rank\left(\mathbf{x}\right)$ represents the current rank value while $cv(\mathbf{x})$ refers to Equation (4). The rank values are obtained from applying the Pareto ranking (Goldberg, 1989) to the swarm population. Refer to Equation (6), the first term indicates the dominant

relationship of the particles comparing the others and it is mapped between zero and one, where zero indicates non-dominated particles and any values greater than zero indicates particle is dominated in various degrees. The purpose is to search for the non-dominated solutions, regardless if the solutions are infeasible, and these solutions will possibly indirectly influence the improvement of the particles in the next iterations in terms of convergence. However, this does not guarantee that the particles will move towards the feasible regions easily since most of the time the searching is spent in the infeasible regions. So, the second term is added to Equation (6) to emphasize the current state of the particles in terms of their feasibility or the degree of infeasibility in the current swarm population. Both terms are considered equally important without any preference. Note that the range of *RC* is between 0 and 2, and a particle with smaller *RC* value indicates better solution in terms of its convergence and feasibility status. In this chapter, the calculation of RC is applied to the particles in the swarm population at every iteration.

The updating procedures for particles' personal best memory, done at every iteration, are summarized below.

If the personal best memory is empty, record all computed RC values of all particles in the current swarm population, including their corresponding positions (*pbest*) and their scalar constraint violations (*pbest_cv*).

If the personal best memory is not empty, their recorded RC values are compared with the computed RC values of their corresponding particles in the current swarm population. Any current particles with smaller RC values will replace the recorded ones, including updating the corresponding RC values, *pbest* , and *pbest_cv* . In any case if the recorded and computed RCs are the same, then one of them is randomly chosen to update the personal best memory.

Once the updating procedure is completed, the feasibility ratio of the particles' personal bests (r_f) is updated via the following equation:

$$r_f = \frac{\text{number of particles' personal bests that are feasible}}{\text{swarm population size}} \cdot$$

(7)

Update Feasible and Infeasible Global Best Archives

Recent studies have shown the advantage of using infeasible solutions to search for global optimal solution (Chafekar *et al.*, 2003; Geng *et al.*, 2006; Yang *et al.*, 2006). One purpose is to promote diversity during the search process through a balance between feasible and infeasible solutions (Cai & Wang, 2006; Wang *et al.*, 2007; 2008). Another purpose is to use the infeasible solutions as the bridge to explore isolated feasible regions in order to search for better feasible solutions and to deal with the case where the proportional feasible region is relatively smaller compared to the entire search space. Hence, we propose two fixed

size global best archives: 1) The feasible global best archive stores only the best feasible solution found so far; while 2) the infeasible global best archive stores the infeasible solutions that have minimum $cv(\mathbf{x})$ found so far. The solutions in both archives serve as potential global best candidates (*Gbest)* for the particle flight update.

To maintain the archives, first the new nondominated particles from the swarm population are found. Then, these new nondominated particles are divided into new feasible nondominated solutions and infeasible nondominated solutions. The procedures to maintain both global best archives are summarized below:

- **Maintaining Feasible Global Best Archive**: At each iteration count, new *feasible* nondominated solutions are compared with respect to any members in the archive. If new feasible solutions are not dominated by any archive members, they are accepted into the archive. Similarly, any archive members dominated by any new feasible solutions are removed from the archive. If the archive population size exceeds the allocated archive size, the dynamic crowding distance's diversity maintenance strategy (Luo *et al.*, 2008) is applied to remove the crowded members among the archive members. The idea of dynamic crowing distance is very similar to Deb's crowding distance in NSGA-II. The equation to calculate the member's dynamic crowding distance is modified to solve the flaw of Deb's crowding distance, which is the crowding distance may not accurately reflect the crowding degrees of the solutions and may end up removing the wrong members.

- **Maintaining Infeasible Global Best Archive**: Initially, if the archive is empty, then any infeasible nondominated solutions and their scalar constraint violation (

$cv(\mathbf{x})$) are immediately recorded in the archive. However, if the archive is not empty, then at each iteration count, two procedures are executed: In the first procedure, the $cv(\mathbf{x})$ of the new infeasible nondominated solution is compared with the largest $cv(\mathbf{x})$ stored in the archive. Those new infeasible nondominated solutions with $cv(\mathbf{x})$ exceeding the largest $cv(\mathbf{x})$ stored in the archive are removed. In the second procedure, the remaining new infeasible nondominated solutions are compared with respect to any members in the archive. If any new solutions are not dominated by any archive members, they are accepted into the archive; and those archive members dominated by any new solutions are removed from the archive. Similarly, the dynamic crowding distance approach (Luo *et al.*, 2008) is applied to remove any crowded members from the overflowed archive population size.

Global Best Selection

Once both feasible and infeasible global best archives are updated, a *Gbest* is selected either from these archives with equal probability. This provides equal probability of utilizing a set of the feasible and infeasible *Gbest*s to guide their particles. Unless one of the archives is empty, then by default all *Gbest* are selected from the remaining nonempty archive. Note that each particle selects its own *Gbest*. The procedure for a particle to select its *Gbest* at every iteration is given below:

Step 1: Two archive members from the selected Global Best Archive are randomly chosen via equal probability.

Step 2: Apply tournament selection: The dynamic crowding distance value of the two randomly chosen archive members are compared. The member with larger dynamic crowd-

ing distance value (Luo *et al.*, 2008) (i.e., less crowded area) wins the tournament and becomes the particle's *Gbest*.

The use of dynamic crowding distance values with tournament selection is a diversity preservation mechanism to encourage more exploration among the particles in the swarm population.

Particle Update Mechanism

In the original PSO equations, the movement of particles is influenced by their past experiences, i.e., their personal past experience (*pbest*) and successful experience attained by their peers (*Gbest*). In (Lu & Chen, 2006) and (Cushman, 2007), the PSO's velocity equation is modified to influence the particles movement towards feasibility. Lu and Chen (2006) replaced the inertial term with personal and global bests in order to restrict the velocity term so that those feasible particles (solutions) will not be moved away from the feasible regions. Cushman (2007) added a global worst term (*Gworst*) with a very low acceleration constant (suggested 0.0001) to nudge the particles away from the center of the least feasible solution.

In our design, the scalar constraint violation ($cv(\mathbf{x})$) and the feasibility ratio (r_f) are incorporated into the velocity equation to guide the particles towards feasibility first and then influence them to search for global optimal solution. The new PSO equation and its new acceleration constants are formulated as follow:

$$v_{i,j}\left(t+1\right) = w \times v_{i,j}\left(t\right) + c_1 \times r_1 \times$$
$$\left(pbest_{i,j}\left(t\right) - x_{i,j}\left(t\right)\right) + c_2 \times r_2 \times \left(Gbest_j\left(t\right) - x_{i,j}\left(t\right)\right)$$
$$(8)$$

$$x_{i,j}\left(t+1\right) = x_{i,j}\left(t\right) + v_{i,j}\left(t+1\right) \qquad (9)$$

where

$$c_1 = \left(1 - r_f\right) + \left(1 - pbest\_cv_i\left(t\right)\right), \qquad (10a)$$

$$c_2 = r_f + \left(1 - Gbest\_cv(t)\right). \qquad (10b)$$

$v_{i,j}\left(t\right)$ is the jth dimensional velocity of particle i in iteration t; $x_{i,j}\left(t\right)$ is the jth dimensional position of particle i in iteration t; $pbest_{i,j}\left(t\right)$ denotes the jth dimensional personal best position of the particle i in iteration t; $pbest\_cv_i\left(t\right)$ is the $cv(\mathbf{x})$ of the personal best of particle i in iteration t, $Gbest_j\left(t\right)$ is the jth dimensional $Gbest$ selected from global best archive in iteration t; $Gbest\_cv\left(t\right)$ represents the $cv(\mathbf{x})$ of the selected $Gbest\left(t\right)$ in iteration t; r_1 and r_2 are random numbers within $\left[0,1\right]$ that are regenerated every time they occur; w is the inertial weight, set to varied between 0.1 to 0.7 (as suggested in (Sierra & CoelloCoello, 2005) to eliminate the difficulty of fine tuning the inertial weight); and c_1 and c_2 are the acceleration constants. Please note the PSO flight equations stress the update mechanism of a particle i (so the iteration variable t and subscript i are used). On the other hand, Equations (3)-(5) emphasizes the $cv(\mathbf{x})$ of a particle with decision vector $\mathbf{x}$. Specifically, $pbest\_cv_i\left(t\right)$ refers to $cv(pbest(\mathbf{x}))$ in iteration t.

Adjustment of acceleration constants: In usual practice, the acceleration constants, c_1 and c_2, are fixed values and are normally set to 2. This means that both second and third terms in Equation (8) are weighted equally. If r_1 and r_2 are equal, the movement of a particle depends on both its personal past experience and the global experiences attained by the whole swarm population. Understand this concept, we proposed using the feasibility ratio of the particles' personal best (r_f), and the amount of scalar constraint violations of the $pbest$ and $Gbest$ to adjust the parameters c_1 and c_2 (see Equations (10a) and (10b)). The idea is to utilize the infeasibility information to influence a particle's movement; hopefully the particle will discover better solution. The movement depends either on its personal past experience (the second term) or the collective global experiences (the third term) or both terms. Table 1 briefly summarizes the effects of r_f, $pbest\_cv$, and $Gbest\_cv$ on the second and third terms in Equation (8). Observe Table 1, we can generally conclude that small r_f will likely influence the particles to favor on searching for feasible regions instead of optimum solution, while with large r_f, the particles are inclined to search for optimum solution. Both $pbest\_cv$ and $Gbest\_cv$ play their role to guide the particles towards feasibility and search for better solution, but in an indirect manner.

Mutation Operation

In this approach, uniform and Gaussian mutation operators are applied. Uniform mutation aims to encourage exploration in the swarm population and is presented in Equation (11), while Gaussian mutation in Equation (12) promotes exploitation among the particles in the swarm population via local search characteristics.

$$x_{i,j}\left(t\right) = x_{i,j}^{\min} + r_3\left(x_{i,j}^{\max} - x_{i,j}^{\min}\right), \qquad (11)$$

$$x_{i,j}\left(t\right) = x_{i,j}\left(t\right) + \beta_i, \qquad (12)$$

where $x_{i,j}\left(t\right)$ is the jth dimensional position of particle i in iteration t; r_3 is a random number

Table 1. Brief summary of the effects of r_f, $pbest\_cv$, and $Gbest\_cv$ on the second and third terms in Equation (8)

r_f	$pbest\_cv$	$Gbest\_cv$	Comments
Small	Small	Small	$c_1 > c_2$; emphasize on the second term (Both terms will guide the particle towards feasibility)
Small	Small	Large	$c_1 >> c_2$; highly emphasize on the second term (Second term guides the particle towards feasibility)
Small	Large	Small	$c_1 \approx c_2$, both terms may have equal emphasis (Both terms will guide the particle towards feasibility and find better solutions)
Small	Large	Large	$c_1 > c_2$; emphasize on the second term (Second term guides the particle towards feasibility)
Large	Small	Small	$c_1 < c_2$; emphasize on the third term (Third term guides the particle to find better solutions)
Large	Small	Large	$c_1 \approx c_2$; both terms may have equal emphasis (Both terms will guide the particle towards feasibility and find better solutions)
Large	Large	Small	$c_1 << c_2$; highly emphasize on the third term (Third term guides the particle to find better solutions)
Large	Large	Large	$c_1 < c_2$; emphasize on the third term (Third term guides the particle to find better solutions)

within $\left[0,1\right]$; $x_{i,j}^{\max}$ and $x_{i,j}^{\min}$ are the jth dimensional upper and lower bounds of particle i; and β_i represents a random number in which it is drawn from the Gaussian distribution, $Gaussian\left(0, P_m\left(x_{i,j}^U - x_{i,j}^L\right)\right)$. Parameter P_m is computed using Equations (13) and (14) (Leong & Yen, 2008; Yen & Leong, 2009).

$$lb = \frac{0.1}{n}, \; n = \text{number of decision variables,}$$

$$P_m = \begin{cases} \left(0.5 - lb\right) \times \left(1 - 2 \times r_f^2 + \dfrac{lb}{0.5 - lb}\right), & 0 \le r_f \le 0.5 \\ \left(0.5 - lb\right) \times \left(2 \times \left(r_f - 1\right)^2 + \dfrac{lb}{0.5 - lb}\right), & 0.5 < r_f \le 1 \end{cases}$$

(14)

The P_m parameter is adaptively determined by the feasibility ratio of the particles' *personal best* (r_f). Figure 2 is the illustration of Equation (14). *lb* represents the minimum allowable P_m and is determined from Equation (13). Smaller

r_f yield larger P_m value and vice versa. If $r_f = 1$, P_m will remain to be lb. This parameter P_m serves two purposes: 1) it controls the particles' local search area by allowing larger mutation area when there are fewer feasible particles (r_f is small) to explore nearby feasible regions, and reduces the mutation area when r_f is larger to encourage finer search for quality solutions; and 2) it represents the mutation probability, in which the mutation probability increases when r_f value decreases. The idea is to increase the chances for infeasible particles to discover potential feasible solutions or feasible particles to escape the sub-optimal solutions.

After the velocity and position of each particle i in iteration t (Equations 8-10) is updated, for each jth dimensional position of particle i, ($x_{i,j}(t)$), the procedure to implement the mutation operator are given.

Step 1: Compute Equations (13) and (14).
Step 2: Generate a random number r_4 with uniform distribution between $[0,1]$. If $r_4 < P_m$, go to Step 3, otherwise go to Step 4.
Step 3: Generate a random number r_5 with uniform distribution between $[0,1]$. If $r_5 < 0.5$, apply uniform mutation (Equation (11)),

otherwise Gaussian mutation (Equation (12)) is used.
Step 4: If the jth dimensional position of particle i is outside of its bounds, i.e. $x_{i,j}(t) \notin \left[x_{i,j}^{\min}, x_{i,j}^{\max}\right]$, the following rule is applied:

$$x_{i,j}(t) = \begin{cases} x_{i,j}(t) = x_{i,j}^{\min}, & \text{if } x_{i,j}(t) < x_{i,j}^{\min} \\ x_{i,j}(t) = x_{i,j}^{\max}, & \text{if } x_{i,j}(t) > x_{i,j}^{\max} \end{cases}.$$
$$(15)$$

COMPARATIVE STUDY

In this section, simulation study is conducted to analyze RCVMOPSO in two aspects: 1) to evaluate and compare its performance with the selected algorithms; and 2) to find out which test problems' characteristics that our approach is having difficulty to solve.

Experimental Setup

Three state-of-the-art constrained MOEAs are chosen and they are NSGA-II (Deb *et al.*, 2002), Geng *et al.* (2006) (indicated as GZHW), and Woldesenbet *et al.* (2009) (indicated as WTY). The reason that all the selected algorithms are

Figure 2. Mutation rate (P_m) versus feasibility ratio of the particles' personal best (r_f)

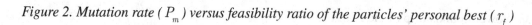
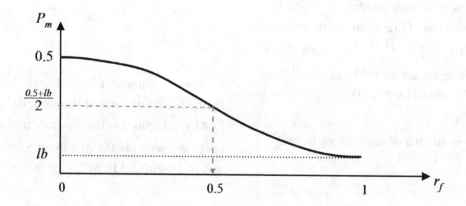

MOEAs is because there exist no prominent constrained MOPSO designed to solve CMOPs. Secondly, these selected MOEAs adopted different *constraint handling techniques*, though their basic building blocks are based on NSGA-II. Each algorithm is set to perform 50,000 fitness evaluations. The parameter configurations for all testing algorithms are summarized in Table 2.

Fourteen minimization benchmark problems with different characteristics are chosen to evaluate the performance of RCVMOPSO with the selected MOEAs. Table 3 presents the summary of the main characteristics of these benchmark problems. It provides the number of objective functions and their types of constraint functions (i.e., linear inequality (LI), nonlinear inequality (NI), linear equality (LE), and nonlinear equality (NE)). The parameter **n** represents the number of decision variables, and parameter **a** represents the number of inequality constraints that are active constraints. The parameter ρ is called feasibility ratio. This ratio is determined by calculating the percentage of feasible solutions out of 1,000,000 randomly generated solutions in the entire search space (Cai & Wang, 2006). If the feasibility ratio is very small, this challenges the algorithms to search for feasible solutions. Among the test problems, the welded beam problem represents a real-world optimization problem (Chafekar *et al.*, 2003). Some of the test problems have continuous Pareto-fronts (i.e., SRN, OSY, CTP1, CTP6, CONSTR, and Welded Beam), while the remaining problems have disjoint Pareto-fronts (i.e., TNK, CTP2-CTP5, CTP7, and CTP8). It is a great challenge to the proposed algorithm to locate disjoint Pareto fronts with alternating feasible and infeasible regions, especially for the CTP8 which possesses multiple, small, and disjoint feasible regions that impose greater difficulty in locating the optimal solutions.

In this chapter, all of the algorithms use a real-number representation for decision variables. For each experiment, 50 independent runs were conducted to collect the statistical results.

Table 2. Parameter configurations for testing algorithms

Algorithms	Parameter Settings
NSGA-II (Deb *et al.*, 2002)	Population size =100; crossover probability = 0.9; mutation probability = $1/n$; SBX crossover parameter = 20; polynomial mutation parameter = 20.
GZHW (Geng *et al.*, 2006)	Population size =100; crossover probability = 0.9; mutation probability = $1/n$; SBX crossover parameter = 20; polynomial mutation parameter = 20; comparison probability = 0.45; penalty parameters, $w_j = 1, \beta = 1$.
WTY (Woldesenbet *et al.*, 2009)	Population size =100; Test Functions CTP1- CTP8, and DTLZ9 Crossover probability = 0.9; mutation probability = $1/n$; SBX crossover parameter = 10; polynomial mutation parameter = 20. Test Functions, SRN, TNK, OSY, CONSTR, and Welded Beam Crossover probability = 0.9; mutation probability = $1/n$; SBX crossover parameter = 5; polynomial mutation parameter = 5.
RCVMOPSO	Population size =100; feasible and infeasible *Gbest* archive size = 100; $\delta = 0.0001$

Table 3. Summary of main characteristics of the 14 benchmark functions

Problems	Objective Functions	n	ρ	LI	NI	LE	NE	a
SRN (Binh & Korn, 1997)	2	2	16.18%	1	1	0	0	0
TNK (Tanaka, 1995)	2	2	5.09%	0	2	0	0	1
OSY (Osyezka & Kundu, 1995)	2	6	3.25%	4	2	0	0	6
CTP1 (Deb *et al.*, 2001)	2	2	99.58%	0	1	0	0	1
CTP2 (Deb *et al.*, 2001)	2	2	78.65%	0	1	0	0	1
CTP3 (Deb *et al.*, 2001)	2	2	76.85%	0	1	0	0	1
CTP4 (Deb *et al.*, 2001)	2	2	58.17%	0	1	0	0	1
CTP5 (Deb *et al.*, 2001)	2	2	77.54%	0	1	0	0	1
CTP6 (Deb *et al.*, 2001)	2	2	0.40%	0	1	0	0	1
CTP7 (Deb *et al.*, 2001)	2	2	36.68%	0	1	0	0	1
CTP8 (Deb *et al.*, 2001)	2	2	17.86%	0	2	0	0	1
CONSTR (Deb *et al.*, 2001)	2	2	52.52%	2	0	0	0	1
Welded Beam (Chafekar *et al.*, 2003)	2	4	18.67%	1	3	0	0	0
DTLZ9 (Deb *et al.*, 2005)	3	30	10.37%	0	2	0	0	2

Performance Metrics

All comparisons are based on qualitative and quantitative measures. Qualitative comparison is based on the plots of the final Pareto fronts in a given run. For quantitative comparison, two performance metrics are taken into consideration to measure the quality of algorithms with respect to dominance relations. The hypervolume indicator (S metric) (Zitzler, 1999) measures how well the algorithm converges and produces nondominated solutions that is well-distributed and well-extent along the Pareto front. The additive binary ε-indicator (Zitzler *et al.*, 2003) indicates whether a non-dominated set produced by an algorithm is better than another. In addition, Wilcoxon rank-sum test is used to measure the significant differences between the two sample sets (Conover, 1999). The null hypothesis (i.e., p-value > α)

suggests that there is *no* significant differences between the two sample sets; while the alternative hypothesis (i.e., p-value ≤ α) indicates otherwise. The symbol, α represents the significant level and is set to 5%.

Performance Evaluation

The box plots of hypervolume indicator (the I_H values) are summarized in Figure 3. The algorithm with higher I_H values indicates better performance in terms of coverage and better distribution of the nondominated solutions along the Pareto front. In Figure 3, the I_H values are normalized for each test problem. So, the highest I_H value will equal one. Table 4 presents the Wilcoxon rank-sum test results of the I_H values for these algorithms. Observe the medians of the box plots in Figure 3 and the results in Table 4, RCVMOPSO yields a better performance than the other three algorithms for test functions CTP3, CTP5, CTP6, and DTLZ9. RCVMOPSO also gains the equal or better performance than NSGA-II and WTY for test function OSY, CTP4 and better performance than GZHW for test functions CTP1 and Welded Beam; while RCVMOPSO has produced comparable results with GZHW for test functions SRN, CTP2, CTP7, and CTP8. Observing Figure 3, RCVMOPSO has the lowest I_H values for test functions SRN, CTP7, CTP8, and TNK, and does not fall short in terms of performance because it has I_H values higher than 0.99 and the differences between its I_H values compared to those achieved by the selected MOEAs are between 0.001 and 0.006. However, on test functions CTP4 and CONSTR, the proposed algorithm's performance is considered worse. In addition, the y-axis in Figure 3 shows that the distributions of RCVMOPSO are consistently low for all of the test functions. This indicates its ability of producing reliable solutions for all of the benchmark functions.

Figures 4 through 11 illustrates the results (summarized in box plots) of additive binary ε-indicator. For each test problem, there are two box plots, i.e., $I_{\varepsilon+}\left(A, B_{1-3}\right)$ and $I_{\varepsilon+}\left(B_{1-3}, A\right)$, in which RCVMOPSO is represented by A and the algorithm B_{1-3} refer to NSGA-II, GZHW, and WTY, respectively. Observed in Figures 4 through 11, neither RCVMOPSO nor the rest of the algorithms dominate each other for test function SRN, TNK, CTP1, CTP2, CTP4, CTP5, CTP6, CTP8, and DTLZ9 since box plots show that $I_{\varepsilon+}\left(A, B_{1-3}\right) > 0$ and $I_{\varepsilon+}\left(B_{1-3}, A\right) > 0$. In addition, the results in Table 5 confirm this analysis and for some of the test functions, RCV-MOPSO shares the same performance with GZHW and NSGA-II for test function CTP1 and CTP8. Based on the mediums in the box plots and results in Figures 12 through 19, RCVMOPSO weakly

dominates GZHW for test function Welded Beam since the $I_{\varepsilon+}\left(A, B_2\right) \approx 0$ and $I_{\varepsilon+}\left(B_2, A\right) > 0$. It also weakly dominates GZHW and WTY for test function CTP7. On the contrary, NSGA-II weakly dominates the proposed algorithm for test functions CTP4, CTP7, and Welded Beam. The same observation also applies to WTY for test functions OSY and Welded beam. The proposed algorithm is weekly dominated by the three algorithms for test function CTP3. In summary, in terms of dominance relationship, RCVMOPSO yields equal performance as the selected MOEAs for the nine test functions, and obtains the best result for DTLZ9 and the worst for CTP3.

For qualitative comparison, the resulted Pareto fronts generated by all the algorithms from a single run given the same initial population are presented in Figures 12 through 19. For every test problem, four plots are presented and the labels (a)-(d) represent the following algorithms: RCVMOPSO, NSGA-II, GZHW, and WTY respectively. In this analysis, the performance is compared by the solutions' distribution and their extendibility along the true Pareto front. The observation indicates that RCVMOPSO is able to produce equal or better Pareto optimal fronts compared to the rest of the MOEAs for test functions SRN, TNK, CTP1, CTP2, CTP3, CTP4, CTP5, CTP6, CTP7, and CTP8. On test function DTLZ9, it produces the best Pareto optimal fronts (i.e., well-distributed and well-extended). However, for test functions OSY, CONSTR, and Welded Beam, it achieves the worst Pareto optimal fronts. These Pareto fronts achieved by the proposed MOPSO are either incomplete (i.e., only cover part of the true Pareto front), such as test functions OSY, Welded Beam, and CONSTR. Based on the results analysis given above, several conclusions are drawn:

- The additive binary ε-indicator results in Figures 4 through 11 and Table 5, and all the Pareto front plots in Figures 12

Figure 3. Box plot of hypervolume indicator (I_H values) for all test functions by algorithms 1-4 represented (in order): RCVMOPSO, NSGA-II, GZHW and WTY

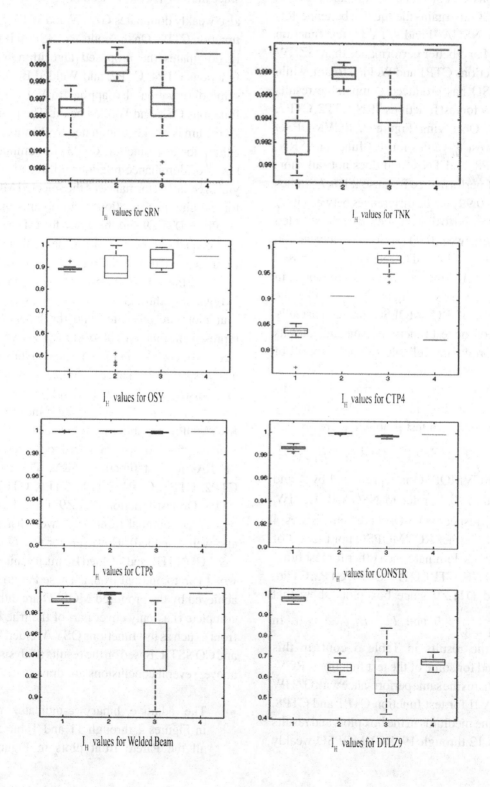

Table 4. The distribution of I_H values tested using Wilcoxon rank-sum test. The numbers in each bracket represents (z values, p-values) with respect to the alternative hypothesis (if p-value $\leq \alpha=0.05$, reject the null hypothesis) for each pair of RCVMOPSO and a selected constrained MOEAs. The distribution of RCVMOPSO is significantly different than those selected constrained MOEAs.

Test Functions	I_H (RCVMOPSO) AND		
	I_H (NSGA-II)	I_H (GZHW)	I_H (WTY)
SRN	(-6.6457, 3.0E-11)	(-1.2197, >0.05) *no difference*	(-7.1040, 1.2E-12)
TNK	(-6.6458, 3.0E-11)	(-4.5314, 5.9E-06)	(-7.1040, 1.2E-12)
OSY	(2.1955, 2.8E-02)	(-4.7680, 1.86E-06)	(3.3644, 7.6E-04)
CTP1	(-6.5865,4.5E-11)	(4.2357,2.2E-05)	(-6.6160, 3.6E-11)
CTP2	(-5.6699, 1.4E-08)	(0.3327, >0.05) *no difference*	(-4.8272, 1.3E-06)
CTP3	(6.6160, 3.6E-11)	(5.4905, 4.0E-08)	(6.6003, 4.1E-11)
CTP4	(-6.6458, 3.0E-11)	(-6.6456, 3.0E-11)	(6.6299, 3.4E-11)
CTP5	(5.4863,4.1E-08)	(5.8820,4.0E-09)	(4.9841,6.2E-07)
CTP6	(5.5075, 3.6E-08)	(6.6460,3.0E-11)	(6.2468, 4.1E-10)
CTP7	(-6.6456,3.0E-11)	(0.4509,>0.05) *no difference*	(-6.6456,3.0E-11)
CTP8	(-6.4980, 8.1E-11)	(-0.1109,, >0.05) *no difference*	(-7.1040, 1.2E-12)
CONSTR	(-6.6459, 3.0E-11)	(-6.6456, 3.0E-11)	(-6.5846, 4.6E-11)
Welded Beam	(-5.8624, 4.6E-09)	(6.3499, 2.2E-10)	(-7.1040, 1.21E-12)
DTLZ9	(8.6138, 7.1E-18)	(8.6138, 7.1E-18)	(8.6139, 7.1E-18)

Figure 4. Box plot of additive binary epsilon indicator ($I_{\varepsilon+}$ values) for SRN (algorithm A refers to RCV-MOPSO; algorithms B_{1-3} are referred to as NSGA-II, GZHW and WTY, respectively)

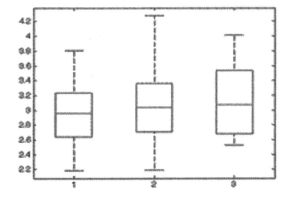
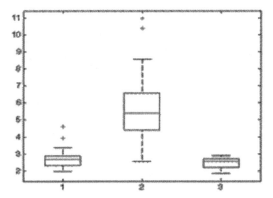

Figure 5. Box plot of additive binary epsilon indicator (I_{e+} values) for TNK (algorithm A refers to RCV-MOPSO; algorithms B_{1-3} are referred to as NSGA-II, GZHW and WTY, respectively)

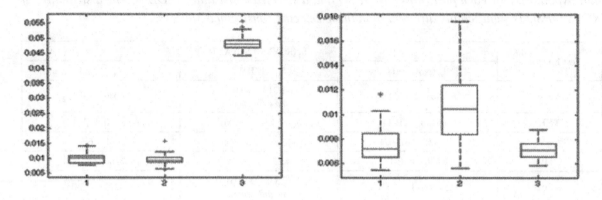

Figure 6. Box plot of additive binary epsilon indicator (I_{e+} values) for OSY (algorithm A refers to RCV-MOPSO; algorithms B_{1-3} are referred to as NSGA-II, GZHW and WTY, respectively)

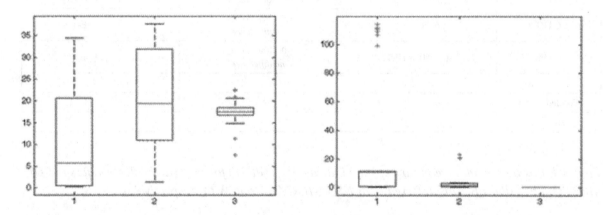

Figure 7. Box plot of additive binary epsilon indicator (I_{e+} values) for CTP4 (algorithm A refers to RCVMOPSO; algorithms B_{1-3} are referred to as NSGA-II, GZHW and WTY, respectively)

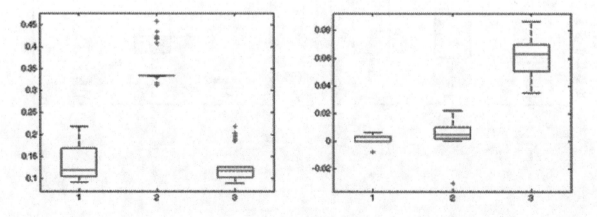

Figure 8. Box plot of additive binary epsilon indicator ($I_{\varepsilon+}$ values) for CTP8 (algorithm A refers to RCVMOPSO; algorithms B_{1-3} are referred to as NSGA-II, GZHW and WTY, respectively)

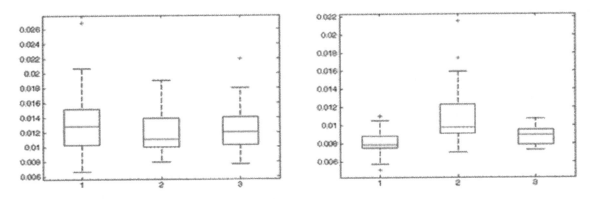

Figure 9. Box plot of additive binary epsilon indicator ($I_{\varepsilon+}$ values) for CONSTR (algorithm A refers to RCVMOPSO; algorithms B_{1-3} are referred to as NSGA-II, GZHW and WTY, respectively)

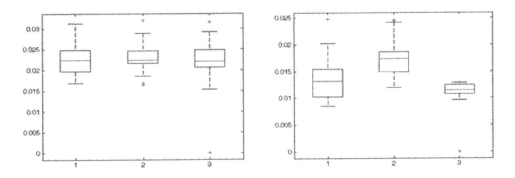

Figure 10. Box plot of additive binary epsilon indicator ($I_{\varepsilon+}$ values) for Welded Beam (algorithm A refers to RCVMOPSO; algorithms B_{1-3} are referred to as NSGA-II, GZHW and WTY, respectively)

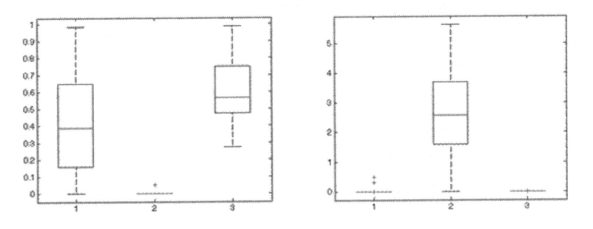

Figure 11. Box plot of additive binary epsilon indicator ($I_{\varepsilon+}$ values) for DTLZ9 (algorithm A refers to RCVMOPSO; algorithms B_{1-3} are referred to as NSGA-II, GZHW and WTY, respectively)

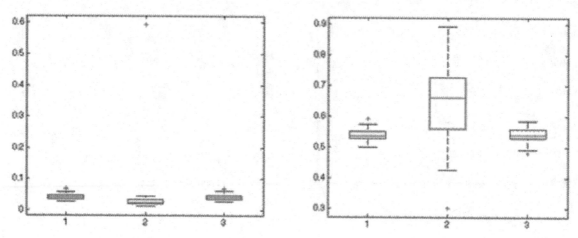

Table 5. The distribution of $I_{\varepsilon+}$ values tested using Wilcoxon rank-sum Test. The numbers in each bracket represents (z values, p-values) with respect to the alternative hypothesis (if p-value $\leq \alpha$=0.05, reject the null hypothesis) for each pair of RCVMOPSO and a selected constrained MOEAs. RCVMOPSO is represented by A, and algorithms B_1, B_2, and B_3 are referred to as NSGA-II, GZHW and WTY, respectively. The distribution of RCVMOPSO is significantly difference than those selected constrained MOEAs unless stated.

Test Functions	$I_{\varepsilon+}$ (A,B1) and $I_{\varepsilon+}$ (B1,A)	$I_{\varepsilon+}$ (A,B2) and $I_{\varepsilon+}$ (B2,A)	$I_{\varepsilon+}$ (A,B3) and $I_{\varepsilon+}$ (B3,A)
SRN	(2.3138, 2.1E-01)	(-5.8916, 3.8E-09)	(4.7828, 1.7E-06)
TNK	(4.7680, 1.9E-06)	(-1.0719, >0.05) *no difference*	(6.6456, 3.0E-11)
OSY	(-1.3528,, >0.05) *no difference*	(4.9750, 6.5E-07)	(6.6456, 3.0E-11)
CTP1	(6.1874,6.1E-10)	(6.4830,8.9E-11)	(6.2169,5.0E-10)
CTP2	(6.0247,1.6E-09)	(3.3487,8.1E-04)	(5.9507,2.6E-10)
CTP3	(7.1040, 1.2E-12)	(7.1040, 1.2E-12)	(7.1040, 1.2E-12)
CTP4	(6.7223, 1.8E-11)	(6.6456, 3.0E-11)	(6.6456, 3.0E-11)
CTP5	(6.6456, 3.0E-11)	(6.3351,2.3E-10)	(5.6403,1.6E-08)
CTP6	(2.4616, 0.0138)	(4.6201,3.8E-06)	(1.4415,>0.05) *no difference*
CTP7	(6.6457,3.0E-11)	(-6.3943,1.6E-10)	(-6.4978, 8.1E-11)
CTP8	(5.4037, 6.5E-08)	(1.7224, >0.05) *no difference*	(5.1524, 2.6E-07)
CONSTR	(6.0099, 1.9E-09)	(4.5166, 6.3E-06)	(6.2095, 5.3E-10)
Welded Beam	(6.1725, 6.7E-10)	(-6.6308, 3.3E-11)	(6.6456, 3.0E-11)
DTLZ9	(-8.6138, 7.1E-18)	(-8.4828, 2.2E-17)	(-8.6139, 7.1E-18)

Figure 12. Pareto fronts for SRN produced by the following algorithms a-d represented (in order): RCVMOPSO, NSGA-II, GZHW and WTY, respectively

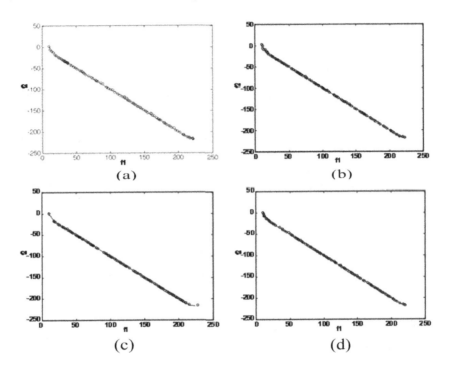

(a) (b)

(c) (d)

Figure 13. Pareto fronts for TNK produced by the following algorithms a-d represented (in order): RCVMOPSO, NSGA-II, GZHW and WTY, respectively

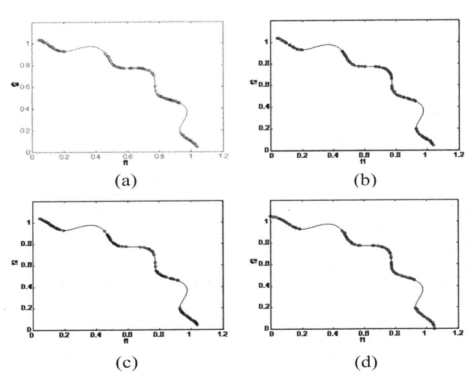

(a) (b)

(c) (d)

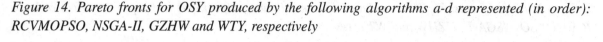

Figure 14. Pareto fronts for OSY produced by the following algorithms a-d represented (in order): RCVMOPSO, NSGA-II, GZHW and WTY, respectively

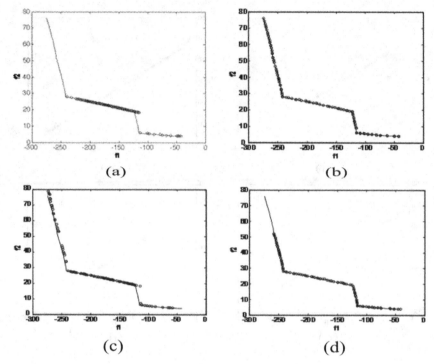

(a) (b)

(c) (d)

through 19 indicate that RCVMOPSO' performance is competitive with respect to NSGA-II, GZHW, and WTY for the fourteen test functions, excluding test functions OSY, CTP7, CONSTR, and Welded Beam. However, the weakness of the proposed approach is diversity maintenance. This conclusion is based on the hypervolume indicator results (i.e., I_H values) presented in Figure 3 and Table 4. The main reason lies on the basic mechanism of PSO algorithm that is designed for better convergence speed than EAs (at the cost of poor diversity), and is modeled with swarm-like characteristic.

- The strength of the proposed algorithm is solving test problems with the following profiles: objective space with infeasible bands or feasible island (e.g., CTP8), and continuous Pareto front with or without active constraints (e.g., SRN and DTLZ9).

For test problems with multiple, isolated, and disconnected Pareto front (e.g., CTP4), RCVMOPSO perform fairly well.

- There are certain problem characteristics that RCVMOPSO is having difficulty in solving. The true Pareto front of test problems such as OSY constitutes of several disjoint regions, in which there is at least one active constraint in each region. For test functions with the curves of the Pareto front that consists of extreme regions, such as the Welded Beam, they also present great challenge to RCVMOPSO.

FUTURE RESEARCH DIRECTIONS

After analyzing the simulated results, it indicates that RCVMOPSO has difficulty solving test functions with certain characteristics, for example,

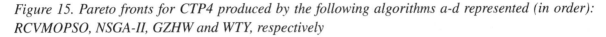

Figure 15. Pareto fronts for CTP4 produced by the following algorithms a-d represented (in order): RCVMOPSO, NSGA-II, GZHW and WTY, respectively

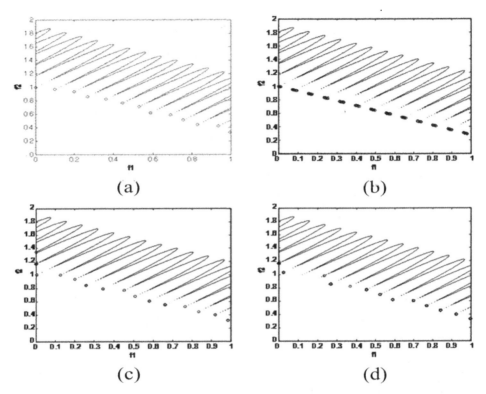

combination of Pareto fronts of several disjoint regions and multiple active constraints. Hence, in our future works we are considering to improve the diversity mechanism in the design elements and include ability to deal with active constraints.

CONCLUSION

This paper proposes a constrained MOPSO (RCVMOPSO) to solve constrained multiobjective optimization problems. The proposed algorithm adopts a multiobjective constraint handling technique. It incorporates the following design features: 1) separate procedures to update the infeasible and feasible personal best in the personal best archive in order to guide the infeasible particles

towards the feasible regions while promote search for better solutions; 2) an infeasible global best archive is adopted to make use of the infeasible nondominated solutions for searching possible isolated feasible regions or a very small feasible region while the feasible global best archive aims to guide the particles to find better solutions; 3) the adjustment of the accelerated constants in the PSO equation is based on the number of feasible personal best in the personal best archive and the scalar constraint violations of personal best and global best. The adjustment will influence the search process either to find more feasible solutions (particles) or to search for better solutions; and 4) the frequency of applying the mutation operators are based on the feasibility ratio of the particles' personal best. This feasibility ratio is exploited

Figure 16. Pareto fronts for CTP8 produced by the following algorithms a-d represented (in order): RCVMOPSO, NSGA-II, GZHW and WTY, respectively

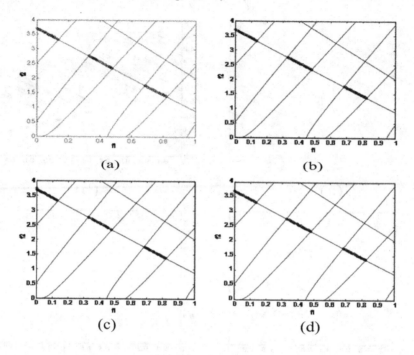

Figure 17. Pareto fronts for CONSTR produced by the following algorithms a-d represented (in order): RCVMOPSO, NSGA-II, GZHW and WTY, respectively

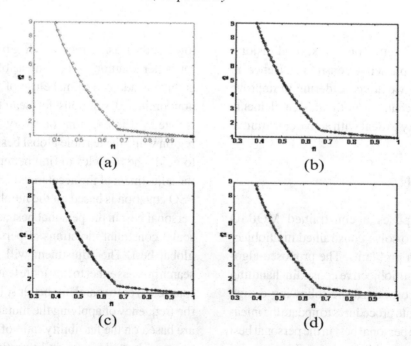

Figure 18. Pareto fronts for Welded Beam produced by the following algorithms a-d represented (in order): RCVMOPSO, NSGA-II, GZHW and WTY, respectively

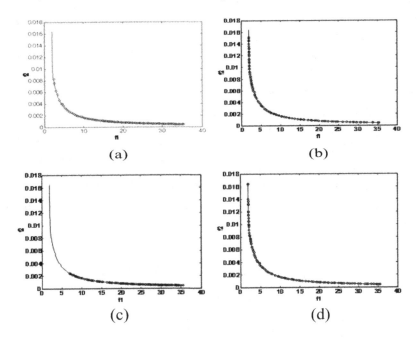

Figure 19. Pareto fronts for DTLZ9 produced by the following algorithms a-d represented (in order): RCVMOPSO, NSGA-II, GZHW and WTY, respectively

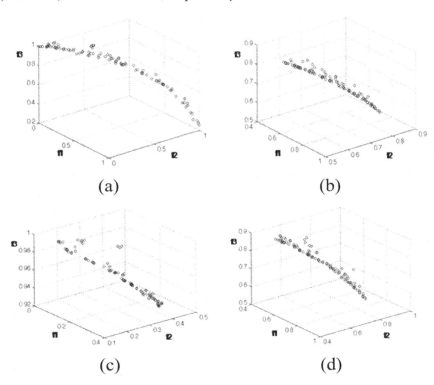

to encourage more exploration characteristic to search for possible feasible regions when there are few feasible particles' personal best, while reduce the exploration rate when most of the particles' personal best are feasible to support convergence towards Pareto optimal front. Both uniform and Gaussian mutation operators are used to facilitate a delicate balance in local and global search. A comparative study of RCVMOPSO and three state-of-the-art constrained MOEAs on fourteen benchmark test functions is presented. The simulation results show the proposed MOPSO is highly competitive and able to obtain quality Pareto fronts for most of the test functions.

REFERENCES

Binh, T., & Korn, U. (1997). *MOBES: A multiobjective evolution strategy for constrained optimization problems*. Paper presented at the 3rd International Conference on Genetic Algorithms. Brno, Czech Republic.

Cai, Z., & Wang, Y. (2006). A multiobjective optimization-based evolutionary algorithm for constrained optimization. *IEEE Transactions on Evolutionary Computation, 10*(6), 658–675. doi:10.1109/TEVC.2006.872344

Chafekar, D., Xuan, J., & Rasheed, K. (2003). *Constrained multi-objective optimization using steady state genetic algorithms*. Paper presented at the Genetic and Evolutionary Computation Conference. Chicago, IL.

Coello, C. A. C., Pulido, G. T., & Lechuga, M. S.Coello Coello. (2004). Handling multiple objectives with particle swarm optimization. *IEEE Transactions on Evolutionary Computation, 8*(3), 256–279. doi:10.1109/TEVC.2004.826067

Coello Coello, C.A., & Pulido, G.T. (2001). *Multiobjective optimization using a micro-genetic algorithm*. Paper presented at Genetic and Evolutionary Computation Conference. San Francisco, CA.

Coello Coello, C. A., & Christiansen, A. D.Coello Coello. (1999). MOSES: A multiobjective optimization tool for engineering design. *Engineering Optimization, 31*(3), 337–368. doi:10.1080/03052159908941377

Conover, W. J. (1999). *Practical Nonparametric Statistics* (3rd ed.). New York: John Wiley & Sons.

Cushman, D. L. (2007). *A particle swarm approach to constrained optimization informed by 'Global Worst*. University Park, PA: Pennsylvania State University.

Deb, K. (2001). *Multi-Objective Optimization Using Evolutionary Algorithms*. New York, NY: John Wiley & Sons.

Deb, K., & Goel, T. (2001). *Controlled elitist non-dominated sorting genetic algorithm for better convergence*. Paper presented at the 1st International Conference on Evolutionary Multi-Criterion Optimization. Zurich, Switzerland.

Deb, K., Pratap, A., Agarwal, A., & Meyarivan, T. (2002). A fast and elitist multiobjective genetic algorithm: NSGA-II. *IEEE Transactions on Evolutionary Computation, 6*(2), 182–197. doi:10.1109/4235.996017

Deb, K., Pratap, A., & Meyarivan, T. (2001). *Constrained test problems for multi-objective evolutionary optimization*. Paper presented at the 1st International Conference of Evolutionary Multi-Criterion Optimization. Zurich, Switzerland.

Deb, K., Thiele, L., Laumanns, M., & Zitzler, E. (2005). Scalable test problems for evolutionary multi-objective optimization. In Evolutionary Multiobjective Optimization: Theoretical Advances and Applications. Springer.

Fonseca, C. M., & Fleming, P. J. (1998). Multiobjective optimization and multiple constraint handling with evolutionary algorithms, I: a unified formulation. *IEEE Transactions on Systems, Man, and Cybernetics, Part A: Cybernetics, 28*(1), 26–37.

Geng, H., Zhang, M., Huang, L., & Wang, X. (2006). *Infeasible elitists and stochastic ranking selection in constrained evolutionary multiobjective optimization.* Paper presented at the 6th International Conference of Simulated Evolution and Learning. Hefei, China.

Goldberg, D. E. (1989). *Genetic Algorithms in Search, Optimization and Machine Learning.* Reading, MA: Addison-Wesley.

Harada, K., Sakuma, J., Ono, I., & Kobayashi, S. (2007). *Constraint-handling method for multiobjective function optimization: Pareto descent repair operator.* Paper presented at the 4th International Conference of Evolutionary Multi-Criterion Optimization. Matsushima/Sendai, Japan.

He, Q., & Wang, L. (2007). A hybrid particle swarm optimization with a feasibility-based rule for constrained optimization. *Applied Mathematics and Computation, 186*(2), 1407–1422. doi:10.1016/j.amc.2006.07.134

Hingston, P., Barone, L., Huband, S., & While, L. (2006). Multi-level ranking for constrained multi-objective evolutionary optimization. In T. R. Runarsson (Ed.), Lecture notes in Computer Science (vol. 4193, pp. 563–572). Berlin: Springer.

Hsieh, M., Chiang, T., & Fu, L. (2011). *A hybrid constraint handling mechanism with differential evolution for constrained multiobjective optimization.* Paper presented at the 2011 IEEE Congress on Evolutionary Computation. New Orleans, LA.

Jan, M. A. (2010). *Zhang.* Colchester, UK: Computational Intelligence.

Jimenéz, F., Gomez-Skarmeta, A. F., Sanchez, G., & Deb, K. (2002). *An evolutionary algorithm for constrained multiobjective optimization.* Paper presented at the Congress on Evolutionary Computation. Honolulu, HI.

Kundu, A. (1995). A new method to solve generalized multi-criteria optimization problems using the simple genetic algorithm. *Structural Optimization, 10*(2), 94–99. doi:10.1007/BF01743536

Kurpati, A., Azarm, S., & Wu, J. (2002). Constraint handling improvements for multiobjective genetic algorithms. *Structure Multidisciplinary Optimization, 23*(3), 204–213. doi:10.1007/s00158-002-0178-2

Leong, W. F., & Yen, G. G. (2008). PSO-based multiobjective optimization with dynamic population size and adaptive local archives. *IEEE transactions on systems, man, and cybernetics. Part B, Cybernetics: a publication of the IEEE Systems, Man, and Cybernetics Society, 38*(5), 1270–1293. doi:10.1109/TSMCB.2008.925757 PMID:18784011

Li, H. (2009). Multiobjective Optimization Problems with Complicated Pareto Sets, MOEA/D and NSGA-II. *IEEE Transactions on Evolutionary Computation, 13*(2), 284–302. doi:10.1109/TEVC.2008.925798

Li, L. D., Li, X., & Yu, X. (2008). *A multi-objective constraint-handling method with PSO algorithm for constrained engineering optimization problems.* Paper presented at the IEEE Congress on Evolutionary Computation. Hong Kong, China.

Liang, J. J., & Suganthan, P. N. (2006). *Dynamic multi-swarm particle swarm optimizer with a novel constraint-handling mechanism.* Paper presented at the IEEE Congress on Evolutionary Computation. Vancouver, Canada.

Liu, H., & Wang, D. (2013), *A Constrained Multiobjective Evolutionary Algorithm based Decomposition and Temporary Register*. Paper presented at the IEEE Congress on Evolutionary Computation. Cancún, México.

Liu, Z., Wang, C., & Li, J. (2008). Solving constrained optimization via a modified genetic particle swarm optimization. Paper presented at the International Workshop on Knowledge Discovery and Data Mining. Adelaide, Australia.

Lu, H., & Chen, W. (2006). Dynamic-objective particle swarm optimization for constrained optimization problems. *Journal of Combinatorial Optimization*, *2*(4), 409–419. doi:10.1007/s10878-006-9004-x

Luo, B., Zheng, J., Xie, J., & Wu, J. (2008). *Dynamic crowding distance-a new diversity maintenance strategy for MOEAs*. Paper presented at the 4th International Conference on Natural Computation. Jinan, China.

Mezura-Montes, E., & CoelloCoello, C.A. (2006). *A survey of constraint-handling techniques based on evolutionary multiobjective optimization* (Technical Report EVOCINV-04-2006). Mexico City, México: Academic Press.

Michalewicz, Z., & Schoenauer, M. (1996). Evolutionary algorithm for constrained parameter optimization problems. *Evolutionary Computation*, *4*(1), 1–32. doi:10.1162/evco.1996.4.1.1

Miyakawa, M., & Sato, H. (2012). *An evolutionary algorithm using two-stage non-dominated sorting and directed mating for constrained multi-objective optimization*. Paper presented at the Joint 6th International Conference on Soft Computing and Intelligent Systems (SCIS) and 13th International Symposium on Advanced Intelligent Systems. Kobe, Japan.

Narayanan, S., & Azarm, S. (1999). On improving multiobjective genetic algorithms for design optimization. *Structural Optimization*, *18*(2-3), 146–155. doi:10.1007/BF01195989

Oyama, A., Shimoyama, K., & Fujii, K. (2007). New constraint-handling method for multi-objective and multi-constraint evolutionary optimization. *Transactions of the Japan Society for Aeronautical and Space Sciences*, *50*(167), 56–62. doi:10.2322/tjsass.50.56

Parsopoulus, K. E., & Vrahatis, M. N. (2002). Particle swarm optimization method for constrained optimization problems. In Technologies- Theory and Applications: New Trends in Intelligent Technologies, (pp. 214-220). Academic Press.

Pulido, G.T., & Coello Coello, C.A. (2004). *A constraint-handling mechanism for particle swarm optimization*. Paper presented at the IEEE Congress on Evolutionary Computation. Portland, OR.

Ray, T., & Won, K. S. (2005). *An evolutionary algorithm for constrained bi-objective optimization using radial slots*. Paper presented at the 9th International Conference of Knowledge-Based Intelligent Information and Engineering Systems. Melbourne, Australia.

Runarsson, T. P., & Yao, X. (2005). Search biases in constrained evolutionary optimization. *IEEE Transactions on System. Man, and Cybernetics, Part C: Applications and Reviews*, *35*(2), 233–243. doi:10.1109/TSMCC.2004.841906

Sierra, M.R. & Coello Coello, C.A. (2005). *Improving PSO-based multi-objective optimization using crowding, mutation and ε–dominance*. Paper presented at the Evolutionary Multi-Criterion Optimization Conference. Guanajuato, Mexico.

Takahama, T., & Sakai, S. (2006). *Constrained optimization by the ε constrained differential evolution with gradient-based mutation and feasible elites*. Paper presented at the IEEE Congress on Evolutionary Computation. Vancouver, Canada.

Tanaka, M. (1995). *GA-based decision support system for multi-criteria optimization*. Paper presented at the International Conference on Evolutionary Multi-Criteria Optimization. Guanajuato, Mexico.

Tessema, B., & Yen, G. G. (2009). An adaptive penalty formulation for constrained evolutionary optimization. *IEEE Transactions on Systems, Man, and Cybernetics. Part A, Systems and Humans*, *39*(3), 565–578. doi:10.1109/TSMCA.2009.2013333

Venkatraman, S., & Yen, G. G. (2005). A generic framework for constrained optimization using genetic algorithms. *IEEE Transactions on Evolutionary Computation*, *9*(4), 424–435. doi:10.1109/TEVC.2005.846817

Wang, Y., Cai, Z., Guo, G., & Zhou, Y. (2007). Multiobjective optimization and hybrid evolutionary algorithm to solve constrained optimization problems. *IEEE Transactions on System, Man, and Cybernetics, Part B. Cybernetics*, *37*(3), 560–575. PMID:17550112

Wang, Y., Cai, Z., Zhou, Y., & Zeng, W. (2008). An adaptive trade-off model for constrained evolutionary optimization. *IEEE Transactions on Evolutionary Computation*, *12*(1), 80–92. doi:10.1109/TEVC.2007.902851

Wei, J., & Wang, Y. (2006). A novel multi-objective PSO algorithm for constrained optimization problems. In T. D. Wang, et al. (Eds.), Lecture notes in Computer Science (vol. 4247, pp. 174–180). Berlin: Springer. doi:10.1007/11903697_23

Woldesenbet, Y. G., Tessema, B. G., & Yen, G. G. (2009). Constraint handling in multiobjective evolutionary optimization. *IEEE Transactions on Evolutionary Computation*, *13*(2), 1–12.

Yang, B., Chen, Y., Zhao, Z., & Han, Q. (2006). *A master-slave particle swarm optimization algorithm for solving constrained optimization problems*. Paper presented at the 6th World Congress on Intelligent Control and Automation. Dalian, China.

Yen, G. G., & Leong, W. F. (2009). Dynamic multiple swarms in multiobjective particle swarm optimization. *IEEE Transactions on Systems, Man, and Cybernetics. Part A, Systems and Humans*, *39*(4), 890–911. doi:10.1109/TSMCA.2009.2013915

Zhang, M., Geng, H., Luo, W., Huang, L., & Wang, X. (2006). A hybrid of differential evolution and genetic algorithm for constrained multiobjective optimization problems. In Simulated Evolution and Learning, (LNCS) (Vol. 4247, pp. 318-327). Berlin: Springer.

Zielinski, K., & Laur, R. (2006). *Constrained single-objective optimization using particle swarm optimization*. Paper presented at the IEEE Congress on Evolutionary Computation. Vancouver, Canada.

Zitzler, E. (1999). *Evolutionary Algorithms for Multiobjective Optimization: Methods and Applications*. (Ph.D. Dissertation). Swiss Federal Institute of Technology, Zurich, Switzerland.

Zitzler, E., Thiele, L., Laumanns, M., Fonseca, C. M., & Fonseca, V. G. (2003). Performance assessment of multiobjective optimizers: An analysis and review. *IEEE Transactions on Evolutionary Computation*, *7*(2), 117–132. doi:10.1109/TEVC.2003.810758

ADDITIONAL READING

Daneshyari, M., & Yen, G. G. (2011). Cultural-based multiobjective particle swarm optimization. *IEEE transactions on systems, man, and cybernetics. Part B, Cybernetics: a publication of the IEEE Systems, Man, and Cybernetics Society, 41*(2), 553–567. doi:10.1109/TSMCB.2010.2068046 PMID:20837447

Daneshyari, M., & Yen, G. G. (2012). Constrained multiple-swarm particle swarm optimization within a cultural framework. *IEEE Transactions on Systems, Man and Cybernetics, Part A. Systems and Human, 42*(2), 475–490. doi:10.1109/TSMCA.2011.2162498

Daneshyari, M., & Yen, G. G. (2012). Cultural based particle swarm for dynamic optimization problems. *International Journal of Systems Science, 43*(7), 1284–1304. doi:10.1080/00207721.2011.605965

Goldstein, M. L., & Yen, G. G. (2005). Using evolutionary algorithms for defining the sampling policy of complex n-partite networks. *IEEE Transactions on Knowledge and Data Engineering, 17*(6), 762–773. doi:10.1109/TKDE.2005.100

Leong, W. F., & Yen, G. G. (2008). PSO-based multiobjective optimization with dynamic population size and adaptive local archives. *IEEE transactions on systems, man, and cybernetics. Part B, Cybernetics: a publication of the IEEE Systems, Man, and Cybernetics Society, 38*(5), 1270–1293. doi:10.1109/TSMCB.2008.925757 PMID:18784011

Lu, H., & Yen, G. G. (2003). Rank-density-based multiobjective genetic algorithm and benchmark test function study. *IEEE Transactions on Evolutionary Computation, 7*(4), 325–343. doi:10.1109/TEVC.2003.812220

Tessema, B., & Yen, G. G. (2009). An adaptive penalty formulation for constrained evolutionary optimization. *IEEE Transactions on Systems, Man, and Cybernetics. Part A, Systems and Humans, 39*(3), 565–578. doi:10.1109/TSMCA.2009.2013333

Venkatraman, S., & Yen, G. G. (2005). A generic framework for constrained optimization using genetic algorithms. *IEEE Transactions on Evolutionary Computation, 9*(4), 424–435. doi:10.1109/TEVC.2005.846817

Woldesenbet, Y. G., & Yen, G. G. (2009). Dynamic evolutionary algorithm with variable relocation. *IEEE Transactions on Evolutionary Computation, 13*(3), 500–513. doi:10.1109/TEVC.2008.2009031

Woldesenbet, Y. G., Yen, G. G., & Tessema, B. G. (2009). Constraint handling in multi-objective evolutionary optimization. *IEEE Transactions on Evolutionary Computation, 13*(3), 514–525. doi:10.1109/TEVC.2008.2009032

Yen, G. G., & Leong, W. F. (2009). Dynamic multiple swarms in multiobjective particle swarm optimization. *IEEE Transactions on Systems, Man and Cybernetics, Part A. Systems and Human, 39*(4), 890–911. doi:10.1109/TSMCA.2009.2013915

Yen, G. G., & Lu, H. (2003). Dynamic multiobjective evolutionary algorithm: Adaptive cell-based rank and density estimation. *IEEE Transactions on Evolutionary Computation, 7*(3), 253–274. doi:10.1109/TEVC.2003.810068

KEY TERMS AND DEFINITIONS

Constrained Optimization: In mathematical optimization, constrained optimization is the process of optimizing an objective function with respect to some variables in the presence of constraints on those variables. The objective function is either a cost function or energy function which is to be minimized, or a reward function or utility function, which is to be maximized. Constraints can be either *hard constraints* which set conditions for the variables that are required to be satisfied, or *soft constraints* which have some variable values that are penalized in the objective function if, and based on the extent that, the conditions on the variables are not satisfied. Constraints could also be presented in either equality or inequality form.

Multiobjective Optimization: Multiobjective optimization (also known as vector optimization, multicriteria optimization, multiattribute optimization, or Pareto optimization) is an area of multiple criteria decision making, that is concerned with mathematical optimization problems involving more than one objective function to be optimized simultaneously. Multi-objective optimization has been applied in many fields of science, including engineering, economics and logistics where optimal decisions need to be taken in the presence of trade-offs between two or more conflicting objectives. For a nontrivial multiobjective optimization problem, there does not exist a single solution that simultaneously optimizes each objective. In that case, the objective functions are said to be conflicting, and there exists a (possibly infinite number of) Pareto optimal solutions. A solution is called nondominated, Pareto optimal, Pareto efficient or noninferior, if none of the objective functions can be improved in value without degrading some of the other objective values. Without additional subjective preference information, all Pareto optimal solutions are considered equally good. Researchers study multi-objective optimization problems from different viewpoints and, thus, there exist different solution philosophies and goals when setting and solving them. The goal may be to find a representative set of Pareto optimal solutions, and/or quantify the trade-offs in satisfying the different objectives, and/or finding a single solution that satisfies the subjective preferences of a human decision maker.

Particle Swarm Optimization: Particle swarm optimization (PSO) is a computational approach that optimizes a problem by iteratively trying to improve a candidate solution with regard to a given measure of quality. PSO optimizes a problem by having a population of candidate solutions and moving these particles around in the search-space according to simple mathematical formulae over the particle's position and velocity. Each particle's movement is influenced by its local best known position but, is also guided toward the best known positions in the search-space, which are updated as better positions are found by other particles. This is expected to move the swarm toward the best solutions. PSO is originally attributed to Kennedy and Eberhart and was first intended for simulating social behavior as a representation of the movement of organisms in a bird flock or fish school.

Section 2
Swarm Intelligence Applications

Chapter 7
Hybrid Swarm Intelligence-Based Biclustering Approach for Recommendation of Web Pages

R. Rathipriya
Periyar University, India

K. Thangavel
Periyar University, India

ABSTRACT

This chapter focuses on recommender systems based on the coherent user's browsing patterns. Biclustering approach is used to discover the aggregate usage profiles from the preprocessed Web data. A combination of Discrete Artificial Bees Colony Optimization and Simulated Annealing technique is used for optimizing the aggregate usage profiles from the preprocessed clickstream data. Web page recommendation process is structured in to two components performed online and offline with respect to Web server activity. Offline component builds the usage profiles or usage models by analyzing historical data, such as server access log file or Web logs from the server using hybrid biclustering approach. Recommendation process is the online component. Current user's session is used in the online component for capturing the user's interest so as to recommend pages to the user for next navigation. The experiment was conducted on the benchmark clickstream data (i.e. MSNBC dataset and MSWEB dataset from UCI repository). The results signify the improved prediction accuracy of recommendations using biclustering approach.

INTRODUCTION

Web usage mining (WUM) systems use data mining algorithms on both usage and clickstream data from one or more websites to discover usage patterns/user profiles. These patterns are analyzed to determine user's behavior and these patterns are used by the recommendation systems to provide the recommendation of appropriate pages to the web users. Web personalization is the process of personalizing web sites or web services according to the specific user's profile to achieve more efficient web browsing. User's browsing efficiency can be increased by altering the web sites' structures, and by employing recommender systems to produce user-tailored recommendations.

DOI: 10.4018/978-1-4666-6328-2.ch007

User profiles or Usage models are the generalization of the collected data about the user behavior from web usage data (such as clickstream data). The main goal of using user profiling is to increase the efficiency of user activities by delivering more personalized information when users interacting the web site. Usage-based Personalized Recommendation systems (Cooley *et al.*, 1997; Srivastava et al., 2000) analyzed the user's navigation pattern to provide personalized recommendations of web pages according to the current interests of the user.

Recently, web usage mining has gained much attention as it is found to fulfill the needs of web personalization. In the literature, various clustering algorithms can be applied to detect the user profiles as well as other web mining techniques such as association rule, have been explored by several research groups. Clustering is the process of grouping the users into clusters such that users within a cluster have high similarity compared to each other but dissimilar to users in other clusters.

The discovery of patterns from usage data by clustering the web transaction into clusters of user sessions or pages, by itself is not sufficient for performing the personalization tasks *(Mobasher et al., 2002)*. The critical step in the recommendation system is the effective derivation of good quality and useful usage profiles from the web usage data. Clustering, in general tries to partition the set of web users according to their browsing interest of all pages of a web site. Assuming that users may show interest only for a particular subset of pages, conventional clustering approaches may not be sensitive and/or specific enough to find and present correlation between users in an appropriate and comprehensive manner.

To address the limitation of traditional clustering, the biclustering method was introduced. In contrast to traditional clustering, a biclustering method produces biclusters, which consists of subset of users and a subset of pages under which these users behave similarly.

Greedy search algorithms are used as the promising approach in the biclustering algorithms. Greedy search algorithms start with an initial solution and find a locally optimal solution by successive transformations that improve some fitness function. Most of the times, the results of biclustering suffer from local optima problem. Meta-heuristics optimization algorithms such as Particle Swarm Optimization (PSO) (Kennedy & Eberhart, 1995) Genetic Algorithm (GA) (Goldberg, 1989) and Simulated Annealing (SA) are used along with greedy biclustering to improve the results because it has potential to escape local optima.

The term Swarm Intelligence (SI) was coined by Beny and Wang in late 1980s in the context of cellular robotics. Swarm Intelligence is a collection of nature based algorithms which has attracted several researchers from the field of pattern recognition, information retrieval and clustering. SI systems are typically made up of a population of simple agents interacting locally with one another and with their environment. The efforts to mimic such behaviors through computer simulation finally resulted into the fascinating field of SI. An example of swarm intelligence is Particle Swarm Optimization (PSO) and it is a very popular SI algorithm for global optimization over continuous search spaces and also for discrete optimization problems.

The search algorithms achieve the two goals that are exploration (diversification) and exploitation (intensification) by using local search methods or global search approaches, or an integration of both global and local strategies, these algorithms are commonly known as hybrid methods. The present study focuses on the hybrid swarm algorithm in which one of the main algorithms is a well known search strategy called Discrete Artificial Bees Colony Optimization (DABC) is combined with Simulated Annealing (SA) technique. SA is a powerful optimization procedure that has been successfully applied to a number of combinatorial optimization problems.

One of the most important challenges in the DABC Optimization algorithm is the neighborhood calculation in the employee bee phase and scout bee phase. To overcome this challenge, Hybrid DABC is proposed in this chapter. Simulated Annealing (SA) algorithm is used as improvisation step in this hybrid DABC to present a suitable solution for generating new neighborhood solution vectors. Therefore, hybrid DABC based biclustering model convergence faster than standard DABC algorithm and it is able to escape from a local optimum with the help of SA. To the best of our knowledge, there is still no study on using hybrid technique based on DABC and SA for biclustering of web usage data. In this chapter, a detailed description of the artificial bee colony optimization algorithms is given. Afterwards, development of a DABC optimization based biclustering model is discussed. It is applied on web usage data in order to find a high volume bicluster with scaling and shifting browsing pattern for the web usage profiling.

The rest of the Chapter is organized as follows. Section Related Work discussed some of the existing works that are related to the biclustering methods, and recommendation systems available in the literature. A brief introduction to the methods and materials required for the proposed work is discussed in Section Methods and Materials. Section Proposed Work describes in detail about the hybrid DABC with SA based biclustering algorithm for user profiling which is followed by the recommending process. The experimental results are presented and discussed in Section Experimental Analysis. Section Conclusions concluded this chapter with possible future work.

RELATED WORK

Various approaches for implementing recommendation system are discussed in (Mobasher *et al.*, 2000; Mobasher *et al.*, 2002; Mobasher *et al.*, 2001; Eirinaki & Vazirgiannis, 2003; Forsati *et*

al., 2009). Collaborative filtering approach using kNN (k-Nearest Neighbor) technique is widely used for e-commerce applications. This technique requires explicit feedback provided by the user or user ratings on items. The current user's interest is matched with online clustering of users with similar interest to provide recommendations. This approach has limitations such as scalability and performance (Mobasher *et al.*, *2002*) due to the lack of adequate user information. To overcome these limitations, recent research has focused on Web Usage Mining approach for Web Personalization (Srivatsav, *et al.*, *2000*). The pattern discovery phase, using various data mining techniques, is performed offline to improve the scalability of collaborative filtering. The discovered patterns or aggregate usage profiles can be used to provide dynamic recommendations based on the current user's interest.

In (AlMurtadha *et al.*, 2010), a model has been developed using K-Means clustering approach for deriving usage profiles which followed by recommender systems to predict the next navigations profile. In (Mobasher *et al.*, 2000) usage based personalization have been discussed using various data mining techniques. In (Gunduz & Ozsu, 2003), model based clustering approach was developed based on the user's interest in a session that are used to recommend pages to the user. Web Personalizer is the usage based web personalization system to provide dynamic recommendations was proposed in (Mobasher *et al.*, 2001).

In (Mobasher *et.al*, 2002), two different techniques were discussed such as PACT based on the clustering of user transactions and Association Rule Hypergraph Partitioning based on the clustering of pageviews for the extraction of usage profiles. An improved web page prediction accuracy by using a novel approach that involves integrating clustering, association rules and Markov models based on certain constraints has been presented in (Forsati *et al.*, 2009). In (Symeonidis *et al.*, 2008), use biclustering approach to provide recommendation to the users based on the user and item similarity of neighborhood biclusters.

Sequential Web Access based Recommender System (called SWARS) was proposed in (Zhou *etal.,* 2004) that uses sequential access pattern mining. Liu and Keselj (*2007*) proposed an approach that classifies the user navigation patterns and predicting users' future requests based on the combined mining of web server logs and the contents of the retrieved web pages. In (Castellano *et al.,* 2011), usage-based web recommendation system is presented that exploits the potential of neuro-fuzzy computational intelligence techniques to dynamically suggest interesting pages to users according to their preferences. (Sankaradass & Arputharaj, 2011) proposed Fuzzy-Temporal Association Rule Mining Algorithm (FTARM) to classify the Web user profiles dataset periodically to know the users behaviors and interests based on temporal pattern analysis. AlMurtadha, Sulaiman, Mustapha, and Udzir (2011) introduced a new method called iPACT, an improved recommendation system using Profile Aggregation based on Custering of Transactions (PACT) which has better recommendation predictions accuracy than the PACT.

However, almost all of these works are user centered prediction engine which concentrate on recommending the next visited pages based on the previous navigation of the user but the accuracy of the predictions still does not meet satisfaction. In these work, for obtaining the usage/user profile from web usage data, clustering and association rules are applied very frequently.

Clustering reveals users behavior similarly over all the pages. Unlike clustering, biclustering captures a subset of users exhibiting pattern similarity across a subset of pages of a website. Biclustering attempts to cluster web user and web pages simultaneously based on the users' behavior recorded in the form of clickstream data. These local browsing patterns play vital role in E-commerce based applications. Biclustering methods based optimization algorithms has potential to produce the optimal results than greedy

based biclustering method. Hybridization of one or more meta-heuristics techniques yields the better results by utilizing the advantages of these techniques. Wang & Li (2004) introduced hybrid technique based on PSO and SA to reconstruct the permittivity profile of dielectric scatterers in free space. In (Premalatha *et al.,* 2010; Idoumghar *et al.,* 2009), a hybrid technique was proposed, which was a combination of SA and PSO algorithm for global optimization problem.

The ABC algorithm was proposed by Karaboga (2007) for unconstrained optimization problems. Later on, the algorithm has been extended by Karaboga & Basturk (2007) for solving constrained optimization problems. This algorithm is good at solving unimodal and multimodal numerical optimization problems. It is very simple and flexible when compared to the other Swarm Based algorithms such as Genetic Algorithm, Particle Swarm Optimization (PSO). It does not require external parameters like mutation and crossover rates, which are hard to determine in prior. It combines local search methods with global search methods and tries to attain a balance between exploration and exploitation.

In this chapter, a new hybrid swarm intelligence (i.e. combination of DABC and SA) based biclustering approach is used for identifying optimal usage profiles based on their browsing interest and thereby provides recommendation of web pages effectively. The proposed approach is tested on msnbc.com and msweb.com dataset. The results indicate that the hybrid swarm intelligence approach can improve the quality of the system for recommendations.

METHODS AND MATERIALS

Data Sources

There are several kinds of data that are potential input to the web personalization pipeline. The data can be divided into four main categories: (1) the data from web access logs, (2) the content data,

(3) web site structure data, and (4) the usage data. The following subsections briefly describe each of the categories.

- **Data from Web Access Logs:** Web logs are maintained by web servers and contain information about users accessing sites. Logs are mostly stored simply as text files, each line corresponding to one access. The most widely used log file formats are, implied by (*Web Server Survey*), the Common Log File format (CLF) (*Logging Control in W3C*) and the Extended Log File format (ExLF) (*Extended Log File Format*). The web log contains the following information: (1) the user's IP address, (2) the user's authentication name, (3) the date-time stamp of the access, (4) the HTTP request, (5) the response status, (6) the size of the requested resource, and optionally (7) the referrer URL (the page the user "came from") and (8) the user's browser identification. Of course, the user's authentication name is not available if the site does not require authentication. In the worst case, the only user identification information included in a log file is his/her IP address. This introduces a problem since different users can share the same IP address and, what is more, one user can be assigned different IPs even in the same session.
- **Content Data:** The content data are all the contents that can be accessed by users.
- **Web Site Structure Data:** The Web site structure data is prepared by the web site designer or by the structure generator which is used to produce user specific structure for more efficient browsing.
- **Web Usage Data:** Web usage data records the user's behavior when the user browses or makes transactions on the web site.

Data Preprocessing

Data preprocessing phase is the first phase of the web usage mining. It is a pre-requisite phase before the mining of web data to obtain useful and hidden interesting browsing patterns. A session file is consists of a sequence of user's request for pages s= $\{p_1, p_2, p_3, ..., p_n\}$ and a set of m sessions, S = $\{s_1, s_2, s_3, ..., s_m\}$ where each si belongs to S.

- **Web Access Data Preparation:** The result of the web access data preparation is a large and sparse user-by-page matrix. For the purposes of web usage mining, sessions or transactions are identified and stored for further processing.
- **Data Cleaning:** Not every access to the content should be taken into consideration. We need to remove accesses to irrelevant items (such as button images), accesses by Web crawlers (i.e. non-human accesses), and failed requests.
- **Efficient User Identification:** Many users can be assigned the same IP address and on the other hand one user can have several different IP addresses even in the same session. A good mean of identifying users is cookies can be used for better user identification. Users can block or delete cookies but it is estimated that well over 90% of users have cookies enabled. Another, user identification is assigning users usernames and passwords. However, requiring users to authenticate is inappropriate for Web browsing in general.
- **Pageviews Identification and Sessionization**: Pageview is a request to load a single page from a web site. A sequence of pageviews by a single user during a single visit is called a session s = $\{p_1, p_2, p_3, ..., p_n\}$. World Wide Web consortium

(W3C) has defined a session as the group of browsing activities performed by a single user from the moment the user starts to the time he/she left. Sessionization is the process of segmenting the activity record of each user into sessions, each representing a single visit to the site.

- **Preprocessing of Clickstream Data:** Clickstream data is cleaned and partitioned into a set of user transactions representing the activities of each user during different visits to the site. This data needs to be transformed and aggregated in to sessions. A session-pageview matrix A(U,P) of size n x m where n is the number of sessions and m is the number of pageviews. Each row represents a session and each column represents a frequency of occurrence of the page view in the session.

In this chapter, the weight of the pageview is determined by evaluating the importance of a page in terms of the ratio of the frequency of visits to the page with respect to the overall page visits in a session. A numerical weight is assigned to each pageview visited with the purpose of measuring its relative importance within the session. If the page has not been visited, the weight of the page is assigned 0. The page visits repeated consecutively have been treated as a single visit to that page. The weights have been normalized to account for variances. Each session si is modeled as a vector over the n dimensional space of pageviews. Each session si is represented as $s_i = \{pf_1, pf_2, pf_3, ..., pf_n\}$ where each pf_j is the relative frequency of pageview j in session i. This type of weight normalization is referred to as transaction normalization which is beneficial since it captures the relative importance/interest of the pageview in a session.

Biclustering Approach for Web Usage Data

Biclustering finds a set of significant biclusters in a matrix (i.e.) identify sub-matrices (subsets of rows and subsets of columns) with interesting properties (Madeira & Oliveira, 2004). Unlike clustering, biclustering identifies groups of users that show similar activity patterns under a specific subset of the pages of a web site. Biclustering is the key technique to use when

- Only a small set of the users visits the subset set of pages
- An interesting users' browsing pattern is exhibit only in a subset of the pages.

Type of Biclustering Evaluation Measures

The type of biclustering evaluation measures is given in Table 1.

Fitness Function

The general goal of the optimization is to find a solution that represents the global maximum or minimum of a fitness function. Fitness for the biclustering problem is usually based on the following

- Mean squared residue (MSR)
- Row variance
- Large volume
- Penalty (exponential)
- Average Correlation Value (ACV)

In this chapter, fitness function based on ACV is used to generate maximal set of users and pages while maintaining the "homogeneity" of the biclusters. ACV measures the homogeneity of the bicluster.

Table 1. Type of biclustering evaluation measures

S.No	Measures	Formula	Value
1	Variance (Hartigan, 1972)	$$VAR(B) = \sum_{i=1}^{n}\sum_{j=1}^{m}(b_{ij} - \overline{b_{ij}})^2$$	0, for prefect bicluster i.e. Constant Bicluster
2.	Mean Squared Residue (MSR) (Cheng & Church, 2000)	$$MSR(B) = \frac{1}{nm}\sum_{i}\sum_{j}(b_{ij} - \overline{b_I} - \overline{b_J} + \overline{b_{ij}})^2$$	0, for high similar bicluster i.e. Constant and Constant Row/ Column Biclusters
3.	Average Correlation Value (ACV) (Tang et al., 2001),	$$ACV(B) = \max\{\frac{\sum_{i=1}^{n}\sum_{j=1}^{n}\left|row_{ij}\right| - n}{n^2 - n}, \frac{\sum_{k=1}^{m}\sum_{l=1}^{m}\left|col_{kl}\right| - m}{m^2 - m}\}$$	1, for highly coherent bicluster

Discrete Artificial Bees Colony Optimization (ABC)

The Artificial Bees Colony (ABC) algorithm uses a colony of artificial bees. The bees are classified into three types:

1. Employed bees
2. Onlooker bees
3. Scout bees

Employed bees go to their food source and come back to hive and dance in this area. The employed bee whose food source has been abandoned becomes a scout and starts to search for finding a new food source. Onlookers watch the dances of employed bees and choose food sources depending on dances.

In the ABC algorithm, the position of a food source represents a possible solution to the optimization problem and the nectar amount of a food source corresponds to the quality (fitness) of the associated solution.

At the first step, the ABC generates a randomly distributed initial population x_i of S_N (food source positions), where S_N denotes the number of employed bees or onlooker bees. Each solution x_i, where $i = 1, 2, ..., n$ is a Dth dimensional vector.

After initialization, the population of the positions (solutions) is subject to repeated cycles, C = 1, 2,..., max_iteration, of the search process of the employed, onlookers and scout bees. An employed bee produces a modification on the position (solution) in their memory and tests the nectar amount (fitness value) of the new source (new solution). If the nectar amount of the new one is higher than that of the previous one, the bee memorizes the new position and forgets the old one. Otherwise, keep the position of the previous one in her memory.

After all employed bees complete the search process, they share the nectar information of the food sources and their position information with the onlooker bees. An onlooker evaluates the nectar information taken from all employed bees and chooses a food source with a probability related to its nectar amount. As in the case of the employed bee, it produces a modification on the position in her memory and checks the nectar amount of the candidate source. Providing that its nectar is higher than that of the previous one, the bees memorize the new position and forget the old one.

When the nectar amount of a food source is abandoned by the bees, a new food source is randomly determined by a scout bee and replaced with the abandoned one. These steps are repeated through a predetermined number of cycles called Maximum Cycle Number (MCN) or until a termination criteria is satisfied.

The main steps of the basic ABC algorithm are given below.

Basic ABC Algorithm:

Step 1: Produce initial population;

Step 2: For iteration = 1 to max_iteration

Step 3: Send the employed bees onto their food sources.

Step 4: Send the onlooker bees onto the food sources depending on their nectar amounts.

Step 5: Send the scout bees to search possible new food sources.

Step 6: Memorize the best food source found so far.

In the Discrete Artificial Bees Colony (DABC) algorithm (Marinakis *et al.*, 2011), the population vectors are formed by binary strings (zeros and ones) and all the points in the search space are possible to be represented. This particular feature of the DABC allows that any problem (combinatorial, discrete or even real-valued) can be treated. Changes in the directions of the population vectors may be represented as probabilities that a bit will take a zero or a one value and this is done by means of a sigmoid function.

In continuous search spaces, changes in directions of population vectors are defined as changes in positions on some number of dimensions. These changes, in fact, define a concept of the neighbourhood because they define a new point (solution) in the neighbourhood. In the discrete model, the binary vectors change directions in a search space restricted to zero and one on each dimension. The probability of a bit in the binary vector taking a value 0 or 1 is calculated using equation (1) and it should be rewritten as:

$$x_i = \begin{cases} 1, & if \; r_3 < S_{sig}\left(v_i\right) \\ 0, & otherwise \end{cases} \tag{1}$$

where r_3 is a uniform random number in the range [0, 1] and

$$S_{sig}\left(V_i\right) = \frac{1}{1 + e^{\left(V_i\right)}}$$

The goal of optimization of biclusters is to find biclusters with highly correlated users and high volume from the web usage data using Discrete Artificial Bees Colony Optimization.

Evaluation of Biclusters: Fitness Function

The aim of this work is to discover the biclusters with shifting and scaling patterns by using following fitness function.

max f(U', P')= | U'| * | P'|

subjected to g(U', P') ≤ μ

where $g(U', P') = (1- \rho(B))$, | U'| and | P'| are the number of users and pages in the bicluster respectively and μ is the correlation threshold. Thus, it has been considered $(1 - \rho(B))$ to identify biclusters with highly-correlated users. Best biclusters are those with the highest value for the fitness function subjected to the given threshold.

Simulated Annealing (SA)

Simulated Annealing is a well established stochastic technique originally developed to model the natural process of crystallisation and later adopted to solve optimization problems (Kirkpatrick *et al.*, 1983). SA is a variant of local neighborhood search .Traditional local search (e.g. steepest descent for minimization) always moves in a direction of improvement whereas SA allows non-improving moves to avoid getting stuck at a local optimum.

It has ability to allow the probabilistic acceptance of changes which lead to worse solutions i.e.

reversals in fitness. The probability of accepting a reversal is inversely proportional to the size of the reversal with the acceptance of smaller reversals being more probable. This probability also decreases as the search continues or as the system cools allowing eventual convergence on a solution. It is defined by Boltzman's equation:

$$\mathbf{P}\Delta E \; \alpha \; \mathbf{e}^{\frac{-\Delta E}{T}} \tag{3}$$

where ΔE is the difference in energy (fitness) between the old and new states and T is the temperature of the system.

In the virtual environment the temperature of the system is lowered after certain predefined number of accepted changes, successes, or total changes, attempts, depending on which is reached first. The rate at which temperature decreases depends on the cooling schedule. In the natural process the system cools logarithmically however this is so time consuming that many simplified cooling schedules have been introduced for practical problem solving; the following simple cooling model is popular:

$$T(k) = T(k - 1) / (1 + \alpha)$$

where T(k) is the current temperature, T(k−1) is the previous temperature and α indicates the cooling rate.

Standard Simulated Annealing Algorithm:

Step 1: Initialize a very high "temperature" and particles.

Step 2: Perturb the placement through a defined move.

Step 3: Calculate the fitness of particle.

Step 4: Depending on the change in score, accept or reject the move. The probability of acceptance depending on the current "temperature" T.

Step 5: Update the temperature value by lowering the temperature. Go back to Step 2.

Each step of the SA algorithm replaces the current solution by a random nearby solution, chosen with a probability that depends on the difference between the corresponding function values and on a global parameter T called the temperature that is gradually decreased during the process.

PROPOSED WORK

Outline of the Proposed Approach

The proposed hybrid swarm intelligence based biclustering for web page recommendation system has 2 components. They are offline and online components. Each component consists of 2 stages (Figure 1).

- Offline Component
    - **Stage 1:** Data Preprocessing.
        - Conversion of Clickstream data patterns from web server log file to User session-by- Pageview Matrix
    - **Stage 2:** Biclustering Process.
        - Biclustering approach is used to identify the optimal user/usage profile using hybrid swarm intelligence. Create the aggregate usage models.
- Online Component
    - **Stage 3:** Identifying the Nearest Usage Model.
        - Using similarity measures identify the 'K' nearest user models to the current user session.
    - **Stage 4:** Recommendation List.
        - Generate the recommendation list of web pages from the 'K' nearest usage models.

Figure1. Overview of recommendation process

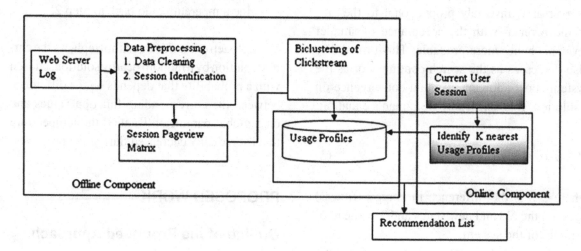

Offline Component: Building the Usage Profiles from Clickstream Data

The proposed work combines DABC and SA for bicluster optimization. One of the challenges in DABC is that it may be trapped into local optima if the neighbourhood position is not changed over a number of iterations. To overcome this shortcoming, this chapter has been presented a new hybrid biclustering optimization method based on DABC and SA, called hybrid DABC. This hybridization takes the benefit from the both approaches that is the advantages of both DABC(that has a strong global-search ability) and SA (that has a strong local-search ability) (Triki *et al.*, 2005).

Simulated Annealing (SA) begins the search for potential solution in a top-down manner with the initial solution (i.e. biclusters) containing; all rows (users) and columns (pages). The solution is then iteratively perturbed by the deletion or addition of users or pages with the fitness being recalculated each time. Each step of the SA algorithm replaces the current solution by a random nearby solution, chosen with a probability that depends on the difference between the corresponding function values

and on a global parameter T called the temperature that is gradually decreased during the process.

The detailed steps of the proposed Hybrid DABC based biclustering model are as follows:

Employed Bee Phase

The employed bee is to perform the local search around a given food source. Therefore, the employed bee takes the exploitation search of the algorithm. In order to generate good quality and diversity neighboring solutions, SA, a local search algorithm is applied for the employed bees in this study. After performing the local search approach using SA, the employed bee obtains a new neighboring food source around the old one. Then the new food source will be evaluated and compared with the old one. The better food source will be kept in the population as in the basic DABC algorithm which performs a greedy selection procedure.

Onlooker Bee Phase

In the hybrid DABC algorithm, each onlooker bee selects a food source based on the probability of the nectar amount of each food source among

Algorithm 1. Hybrid DABC based biclustering algorithm

```
Input: Session Matrix A, k_u, k_p, T, α
Output: Optimized Biclusters
Step 1 Set the system parameters. //Initialization Phase
Step 2 Produce the initial population x={x_1, x_2, …, x_n} using either Two-Way K-
Means Clustering or Greedy Biclustering.
Step 3 If the stopping criterion is satisfied, output the optimal solution;
        otherwise, perform steps 4 to14.
// Employed bee phase
Step 4 For each employed bee,
        v_i = SA_population (A, x_i) // generate a new neighbouring solution
using SA.
Step 5 Evaluate the new neighbouring solution.
Step 6 Record the better solution among the new solution and the old one as
the current solution and put it into the population.
Step 7 If a solution has not been improved through cycles, then the corre-
sponding employed bee becomes a scout bee and perform step 6.
Step 8 Evaluate each solution corresponding to each employed bee.
// Onlooker bee phase
Step 9 For each onlooker bee, calculate its probability using equation (7.3).
Step 10 Perform local search for the selected food source.
Step 11 Apply greedy selection procedure to record the better solution in the
population.
Step 12 Evaluate solution corresponding to each onlooker bee.
// Scout bee phase
Step 13 The scout bees select a food source randomly and perform local search
operator in the predefined region. After generating a new solution, performs
greedy selection procedure.
Step 14 Evaluate solution corresponding to each scout bee,
Step 15 Return optimized biclusters.
```

the total nectar amounts. Then the food source with highest probability will be selected by the onlooker bee. After selecting the food source, each onlooker bee performs local search for the selected food source using SA and produce a new neighboring food source. The better food source between the old one and the new neighboring one will be memorized in the population.

Scout Bee Phase

A scout bee performs randomly search in the simple DABC algorithm. This will increase the population diversity and suffers from local optima, whereas this will also decrease the search efficacy. Therefore, in the hybrid DABC algorithm, the scout bees perform search in the predefined search

Function 1. SA_population(A, x)

```
Input: A, x, T, α
Output: sbest,  set of optimal biclusters
Step 7.             Initialize T, α, Tmin
Step 8.             initial particles (s) = x    // Initialize the initial
solution
Step 9.             e = fitness(s)
Step 10.             ebest = max(e)
Step 11.             while (T < Tmin)
      snew = generate neighbour of s //Pick some neighbour.
       enew = fitness(snew)              // Compute its fitness.
      if enew > ebest then
      sbest = snew
      ebest = enew
      elseif  exp(-(e - enew)/T) > random() then
      sbest = snew
      ebest = enew
      else
      T=T/(1+ α)// Reduce the temperature       End (while)
Step 12.        Return sbest
```

space using SA. In the hybrid DABC algorithm, at least 5% – 10% of the population is scout bees.

The weight of each page in the bicluster is calculated using following formula *(Obasher et al., 2002)*

$$w(p) = \frac{\sum_{i \in I} b(i, p)}{nU} \qquad (5)$$

where p is the index of the page, I is the set of users in the bicluster and nU is the number of users in the bicluster. The value of w(p) falls between 0 and 1.

Aggregated usage profile is defined as a set of pairs of pageview and weight.

Usage profile = { p, w(p) | p∈P, w(p) ≥ min_weight }

where $P = \{p_1, p_2, \ldots, p_n\}$, a set of n pageviews and each pageview uniquely represented by its

associated URL and the w(p) is the (mean) value of the attribute's weights in the bicluster.

Online Component: Matching the Current Session to Usage Profiles

When the user browses the internet, the web server will start to keep his logs on a file. This file can be accessed to extract the current active navigation web pages called the Active Session/ Current Session. Using this active session, the online component is responsible for identifying the best navigation profile for the current session where by a recommendation list is to be created and attached to the user navigation list.

If user navigates through the web site, the active session window is compared to the aggregate usage profiles generated by using Algorithm-3. Profiles having a similarity greater than a similarity score threshold β are selected as K nearest biclusters. These nearest biclusters can be used

Algorithm 2. Generation of Aggregate Usage Profile

```
Input: Set of optimal biclusters, min_weight
Output: Set of Aggregate usage profile
Step 1.         For all pages p in global optimal bicluster
1) Calculate the weight of the page p using equation (6)
2) If w(p) > min_weight
            profile= Union(profile, p)
                        end(if)
                  end(for)
     Step 2.        Return the aggregate usage profile
```

for recommending pages instantaneously which have not been visited by the user.

EXPERIMENTAL ANALYSIS

About Datasets

The web log files of msnbc.com web site have been used to evaluate the performance of the proposed algorithm. The web site includes the page visits of users who visited the msnbc.com web site on 28/9/99. The visits are recorded at the level of URL category (for example sports, news and so on) and are recorded in time order. It includes visits to 17 categories. The data is obtained from IIS logs for msnbc.com and news-related portions of msn.com.

Each sequence in the dataset corresponds to a user's request for a page. The 17 categories are:

1. Frontpage
2. News
3. Tech
4. Local
5. Opinion
6. On-air
7. Misc
8. Weather
9. Health
10. Living
11. Business
12. Sports
13. Summary
14. BBS
15. Travel

Algorithm 3. Recommendation algorithm

```
Input: Active user session A, Set of usage profiles, Similarity score thresh-
old β. K=0
Output: Recommendation Set R
Step 1. For each usage profile 'up'
          cp= Find common pages in 'up' with respect to A.
        ncp=Find not common pages in 'up' with respect to A.
        Sim_score(up)= cp / (cp+ncp).
        End(for)
Step 2. Recommend the pages in K nearest usage profile whose Sim_score>β
Step 3. Return R as Recommendation set
```

16. Msn-news
17. Msn-sports

Example:

```
1 1
2
3 2 2 4 2 2 2
```

The above clickstream is a sequence of visits. The first row indicates that the user has visited category 1 twice. The second row indicates that a user has visited category 2 once. The third row indicates that the user visited category 3 once, category 2 visited consecutively, then visited category 4 once and finally visited category 2 consecutively three times. Convert these sequences into the user-by-page matrix A using equation (7). The element a_{ij} of A(U,P) represents frequency visit of the p_j of P by user u_i of U during a given period of time.

$$a_{ij} = \begin{cases} Hits\,(i,j), & if\ p_j\ is\ visited\ by\ u_i \\ 0, & otherwise \end{cases}$$

(7)

where Hits(i,j) is the frequency of visit of page p_j of P by the user u_i of U

The *MSWEB* dataset is taken from the UCI KDD archive http://kdd.ics.uci.edu/databases/msweb/msweb.html) and records the logs within www.microsoft.com that users visited in one-week time frame during February 1998. Two separate data sets are provided, a training set and a test set. It consist of 32711 sessions and 285 pages. For preprocessing MSWEB dataset, only root pages were considered as the pageview of a session. This preprocessing step resulted in total of 20 categories namely "library", "developer", "home", "finance", "repository", "gallery", "catalog", "mail", "ads", "education", "magazine", "support", "ms", "technology", "search", "country", "business", "entertainment", "news", "feedback".

Data Preparation

In dataset, the length of the record having less than 5 is considered as a short and record length greater than 15 is considered as a long. During data filtering process, short and long records are removed from the dataset. After data filtering process, number of records in the MSNBC dataset is reduced to 3386 from 9 lakh records. In case of MSWEB, number of user sessions taken for the study is 5000. The size of the MSNBC and MSWEB datasets taken for the evaluation of the proposed algorithm is 3386 x 17 and 5000 x 20 respectively.

Result

The performance of the Discrete ABC based biclustering model is studied by conducting experiment on the MSNBC and MSWEB datasets. Different types of initial population for each dataset are generated by using Two-Way K-Means clustering and Greedy Biclustering method (Rathipriya & Thangavel, 2011)

The results of the Two-Way K-Means clustering are given as the input to DABC based biclustering model to extract the optimal bicluster from above mentioned datasets. The characteristics of the global optimal bicluster for each dataset such as Volume, ACV, Number of Users and Pages in the bicluster are recorded in the Table 2.

From the values recorded in the Table 3, it is clear that DABC is combined with Greedy biclustering extracts the high volume optimal bicluster than it is coupled with Two-Way K-Means clustering. The rate of convergence of global optimal bicluster is also better than DABC + Two-Way K-Means clustering.

The results of hybrid DABC based biclustering model for each dataset are recorded in Table 4 and 5. The output of the Greedy Biclustering is given as input to the hybrid DABC based biclustering model, it extracts the high user coverage bicluster subjected to the given ACV threshold. The con-

Table 2. Performance of two-way K-Means clustering + DABC based biclustering model

	MSWEB	MSNBC
Volume	1870	5888
ACV	0.9026	0.9054
No. of Users	187	736
No. of Pages	10	8

Table 3. Performance of greedy clustering + DABC based biclustering model

	MSWEB	MSNBC
Volume	7890	9888
ACV	0.9362	0.9305
No. of Users	789	1236
No. of Pages	10	8

Table 4. Performance of two-way K-Means clustering + hybrid DABC based biclustering model

	MSWEB	MSNBC
Volume	9810	11120
ACV	0.9130	0.9081
No. of Users	1090	1390
No. of Pages	9	8

vergence rate of optimal bicluster is fast in Hybrid DABC than simple DABC based biclustering model. The comparison of Hybrid DABC and Simple DABC based biclustering models for each dataset is given in Table 6. It is observed that, to extract high user coverage bicluster for a subset of pages with high degree of correlation, hybrid DABC is coupled with Greedy Biclustering. It gives fast rate of convergence of optimal bicluster.

Figure 2 shows comparison of hybrid DABC and Simple DABC based Biclustering model based on the number of iterations taken by each dataset for convergence of global optimal bicluster. From this, it is concluded that hybrid DABC converged quickly than simple DABC. It is obvious from

Figure 3, percentage of User Coverage in optimal bicluster for each dataset is high in hybrid DABC than simple DABC based Biclustering model.

In this chapter, usage profiles extracted from MSNBC dataset is taken for online component i.e. recommendation process. Table 7 and 8 show list of pageview index for each aggregated usage profile of MSNBC dataset using simple and hybrid DABC based biclustering model respectively. The weight of each pageview in the aggregated usage profile is calculated and tabulated. Percentage of the users in the global optimal bicluster is high in hybrid DABC so that weight of the pageview in the corresponding aggregated usage profile is also high.

Measures to Evaluate the Recommendation System

The current user is anonymous to the recommender system with no previous navigation history, hence a sliding window technique over the current user session was used to represent the user history. To do so, the user current session is broken into two parts; the first part with size n pages is used as the surrogate user history which is matched against the web navigation profiles then produces a recommendation list from the selected profile. The remaining pages form the second part which is used for the comparison purpose to evaluate the recommendation accuracy.

In this chapter, precision, coverage and F1 measure are used to evaluate the recommendation effectiveness (AlMurtadha *et al.,* 2010). Let A be active current session taken from the evaluation set and *R be* a recommendation set generated by using the proposed system over the navigation profiles. *W* represents the items that already visited by the user in *A*. The precision is defined as:

$$\text{Precision(R,A)} = \frac{\left| R \bigcap (A - W) \right|}{\left| R \right|}$$

Table 5. Performance of Greedy Biclustering + Hybrid DABC based biclustering model

	MSWEB	MSNBC
Volume	11619	14336
ACV	0.9435	0.9401
No. of Users	1291	1792
No. of Pages	9	8

Table 6. Comparison of DABC and hybrid DABC based biclustering model

	MSWEB		MSNBC	
	Hybrid	Normal	Hybrid	Normal
No .of user	1291	789	1792	1236
No. of pages	9	10	8	8
User Coverage %	50.96	41.16	52.86	47.27
Optimal ACV	0.9435	0.9362	0.9401	0.9305

$$\text{Coverage (R,A)} = \frac{\left| R \cap (A - W) \right|}{\left| (A - W) \right|}$$

$$\text{F1 measure} = \frac{2 * \text{Precision} * \text{Coverage}}{\text{Precision} + \text{Coverage}}$$

In this chapter, window (W=2 to 4) size is used to represent the surrogate user history and the rest pages are used for the evaluation of the recommendation system. Table 9 shows the pageview categories in the active user session and their corresponding recommended pages.

Table 10 and Table 11 consists of performance measures for recommendation system using standard DABC and Hybrid DABC in which hybrid DABC based recommendation system has high precision than other.

F1 measure is tabulated in Table 10 and Table 11 for DABC and Hybrid DABC. It shows that hybrid DABC performs better and achieves

Figure 2. Comparison of hybrid and simple DABC based biclustering model

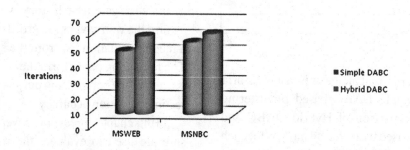

Figure 3. User coverage percentage of optimal biclusters

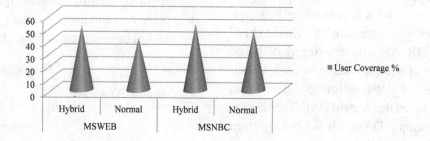

Table 7. Aggregate usage profiles of MSNBC dataset using DABC

S.No	Aggregate Usage Profile	List of Pages	Weights of Each Page in the Profile
1	1	3,6,10,11,12,14	0.6790, 0.7819, 0.6533, 0.7295, 0.7048, 0.6190
2	2	1,4,7	0.7421, 1.0000, 0.8507
3	3	2,6,11,12,14	1.0000, 0.6804, 0.8041, 0.6701, 1.0000
4	4	2,3,5,6,11,12	0.8325, 0.6649, 1.0000, 0.6911, 0.6859, 0.6702
5	5	1,5	0.6415, 1.0000
6	6	1,4	1, 0.7943

Table 8. Aggregate usage profiles of MSNBC dataset using hybrid DABC

S.No	Aggregate Usage Profile	List of Pages	Weights of Each Page in the Profile
1	1	3,6,10,11,12,14, 17	0.7819, 0.6533, 0.7295, 0.7048, 0.6190,0.6023,0.6003
2	2	1,4,7	0.7421 1.0000 0.8507
3	3	2,6,11,12,14	1.0000, 0.6804, 0.8041, 0.6701, 1.0000
4	4	2,6,10,11,12	0.8929, 0.8304, 1.0000, 0.6161, 0.6339
5	5	2,3,6,10,11	0.9408, 0.6250,1.0000, 0.6842, 0.6974
6	6	1,4	1.0000, 0.7307
7	7	8,9,17	0.6900,0.6123,0.6063

Table 9. Recommendation set using hybrid DABC

Active Session (w)	Recommended Pages (R)
1,6	3,10,11,12
1,2	4,7,8
1,2,17	4,7,8,9
1,4,6,10	2,3,11,12

higher prediction accuracy than standard DABC. This improvement is due to the hybrid swarm intelligence based biclustering process is applied to extract coherent usage profiles in the offline component which is followed by the prediction of next navigation profiles to the user based on their current browsing session.

Table 10. Evaluation measure for A(=1,2,4,7,9,10,12,17) using DABC

S.No	Window Size	Pages id in W	Recommendation Set R	Precision	Coverage	F1measure
1	2	1,2	4, 8	0.5	0.16	0.2424
2	3	1,2,17	4, 8,9	0.667	0.28	0.3944
3	4	1,4,9, 10	11,12	0.5	0.16	0.2424

Table 11. Evaluation measure for A(=1,2,4,7,9,10,12,17) using hybrid DABC

S.No	Window Size	Pages id in W	Recommendation Set R	Precision	Coverage	F1measure
1	2	1,2	4,7,8	0.667	0.28	0.3944
2	3	1,2,17	4,7,8,9	0.75	0.6	0.6667
3	4	1,4,9, 10	2,11,12	0.5	0.5	0.5

CONCLUSION

Hybrid Swarm Intelligence Based Biclustering algorithm is proposed in this chapter to generate the optimal usage profiles and to recommend the set of web pages for next navigation based on their preformed navigation profiles for similar interested users. The ability of predicting the next visited pages and recommending it to the user is highly recommended especially in e-commerce applications. The results show that the proposed work has higher prediction accuracy. The results also show that biclustering technique has the ability to build recommendation system for the anonymous user based on their early navigation which is ideal for e-commerce applications.

REFERENCES

AlMurtadha, Y.M., Sulaiman, M.N.B., Mustapha, N., & Udzir, N.I. (2010). Mining web navigation profiles for recommendation system. *Information Technology Journal, 9*, 790-796.

AlMurtadha, Y.M., Sulaiman, M.N.B., Mustapha, N., & Udzir, N. I. (2011). IPACT: Improved Web Page Recommendation System Using Profile Aggregation Based On Clustering of Transactions. *American Journal of Applied Sciences, 8*(3), 277–283. doi:10.3844/ajassp.2011.277.283

Castellano, G., Fanelli, A. M., & Torsello, M. A. (2011). NEWER: A system for NEuro-fuzzy WEb Recommendation. *Applied Soft Computing, 11*(1), 793–806. doi:10.1016/j.asoc.2009.12.040

Cheng, Y., & Church, G. M. (2000). Biclustering of Expression Data. In Proceeding of International Conference of Intelligent. System Molecular Biology, 8, 93-103.

Cooley, R., Mobasher, B., & Srivastava, J. (1997). Web Mining: Information and Pattern Discovery on the World Wide Web. In *Proceedings of Ninth IEEE International Conference on Tools with Artificial Intelligence* (pp. 558-567). IEEE.

Eirinaki, M., & Vazirgiannis, M. (2003). Web mining for web personalization. *ACM Transactions on Internet Technology, 3*(1), 1–27. doi:10.1145/643477.643478

Forsati, R., Meybodi, M. R., & Neiat, A. G. (2009). Web Page Personalization Based on Weighted Association Rules. In *Proceeding of International Conference on Electronic Computer Technology,* (pp. 130-135). Academic Press.

Goldberg, D. E. (1989). *Genetic algorithms in search, optimization, and machine learning*. Reading, MA: Addison-Wesley Pub. Co.

Gunduz, S., & Ozsu, M. (2003). A user interest model for web page navigation. In *Proceedings of International Workshop on Data Mining for Actionable Knowledge* (DMAK), (pp. 46-57). DMAK.

Hartigan, J. A. (1972). Direct clustering of a data matrix. *Journal of the American Statistical Association, 67*(337), 123–129. doi:10.1080/0162 1459.1972.10481214

Idoumghar, L., Melkemi, M., & Schott, R. (2009). A novel hybrid evolutionary algorithm for multimodal function optimization and engineering applications. In *Proceeding of International Conference on Artificial Intelligence and Soft Computing,* (pp. 87-93). Academic Press.

Karaboga, D., & Basturk, B. (2007). Artificial bee colony (ABC) optimization algorithm for solving constrained optimization problems. In *Proceedings of the 12th International Fuzzy Systems Association world congress on Foundations of Fuzzy Logic and Soft Computing* (IFSA '07). Berlin: Springer.

Kennedy, J. N., & Eberhart, R. C. (1995). Particle swarm optimization. In *Proceedings of IEEE International Conference on Neural Networks*, (vol. 4, pp. 1942-1948). IEEE.

Kirkpatrick, S., Vecchi, M. P., & Gelatt, C. D. (1983). Optimization by Simulated Annealing. *Science, 220*(4598), 671–680. doi:10.1126/science.220.4598.671 PMID:17813860

Madeira, S. C., & Oliveira, A. L. (2004). Biclustering Algorithms for Biological Data Analysis: A Survey. *IEEE/ACM transactions on computational biology and bioinformatics / IEEE, ACM, 1*(1), 24–45. doi:10.1109/TCBB.2004.2 PMID:17048406

Marinakis, Y., Marinaki, M., Matsatsinis, N. F., & Zopounidis, C. (2011). Discrete Artificial Bee Colony Optimization Algorithm for Financial Classification Problems. *International Journal of Applied Metaheuristic Computing, 2*(1), 1–17. doi:10.4018/jamc.2011010101

Mobasher, B. (2001). *WebPersonalizer: A Server-Side Recommender System Based on Web Usage Mining* (Technical Report). Telecommunications and Information Systems.

Mobasher, B., Cooley, R., & Srivastava, J. (2000). Automatic personalization based on Web usage mining. *Communications of the ACM, 43*(8), 142–151. doi:10.1145/345124.345169

Mobasher, B., Dai, H., Luo, T., & Nakagawa, M. (2001). Improving the Effectiveness of Collaborative Filtering on Anonymous Web Usage Data. In *Proceedings of the IJCAI 2001 Workshop on Intelligent Techniques for Web Personalization* (ITWP01). Seattle, WA: IJCAI.

Mobasher, B., Dai, H., Luo, T., & Nakagawa, M. (2002). Discovery and Evaluation of Aggregate Usage Profiles for Web Personalization. *Data Mining and Knowledge Discovery, 6*(1), 61–82. doi:10.1023/A:1013232803866

Premalatha, K., & Natarajan, A. M. (2010). Combined Heuristic Optimization Techniques for Global Minimization. *International Journal of Advance. Soft Computing Application, 2*, 85–99.

Rathipriya, R., & Thangavel, K. (2012). A Discrete Artificial Bees Colony Inspired Biclustering Algorithm. *International Journal of Swarm Intelligence Research, 3*(1), 30–42. doi:10.4018/jsir.2012010102

Sankaradass, V., & Arputharaj, K. (2011). An Intelligent Recommendation System for Web User Personalization with Fuzzy Temporal Association Rules. *European Journal of Scientific Research, 51*(1), 88–96.

Srivastava, J., Cooley, R., Deshpande, M., & Tan, P. (2000). Web Usage Mining: Discovery and Applications of Usage Patterns from Web Data. *SIGKDD Explorations, 1*(2), 12–23. doi:10.1145/846183.846188

Symeonidis, P., Nanopoulos, A., Papadopoulos, A. N., & Manolopoulos, Y. (2008). Nearest-biclusters collaborative filtering based on constant and coherent values. *Information Retrieval, 11*(1), 51–75. doi:10.1007/s10791-007-9038-4

Tang, C., Zhang, L., Zhang, A., & Ramanathan, M. (2001). Interrelated Two-way Clustering: An Unsupervised Approach for Gene Expression Data Analysis. In *Proceedings in Second IEEE International Symposium. Bioinformatics and Bioeng.*, (vol. 14, pp. 41-48). IEEE.

Triki, E., Collette, Y., & Siarry, P. (2005). A theoretical study on the behavior of simulated annealing leading to a new cooling schedule. *European Journal of Operational Research, 166*(1), 77–92. doi:10.1016/j.ejor.2004.03.035

Wang, X., & Li, J. (2004). Hybrid particle swarm optimization with simulated annealing. In *Proceedings of 2004 International Conference on Machine Learning and Cybernetics*, (Vol.4, pp.2402-2405). Academic Press.

Zhou, B., Hui, S. C., & Chang, K. (2004). An intelligent recommender system using sequential web access patterns. In *Proceedings of IEEE Conference on Cybernetics and Intelligent Systems*, (vol. 1, pp. 393-398). IEEE.

KEY TERMS AND DEFINITIONS

Biclustering: Biclustering, co-clustering, subspace clustering or two-way clustering is a data mining technique which allows simultaneous clustering of the rows and columns of a matrix. The term was first introduced by Mirkin. Given a m x n matrix, the biclustering algorithm generates biclusters which is a subset of rows which exhibit similar behavior across a subset of columns, or vice versa.

Clickstream Data: Clickstream data is a natural byproduct of a user accessing web pages, and refers to the sequence of pages visited and the time these pages were viewed.

Discrete ABC Optimization: Artificial Bees Colony (ABC) Optimization is the recently developed swarm intelligence technique. It is a meta-heuristic approach motivated by foraging behavior of honeybees and it is based on the concept of cooperation. It has the capability through the information exchange and recruiting process, to intensify and diversify the search in the promising regions of the solution space. In the Discrete Artificial Bees Colony (DABC) algorithm, the population vectors are formed by binary strings (zeros and ones) and all the points in the search space are possible to be represented.

Simulated Annealing (SA): Simulated Annealing is a well established stochastic technique originally developed to model the natural process of crystallization and later adopted to solve optimization problems.

Web Personalization: Web personalization is the process of personalizing web sites or web services according to the specific user's profile to achieve more efficient web browsing.

Web Usage Profile: Web user profile or web usage model is the generalization of the collected data about the user behavior from web usage data.

Web Usage Mining: Web usage mining (WUM) systems use data mining techniques on web usage data (such as web log file, clickstream data and etc.,) to extract the knowledge from it.

Chapter 8
Optimization of Drilling Process via Weightless Swarm Algorithm

T. O. Ting
Xi'an Jiaotong-Liverpool University, China

ABSTRACT

In this chapter, the main objective of maximizing the Material Reduction Rate (MRR) in the drilling process is carried out. The model describing the drilling process is adopted from the authors' previous work. With the model in hand, a novel algorithm known as Weightless Swarm Algorithm is employed to solve the maximization of MRR due to some constraints. Results show that WSA can find solutions effectively. Constraints are handled effectively, and no violations occur; results obtained are feasible and valid. Results are then compared to previous results by Particle Swarm Optimization (PSO) algorithm. From this comparison, it is quite impossible to conclude which algorithm has a better performance. However, in general, WSA is more stable compared to PSO, from lower standard deviations in most of the cases tested. In addition, the simplicity of WSA offers abundant advantages as the presence of a sole parameter enables easy parameter tuning and thereby enables this algorithm to perform to its fullest.

In this chapter, the main objective of maximizing the Material Reduction Rate (MRR) in the drilling process is carried out. The model describing the drilling process is adopted from the authors' previous work. With the model in hand, a novel algorithm known as Weightless Swarm Algorithm is employed to solve the maximization of MRR due to some constraints. Results show that WSA can find solutions effectively. Constraints are handled effectively, and no violations occur; results obtained are feasible and valid. Results are then compared to previous results by Particle Swarm Optimization (PSO) algorithm. From this comparison, it is quite impossible to conclude which algorithm has a better performance. However, in general, WSA is more stable compared to PSO, from lower standard deviations in most of the cases tested. In addition, the simplicity of WSA offers abundant advantages as the presence of a sole parameter enables easy parameter tuning and thereby enables this algorithm to perform to its fullest.

DOI: 10.4018/978-1-4666-6328-2.ch008

INTRODUCTION

The drilling optimization is the utilization of an existing model to predict an unknown parameter aiming to assist in decision-making. In the manufacturing, drilling has been crucial process as it consumes significant costs in drilling tools. Therefore, an accurate model is crucial in the manufacturing process. However, the model would not have been useful without the presence of a reliable algorithm to seek for unknown parameters in this model. As drilling is an extremely common process in manufacturing industry, the materials removing due to degraded or wear out drills, which are frequent events in the manufacturing process. It is by no doubt that one-third of the material removal process is due to drilling operations.

Hence, the maximization of the so-called Material Removal Rate is done in this work. The drilling operation is a basic operation for many processes such as boring, tapping, and reaming. This complex cutting operation holds a substantial portion for all metal cutting operations, and the largest amount of money spent on any class of the cutting tool (Ting & Lee, 2012). In short, drilling is crucial from the viewpoint of cost, productivity and manufacturing. As a matter of fact, effective drilling also significantly reduces the down-time of the manufacturing processes. In order to overcome this inevitable drawback, constant monitoring is performed in the cutting process to determine the right time to change the relevant tool. Alternatively, one can optimize the relevant parameter in the drilling process. This improves the tool life and apparently increases the cutting period in the prolonged lifetime. Hence, is the motivation of the work being done here.

Many methods were introduced in the past. For instance, Li and Wu (1998) have introduced a new approach for online monitoring of drill wears by using a fuzzy approach, which was known as fuzzy c-means algorithm. From their results, the wear conditions can be categorized into a few fuzzy grades. Dutta et al. (2000) proposed machining features in tool condition monitoring during the drilling process, in which process parameters are related to the machining responses and experimental observations provide a basis for monitoring the tool wear. Yao et al. (1999) have proposed tool wear detection by fuzzy classification and wavelet fuzzy network. In the work done by El-wardany et al. (1996), vibration analysis is carried out to predict the conditions of drills.

More interestingly, drilling wear prediction and monitoring based on current signals was proposed by Li and Tso (1999). Thangaraj and Wright (1998) used change rate of thrust force for drilling failure monitoring. Liu and Wu (1990) applied sensor fusion methods in estimating drill wear. Further, Singh et al. (2006) used an artificial neural network to learn the drilling process based on experimental data in order to predict drill wear. The results from the ANN is found to be satisfactory and reliable. The ant algorithm was applied by Ghaiebi and Solimanpur (2007) to optimize drill-making operation using tool airtime and tool switch time as the objective function. On the other hand, Lee et al. (1998) used the abductive network for modeling and optimization of the drilling process. Once the process parameters such as drill diameter, cutting speed and feed are given, the drilling performance such as tool life, removal rate and thrust force can be predicted by the proposed network. This was successfully done in the work by Ting and Lee (2012).

In terms of process optimization related to machining processes, many methods were applied in the literature. These are the deterministic optimization approaches (Wang, Kuriyagawa, Wei, & Guo, 2002) (Armarego, Smith, & Wang, 1993) which were applied to turning and peripheral milling processes. For turning process, Gopalakrishnak (1991) and Fang (1994) introduced the polynomial geometric programming for turning process. Subsequently, Gopal and Rao (2003) applied the genetic algorithm to tackle grinding process optimization. Subsequently, Lee, Ting, Lin, & Than (2006) solved the similar problem via particle swarm optimization. The rest of the paper is organized as follows. The following section presents the formulation of the optimization problem as the objective function in the algorithm, followed by descriptions on Weightless Swarm Algorithm. Then, parameter sensitivity analysis is carried out to determine the optimal parameter for best performance, followed by result and comparison and lastly is the conclusion.

THE FORMULATION OF OPTIMIZATION PROBLEM

The objective of the optimization problem of the drilling process is the maximization of the material removal rate MRR subjected to a set of constraints on surface roughness, tool wear and input variables. This formulation is similar to the previous work (Ting & Lee, 2012). The MRR for drilling process optimization is defined as

$$MRR = \frac{\pi \cdot D^2 \cdot f \cdot N \cdot m}{4} \qquad (1)$$

where

f is the feed of the drilling [mm/rev]
D is the diameter of the drill [mm]
N is the spindle speed of drilling machine [rpm]
m is the number of holes to be drilled

Hereby, the spindle speed N is related to the cutting speed S [m/min] by Equation (2).

$$N = \frac{1000 \cdot S}{\pi \cdot D} \qquad (2)$$

By applying D=10mm in (1) and substituting (2) into (1) we further simplify the objective function

$$MRR = 250 \cdot D \cdot S \cdot f \cdot m \qquad (3)$$

With the equation (3) as the objective function in this drilling process optimization, some constraints should be satisfied. These constraints can be divided into 2 categories:

1. **Process inequality constraints:**
    a. Allowable surface roughness limit, R_a [μm]

$$R_a \leq R_{a(\max)}$$
$$R_a = 0.00015 \cdot S^{0.1767} \cdot f^{0.0075} \cdot t^{0.0808} \cdot F_c^{1.3686}$$
$$(4)$$

    b. Allowable tool wear limit, T_w [mm]

$$T_w \leq T_{w(\max)}$$
$$T_w = 0.26830 \cdot S^{2.8306} \cdot f^{0.2013} \cdot t^{1.2385} \cdot F_c^{-1.1250}$$
$$(5)$$

2. **Physical boundary constraints:**
    a. Cutting speed, S [m/min]

$$10.27 \leq S \leq 12.69 \qquad (6)$$

    b. Feed, f [mm/rev]

$$0.200 \leq f \leq 0.285 \qquad (7)$$

    c. Thrust force, F_c [N]

$$1307 \leq F_c \leq 1762 \qquad (8)$$

    d. Number of drilled holes m (integer number)

$$1 \leq m \leq 30 \qquad (9)$$

    e. Machining time, t [min]

$$0.25 \leq t \leq 12.90 \tag{10}$$

whereby machining time t is given by

$$t = \frac{L \cdot m}{N \cdot f} \tag{11}$$

where L is the tool traveled length and is equal to 28.4 mm in this investigation and diameter of the drill D is equal to 10mm. The spindle speed N is given in Equation (11). The machining time above is not reflected in the objective function in (1). However, from Equation (11) t is in fact a dependent variable in which its value depends on variables m, L, N and f. Again by substitution of dependent variable N from (2) into (11) thus we have

$$t = \frac{L \cdot D \cdot m \cdot \pi}{1000 \cdot S \cdot f} \tag{12}$$

Further, we transformed this constrained optimization problem into a single objective function by inclusion of all the penalized absolute values due to the violations by

$$f(x) = 250 \cdot D \cdot S \cdot f \cdot m -$$
$$\left(penalty \cdot \sqrt{\left(R_a - R_{a(max)} \right)^2 + \left(T_w - T_{w(max)} \right)^2} \right) \tag{13}$$

whereby *penalty* is a very large positive value set to 1×10^{11} in the simulation program. Thus, an optimization algorithm seeks to maximize the above function that takes into account both surface roughness and tool wear constraints specified by Equation (4) – Equation (5).

WEIGHTLESS SWARM ALGORITHM

WSA has the same form as the canonical PSO (Kennedy J. and Eberhart R.C., 1995). Without the inertia weight, the updated equation is simplified from two-line equation to a single line:

$$X_{i,d}^{t+1} = X_{i,d}^{t} + r_1 c_1 \left(Gbest_{i,d} - X_{i,d}^{t} \right) + r_2 c_2 \left(Pbest_{i,d} - X_{i,d}^{t} \right) \tag{14}$$

whereby $X_{i,d}$ is the position of dth dimension of the ith particle. *Pbest* is the best position found in the search history of a particle whereas *Gbest* is the best solution found in the entire search history. r_1 and r_2 are two independent uniform random number generators within [0, 1]. The acceleration coefficient, c_1 and c_2 are both sets to 1.7. Using Equation (14) works effectively as swapping is done during the update of *Pbest* and *Gbest* values; many X values are the previous *Pbest* values. Hence, it is not necessary to learn from oneself. Therefore, in WSA, several parameters prominent in PSO are omitted. The well-known inertia weight w is now not present. Hence, it means that the velocity, V is also unnecessary. Without V, the user also discards the concern of the bound for this parameter, namely V_{max} and V_{min}. Thus, the proposed algorithm has a much simpler form compared to canonical PSO. By this form of an algorithm, the complexity present is greatly reduced and we only need to tune c_1 for optimal performance; this has been done successfully in this work.

The implementation of WSA is pretty simple and can be implemented from any existing PSO algorithm with the following steps (Ting, T.O. et al., 2012):

1. Set inertia weight = 0,
2. Discard the Pbest term by setting c_1 in equation (1) to zero.

3. Use swapping strategy during Pbest update. The swapping for Gbest may not be necessary as in many algorithm implementations; one of the Pbest values is the Gbest.

The above three steps are simple yet they improve the performance of the algorithm drastically without the need of inertia weight. This simple strategy can be implemented easily into any existing PSO algorithm.

PARAMETER SENSITIVITY ANALYSIS (PSA)

In order to ensure the optimal performance of the algorithm, parameter sensitivity analysis is crucial and should be carried out to determine the optimal value of a known parameter for optimal performance. This PSA is carried out for parameter c_1 as mention in the previous section. Assuming the nature of the problem is similar for all cases specified in Table 1, only one case is appropriate to determine the optimal c_1. From previous experience, c_1 takes a value from 2.5 to 3.5. Therefore, the algorithm is run starting with $c_1 = 2.5$ on a step size of 0.1 until 3.5. Figure 1 plots and portray the changes in MRR values versus. Other parameter settings are available from the program's screenshot given in Figure 2. Based on this graph, it is easy to conclude that the optimal c_1 is 2.7.

RESULTS AND COMPARISON

A screen shot of a computer program (in Visual Basic 6.0) is shown in Figures 3 through 5. The parameter settings for WSA is as observed in this Figure (population size = 100, maximum generation = 1000). The statistical results of the drilling process optimization via WSA are recorded in Table 1. As WSA is a non-deterministic approach, results are tabulated in the form of best, mean and worst solutions out of 50 trials. There are six different parameter settings to test the efficiency of the algorithm. From Table 1, the WSA algorithm seems to stabilize when the allowable surface roughness limit, $R_{a(max)}$ is increased from 5 μm to 7 μm. This is shown by a closer gap between the best, mean and worst for both 0.3 mm and 0.6 mm of allowable tool wear limit $T_{w(max)}$.

Here, it is worth mentioning that in all trials, there is no violation to any of the available constraints. It means that the error calculated is zero in all six cases; the solution has calculated constraints right at the limit boundary. With different parameter settings, the Material Removal Rate MRR has different values. Results adopted from previous work (Ting & Lee, 2012), given as Table 2 is included here for comparison purposes. From this table, the mean value obtained by WSA is better for cases 1 and 2. However, this trend is not significant for other cases. Hence, it is difficult to conclude either WSA or PSO is more stable. By careful comparison of the best values

Table 1. Statistical results of drilling process optimization via WSA (50 trials)

No	Constraints		MRR		
	$T_{w(max)}$ [mm]	$R_{a(max)}$ [μm]	Best	Mean	Worst
1	0.30	5	110934.80	110927.97	110918.80
2	0.30	6	124717.82	124658.66	124395.38
3	0.30	7	136237.98	136228.98	136209.22
4	0.60	5	187854.80	187699.62	185433.18
5	0.60	6	212273.05	211995.12	210596.19
6	0.60	7	230702.56	230685.79	230650.42

Figure 1. Parameter sensitivity analysis on case 1

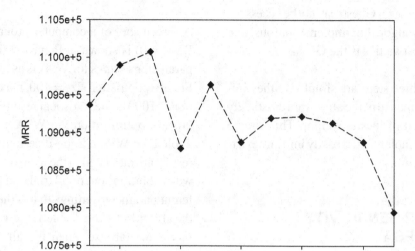

Figure 2. Settings for PSA

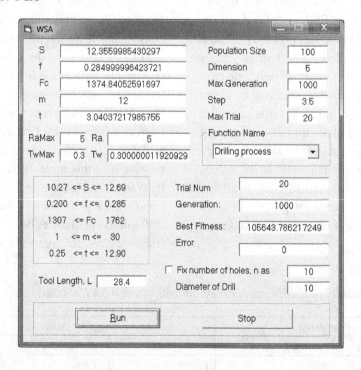

for both algorithms, PSO is slightly better for most cases except for Case 5 (WSA's=212273.05 and PSO's =212261.44). It is suspected that this performance is due to the swapping strategy in WSA. When particles are swapped, the diversity in the population decreases alongside increment of generation. Further works to overcome this premature convergence will be investigated in future.

Figure 3. Screen shot of a program run for Case 1

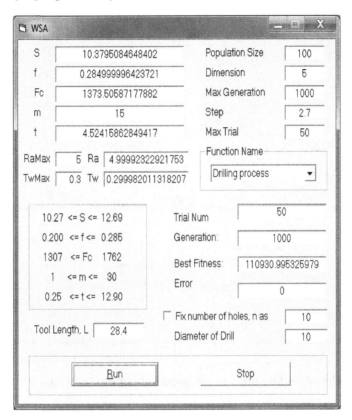

Figure 4. Screen shot of a program run for Case 2

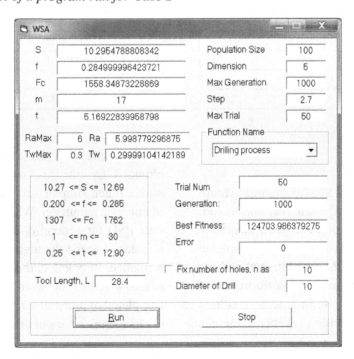

Figure 5. Screen shot of a program run for Case 3

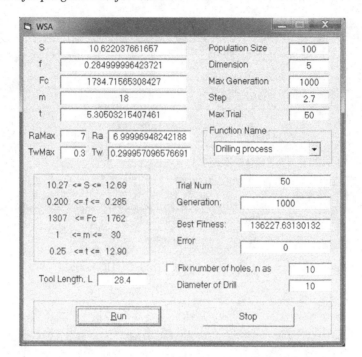

Table 2. Statistical results of drilling process optimization via PSO (50 trials)

No	Constraints		MRR		
	$T_{w(max)}$ [mm]	$R_{a(max)}$ [μm]	Best	Mean	Worst
1	0.30	5	110935.82	110769.42	109271.90
2	0.30	6	124718.71	124471.93	123073.44
3	0.30	7	136239.58	136239.59	136239.59
4	0.60	5	187855.60	187855.61	187855.61
5	0.60	6	212261.44	211996.45	210648.41
6	0.60	7	230704.31	230704.32	230704.32

CONCLUSION

In this work, Weightless Swarm Algorithm is applied to search for optimal drilling parameters subject to an objective function with some inequality constraints. The objective function is formulated as the maximization of Material Reduction Rate (MRR). We then compared the performance of WSA with PSO algorithm. In general, it is hard to conclude which algorithm is better as there is no significant proof from the experimental results obtained. Despite this fact, we have proven that with a much simpler structure and the presence of only one parameter, WSA offers more benefits over PSO for general optimization problems as it is easy to tune the algorithm for optimal performance. In practice, this program can be used to estimate the time taken for drilling work to be completed or assist in determining the right time to change the wear out drill, etc.

REFERENCES

Al-Khayyal, B. (1991). Machine Parameter selection for turning with constraints: An analytical approach based on geometric programming. *International Journal of Production Research, 29*(9), 1897–1908. doi:10.1080/00207549108948056

Armarego, E. J. A., Smith, A. J. R., & Wang, J. (1993). Constrained optimization strategies and CAM software for single-pass peripheral milling. *International Journal of Production Research, 31*(9), 2139–2160. doi:10.1080/00207549308956849

Clerc, M., & Kennedy, J. (2002). The particle swarm – explosion, stability and convergence in a multidimensional complex space. *IEEE Transactions on Evolutionary Computation, 6*(1), 58–73. doi:10.1109/4235.985692

Dutta, R. K., Kiran, G., Paul, S., & Chattopadhyay, A. B. (2000). Assessment of machining features for tool condition monitoring in face milling using an artificial neural network. *Proceedings - Institution of Mechanical Engineers, 214*(7), 535–546. doi:10.1243/0954405001518233

El-Wardany, T. I., Gao, D., & Elbestawi, M. A. (1996). Tool condition monitoring in drilling using vibration signature analysis. *International Journal of Machine Tools & Manufacture, 36*(6), 687–711. doi:10.1016/0890-6955(95)00058-5

Fang, X. D., & Jawahir, I. S. (1994). Predicting total machining performance in finish turning using integrated fuzzy-set models of the machinability parameters. *International Journal of Production Research, 32*(4), 833–849. doi:10.1080/00207549408956974

Ghaiebi, H., & Solimanpur, M. (2007). An ant algorithm for optimization of hole-making operations. *Computers & Industrial Engineering, 52*(2), 308–319. doi:10.1016/j.cie.2007.01.001

Gopal, A. V., & Rao, P. V. (2003). The optimisation of the grinding of silicon carbide with diamond wheels using genetic algorithms. *International Journal of Advanced Manufacturing Technology, 22*(7-8), 475–480. doi:10.1007/s00170-002-1494-9

Hines, W. W., Montgomery, D. C., Goldman, D. H., & Borror, C. M. (2008). *Probability and statistics in engineering*. John Wiley & Sons.

Kennedy, J., & Eberhart, R. C. (1995). Particle swarm optimization. In *Proceedings of IEEE International Conference on Neural Networks*, (vol. 4, pp. 1942). Perth, Australia: IEEE.

Lee, B. Y., Liu, H. S., & Tarng, Y. S. (1998). Modeling and optimization of drilling process. *Journal of Materials Processing Technology, 74*(1-3), 149–157. doi:10.1016/S0924-0136(97)00263-X

Lee, T. S., Ting, T. O., Lin, Y. J., & Than, H. (2007). A particle swarm approach for grinding process optimisation analysis. *International Journal of Advanced Manufacturing Technology, 33*(11-12), 1128–1135. doi:10.1007/s00170-006-0538-y

Li, P. G., & Wu, S. M. (1988). Monitoring drilling wear states by a fuzzy pattern recognition technique. *ASME Journal of Engineering for Industry, 110*(3), 297–302. doi:10.1115/1.3187884

Li, X., & Tso, S. K. (1999). Drill wear monitoring based on current signals. *Wear, 231*(2), 172–178. doi:10.1016/S0043-1648(99)00130-1

Liu, T. I., & Wu, S. M. (1990). On-line detection on tool wear. *ASME Journal of Engineering for Industry, 112*(3), 299–302. doi:10.1115/1.2899590

Shi, Y., & Eberhart, R. C. (1998) A modified particle swarm optimizer. In *Proceedings of the IEEE International Conference on Evolutionary Computation*. Anchorage, AK: IEEE.

Singh, A. K., Panda, S. S., Pal, S. K., & Chakraborty, D. (2006). Predicting drill wear using an artificial neural network. *International Journal of Advanced Manufacturing Technology, 28*(5-6), 456–462. doi:10.1007/s00170-004-2376-0

Tandon, V., El-Mounary, H., & Kishawy, H. (2002). NC end milling optimization using evolutionary computation. *International Journal of Machine Tools & Manufacture, 42*(5), 595–605. doi:10.1016/S0890-6955(01)00151-1

Thangaraj, A., & Wright, P. K. (1988). Computer-assisted prediction of drill failure using in-process measurements of thrust force. *ASME Journal of Engineering Industry, 110*(2), 192–200. doi:10.1115/1.3187869

Ting, T. O., & Lee, T. S. (2012). Drilling optimization via particle swarm optimization. *International Journal of Swarm Intelligence Research, 3*(1), 43–54. doi:10.4018/jsir.2012010103

Ting, T. O., Man, K. L., Guan, S.-U., Nayel, M., & Wan, K. Y. (2012). Weightless swarm algorithm (wsa) for dynamic optimization problems. In J. J. Park, A. Zomaya, S. Yeo, & S. Sahni (Eds.), *Network and Parallel Computing: Proceedings of 9th IFIP International Conference (NPC 2012)* (LNCS) (vol. 7513, pp. 508–515). IFIP.

Wang, J., Kuriyagawa, T., Wei, X. P., & Guo, D. M. (2002). Optimization of cutting conditions for single pass turning operations using a deterministic approach. *International Journal of Machine Tools & Manufacture, 42*(9), 1023–1033. doi:10.1016/S0890-6955(02)00037-8

Yao, Y., Li, X., & Yuan, Z. (1999). Tool wear detection with fuzzy classification and wavelet fuzzy neural network. *International Journal of Machine Tools & Manufacture, 39*(10), 1525–1538. doi:10.1016/S0890-6955(99)00018-8

KEY TERMS AND DEFINITIONS

Boring: A machining process of enlarging a hole that has been drilled.

Feed: The length of drilled hole with respect to drilling revolution, measured in [mm/rev].

Material Reduction Rate: The frequency of removing flawed raw materials due to machining process.

Reaming: The process of enlarging previously formed hole by small amount for smooth sides.

Tapping: Cutting process to create screw thread, also known as threading.

Wear Out: The degradation of the sharpness of a drill.

Chapter 9
Artificial Insect Algorithms for Routing in Wireless Sensor Systems

Li-Minn Ang
Edith Cowan University, Australia

Adamu Murtala Zungeru
Federal University of Oye-Ekiti, Nigeria

Kah Phooi Seng
Edith Cowan University, Australia

Daryoush Habibi
Edith Cowan University, Australia

ABSTRACT

Social insect communities are formed from simple, autonomous, and cooperative organisms that are interdependent for their survival. These communities are able to effectively coordinate themselves to achieve global objectives despite a lack of centralized planning. This chapter presents a study of artificial insect algorithms for routing in wireless sensor networks, with a specific focus on simulating termites and their behaviours in their colony. The simulating behaviour demonstrates how the termites make use of an autocatalytic behaviour in order to collectively find a solution for a posed problem in reasonable time. The derived algorithm termed Termite-Hill demonstrates the principle of the termite behavior for solving the routing problem in wireless sensor networks. The performance of the algorithm was tested on static and dynamic sink scenarios. The results were compared with other routing algorithms with varying network density and showed that the proposed algorithm is scalable and improved on network energy consumption with a control over best-effort service.

DOI: 10.4018/978-1-4666-6328-2.ch009

INTRODUCTION

Social insect communities are formed from simple, autonomous and cooperative organisms that are able to effectively coordinate themselves to achieve global objectives despite a lack of centralized planning. This chapter focuses on simulating termite behaviours in their colony for the problem of routing in wireless sensor networks (WSNs). A WSN is a distributed infrastructure composed of a large collection of nodes with the ability to instrument and react to events and phenomena in a specific environment (Saleem et al., 2010; Zungeru et al., 2012b; Akyildiz et al., 2002). WSNs are collections of compact-size, relatively inexpensive computational nodes that measure local environmental conditions or other parameters and relay the information to a central point for appropriate processing using wireless communications. Each sensor node is equipped with embedded processors, sensor devices, storage devices and radio transceivers. The critical factor in the design of WSNs is to maximize the lifetime of the sensor nodes which are battery-powered and have a limited energy supply. A key element that determines the lifetime in a WSN is the way that information is transmitted or routed to a destination node (called sink). A node with information to send to the sink does not transmit the information directly to the sink (single-hop network) (a situation when the sink is not a neighbor of the source node) because this will require a very high transmission power. Rather, the node sends the information to a neighbouring node which is closer to the sink which in turn sends to its neighbour and so on until the information arrives at the sink (multi-hop network). This process is known as routing. An important problem in WSN is how to design a routing protocol which is not only energy efficient, scalable, robust and adaptable, but also provides the same or better performance than that of existing state-of-the-art routing protocols.

Termites are relatively simple insects. Their small size and small number of neurons makes them incapable of dealing with complex tasks individually. On the other hand, the termite colony can be seen as an intelligent entity for its high level of self-organization and the complexity of tasks it can perform to achieve global objectives despite a lack of centralized planning and direct communications. One way termites communicate is by secreting chemical agents that will be recognized by receptors on the bodies of other termites. A termite is capable of determining if another termite is a member of its own colony by the smell of its body. One of the most important of such chemical agents is the pheromone. Pheromones are molecules released from glands on the termite body. Once deposited on the ground they start to evaporate, releasing the chemical agent into the air. Individual termites leave a trail of such scents, which stimulates other termites to follow that trail, dropping pheromones while doing so (Matthews & Mattheus, 1942). This use of the environment as a medium for indirect communication is called stigmergy. This process will continue until a trail from the termite colony to the food source is established. While following very basic instincts, termites accomplish complex tasks for their colonies in a demonstration of emergent behaviour. In the foraging example, one of the characteristics of the pheromone trail is that it is highly optimized, tending toward the shortest path between the food source and the termite nest or hill. This creation of a trail with the shortest distance from the nest to the food source is a side effect of their behaviour, which is not something they have as an *a priori* goal.

In this chapter, we will focus on how termite colonies use pheromone trails to accomplish complex tasks and show the similarity between termite colonies and WSNs. We also show the relationship between the stigmergic behaviour utilizing pheromones and the process of representation in a complex system which in our case is the WSN. From the WSN perspective, social insect communities have many desirable properties as surveyed in (Zungeru et al., 2012b; Saleem et al., 2010). These communities are formed from simple, autonomous, and cooperative organisms that are interdependent for their survival. Social insect communities are able to effectively coordinate themselves to achieve global objectives. The behaviors which accomplish these tasks are emergent from much simpler behaviors or rules that the individuals are following. The coordination of behaviors is adaptive, flexible and robust, and necessary in an unpredictable world which is capable of solving real world problems (Roth & Wicker, 2003; Hölldobler & Wilson, 1990). The characteristics described above are desirable in the context of WSNs. Such wireless systems may be composed of simple nodes working together to deliver messages, while remaining resilient against changes in its environment. The sensor network environment may include anything from its own topology to physical layer effects on the communications links, to traffic patterns across the network. A noted difference between biological and engineered networks is that the former have an evolutionary incentive to cooperate, while engineered networks may require alternative solutions to force nodes to cooperate (Buttyan & Hubaux, 2000; Mackenzie & Wicker, 2001).

Such self organization of biological species is known as swarm intelligence. Research in this field of swarm intelligence has focused on working principles of ant colonies (Bonabeau et al., 1999; Dorigo & Di Caro, 1998), slime mold (Li et al., 2011) and honey bees (Saleem & Farooq, 2005). To the best of our knowledge, less attention has been paid in utilizing the organization and behavioral principles of other swarms such as termites to solve real world problems. In this approach, termite agents are modeled to suit the energy resource constraints in WSNs for the purpose of finding the best paths between sites as a function of the number of visited nodes and the energy of the path, by borrowing from the principles behind the termite communication. Since communication is an energy expensive function, given a network and a source-destination pair, the problem is to

route a packet from the source to the destination node using a minimum number of nodes, low energy, and limited memory space so as to save energy. This implies that when designing a routing protocol for WSN, it is important to consider the path length as well as the energy of the path along which the packet is to traverse before its arrival at the sink, while also maintaining low memory usage at the network nodes. In Termite-hill, termite agents are considered as packets that travel the network changing routing information in order to find the best path towards the termite-hill, in this case towards the sink node. We will show that the Termite-hill routing algorithm is scalable, robust, adaptable and energy efficient with low latency. The remainder of this chapter is organized as follows. Section Artificial Insect-Based Routing Algorithm in WSN discusses related work and current research findings for artificial insect-based routing algorithms for WSNs. Section Simulating the Behavior of Termites presents a description of simulating the behaviors of termites. In Section the Termite-Hill Routing Algorithm, we describe the Termite-hill routing algorithm. Section Performance Evaluation evaluates the performance of Termite-hill and compares with other routing protocols. Section Conclusions and Future Works concludes the chapter with comments for future work.

ARTIFICIAL INSECT-BASED ROUTING ALGORITHMS IN WSN

The idea of using a swarm paradigm to establish routes in communication networks has been investigated by many researchers. Examples of proposed swarms include social insect communities like ants and bees. Optimization techniques using artificial ant colonies have been extensively researched. Researchers have successfully applied ant-based algorithms to the solutions of difficult combinatorial problems such as the travelling salesman problem and the job scheduling problem (Dorigo et al., 1999). In (Ramos & Almeida, 2000) and (Semet et al., 2004), the ant colony approach is used to perform image segmentation. Heusse et al. (1998) and Merloti (2004) applied the concepts of ant colonies on routing of network packages. These and other works show that the ant colony behavior offers a clear demonstration of the notion of emergence with complex systems of which coordinated behaviors can arise from the local interactions of many relatively simple agents. This concept is known as stigmergy and appears to the viewer almost intentional, as if it were a representation of aspects of a directed situation. Yet, the individuals creating this phenomenon have no awareness of the larger process in which they are participating. This is typical of self-organizing properties which are visible at one level of the system and not at another. Considering this, Lawson & Lewis (2004) have suggested that representation emerges from the behavioral coupling of emergent processes with their environments.

The basic ant-based routing algorithm and its main characteristics (Dorigo & Cara, 1998) can be summarized into the following steps:

1. At regular intervals along with the data traffic, a forward ant is launched from the source node towards the sink node.
2. Each agent (forward ant) tries to locate the destination with equal probability by using neighboring nodes with minimum cost (fewer hops) joining its source and sink.
3. Each agent moves step-by-step towards its destination node. At each intermediate node a greedy stochastic policy is applied to choose the next node to move to. The policy makes use of three sources of information: (i) local agent-generated and maintained information, (ii) local problem-dependent heuristic information, and (iii) agent-private information.

4. During the movement, the agents collect information about the time length, the congestion status and the node identifiers of the followed path.
5. Once the destination is reached, a backward ant is created which takes the same path as the forward ant, but in an opposite direction.
6. During this backward travel, local models of the network status and the local routing table of each visited node are modified by the agents as a function of the path they followed and of its goodness.
7. On returning to the source node, the agents die.

In Sensor driven and Cost-aware ant routing (SC) (Zhang et al., 2004), it is assumed that ants have sensors so that they can smell where there is food at the beginning of the routing process so as to increase the possibility of sensing the best direction that the ant will go initially. In addition to the sensing ability, each node stores the probability distribution and the estimates of the cost of destination from each of its neighbors. In their extended work, Flooded Forward ant routing (FF), Zhang et al. (2004) argued the fact that ants even augmented with sensors, can be misguided due to the obstacles or moving destinations. This protocol is based on flooding of ants from source node to the sink node. In cases where the destination is not known at the beginning or the cost cannot be estimated, the algorithm simply uses the broadcast method of sensor networks so as to route packets to the destination. The probabilities are updated in the same way as the basic ant routing.

Beesensor (Saleem and Farooq, 2007) is an algorithm based on the foraging principles of honey bees with an on-demand route discovery. The algorithm works with three types of agents: packers, scouts and foragers. Packers locate appropriate foragers for the data packets at the source node. Scouts are responsible for discovering the path to a new destination using the broadcasting principle. Foragers are the main workers of beesensor which follow a point-to-point mode of transmission and carry the data packets to a sink node. When a source node detects an event and does not have a route to the sink node, it launches a forward scout and queues the event. A forward scout is propagated using the broadcasting principle to all neighbors of a node. Each forward scout has a unique identification with the detected event in its payload. Intermediate nodes at a distance of two hops or fewer always broadcast the forward scout while the rest of the nodes stochastically decide whether to broadcast it further or not. The forward scouts do not create a source header in which a complete sequence of the traversed nodes up to the sink node is saved. Hence their size is fixed and is independent of the length of the followed path. The approach is based on the interactions of scouts and source routing in which small forwarding tables are built during the return of a scout.

SIMULATING THE BEHAVIOR OF TERMITES

Computer simulations attempt to imitate real-world systems or processes as accurately as possible. In many cases, computer simulations are used to make predictions about real-world processes. In this section, we simulate artificial termites so as to investigate their termite-like behaviors. The objective is to simulate the termite world and this will probe some challenges that will be helpful in solving the routing problem in WSNs. The behavior of termites can be viewed as a prototypical example of how complex group behavior can arise from simple individual behaviors. As such, the relationship between the colony and termites can be seen as an illuminating model, or an inspiring metaphor for thinking about other group or individual relationships, such as the relationship between an organ and its cells, a cell and

its macromolecules, a corporation and its employees, or a country and its citizens (Resnick, 1994, 1997). Each termite colony has a queen. Unlike other insects, the queen does not give directives to the workers. On the termite hill building site, the termites have no leader and there is no one to take control of the master plan. Each individual termite carries out a specific simple task. Being practically blind, their interaction is through their senses of smell and touch. The principle of hill building, through cooperative behavior without a leader to give directives makes them well-suited for solving the routing problem in WSN where information is expected to be gathered in one place (sink). This means that simulating the construction of an entire termite nest will give more insight on their behavior, and thus can easily be mapped to simulating the sensor network. As such, in this section, we program some artificial termites to collect wood samples and the wood samples are expected to be gathered into particular sites (hills).

The main challenge which is the motivating factor in this task is to figure out a decentralized strategy for adding some order to a disordered collection of wood samples. Initially, the wood samples are randomly distributed throughout the termite environment. As the program runs and simulation time passes, the termites are expected to organize the wood samples into a few orderly piles. This model could be mapped to a sensor network environment where sensor nodes are distributed randomly with the aim to sense their environment and to gather the sensed event into one place (sink). Following the four rules bounded by each termite as proposed in (Zungeru et al., 2012a), we then program the termites to gather the disordered wood samples into an ordered form and into fewer piles. The four rules are as follows:

1. A termite moves randomly, but is biased towards the locally observed pheromone gradient. If no pheromone exists, a termite moves uniformly randomly in any direction.

2. Each termite may carry only one wood at a time.

3. If a termite is not carrying a wood and it encounters one, the termite will pick it up.

4. If a termite is carrying a wood and it encounters one, the termite will put the wood down. The wood will be infused with a certain amount of pheromone.

In this program of termites piling up the disordered wood samples into order, we wrote a set of programs for different functions. This set of functions include: (1) defining sets of variables and initializing the global variables and functions. This includes the number of woods needed in the termite world to the dimensions of the termite environment. In this environment, the number of woods equals the number of potential hills in the environment. (2) A function to distribute the wood and termites in the simulation environment. (3) Function definitions. (4) A function to make the termites move in the simulation environment, and (5) a function to make termites pick up and put down the woods in piles. As the termites pick up woods and look for piles, they do so in an orderly manner in which they put down wood samples only at a place where there exist at least a sample of wood. That is to say that they do not put down the wood samples in an empty space. This process leads to the gathering of woods into fewer piles. If all of the wood samples from a particular pile are by chance removed completely, it then means that termites will never drop any wood sample in that spot with the consequence that the particular hill will not grow again. If there happen to be an existence of a pile or hill, its size will have the probability of increasing or decreasing. With this behavior, termites are able to gather the disordered wood into ordered forms. As an example of this behavior, we simulated 200 termites and 100 wood samples in a 200m by 200m application environment, and we further increased the number of termites up to 500 in the environment. Figure 1 shows the results from the simulations. The graph shows the termite behaviors with respect

to simulation time and the number of termites in the environment to gather the widely dispersed woods. The following pseudo-code (Code 1.0) explains the process of the program.

In the simulation scenario, termites put down the wood samples next to other wood samples, rather than on top of other samples as in the normal hill building. This is still fine as long as the wood samples are gathered into one or fewer piles. Initially, the wood samples are gathered into many small piles, but as the simulation proceeds, the number of samples per pile increases while the number of piles in the environment decreases. This action can be seen in Figure 1(a-d). It was also observed that after 1000 seconds of simulation time with 200 termites randomly distributed along with 100 wood samples in the environment, there were about 20 piles of woods out of the initial piles of 100 with a total of 72 woods. After 5000 seconds, 9 piles were recorded with a total of 97 woods. As the simulation time proceeds to 7000 seconds, 4 piles were recorded and a total of 100 woods were also recorded. With more simulation time, the number of piles shrink to just a single whole pile. Also, the number of woods gathered (success rate) tends to 100%. This is shown in Figure 1(a) and (b). We then increased the number of termites to 500 as against the original 200. In this case, after 1000 seconds, we recorded 18 piles with a total of 38 woods, and after 5000 seconds, we recorded 2 piles with a total of 81 woods, and at 7000 seconds, a large pile of 1 was recorded with 92 woods, which implies that 8 woods were still carried by some termites. This is expected since in most cases, with a high population of termites in the environment, the piles shrink faster. The ability of termites to gather woods into fewer piles demonstrates the convergence of the network when we have more termites in the environment. It was also observed in the simulation that as we increased the number of termites above five times the number of wood samples, the environment gets congested and all woods are carried by the termites when it becomes difficult for them to form any reasonable pile. Using this behavior and

Figure 1. Behavioral pattern of termites gathering wood samples in the presence of variation in simulation time with respect to: (a) fewer termites and number of hills built (b) fewer termites and number of woods gathered (c) more termites and number of hills built and (d) more termites and number of woods gathered.

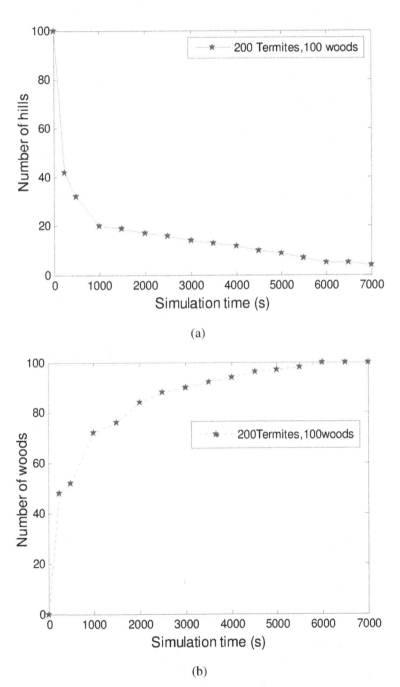

(a)

(b)

Code 1. Simulation of artificial termites in a wood gathering environment

```
1.        //Termite's real world behaviour:
2.        //Define variable and initialization
3.        int Termite = 200;
4.        int woodchip = 100;
5.        pile-name;
6.        Pile-wood-count;          //indicates the number of woods each pile
is constructed with.
7.        int Number-of-pile ;
8.        Int x=200, y=200;          // the environment in which termite and
wood chips are distributed.
9.        //functions' prototype
10.       Distribute_wood (wood_chip,x,y);
11.       View_wood ();
12.       Distribute_termite (Termite,Distribute_wood,x,y);
13.       Termite-move();
14.       //main
15.       Void main (){
16.          Distribute_wood;
17.          Distribute_Termite;
18.          //call Distribute_wood function for distributing woods randomly
19.          Distribute_wood=Distribute_wood (wood_chip,x,y);
20.          //Distribute_ termite function is in charge of distributing ter-
mite and pick up and put
21.          down the woods
22.          Distribute_termite=Distribute_termite (Termite,Distribute_
wood,x,y);
23.          Print ("number of pile = " number-of-pile);
24.          Print (Pile$i,Pile$i.pile-wood-count)
25.          Wood-in-piles=0
26.          For (c=0;c<number-of-pile,c++){
27.                  Int Wood-in-piles =Wood-in-piles +Pile$c.pile-wood-
count
28.             }
29.          Print Wood-in-piles;
30.       }
31.       // Functions' definition:
32.       Function Distribute_wood (wood_chip,x,y){
33.          int number-of-wood=0;
34.          for(int i = 1; i <= woodchip; i++)
35.          {
36.                  L1:        int wood-x ← choose random number between 0
to x;
```

continued on following page

Code 1. Continued

```
37.                            int wood-y  ← choose random number between
0 to y;
38.                          check (x,y) ;
39.                            if  the place is empty{
40.                                put wood there
41.                                number-of-wood=number-of-wood++;
42.                                Number-of-pile =   number-of-wood;
43.                                   /*in the initialization step, each
wood determines a pile, and therefore,
44.                                when we find an empty place for wood,
45.                                we should keep the coordinate in the array
for storing the
46.                            pile's location*/
47.                                  matrix[wood-x][wood-y]="Pile$i";
48.                                  pile-name[i] = "Pile$i";
49.                                pile-wood-count[$i] = 1;
50.                                }
51.                              else
52.                                  goto L1;
53.              }
54.         Return   number-of-wood;
55.         }
56.       Function Distribute_termite (Termite,Distribute_wood,x,y){
57.         int  pick_up_wood = 0 ; //indicate how many woods are been car-
ried by termites
58.         // distributes the termite in the environment
59.         For(i= 0 ; i<Termite;i++){
60.                   L2:   int Termite-x  ← choose random number between
0 to x;
61.                            int Termite-y  ← choose random number
between 0 to y;
62.                          check (x,y) ;
63.                          if the place is empty Put termite in (x,y)
64.                           else goto L2 ;
65.             }
66.       While (simulation's time > 0){
67.         //Termites should keep moving until they find a wood
68.          Termite-move();
69.         // termite find a wood
70.         pick_up_wood = pick_up_wood + 1;
71.         Pile$i.pile-wood-count=Pile$i.pile-wood-count - 1;
```

continued on following page

Code 1. Continued

```
72.          If (Pile$i.pile-wood-count < 1){
73.             Delete Pile$i;
74.             Number-of-pile = Number-of-pile-1;
75.            }
76.        // termite should keep a random movement until they find another
wood and put down this
77.          one near it.
78.          Termite-move();
79.          Select the nearest empty place
80.          Put the wood;
81.          Pile$i.pile-wood-count=pile-wood-count+1;
82.         Termite-move();
83.        }
84.        Function Termite-move(){
85.        Int row = Termite-x;
86.        Int col  = Termite-y;
87.        L4:
88.               For (row; row<x;row++){
89.               For (col;col<y;col++){
90.                   If ((row,col) == (wood-x,wood-y)){
91.                        Return (Pile$i);
92.                          Break;
93.                   }
94.                }
95.           }
96.        // that means termite did not find wood and it reaches (200,200)
97.        Col=0;
98.        Row=0;
99.        Goto L4;
100.        }
```

observations, we then map our findings into the routing problem for WSN which will be described in Section 4.

THE TERMITE-HILL ROUTING ALGORITHM

Termite-hill is a routing algorithm for WSNs that is inspired by the termite behaviors. Preliminary results of this algorithm have been reported in (Zungeru et al., 2012a). Analogous to the termite ad-hoc networking (Roth and Wicker, 2003), each node serves as router and source, and the hill is a specialized node called the sink. There can be one or more sinks depending on the network size. Termite-hill discovers routes only when they are required. When a node has some events or data to be relayed to a sink node and it does not have the valid routing table entry, it generates a *forward soldier* and broadcasts it to all its neighbors. When an intermediate node receives this *forward soldier*, it searches its local routing table for a valid route to the requested destination. If the search is successful, the receiving node then generates a *backward soldier* packet, which is then sent as a unicast message back to the source node where the original request was originated using the reverse links. If the node has no valid route to the destination, it sets up a reverse link to the node from which the *forward soldier* was received and further broadcasts the *forward soldier* packet. When the destination node receives the *forward soldier* packet, it generates a *backward soldier* packet which is also unicast back to the source node. On reception of the *backward soldier* packet, each intermediate node updates its routing table to set up a forward pointer and relays the *backward soldier* message to the next hop using the reverse pointer. The process continues till the *backward soldier* is received by the original source node. The algorithm does not use *HELLO* packets to detect link failures. Rather it uses feedback from the link layer (MAC) to achieve the same objective. Intermediate nodes do not generate *backward soldier* packets even if they have a valid route which avoids the overhead of multiple replies. It also employs cross layer techniques to avoid paths which have high packet loss.

In the course of the algorithm design, the following assumptions were also made:

1. Each node is linked to one or more nodes in the network (neighbors).
2. A node may act as a source, a destination, or a router for a communication between different pair of nodes.
3. Neither network configuration nor adjacency information is known before hand.
4. The same amount of power is required for sending a message between any pair of adjacent nodes throughout the network.

The Pheromone Table

The pheromone table keeps the information gathered by the forward soldier. Each node maintains a table keeping the amount of pheromone on each neighbor path. The node has a distinct pheromone scent, and the table is in the form of a matrix with destination nodes listed along the side and neighbor nodes listed across the top. Rows correspond to destinations and columns to neighbors. An entry in the pheromone table is referenced by $T_{n,d}$ where n is the neighbor index and d denotes the destination index. The values in the pheromone table are used to calculate the selecting probabilities of each neighbor. From Figure 2, when a packet arrives at node G from previous hop S, i.e. the source, the source pheromone decay, and pheromone is added to link $\overrightarrow{SG}$. A *backward soldier* on its way back from the sink node is more likely to take the path through G, since it is the shortest path to the destination i.e. $\overrightarrow{SGED}$. The pheromone table of node G is shown in Figure 2 with nodes A, S, F, and E as its neighbors. It is worth noting that all neighbors are potential destinations. At node G, the total probability of selecting links $\overrightarrow{ED}$, $\overrightarrow{FE}$, $\overrightarrow{AC}$ or $\overrightarrow{SB}$ to the destination node is equal to unity (1) i.e. $\sum T_{ED} + T_{SD} + T_{AD} + T_{FD} = 1$. It will then be observed that, since link $\overrightarrow{GED}$ is shorter to the destination for a packet at node G, more pheromone will be present on it and hence, soldiers are more likely to take that path.

Pheromone Update

When a packet arrives at a node, the pheromone for the source of the packet is incremented by γ, where γ is the reward. Only packets addressed to a node will be processed. A node is said to be addressed if it is the intended next hop recipient of the packet. Equation (1) describes the pheromone update procedure when a packet from source s is delivered from previous hop r. A prime indicates the updated value.

Figure 2. Description of pheromone table of node G

Destination ＼ Neighbor	A	S	F	E
C	$T_{A,C}$	$T_{S,C}$	$T_{F,C}$	$T_{E,C}$
B	$T_{A,B}$	$T_{S,B}$	$T_{F,B}$	$T_{E,B}$
E	$T_{A,E}$	$T_{S,E}$	$T_{F,E}$	$T_{E,E}$
D	$T_{A,D}$	$T_{S,D}$	$T_{F,D}$	$T_{E,D}$
S	$T_{A,S}$	$T_{S,S}$	$T_{F,S}$	$T_{E,S}$
A	$T_{A,A}$	$T_{S,A}$	$T_{F,A}$	$T_{E,A}$
F	$T_{F,A}$	$T_{S,F}$	$T_{F,F}$	$T_{E,F}$

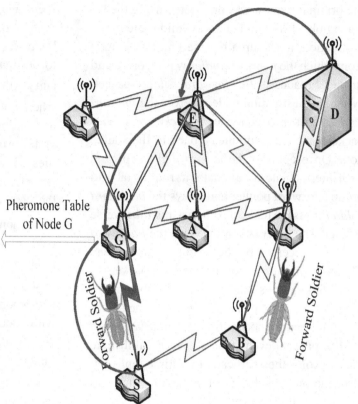

Pheromone Table of Node G

$$T'_{r,s} = T_{r,s} + \tilde{a} \qquad (1)$$

and

$$\tilde{a} = \frac{N}{E - \left(\dfrac{E_{min} - N_j}{E_{av} - N_j} \right)} \qquad (2)$$

where E is the initial energy of the nodes and, E_{min}, E_{av} are the minimum and average energy respectively of the path traversed by the forward soldier as it moves towards the hill. The values of E_{min} and E_{av}, depends on the number of nodes on the path and the energy consumed by the nodes on the path during the transmission and reception of packets. The minimum energy of the path (E_{min}) can be less than the number of nodes

visited by the forward soldier, but the average energy of the path (E_{av}) can never be less than the number of visited nodes. N_j represents the number of nodes that the forward soldier has visited, and N is the total number of network nodes.

Pheromone Evaporation

Pheromone is evaporated so as to build a good solution in the network. Each value in the pheromone table is periodically multiplied by the evaporation factor $e^{-\tilde{n}}$. The evaporation rate is $\tilde{n} \geq 0$. A high evaporation rate will quickly reduce the amount of remaining pheromone, while a low value will degrade the pheromone slowly. The pheromone evaporation interval is one second;

this is called the decay period. Equation (3) describes the pheromone decay.

$$T'_{n,d} = T'_{n,d} * e^{-\tilde{n}} \qquad (3)$$

Applications requiring robustness and flexibility need a slow decay rate, and some applications like security and target tracking applications need a fast decay process. The value of ρ and x in equation (4) depends on the application area. To account for the pheromone decay each value in the pheromone table is periodically subtracted by a percentage of the original value as shown in equation (4).

$$T'_{n,d} = \left(1 - x\right) T'_{n,d} \qquad (4)$$

where $0 \leq x \leq 1$. If all of the pheromone for a particular node has been removed, then the corresponding row and/or column are removed from the pheromone table. The removal of an entry from the pheromone table indicates that no packet has been received from that node for quite some time. It has likely become irrelevant and no route information needs to be maintained. A column (destination) is considered decayed if all of the pheromone in that column is equal to a minimum value. If that particular destination is also a neighbor then it cannot be removed unless all entries in the neighbor row are also decayed. A row is considered decayed if all of the pheromone values on the row are equal to the pheromone floor. Neighbor nodes must be specially handled because they can forward packets as well as originate packets. A decayed column indicates that no traffic has been seen which was sourced by that node. Since neighbors can also forward traffic, their role as traffic sources may become secondary to their role as traffic relays. Thus, the neighbor row must be declared decayed before the neighbor node can be removed from the pheromone table. If a neighbor is determined to

be lost by means of communications failure (the neighbor has left communications range), the neighbor row is simply removed from the pheromone table.

Pheromone Limits

The limit of the pheromone table is bounded by three values which are: (1) the *upper pheromone*, (2) the *lower pheromone*, and (3) the *initial pheromone*. When a data packet is received at a node from the node that is not known to it, an entry for it is created in that receiving node pheromone table. The entries consist of a column and a row. If the information received about the node tells that it is a neighbor, a column in addition to a row is created for it, otherwise, only a row is created in the case that it is not a neighbor. The cells created will be initialized with the initial pheromone values. When pheromone is to be evaporated, the value is never allowed to enter the critical value which is normally the lowest pheromone value. This is done to make sure that nodes that are hardly used are detected. Also, no value is permitted to be more than the upper value. These limits help in safeguarding the pheromone difference from affecting the calculation of the probabilities of the next hop selection. Though, each parameter may be chosen based on the network environments and requirements.

Route Selection

Each of the routing tables of the nodes is initialized with a uniform probability distribution given as

$$P_{s,d} = \frac{1}{N} \qquad (5)$$

where $P_{s,d}$ is the initial probability of each source node, and represents the probability by which an agent at source node s will take to get to node d (destination), and N is the total number of nodes in the network. Equation (6) details the transformation of pheromone for d on link s $T_{s,d}$ into the probability $P_{s,d}$ that the packet will be forwarded to d.

$$P_{s,d} = \frac{(T_{s,d} + \acute{a})^{\hat{a}}}{\sum_{i=1}^{N}(T_{i,d} + \acute{a})^{\hat{a}}} \qquad (6)$$

As shown in Figure 2, the summation of the probabilities of taking all paths leading to the destination node is unity (1). The parameters $\acute{a}$ and $\hat{a}$ are used to fine tune the routing behavior of Termite-hill. The value of $\acute{a}$ determines the sensitivity of the probability calculations to small amounts of pheromone, $\acute{a} \geq 0$ and the real value of $\acute{a}$ is zero. Similarly, $0 \leq \hat{a} \leq 2$ is used to modulate the differences between pheromone amounts, and the real value of $\hat{a}$ is two. For each of the N entries in the node k routing table, it will be N_k (where N_k represents neighboring nodes of node k) values of $P_{s,d}$ subject to the condition:

$$\sum_{s \in N_k} P_{s,d} = 1; \ d = 1, ..., N \qquad (7)$$

Termite-Hill Agent Model and Module Design

The termites evaluate the quality of each discovered path to a hill by the pheromone contents of the pebbles on the path. This means that not all the discovered path receives reinforcement. *Termite-hills* works with three types of agents: reproductive, soldiers and workers. The algorithm is designed to function as three main modules: *route discovery, seed, and data.* The pseudocode describing the operation of the algorithm is divided into four parts as shown in Pseudo-codes 2 to 5.

PERFORMANCE EVALUATION

This section evaluates the performance of the Termite-hill routing algorithm using the Routing Modeling Application Simulation Environment (RMASE) (PARC, 2006; Zhang et al., 2006; Zhang, 2005). RMASE is a simulation framework implemented as an application in the Probabilistic Wireless Network Simulator (PROWLER) (Sztipanovits, 2004). The simulator is written and runs under Matlab, thus providing a fast and easy way to prototype applications and having nice visualization capabilities for the experimental and comparison purposes. The simulation parameters used are as shown in Table 1. We used the following metrics to evaluate the performance.

- **Success Rate:** It is a ratio of total number of events received at the destination to the total number of events generated by the nodes in the sensor network (%).
- **Energy Consumption:** It is the total energy consumed by the nodes in the network during the period of the experiment (Joules).
- **Energy Utilization Efficiency:** It is a measure of the ratio of total packet delivered at the destination to the total energy consumed by the network's sensor nodes (Kbits/Joules).

Performance of Termite-Hill with Static Sink

We evaluated the performance of Termite-hill and compared with other routing protocols with a static sink. In this scenario, we assumed that the sink node is fixed at a particular destination. Figure 3 shows the performance in terms of the success rate of events generated in the network, energy consumption of nodes and energy utiliza-

Code 2. Route discovery pseudocode

```
1.      Required:        A copy of Forward Soldier (FS)
2.      if       (SinkNode)               then
3.                  // Upload Payload and pass to application layer
4.                  PayloadToApplication (FS);
5.                  UpdateForwardingTable (FS.From, NodeID, PathID);
6.                  // Construct a Backward Soldier and forward to FS.From
7.                  BS ← ConstructBackwardSoldier (BS);
8.                  Forward (BS, FS.From);
9.      else if         (NotSeenBefore (FS))          then
10.                 Nj ← FS.Hops ← FS.Hops + 1;
11.                 if       (FS.Hops ≤ Hmax)          then
12.                         // Set Broadcast Flag
13.                         BFlag ← 1;
14.                 else
15.                         BFlag ← StochasticForwarding ();
16.                 end if
17.                 N ← TotalNetworkNodes ← (Node.Total);
18.                 E ← InitialNodesEnergy ← (Node.Energy);
19.                 Emin ← FS.MinEnergy ← Min (FS.MinEnergy, Node.Energy.Min);
20.                 Eav ← FS.AvEnergy ← Av (FS.AvEnergy, Node.Energy.Av);
```

21.
$$2 \leftarrow \frac{N}{E - \left(\dfrac{E_{min} - N_j}{E_{av} - N_j} \right)} ;$$

```
22.                 UpdateSoldierCache (FS.From, FS.SourceID, FS.SoldierID,
BFlag, β);
23.                 if       (BFlag)          then
24.                         Broadcast (FS);
25.                 else
26.                         DeleteForwardSoldier (FS);
27.                 end if
28.         else
29.                 if         (Forwarded(FS))          then
30.                         Nj ← FS.Hops ← FS.Hops + 1;
31.                         Emin ← Min (FS.MinEnergy, Node.Energy.Min);
32.                         Eav ← Av (FS.AvEnergy, Node.Energy.Av);
```

33.
$$2 \leftarrow \frac{N}{E - \left(\dfrac{E'_{min} - N_j}{E_{av} - N_j} \right)} ;$$

```
34.                         if         (β > RewardInSoldierCache
())      then
```

continued on following page

Code 2. Continued

```
35.                         UpdateSoldierCache (FS.From, FS.SourceID, FS.
SoldierID, BFlag, β);
36.                    end if
37.              end if
38.              DeleteForwardSoldier (FS);
39.         end if
```

Code 3. Route update pseudocode

```
1.       Required:        A copy of Backward Soldier (BS)
2.       if        (SourceNode)        then
3.                 T_rs ← CalculatePheromoneValue (BS.Pheromone);
4.                 // Update the pheromone and probability tables
5.                 UpdatePheromoneTable (BS.From, BS.SinkID, BS.PathID, T_rs);
6.                 UpdateProbabilityTable (P_sd);
7.                 DeleteBackwardSoldier (BS);
8.                 // announce path to the neighbors
9.                 BroadcastBeacon ();
10.      else
11.                // Check for matching BS if earlier forwarded
12.                if        (MatchInSoldierCache(BS))        then
13.                    // Update the forwarding table
14.                    UpdateForwardingTable (BS.From, SoldierCache,
PrevHop, BS.PathID);
15.                    Forward (BS, SoldierCache.PrevHop);
16.                    DeleteSoldierCacheEntry (BS);
17.                    BS.Pheromone ← (BS.Pheromone, Path.Pheromone);
18.                else
19.                    DeleteBackwardSoldier (BS);
20.                end if
21.      end if
```

tion efficiency of the respective algorithms with varied network density. In terms of the number of successful packets delivered at the sink node, it was observed that Termite-hill had a maximum success rate when the number of network nodes were still few in number (9 nodes) corresponding to the value of 96.4%. This value decreases a little with an increase in the number of network nodes. When the number of nodes in the network approached the value of 100, the success rate approached 80%. By comparison, the AODV performance is better than SC when the network density increases due to an increase in the number of nodes. At the value of 100 nodes in the network, SC had a success rate of 51% as against 69% of AODV. The poor performance of these two algorithms were due

Code 4. Working group pseudocode

```
1.          Required: A Phenomenon for Transportation to Sink Node
2.     for all          Phenomenon received from Application layer   do
3.               W = Worker ();
4.          if        (W = = NULL)   then
5.                    if       (RouteDiscoveringInProgress())  then
6.                         // Route discovery in progress, wait in
cache
7.                             StorePayloadInCache (P);
8.                    else
9.                         // Route required, initiate forward sol-
dier
10.                            LaunchForwardSoldier (FS);
11.                 end if
12.            else
13.                 //Worker found, forward to next hop
14.                 Forward (W, NextHop);
15.            end if
16.     end for
```

Code 5. Working group at intermediate nodes pseudocode

```
1.          Required:        A Worker
2.     if      SinkNode()            then
3.               PassToApplication (W.P);
4.               AddToWorkersList (W);
5.      else
6.               Next ← GetNextHop (W.PathID);
7.               Forward (W, Next);
8.          end if
```

to flooding of route discovery packets as most of its data packets do not actually get to the sink even when generated by the source nodes. The performance of FF which was designed for high success rate is still below that of Termites-hill as shown in Figure 3. In overall, the Termite-hill performance was higher in terms of high reliability (high success rate) and its performance in terms of energy consumption was better than the other algorithms, making it the most energy efficient.

The Termite-hill algorithm achieved both high packet successful delivery and energy utilization efficiency as compared to SC, FF, and AODV due to some of its important features. First, the launching of its soldier carrying the first generated event would in most cases be able to find routes to the destination in the first attempt. Second, it makes use of restrictive flooding which results in quick convergence of the algorithm. Third, it maintains a small event cache to queue events while route discovery is in progress. Fourth, it

Table 1. Simulation parameters

Parameters	Values
Routing Protocol	SC, FF, AODV, Termite-hill
Size of Topology (A)	100 x 100
Distribution of Nodes	Random distribution
Number of Nodes (N)	100
Maximum number of Retransmission (n)	3
Transmission Range (R)	35 m
Data Traffic	Constant Bit Rate (CBR)
Data Rate	250 kbps
Propagation model	Probabilistic
Energy consumption	Waspmote-802.15.4
Time of topology change	2 s
Simulation Time	360s
Average Simulation times	10

utilizes a simple packet switching model in which intermediate nodes do not perform complex routing table lookup as in other schemes. Rather packets are switched using a simple forwarding table at a faster rate, and fifth, the updating rule takes into consideration the path energy, hence the probability of route selection is also a function of the paths remaining energy.

Performance of Termite-Hill with a Dynamic Sink

In this section, we evaluate the performance of Termite-hill with other routing algorithms in a dynamic network. In this scenario, we also assumed that the sink can change its location at any given time. The change is not along a path, but in any direction making it different from the mobility scenario. This is a target tracking scenario. The target in the region of interest has to be monitored, but sometimes, it gets out of the transmission range of almost all the nodes and the use of a dynamic sink becomes very important. Also, sensor nodes would need fewer hops to get

to the sink so as to reduce energy consumption. We simulated the algorithms over long duration of time with fixed speed of sink as shown in Figure 4. In this scenario, Termite-hill performance in terms of successful packet delivery was still higher than the other algorithms. With its high packet delivery rate, Termite-hill had the highest energy utilization efficiency as compared to all the algorithms. To further test its performance, we adapted all the routing algorithms in the dynamic scenario with varying network density as shown in Figure 4. In this case, Termite-hill performance in terms of successful packet delivery rate and energy utilization efficiency is higher, with less energy consumption. It will also be observed that though the success rate of each of the routing protocols tends to decrease with an increasing number of network nodes, the energy consumption of all the algorithms also increases as more packets are delivered at the sink node since the average remaining energy keeps on dropping. The poor performance of FF in terms of high energy consumption is due to its pure flooding of Route Request (RREQ) packets (ants), which make it to have unnecessary overhead in the network.

CONCLUSION AND FUTURE WORKS

This chapter proposed the application of the termite colony optimization metaheuristic to solve the routing problem in wireless sensor networks. A basic termite based routing protocol was proposed. Several factors and improvements inspired by the features of wireless sensor networks (low energy level, low memory and processing capabilities) were considered and implemented. The resulting routing protocol termed Termite-hill was designed to function in three modules: route discovery, route maintenance and data packet module. The algorithm uses backward and forward soldiers for route discovery and updating between the sensor nodes and the sink node, which are optimized in terms of the distance and energy level of each

Figure 3. Performance evaluation in static scenario among routing protocols: (a) Success rate (b) Energy consumption (c) Energy Efficiency

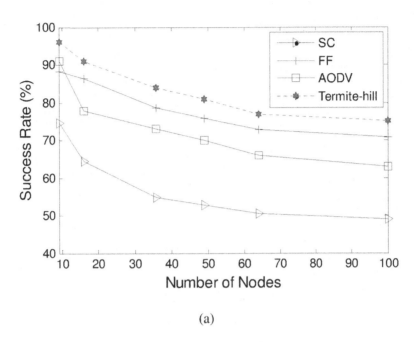

(a)

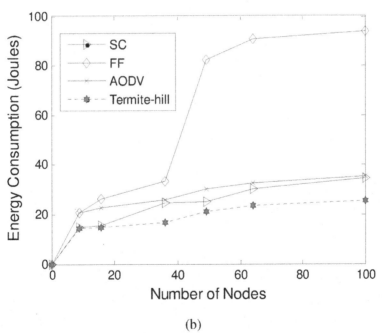

(b)

Figure 4. Performance evaluation in Target tracking scenario among routing protocols: (a) Success rate (b) Energy consumption (c) Energy Efficiency

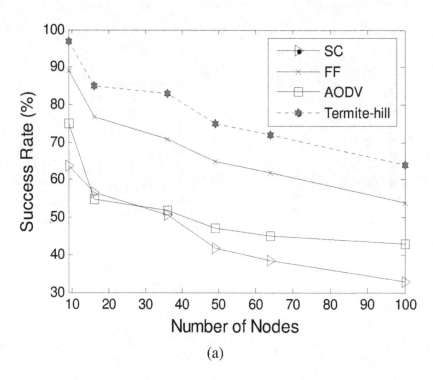

(a)

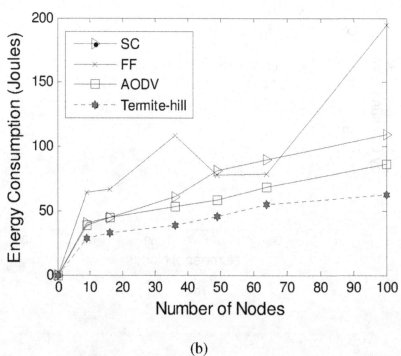

(b)

path. The algorithm minimizes network overhead by on-demand routing, and maximizes network reliability and energy savings, which contribute to improving the lifetime of the sensor network. The experimental results showed that the algorithm leads to very good results in different network scenarios and the algorithm is scalable, robust and more energy efficient in comparison with other routing protocols.

REFERENCES

Akyildiz, I. F., Su, W., Sankarasubramaniam, Y., & Cayirci, E. (2002). Wireless sensor networks: A survey. *Computer Networks*, *38*(4), 393–422. doi:10.1016/S1389-1286(01)00302-4

Bonabeau, E., Dorigo, M., & Theraulaz, G. (1999). *Swarm intelligence: From natural to artificial systems*. London, UK: Oxford University Press.

Buttyan, L., & Hubaux, J.-P. (2000). Enforcing service availability in mobile ad-hoc WANs. In Mobile and Ad Hoc Networking and Computing, (pp. 87-96). doi:10.1109/MOBHOC.2000.869216

Camilo, T., Carreto, C., Silva, J. S., & Boavida, F. (2006). An energy-efficient ant based routing algorithm for wireless sensor networks. In *Proceedings of 5th International Workshop on Ant Colony Optimization and Swarm Intelligence*, (pp. 49-59). Academic Press.

Çelik, F., Zengin, A., & Tuncel, S. (2010). A survey on swarm intelligence based routing protocols in wireless sensor networks. *International Journal of the Physical Sciences*, *5*(14), 2118–2126.

Dorigo, M., & Di Caro, G. (1998). AntNet: Distributed stigmergetic control for communications networks. *Journal of Artificial Intelligence Research*, *9*, 317–365.

Dorigo, M., Di Caro, G., & Gambardella, L. M. (1999). Ant Algorithms for Discrete Optimization. *Artificial Life*, *5*(2), 137–172. doi:10.1162/106454699568728 PMID:10633574

Heusse, S. G., Snyers, D., & Kuntz, P. (1998). *Adaptive Agent-driven Routing and Load Balancing. Communication Networks* (Technical Report RR-98001-IASC). Department Intelligence Artificielle et Sciences Cognitives, ENST Bretagne.

Hölldobler, B., & Wilson, E. O. (1990). The Ant. Harvard University Press.

Lawson, B. J., & Lewis, J. (2004). Representation emerges from coupled behavior. In *Self-Organization, Emergence, and Representation Workshop, Genetic and Evolutionary Computation Conference Proceedings*. Springer-Verlag.

Li, K., Torres, C. E., Thomas, K., Rossi, L. F., & Shen, C.-C. (2011). Slime mold inspired routing protocols for wireless sensor networks. *Swarm Intelligence*, *5*(3-4), 183–223. doi:10.1007/s11721-011-0063-y

MacKenzie, A. B., & Wicker, S. B. (2001). Game theory in communications: motivation, explanation, and application to power control. In *Proceedings of GLOBECOM'01, IEEE Global Telecommunications Conference*, (vol. 2, pp. 821-826). IEEE.

Matthews, R. W., & Mattheus, J. R. (1942). *Insect Behavior*. New York: Wiley-Interscience.

Merloti, P. E. (2004). Optimization algorithms inspired by biological ants and swarm behavior. San Diego State University.

Olugbemi, B. O. (2010). Influence of food on recruitment pattern in the termite, Microcerotermes fuscotibialis. *Journal of insect science (Online)*, *10*(154), 1–10. doi:10.1673/031.010.14114 PMID:20569122

PARC. (2006). RMASE: Routing Modeling Application Simulation Environment. Available at http://webs.cs.berkeley.edu/related.html

Perkins, C., & Royer, E. (1999). Ad-hoc on-demand distance vector routing. In *Proceedings of Second IEEE Workshop on Mobile Computing Systems and Applications* (pp. 90-100). IEEE. doi:10.1109/MCSA.1999.749281

Ramos, V., & Almeida, F. (2000). Artificial ant colonies in digital image habitats – A mass behavior effect study on pattern recognition. In *Proceedings of ANTS'2000, 2nd International Workshop on Ant Algorithms,* (pp. 113-116). ANTS.

Reinhard, J., & Kaib, M. (2001). Trail communication during foraging and recruitment in the subterranean termite Reticulitermes santonensis De Feytaud (Isoptera, Rhinotermitidae). *Journal of Insect Behavior, 14*(2), 157–171. doi:10.1023/A:1007881510237

Resnick, M. (1994). Learning About Life. *Artificial Life, 1*(1-3), 229–242.

Resnick, M. (1997). *Turtles, termites, and traffic jams: Explorations in massively parallel microworlds.* Cambridge, MA: MIT Press.

Roth, M., & Wicker, S. (2003). Termite: Ad-hoc networking with stigmergy. In *Proceedings of GLOBECOM '03, IEEE Global Telecommunications Conference* (vol. 5, pp. 2937-2941). IEEE.

Saleem, M., Di Caro, G. A., & Farooq, M. (2011). Swarm intelligence based routing protocol for wireless sensor networks: Survey and future directions. *Information Sciences, 181*(20), 4597–4624. doi:10.1016/j.ins.2010.07.005

Saleem, M., & Farooq, M. (2005). Beesensor: A bee-inspired power aware routing algorithms. In Proceedings EvoCOMNET (LNCS) (vol. 3449, pp. 136-146). Berlin: Springer.

Semet, Y., O'Reilly, U., & Durand, F. (2004). An interactive artificial ant approach to non-photorealistic rendering. In Proceedings of GECCO 2004, (LNCS) (vol. 3102, pp. 188-200). Berlin: Springer.

Sztipanovits, J. (2004). Probabilistic wireless network simulator (Prowler). Retrieved from http://www.isis.vanderbilt.edu/Projects/nest/prowler/

Turner, J. S. (2011). Termites as models of swarm cognition. *Swarm Intelligence, 5*(1), 19–43. doi:10.1007/s11721-010-0049-1

Zhang, Y. (2005). Routing Modeling Application Simulation Environment (RMASE). Available at https://docs.google.com/file/d/0B-29IhEITY3bb-GY2VVo2SGxxRFE/edit

Zhang, Y., Kuhn, L. D., & Fromherz, M. P. J. (2004). Improvements on ant routing for sensor networks. In M. Dorigo, et al. (Eds.), ANTS 2004, (LNCS) (vol. 3172, pp. 154–165). Berlin: Springer. doi:10.1007/978-3-540-28646-2_14

Zhang, Y., Simon, G., & Balogh, G. (2006). High-level sensor network simulations for routing performance evaluations. In *Proceedings of 3rd International Conference on Networked Sensing Systems.* Chicago: Academic Press.

Zungeru, A. M., Ang, L.-M., & Seng, K. P. (2012a). Performance of termite-hill routing algorithm on sink mobility in wireless sensor networks. In Advances in Swarm Intelligence, (LNCS) (vol. 7332, pp. 334-343). Berlin: Springer.

Zungeru, A. M., Ang, L.-M., & Seng, K. P. (2012b). Classical and swarm intelligence based routing protocols for wireless sensor networks. *Journal of Network and Computer Applications, 35*(5), 1508–1536. doi:10.1016/j.jnca.2012.03.004

KEY TERMS AND DEFINITIONS

Dynamic Sink: In a dynamic sink scenario, the sink can change its location at any given time. This can also be described as a target tracking scenario.

Pheromone: These are chemical scents used by insects to direct each other through their environment. Individual insects leave a trail of such scents, which stimulates other insects to follow that trail, dropping pheromones while doing so.

Routing: In a network which consists of hundreds or thousands of nodes, the role of a routing protocol is to identify or discover one or more paths connecting a pair of nodes under a given set of constraints. The discovered paths can then be used for information exchange.

Static Sink: In a static sink scenario, the sink node is always in a fixed position. All the traffic destined to it must pass through the nodes closer to it, which will make them to deplete their energy resources faster.

Stigmergy: This is the indirect communications between individuals of the social insect, generally through their environment. Complexity in stigmergic systems is due to the fact that individuals do not interact directly with each other but rather they do so through their environment.

Wireless Sensor Network: A wireless sensor network is a collection of nodes organized into a cooperative network. Each node consists of processing capability (e.g. microcontrollers), memory, a RF transceiver, a power source (e.g., batteries and solar cells), and accommodate various sensors and actuators.

Chapter 10
Coverage Path Planning Using Mobile Robot Team Formations

Prithviraj Dasgupta
University of Nebraska – Omaha, USA

ABSTRACT

The multi-robot coverage path-planning problem involves finding collision-free paths for a set of robots so that they can completely cover the surface of an environment. This problem is non-trivial as the geometry and location of obstacles in the environment is usually not known a priori by the robots, and they have to adapt their coverage path as they discover obstacles while moving in the environment. Additionally, the robots have to avoid repeated coverage of the same region by each other to reduce the coverage time and energy expended. This chapter discusses the research results in developing multi-robot coverage path planning techniques using mini-robots that are coordinated to move in formation. The authors present theoretical and experimental results of the proposed approach using e-puck mini-robots. Finally, they discuss some preliminary results to lay the foundation of future research for improved coverage path planning using coalition game-based, structured, robot team reconfiguration techniques.

INTRODUCTION

Automated exploration of an unknown environment using a multi-robot system is an important topic within robotics that is relevant in several applications of robotic systems. These applications include automated reconnaissance and surveillance operations, automated inspection of engineering structures, and even domestic applications such as automated lawn mowing and vacuum cleaning. An integral part of robotic exploration is coverage path planning - how to enable robots to cover an initially unknown environment using a distributed terrain or area coverage algorithm. The coverage algorithm should ensure that every portion of the environment is covered by the coverage sensor or tool of at least one robot. Simultaneously, to ensure that the coverage is efficient, the coverage algorithm should prevent robots from repeatedly covering the same regions that have already been covered by themselves or by other robots. In most of the current multi-robot area coverage techniques, each robot performs and coordinates its motion individually. While individual coverage has shown promising results in many domains, there are a significant number of scenarios for multi-robot exploration such as

DOI: 10.4018/978-1-4666-6328-2.ch010

extra-terrestrial exploration, robotic demining, unmanned search and rescue, etc., where the system can perform more efficiently if multiple robots with different types of sensors or redundant arrays of sensors can remain together as single or multiple cohesive teams (Cassinis, 2000; Chien *et al.*, 2005; De Mot, 2005). For example, in the domain of robotic demining (Bloch, Milisavljevc & Acheroy, 2007), where autonomous robots are used to detect buried landmines, the incidence of false positive readings from underground landmines can be significantly reduced if robots with different types of sensors such as ground penetrating radar (GPR), IR (infra-red) sensors and metal detectors are able to simultaneously analyze the signals from potential landmines. In such a scenario, it would benefit if robots, each provided with one of these sensors, are able to explore the environment while maneuvering themselves together as a team. Multi-robot formation control techniques provide a suitable mechanism to build teams of robots that maintain and dynamically reconfigure their formation, while avoiding obstacles along their path (Mastellone, Stipanovic, Graunke, Intlekofer & Spong, 2008; Olfati Saber, 2006; Smith, Egerstedt & Howard, 2009). However, these techniques are not principally concerned with issues related to area coverage and coverage efficiency. To address this deficit, in this paper, we investigate whether multi-robot formation control techniques and multi-robot area coverage techniques can be integrated effectively to improve the efficiency of the area coverage operation in an unknown environment by maintaining teams of multiple robots.

Recently, miniature robots that have a small footprint size are being used for applications such as automated exploration of engineering structures (Rutishauser, Corell & Martinoli, 2009; Tache *et al.*, 2009). Similarly, unmanned aerial vehicles (UAVs) and micro-helicopters that have memory and computation capabilities comparable to these mini-robots are being widely used in several domains such as aerial reconnaissance

for homeland security, search and rescue following natural disasters, monitoring forest fires, wildlife monitoring, etc (Boccalate *et al.*, 2013). Mini-robots are attractive because they are relatively inexpensive to field and a swarm of several mini-robots can be fielded at a cost comparable to fielding one or a few large robots. A multi-robot system that consists of several mini-robots also improves the robustness of the system. However, coordinating the actions of mini-robots to make them work cooperatively (e.g., move in formation) in a distributed manner becomes a challenging problem. We have approached this problem using a flocking-based technique (Gokce & Sahin, 2009; Balch & Arkin, 1998) to control the movement of robots so that they can move in formation. We have theoretically analyzed our team-formation techniques and identified certain conditions under which team formation improves the efficiency of distributed area coverage. We have also verified our techniques through extensive experiments on the Webots robotic simulation platform as well as using physical robots within an indoor environment. Our analytical and experimental results show that our team-based coverage techniques for distributed area coverage can perform comparably with other coverage strategies where the robots are coordinated individually. We also show that various parameters of the system such as the size of the robot teams, the presence of localization noise and wheel slip noise (error in the wheel's encoder readings caused by the slippage of the wheels on the floor), as well as environment-related features like the size of the environment and the presence of obstacles and walls significantly affect the performance of the area coverage operation. Finally, we discuss a promising future direction to improve the quality of coverage by multi-robot teams by using a coalition game-based technique for systematically restructuring robots teams through splitting and merging, based on the geometry of obstacles perceived by the robots while moving in the environment.

BACKGROUND

Much of the formation control research with multi-robot teams (Bahceci, Soysal & Sahin, 2003; Gokce & Sahin, 2009; Olfati Saber 2006; Sahin & Zergeroglu, 2008; Turgut, Celikkanat, Gokce & Sahin, 2008) has been based on Reynolds' model for the mobility of flocks (Reynolds, 1987). Reynolds prescribes three fundamental operations for each team member to realize flocking - *separation, alignment* and *cohesion*. In the flocking model, each robot in a robot team adapts its motion and position based on the current position and heading of other team members such as a team leader or an immediate neighbor(s). This allows the robot team to remain in formation while moving as well as adapt its formation while avoiding obstacles. Following Reynolds' model, Chen & Luh (1994) and Wang (1989) describe mechanisms for robot-team motion while maintaining specific formations where individual robots determine their motion strategies from the movement of a team leader or neighbor(s). In (Balch & Arkin, 1998), the authors describe three reactive behavior-based strategies for robot teams to move in formation, viz., unit-center-referenced, neighbor-referenced, or leader-referenced. In contrast to these approaches, Fredslund & Mataric (2002) describe techniques for robot team formation without using global knowledge such as robot locations, or the positions/headings of other robots, while using little communication between robots. Smith, Egerstedt & Howard (2009) have used a combination of graph theory and control theory-based techniques to effect multi-robot formations. Complementary to these approaches Spears, Kerr & Spears (2006) have used physics-based approaches to form and navigate multi-robot teams. More recently, a technique based on a method called Voronoi Fast Marching (VFM) that determines the path and motion constraints for a team of robots moving in formation by propagating a wave over the robots' workspace represented as a viscosity map has been proposed (Garrido, Morena & Lima, 2011). Fine

and Shell (Fine & Shell, 2011) propose a technique for navigating robot flocks guided by Hamilton's aggregation rule (Hamilton, 1971) while using low level sensor data from a laser sensor to maintain the flock's formation constraints. However, in most of these approaches, the main objective is to achieve and maintain a certain formation and not to ensure the efficiency of tasks, like area coverage, being performed by the robots.

Distributed area coverage of an unknown environment using a multi-robot system has been an active area of research for over a decade and excellent overviews of this area are given in (Choset, 2001; Stachniss, Mozos & Burgard, 2008, Galceran & Carreras, 2013). Subsequently, several techniques for multi-robot coverage such as using Boustrophedon decomposition (Rekleitis, New, Rankin & Choset, 2008; Mannadiar & Rekleitis, 2010), using occupancy grid maps (Burgard, Moors, Fox, Simmons & Thrun, 2005), using probabilistic Bayesian models of the coverage map, information gain-based heuristics and graph segmentation techniques (Wurm, Stachniss & Burgard, 2008), ant-based coverage algorithms (Koenig, Szymanski & Liu, 2001; Wagner, Altshuler, Yanovski & Bruckstein, 2008) have also been proposed. Tzanov (Tzanov, 2006) provides techniques that can be used by a group of robots to cover an initially unknown environment using either a frontier expansion method when the robots have perfect localization, or, using depth first traversal proceeding along triangulations of the environment when the robots localize themselves only with respect to each other. Several techniques have been proposed in literature where robots incrementally build a map of the environment, using a graph traversal technique (Gabriely & Rimon, 2001) and store the map either within the memory of each robot (Cheng & Dasgupta, 2007, Kaminka, Schechter & Sadov, 2008; Rutishauser, Correll & Martinoli, 2009) or at a central location that can be accessed by all robots (Koenig, Szymanski & Liu, 2001). Recently, authors (Puig, Garcia & Wu, 2011) have proposed a multi-robot exploration strategy that improves on previously existing techniques by balancing the frequency with which different regions of the environment are explored by the robots, using a K-means based region-partitioning algorithm. However, in this technique the robots do not maintain formation while exploring the environment. The problem of robotic exploration of initially unknown areas has also been addressed by deploying local sensor tags in the environment by robots which facilitate the information exchange and coordination between robots for the exploration task (Ferranti, Trigoni & Levene, 2009). Xu (Xu, 2011) presented a technique for coverage planning in environments that can be represented as graphs while allowing for dynamic replanning of paths due to obstacles encountered along the graph edges. Most of the existing literature on robotic coverage requires robots to cover the environment while minimizing the overlap between their covered regions. In contrast, authors have recently addressed problem of repeated coverage under different constraints such as the environment's representation and the robots' perception range (Fazli, Davoodi & Mackworth, 2013). They propose graph-based coverage algorithms where the environment is partitioned into overlapping regions called clusters with one cluster allocated to each robot. Robots then calculate the shortest tour through the clusters and successively visit the clusters to perform repeated coverage. However, these works principally focus on controlling robots individually and designing different coordination strategies between them so that the robots can cover the environment while reducing repeated coverage among the regions covered by different robots. In contrast, our work focuses on achieving area coverage while coordinating teams of robots in a distributed manner instead of coordinating each robot's movements individually.

Recently, robotic exploration of unknown environments has also been successfully demonstrated for several robot platforms and domains such as constructing bathymetric maps and area coverage for under-water exploration (Galceran & Carreras, 2013; Yan & Zhu, 2011), aerial surveillance using unmanned aerial vehicles (Xu, Virie & Rekleitis, 2011), inspection of complex structures (Englot & Hover, 2012), and cooperative localization by a robot team using a leap-frog mechanism (Tully, Kantor & Choset, 2010). The techniques discussed in this chapter for mini-robots could also be adapted to larger robot platforms that are suitable for the different application domains mentioned above.

MULTI-ROBOT DISTRIBUTED AREA COVERAGE

We consider a scenario where R mobile robots are deployed into an initially unknown two-dimensional environment. Without loss of generality, we assume that the environment is a square with each side of length D. The obstacles in the environment are assumed to be convex shaped. and the location of these obstacles are not known initially by the robots. Let O be the area within the environment that is inaccessible to the robots because those areas are either occupied by obstacles or too tight for a single robot to fit into. The area of the environment to be covered by robots is given by $D^2 - O$ sq. units. Each robot is equipped with a square coverage tool with a width $d << D$. We define the duration of a single timestep as the time required by a robot to travel a distance equal to the length of its own footprint measured in the direction of its motion. Let a_r^t denote the action performed by a robot $r \in R$ during a timestep t that results in the robot's motion. Let c_r^t denote the corresponding area covered by robot r's coverage tool because of its motion during the timestep t. The objective of the distributed area coverage problem is to find a sequence of actions for each robot that ensures the following criteria:

- **Maximum Coverage Criterion:** The area of the environment covered by the coverage tool of at least one robot is maximized, i.e., $max\{\cup_{r \in R} \cup_{t=1...T} c_r^t\} \cap \{D^2 - O\}$.

- **Minimum Overlap Criterion:** The overlap between the regions covered by different robots is minimized, i.e., $min \cap_{r \in R} \cap_{t=1...T} c_r^t$. This criterion ensures that the system performs efficiently and robots do not expend time and energy to revisit regions that have already been covered by other robots.

- **Distributed Behavior Criterion:** Each robot should determine its actions autonomously, in a completely distributed manner, so that the system can be scalable and robust.

Each robot in our system is a two-wheeled robot equipped with forward-facing distance sensors to avoid obstacles and is capable of wireless communication. Each robot is also provided with a local positioning system (a GPS node in the simulator or an overhead camera-based positioning system in the physical experiments) to determine its position in the environment.

Team Representation

We have defined a robot team as a set of robots (>=2) that are able to navigate within an environment while avoiding obstacles and while preserving the team's shape and configuration. The essential parameters related to a robot team are described as follows: (1) Team Leader. Our robot team formation technique is inspired by the leader-referenced motion described in Reynolds' flocking model (Reynolds, 1987). In the leader referenced motion, one robot in a team of robots is selected as the leader. The leader robot guides the motion of the rest of the robots in the team by communicating its direction of movement to all other team members. A robot that is not the team leader is called a follower robot. (2) Team Position Identifiers. To interact with the follower robots in a team, each leader robot assigns a local

position identifier to each robot within the team. The leader robot's position identifier is 0, robots to the left of the leader robot are assigned odd integer identifiers starting from 1, while robots to the right of the leader robot are assigned even integer identifiers starting from 2. (3) Team Shape. To enable efficient movement of a team, the number of follower robots that are located on either side of a leader robot in a team are equally balanced. The angular separation between the two sets of followers robots, denoted by $u \in [0,\pi]$, denotes the shape of the team, where u is measured in radians. When $u = 0$, the team is organized into a vertical line-shape, when $u = \pi$, the team is organized into a horizontal line-shape, and when $0 \leq u \leq \pi$, we get a V-shape formation in the team, as shown in Figure 1. (4) Team Configuration. To maintain the shape of the team while in motion, each robot has to ensure that its relative position within the team does not change when the team moves. To achieve this, every pair of robots in the team maintains a separation of d_{sep} units between each other.

Single-Team Flocking

In our single-team flocking technique, the leader robot communicates the direction it is moving as the prescribed direction of motion for each fol-

Figure 1. A robot team showing the position identifiers of each robot. The angular separation in the team is u, the separation between adjacent robots is d_{sep} and α is the heading of the team.

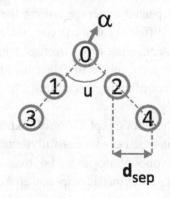

lower robot in the team. Each follower robot then attempts to move in the prescribed direction. If any follower robot fails to move in this direction, it stops and communicates to the leader robot that its motion failed. Depending on the position of the follower robot in the team and its attempted direction of motion, the team leader then selects a new direction of motion that would possibly allow the affected follower robot to avoid the obstruction in its path. The team leader then broadcasts this newly selected direction as the prescribed direction for the next time step to all the follower robots in the team. In some scenarios, due to communication noise, a follower robot might fail to receive the communication containing the prescribed direction of motion from the leader robot. Then the follower robot just continues to move in the same direction it moved during its previous time step. The pseudo-code algorithm used by a team of robots in the leader-referenced motion strategy is described in Figure 2.

Formation Maintenance: When a team of robots moves in formation, the wheel slip noise and encoder readings can cause one or more of the team members to lose their desired positions which destroys the configuration in the team. To address this problem, a leader robot uses a dynamic formation maintenance protocol to ensure that each follower robot retains its position in the team. In this protocol, the team leader first calculates the desired positions (DP_i) of every follower robot i relative to its own position and sends it to follower robot i. Each follower robot i compares its desired position DP_i with its actual position AP_i. A follower robot i adjusts its speed (move faster or slower) proportionally to $\|AP_i - DP_i\|$ so that it can reach its desired position and maintain the configuration of the team. The calculation of DP_i for follower robot i is given below. In these formulae, the actual position AP_i is represented by (x_{AP_i}, y_{AP_i}), the desired position DP_i is represented by (x_{DP_i}, y_{DP_i}), α is the direction of motion of the team, u is the angular separation

Figure 2. Algorithm used by a robot to realize the leader-referenced formation control

```
function LeaderReferencedMotion
    ac^{t-1} ← action(movement direction) performed during
                last time step t - 1;
    if (I am not the leader)
        Ac_{leader} ← movement direction received from leader;
        if (Ac_{leader} ≠ NULL)
            ac^t ← Ac_{leader};
        else ac^t ← ac^{t-1}
        execute ac^t;
        if (ac^t fails due to obstacle)
            STOP;
        sendMessage (MotionFailed, local id in team, leader);
    else // I am the leader
        ac^t ← ac^{t-1}
        execute ac^t;
        if (ac^t fails due to obstacle)
            STOP;
            broadcastMessage (selectNewLeader);
        if (received MotionFailed message from follower robot)
            newAction ← An new direction of motion that will
                allow the follower robot to avoid the obstacle
                in the next step
            ac^t ← newAction;
            broadcastMessage(nextAction, ac^t);
```

in the team, d_{sep} is the linear separation between adjacent robots and i is the local identifier of a follower robot in a team:

Case 1: $0 \leq a < \pi$

$$x_{DP_i} = \begin{cases} x_{AP_i} - \dfrac{i}{2} \times d_{sep} \times \cos(\alpha - \dfrac{u}{2}) \text{ if } i \text{ is odd} \\ x_{AP_i} + \dfrac{i}{2} \times d_{sep} \times \cos(\alpha - \dfrac{u}{2}) \text{if } i \text{ is even} \end{cases}$$

$$y_{DP_i} = y_{AP_i} - \frac{i}{2} \times d_{sep} \times \sin\left(\alpha - \frac{u}{2}\right)$$

Case 2: $\pi < a \leq 2\pi$

$$x_{DP_i} = \begin{cases} x_{AP_i} + \dfrac{i}{2} \times d_{sep} \times \cos(\alpha - \dfrac{u}{2}) \text{ if } i \text{ is odd} \\ x_{AP_i} - \dfrac{i}{2} \times d_{sep} \times \cos(\alpha - \dfrac{u}{2}) \text{if } i \text{ is even} \end{cases}$$

$$y_{DP_i} = y_{AP_i} + \frac{i}{2} \times d_{sep} \times \sin(\alpha - \frac{u}{2})$$

Team Reconfiguration: A leader robot that encounters an obstacle ahead of it will fail to move in its direction of motion. In such a scenario, the team leader stops and communicates to the follower robots to stop moving. Then, the leader robot selects a new leader. If the obstacle is encountered by the old leader using its forward-facing distance sensors on its righthand (lefthand) side going clockwise from current heading, then the follower robot that is farthest from the leader on its lefthand (righthand) side is selected as the new leader. If the old leader robot approaches the obstacle orthogonally resulting in comparable readings on both pairs of the forward-facing (left and right) distance sensors, then one of the two follower robots that is farthest from the old leader robot and has the lowest identifier is selected to become the new leader. Sometimes a team of robots may end up in a tight space such as concave shape where two walls of an obstacle converge. Such scenarios are difficult for reformation because the team is surrounded by obstacles on both its left and right sides. To handle such scenarios, when the leader robot encounters an obstacle the entire team stops and all the robots in the team back up a certain distance by reversing the direction of rotation of their wheels but not changing their heading. The team attempts to reform only after backing up a fixed distance after none of the robots in the team pick up an obstacle on their IR proximity sensors.

A scenario illustrating team reconfiguration is shown in Figure 3. One of the principal objectives of the team reconfiguration is to enable rapid reconfiguration of the team when the leader encounters an obstacle. To enable this, the follower robots between and including the new and old leader robots do not change their relative position in the team while reconfiguring (Figure 3(b)). The old leader then calculates the relative positions of the remaining follower robots in the new team so that the sum of the distances traveled by these robots to get into their desired positions under the new team leader is minimized. (Figure

3(c)). It then communicates these desired positions to the respective follower robots. The new leader robot also selects a new heading for itself and the team based on a Braitenberg controller that uses the perceived location of the obstacle on the old leader robot's sensor and calculates an appropriate turning angle to ensure that the team turns away from the obstacle and does not encounter it again after forming a new team The new leader robot adds a certain amount of random noise to the new direction calculated by the Braitenberg controller - if α is the turning angle calculated, it selects a value in the range of $\alpha \pm \beta$, where $\beta \in$ U[0, 10] degrees.

In certain scenarios, the obstacles encountered by the robot team might have a complex shape. This can result in the desired positions of one or more the follower robots being unreachable or being occupied by an obstacle and the robots might have to re-attempt several times, perhaps unsuccessfully to get into the desired configuration. To avoid repeated looping by the follower robots to get into their desired position and thereby reduce the stoppage time of the team following reconfiguration, the new leader and the follower robots do not wait to get into their new positions before start to move as a new team. Instead, as soon as the new leader robot reaches its desired position, it starts to move in its new direction. If the path of the follower robots to their desired positions while reconfiguring is occluded or occupied by an obstacle, the robots attempt to avoid the obstacle by turning away from the obstacle using the perceived location of the obstacle from their IR distance sensors, moving a random distance away from the obstacle, and reattempting to resume its desired motion as the team. The new leader robot adjusts its speed to give the follower robots that have not yet reached their desired positions more time to catch up with the rest of the team. After starting to move in its new direction, the new leader updates and communicates the desired positions of the follower robots so that they can move directly

Figure 3. (a) The leader robot (id=0) in a team of five robots encounters an obstacle. (b) A new leader is selected (id=3); robots (id=2, 4) are the robots that have to move the minimum distance to get into the new formation (c) New robot id-s are assigned and the new leader robot selects its heading from randomly between −α±β.

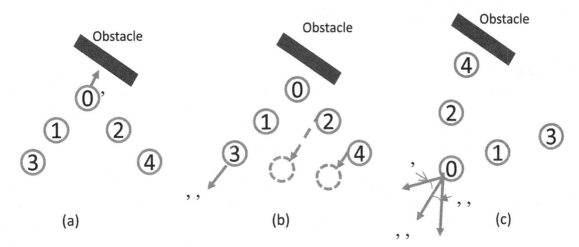

towards their new position and retain the formation of the new team. Finally, if the new leader is unable to reach its desired position after repeated tries, it aborts the movement and attempts to go in a direction in which it does not perceive any obstacles. It moves for a random distance in this new direction and tries to reform the team from its new position.

Single-Team Coverage Technique

After a team of multiple robots is assimilated using the technique described above, the next step is to enable the team to cover the environment using a coverage technique. The coverage technique for a robot team is implemented by the team's leader robot. Each robot in the team, including the leader robot records the coordinates of the locations it has covered over the last H time steps within a data structure called its coverage history. Each follower robot communicates this coverage information at intervals of H time steps to the leader robot. The finite size H of the coverage information recorded makes the coverage technique amenable to implementation within on-board memory limitations of

robots. To combine the coverage information of the team, the leader robot uses a node counting technique (Koenig, Szymanski & Liu, 2001). In the node-counting technique, the leader robot uses a data structure called a coverage map that contains the locations or coordinates visited by itself and the follower robots. Each location is associated with a real number that is initialized to zero. Every time a location appears in the coverage history of the leader robot or one of the follower robots, the number associated with the location is incremented. This results in the formation of a landscape within the leader robot's coverage map. Locations associated with large number or a 'high altitude' on this landscape indicate regions that have been covered multiple times, while regions with a smaller number or zero associated with them denote infrequently visited and unvisited regions respectively. To navigate the team, the leader robot selects a direction that will take it towards the lowest (least covered) point on this coverage landscape. A detailed description of the coverage technique used by the team leader to navigate a single team is given in (Cheng & Dasgupta, 2007). When the leader robot of a team has to change because the team encountered an obstacle, the old leader robot communicates its coverage history to the new leader robot so that it can continue efficient coverage without re-covering regions already covered by the team in its previous configuration.

Multi-Team Distributed Coverage Technique

The single-team coverage technique described above provides a mechanism for multiple robots to move together as a single team. However, when team sizes are large (for example, greater than 10 robots per team), it becomes challenging for the robots to maintain the configuration of the follower robots in the team because of frequent reformations of the team to avoid obstacles, and the motion and communication noise in the follower robots. To prevent the formation of large teams, we limit the maximum allowable size of a team to T_{max} robots. We then use multiple teams to perform the coverage operation in the environment.

These multiple teams of robots need to be co-ordinated appropriately, in a distributed manner, to ensure that each team covers the environment efficiently while reducing the overlap of regions previously covered by that and other teams. We have used a *potential field-based navigation* strategy that also uses the recent coverage history of the teams' leader robots to enable multiple teams navigate themselves and perform coverage of the environment. In this strategy, each leader robot of a team has a *virtual potential field* of radius χ_r around it. When the leader robots of two teams get within the communication range χ_r of each other the leader robots of the teams exchange their current coverage maps, including the maps received from their respective follower robots, with each other. They then fuse each other's coverage information using the node counting technique described in the previous section. Finally, each team leader selects the region that closest to its team that has been least visited, and adjusts its heading to

move towards that region. The pseudo-code of the algorithm for implementing the multi-team coverage technique is shown in Figure 4.

ANALYSIS

In this section, we investigate analytically whether area coverage using multiple robots organized as a team is more efficient than an area coverage technique that uses the same number of robots that are not configured into teams and perform coverage individually. We refer to this latter scenario as coverage with individually coordinated robots. Using the notation introduced in the section titles "Multi-Robot Distributed Area Coverage", we consider a square environment where D is the length of a side of a square, O is the area within the environment occupied by obstacles and $d << D$ is the width of the coverage tool of a robot. We let D_{free} denote the area of the free space in the environment that needs to be covered by the robots, i.e., $D_{free} = D^2 - O$, As mentioned before, the values of D, O and D_{free} are unknown to each robot. To simplify our analysis, we consider that covering the surface of an environment with a coverage tool of width d is analogous to painting stripes in a two dimensional space with a "brush" of width d. The actual length of each such stripe depends on the number of obstacles and the number of robots in the environment. For our analysis, we let l denote the average length of a stripe.

Proposition 1: Coverage using a single robot. With a single robot performing the coverage of the environment, there is no guarantee of the robot covering previous uncovered terrain after it has made

$$\frac{41}{d} - 1$$

stripes.

Figure 4. Algorithm used by a leader robot to disperse from other teams in the multi-team coverage technique

```
function PotentialFieldNavigation
    if (I am the leader)
        if (there is another leader robot within radius χᵣ)
            Receive location, heading and coverage map
                from the leader robot of the other team
            Select a new direction to move that has
                the least overlap with the coverage history
                of my team and that obtained from the other team
            Perform team reconfiguration
        else
            Use single-team coverage technique to navigate
                until an obstacle is encountered
```

Proof: We consider that the single robot travels in a straight line until it encounters a wall or an obstacle. It then turns away from the wall at an angle determined by the Braitenberg controller from the sensor data of its proximity sensors. Using this technique, when the robot starts the i-th stripe, it has already encountered $(i-1)$ walls or obstacles. This means that there are $(i-1)$ points along the boundaries of the environment or on the obstacles within the environment that have been encountered by the robot. The i-th stripe partitions this set of $(i-1)$ points into two disjoint subsets, one subset lying to the left (or counter-clockwise) from the endpoint of the i-th stripe, and the other subset lying to the right (or clockwise) from the endpoint of the i-th stripe. We denote these two subsets of points on either side of the i-th stripe as CCW_i and CW_i respectively. Let $|CW_i| = p_k$, and, consequently, $|CCW_i| = (i-1)-p_k$. Now, if the $(i+1)$-th stripe is made to the left of the i-th stripe, then the $(i+1)$-th stripe will intersect the points in CCW_i. The expected number of intersects the $(i+1)$-th stripe will have is given by: $E(intersects^{i+1}) = |p_k| \times 2 - E(\text{stripes in } CCW_i)$. Now, because the angle at which a robot turns is distributed uniformly over $[0, \pi]$, we can assume that the robot has an equal probability of 0.5 of making the $(i+1)$-th stripe to the left or to the right of the i-th stripe. This gives us $|p_k| = [i/2]$. Also, the uniform distribution of the turning angle implies that the average number of stripes made by the robot in each of the sets CW_i and CCW_i are equal. Therefore, we can write $E(\text{stripes in } CCW_i) = [i/2]$. Therefore, $E(intersects^{i+1}) = [i/2] \times 2 - [i/2] = [i/2]$. Then, the expected number of intersects between the i-th stripe and previous stripes is given by $[1/2] + [2/2]+[3/2]+....[i/2] = [1/2] \times [(i(i+1))/2] = [(i(i+1))/4]$ Because each stripe is of width d, every time two stripes intersect there is an overlap of d^2 square units. Correspondingly, the area overlap between the i-th stripe and previous stripes is given by: $d^2 \times [(i(i+1))/4]$. In general, if the average stripe length is l, then the area of the new region covered till the i-th stripe by the single robot is given by:

$$R^i_{new,} SR = \left(i \times l \times d \right) - \left(d^2 \times \frac{i(i+1)}{4} \right) \qquad (1)$$

In Equation 1, the first term on the r.h.s. indicates the area of the region covered until the i-th stripe while the second term indicates the area of the region over which there was repeated coverage until the i-th stripe. The value of i after which the second term exceeds the first indicates the number of stripes after which a single robot performs more repeated coverage than covering new region. To find the duration in number of stripes (denoted by $\hat{i}_{SR}$) when this happens, we differentiate the expression in Equation 1 w. r. t. i and set the differential equal to zero. This gives us

$$\hat{i}_{SR} = \frac{4l}{d} - 1 .$$

Proposition 2: Multi-robot Non-flocking Coverage. When multiple memoryless robots are coordinated individually to perform distributed coverage in an unknown environment, increasing the number of robots by a factor R results in a speedup that is less than R.

Proof: Consider R robots, each with a coverage tool of width d. As before, let l denote the average length of a stripe if there was a single robot in the environment. The robots use the navigation strategy described in the previous section to cover the environment. For this multi-robot scenario, let i_{enc} denote the frequency with which any two robots encounter each other and let l_{frac} denote the average length of the incomplete stripe for each robot at that point. The proof follows in a manner similar to the proof of Proposition 1. In the multi-robot case, when a robot does not encounter another robot it makes a stripe of average length l. Since the frequency of encountering another robot is $[1/(i_{enc})]$, therefore, out of i stripes, there are $1 - [1/(i_{enc})]$ stripes of length l. The new area covered by these stripes can be obtained by substituting i with $i \times (1 - [1/(i_{enc})])$ in Equation 1. For, the remaining $[i/(i_{enc})]$ stripes, a robot encounters another robot after doing an incomplete stripe of average length l_{frac} and moves away from the robot, thereby starting a new stripe. Combining these $i \times (1 - [1/(i_{enc})])$

complete and $[i/(i_{enc})]$ incomplete stripes, we can get $R_{new,MR}{}^{i}$, the amount of new area covered till the i-th stripe in the multi-robot case as:

$$R_{new,MR}^{i} = \left(i - \left\lfloor \frac{i}{i_{enc}} \right\rfloor\right) \times l \times d \times R$$

$$\frac{\left(i - \left\lfloor \frac{i}{i_{enc}} \right\rfloor\right)\left(i - \left\lfloor \frac{i}{i_{enc}} \right\rfloor + 1\right)}{4} \times d^2 R$$

$$+ \left\lfloor \frac{i}{i_{enc}} \right\rfloor \times l_{frac} \times d \times R$$

$$- \frac{\left(\left\lfloor \frac{i}{i_{enc}} \right\rfloor\right)\left(\left\lfloor \frac{i}{i_{enc}} \right\rfloor + 1\right)}{4} \times i_{enc} \times d^2 R \qquad (2)$$

The stripe $\hat{i}_{MR}$ in the multi-robot case after which a robot covers more previously covered region than new region can be obtained by differentiating the expression in Equation 2 w. r. t. i and setting the differential equal to zero. This gives:

$$\hat{i}_{MR} = \frac{4\left(1 - \frac{1}{i_{enc}}\right)l + 4\frac{-l_{frac}}{i_{enc}} - \left(2 - \frac{1}{i_{enc}}\right)d}{2d\left(\left(1 - \frac{1}{i_{enc}}\right)^2 + \frac{1}{i_{enc}}\right)}$$

$$(3)$$

Comparing the values of the time measured in number of stripes after which a robot covers more previously covered region than previously uncovered region for the single and multi-robot cases, we can get an estimate of the speedup between these two settings. The speedup is given by the following expression:

$$speedup_{MR-SR} = \frac{\hat{i}_{MR}}{R \times \hat{i}_{SR}}$$

$$= \frac{1}{R} \times \left[\frac{(1 - \frac{1}{i_{enc}}) + \frac{\frac{4l_{frac}}{i_{enc}} - d}{4l - d}}{2\left((1 - \frac{1}{i_{enc}})2 + \frac{1}{i_{enc}}\right)} \right] \qquad (4)$$

Since, the average stripe length $\bar{l}$ is greater than the d ($l > d$), and, the factor within square brackets in the above expression is <1. Consequently, we get sub-linear speedup by increasing the number of robots by a factor of R.

The result of sublinear speedup obtained above can be attributed to the fact that when the number of robots is increased, although they are able to cover more region in less time, the repeated coverage done by the robots over regions previously covered by other robots also increases.

Proposition 3: Multi-robot, Multi-Team Flocking-based Coverage. When multiple robots are organized to form teams to perform distributed coverage in an unknown environment, the coverage improves by a factor proportional to the size of each team τ.

Proof: Let us suppose that R robots are organized to form teams of size τ. This yields

$$\frac{R}{\tau}$$

teams. The footprint of each team is then $d \times \tau$. This setting is similar to the multi-robot case analyzed in proposition 2, with the following

changes - each 'unit' of coverage is not a single robot but a team of τ robots with a footprint of $d \times \tau$, the number of teams is

$$\frac{R}{\tau}$$

and the teams encounter each other after every $\tau \times i_{enc}$ stripes, where i_{enc} is number of stripes after which two robots encounter each other in the individually coordinated multi-robot case. The values of the new region covered till the i-th stripe, $R^i_{new,team}$ and the stripe after which a robot covers more previously covered region than previously uncovered region,, can be obtained from the corresponding values in the multi-robot case given in Proposition 2, as shown below:

$$R^i_{new,team}$$

$$\left(i - \left\lfloor \frac{i}{\tau \times i_{enc}} \right\rfloor\right) \times l \times d \times \tau \times \frac{R}{\tau}$$

$$\frac{\left(i - \left\lfloor \frac{i}{\tau \times i_{enc}} \right\rfloor\right)\left(i - \left\lfloor \frac{i}{\tau \times i_{enc}} \right\rfloor + 1\right)}{4} \times (d\tau)^2 \times \frac{R}{\tau}$$

$$+ \left\lfloor \frac{i}{\tau \times i_{enc}} \right\rfloor \times l_{frac} \times d \times \tau \times \frac{R}{\tau}$$

$$- \frac{\left(\left\lfloor \frac{i}{\tau \times i_{enc}} \right\rfloor\right)\left(\left\lfloor \frac{i}{\tau \times i_{enc}} \right\rfloor + 1\right)}{4} \times \tau \times i_{enc}(d \times \tau)^2 \frac{R}{\tau}$$

$$\qquad (5)$$

and,

$$\hat{i}_{team} =$$

$$\frac{4(1 - \dfrac{1}{\tau \times i_{enc}})l + \dfrac{4l_{frac}}{\tau \times i_{enc}} - (2 - \dfrac{1}{\tau \times i_{enc}}) \times \tau \times d}{\tau \times 2d \left[(1 - \dfrac{1}{\tau \times i_{enc}})^2 + \dfrac{1}{\tau \times i_{enc}} \right]}$$

$$(6)$$

Figures 5(a) and (b) show the improvement in coverage for different team sizes with 20 and 48 robots in the environment for different team sizes. We observe that as the team size increases but the total number of robots in the environment remains fixed, the robots are able to cover more previously uncovered region. The second derivative of $R^i_{new,team}$ from Equation 5 is proportional to

$$2\tau \left(1 - \frac{1}{\tau \times i_{enc}} \right)^2 - \frac{2}{i_{enc}}$$

Although our analyses presented in this section provide insights into the behavior of our system there are several characteristics of the system such as the effect of the frequency with which teams encounter each other on the performance of the system, the effect of team reformation delays due

to physical characteristics that were not mathematically modeled such as the localization error and wheel slip noise, the effect of dynamic change in team configurations due to obstacles encountered by the teams, etc.., which are not directly amenable to theoretical analysis. To understand the behavior of our system further, we provide several empirical analyses of the performance of our system under different values of system parameters and different environment and operational constraints in the following section.

EXPERIMENTAL RESULTS

We have evaluated our team-based, multi-robot flocking and area coverage techniques through extensive experiments using simulated robots as well as on physical *e-puck* robots. An e-puck robot has a diameter of 7 cm and a memory capacity of 144 KB including RAM and Flash memory. Each wheel is 4.1 cm in diameter and is capable of a maximum speed of about 12cm/s. We have used the following sensors that are available on the e-puck robot: (1) Eight infra-red distance sensors measur-

Figure 5. Area of new region covered by robots for different team sizes. (a) With 20 robots in the environment. (b) With 48 robots in the environment.

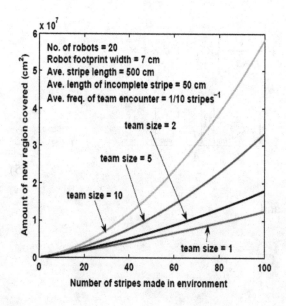
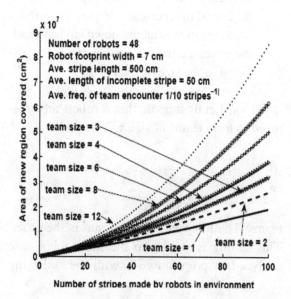

ing ambient light and proximity of obstacles in a range of 4 cm, and, (2) Bluetooth capability for wireless communication. Each e-puck robot is also provided with a local positioning system (a GPS node in the simulator or an overhead camera-based positioning system in the physical experiments) to determine its position in the environment within a 2-D coordinate system. A photograph of the e-puck robot is shown in Figure 6(a). For all our simulations, the inter-robot separation between a pair of follower robots in a team is set to 20 cm. For multi-team coverage, the radius for the potential field-based navigation (χ_r) is set to 1.1 m.

Simulations in Webots

The first objective of our experiments is to understand the behavior of a multi-robot system using the coverage techniques described in this paper, and, to quantify the performance of those techniques while varying the different system and environment related parameters. To achieve this objective we have used extensive multi-robot simulations that allows us to analyze the robots' coverage performance within different experimental settings. We have used the **Webots** simulation platform (Michel, 2004) for our experi-

ments under this category. Webots is a powerful robotic simulation platform that allows realistic modeling of robots and environments including the parameters of different sensors on robots and the physics of the environment. Each robot in our simulated system is modeled as an e-puck robot with accurate models of the features and characteristics of the physical e-puck robot, as shown in Figures 6 (a) and (b).

We have used four metrics to evaluate the performance of our multi-robot team-based area coverage techniques which are given below:

1. The percentage of the area of an environment covered during 2 hours of real time.
2. The percentage of time spent in reformations by a multi-robot team. This metric measures the direct overhead in terms of time of team-based coverage vs. covering the environment individually.
3. The competitive ratio (CR) of the distributed coverage compared to an optimal offline coverage technique. To calculate the competitive ratio(CR), we first calculate the amount of redundancy or repeated coverage of the environment given by:

Figure 6. (a) An actual e-puck robot (Photograph courtesy: http://www.e-puck.org) (b) The model of the e-puck robot in the Webots simulator used for our simulations.

(a)
(b)

$$WR = \sum_i i \times \text{ Area of the region visited } i \text{ times}$$

The competitive ratio (CR) is given by:

$$CR = \frac{\text{Free area of the environment}}{WR}$$

A higher value of CR (near 1) indicates near-optimal coverage while smaller values of CR (approaching 0) indicate increased repeated coverage of the same region by multiple robots that degrades the performance of the system.

4. The number of obstacles (including walls) encountered by the leader and follower robots in a team. This metric measures the overhead of having larger sized teams because larger (wider) teams encounter obstacles more frequently than smaller ones.

For evaluating the efficacy of team-based coverage, we have compared each of the results obtained using multi-robot teams with an identical scenario where the same number of robots cover the environment individually without forming teams. Each scenario was allowed to run for a duration of 2 hours of real time and results were averaged over 10 runs for each scenario. We have divided our experiments into four categories to verify the performance of area coverage while using different configurations of robot teams, and to understand the effect of different types of environments and noise on the performance of the system.

Effect of Varying Number of Robots and Robot Team Size

In our first set of experiments we quantify the effect of changing the number of robots, number of teams and the team sizes of the robots covering the environment on the performance of our metrics. Our simulation and physical robot experiments are done with different numbers of robot teams,

where the size of each team is either 1 robot (individual), 3 robots, 5 robots, 7 robots or 9 robots (controlling teams larger than 9 robots is difficult with the current hardware capabilities including Bluetooth communication available on the robots). With these sizes for each robot team, we tested our algorithms with three different population sizes of robots within the environment 15, 27 and 48 robots. These population sizes ensure that the robots can be divided into the desired size for each team (3, 5, 7 or 9 robots) while approximately doubling the total number of robots in the environment from one population size to the next. The numbers of different sized teams for each population size are shown in the first column of Table 1. The circled multiplicand (e.g. ⑤ denotes the number of robots in a team, while the multiplier denotes the number of teams. Using this convention, the notation 3× ⑤ denotes 3 teams with 5 robots in each team. The last configuration within each set denoted by *number of robots* ×① considers robots moving individually without forming teams and provides a comparison along the different metrics between forming and not forming teams while using the same number of robots. The results of varying the number of robots, number of teams and the sizes of the teams on the metrics used for our experiments are shown in Table 1. We observe that the percentage of environment covered by the robots increases with the number of robots - ranging from an average value of 81.2% with 15 robots to 86.98% with 27 robots and finally to 93.61% with 48 robots. However, the increase in the amount area covered is sublinear in the number of robots because with more robots, robot teams encounter each other more often and spend more time in reformations to avoid colliding with each other. Further analysis of the values in Table 1 shows that with 15 robots in the environment, when the average team size changes from 5 to 3 robots, the coverage improves by

$$\frac{82.95 - 76.13}{76.13} \times 100 = 8.96\%$$

Table 1. Effect of changing number of robots, number of teams and team sizes with 15, 27 and 48 robots on the different metrics used in our experiments. All results shown are for the office environment shown in Figure 7(c).

No. of robots and their configurations	Average team size	% of env. covered		% of time spent in reformations		CR
15 robots		Mean	Std. Dev.	Mean	Std. Dev.	
{3× ⑤}	5	76.59	4.29	70.82	6.95	0.30
{1× ③, 1× ⑤, 1× ⑦}	5	76.13	5.49	66.14	4.85	0.31
{5× ③}	3	82.95	1.97	59.36	2.28	0.29
{15× ①}	1	89.13	0.83	39.65	1.36	0.26
27 robots						
{3× ⑨}	9	76.91	5.70	78.23	3.05	0.27
{1× ③, 2× ⑤, 2× ⑦}	5.4	87.18	2.26	70.82	3.10	0.22
{4× ③, 3× ⑤}	3.85	90.21	1.06	64.90	2.15	0.20
{27× ①}	1	93.60	0.15	43.09	1.27	0.16
48 robots						
{4× ⑤, 4× ⑨}	6	91.95	1.92	71.46	1.72	0.22
{6× ③, 6× ⑤}	4	93.56	0.62	68.83	2.63	0.22
{16× ③}	3	94.45	0.39	63.13	1.61	0.21
{48× ①}	1	94.48	0.12	40.71	1.03	0.19

With 27 robots, when the average team size drops from 9 to 3.85 robots, the improvement in coverage becomes

$$\frac{90.21 - 76.91}{76.91} \times 100 = 17.29\%$$

Finally, the improvement in coverage from a team size of 6 to a team size of 3 robots is

$$\frac{94.45 - 91.95}{91.95} \times 100 = 2.72\%$$

These numbers indicate the smaller team sizes are able to achieve better coverage. To further validate this hypothesis, we performed a regression analysis between the average team size and the percentage of environment covered from the data reported in Table 1. The correlation coefficient for different numbers of robots in the environment are shown in Table 2. We observe that a strong inverse correlation exists between the average size of the robot teams and the percentage of environment covered. Overall, the results of the percentage of environment covered for different robot team sizes indicate that smaller team sizes are able to achieve better coverage. This is in contrast to the result from Proposition 3 that the coverage performance is proportional to the robot team size. The anomaly in the analytical and experimental results can be explained by the fact that the analytical model does assume 'instantaneous' reformation when the team leader encounters an obstacle. On the other hand,

Table 2. Table showing the correlation coefficient between the average size of robot team and the percentage of environment covered for a different numbers of robots in the environment.

No. of robots	Correl(team size,
in env.	% of env. covered)
15	−0.999
27	−0.977
48	−0.914

the experiments include physical characteristics of the setting such as localization errors, wheel slip noise and follower robots encountering obstacles. All of these characteristics force the team to reform and these additional reformation times degrade the coverage performance of larger robot teams.

The better performance of smaller robot teams due to rapid reformation times can also be explained by analyzing the 'percentage of time spent in reformations column of Table 1. We observe that smaller teams with a size of 3 robots spend about 60% of their total time of operation in reformations. This value increases to as much as 78.23% for a team size of 9 robots. To further validate the correlation between team size and time spent in reformations, we performed a linear regression test between the team size as the independent variable and the percentage of time spent in reformations as the independent variable, from the data reported in Table 1. The correlation coefficient between the team size and the percentage of time spent in reformations is 0.92, the slope of the linear curve is 5.06 and its y-coefficient is 41.49 - confirming our hypothesis that team size affects the time spent in reformations by a team. The larger reformation times for larger robot teams follows intuitively too because when a larger team encounters an obstacle, more robots have to get into new positions before the team can regain formation and start moving in a new direction. When robots move individually, the

reformation times are the lowest because a single robot only has to turn itself to avoid an obstacle without worrying about getting all follower robots into correct positions to regain team formation after avoiding an obstacle.

Among the experimental results reported in Table 1, individually moving robots also appear to achieve better or comparable coverage than robots that move together as a team, irrespective of the team size. The inferior coverage performance of larger teams together with longer reformation times leads us to the question - are larger teams always worse for team-based area coverage? The answer to this question can be inferred from the results in the competitive ratio (CR) column of Table 1. The competitive ratio expresses the efficiency of the coverage performed by the robots by incorporating the amount of repeated, and hence, unnecessary coverage of previously covered regions done by the robots. The repeated coverage happens in our system because leader robots refresh their coverage histories after H steps. We observe that although robots that move individually are able to cover a marginally higher percentage of the total environment than team-based robots, the competitive ratio of robots that move individually is lower than that of robots moving in teams. This indicates that robots that move individually sacrifice a significant amount of the advantage of their lower reformation times by performing repeated coverage of previously covered regions. The lower competitive ratio for area coverage by the individually moving robots can be attributed to the fact that individual coordination between robots requires each robot to exchange and fuse coverage information from more robots, more frequently. In contrast, with team-based coverage only leader robots aggregate the team's coverage information and exchange it with each other. This results in more efficient information exchange and judicious decision making by robot teams to avoid repeated coverage of previously covered regions.

Effect of Different Environments

For our next set of experiments we vary the environment in which the robots operate and observe the effect on the performance of the system. We consider three different environments with different geometric features and different numbers of obstacles in the environment as shown in Figure 7. The results of this experiment for different team sizes while using 27 robots are shown in Figure 8(a)-(d). We observe that for the square environment with no obstacles, the percentage of the environment covered by the robots shown in Figure 8(a) and the competitive ratio shown in Figure 8(c) are not significantly affected by changing the team size. This is substantiated by the high correlation coefficient of 0.97 and 0.98 respectively, but a very small slope of the linear best-fit curve, 0.23 and 0.003 respectively, for these cases obtained by a linear regression analysis of the data. These results are in contrast to the analytical results mentioned in Proposition 3 which state that the area of the previously uncovered region increases proportionally with the robot team size. However, the mathematical model of the robots did not account for physical characteristics such as the localization error and wheel slip noise, which cause the performance of the area coverage to get adversely affected in the experimental results. For the more complex environments of the corridor and the office, the robot team size adversely affects the percentage of the area of the environment that gets covered as shown in Figure 8(a). This relationship between the average team size and coverage performance is confirmed by the high negative value of the correlation coefficient −0.89 and −0.97 respectively, coupled with a considerable slope of the linear best-fit curve at −1.35 and −2.11 respectively, as shown in Figure 8(a). The decrease in coverage can be attributed to the longer reformation times of larger teams as shown in Figure 8(b) - larger robot teams spend longer times to reconfigure after encountering an obstacle, and therefore,

have lesser time to perform coverage of the environment. The competitive ratio of the robots in the corridor and office environments increases marginally with larger sized robot teams as shown by the positive slope of the linear best-fit curve of 0.02 and 0.01 respectively in Figure 8(c). But this improvement comes at the expense of lower coverage in the environment. Finally, Figure 8(d) shows the number of obstacles encountered by the leader and follower robots in robot teams for different team sizes. We observe in this graph that as the team size gets larger, follower robots evidently encounter more obstacles because of the larger physical width of the team. This further aggravates the reformation time for larger teams as evidenced in Figure 8(b), and reduces the coverage efficiency for large sized teams in environments with a considerable number of obstacles like the corridor and office environments.

Effect of Noise on the System

In our final set of experiments we quantify the effect of noise on the coverage performance of the robots. We consider two sources of noise: a) wheel slip noise that depends on the friction between the robot's wheels and floor of the environment, and, b) localization noise that is introduced due to the local positioning mechanism used by the robots in our system.

For determining the wheel slip noise, we performed 5 sets of trials by moving a physical e-puck robot from a fixed start location to a target location. Each trial set consisted of 10 individual runs and in each trial set, the robot was moved through a distance of 3.85 m at different angles (0, 30, 45, 60 and 90 degrees) relative to the local coordinate system in the environment. For each trial, we measured the difference in distance between the actual location reached by the robot and its target location. The error due to wheel slip noise, obtained by averaging the results of these trials, was calculated as 0.1339 in the x-axis and 0.1261 in the y-axis of the environment's coor-

Figure 7. The three different types of environment used in our experiments. (a) A 4×4 m square environment with no obstacles, (b) A corridor environment consisting of two diamond shaped regions, joined by a corridor that is 8 m long and 1 m wide, and, (c) A 4 m ×2 m office environment that is occupied by furniture.

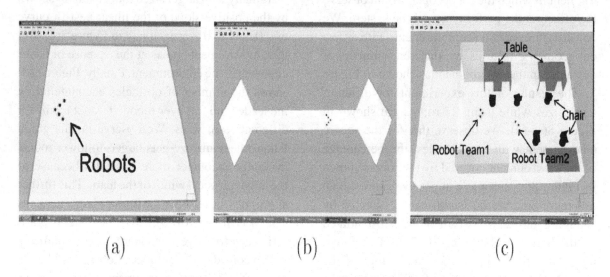

(a) (b) (c)

dinate system. We averaged these two values to set a wheel slip noise of 0.13 for each simulated e-puck robot inside Webots. The effects of the wheel slip noise of the coverage metrics is shown in Figure 9(a)-(d) with different configurations of 15 robots moving in the three environments shown in Figure 7. We observe that the effect of the wheel slip noise on the different metrics used for our experiments is nominal in the case of the square and the office environments. However, the wheel slip noise results in a more pronounced effect on these metrics when the robots move in the corridor environment. Specifically, for the configurations {3×,⑤} and {1×③ 1×⑤ 1×⑦} in the corridor environment, we observe that the wheel sleep noise adversely affects the coverage performance, the competitive ratio and the number of obstacles encountered by follower robots. The reason for this behavior can be understood by analyzing the effect of wheel slip noise and the space of the corridor. The wheel slip noise we observed on the physical robots causes each wheel to turn at a different speed than was set by the wheel encoders, due to friction with the

floor's surface. This causes the robots to drift intermittently from their planned paths instead of moving in a straight line. In the corridor, that is 1 m wide, the wheel slip noise causes the robots, especially the follower robots to drift from their planned path through the corridor and encounter the walls of the narrow corridor. This results in the higher number of obstacles encountered by the follower robots with the {1×③ 1×⑤ 1×⑦} configuration in the corridor environment as shown in Figure 9(d).

We further performed 2-way and 1-way ANOVA (analysis of variance) tests at 95% confidence interval to validate our conclusions for each of the data sets shown in Figures 9 (a) - (d). The results show that, when considered together with the team size variable (in column 2 of Table 4), slip noise does not have a significant effect on the first three metrics - percentage of environment covered by the robots, percentage of time spent in reformations, and competitive ratio. However, for the last metric - number of obstacles encountered by follower robots, the wheel slip noise does make a significant impact. The marginal impact of the

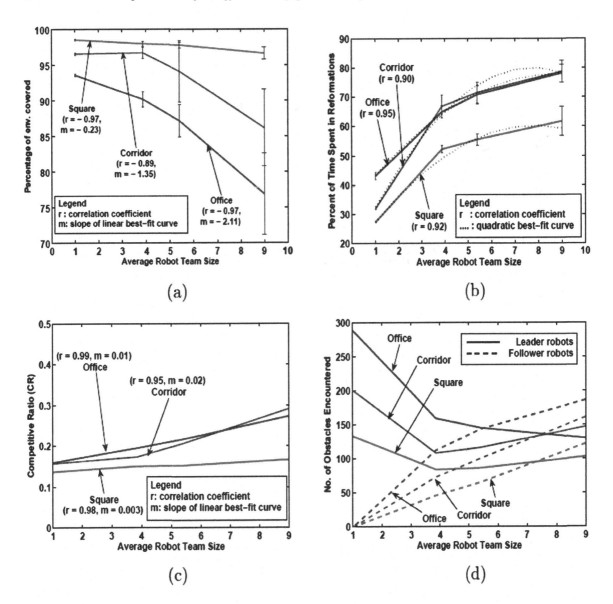

(a)   (b)

(c)   (d)

wheel slip noise is in accordance with the results shown in Figures 9(a)-(c), where the graphs for the metrics with and without slip noise are almost identical. To further analyze our results we also performed 1-way ANOVA tests with the variables team size and wheel slip noise respectively. As noted previously in this section, we once again observe from the significance results that the team size variable affects the performance of the first three metrics. The wheel slip noise is a significant variable only for the percentage of environment covered and the number of obstacles encountered by follower robots metrics. These results can be explained by the fact that when the follower robots are closer to walls of obstacles, especially for the narrow channel connecting the

Figure 9. Effect of incorporating wheel slip noise within the three types of environments considered on the different metrics used for our experiments. The results reported are for different configurations of 15 robots.

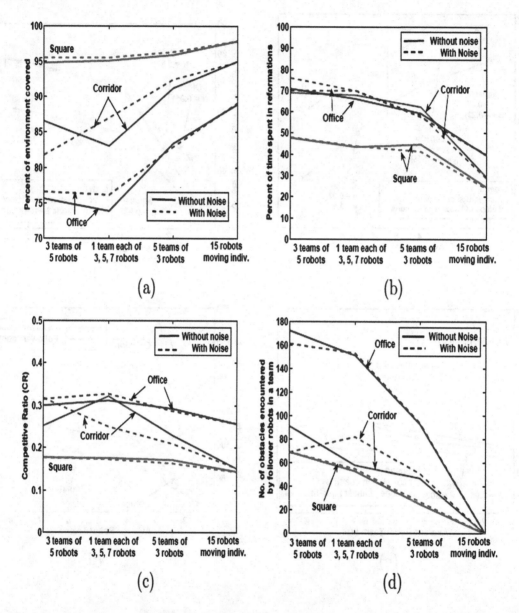

two rooms in the corridor environment, the wheel slip noise causes the robots to deviate from their desired locations within the team and encounter the walls more often. Without wheel slip noise added to their motion, the robots deviate from their positions less frequently, and, therefore, they encounter obstacles less frequently. More

obstacles should result in more reformation time. However, the percentage of reformation times shown in Figure 9(b) is not affected significantly by the wheel slip noise. An increased number of obstacles encountered, but unchanged number of reformations indicate that robot teams are able to avoid obstacles encountered by followers without reforming. In other words, teams are able to continue coverage despite follower robots encountering obstacles. This behavior in turn translates to a slight improvement in the amount of coverage achieved by the robots, while considering wheel slip noise, as shown in Figure 9(a).

Localization noise in our system is caused mainly by the image processing algorithm that processes the video stream of the robots' movement captured by the overhead camera overlooking the experiment arena and calculates each robot's coordinates in the local coordinate system. For calculating the localization noise, we used five physical e-puck robots and tracked their paths over a distance of 3.85 m for 5 trials. Each robot was fitted with uniquely colored marker on its top that showed its heading relative to the local coordinate system. The error in the location and heading of the different robots is shown in Table 3. We added these noise values to the "accurate" GPS readings provided by Webots (using the GPSNode class) to simulate the effect of localization noise in our simulations. The results are reported in Table 5 for a team of 5 robots moving in the

square environment with and without localization noise added to its coordinates. We observe that localization noise marginally affects the coverage and competitive ratio metrics. To validate this observation, we performed the Kruksal-Wallis analysis of variance test to determine if localization noise had a significant effect on the metrics used in our experiments. The results of the tests are reported in Table 6. For each of the metrics, the p-value of the data set is found to be greater than the confidence level $\alpha=0.05$, indicating that the medians of the distributions with and without localization noise are identical at 95% confidence interval. This implies that the localization noise only has a marginal effect on percentage of the environment covered, the time spent in reformations and the competitive ratio.

Experiments on E-Puck Robots

To test the performance of our team-based coverage algorithm on physical e-puck robots, we performed coverage within a 2.31×2.31 m environment using 3 e-puck robots that moved together as

Table 3. Localization error due to image processing errors for five experiments

Parameter	X (cm)	Y (cm)	Θ (Degrees)
	The E-Puck with a Red Hat		
Mean Error	0.25	0.088	-3.49
Standard Deviation	0.33	0.15	2.38
	The E-Puck with a Blue Hat		
Mean Error	0.68	0.62	3.05
Standard Deviation	0.15	0.148	0.3
	The E-Puck with a Green Hat		
Mean Error	-0.07	-0.18	-1.43
Standard Deviation	0.12	0.147	5.72
	The E-Puck with a Pink Hat		
Mean Error	-0.02	-0.089	4.85
Standard Deviation	0.19	0.14	1.75
	The E-Puck with a Purple Hat		
Mean Error	-0.29	-0.398	5.69
Standard Deviation	0.18	0.137	2.17

Table 4. Analysis of variance of the results with slip noise for different metrics used in our experiments shown in Figures 9(a)-(d). The significance level α is set to α=0.05 (95% confidence intervals). The abbreviation "sig." stands for significant.

Metric	Sig. Value with 2-Way ANOVA (Team Size * Slip Noise)	Sig. Value with 1-Way ANOVA (Team Size)	Sig. Value with 1-Way ANOVA (Slip Noise)
% of env.	0.974	0	0.05
covered	(not sig.)	(sig.)	(sig.)
% of time	0.992	0	0.974
in reform	(not sig.)	(sig.)	(not sig.)
CR	0.956	0	0.969
	(not sig.)	(sig.)	(not sig.)
No. of obst.	0.05	0.679	0.05
(followers)	(sig.)	(not sig.)	(sig.)

Table 5. Effect of localization noise on the different metrics used for our experiments. The results are reported for navigating a team of 5 robots in the square environment.

Environment	% of env. covered		% of time spent in reformations		CR
	Mean	Std. Dev.	Mean	Std. Dev.	
1 team of 5 robots WITHOUT localization noise					
Square	75.13	3.90	26.56	4.56	0.43
Corridor	70.57	5.67	45.23	4.66	0.46
Office	45.42	7.35	62.09	7.77	0.79
1 team of 5 robots WITH localization noise					
Square	78.56	3.64	38.33	4.78	0.44
Corridor	59.81	10.52	60.42	10.31	0.60
Office	43.44	8.82	67.19	9.86	0.82

a team. We compared the metrics obtained from this scenario with a scenario where the robots are coordinated to move individually. The environment either had no obstacles, or had 10% of its area covered by obstacles. Each scenario was run for 60 minutes and five runs were conducted for each scenario. A snapshot of the 3 e-puck robots within the image processing software's user interface and a photograph of the robots within our experiment arena is shown in Figure 10. A video of a simulation run from the e-puck robot experiments is available at http://www.youtube.

Table 6. Different metrics and corresponding p-values from Kruksal-Wallis Test on the data with and without localization noise reported in Table 5

Metric	p-Value
% of env. covered	0.873
% of time in reform	0.513
CR	0.513

com/watch?v=jmyhURYq5Uc. We observed that in the individually coordinated case robots obtain 7% to 20% more coverage than the team-based coverage at the different running times. Due to the localization error and wheel slip noise, the robot team needs to reform its shape approximately every 2 minutes, and spends about 35-40 seconds to get the team reconfigured. This results in about 2/3 of its total runtime being spent by the robot team to perform coverage while the remaining 1/3 is spent in reconfigurations. However, we observed that when robots are individually coordinated, they encounter 10 times more obstacles than the team-based coverage. The team based coverage performs especially better than the individually coordinated strategy when the robots are at a

corner. The individual robot gets "stuck" for some time oscillating between the two walls of the corner, while the robot team, because of its wider coverage "swathe" can navigate out of the corner more efficiently.

FUTURE DIRECTION: BEYOND FIXED ROBOT TEAMS WITH DYNAMIC FORMATION MAINTENANCE FOR AREA COVERAGE

In the formation maintenance techniques discussed till now, a robot team avoids obstacles by adjusting its configuration or movement direction, but the constitution of the team remains unchanged. In other words, robots do not join and leave teams while they are performing coverage in the environment. Maintaining a fixed set of team members throughout the robots' operation is definitely straightforward. However, there are certain situations where keeping the team members and team size fixed, can adversely affect the coverage performance. An example is shown in Figure 11 (a), using a coverage technique without

Table 7. Experimental results showing the different metrics for coverage with 3 e-puck robots

	Percentage of Coverage (%)			
	15 min.	30 min.	45 min.	60 min.
Ind. no obs.	20.1	32.5	48.3	53.4
Team, no obs.	13.4	18.6	29.6	42.9
Ind. 10% obs.	20.39	33.17	49.6	55.7
Team, 10% obs.	16.44	21.78	30.67	45.33
	No. of Times Obstacle Encountered			
Ind., no obs.	16	44	69	99
Team, no obs.	2	5	7	8
Ind., 10% obs.	21	46	78	107
Team, 10% obs.	2	6	7	10
	Avg. Reformation Time			
Team, no obs.	34.7	39.15	39.33	38.08
Team, 10% obs.	33.94	37.13	36.57	37.55

Figure 10. (a) Screen shot of three e-pucks within our experiment arena in the image processing software's user console. (b) A photo of three e-pucks in a V-shape formation within the experiment arena.

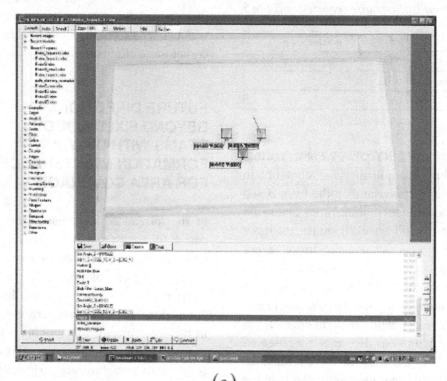

(a)

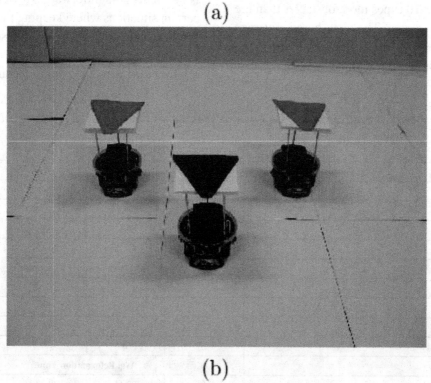

(b)

reconfiguration, when a 5-robot team encounters a T-shaped obstacle, it would have to change its configuration to a narrow formation and cover the free space to the left of the obstacle, encounter the 'top' of the T-shaped obstacle and reverse the direction of all the robots to continue coverage. In contrast, better coverage would be afforded around the obstacle, if the 5-robot team could intelligently split into three smaller teams, with two teams continuing coverage in the free spaces to the left and right of the obstacle respectively, while one of the teams – that is blocked by the obstacle, reverses its direction to continue coverage, as shown in Figure 11(b). Similarly, when two teams heading towards each other, get in close proximity of each other with obstacle-free space around them, they should be able to merge into a larger team to perform their coverage together, instead of trying to adjust their configuration to avoid each other, as shown in Figures 11(c) and (d). In summary, better and more efficient coverage, with fewer reconfigurations and movement direction adjustments can be achieved if robot teams are equipped with intelligent decision making

capabilities so that they can split and merge into new teams depending on the perceived obstacles and robot in the vicinity.

To pursue this direction, we envisage that techniques from the field of economics called coalition game theory (Hadjukova, 2004) can be suitably adapted on multi-robot teams to provide a structured way of dynamic reconfiguration. Coalition games provide a set of rules for partitioning a group of humans or agents, called the game's players, into subsets that are called coalitions. The game's rules ensure that the value that each player gets in its coalition is at least as large as what it would get if the group had stayed together. This in turn guarantees that coalitions are stable, that is, players in a coalition do not have any incentive to leave the current coalition and join another coalition or form new coalitions. For our setting, each robot is provided with a software agent that performs the coalition game related calculations on its behalf. Specifically, a form of coalition game called a weighted voting game (WVG) (Shoham & Leyton Brown, 2008) has been proposed as a succinct representation for

Figure 11. Dynamic reconfiguration by a team of mobile robots. (a) – (b) shows a 5-robot team reconfiguring by splitting into three new teams around an obstacle they encounter; (c) – (d) shows two 5-robot teams heading towards each other, merging to form a larger, 10-robot team. The new team moves in a new direction that has not been covered by the teams before merging.

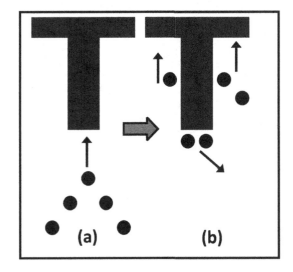 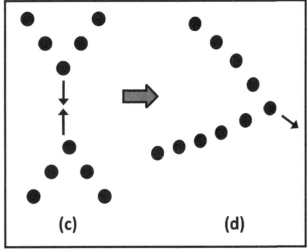

general coalition games. The general schematic for using a coalition game to reconfigure robot teams moving using flocking based formation control is shown in Figure 12 (a) – the formation control of the robots is done using the flocking-based controller while reconfiguration is handled by the higher-level, coalition game layer. To realize a weighted voting game, each robot in a team is provided with a numerical 'weight' that represents how well the robot has performed its task of coverage in the recent past; higher values of weight indicate better performance. To form a new team, a threshold weight value called a quota is provided. To be able to be part of the new team, a set of robots must have sufficient weight among themselves to just reach the threshold weight set as the new team's quota. The condition of 'just reaching' the weight in the quota guarantees that team members that have been performing poorly, e.g., due to obstacles in their path in the recent past

end up getting a low weight and are not included in the new team. These robots can then continue covering the environment individually, or, possibly merge into another team later on. Figures 12 (b) and (c) show an example illustrating the formation of a new team by splitting an existing 6-robot team into two smaller teams using a WVG. The weights of the robots are shown inside the circles representing the robots and the threshold weight or quota is set to 3.5. Note that there are two ways to reach the quota as shown by the sets MWC1 and MWC2 in Figure 12 (b). Out of these, MWC1 is selected as the robot directions are more aligned with each other in this set, as shown in Figure 12(c). We have also performed some preliminary research in this direction to implement a WVG-based robot team reconfiguration mechanism. The important results from this research are shown in Figures 13-15.

Figure 12. (a) The hierarchical approach to multi-robot team reconfiguration using a coalition game based technique; (b) A 6-robot team splitting using a weighted-voting game technique. The weights of the robots are shown inside the circular robots and the quota is set to 3.5. There are two subsets of robots denoted by MWC1 and MWC2 that can reach the quota; (c) The subset MWC1, denoted as BMWC, is selected as the new team to form because the robots in this set are more aligned with each other than in MWC2.

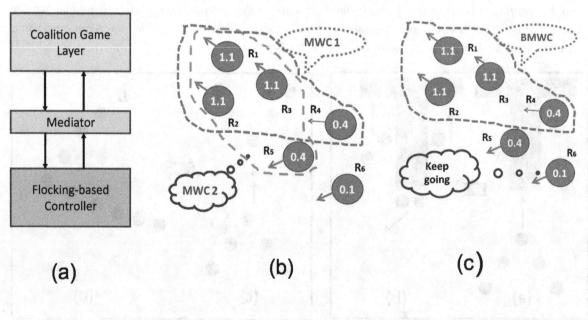

Figure 13. Two 2 X 2 m² environments with 10% and 20% of the free space in the environment occupied by obstacles; (c) Percentage of the environment covered by a 5-robot team with and without WVG-based reconfiguration. Each experiment was run over a period of 30 mins.

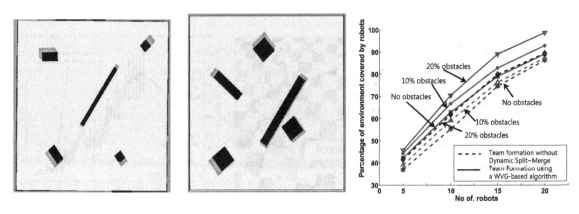

Figure 14. (a) A 5-robot team approaching an obstacle where the motion of only three team members is occluded by the obstacle; (b) the team splits into two new teams using a WVG-based algorithm based on the robots that were not occluded and occluded by the obstacle respectively in (a). The two new teams continue moving in two different directions to perform coverage; (c) Time taken by the WVG-based reconfiguration algorithm including the time taken by the two new teams to regain formation after reconfiguring. The y-axis shows the mean error of the team members from their desired position in formation – a low value denotes that the team has achieved formation.

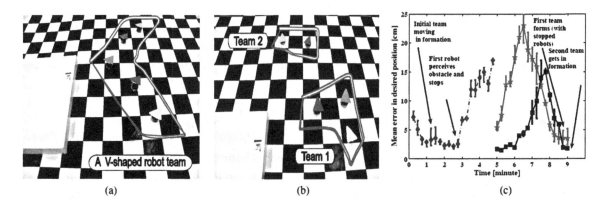

CONCLUSION AND FUTURE WORK

In this chapter, we have described a technique for multi team flocking for distributed area coverage. We have shown that with many small sized teams, team-based coverage performs comparably with coverage when the robots are individually coordinated. Our techniques hold promise in sce-

narios where a suite of robots have to maneuver themselves as a cohesive team to provide an array of sensors located on the different robots of the team or to provide redundancy in the sensor measurements. We also provided a future direction showing that basic flocking based formation for robot coverage can be enhanced if the teams can dynamically split and merge depending on

Figure 15. (a) Two 3-robot teams approaching towards each other (b) the teams merge into one new team using a WVG-based algorithm. The new team continues moving in a new direction that is different from the region covered by the teams before merging to avoid repeated coverage; (c) Time taken by the WVG-based reconfiguration algorithm to merge the two 3-robot teams.

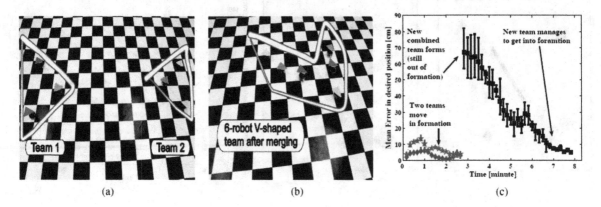

(a)   (b)   (c)

the constraints perceived in the environment such as obstacles and other robot teams. We are currently enhancing the team-based reconfiguration techniques for coverage to dynamically determine the size of the teams within a weighted voting game, instead of using a fixed threshold weight value for the quota. We are also investigating machine learning techniques that will enable robot teams to learn 'good' formations for specific obstacle geometries from their own past actions or previous domain knowledge instead of running a reconfiguration algorithm every time they encounter obstacles. Finally, we are implementing the techniques discussed in this chapter for real-life applications such as robotic landmine detection and robotic exploration of environments that are difficult for humans to maneuver in. In summary, we envisage the formation-based coverage along with dynamic team reconfiguration techniques will considerably enhance the state-of-the-art techniques for multi-robot coverage and will allow robots to replace humans with more efficient yet safe operation in many commercial and domestic application domains.

ACKNOWLEDGMENT

The research reported in this paper has been supported as part of the COMRADES project, sponsored by the U.S. Office of Naval Research, grant no. N000140911174.

We are grateful to Prof. Lotfollah Najjar of the Information Systems and Quantitative Analysis Department, University of Nebraska at Omaha for his help with statistical analysis of our test results reported in this chapter.

A preliminary version of this chapter appeared as the following papers: Dasgupta, P., Whipple, T., & Cheng, K. (2011). Effects of Multi-Robot Team Formation on Distributed Area Coverage. *International Journal on Swarm Intelligence Research, 2*(1), pp. 44-69, and Dasgupta P., & Cheng, K. (2010, November). Robust Multi-robot Team Formations using Weighted Voting Games. Presented at 10th International Symposium on Distributed Autonomous Robotic Systems (DARS) at Lausanne, Switzerland,.

REFERENCES

Bahceci, E., Soysal, O., & Sahin, E. (2003). Review: Pattern formation and adaptation in multi-robot systems. *CMU Tech. Report no. CMU-RI-TR-03-4*. Carnegie Mellon University.

Balch, T., & Arkin, R. (1998). Behavior-based formation control of multi-robot teams. *IEEE Transactions on Robotics and Automation, 14*(6), 926–939. doi:10.1109/70.736776

Bloch, I., Milisavljevc, N., & Acheroy, M. (2007). Multisensor Data Fusion for Spaceborne and Airborne Reduction of Mine Suspected Areas. *International Journal of Advanced Robotic Systems, 4*(2), 173–186.

Boccalatte, M., Brogi, F., Catalfamo, F., Maddaluno, S., Martino, M., & Mellano, V. et al. (2013). A Multi-UAS Cooperative Mission Over Non-Segregated Civil Areas. *Journal of Intelligent & Robotic Systems, 70*(1-4), 275–291. doi:10.1007/s10846-012-9706-5

Burgard, W., Moors, M., Fox, D., Simmons, R., & Thrun, S. (2005). Collaborative multi-robot exploration. *IEEE Transactions on Robotics, 21*(3), 376–386. doi:10.1109/TRO.2004.839232

Cassinis, R. (2000, June). *Multiple single sensor robots rather than a single multi-sensor platforms: a reasonable alternative*. Paper presented at the International Conference on Explosives and Drug Detection Techniques. Crete, Greece.

Chen, Q., & Luh, J. (1994). Coordination and control of a group of small mobile robots. In *Proceedings of International Conference on Robotics and Automation* (pp. 2315-2320). Piscataway, NJ: IEEE Press.

Cheng, K., & Dasgupta, P. (2007). Dynamic area coverage using faulty multi-agent swarms. In *Proceedings of IEEE/WIC/ACM International Conference on Intelligent Agent Technology* (pp. 17-24). Piscataway, NJ: IEEE Press.

Chien, S., Sherwood, R., Tran, D., Cichy, B., Rabideau, G., & Castano, R. et al. (2005). Using Autonomy Flight Software to Improve Science Return on Earth Observing One. *Journal Of Aerospace Computing, Information, And Communication, 2*(4), 196–216. doi:10.2514/1.12923

Choset, H. (2001). Coverage for robotics: A survey of recent results. *Annals of Math and AI, 31*, 113–126.

De Mot, J. (2005). *Optimal agent cooperation with local information*. (Doctoral Dissertation). Massachusetts Institute of Technology, Cambridge, MA.

Dudenhoefer, D., & Jones, M. (2000). A formation behavior for large-scale micro-robot force. In *Proceedings of 32nd Winter Simulation Conference* (pp. 972-982). Academic Press.

Englot, B., & Hover, F. (2012). Sampling-based coverage path planning for inspection of complex structures. In *Proceedings of International Conference on Automated Planning and Scheduling*. San Francisco, CA: AAAI Press.

Fazli, P., Davoodi, A., & Mackworth, A. (2013). Multi-robot repeated area coverage. *Autonomous Robots, 34*(4), 251–276. doi:10.1007/s10514-012-9319-7

Ferranti, E., Trigoni, N., & Levene, M. (2009). Rapid exploration of unknown areas through dynamic deployment of mobile and stationary sensor nodes. *Autonomous Agents and Multi-Agent Systems, 19*(2), 210–243. doi:10.1007/s10458-008-9075-4

Fine, B., & Shell, D. (2011). Flocking: Don't need no stinkin' robot recognition. In *Proceedings of International Conference on Intelligent Robots and Systems* (pp. 5001-5006). Piscataway, NJ: IEEE Press.

Fischer, F., Caprari, W., Siegwart, G., Moser, R., & Mondada, R. (2009). Magnebike: A magnetic wheeled robot with high mobility for inspecting complex-shaped structures. *Journal of Field Robotics, 26*(5), 453–476. doi:10.1002/rob.20296

Fredslund, J., & Mataric, M. (2002). A general algorithm for robot formations using local sensing and minimal communication. *IEEE Transactions on Robotics and Automation, 18*(5), 837–846. doi:10.1109/TRA.2002.803458

Gabriely, Y., & Rimon, E. (2001). Spanning-tree based coverage of continuous areas by a mobile robot. *Annals of Math and AI, 31*(1-4), 77–98.

Galceran, E., & Carreras, M. (2013). Planning coverage paths on bathymetric maps for indetail inspection of the ocean floor. In *Proceedings of International Conference on Robotics and Automation* (pp. 4159-4164). Piscataway, NJ: IEEE Press.

Galceran, E., & Carreras, M. (2013). A Survey on Coverage Path Planning for Robotics. *Robotics and Autonomous Systems, 61*(12), 1258–1276. doi:10.1016/j.robot.2013.09.004

Garrido, S., Moreno, L., & Lima, P. (2011). Robot Formation Motion Planning using Fast Marching. *Robotics and Autonomous Systems, 59*(9), 675–683. doi:10.1016/j.robot.2011.05.011

Gokce, F., & Sahin, E. (2009). To flock or not to flock: the pros and cons of flocking in long-range migration of mobile robot swarms. In *Proceedings of 8th International Conference on Autonomous Agents and MultiAgent Systems (AAMAS)* (pp. 65-72). AAMAS.

Hadjukova, J. (2004). Coalition formation games: A survey. *International Game Theory Review, 8*, 613–641.

Kaminka, G., Schechter, R., & Sadov, V. (2008). Using Sensor Morphology for Multirobot Formations. *IEEE Transactions on Robotics, 24*(2), 271–282. doi:10.1109/TRO.2008.918054

Koenig, S., Szymanski, B., & Liu, Y. (2001). Efficient and Inefficient Ant Coverage Methods. *Annals of Mathematics and Artificial Intelligence, 31*(1/4), 41–76. doi:10.1023/A:1016665115585

Mannadiar, R., & Rekleitis, I. (2010). Optimal coverage of a known arbitrary environment. In *Proceedings of International Conference on Robotics and Autonomous Systems* (pp. 5525-5530). Piscataway, NJ: IEEE Press.

Mastellone, S., Stipanovic, D., Graunke, C., Intlekofer, K., & Spong, M. (2008). Formation control and collision avoidance for multi-agent non-holonomic systems: Theory and experiments. *The International Journal of Robotics Research, 27*(1), 107–126. doi:10.1177/0278364907084441

Michel, O. (2004). Webots: Professional mobile robot simulation. *International Journal of Advanced Robotic Systems, 1*(1), 39–42.

Olfati-Saber, R. (2006). Flocking for multi-agent dynamic systems: Algorithms and theory. *IEEE Transactions on Automatic Control, 51*(3), 401–420. doi:10.1109/TAC.2005.864190

Puig, D., Garcia, M., & Wu, L. (2011). A new global optimization strategy for coordinated multi-robot exploration. *Robotics and Autonomous Systems, 59*(9), 635–653. doi:10.1016/j.robot.2011.05.004

Rekleitis, I., New, A., Rankin, E., & Choset, H. (2008). Efficient boustrophedon multi-robot coverage: An algorithmic approach. *Annals of Mathematics and Artificial Intelligence, 52*(2-4), 109–142. doi:10.1007/s10472-009-9120-2

Reynolds, C. (1987). Flocks, herds and schools: A distributed behavioral model. *Computer Graphics, 21*(4), 25–34. doi:10.1145/37402.37406

Rutishauser, S., Correll, N., & Martinoli, A. (2009). Collaborative coverage using a swarm of networked miniature robots. *Robotics and Autonomous Systems, 57*(5), 517–525. doi:10.1016/j.robot.2008.10.023

Sahin, T., & Zergeroglu, E. (2008). Mobile dynamically reformable formations for efficient flocking behavior in complex environments. In *Proceedings of IEEE International Conference on Robotics and Automation* (pp. 1910-1915). Piscataway, NJ: IEEE Press.

Shoham, Y., & Leyton-Brown, K. (2008). *Multiagent systems*. MIT Press.

Smith, B., Egerstedt, M., & Howard, A. (2009). Automatic generation of persistent formations for multi-agent networks under range constraints. *Mobile Networks and Applications Journal, 14*(3), 322–335. doi:10.1007/s11036-009-0153-x

Spears, D., Kerr, W., & Spears, W. (2006). Physics-based robot swarms for coverage problems. *International Journal of Intelligent Control and Systems, 11*(3), 124–140.

Stachniss, C., Mozos, O., & Burgard, W. (2008). Efficient exploration of unknown indoor environments using a team of mobile robots. *Annals of Math and AI, 52*(2-4), 205–227.

Tully, S., Kantor, G., & Choset, H. (2010). Leapfrog path design for multi-robot cooperative localization. *Field and Service Robotics. Springer Tracts in Advanced Robotics, 62*, 307–317. doi:10.1007/978-3-642-13408-1_28

Turgut, A., Celikkanat, H., Gokce, F., & Sahin, E. (2008). Self-organized flocking with a mobile robot swarm. In *Proceedings of International Conference on Autonomous Agents and MultiAgent Systems* (pp. 39-46). Academic Press.

Tzanov, V. (2006). *Distributed area search with a team of robots*. (Master's Thesis). Massachusetts Institute of Technology, Cambridge, MA.

Wagner, I., Altshuler, Y., Yanovski, V., & Bruckstein, A. (2008). Cooperative cleaners: A study in ant robotics. *The International Journal of Robotics Research, 27*(1), 127–151. doi:10.1177/0278364907085789

Wang, P. (1989). Navigation strategies for multiple autonomous mobile robots. In *Proceedings of IEEE/RSJ International Workshop on Intelligent Robots & Systems* (pp. 486-493). Piscataway, NJ: IEEE Press.

Wurm, K., Stachniss, C., & Burgard, W. (2008). Coordinated multi-robot exploration using a segmentation of the environment. In *Proceedings of IEEE/RSJ International Conference on Intelligent Robots and Systems (IROS),* (pp. 1160-1165). Piscataway, NJ: IEEE Press.

Xu, A., Virie, P., & Rekleitis, I. (2011). Optimal complete terrain coverage using an unmanned aerial vehicle. In *Proceedings of IEEE International Conference on Robotics & Automation* (pp. 2513-2519). Piscataway, NJ: IEEE Press.

Xu, L. (2011). *Graph planning for environmental coverage*. (Doctoral Dissertation). Carnegie Mellon University, Pittsburgh, PA.

ADDITIONAL READING

Acar, E., Choset, H., Zhang, Y., & Schervish, M. (2003). Path Planning for Robotic Demining: Robust Sensor-based Coverage of Unstructured Environments and Probabilistic Methods. *The International Journal of Robotics Research, 22*(7-8), 441–466. doi:10.1177/02783649030227002

Ahmadi, M., & Stone, P. (2006). *A multi robot system for continuous area sweeping tasks. Intl. Conf. on Robotics and Automation* (pp. 1724–1729). Piscataway, NJ, USA: IEEE Press.

Altshuler, Y., Bruckstein, A., & Wagner, I. A. (2005). Swarm robotics for a dynamic cleaning problem. *IEEE Swarm Intelligence Symposium.* (pp. 209-216). Piscataway, NJ, USA: IEEE Press.

Arkin, E., Fekete, S., & Mitchell, J. (2000). Approximation algorithms for lawn mowing and milling. *Computational Geometry, 17*(1-2), 25–50. doi:10.1016/S0925-7721(00)00015-8

Batalin, M., & Sukhatme, G. (2002). *Spreading out: A local approach to multi-robot coverage* (pp. 373–382). Intl. Symp. on Distributed Autonomous Robotic Systems.

Choset, H., Lynch, K., Hutchinson, S., Kantor, G., & Burgard, W. (2005). *Kavraki. L., & Thrun, S.* Cambridge, MA, USA: MIT Press.

Correll, N., & Martinoli, A. (2007). *Robust distributed coverage using a swarm of miniature robots. Intl. Conf. on Robotics and Automation* (pp. 379–384). Piscataway, NJ, USA: IEEE Press.

Gasparri, A., Krishnamachari, B., & Sukhatme, G. (2008). A framework for multi-robot node coverage in sensor networks. *Annals of Math and AI, 52*, 281–305.

Hazon, N., & Kaminka, G. (2008). On Redundancy, Efficiency, and Robustness in Coverage for Multiple Robots. *Robotics and Autonomous Systems, 56*(12), 1102–1114. doi:10.1016/j.robot.2008.01.006

Howard, A., Mataric, M., & Sukhatme, G. (2002). *Mobile sensor network deployment using potential fields: A distributed, scalable solution to the area coverage problem* (pp. 299–308). Intl. Symp. on Distributed Autonomous Robotic Systems.

Jager, M., & Nebel, B. (2002). *Dynamic decentralized area partitioning for cooperating cleaning robots. Intl. Conf. on Robotics and Automation* (pp. 3577–3582). Piscataway, NJ, USA: IEEE Press.

Maza, I., & Ollero, A. (2004). Multiple UAV cooperative searching operation using polygon area decomposition and efficient coverage algorithms. *7th International Symposium on Distributed Autonomous Robotic Systems.* (pp. 291-301).

O'Hara, K., & Balch, T. (2004). Pervasive sensorless networks for cooperative multi-robot tasks. *7th International Symposium on Distributed Autonomous Robotic Systems.* pp. 291-301.

Parker, L. (1998). ALLIANCE: An architecture for fault tolerant multi-robot cooperation. *IEEE Transactions on Robotics and Automation, 14*(2), 220–240. doi:10.1109/70.681242

Parker, L. (1999). Adaptive heterogeneous multi-robot teams. *Neurocomputing, 28*(1-3), 75–92. doi:10.1016/S0925-2312(98)00116-7

Parker, L. (2002). Distributed algorithms for mult robot observation of multiple moving targets. *Autonomous Robots, 12*(3), 231–255. doi:10.1023/A:1015256330750

Pearce, J., Powers, B., Hess, C., Rybski, P., Stoeter, S., & Papanikolopoulos, N. (2006). Using virtual pheromones for dispersing a team of multiple miniature robots. *Robotics and Autonomous Systems, 45*(4), 307–321.

Stachniss, C., & Burgard, W. (2003). *Exploring unknown environments with mobile robots using coverage maps. Intl. Joint Conf. on Artificial Intelligence* (pp. 1127–1134). San Francisco, CA, USA: AAAI Press.

Svennebring, J., & Koenig, S. (2003). *Trail-laying robots for robust terrain coverage. Intl. Conf. On Robotics and Automation* (pp. 75–82). Piscataway, NJ, USA: IEEE Press.

Wagner, I., Lindenbaum, M., & Bruckstein, A. (1999). Distributed covering by ant-robots using evaporating traces. *IEEE Transactions on Robotics and Automation, 15*(5), 918–933. doi:10.1109/70.795795

KEY TERMS AND DEFINITIONS

Coalition Game: A technique from the field of game theory in micro-economics that gives rules for a set of humans to divide themselves into teams. The rules should guarantee that the teams that are finally formed are stable, that is, after the final teams are formed, no one should be able to gain by switching to a different team. A numerical measure called *value* is used to measure and compare how well-off different teams are with respect to each other while possible teams are inspected during the team formation process.

Coverage Path Planning: Computational techniques and algorithms used to determine a path for a robot which guarantees that the entire surface of the environment passes under the footprint or sensor swathe of the robot when the robot follows the path.

Distributed Area Coverage: Computational technique used to ensure that the surface area of an environment is entirely covered by a set of robots. Each robot's coverage path plan is calculated by the robot itself and coordinated with other robots in a distributed manner, that is, without using a central authority to control or exchange information between the robots. A desirable outcome of the technique should be to ensure that the combination of the paths covered by all the robots has minimal or no overlap.

Flocking: A type of team formation where the robots in the team maintain a certain separation in terms of distance and orientation with each other. It is similar to collective motion observed in certain species of birds. Reynolds proposed a set of simple rules to computationally simulate flocking, which are widely used at present.

Multi-Robot System: A system comprising of multiple robots where the robots are usually coordinated with each other to coherently perform operations towards accomplishing a task that has been assigned to them.

Swarm Robotics: Robotic systems that involve miniature robots with very limited computational, sensing and communication capabilities. The operations performed by these robots are usually realized through very simple rules such as taxis (moving towards stimulus provided by a light or odor source), attraction and repulsion, etc.

Team Formation: Rules used by a set of robots to maintain either a geometric shape such as single file, arrow, circle, etc. or any arbitrarily-defined shape between themselves while they are moving.

Chapter 11
Path Relinking Scheme for the Max–Cut Problem

Volodymyr P. Shylo
V. M. Glushkov Institute of Cybernetics (IC), Ukraine

Oleg V. Shylo
University of Tennessee, USA

ABSTRACT

In this chapter, a path relinking method for the maximum cut problem is investigated. The authors consider an implementation of the path-relinking, where it is utilized as a subroutine for another meta-heuristic search procedure. Particularly, the authors focus on the global equilibrium search method to provide a set of high quality solutions, the set that is used within the path relinking method. The computational experiment on a set of standard benchmark problems is provided to study the proposed approach. The authors show that when the size of the solution set that is passed to the path relinking procedure is too large, the resulting running times follow the restart distribution, which guarantees that an underlying algorithm can be accelerated by removing all of the accumulated data (set P) and re-initiating its execution after a certain number of elite solutions is obtained.

INTRODUCTION

The maximum cut problem is a well-known to be NP-hard (Karp, 1972), which recently gathered a lot of interest due to a number of important practical applications (Barahona, Grotschel, Junger & Reinelt, 1988; Chang & Du, 1988). The input for the maximum cut problem is an undirected graph $G = G(V,E)$, where each edge $(i,j) \in E$ is assigned a certain weight w_{ij}. Let (V_1,V_2) be a partition of the set of vertices V into two disjoint subsets. A cut (V_1,V_2) in G is any subset of edges $(i,j) \in E$, such that $i \in V_1$ and $j \in V_2$. The maximum cut problem consists in finding a cut in graph G with the maximum sum of the edge weights.

In the current chapter we describe an extension of the algorithm for the maximum cut problem based on the global equilibrium search (GES) method. Earlier comparison with available algorithms using a set of benchmark problems show that GES performs favorably compared to other approaches in terms of computational speed and

DOI: 10.4018/978-1-4666-6328-2.ch011

solution quality (Shylo & Shylo, 2010). The GES method maintains a set of solutions, which are used to prevent algorithm from converging to previously visited areas in the search space. Since this set contains high quality solutions, it is desirable to utilize this set more efficiently, instead of using it just to prevent visiting the same search space areas. Assuming that these high quality solutions share some common structure, one can combine their components in an attempt to find an enhanced solution, or restrict the search to some subset of solutions defined by them. In the current chapter, we describe a scheme where a path relinking procedure is embedded within the GES method to provide such functionality.

BACKGROUND

Path relinking method searches for solutions of an optimization problem along the trajectories that connect solutions from a given set (Glover, Laguna & Marti, 2000). The most common path relinking scheme involves a pair of solutions: an initiating solution and a guiding solution. A set of moves (transformations) are applied starting in the initiating solution that sequentially introduce the attributes of the guiding solution. Usually, such moves result in a sequence of solutions that lie on a path between the initial solution pair.

Assuming that the weights of the graph edges are non-negative, the maximum cut problem can be formulated by the following mixed-integer program (Kahruman, Kolotoglu, Butenko & Hicks, 2007):

$$\sum_{i,j=1,i<j}^{n} w_{ij} y_{ij}$$
$$s.t. \quad y_{ij} - x_i - x_j \leq 0 \quad i,j = 1,...,n, \quad i < j$$
$$y_{ij} + x_i + x_j \leq 2 \quad i,j = 1,...,n, \quad i < j$$
$$x \in \{0,1\}^n$$

The optimal solution vector x defines a graph partition $\{V_1, V_2\}$ (if $x_i = 1$ then $v_i \in V_1$, otherwise $v_i \in V_2$) that has the maximum cut value, the sum of weight of edges connecting different partititions. Let $f(x)$ denote a cost of a cut corresponding to the solution vector x.

Local search based methods for the max-cut problem require an initial solution $x \in \{0,1\}^n$ to start the chain of local improvements until the local optimum is obtained. GES provides an intelligent mechanism of generating initial solutions for local search based methods and it proved to be efficient for a variety of combinatorial problems (Pardalos, Prokopyev, Shylo & Shylo, 2008; Shylo, Prokopyev & Shylo, 2008). The variation of the global equilibrium search for the Max-Cut problem that does not depend on the path-relinking methodology can be found in (Shylo et al, 2012).

PATH RELINKING AND GLOBAL EQUILIBRIUM SEARCH

The generation probabilities in GES are defined by some subset S of previously visited solutions (e.g., a set of local optima). These probabilities are parameterized by an ordered set of temperature values $0 \leq \mu_0 < \mu_1 < ... < \mu_K$, which bear the same function as a cooling schedule in the simulated annealing method (Aarts & *Korst, 1989*). The search process is organized as a repeating sequence of K temperature stages, one for each temperature value. A fixed number of initial solutions are generated at each temperature stage to be used as starting solutions for some local search based method. In case of binary decision variables, the generation procedure at temperature stage k sets jth component to 1 (or 0) with probability given by $p_j(\mu_k)(1 - p_j(\mu_k))$:

$$p_j(\mu_k) =$$

$$\left[1 + \exp\left\{\sum_{i=0}^{k-1} \frac{\mu_{i+1} - \mu_i}{2}(E_{ij}^0 + E_{i+1j}^0 - E_{ij}^1 - E_{i+1j}^1)\right\}\right]^{-1},$$

$$(1)$$

where E_{kj}^1 (E_{kj}^0) is a weighted sum of objective values, that corresponds to solutions in S, such that $x_j = 1$ ($x_j = 0$):

$$E_{kj}^1 =$$

$$\begin{cases} \dfrac{\displaystyle\sum_{x \in S, x_j=1} f(x)\exp(\mu_k f(x))}{\displaystyle\sum_{x \in S, x_j=1} \exp(\mu_k f(x))}, & \text{if } \exists x \in S, \text{ s.t. } x_j = 1 \\[4mm] 0, & \text{otherwise.} \end{cases}$$

$$(2)$$

These formulas are derived from an approximation of the Boltzmann distribution defined on all feasible solutions (Pardalos et al., 2008). Intuitively, they guarantee that the generated solutions are more likely to resemble the solutions in the set S that have high objective values.

It is worth noting, that there is no need to store the whole set S in memory, since E_{kj}^1 and E_{kj}^0 can be easily updated by simple addition if the denominator and the numerator in (2) are stored separately.

If the initial temperature μ_0 is set to zero, the solutions generated at zero-stage are completely random (no bias). The rest of the temperature values can be defined as: $\mu_k = \alpha^{k-1}\beta$ for $k = 1,...,K$. The multiplier α and the initial value β have to be chosen in such a way that the probability of generating a solution x at the last temperature stage (K), such that $x_j = 1$, is approximately equal to the binary value of jth component in the best known solution:

$$\left\|\arg\max\{f(x) : x \in S\} - p(\mu_K)\right\| \approx 0$$

The same temperature vector was used for all considered benchmark problems.

The pseudo-code for the algorithm is presented in Algorithm 1. The algorithm generates a set of initial solutions within a temperature cycle (Algorithm 1, lines 8-22) that consists of K temperature stages. A temperature at kth stage is defined by a kth component of the temperature vector $\mu = [\mu_0, \mu_1..., \mu_K]$. The generation probabilities are calculated in (1) and are used to construct initial solutions for the local search procedure (Algorithm 1, line 9). All the components of the current best solution are perturbed according to these probabilities (each independently). The implementation described in this chapter utilizes a local search procedure based on one-move operator: given a solution x, the local neighborhood consists of all solutions that differ from x by at most one component. The search method based on this neighborhood is referred to as "1-opt" local search (see Algorithm 2). The local search procedure sequentially evaluates solutions from the neighborhood in a random order. If a solution from the neighborhood has a cost function of the same or better quality than the current solution (Algorithm 2, line 6), it becomes a new current solution (Algorithm 2, line 8). The changes to the components of the solution vector are followed by a recalculation of a so-called vector of gains $g(x)$ (Algorithm 2, line 9). The change of cost resulting from changing jth component of x is given by $g_j(x)$:

$$g_{j(x)} = f(x_1,...,x_{j-1},1 - x_j, x_{j+1},...,x_n) - f(x_1,...,x_{j-1},x_j, x_{j+1},...,x_n)$$

Maintaining $g(x)$ throughout all the algorithmic steps allows us to accelerate the evaluation of the move costs in the local search procedure.

The locally-optimal solutions provided by the local search are used to update the set of known

Algorithm 1. GES with path relinking for the max-cut problem

Input: μ – vector of temperature values, K – number of temperature stages, *ngen* – # of solutions generated during each stage

Function:

```
1:  P = ∅;
2:  while stopping criterion = FALSE do
3:      x  = construct random solution
4:      x^max = x; x^best= x
5:      loop
6:          x^old = x^max
7:          S = {x^max} (set of known solutions)
8:          for k = 0 to K do
9:              calculate generation probabilities p(μ_k)
10:             for g = 0 to ngen do
11:                 x =  generate solution(x^max, p(μ_k))
12:                 x^loc = 1-opt local search (x, x^best)
13:                 S = S ∪ {x^loc}\P
14:                 x^new = argmax{f(x): x ∈ S}
15:                 if f(x^new) > f(x^max) then
16:                     x^max = x^new
17:                     if f(x^max) > f(x^best) then
18:                         x^best= x^max
19:                     end if
20:                 end if
21:             end for
22:         end for
23:         if f(x^max) < f(x^best) - H then
24:             break; {exit loop}
25:         end if
26:         if f(x^old) ≥ f(x^max) then
27:             break; {exit loop}
28:         end if
29:     end loop
30:     P = P ∪ {x^max};
31:     Path relinking(P, x^max, S)
32: end while
33: return x^best
```

solutions S (Algorithm 1, lines 12-13) that is used to calculate generation probabilities at the subsequent stages. In order to prevent convergence to the same solutions, we define a set of prohibited solutions P, which can contain the best solutions found during the main cycle (Algorithm 1, line 30). If a new solution belongs to the set of the prohibited solutions, it is excluded from further

Algorithm 2. Local Search 1-opt

```
Input: x - solution, gains(x) - the vector of gains
Function:
 1:  repeat
 2:      Generate random permutation RP of the set {1,. . ., n}
 3:      Δ = 0
 4:      for k = 1 to n do
 5:          j =RP[k]
 6:          if g_j(x) ≥ 0 then
 7:              Δ = Δ + g_j(x)
 8:              x_j = 1- x_j
 9:              g(x) = recalculate gains(x)
10:         end if
11:     end for
12: until Δ >0
13: return  x
```

consideration (Algorithm 1, line 13). The set P can be quite large, thus there is a desire to utilize valuable information about the search space that is provided by the solutions from this set. Path relinking provides a perfect framework to achieve this goal.

The traditional implementations of the path relinking method populate the elite set with a predefined number of solutions before initiating the path relinking. In our work, the path relinking procedure is used to explore the paths that connect every new solution generated by GES to the solutions generated at the previous solution cycles (set of prohibited solutions P). The solution is included in the set P only if the Hamming distance to other solutions in P is less than a predefined value $d_{div} (d_{div} = 50)$. This allows us to maintain a certain level of diversity of the solutions involved in path relinking.

Usually, within the path relinking method, pairs of high quality solutions are connected with a single path, which may lead to a solution of improved quality. However, computational

experiments with this scheme reveal that such improvement is probable only for initial solutions of bad quality. Since the set of prohibited solutions P provided by GES typically contains high-quality solutions, an application of path relinking via single path construction almost never succeeds. Therefore, we can search for an improvement along all the possible paths between two initial solutions. A truncated version of GES can be used to provide an effective search space exploration in this restricted domain.

Given two binary solutions sol^1 and sol^2, let J be a subset of indices of solution components that are identical in both solutions:

$$J = \{j \in \{1,...,n\} : sol_j^1 = sol_j^2\}$$

Now, there are two minor changes that need to be made to GES scheme presented in Algorithm 1. Firstly, the generation probabilities (Algorithm 1, line 9) should be fixed for all components in J, i.e., $p_j(\mu_k) = sol_j^1 = sol_j^2$ for all temperature stages k and $j \in J$. Secondly, the set J should be excluded from the initial random permutation RP in the local search method (Algorithm 2, line 2): $RP = RP\backslash J$. Let GES^{tr} denote this truncated version of the global equilibrium search.

In this chapter, we will focus on the scheme where the path relinking procedure is invoked after completion of the main cycle of GES (Algorithm 1, line 31). The steps of this procedure are outlined in Algorithm 3. Given the best found solution x^{max} from the main cycle, the path relinking procedure sequentially selects solutions from P (in a random order) to form an initializing/guiding solution pair. These two solutions are used to initialize the set of known solutions S to be used within GES^{tr} that was discussed above. Their cost functions (as used in (2) to calculate generation probabilities) are artificially adjusted to avoid early convergence (Algorithm 3, line 6). The choice of the maximum size of the set P is discussed in the section on computational experiments. Upon reaching this maximum size, the algorithm is restarted by deleting all the solutions from P. If the path relinking routine finds a new best solution, x^{best}, the regular implementation of GES (not GES^{tr}) is initiated with $S = \{ x^{best} \}$.

COMPUTATIONAL STUDY

There are a number of benchmark instances that were suggested for testing and evaluating the efficiency of algorithms for the Max-Cut problem, however two sets of problems dominated the recent studies on the Max-Cut problem (Goemans &Williamson, 1995; Marti, Duarte & Laguna, 2009; Burer, Monteiro & Zhang, 2002; Festa, Pardalos, Resende & Ribeiro, 2002; Palubeckis and Krivickiene, 2004):

1. 24 problems that were suggested by Helmberg and Rendl (1999): G1,G2,G3,G11 - G16, G22, G23, G24, G32 - G37, G43, G44, G45, G48, G49 and G50. These problems consist of planar, toroidal and random graphs with number of vertices from 800 to 3000. The weights of the edges belong to the set {-1, 0, 1}.

2. 20 problems that were considered by Burer et al. (2002): sg3dl101000 – sg3dl1010000 and sg3dl141000 – sg3dl1410000. These graphs are based on cubic lattices with 10 instances having 1000 vertices and another 10 instances having 2744 vertices. The weights of the edges belong to the set { - 1, 0,1}.

The optimal size of the elite set (the set P in our case) used by the path relinking is difficult to characterize. Empirically, it can be shown that the large size of the elite set leads to the restart distribution of the algorithm running times (Luby, Sinclair & Zuckerman, 1993), the algorithm can be accelerated by simply removing all of the accumulated data (set P) and re-initiating its execution after a certain number of elite solutions is obtained.

An extensive set of experiments was performed to evaluate the best choice of the maximum size for the elite set P. This study revealed that the algorithmic performance degrades after accumulating a certain number of solutions in the elite set. Figure 1 illustrates these observations, based on 300 independent runs on the problem G37. Each run was terminated as soon as the solution quality of 7688 or better was achieved, and the distribution of the running times until termination is provided for analysis. Comparing the algorithm with no restriction on the maximum elite set size (G37∞) with the algorithm that is restarted after reaching 27 solutions in the elite set (G37 27), one can see that the overall performance is clearly

Algorithm 3. Path relinking

Input: x^{max} – new initial solution for path relinking, P – set of prohibited solutions, S – set of known solutions.

1:      Generate random permutation RP of the set $\{1,\,.\,.\,.,\,|P|\}$
2:      $x^{new} = x^{max}$
3:      **for** $k = 1$ to $|P|$ **do**
4:          $i = RP[k]$
5:          $\tilde{S} = x^{new} \cup P[i]$;
6:          $f(x^{max}) := f(P[i]) := \sum_{x \in S} f(x) \exp(-\mu_2 f(x)) / \sum_{x \in S} \exp(-\mu_2 f(x))$
7:          $x^{max} = GES^{tr}(\tilde{S})$
8:          **if** $\mathrm{f}(\mathrm{x}^{max}) \geq \mathrm{f}(\mathrm{x}^{new})$ **then**
9:              $\mathrm{x}^{new} = \mathrm{x}^{max}$
10:         **end if**
11:     **end for**
12:     $\mathrm{P} = \mathrm{P} \cup \ \mathrm{x}^{max}$
13:     **return** P

improved in the latter case. The algorithm without the path relinking (G37 0) is dominated by other approaches. Based on experiments with varying sizes, the maximum size of the set P was fixed to 32 solutions in this study; this setting was used in all consequent experiments.

Figure 1. The probability of finding the target solution ($f^{target}= 7688$) for the problem G37 as a function of computational time

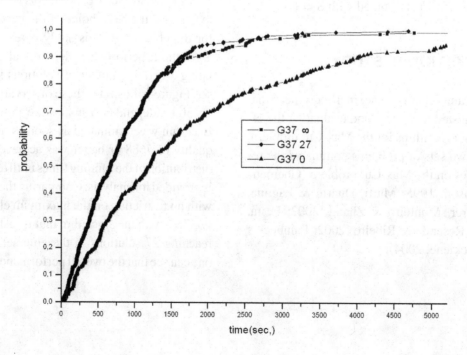

Table 1. Computational results

Problem	Size	BKS	Time (Seconds)		Average		BFS	
			GES-PR	GES	GES-PR	GES	GES-PR	GES
G1	800	11624	10.73	13.72	11624.0	11624.0	11624	11624
G2	800	11620	9.97	9.26	11620.0	11620.0	11620	11620
G3	800	11622	2.63	2.56	11622.0	11622.0	11622	11622
G11	800	564	2.43	2.44	564.0	564.0	564	564
G12	800	556	7.30	7.83	556.0	556.0	556	556
G13	800	582	1.51	1.52	582.0	582.0	582	582
G14	800	3063	707.24	509.94	3064.0	3063.6	3064	3064
G15	800	3050	14.33	10.56	3050.0	3050.0	3050	3050
G16	800	3052	43.10	40.48	3052.0	3052.0	3052	3052
G22	2000	13358	647.28	722.98	13358.9	13356.5	13359	13358
G23	2000	13329	293.36	170.95	13342.0	13342.0	13342	13342
G24	2000	13331	310.53	847.71	13337.0	13335.1	13337	13337
G32	2000	1402	66.35	87.68	1410.0	1410.0	1410	1410
G33	2000	1376	315.89	494.84	1382.0	1381.8	1382	1382
G34	2000	1372	97.50	72.89	1384.0	1384.0	1384	1384
G35	2000	7672	937.83	616.08	7684.8	7682.9	7686	7685
G36	2000	7680	861.02	943.84	7675.7	7673.9	7677	7675
G37	2000	7681	916.74	763.45	7688.7	7687.6	7691	7690
G43	1000	6660	48.69	395.53	6660.0	6660.0	6660	6660
G44	1000	6650	6.33	11.22	6650.0	6650.0	6650	6650
G45	1000	6654	146.42	744.34	6654.0	6653.5	6654	6654
G48	3000	6000	0.12	0.12	6000.0	6000.0	6000	6000
G49	3000	6000	0.16	0.16	6000.0	6000.0	6000	6000
G50	3000	5880	11.82	11.48	5880.0	5880.0	5880	5880
Total sum:		**150803**	**5459.28**	**6481.58**	**150841.1**	**150830.9**	**150845**	**150841**
sg3dl101000	1000	896	77.44	128.25	896.0	896.0	896	896
sg3dl102000	1000	900	3.04	2.98	900.0	900.0	900	900
sg3dl103000	1000	892	9.80	9.73	892.0	892.0	892	892
sg3dl104000	1000	898	13.96	13.62	898.0	898.0	898	898
sg3dl105000	1000	886	130.10	106.4	886.0	886.0	886	886
sg3dl106000	1000	888	4.07	4.28	888.0	888.0	888	888
sg3dl107000	1000	900	108.68	114.96	900.0	900.0	900	900
sg3dl108000	1000	882	121.25	162.67	882.0	882.0	882	882
sg3dl109000	1000	902	36.98	25.04	902.0	902.0	902	902
sg3dl1010000	1000	894	6.73	8.93	894.0	894.0	894	894
sg3dl141000	2744	2446	643.20	714.53	2445.2	2443.6	2446	2446
sg3dl142000	2744	2458	278.61	552.15	2458.0	2457.6	2458	2458
sg3dl143000	2744	2442	609.80	642.61	2441.2	2439.8	2442	2442

continued on following page

Table 1. Continued

Problem	Size	BKS	Time (Seconds)		Average		BFS	
			GES-PR	GES	GES-PR	GES	GES-PR	GES
sg3dl144000	2744	2450	847.39	633.33	2449.0	2447.6	2450	2448
sg3dl145000	2744	2446	259.69	486.88	2446.0	2446.0	2446	2446
sg3dl146000	2744	2450	648.79	360.03	2450.8	2450.2	2452	2452
sg3dl147000	2744	2444	604.55	614.73	2443.8	2443.8	2444	2444
sg3dl148000	2744	2446	617.13	587.98	2445.6	2444.8	2448	2446
sg3dl149000	2744	2424	670.98	659.87	2425.6	2425.4	2426	2426
sg3dl1410000	2744	2458	380.96	539.63	2457.0	2455.8	2458	2456
Total sum:		**33402**	**6073.15**	**6368.6**	**33400.2**	**33392.6**	**33408**	**33402**

The same algorithmic parameters of the algorithm are chosen similarly to those described by Shylo (2010). Each problem from the benchmark set was solved 10 times with a time limit set to 30 minutes. The results of these runs are presented in Table 1. The problem size and the best known solution value (BKS) in the literature (excluding the results reported by Shylo (2010)) are reported for each benchmark instance. The best found solutions (column "BFS") among all 10 runs obtained within the 30 minute interval reveal the overall superiority of the approach, which utilizes the path- relinking scheme (GES-PR) compared to GES without path relinking (see the results for G22, G35, G36, sg3dl144000, sg3dl148000 and sg3dl1410000). The average best found solutions (within the 30 minute time limit) were better for GES-PR on all benchmark problems (column "Average"). The average times (column "Time") to the best found solution for each run (average out of 10) indicate that on many problems GES-PR

not only provides better solutions, but also requires less computational time. All computational experiments presented in this section were performed on a personal computer with a 2.83GHz Intel Core Quad Q9550 processors with 3.0GB of RAM.

CONCLUSION

The path relinking methodology has been shown to provide efficient search strategies for a variety of optimization problems. This chapter illustrates an alternative use of the path relinking methodology ideas, where the path relinking is employed to explore a given subset of solutions. A detailed implementation of the modified GES method incorporating those ideas illustrates effectiveness of this methodology for the Max-Cut problem. The potential of the embedded path-relinking scheme is highlighted through the computational results on a set of standard benchmark problems.

REFERENCES

Aarts, E., & Korst, J. (1989). *Simulated annealing and Boltzmann machines: a stochastic approach to combinatorial optimization and neural computing.* New York, NY: John Wiley & Sons, Inc.

Barahona, F., Grotschel, M., Junger, M., & Reinelt, G. (1988). An application of combinatorial optimization to statistical physics and circuit layout design. *Operations Research, 36*(3), 493–513. doi:10.1287/opre.36.3.493

Burer, S., Monteiro, R. D. C., & Zhang, Y. (2002). Rank-two relaxation heuristics for max-cut and other binary quadratic programs. *SIAM Journal on Optimization, 12*(2), 503–521. doi:10.1137/S1052623400382467

Chang, K. C., & Du, H. C. (1988). Layer assignment problem for three-layer routing. *IEEE Transactions on Computers, 37*(5), 625–632. doi:10.1109/12.4616

Duarte, R., & Laguna, A. (2009). Advanced scatter search for the max-cut problem. *INFORMS Journal on Computing, 21*(1), 26–38. doi:10.1287/ijoc.1080.0275

Festa, P., Pardalos, P. M., Resende, M. G. C., & Ribeiro, C. C. (2002). Randomized heuristics for the max-cut problem. *Optimization Methods and Software, 17*(6), 1033–1058. doi:10.1080/1055678021000090033

Glover, F., Laguna, M., & Marti, R. (2000). Fundamentals of scatter search and path relinking. *Control and Cybernetics, 39*, 653–684.

Goemans, M. X., & Williamson, D. (1995). Improved approximation algorithms for maximum cut and satisfiability problems using semidefinite programming. *Journal of the ACM, 42*(6), 1115–1145. doi:10.1145/227683.227684

Helmberg, C., & Rendl, F. (2000). A spectral bundle method for semidefinite programming. *SIAM Journal on Optimization, 10*(3), 673–696. doi:10.1137/S1052623497328987

Kahruman, S., Kolotoglu, E., Butenko, S., & Hicks, I. V. (2007). On greedy construction heuristics for the max-cut problem. *Int. J. Comput. Sci. Eng., 3*(3), 211–218.

Karp, R. (1972). Reducibility among combinatorial problems. In R. Miller, & J. Thatcher (Eds.), *Complexity of Computer Computations* (pp. 85–103). Plenum Press. doi:10.1007/978-1-4684-2001-2_9

Luby, M., Sinclair, A., & Zuckerman, D. (1993). Optimal speedup of Las Vegas algorithms. *Information Processing Letters, 47*(4), 173–180. doi:10.1016/0020-0190(93)90029-9

Palubeckis, G., & Krivickiene, V. (2004). Application of multistart tabu search to the max-cut problem. *Informaacines Technologijos Ir Valdymas, 2*(31), 29–35.

Pardalos, P. M., Prokopyev, O. A., Shylo, O. V., & Shylo, V. P. (2008). Global equilibrium search applied to the unconstrained binary quadratic optimization problem. *Optimization Methods Software, 23*(1), 129–140. doi:10.1080/10556780701550083

Shylo, O. V., Prokopyev, O. A., & Shylo, V. P. (2008). Solving weighted max-sat via global equilibrium search. *Operations Research Letters, 36*(4), 434–438. doi:10.1016/j.orl.2007.11.007

Shylo, V. P., & Shylo, O. V. (2010). Solving the maxcut problem by the global equilibrium search. *Cybernetics and Systems Analysis, 46*(5), 744–754. doi:10.1007/s10559-010-9256-4

Shylo, V. P., Shylo, O. V., & Roschyn, V. A. (2012). Solving weighted max-cut problem by global equilibrium search. *Cybernetics and Systems Analysis, 48*(4), 563–567. doi:10.1007/s10559-012-9435-6

KEY TERMS AND DEFINITIONS

Elite Set of Solutions: Usually a diverse set of high-quality feasible solutions of an optimization problem.

Local M Move: A change of attributes of a given solution that creates a new solution, where the set of attributes involved and all possible changes are fixed for every solution.

Local Search: Any search procedure that iteratively transforms one solution into another by modifying its attributes using a sequence of local moves.

Metaheuristic: An optimization procedure that exploits, guides or parameterizes lower-level heuristics.

Restart Distribution: The distribution of algorithm runtime that allows improving an average running time by restarting the algorithm after a predefined number of iterations.

Temperature Parameter: A value that parameterizes the Boltzmann Distribution or its approximations.

Temperature Schedule: A vector of temperature parameters corresponding to the temperature stages.

Chapter 12
Image Segmentation Based on Bio-Inspired Optimization Algorithms

Hongwei Mo
Harbin Engineering University, China

Lifang Xu
Harbin Engineering University, China

Mengjiao Geng
Harbin Engineering University, China

ABSTRACT

This chapter addresses the issue of image segmentation by clustering in the domain of image processing. Fuzzy C-Means is a widely adopted clustering algorithm. Bio-inspired optimization algorithms are optimal methods inspired by the principles or behaviors of biology. For the purpose of reinforcing the global search capability of FCM, five Bio-Inspired Optimization Algorithms (BIOA) including Biogeography-Based Optimization (BBO), Artificial Fish School Algorithm (AFSA), Artificial Bees Colony (ABC), Particle Swarm Optimization (PSO), and Bacterial Foraging Algorithm (BFA) are used to optimize the objective criterion function, which is interrelated to centroids in FCM. The optimized FCMs by the five algorithms are used for image segmentation, respectively. They have different effects on the results.

INTRODUCTION

Image segmentation is one of the central problems in computer vision and pattern recognition. It refers to the process of assigning a label to every pixel in an image such that pixels with the same label share certain visual characteristics. The result of image segmentation is a set of segments (sets of pixels) that collectively cover the entire image. Pixels in the same region are similar with respect to some characteristics or computed properties, such as color, intensity, and texture. Adjacent regions are significantly different with respect to the same characteristics. The goal of segmentation is to simplify and/or change the representation of

DOI: 10.4018/978-1-4666-6328-2.ch012

an image into something that is more meaningful and easier to analyze (Shapiro & Stockman, 2001).

There are many general-purpose approaches available for image segmentation such as threshold methods (Mardia & Hainsworth, 1988), edge-based methods (Perona & Malik, 1990), region-based methods (Hijjatoleslami & Kitter, 1998), and graph-based methods (Felzenszwalb & Huttenlocher, 2004). In contrast to the heuristic nature of these methods, one would formalize an objective criterion for evaluating a given segmentation. This would allow us to formulate the segmentation problem as an optimization problem. The objective function that one would seek to optimize is the interclass variance that is used in cluster analysis. An optimizer can lead to efficient solutions for optimal segmentation. But the objective function is usually not a monotone chain, therefore the problem is general NP-hard. Following this way, some clustering methods have been applied to solve image segmentation problems.

Clustering techniques represent the non-supervised pattern classification in groups (Jain et al., 1999). Considering the image context, the clusters correspond to some semantic meaning in the image, which is, objects. Among the many methods for data analysis through clustering and unsupervised image segmentation is: Nearest Neighbor Clustering, Fuzzy C-Means (FCM) clustering and Artificial Neural Networks for Clustering (Jain et al., 1999). Such bio and social-inspired methods try to solve the related problems using knowledge found in the way nature solves problems. Social inspired approaches intend to solve problems considering that an initial and previously defined weak solution can lead the whole population to find a better or a best so far solution.

Among them, the most successful image segmentation algorithm into homogeneous regions is fuzzy c-means algorithm (Bezdek, 1981). There are a lot of visual applications reporting the use of fuzzy c-means, e.g. in medical image analysis, soil structure analysis, satellite imagery (Felzen-

szwalb & Huttenlocher, 2004; Hijjatoleslami & Kitter, 1998; Mardia & Hainsworth, 1988; Perona & Malik, 1990). Many variations of approaches have been introduced over last 20 years, and image segmentation remains an open-solution problem. As global optimization techniques, evolutionary algorithms (EAs) are likely to be good tools for image segmentation task. In the past two decades, EAs have been applied to image segmentation with promising results (Andrey, 1999; Bhandarkar & Zhang, 1999; Bhanu et al., 1995; Gong et al., 2008; Koppen et al., 2003; Maulik, 2009; Melkemi et al., 2006; Veenman et al., 2003). These algorithms exploited the metaphor of natural evolution in the context of image segmentation.

The original FCM algorithm, due to its drawbacks such as poor ability of global searching, easy sticking at local optimal solution, is often improved by combining with other optimal algorithm and then used in image segmentation. In this paper, we adopt five bio-inspired optimization algorithms to search the center of cluster for FCM. The paper is organized as follows. At first, the FCM and image segmentation are introduced respectively. Second, BBO, AFSA, ABC, PSO and BFOA are introduced. Third, the hybrid clustering methods of the five BIOAs and FCM are tested on some standard images from the USC-SIPI Image Database and the simulation results are analyzed. At last, the conclusions are drawn.

BACKGROUND

Recently there has been an increase in the presence of bio-inspired optimization algorithms (BIOA) of image segmentation. Most of them focus on searching the right center of cluster for FCM. Yang et al. (2007) proposed a FCM based on Ant Colony Algorithm. Tian et al. (2008) applied the FCM optimized by PSO to segment SAR images and its experimental results on the MSTAR dataset had demonstrated that the proposed method was capable of effectively segmenting SAR images and achieving better results than the improved FCM (IFCM) algorithm. Yang et al. (2008) had proposed a three-level tree model which was inspired from the ants' self-assembling behavior to make the clustering structure more adaptive for image segmentation. In order to increase the segmentation precision of brain tissues in MR images to solve some problems existing in the present genetic fuzzy clustering algorithm, Nie, et al. (2008) had proposed an improved genetic fuzzy clustering algorithm. Experiment results showed that higher segmentation accuracy was obtained using the proposed segmentation method comparing with the fast FCM algorithm and the conventional genetic fuzzy clustering algorithm. Zeng et al. (2008) directly unified GA in the magnetic resonance images (MRI) segmentation and the global optimum in MRI segmentation was obtained. Swagatam, et al.(2010) had presented a modified differential evolution (DE) algorithm for clustering the pixels of an image in the grayscale intensity space in their paper and extensive comparison results has indicated that the proposed algorithm has an edge over a few state-of-the-art algorithms for automatic multi-class image segmentation. Sowmya et al. (2011) had used a competitive neural network (CNN) and fuzzy clustering techniques to segment color images.

In Sathya(2011), MBF algorithm for solving the multilevel thresholding for image segmentation is proposed. The proposed method considers the two objective functions of the Kapur's and Otsu's methods. The feasibility of the proposed method is demonstrated for fourteen different images and compared with BF, PSO and GA methods. The results show that the proposed MBF algorithm can significantly outperform the other evolutionary techniques, on the basis of the solution quality, stability and computation efficiency.

In Sathya(2011), the authors propose a new optimization approach to solve multilevel thresholding using the adaptive bacterial foraging (ABF) technique.

Balasubramani(2013) used Artificial Bee Colony Algorithm to improve the efficieny of FCM on abnormal brain image.

IMAGE SEGMENTATION AND FCM

The State-of-the-Art

In general, image segmentation techniques can be classified in:

1. **Threshold-Based Techniques**: Are generally used for gray level images. A threshold value T is defined to split the image in two parts: foreground and background based on pixel value.
2. **Histogram-Based Techniques:** The histogram of all the pixels is calculated, and according to peaks and valleys different clusters are formed.
3. **Edge Detection Techniques:** First and second order derivatives are used for detection of edges. Edges are divided in two categories: intensity edges and texture edges.
4. **Region-Based Techniques:** Uses region growing and region splitting-merging procedures. Region growing procedure groups pixels or sub regions into large regions based on predefined criteria. Region split-merge divides image into disjoint regions and then either merge and/or split to satisfy prerequisite constraints.
5. **Watershed Transformation Techniques:** Considered to be more stable than the previous techniques, it considers the gradient magnitude of an image (GMI) as a topographic surface. Pixels having the highest GMI correspond to watershed lines, which represent region boundaries.

In summary, image features may contain concepts (definitions of things) and relations between concepts.

This chapter is located in this context of optimization techniques. We present some new techniques to solve clustering and image segmentation problems and discussion about experiments and results.

The FCM

Clustering is the most popular method for medical image segmentation, with fuzzy c-means(FCM) clustering and expectation– maximization (EM) algorithms being the typical methods. A common disadvantage of EM algorithms is that the intensity distribution of brain images is modeled as a normal distribution, which is not the fact for noisy images. FCM is a kind of simple mechanical clustering method based on exploring minimum value of the objective function (Wu & Yang, 2002). The objective function proposed by Dunn is called the clustering criterion function, namely error squares function. Historically, FCM clustering algorithm introduced by Bezdek (Bezdek,1981) is based on minimizing an objective function, with respect to the fuzzy membership and set of cluster centroids. It has the drawback of increasing insensitivity of the membership function to noise. If an image contains noise or is affected by artifacts, their presences can change the pixel intensities, which will result in an improper segmentation.

Let $X = [x_1, x_2, \cdots, x_n]$ be the n dimension sample space. The criterion function is shown by (1):

$$J(X;U,V) = \sum_{i=1}^{c} \sum_{k=1}^{N} (\mu_{ik})^m \left\| x_k - v_i \right\|_A^2 \quad (1)$$

where $V = [v_1, v_2, \cdots, v_c], v_i \in R^n$, V is the clustering center.

The Euclidean distance between data set x_k and clustering center v_i is

$$D_{ikA}^2 = \left\| x_k - v_i \right\|_A^2 = (x_k - v_i)^T A(x_k - v_i)$$

$$(2)$$

where μ_{ik} is the membership function that the ith sample belongs to k^{th} clustering center. It is defined by equation (3)

$$\mu_{ik} = \frac{1}{\sum_{j=1}^{c} (D_{ikA} / D_{jkA})^{2/(m-1)}}, 1 \leq i \leq c, 1 \leq k \leq N$$

$$(3)$$

FCM is described as follows:

Step1: Select $e > 0$, initialize clustering centre v_0, let $g = 1$.

Step 2: Calculate the fuzzy matrix U^g based on equation (3).

Step 3: If $\exists i$ and r make $\mu_{ir}(g) = 1$ and $k \neq r$, then let $\mu_{ir}(g) = 0$.

Step 4: Update the clustering center following equation (4):

$$v_i = \frac{\sum_{k=1}^{N} \mu_{ik}^m x_k}{\sum_{k=1}^{N} \mu_{ik}^m}, 1 \leq i \leq c \quad (4)$$

Step 5: If $\left\| v^{(k)} - v^{(k+1)} \right\| < e$, stop iteration, else let $g = g + 1$ and return to step 1.

BIO-INSPIRED OPTIMIZATION ALGORITHMS

Biogeograpy Based Optimization

BBO is a new population-based optimization algorithm (Simon, 2008), which mimics how animals migrate from one habitat to another, how new species arise, and how species become extinct. These biological behaviors are modeled into search methods for optimization. In BBO, the variables that characterize habitability are called suitability index variables (SIVs), which are similar to genes of genetic algorithms (GAs). Each individual is considered as a habitat with a habitat suitability index (HSI), which is similar to the fitness of GAs. A good solution is analogous to a habitat with a high HSI and shares its good SIVs with low HSI solution. Low HSI solutions accept a lot of new features from high HSI solutions to raise their quality.

The main feature of BBO which differs from the other EAs lies in its migration strategy or migration operation. In BBO, each individual has its own emigration rate and immigration rate, which are the functions of the number of species in the habitat. Mathematically, the concept of emigration and immigration can be represented by a probabilistic model. Suppose that the number of an individual's species is k ($k = 1, 2, ..., S_{max}$ where S_{max} is the maximum number of species), and then immigration rate λ_k and emigration rate μ_k can be calculated as:

$$\lambda_k = I(1 - \frac{k}{S_{max}}) \tag{5}$$

$$\mu_k = \frac{Ek}{S_{max}} \tag{6}$$

where I and E are the maximum possible immigration and emigration rate, respectively.

If a given solution is selected to be modified, its immigration rate λ is used to probabilistically decide whether or not to modify each SIV in that solution. If a given SIV in a given solution X_i is selected to be modified, the emigration rates μ of the other solutions is used to probabilistically decide which solution X_j should migrate

a randomly selected SIV to the solution S_i. Migration is written as

$$X_i(SIV) \leftarrow X_j(SIV) \tag{7}$$

After migration is completed, mutation is used to increase the diversity of the population to get better solutions. Mutation changes a habitat's SIV randomly based on mutation rate, just as in other EAs.

Suppose that N is the size of the population P, T is the iteration generation and g_{max} is maximum number of generation, the pseudo-code of BBO is given in Algorithm 1.

Artificial Fish School Algorithm

The models imitate the fish swarm series of behavior in nature which can be defined as (Rocha, 2011):

1. Random behavior
2. Searching behavior
3. Swarming behavior
4. Chasing behavior
5. Leaping behavior

The next behavior of artificial fish depends on its current state and environmental state. Random behavior can be presented as the initialization phase of the algorithm. The crucial step in the AFS algorithms is a "visual scope". A basic biological behavior of any animal is to discover a region with more food, by vision or sense. Depending on the current position of the individual in the population, marked as $x_i \in R_n$, three possible situations may occur:

1. When the "visual scope" is empty, and there are no other individuals in its neighborhood to follow, individual x_i moves randomly searching for a better region

Algorithm 1. BBO algorithm

```
Initialize parameters: N , g_max
Evaluate the fitness for each habitat in population P
While T ≤ g_max do
bitat            For each habitat do
Map the HSI to number of species k, λ and μ according to (6) and (7)
     Probabilistically choose the immigration habitat based on λ
If immigrating then
Probabilistically choose the emigration habitat based on μ
X_i(SIV) ← X_j(SIV)
End if
     End for
  Probabilistically decide whether to mutate each habitat in population P
population Pt in rithm I.Evaluate the fitness for each habitat in population
P
T = T +1
End while
```

2. When the "visual scope" is crowded, the xi individual has difficulty to follow any particular individual, and searches for a better region choosing randomly another location from the "visual scope".

3. When the "visual scope" is not crowded, the xi individual can choose between two option: to swarm moving towards the central or to chase moving towards the best location. The condition that determines the crowd issue of xi individual in the 'visual scope' is given in Equation 8:

$$\frac{np^i}{m} \leq \theta \tag{8}$$

where $\theta \in (0,1]$ is the crowd parameter, m is the number of individuals in the population and np^i is the number of individuals in the "visual scope". In the searching behavior phase, an individual is randomly chosen in the "visual scope" of x_i and a movement towards it is carried out if it improves current x_i location. Otherwise, the individual x_i moves randomly. The swarming behavior is characterized by a movement towards the central point in the "visual scope" of x_i. The swarming behavior is progressive stage that is activated only if the central point has a better function value than the current x_i. Otherwise, the point x_i follows the searching behavior. The chasing behavior presents a movement towards the point that has the last function value x_{min}. The swarm and chase behavior can be considered as local search. Leaping behavior solves the problem when the best objective function value in the population does not change for a certain number of iterations. In this case the algorithm selects random individual from the population. This process empowers algorithm for obtaining better results in solving numerous problems.

Artificial Bee Colony Optimization

As mentioned before, Karaboga (2005) developed an algorithm based on the behavior of honey bees, called ABC. The ABC pseudo code is shown next:

1. Initialize food sources
2. Repeat
3. Each employed goes to a food source in its memory
   a. Determines a neighbor source
   b. Evaluates nectar
   c. Return to hive and dances
4. Each onlooker watches the dance
   a. Chooses one of the sources, considering the intensity of dance
   b. Goes to the food source selected
   c. Determines a neighbor source
   d. Evaluates nectar
5. The food sources abandoned are determined
   a. Abandoned food sources are replaced by new ones discovered by scouts
6. The best food source until this iteration is saved
7. Go to step 2 until a certain criteria is reached.

The initial food sources are randomly initialized, by the formula:

$$x_{i,j}^k = x\_low_j + rand()(x\_high_j - x\_low_j) \quad (9)$$

$$j = 1, 2, ..., D; i = 1, 2, ..., N_{fs}; k = 0$$

being considered that x_high_j and x_low_j are the upper and lower limits where the function to optimize is defined; N_{fs} is the number of food sources, D states for dimensions and k is the actual iteration. Next in the algorithm, each employed bee is sent to a randomly selected food source and a neighbor is determined.

Both, the source in memory and the modified one are evaluated; the bee memorizes the new position and forgets the old one. Later, employed bees return the hive and dances; and onlooker bees will choose a food source to exploit according to a probability's function:

$$q_i = \frac{fit_i}{\sum_{j=1}^{N_{fs}} fit_j} \quad (10)$$

where fit_i represents the fitness of solution i, evaluated by the employed i, calculated by:

$$fit_i = \begin{cases} \dfrac{1}{f(x_i) + 1} & if\ f(x_i) \geq 0 \\ 1 + abs(f(x_i)) & elsewhere \end{cases} \quad (11)$$

Later, again a neighbor is determined by the onlooker, both food sources are evaluated and the best is memorized. Finally, one scout is generated at the end of each iteration in order to explore for new food sources. The cycle is repeated both until a minima distance is reached or a maximum iterations number.

Particle Swarm Optimization

Particle Swarm Optimization (PSO) was created as a general purpose optimizer in 1995, when Kennedy and Eberhart joined their efforts in order to simulate the social behavior of some species; those efforts evolved until the simulation became a general purpose optimizer whose main idea lies behind the individuals in a swarm (Kennedy & Eberhart, 1995). In this work we have used a modification of Clerc's PSO (Clerc, 1999), where a constriction parameter is used. In that PSO version, the two main governing equations are:

$$v_i^{k+1} = \omega_k \cdot (v_i^k + c1 \cdot rand() \cdot (p\_best_i - x_i^k) + c2 \cdot rand() \cdot (g\_best - x_i^k))$$

(12)

$$x_i^{k+1} = v_i^{k+1} + x_i^k$$

(13)

In the first part of the algorithm, the particles' positions and velocities are randomly initialized:

$$x_{i,j}^k = x\_low_j + rand()(x\_high_j - x\_low_j)$$

(14)

$$v_{i,j}^k = v\_low_j + rand()(v\_high_j - v\_low_j)$$

(15)

$$j = 1, 2, ..., D; i = 1, 2, ..., N_p; k = 0$$

Considering $rand()$ is a uniformly distributed random number, x_high_j and v_high_j are the superior limits that positions and velocities can reach; x_low_j and v_low_j are the respective inferior limits, and N_p states the particle's number. The next part deals with knowing p_best_i known as the best particle found at i-th position until iteration k, and g_best represents the best global particle found so far, considering all the population. Once the aforementioned values are found, velocities and position of all particles are actualized by using Equation (13), taking into account that ω_k is the constriction parameter as proposed in (Wei & Kangling, 2008), modified with:

$$\omega_k = \omega_0 \cdot \exp\left(\frac{-\rho \cdot k}{N_{max}}\right)$$

Usually $c1 \approx c2 \approx 2$. It is important to notice that the dynamic constriction parameter is a slightly difference to the original Clerc's algorithm, in which the constriction parameter is static. In this case, ω_0 is an initial constriction value, ρ is a control value, k is the actual iteration and N_{max} represents the maximum number of iterations.

Bacterial Foraging Optimization Algorithm

Passino (2002) proposed a new kind of bionic algorithm-- Bacteria Foraging Optimization Algorithm (BFOA) which is based on the behavior that E. coli engulfs food in human's intestinal. In this algorithm, each individual in the colony is independent. They continuously change direction and step length to find out the local point with the most abundant food in the search space which is equivalent to the optimal solution in algorithm. Meanwhile, in order to enhance the searching accuracy, this algorithm contains replication and elimination processes to find the global optimal solution. Besides very strong global search ability, BFOA also has fine local search capability (Chu et al., 2008). The basic procedures of BFOA are demonstrated as follows:

Step 1: Initialization.
$n, S, N_C, N_S, N_{re}, N_{ed}, P_{ed}, C(i) \, i = (1, 2, \cdots S)$
are the main parameters, where
n: Dimension of the search space,
S: The number of bacteria in the colony,
N_C: Chemotactic steps,
N_S: Swim steps,
N_{re}: Reproductive steps,
N_{ed}: Elimination and dispersal steps,
P_{ed}: Probability of elimination,
$C(i)$: Run-length unit.
Step 2: Elimination-dispersal loop: $l = l + 1$.
Step 3: Reproduction loop: $k = k + 1$.
Step 4: Chemotaxis loop: $j = j + 1$.
    a.   For $i = 1, 2, \cdots S$, take a chemotactic step for bacterium i as follows.
    b.   Compute fitness function, $F(i, j, k, l)$.

c. Let $M_{last} = F(i, j, k, l)$ to save this value since we may find a better value via a swim.

d. Tumble: Generate a random vector $\Delta(i) \in R^n$ with each element $\Delta m(i)$, $m = 1, 2, \cdots n$, a random number in $[-1, 1]$.

e. Move: Let

$$\varphi^i(j+1, k, l) = \varphi^i(j, k, l) + C(i) \frac{\Delta(i)}{\sqrt{\Delta^T(i)\Delta(i)}} \quad (17)$$

This results in a step of size $C(i)$ in the direction of the tumble for bacterium i.

f. Compute $F(i, j, k, l)$ with $\varphi^i(j+1, k, l)$.

g. Swim:

   i. Let $m = 0$ (counter for swim length).

   ii. While $m < N_s$

Let $m = m + 1$.

If $F(i, j+1, k, l) < F_{last}$,

let $F_{last} = F(i, j+1, k, l)$,

then another step of size in this same direction will be taken as (5) and use the new generated $\varphi^i(j+1, k, l)$ to compute the new $F(i, j+1, k, l)$.

Else let $m = N_s$.

h. Go to next bacterium $i + 1$ .if $i \neq S$, go to sub-step b) to process the next bacterium.

Step 5: If $j < N_C$, go to step 3. In this case, continue chemotaxis since the life of the bacteria is not over.

Step 6: Reproduction

For the given k and l, and for each $i = 1, 2, \cdots S$, let:

$$F_{health}^i = \sum_{j=1}^{N_c+1} F(i, j, k, l) \quad (18)$$

be the health of the bacteria. Sort bacteria in order of ascending values (F_{health}).

The S_r bacteria with the highest Fhealth values die and the other S_r bacteria with the best values split and the copies are placed at the same location as their parent.

Step 7: If $k < N_{re}$, go to step 2. In this case the number of specified reproduction steps is not reached and start the next generation in the chemotactic loop.

Step 8: Elimination–dispersal. For $i = 1, 2, \cdots S$, with probability P_{ed}, eliminate and disperse each bacterium, which results in keeping the number of bacteria in the population constant. To do this, if a bacterium is eliminated, simply disperse one to a random location on the optimization domain. If $l < N_{ed}$, then go to step 2, otherwise ends.

In the BFOA, run-length unit is the size of the step taken in each swim or tumble. In order to use it to solve the problem of clustering, the run-length is changed to be adaptive. Here, we define $C(i)$ as follows:

$$C(i, j+1) = 0.00001 * Mlast * C(i, j) \quad (19)$$

where i represents the ith bacterium, j the jth chemotaxis, $Mlast$ the fitness value of the ith bacterium in j^{th} chemotaxis.

BF-FCM Algorithm

In this section, for example, we combine BFOA and FCM to implement clustering. We use BFOA to optimize clustering criterion function of FCM algorithm.

The clustering criterion function in FCM algorithm is taken as the fitness function $F(i, j, k, l)$ in BF-FCM. That is,

$$F(i, j, k, l) =$$
$$J(X; U, V) = \sum_{i=1}^{c} \sum_{k=1}^{N} (\mu_{ik})^m \left\| x_k - v_i \right\|_A^2$$

The main steps of BF-FCM are:

Step 1: According to the clustering category number c, set the bacteria number as its 10 times, which is $S = 10 * c$.

Step 2: Select $e > 0$, initialize clustering center v_0 based on equation (4), let $g = 1$.

Step 3: Initialize parameters
$n, S, N_C, N_S, N_{re}, N_{ed}, P_{ed}, C(i)$

Step 4: Calculate fuzzy matrix U^g according to the equation (3).

Step 5: Compute the minimum value of the fitness function.

Step 6: If $\left\| v^{(k)} - v^{(k+1)} \right\| < e$, stop iteration, else let $g = g + 1$ and return to step 1.

Step 7: After the iteration in step 6, take the position of bacteria as the cluster centers. Then start clustering by FCM.

Step 8: When FCM finishes clustering, then BF-FCM ends.

IMAGE SEGMENTATION EXPERIMENTS

Experiments Evaluation

The experiments rely on evaluate numerical results of clustering algorithms based on BBO, AFSA, ABC, PSO and BFOA. We define the following algorithms variations:

1. BBO-FCM
2. AFSA-FCM
3. ABC-FCM
4. PSO-FCM
5. BFOA-FCM

In order to evaluate the effectiveness of clustering, Cluster Validation Indexes(CVI) was used to obtain numerical results including Partition Coefficient (PC), Classification Entropy (PE), Separation (S), Separation Coefficient (SC), Xie and Beni index (XB). These indexes are shown as the following:

Partition Coefficient (PC): PC is used to measure the overlap between classes. It is defined by

$$PC(c) = \frac{1}{N} \sum_{i=1}^{c} \sum_{j=1}^{N} (\mu_{ij})^2 \qquad (21)$$

where μ_{ij} is the membership of data point j in category i.

Partition Entropy (PE): PE measures the fuzzy degree of the category and its definition is as follows:

$$PE(c) = -\frac{1}{N} \sum_{i=1}^{c} \sum_{j=1}^{N} \mu_{ij} \log(\mu_{ij}) \qquad (22)$$

Separation and Compactness (SC): What SC measures is the firmness sum between categories.

$$SC(c) = \sum_{i=1}^{c} \frac{\sum_{j=1}^{N} (\mu_{ij})^m \left\| x_j - v_i \right\|^2}{N_i \sum_{k=1}^{c} \left\| v_k - v_i \right\|^2} \qquad (23)$$

Separation index (S): On contrary to SC, the minimize distance is employs by S to classify data and it is defined by

$$S(c) = \frac{\sum_{i=1}^{c} \sum_{j=1}^{N} (\mu_{ij})^2 \left\| x_j - v_i \right\|^2}{N \min_{i,k} \left\| v_k - v_i \right\|^2} \qquad (24)$$

Xie and Beni index (XB): XB is a validation function proposed by Xie and Beni and it is defined by:

$$XB(c) = \frac{\sum_{i=1}^{c}\sum_{j=1}^{N}(\mu_{ij})^m \left\| x_j - v_i \right\|^2}{N \min_{i,k} \left\| x_j - v_i \right\|^2} \qquad (25)$$

For a review on CVI refer to (El-Melegy et al., 2007).

Parameters Settings

For general comparison purpose, we don't consider the effect of different parameters settings on the performance of image segmentation. We use the common parameters settings as follows:

- **BBO Settings:** For BBO, we use the following parameters: habitat modification probability is 1, immigration probability bounds per gene are [0,1], step size for numerical integration of probabilities, maximum immigration and migration rates for each island are 1, and mutation probability is 0.
- **AFSA Settings:** The main parameters are maximal try_number=100, sense distance=4000, crowd factor δ =0.618, swimming step=300.
- **ABC Settings:** Limit=100, which is a control parameter in order to abandon the food source.

PSO Settings: In our experiments cognitive and social components are both set to 2. Inertia weight, which determines how the previous velocity of the particle influences the velocity in the next iteration, is 0.8.

The parameters of BF-FCM are given in Table1. The number of clustering center of BF-FCM

is the same as that of FCM. Amongst these parameters, e is the convergence indicator.

The procedure of image segmentation of BIOA-FCM is described as follows:

Step 1: Selecting an image, and turn it into gray image

Step 2: Calculate roughness according to equation (14).

Step 3: Construct two-dimensional features data sets based on gray value and roughness

Step 4: Initialize parameters of BIOA-FCM, and run it.

Step 5: Display image segmentation results after this algorithm is finished.

Experiments Results

The dataset used in image segmentation experiments was obtained from the USC-SIPI Image Database (http://sipi.usc.edu/database/). They are Lena, Baboon, Woman, Peppers, Milkdrop, Camera, Bridge and Airplane.

For comparison purposes experiments were taken for classical Fuzzy C-means and the other five BIOA-FCMs, considering 100 rounds – with maximum 100 iterations each.

Tables 1 and Figure 1 to 16 present quantitative and qualitative image segmentation results, respectively. For these datasets there is no ground truth (no true labels). Thus, the evaluation about how measure/approach has the best result need to

Table 1. The parameters of BF-FCM

Parameters	Values
n	2
c	9
e	0.000001
S	90
N_c	50

be made through quantitative and qualitative results. Best quantitative results are bolded in tables.

Figure 1,3,5,7,9,11,13 and 15 show qualitative results for FCM and the other five BIOA-FCMs, respectively. Figure 2,4,6,8,10,12,14,16 show the equipotential lines for the images.

The number of clusters of Lena is 6. From the results in Figure1, it can be seen that BF-FCM has the best results. From the results in Figure 2, it can seen that the clustering centers of ABC-FCM and PSO-FCM fall into local optimum.

The number of clusters of Baboon is 4. From the results in Figure 3, it can be seen that the six algorithms obtain similar results. From the results in Figure 4, it can be seen that the clustering centers of ABC-FCM are close to each other.

The number of clusters of Woman is 5. BBO-FCM, AFSA-FCM and ABC-FCM can identify woman and background. ABC-FCM falls into local optimum.

The number of clusters of Peppers is 5. From the Figure 7, it can be seen that BBO-FCM can identify the peppers with similar gray value. And the type lines of peppers are also continuously. The results of the other algorithms are not as good as that of BBO-FCM. From Figure 8, it can be seen that ABC-FCM falls into local optimum again.

The number of clusters of Milkdrop is 4. From Figure 9, It can be seen that BBO-FCM separate all the milk drops with clear type. The edges of these drops are very clear. ABC-FCM separates the inverted images and inner loop of milk drops. From Figure 10, it can be seen the PSO-FCM,AFSA-FCM, BF-FCM and FCM obtain similar clustering centers.

The number of clusters of camera is 4. From Figure 11, it can be seen that none of the algorithms identify the camera and background successfully. But BF-FCM has relative better results than the other algorithms. From Figure 12, it can be seen that all the algorithms didn't identify correctly any of the classes.

The number of clusters of bridge is 4. From Figure 13 and Figure 14, it can be seen that PSO-

Figure 1. Qualitative image segmentation results for Lena image

Lena(original image)

FCM   BBO-FCM   AFSA-FCM

ABC-FCM   PSO-FCM   BF-FCM

Figure 2. Equipotential lines for Lena

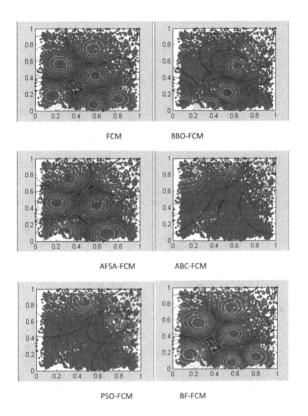

Figure 3. Qualitative image segmentation results for baboon image

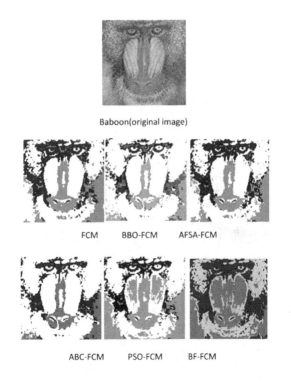

Figure 4. Equipotential lines for Baboon

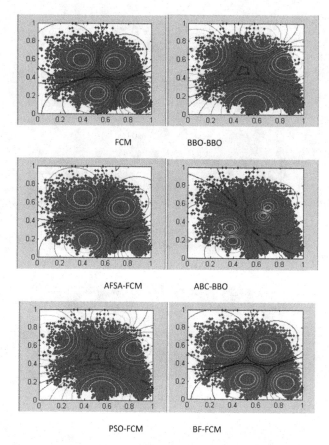

FCM   BBO-BBO

AFSA-FCM   ABC-BBO

PSO-FCM   BF-FCM

Figure 5. Qualitative image segmentation results for woman image

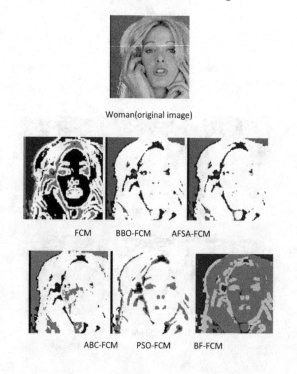

Woman(original image)

FCM   BBO-FCM   AFSA-FCM

ABC-FCM   PSO-FCM   BF-FCM

Figure 6. Equipotential lines for woman

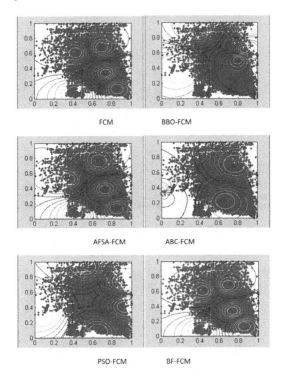

Figure 7. Qualitative image segmentation results for peppers image

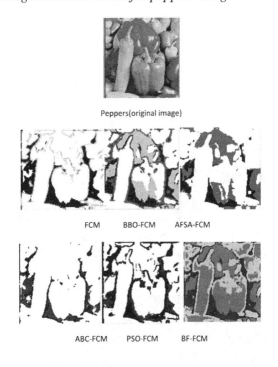

Figure 8. Equipotential lines for peppers

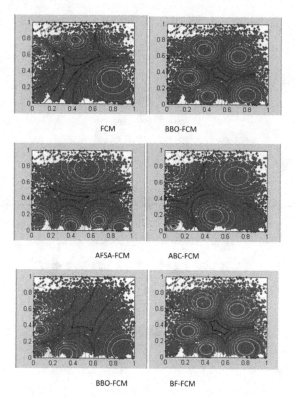

Figure 9. Qualitative image segmentation results for milkdrop image

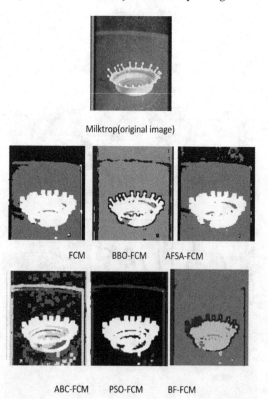

Figure 10. Equipotential lines for milkdrop

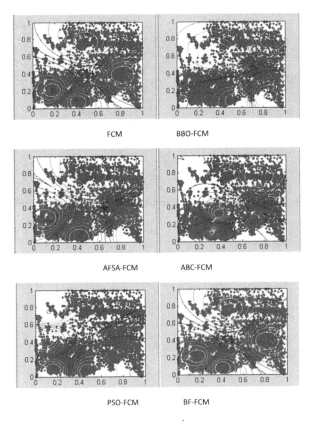

Figure 11. Qualitative image segmentation results for camera image

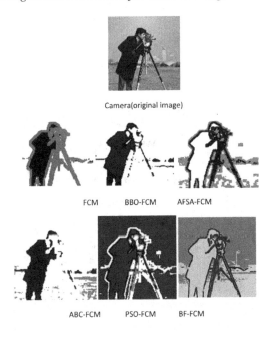

Figure 12. Equipotential lines for camera

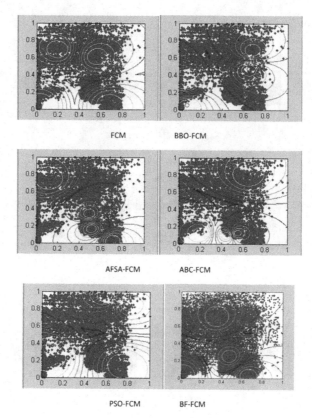

Figure 13. Qualitative image segmentation results for bridge image

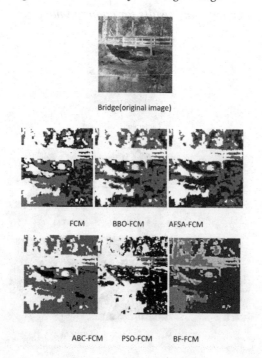

Figure 14. Equipotential lines for bridge

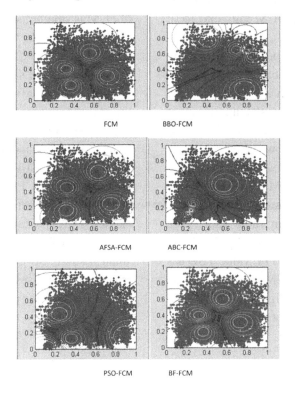

Figure 15. Qualitative image segmentation results for plane image

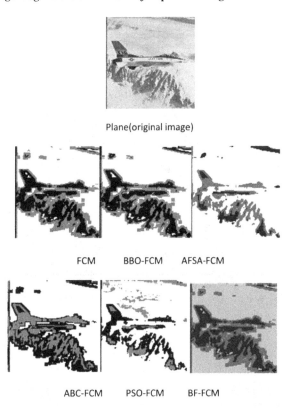

FCM has the worst results. The other algorithms have similar results. ABC-FCM falls into local optimum.

The number of clusters of plane is 3. From Figure 15 and Figure 16, it can be seen that all the algorithms cannot obtain good results. FCM and ABC-FCM have worse results than the other algorithms.

Basically, BBO-FCM shows better results on all the images since it can search the clustering centers accurately. ABC-FCM is easy to fall into local optimum in the experiments (Table 2).

According to results from Table 1, for Lena, BBO-FCM got best results considering XB and CE for Lena. But it has smaller PC value. PSO has bigger PC value so PSO-FCM can separate the image simply and clearly in Figure 1. For Baboon, BBO-FCM doesn't have the best results consider-

ing all the measures. XB of FCM is bigger and S of FCM is smaller, so it cannot identify different classes clearly. For Woman image, FCM has the worst value of XB index and S index. BBO-FCM has smaller CE and XB. So BBO-FCM can identify the detail of the woman. For Pepper image, all the algorithms have similar indices. BBO-FCM has the best results in Fig .7 qualitatively. So it is necessary to justify the results subjectively when the quantitative and qualitative evaluation are not consistent. For Milldrop, Camera, Bridge and Plane, all of them are difficult to separate the classes. The classical FCM has similar evaluation values for the four images. It has big XB value and small S value. So it cannot identify single class from the total classes. For the other BIOA-FCMs, BBO-FCM has one or two better indices than the other algorithms.

Figure 16. Equipotential lines for plane

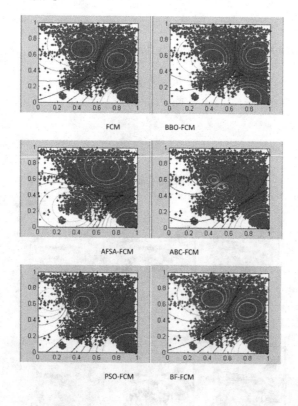

Table 2. CVI results for FCM and BIOA-FCMs

Images	C	CVI	FCM	BBO-FCM	AFSA-FCM	ABC-FCM	PSO-FCM	BF-FCM
Lena	6	SC	1.0684	1.2735	2.2694	0.5670	5.3410	1.0684
		XB	24.0430	2.5015e-011	0.3532	0.8996	0.3839	24.0430
		CE	0.9850	8.5050e-005	2.0446	1.3544	2.0900	0.9850
		S	1.0742e-004	0.2792	0.5505	0.1458	1.4035	1.0742e-004
		PC	0.5316	2.4880e-011	0.3345	0.0608	0.3925	0.5316
Baboon	4	SC	1.6070	2.3520	0.9615	1.3006	2.0409	1.6070
		XB	21.4599	0.1404	1.7361	1.7443	0.0068	21.4599
		CE	0.8059	1.3955	1.2642	1.2428	0.4557	0.8059
		S	1.2310e-004	0.6720	0.2963	0.3898	0.6082	1.2310e-004
		PC	0.5787	0.1277	1.0262	0.1397	0.0066	0.5787
Woman	5	SC	1.0935	2.0527	3.3291	1.0265	1.0960	1.0935
		XB	21.3590	1.7466e-004	7.3913e-009	0.0829	0.7431	21.3590
		CE	0.8125	0.0673	1.5325	1.1775	1.1352	0.8125
		S	1.0990e-004	0.6389	1.2594	0.2468	0.2729	1.0990e-004
		PC	0.5971	1.3606e-004	0.1623	0.1735	0.2775	0.5971
Peppers	5	SC	1.0958	2.3896	1.6854	2.1809	1.5536	1.0977
		XB	40.9849	0.0802	0.0077	1.4853e-008	0.1991	25.3268
		CE	0.8200	1.1923	0.5067	0.0018	1.4625	1.4625
		S	3.7783e-05	0.6942	0.4192	0.5278	0.4581	7.4988e-05
		PC	0.6001	0.0600	0.0072	8.8651e-009	0.1393	0.1393
Milkdrop	4	SC	0.8783	2.2456	2.1409	2.7977	1.3039	0.8783
		XB	32.0841	0.0376	0.0092	0.4249	0.4699	32.0841
		CE	0.5669	1.0485	0.4935	0.5706	0.9533	0.5669
		S	6.3765e-005	0.7221	0.7398	1.0784	0.2913	6.3765e-05
		PC	0.7067	0.0906	0.0088	0.2413	0.2349	0.7067
Camera	4	SC	0.6968	2.0697	0.2741	2.6505	2.0099	0.6654
		XB	27.6367	0.2346	3.9648	0.0011	0.4228	35.0630
		CE	0.4384	1.3535	0.1371	0.5452	1.4608	1.4608
		S	7.0817e-005	0.6152	0.1061	0.8594	0.6512	1.7243e-05
		PC	0.7797	0.2141	3.7258	1.8678	0.4219	0.4219
bridge	4	SC	2.0561	0.3657	1.0919	7.5019	2.2020	2.0561
		XB	31.1346	4.6177	1.6310	0.0465	0.3462	31.1346
		CE	0.8622	0.1074	0.8393	1.1978	1.2324	0.8622
		S	1.5511e-004	0.1337	0.3467	2.7663	0.6170	1.5511e-004
		PC	0.5439	1.0463e-004	0.0408	0.1151	0.1602	0.5439
Plane	3	SC	1.1305	1.6043	0.9088	1.2301	1.4111	1.1305
		XB	35.0280	0.6743	0.2734	1.4699	0.4936	35.0280
		CE	0.4030	1.0634	0.8401	0.7791	1.4306	0.4030
		S	9.8403e-005	0.6294	0.2610	0.5571	0.4654	9.8403e-005
		PC	0.7768	0.6578	0.2441	1.4033	0.3932	0.7768

FUTURE RESEARCH DIRECTIONS

For the image segmentation, it only takes gray scale images into account and adopts gray value and roughness as features for segmentation. In future research, it is necessary to testify it on color images and consider the other image character-istics, like texture, region and borders in future research. And we will apply more nature inspired computing methods on image segmentation in order to show whether and how the nature inspired computing methods can be adaptively applied to what kinds of images.

CONCLUSION

In this chapter, we proposed five hybrid algorithms, AFS-FCM, BBO_FCM, BF-FCM, ABC-FCM, PSO-FCM, which are bio-inspired optimization algorithms combined with the standard FCM. These new approaches aim at optimizing the cluster criterion function directly related to the cluster centers of FCM to improve the quality of clustering. Two kinds of experiments are conducted. Qualitative and quantitative results are obtained in order to evaluate the clustering effectiveness. All the experiments results are compared to those obtained by standard FCM and quantitative and qualitative analysis shows that the BBO-FCM have relative better performance than ABC-FCM, AFS-FCM, PSO-FCM and FCM on the images used in the chapter.

ACKNOWLEDGMENT

This work is partially supported by the National Natural Science Foundation of China under Grant No. 61075113, the Excellent Youth Foundation of Heilongjiang Province of China under Grant No. JC201212, the Fundamental Research Funds for the Central Universities No. HEUCFZ1209, and Harbin Excellent Discipline Leader, No. 2012RFXXG073.

REFERENCES

Aeberhard, S., Coomans, D., & Vel, O. D. (1992). *Comparison of classifiers in high dimensional settings* (Tech. Rep. No. 92-02). North Queensland, Australia: James Cook University of North Queensland, Dept. of Computer Science and Dept. of Mathematics and Statistics.

Anderson, E. (1935). The irises of the gaspe peninsula. *Bulletin of the American Iris Society*, *59*, 2–5.

Andrey, P. (1999). Selectionist relaxation: Genetic algorithms applied to image segmentation. *Image and Vision Computing*, *17*(3-4), 175–187. doi:10.1016/S0262-8856(98)00095-X

Balasubramani, K., & Marcus, K. (n.d.). Artificial bee colony algorithm to improve brain MR image segmentation. *International Journal on Computer Science and Engineering, 5*(1), 31-36.

Bastos, F., Carmelo, J. A., Lima, N., & De Fernando, B. (2002). A novel search algorithm based on fish school behavior. In Proceedings of IEEE Int Conf on Systems, Man, and Cybernetics. Cingapura.

Bezdek, J. C. (1981). *Patten Recognition with Fuzzy Objective Function Algorithm*. New York: Plenum Press. doi:10.1007/978-1-4757-0450-1

Bhandarkar, S. M., & Zhang, H. (1999). Image segmentation using evolutionary computation. *IEEE Transactions on Evolutionary Computation*, *3*(1), 1–21. doi:10.1109/4235.752917

Bhanu, Lee, S., & Ming, J. (1995). Adaptive image segmentation using a genetic algorithm. *IEEE Transactions on Systems, Man, and Cybernetics*, *25*(12), 1543–1567. doi:10.1109/21.478442

Chabrier, S., Emile, B., Rosenberger, C., & Laurent, H. (2006). Unsupervised Performance Evaluation of Image Segmentation. *EURASIP Journal on Applied Signal Processing*, 1–13. doi:10.1155/ASP/2006/96306

Charalampidis, D., & Kasparis, T. (2002). Wavelet-based rotational invariant roughness features for texture classification and segmentation. *IEEE Transactions on Image Processing*, *11*(8), 825–837. doi:10.1109/TIP.2002.801117 PMID:18244677

Chen, J. S, & Wei, G. (2002). A hybrid clustering algorithm incorporating fuzzy c-means into canonical genetic algorithm. *Journal of Electronics & Information Technology*, 24(2), 102-103.

Coleman, G. B., & Andrews, H. C. (1979). Image Segmentation by Clustering. *Proceedings of the Institute of Electrical and Electronics Engineers, 67*, 773–785. doi:10.1109/PROC.1979.11327

Das, S., & Sila, S. (2010). Kernel-induced fuzzy clustering of image pixels with an improved differential evolution algorithm. Information Sciences, 180(8), 1237-1256.

EL-Melegy, M., Zanaty, E. A., Abd-Elhariez, W. M., & Farag, A. (2007). On cluster validity index in fuzzy and hard clustering algorithms for image segmentation. In *Proceedings of IEEE International Conference on Image Processing,* (vol. 6, pp. 5-8). IEEE.

Felzenszwalb, P. F., & Huttenlocher, D. P. (2004). Efficient graph-based image segmentation. *International Journal of Computer Vision, 59*(2), 167–181. doi:10.1023/B:VISI.0000022288.19776.77

Gong, M. G., Jiao, L. C., Bo, L. F., Wang, L., & Zhang, X. G. (2008). Image texture classification using a manifold distance based evolutionary clustering method. *Optical Engineering (Redondo Beach, Calif.), 47*(7), 1–10. doi:10.1117/1.2955785

Jain, A. K., Murty, M. N., & Flynn, P. J. (1999). Data clustering: a review. *ACM Computing Surveys, 31*(3), 264–323. doi:10.1145/331499.331504

Karaboga, D. (2005). *An idea based on honey bee swarm for numerical opitmization* (Technical Report-TR06). Erciyesniversity, Engineering Faculty, Computer Engineering Deparment.

Kennedy, J., & Eberhart, R. (1995). *Particle swarm optimization*. Piscataway, NJ: IEEE Int Conf on Neural Networks.

Hojjatoleslami, S. A., & Kitter, J. (1998). Region growing: A new approach. IEEE Transactions on Image Processing, 7(7), 1079–1084. PubMed doi:10.1109/83.701170 PubMed

Koppen, M. X., Franke, M., & Vicente-Garcia, R. (2006). Tiny GAs for image processing applications. *IEEE Computational Intelligence Magazine, 1*(2), 17–26. doi:10.1109/MCI.2006.1626491

Liu, L. P., & Meng, Z. Q. (2004). An initial centrepoints selection method for k-means clustering. *Computer Engineering and Application, 40*(8), 179–180.

Mardia, K. V., & Hainsworth, T. J. (1988). A spatial thresholding method for image segmentation. *IEEE Transactions on Pattern Analysis and Machine Intelligence, 10*(6), 919–927. doi:10.1109/34.9113

Maulik, U. (2009). Medical image segmentation using genetic algorithms. *IEEE Transactions on Information Technology in Biomedicine, 13*(2), 166–173. doi:10.1109/TITB.2008.2007301 PMID:19272859

Melkemi, K. E., Batouche, M., & Foufou, S. (2006). A multiagent system approach for image segmentation using genetic algorithms and extremal optimization heuristics. *Pattern Recognition Letters, 27*(11), 1230–1238. doi:10.1016/j.patrec.2005.07.021

Nie, S. D., Zhang, Y. L., & Chen, Z. X. (2008). Improved genetic fuzzy clustering algorithm and its application in segmentation of MR brain images. *Chinese Journal of Biomedical Engineering, 27*(6).

Nikhil, R. P., & Bezdek, J. C. (1995). On cluster validity for the fuzzy c-means model. *IEEE Transactions on Fuzzy Systems, 3*(3), 370–379. doi:10.1109/91.413225

Pal, N. R., & Pal, S. K. (1993). A review on image segmentation techniques. *Pattern Recognition, 26*(9), 1277–1294. doi:10.1016/0031-3203(93)90135-J

Passino, K. M. (2002). Biomimicry of bacterial foraging for distributed optimization and control. *Control Systems Magazine of the Institute of Electrical and Electronics Engineers, 22*(3), 52–67.

Perona, P., & Malik, J. (1990). Scale-space and edge detection using anisotropic diffusion. *IEEE Transactions on Pattern Analysis and Machine Intelligence, 12*(7), 629–639. doi:10.1109/34.56205

Rocha, A. M. A. C., Fernandes, E. M. G. P., & Martins, T. F. M. C. (2011). Novel fish swarm heuristics for bound constrained global optimization problems, comp. In *Proceedings of Science and its App. -ICCSA 2011* (LNCS) (vol. *6784*, pp. 185–199). Berlin: Springer. doi:10.1007/978-3-642-21931-3_16

Tian, X. L., Jiao, L. C., & Gou, S. P. (2008). SAR image segmentation based on spatially constrained FCM optimized by particle swarm optimization. *Acta Electronica Sinica, 36*(3), 453–457.

Sathya, P. D., & Kayalvizhi, R. (2011). Modified bacterial foraging algorithm based multilevel thresholding for image segmentation. *Engineering Applications of Artificial Intelligence, 24*, 595–615. doi:10.1016/j.engappai.2010.12.001

Sathya, P. D., & Kayalvizhi, R. (2011). Optimal segmentation of brain MRI based on adaptive bacterial foraging algorithm. *Neurocomputing, 74*, 2299–2313. doi:10.1016/j.neucom.2011.03.010

Shao, Y., & Chen, H. N. (2009). Cooperative bacterial foraging optimization. In *Proceedings of International Conference on Future BioMedical Information Engineering* (pp. 486-488). Academic Press.

Shapiro, L. G., & Stockman, G. C. (2001). *Computer vision*. Prentice-Hall.

Simon, D. (2008). Biogeography-based Optimization. *IEEE Transactions on Evolutionary Computation, 12*, 702–713. doi:10.1109/TEVC.2008.919004

Sowmya, B., & Sheela Rani, B. (2011). Colour image segmentation using fuzzy clustering techniques and competitive neural network. *Applied Soft Computing, 11*(3), 3170–3178. doi:10.1016/j.asoc.2010.12.019

Veenman, C. J., Reinders, M. J. T., & Backer, E. (2003). A cellular coevolutionary algorithm for image segmentation. *IEEE Transactions on Image Processing, 12*(3), 304–316. doi:10.1109/TIP.2002.806256 PMID:18237910

Wolberg, W. H., & Mangasarian, O. L. (1990). Multisurface method of pattern separation for medical diagnosis applied to breast cytology. *Proceedings of the National Academy of Sciences of the United States of America, 87*(23), 9193–9196. doi:10.1073/pnas.87.23.9193 PMID:2251264

Wu, K. L., & Yang, M. S. (2002). Alternative c-means clustering algorithms. *Pattern Recognition, 35*(10), 2267–2278. doi:10.1016/S0031-3203(01)00197-2

Yang, L. C., Zhao, L. N., & Wu, X. Q. (2007). Medical image segmentation of fuzzy C-means clustering based on the ant colony algorithm. *Journal of ShanDong University, 37*(3).

Yang, X. C., Zhao, W. D, Chen, Y. F, & Fang, X. (2008). Image segmentation with a fuzzy clustering algorithm based on Ant-Tree. Signal Processing, *88*(10), 2453-2462.

Ying, C., Shao, Z. B., Mi, H., & Wu, Q. H. (2008). An application of bacterial foraging algorithm in image compression. *Journal of ShenZhen University (Science & Engineering), 25* (2).

Yue, X. D., Miao, D. Q., & Zhong, C. M. (2010). Roughness Measure Approach to Color Image Segmentation. *Acta Automatica Sinica, 36*(6), 807–816. doi:10.3724/SP.J.1004.2010.00807

Zeng, L., Wang, M. L., & Chen, H. F. (2008). Genetic Fuzzy C-Means Clustering Algorithm for Magnetic Resonance Images Segmentation. *Journal of University of Electronic Science and Technology of China, 37*(4), 627–629.

ADDITIONAL READING

Araújo, D., Neto, A. D., & Martins, A. (2013). Information-theoretic clustering: A representative and evolutionary approach. *Expert Systems with Applications, 40*, 4190–4205. doi:10.1016/j.eswa.2013.01.027

Balasubramani, K., & Marcus, K. (2013, January). Artificial Bee Colony Algorithm to improve brain MR Image Segmentation. *International Journal on Computer Science and Engineering, 1*(5), 0975-3397.

Bhandari, A. K., Singh, V. K., Kumar, A., & Singh, G. K. (2013). Cuckoo search algorithm and wind driven optimization based study of satellite image segmentation for multilevel thresholding using Kapur's entropy. *Expert Systems with Applications*. doi:10.1016/j.eswa.2013.10.059

Castillo, O., Rubio, E., Soria, J., & Naredo, E. (2012, February). *Optimization of the Fuzzy C-Means Algorithm using Evolutionary Methods.* Engineering Letters, 20:1, EL_20_1_08, Advance online publication, 27.

Chabrier, S., Rosenberger, C., Emile, B., & Laurent, H. (2008). Optimization Based Image Segmentation by Genetic Algorithms. *EURASIP journal on Video and Image processing,* 1-23.

Ding, Z., Sun, J., & Zhang, Y. (2013, January). FCM Image Segmentation Algorithm Based on Color Space and Spatial Information. *International Journal of Computer and Communication Engineering, 1*(2).

Epitropakis, M. G., Plagianakos, V. P., & Vrahatis, M. N. (2012). Evolving cognitive and social experience in Particle Swarm Optimization through Differential Evolution: A hybrid approach. *Information Sciences, 216*, 50–92. doi:10.1016/j.ins.2012.05.017

Fagbola, T. M., Babatunde, R. S., & Oyeleye, C. A. (2013, February). Image Clustering using a Hybrid GA-FCM Algorithm. *International Journal of Engineering and Technology, 2*(3), 2049–3444.

Ganesh, M., & Palanisamy, V. (2012, October). A Modified Adaptive Fuzzy C-Means Clustering Algorithm For Brain MR Image Segmentation. *International Journal of Engineering Research & Technology, 8*(1), 2278–0181.

Hiziroglu, A. (2013). Soft computing applications in customer segmentation: State-of-art review and critique. *Expert Systems with Applications, 40*, 6491–6507. doi:10.1016/j.eswa.2013.05.052

Izakian, H., & Abraham, A. (2011). Fuzzy C-means and fuzzy swarm for fuzzy clustering problem. *Expert Systems with Applications, 38*, 1835–1838. doi:10.1016/j.eswa.2010.07.112

Izakian, H., Abraham, A., & Snášel, V. (2009). *Fuzzy Clustering Using Hybrid Fuzzy c-means and Fuzzy Particle Swarm Optimization.* World Congress on Nature & Biologically Inspired Computing.

Jassim, F. A. (2012, November). Hybrid Image Segmentation using Discerner Cluster in FCM and Histogram Thresholding. *International Journal of Graphics & Image Processing, 4*(2).

Ramezani, F., & Lotfi, S. (2013). Social-Based Algorithm (SBA). *Applied Soft Computing, 13*, 2837–2856. doi: doi:10.1016/j.asoc.2012.05.018

Mullen, R. J., Monekosso, Dorothy N., & Remagnino P. (2013). Ant algorithms for image feature extraction. *Expert Systems with Applications, 40*, 4315–4332. doi:10.1016/j.eswa.2013.01.020

Osuna-Enciso, V., Cuevas, E., & Sossa, H. (2013). A comparison of nature inspired algorithms for multi-threshold image segmentation. *Expert Systems with Applications, 40*, 1213–1219. doi:10.1016/j.eswa.2012.08.017

Raju, N. G., & Nageswara Rao, P. A. (2013, Nov-Dec). Particle Swarm Optimization Methods for Image Segmentation Applied In Mammography. *Journal of Engineering Research and Applications, 6*(3), ISSN: 2248-9622, pp.1572-1579.

Selvy, P. T., Palanisamy, V., & Radhai, M. S. (2013, April). An Improved MRI Brain Image Segmentation to Detect Cerebrospinal Fluid Level Using Anisotropic Diffused Fuzzy C Means. *Wseas Transactions on Computers, 4*(12).

Liang Shan. *Clustering Techniques and Applications to Image Segmentation.* Unpublised.

Zhenghao Shi, Yuyan Chao, Lifeng He, Nakamura, T., & Itoh, H. (2007). Rough Set Based FCM Algorithm for Image Segmentation. *International Journal of Computation Science, 1*(1), 58 - 68. 1992-6669(Print), 1992-6677(Online).

Shokouhifar, M., & Abkenar, G. S. (2011). An Artificial Bee Colony Optimization for MRI Fuzzy Segmentation of Brain Tissue. *International Conference on Management and Artificial Intelligence, IPEDR vol.6,* IACSIT Press, Bali, Indonesia.

Soesanti, I., Susanto, A., Widodo, T. S., & Tjokronagoro, M. (2011, August). MRI Brain Images Segmentation Based on Optimized Fuzzy Logic and Spatial Information. *International Journal of Video & Image Processing and Network Security, 4*(11).

Sutar, M., & Janwe, N. J. (2011, March). A Swarm-based Approach to Medical Image Analysis. *Global Journal of Computer Science and Technology, 3*(11), http://creativecommons.org/licenses/by-nc/3.0/)

Venkatesan, A., & Parthiban, L. (2013, February). Hybridized Algorithms for Medical Image Segmentation. *International Journal of Engineering and Advanced Technology, 3*(2), 2249–8958.

Venkateswaran, R., & Muthukumar, S. (2010). Genetic Approach on Medical Image Segmentation by Generalized Spatial Fuzzy C- Means Algorithm. *IEEE International Conference on Computational Intelligence and Computing Research.*

Kehong Yuan, et al. *A novel fuzzy C-means algorithm and its Application.* Unpublished.

KEY TERMS AND DEFINITIONS

Bacteria Foraging Optimization Algorithm (BFOA): BFOA is a kind of BIOA based on the behavior that E. coli engulfs food in human's intestinal.

Biogeograpy Based Optimization (BBO): BBO is a new population-based optimization algorithm, which mimics how animals migrate from one habitat to another, how new species arise, and how species become extinct.

Bio-Inspired Optimization Algorithms (BIOA): It means the optimization approaches inspired by the principles of biology or biologic behaviors in nature.

Cluster Validation Indexes (CVI): Cluster Validation Indexes are the criteria in order to evaluate the effectiveness of clustering.

Clustering: Clustering techniques represent the non-supervised pattern classification in groups.

Fuzzy C-Means (FCM): FCM is a kind of simple mechanical clustering method based on exploring minimum value of the objective function.

Image Segmentation: Image segmentation is one of the central problems in computer vision and pattern recognition. It refers to the process of assigning a label to every pixel in an image such that pixels with the same label share certain visual characteristics.

Chapter 13
Swarm Intelligence for Dimensionality Reduction:
How to Improve the Non-Negative Matrix Factorization with Nature-Inspired Optimization Methods

Andreas Janecek
University of Vienna, Austria

Ying Tan
Peking University, China

ABSTRACT

Low-rank approximations allow for compact representations of data with reduced storage and runtime requirements and reduced redundancy and noise. The Non-Negative Matrix Factorization (NMF) is a special low-rank approximation that allows for additive parts-based, interpretable representation of the data. Various properties of NMF are similar to Swarm Intelligence (SI) methods: indeed, most NMF objective functions and most SI fitness functions are non-convex, discontinuous, and may possess many local minima. This chapter summarizes efforts on improving convergence, approximation quality, and classification accuracy of NMF using five different meta-heuristics based on SI and evolutionary computation. The authors present (1) new initialization strategies for NMF, and (2) an iterative update strategy for NMF. The applicability of the approach is illustrated on data sets coming from the areas of spam filtering and email classification. Experimental results show that both optimization strategies are able to improve NMF in terms of faster convergence, lower approximation error, and/or better classification accuracy.

DOI: 10.4018/978-1-4666-6328-2.ch013

INTRODUCTION

Low-rank approximations are utilized in several content based retrieval and data mining applications, such as text and multimedia mining, web search, etc. and achieve a more compact representation of the data with only limited loss in information. They reduce storage and runtime requirements, and also reduce redundancy and noise in the data representation while capturing the essential associations. The Non-negative Matrix Factorization (NMF, (Lee and Seung 1999)) leads to a low-rank approximation which satisfies non-negativity constraints. NMF approximates a data matrix A by $A \approx WH$, where W and H are the *NMF factors*. NMF requires *all entries* in A, W and H to be zero or positive. Contrary to other low-rank approximations such as the Singular Value Decomposition (SVD), these constraints force NMF to produce so-called "additive parts-based" representations. This is an impressive benefit of NMF, since it makes the interpretation of the NMF factors much easier than for factors containing positive and negative entries (Berry, Browne et al. 2007) (Janecek and Gansterer 2010) (Lee and Seung 1999).

The NMF is usually not unique if different initializations of the factors W and H are used. Moreover, there are several different NMF algorithms which all follow different strategies (e.g. mean squared error, least squares, gradient descent, etc.) and produce different results. Mathematically, the goal of NMF is to find a "good" (ideally the best) solution of an optimization problem with bound constraints in the form $\min_{x \in \Omega} f(x)$, where $f : \mathbb{R}^N \to \mathbb{R}$ is the nonlinear objective function of NMF, and Ω is the feasible region (for NMF, Ω is restricted to non-negative values). f is usually not convex, discontinuous and may possess many local minima (Stadlthanner, Lutter et al. 2007). Since meta-heuristic optimization algorithms are known to be able to deal well with such difficulties they seem to be a promising

choice for improving the quality of NMF. Over the last decades nature-inspired meta-heuristics, including those based on swarm intelligence, have gained much popularity due to their applicability for various optimization problems. They benefit from the fact that they are able to find acceptable results within a reasonable amount of time for many complex, large and dynamic problems (Blackwell 2007). Although they lack the ability to guarantee the optimal solution for a given problem (comparably to NMF), it has been shown that they are able to tackle various kinds of real-world optimization problems (Chiong 2009). Meta-heuristics as well as the principles of NMF are in accordance with the *law of sufficiency* (Eberhart, Shi et al. 2001): If a solution to a problem is good enough, fast enough and cheap enough, then it is sufficient.

In this chapter we present two different strategies for improving the NMF using five optimization algorithms based on swarm intelligence and evolutionary computing: Particle Swarm Optimization (PSO), Genetic Algorithms (GA), Fish School Search (FSS), Differential Evolution (DE), and Fireworks Algorithm (FWA). All algorithms are population based and can be categorized into the fields of *swarm intelligence* (PSO, FSS, FWA), *evolutionary algorithms* (GA), and a combination thereof (DE). The goal is to find a solution with smaller overall error at convergence, and/or to speed up convergence of NMF (*i.e.* smaller approximation error for a given number of NMF iterations) compared to identical NMF algorithms without applied optimization strategy. Another goal is to increase the classification accuracy in cases where NMF is used as dimensionality reduction method for machine learning applications. The concepts of the two optimization strategies are the following: In the first strategy, meta-heuristics are used to initialize the factors W and H in order to minimize the NMF objective function *prior* to the factorization. The second strategy aims at iteratively improving the approximation quality of NMF during the first iterations.

The proposed optimization strategies can be considered successful if they are able to improve the NMF in terms of either (*i*) faster convergence (*i.e.* better accuracy per runtime) (*ii*) lower final approximation error, (*iii*) or better classification accuracy. The optimization of different rows of W and different columns of H can be split up into several partly independent sub-tasks and can thus be executed concurrently. Since this allows for a parallel and/or distributed computation of both update strategies, we also discuss parallel implementations of the proposed optimization strategies. Experimental results show that both strategies, the initialization of NMF factors as well as an iterative update during the first iterations, are able to improve the NMF in terms of faster convergence, lower approximation error, and/or better classification accuracy.

Related Work

The work by Lee and Seung (Lee and Seung 1999) is known as a standard reference for NMF. The original *Multiplicative Update* (MU) algorithm introduced in this article provides a good baselines against which other algorithms (e.g. the *Alternating Least Squares* algorithm (Paatero and Tapper 1994), the *Gradient Descent* algorithm (Lin 2007), ALSPGRAD (Lin 2007), quasi Newton-type NMF (Kim and Park 2008), fastNMF and bayes-NMF (Schmidt and Laurberg 2008), etc.) have to be judged. While the MU algorithm is still the fastest NMF algorithm per iteration and a good choice if a very fast and rough approximation is needed, ALSPGRAD, fastNMF and bayesNMF have shown to achieve a better approximation at convergence compared to many other NMF algorithms (Janecek, Schulze-Grotthoff et al. 2011).

NMF initialization. Only few algorithms for non-random NMF initialization have been published. (Wild, Curry et al. 2004) used spherical k-means clustering to group column vectors of A as input for W. A similar technique was used in (Xue, Tong et al. 2008). Another clustering-based method of structured initialization designed to find spatially localized basis images can be found in (Kim and Park 2008). (Boutsidis and Gallopoulos 2008) used an initialization technique based on two SVD processes called *nonnegative double singular value decomposition* (NNDSVD). Experiments indicate that this method has advantages over the centroid initialization in (Wild, Curry et al. 2004) in terms of faster convergence.

NMF and meta-heuristics. So far, only few studies can be found that aim at combining NMF and meta-heuristics, most of them are based on Genetic Algorithms (GAs). In (Stadlthanner, Lutter et al. 2007), the authors have investigated the application of GAs on sparse NMF for microarray analysis, while (Snásel, Platos et al. 2008) have applied GAs for boolean matrix factorization, a variant of NMF for binary data based on Boolean algebra. However, the methods presented in these studies are barely connected to the techniques presented in this chapter. In two preceding studies (Janecek and Tan 2011), (Janecek and Tan 2011) we have introduced the basic concepts of the proposed update strategies. Very recently, the study in (LI, YANG et al. 2013) proposed to replace the two NMF algorithm presented in (Lee and Seung 1999) with the quantum-behaved PSO (QPSO) for speech signal processing. QPSO is used to extract non-negative components with low cross-talk error and high SNR. Although the authors mention that QPSO is able to achieve better results than the two classic NMF algorithms, unfortunately no runtime comparisons are performed to check whether approximation per runtime can be improved. We performed similar experiments and found that when the complete NMF is replaced with SI methods the runtime increases significantly. Thus, we expect a significant growth of computation time also in the case of QPSO. Another very recent study (DAI 2013) uses an approach very similar to the NMF initialization presented in this chapter. We note that our first publication on this topic (Janecek and Tan 2011) appeared two years earlier. In their abstract, the authors mention that their approach uses the output of nonsmooth NMF as initial values for PSO to avoid blind search. However, at the moment this article is only available in Chinese characters. Similarly to the study (DAI 2013), no runtime measurements are available.

In this chapter we extend our preliminary work in several ways by the following new contributions. At first, we evaluate our methods on synthetic data as well as on data sets coming from the areas of spam filtering/email classification. This allows us to evaluate the proposed methods in the application context of the applied data sets. In other words, we are now able to investigate the quality of the NMF not only in terms of approximation accuracy but also in terms of *classification* accuracy achieved with the approximated data sets as well as with the basic vectors of the NMF factor W. Within this evaluation process we consider two different classification settings, a static setting where NMF is computed on the complete data set (training and test data), and a dynamic setting where NMF can be applied dynamically to new data. Moreover, we present a detailed evaluation of the runtime performance of the proposed update strategies, and, finally, we are able to compare the performance of our strategies with each other using the same parameter settings, data sets, and hardware set-up.

Notation

A matrix is represented by an uppercase italic letter (A, B, Σ, ...), a vector by a lowercase bold letter ($\mathbf{u}$, $\mathbf{x}$,, $\mathbf{q}_1$, ...), and a scalar by a lowercase Greek letter (λ, μ, ...). The ith row vector of a matrix D is represented as $\mathbf{d}_i^r$, and the jth column vector of D as $\mathbf{d}_j^c$. Matrix-matrix multiplications are denoted by "*", element-wise multiplications by "·", and element-wise divisions by "./".

Synopsis

In the following section we briefly review low-rank approximations and NMF algorithms. Then, we summarize the swarm intelligence algorithms used in this chapter, and present the proposed optimization strategies for NMF based on them. Moreover, we discuss different classification methods based on NMF. Finally, we evaluate our methods, discuss the achieved results, and conclude our work and summarize ongoing and future research activities in this area.

LOW RANK APPROXIMATIONS

Given a data matrix $A \in \mathbb{R}^{m \times n}$ whose n columns represent instances and whose m rows contain the values of a certain feature for the instances, most low-rank approximations reduce the dimensionality by representing the original data as accurately as possible with linear combinations of the original instances and/or features. Mathematically, A is replaced with another matrix A_k with usually much smaller rank. In general, a closer approximation means a better factorization. However, it is highly likely that in some applications specific factorizations might be more desirable compared to other solutions.

The most important low-rank approximation techniques are the Singular Value Decomposition (SVD, (Berry 1992)) and the closely related Principal Component Analysis (PCA, (Jolliffe 2002)). Traditionally, the PCA uses the eigenvalue decomposition to find eigenvalues and eigenvectors of the covariance matrix Cov(A) of A. Then the original data matrix A can be approximated by $A_k := A Q_k$, with $Q_k = [\mathbf{q}_1,...,\mathbf{q}_k]$, where $\mathbf{q}_1,...,\mathbf{q}_k$ are the first k eigenvectors of Cov(A). The SVD decomposes A into a product of three matrices such that $A = U\Sigma V^\top$, where

Σ contains the singular values along the diagonal, and U and V are the singular vectors. The reduced rank SVD to A can be found by setting all but the first k largest singular values equal to zero and using only the first k columns of U and V, such that $A_k := U_k \Sigma_k V_k^\top$. Other well-known low-rank approximation techniques comprise Factor Analysis, Independent Components Analysis, Multidimensional Scaling such as Fastmap or ISOMAP, or Locally Linear Embedding (LLE), which are all summarized in (Tan, Steinbach et al. 2005).

Amongst all possible rank k approximations, the approximation A_k calculated by SVD and PCA is the best approximation in the sense that $|| A - A_k ||_F$ is as small as possible (cf. (Berry, Drmac et al. 1999)). In other words, SVD and PCA give the closest rank k approximation of a matrix, such that $|| A - A_k ||_F \leq || A - B_k ||_F$, where B_k is *any* matrix of rank k, and $|| . ||_F$ is the Frobenius norm, which is defined as $\left(\sum |a_{ij}|^2 \right)^{1/2} = || A ||_F$. However, the main drawback of PCA and SVD refers to the interpretability of the transformed features. The resulting orthogonal matrix factors generated by the approximation usually do not allow for direct interpretations in terms of the original features because they contain positive *and* negative coefficients (Zhang, Berry et al.). In many application domains, a negative quantification of features is meaningless and the information about how much an original feature contributes in a low-rank approximation is lost. The presence of negative, meaningless components or factors may influence the entire result. This is especially important for applications where the original data matrix contains only positive entries, e.g. in text-mining applications, image classification, etc. If the factor matrices of the low-rank approximation were constrained to contain only positive or zero values, the original meaning of the data could be preserved better.

Non-Negative Matrix Factorization (NMF)

The NMF leads to special low-rank approximations which satisfy these non-negativity constraints. NMF requires that all entries in A, W and H are zero or positive. This makes the interpretation of the NMF factors much easier and enables NMF a non-subtractive combination of parts to form a whole (Lee and Seung 1999). The NMF consists of reduced rank *nonnegative* factors $W \in \mathbb{R}^{m \times k}$ and $H \in \mathbb{R}^{k \times n}$ with $k \ll min\{m, n\}$ that approximate a matrix $A \in \mathbb{R}^{m \times n}$ by $A \approx WH$, where the approximation WH has rank at most k. The nonlinear optimization problem underlying NMF can generally be stated as

$$\min_{W,H} f(W,H) = \min_{W,H} \frac{1}{2} || A - WH ||_F^2 .$$

(1.1)

The Frobenius norm $|| . ||_F$ is commonly used to measure the error between the original data A and the approximation WH, but other measures such as the Kullback-Leibler divergence are also possible (Lee and Seung 2001)). The error between A and WH is usually stored in a distance matrix $D = A - WH$ (cf. *Figure 1*). Unlike the SVD, the NMF is not unique, and convergence is not guaranteed for all NMF algorithms. If they converge, then usually to local minima only (potentially different ones for different algorithms). Nevertheless, the data compression achieved with only local minima has been shown to be of desirable quality for many data mining applications (Langville, Meyer et al. 2006). Moreover, for some specific problem settings a smaller residual $D = A - WH$ (a smaller error) may not necessarily improve of the solution of the actual application (e.g. classification task) compared to a rather coarse approximation. However, as analyzed in (Janecek and Gansterer 2010) a closer NMF approximation leads to qualitatively better clas-

Figure 1. Scheme of very coarse NMF approximation with very low rank k. Although k is significantly smaller than m and n, the typical structure of the original data matrix can be retained (note the three different groups of data objects in the left, middle, and right part of A).

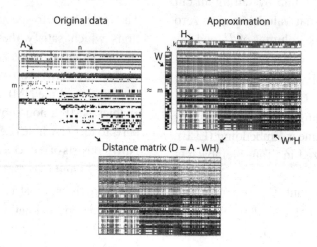

sification results and turns out to achieve significantly more stable results.

NMF Initialization: Algorithms for computing NMF are iterative and require initialization of the factors W and H. NMF unavoidably converges to local minima, probably different ones for different initialization (cf. (Boutsidis and Gallopoulos 2008)). Hence, random initialization makes the experiments unrepeatable since the solution to Equ.1.1 is not unique in this case. A proper non-random initialization can lead to faster error reduction and better overall error at convergence. Moreover, it makes the experiments repeatable. Although the benefits of good NMF initialization techniques are well known in the literature, most studies use random initialization (cf. (Boutsidis and Gallopoulos 2008). Since some initialization procedures can be rather costly in terms of runtime the trade-off between computational cost in the initialization step and the computational cost of the actual NMF algorithm need to be balanced carefully. In some situations, an expensive preprocessing step may overwhelm the cost savings in the subsequent NMF update steps.

General structure of NMF: In the basic form of NMF (see *Algorithm 1*), W and H are initialized randomly and the whole algorithm is repeated several times (*maxrepetition*). In each repetition, NMF update steps are processed until a maximum number of iterations is reached (*maxiter*). These update steps are algorithm specific and differ from one NMF variant to the other. Termination criteria: If the approximation error drops below a pre-defined threshold, or if the shift between two iterations is very small, the algorithm might stop before all iterations are processed.

Multiplicative update (MU) algorithm: To give an example of the update steps for a specific NMF MU algorithm we provide the update steps for the MU algorithm in *Algorithm 2*. MU is one of the two original NMF algorithms presented in (Lee and Seung 1999) and still one of the fastest NMF algorithms per iteration. The update steps are based on the mean squared error objective function and consist of multiplying the current factors by a measure of the quality of the current approximation. The divisions in *Algorithm 2* are to be performed *element-wise*. ε is used to avoid division by zero ($\varepsilon \approx 10^{-9}$).

Algorithm 1. General structure of NMF algorithms

```
1: given matrix A ∈ ℝ^{m×n} and k ≪ min{m, n}:
2: for rep = 1 to maxrepetition do
3:     W = rand(m, k);
4:     (H = rand(k, n);)
5:     for i = 1 to maxiter do
6:         perform algorithm specific NMF update steps
7:         check termination criterion
8:     end for
9: end for
```

SWARM INTELLIGENCE OPTIMIZATION

Optimization techniques inspired by swarm intelligence (SI) have become increasingly popular and benefit from their robustness and flexibility (Chiong 2009). Swarm intelligence is characterized by a decentralized design paradigm that mimics the behavior of swarms of social insects, flocks of birds, or schools of fish. Optimization techniques inspired by swarm intelligence have shown to be able to successfully deal with increasingly complex problems (Blackwell 2007). In this chapter we use five different optimization algorithms. Particle Swarm Optimization (PSO, (Kennedy and Eberhart 1995)) is a classical swarm intelligence algorithm, while Fish School Search (FSS, (Bastos Filho, Lima Neto et al. 2009)) and Fireworks Algorithm (FWA, (Tan and Zhu 2010)) are two recently developed swarm intelligence methods. These three algorithms are compared to a Genetic Algorithm (GA, (Haupt and Haupt

2005)), a classical evolutionary algorithm, and Differential Evolution (DE, (Price, Storn et al. 2005)), which shares some features with swarm intelligence but can also be considered as an evolutionary algorithm. Since PSO, GA and DE are well known optimization techniques we will not summarize them here; instead the interested reader is referred to the references given above.

Fish School Search is a recently developed swarm intelligence algorithm that mimics the movements of schools of fish. The main operators are *feeding* (fish can gain/lose weight, depending on the region they swim in) and *swimming* (there are three different swimming movements).

The *Fireworks Algorithm* is a novel swarm intelligence algorithm that is inspired by observing fireworks explosion. Two different types of explosion (search) processes are used in order to ensure diversity of resulting sparks, which are similar to particles in PSO or fish in FSS.

IMPROVING NMF WITH SWARM INTELLIGENCE OPTIMIZATION

Before describing our two optimization strategies for NMF based on swarm intelligence, we discuss some properties of the Frobenius norm (cf. (Berry, Drmac et al. 1999)). We use the Froben-

Algorithm 2. Update steps of the multiplicative update algorithm

```
1: H = H .* (W^⊤ A) ./ (W^⊤ W H + ε);
2: W = W .* (A H^⊤) ./ (W H H^⊤ + ε);
```

Algorithm 3. Pseudo code of the fish school search algorithm

1: Randomly initialize locations (x_i) of all fish, set all weights (w_i) to 1;

2: **repeat**

3:   *Swimming 1:* Compute random individual movement for each fish;

4:   *Feeding:* update weights for all fish based on new locations;

5:   *Swimming 2:* Collective instinctive movement towards overall direction;

6:   *Swimming 3:* Collective volitive movement dilation/contraction;

7: **until** termination (time, max. number of fitness evals., convergence, ...)

---

ius norm (1.1) as NMF objective function (*i.e.* to measure the error between A and WH) because it offers some properties that are beneficial for combining NMF and optimization algorithms. The following statements about the Frobenius norm are valid for any real matrix. However, in the following we assume that D refers to a distance matrix storing the distance (error of the approximation) between the original data and the approximation, $D = A - WH$. The Frobenius norm of a matrix $D \in \mathbb{R}^{m \times n}$ is defined as

$$\| D \|_F = \left(\sum_{i=1}^{min(m,n)} \sigma_i \right)^{1/2} = \left(\sum_{i=1}^{m} \sum_{j=1}^{n} |\mathbf{d}_{ij}|^2 \right)^{1/2} , \quad (1.2)$$

where σ_i are the singular values of D, and $\mathbf{d}_{ij}$ is the element in the ith row and j^{th} column of D. The Frobenius norm can also be computed row wise or column wise. The *row wise* calculation is

$$\| D \|_F^{RW} = \left(\sum_{i=1}^{m} |\mathbf{d}_i^r|^2 \right)^{1/2} , \quad (1.3)$$

where $|\mathbf{d}_i^r|$ is the norm of the ith row vector of D, *i.e.* $|\mathbf{d}_i^r| = (\sum_{j=1}^{n} |r_j^i|^2)^{1/2}$, and r_j^i is the jth element in row i. The *column wise* calculation is

$$\| D \|_F^{CW} = \left(\sum_{j=1}^{n} |\mathbf{d}_j^c|^2 \right)^{1/2} , \quad (1.4)$$

Algorithm 4. Pseudo code of the fireworks algorithm

1: Randomly initialize locations (x_i) of n fireworks;

2: **repeat**

3:   Set off n fireworks respectively at the n locations

4:   Calculate number $\hat{s}_i$ and location of sparks for each x_i

5:   Generate $\hat{m}$ specific sparks, each for a randomly selected firework

6:   Keep best location and select $n - 1$ locations for next iteration

7: **until** termination (time, max. number of fitness evals., convergence, ...)

---

with $|\,\mathbf{d}_j^c\,|$ being the norm of the jth column vector of D, *i.e.* $|\,\mathbf{d}_j^c\,| = (\sum_{i=1}^{m}|c_i^j|^2)^{1/2}$, and c_i^j being the ith element in column j. Obviously, a reduction of the Frobenius norm of any row or any column of D leads to a reduction of the total Frobenius norm $||\,D\,||_F$.

In the following we exploit these properties of the Frobenius norm for the proposed NMF optimization strategies. While strategy 1 aims at finding heuristically optimal starting points for the NMF factors, strategy 2 aims at iteratively improving the quality of NMF during the first iterations. All meta-heuristics mentioned in Section 0 can be used within both strategies. Before discussing the optimization strategies we illustrate the basic optimization procedure for a specific

row (row l) of W in Figure 2. This procedure is similar for both optimization strategies.

Parameters: Global parameters used for all optimization algorithms are upper/lower bound of the search space and the initialization, the number of particles (chromosomes, fish, ...), and maximum number of fitness evaluations. Parameter settings are discussed in Sections 0. For all meta-heuristics, the problem dimension is equal to the rank k of the NMF. *I.e.* if, for example, k = 10, a row/column vector with 10 continuous entries is returned by the optimization algorithms.

Optimization Strategy 1: Initialization

The goal of this optimization strategy is to find heuristically optimal starting points for the rows of W and the columns of H respectively, *i.e.*

Figure 2. Illustration of the optimization process for row l of the NMF factor W. The l^{th}row of A (a_l^r) and all columns of H0 are the input for the optimization algorithms. The output is a row-vector w_l^r (the l^{th}row of W) which minimizes the norm of d_l^r, the l^{th}row of the distance matrix D. The norm of d_l^r is the fitness function for the optimization algorithms (minimization problem).

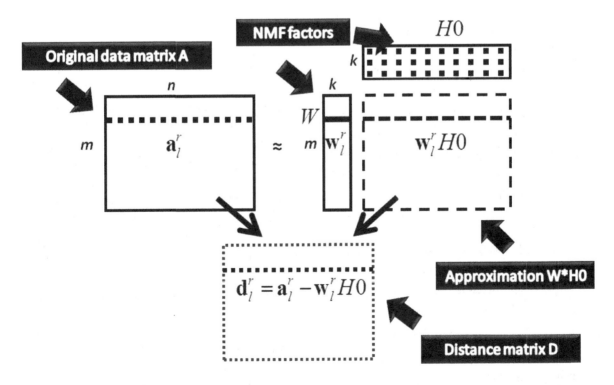

Algorithm 5. Pseudo code for the initialization procedure for NMF factors W and H. The two for-loops in lines 4 and 10 can be executed concurrently. SIO = Swarm Intelligence Optimization.

1: Given matrix $A \in \mathbb{R}^{m \times n}$ and $k \ll min\{m, n\}$;

2: $H0 = \text{rand}(k, n)$;

3: % Compute in parallel

4: **for** $i = 1$ to m **do**

5:     Use SIO to find $\mathbf{w}_i^r$ that minimizes $||\mathbf{a}_i^r - \mathbf{w}_i^r H0||_F$, (min $||.||_F$ of row i of D);

6: **end for**;

7: % Gather

8: $W = [\mathbf{w}_1^r; \ldots; \mathbf{w}_m^r]$;

9: % Compute in parallel

10: **for** $j = 1$ to n **do**

11:     Use SIO to find $\mathbf{h}_j^c$ that minimizes $||\mathbf{a}_j^c - W\mathbf{h}_j^c||_F$, (min $||.||_F$ of col j of D);

12: **end for**

13: % Gather

14: $H = [\mathbf{h}_1^c, \ldots, \mathbf{h}_n^c]$;

---

prior to the factorization process. *Algorithm 5* shows the pseudo code for the initialization procedure. In the beginning, $H0$ needs to be initialized randomly using a non-negative lower bound (preferably 0) for the initialization. In the first loop, W is initialized row wise, *i.e.* row $\mathbf{w}_i^r$ is optimized in order to minimize the Frobenius norm of the ith row $\mathbf{d}_i^r$ of D, which is defined as $\mathbf{d}_i^r = \mathbf{a}_i^r - \mathbf{w}_i^r H0$. Since the optimization of any row of W is independent to the optimization of any other row of W, all $\mathbf{w}_i^r$ can be optimized concurrently. In the second loop, the columns of H are initialized using on the previously computed and already optimized rows of W, which need to be gathered beforehand (in line 7 of the algorithm). H is initialized column wise, *i.e.* column $\mathbf{h}_j^c$ is optimized in order to minimize the Frobenius norm of the jth column $\mathbf{d}_j^c$ of D, which is defined as $\mathbf{d}_j^c = \mathbf{a}_j^c - W\mathbf{h}_j^c$. The optimization of the columns of H can be performed concurrently as well.

Optimization Strategy 2: Iterative Optimization

The second optimization strategy aims at iteratively optimizing the NMF factors W and H *during the first iterations* of the NMF. Compared to the first strategy not all rows of W and all columns of H are optimized – instead the optimization is only performed on selected rows/columns. In order to improve the approximation as fast as possible we identify rows of D with highest norm (the approximation of this row is worse than for other rows of D) and optimize the corresponding rows of W. The same procedure is used to identify the columns of H that should be optimized. Our experiments showed that not all NMF algorithms are suited for this iterative optimization procedure. For many NMF algorithms there was no improvement with respect to the convergence or a reduction of the overall error after a fixed number of iterations. However, for the multiplicative update (MU) algorithm – which is one of the most widely used NMF algorithms

Algorithm 6. Pseudo code for the iterative optimization for the Multiplicative Update algorithm. SIO = Swarm Intelligence Optimization. The methods used in this algorithm are explained below.

```
1: for iter = 1 to maxiter do
2:     % perform MU specific update steps
```
3:     $W = W \cdot (AH^\top)./(WHH^\top + \varepsilon);$

4:     $H = H \cdot (W^\top A)./(W^\top WH + \varepsilon);$

5:     **if** $(iter < m)$ **then**

6:       % Update rows of W ++

7:         $\mathbf{d}_i^r$ is the ith row vector of $D = A - WH$;

8:         $[Val, IX\_W] = sort(norm(\mathbf{d}_i^r),' descend');$

9:         $IX\_W = IX\_W(1:c);$

10:       % Compute in parallel

11:         $\forall i \in IX\_W:$

12:           Use SIO to find $\mathbf{w}_i^r$ that minimizes $||\mathbf{a}_i^r - \mathbf{w}_i^r H0||_F;$

13:       % Gather

14:         $W = [\mathbf{w}_1^r; \ldots; \mathbf{w}_m^r];$

15:     % Update columns of H ++

16:         $\mathbf{d}_j^c$ is the jth column vector of $D = A - WH$;

17:         $[Val, IX\_H] = sort(norm(\mathbf{d}_j^c),' descend');$

18:         $IX\_H = IX\_H(1:c);$

19:       % Compute in parallel

20:         $\forall j \in IX\_H:$

21:           Use SIO to find $\mathbf{h}_j^c$ that minimizes $||\mathbf{a}_j^c - W\mathbf{h}_j^c||_F;$

22:       % Gather

23:         $H = [\mathbf{h}_1^c, \ldots, \mathbf{h}_n^c];$

24:       $c = c - \Delta c;$

25:     **end if**

26: **end for**

– this strategy is able to improve the quality of the factorization. Hence, *Algorithm 6* shows the pseudo code for the iterative optimization of the NMF factors during the first iterations using the update steps of the MU algorithm described in Section 0. As shown in Section 0, this update strategy is able to significantly reduce the approximation error per iteration for the MU algorithm. Due to the relatively high computational cost of the meta-heuristics the optimization procedure is only applied in the first m iterations and only on c selected rows/columns of the NMF factors. Similar to strategy one the optimization of all rows of W are independent from each other (identical for columns of H), which allows for a parallel implementation of the proposed method.

In the following we describe the variables and functions (for updating rows of W) of *Algorithm 6*. Updating columns of H is similar to updating the rows of W.

- m: The number of iterations in which the optimization using meta-heuristics is applied
- c: The number of rows and/or columns that are optimized in the current iteration.
- Δc: The value of c is decreased by Δc in each iteration. $\Delta c = round(c_{initial} / m)$
- $[Val, IX\_W] = sort(norm(\mathbf{d}_i^r), 'descend')$ Returns the values Val and the corresponding indices (IX_W) of the norm of all row vectors $\mathbf{d}_i^r$ of D in descending order.
- $IX\_W = IX\_W(1:c)$: Returns only the first c elements of the vector IX_W.
- minimize $\| \mathbf{a}_i^r - \mathbf{w}_i^r H \|_F$: See Figure 2 and optimization strategy 1

Using NMF for Classification Problems

As already mentioned before, we also investigate the performance of NMF when applied for classification tasks. In this article, we use two different classification methods for evaluating the classification accuracy of NMF based on the optimization strategies discussed in Sections 0 and 0. Both classification methods have shown to work well for different application areas (Janecek 2010).

Static classification: In the first approach we analyze the classification accuracy achieved with the basis vectors (*i.e.* features in W). In this setting the NMF needs to be computed on the complete dataset (training and test data) which makes this technique only applicable on test data that is already available before the approximation/classification. However, the advantage of this approach

is that any freely chosen classification method can be applied on the basis features.

If the original data matrix $A \in \mathbb{R}^{m \times n}$ is an instance $\times$ feature matrix, then the NMF factor W is a $m \times k$ matrix, where every instance is described by k basis *features, i.e.* every column of W corresponds to a basis feature. Note that this setup is different to the one discussed at the beginning of Section 0! By applying a classification algorithm on the rows of W instead on the rows of A we can significantly reduce the dimension of the classification problem and thus decrease the computational cost for both, building the classification model and testing new data.

Dynamic classification: The second approach can be applied dynamically to new data. Here the factorization of the data (NMF) and the classification process are separated from each other (*i.e.* the NMF is performed on labeled training data – the unlabeled test data does not have to be available at the time of performing the NMF). This approach is called *NMF-LSI* and is based on an adaptation of latent semantic indexing which is a variant of the well-known vector space model.

A *vector space model* (VSM, (Raghavan and Wong 1999)) is a widely used algebraic model for representing objects as vectors in a potentially very high dimensional metric vector space. The distance of a query vector $\mathbf{q}$ to all objects in a given *feature* $\times$ *instance* matrix A are usually measured in terms of the cosines of the angles between $\mathbf{q}$ and the columns of A such that

$$cos\varphi_i = \frac{e_i^\top A^\top q}{\| A e_i \|_2 \| q \|_2}.$$

Latent semantic indexing (LSI, (Berry, Drmac et al. 1999)) is a variant of the basic VSM that replaces the original matrix A with a low-rank approximation A_k of A. In the standard version of LSI the SVD (see Section 0) is used to construct A_k, and $cos\varphi_i$ can be approximated as

$$cos\varphi_i \approx \frac{e_i^\top V_k \Sigma_k U_k^\top q}{\|\, U_k \Sigma_k V_k^\top e_i \,\|_2 \|\, q \,\|_2}.$$

LSI has computational advantages resulting in lower storage and computational cost, and often gives a cleaner and more efficient representation of the (latent) relationship between data elements.

NMF-LSI: The approximation within LSI can be replaced with other approximations. Instead of using the truncated SVD ($A_k := U_k \Sigma_k V_k^\top$), we approximate A with $A_k := W_k H_k$ (the NMF). When using NMF, the value of k must be fixed prior to the approximation. The cosine of the angle between $\mathbf{q}$ and the ith column of A can then be approximated as

$$cos\varphi_i \approx \frac{e_i^\top H_k^\top W_k^\top q}{\|\, W_k H_k e_i \,\|_2 \|\, q \,\|_2}.$$

In order to save computational cost, the left term in the numerator ($e_i^\top H_k^\top$) and the left part of the denominator ($\|\, W_k H_k e_i \,\|_2$) can be computed a priori. In all three methods (VSM and both LSI variants) a query instance $\mathbf{q}$ is assigned to the same class as the majority of its k-closest (in terms of cosine similarity) instances in A.

SETUP

Software: All software is written in Matlab. We used only publicly available NMF implementations: Multiplicative Update (MU, Matlab's Statistics Toolbox since v6.2, *nnmf()*). ALS using Projected Gradient (ALSPG, (Lin 2007)), BayesNMF and FastNMF (both (Schmidt and Laurberg 2008)). Matlab code for NNDSVD (Section 0) is also publicly available (cf. (Boutsidis

and Gallopoulos 2008)). Codes for PSO and DE were adapted from (Pedersen 2010), and code for GA from the appendix of (Haupt and Haupt 2005). For FWA we used the same implementation as in the introductory paper (Tan and Zhu 2010), and FSS was self-implemented following the algorithm provided in (Bastos Filho, Lima Neto et al. 2009).

Hardware: All experiments were performed on a SUN FIRE X4600 M2 with eight AMD Opteron quad-core processors (32 cores overall) with 3.2 GHz, 2MB L3 cache, and 32GB of main memory (DDR-II 666).

Parallel implementation: We implemented parallel variants of the optimization algorithms exploiting Matlab's parallel computing potential. Matlab's Distributed Computing Server (which requires a separate license) allows for parallelizing the optimization process over a large number (currently up to 64) of workers (threads). These workers can be nodes in multi-core computers, GPUs, or a node in a cluster of simple desktop PCs. Matlab's Parallel Computing Toolbox (which is included in the basic version of Matlab) allows to run up to eight workers concurrently, but is limited to local workers, *i.e.* nodes on a multi-core machine or local GPUs, but no cluster support.

Parameter setup: The dimension of the optimization problem is always identical to the rank k of the NMF (cf. Section 0). The upper/lower bound of the search space was set to the interval $[0, (4 * max(A))]$ and upper/lower bound of the initialization to $[0, max(A)]$. In order to achieve fair results which are not biased due to excessive parameter tuning we used the same parameter settings for all data sets. These parameter settings were found by running a self-written benchmark program that tested several parameter combinations on randomly generated data. For some optimization strategies (PSO, FSS and FWA) the recommended parameter settings from the literature worked fine. However, for GA and DE the parameter settings that were used in most studies in the literature did not perform very well. For

GA we found that a very aggressive (high) mutation rate highly improved the results. For DE we observed a similar behavior and found that the maximum crossover probability (1) achieved the best results. For all experiments in this paper, the following parameter settings were used:

GA: Mutation rate of 0.5; selection rate of 0.65

PSO: (G_{best} topology) following (Bratton and Kennedy 2007) $\omega = 0.8$, and $c_1 = c_2 = 2.05$

DE: crossover probability (pc) set to upper limit 1

FSS: $step_{ind\_initial} = 1$, $step_{ind\_final} = 0.001$, $W_{scale} = 10$

FWA: Number of sons (*sonnum*) set to 10

Data sets: We used three different data sets to evaluate our methods. *DS-RAND* is a randomly created, fully dense 100×100 matrix which is used in order to provide unbiased results. To evaluate the proposed methods in a classification context we further used two data sets from the area of email classification (spam/phishing detection). Data set *DS-SPAM1* consists of 3000 e-mail messages described by 133 features, divided into three groups: spam, phishing and legitimate email.

An exact description of this data set can be found in (Janecek and Gansterer 2010). Data set *DS-SPAM2* is the *spambase* data set taken from (Kjellerstrand 2011) which consists of 1813 spam and 2788 non-spam messages. DS-SPAM1 represents a ternary classification problem; DS-SPAM2 represents a typical binary classification problem.

EXPERIMENTAL EVALUATION

The evaluation is split up into two parts. First we evaluate the two optimization strategies proposed in Section 0 and Section 0, then we evaluate the quality of NMF in a classification context.

Evaluation of Optimization Strategy 1

Initialization: Before evaluating the improvement of the NMF approximation quality as such, we first measure the initial error after initializing W and H (*before* running the NMF algorithm). Figure 3 and Figure 4 show the average approximation error (*i.e.* Frobenius norm / fitness) per row (left) and per column (right) for data set DS-RAND.

Figure 3. Left hand-side: average approximation error per row (after initializing rows of W). Right hand-side: average approximation error per column (after initializing of H). NMF rank k = 5. Legends are ordered according to approximation error (top = worst, bottom = best).

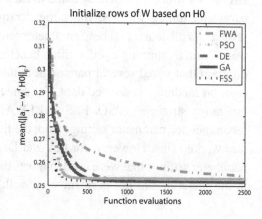
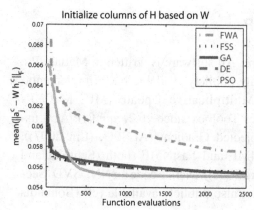

Figure 4. Similar information as for Figure 3, but for NMF rank k = 30.

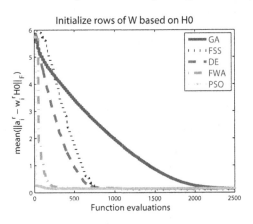 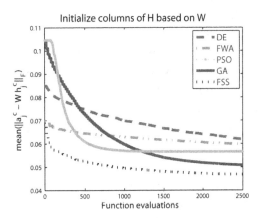

The figures on the left side show the *average* (mean) approximation error per *row* after initializing the rows of W (first loop in *Algorithm 5*). The figures on the right side show the *average* (mean) approximation error per *column* after initializing the columns of H (second loop in *Algorithm 5*). The legends are ordered according to the average approximation error achieved after the maximum number of function evaluations for each figure (top = worst, bottom = best). When the NMF rank k is small (see *Figure 3*, k=5) all optimization algorithms except FWA achieve similar results. Except FWA, all optimization algorithms quickly converge to a good result. With increasing complexity (*i.e.* increasing rank k) FWA clearly improves its results, as shown in Figure 4. The gap between the optimization algorithms is much bigger for larger rank k. Note that GA needs more than 2000 evaluations to achieve a low approximation error for initializing the rows of W. When initializing the columns of H, PSO and GA suffer from their high approximation error during the first iterations, which is caused by the relatively sparse factor matrix W for PSO and GA. Although PSO is able to reduce the approximation error significantly during the first 500 iterations, FSS and GA achieve slightly better final results. Generally, FSS achieves the best approximation accuracy after the initialization procedure for large k. However, as shown later

the initial approximation error is *not necessarily an indicator* for the approximation quality of NMF or the resulting classification accuracy.

Runtime performance: When parallelizing a sequential algorithm over p processors the speed-up indicates how much the parallel algorithm can perform specific tasks faster than the sequential algorithm. Speed-up is defined as $S_p = ET_{sequential} / ET_{parallel}$, where ET is the execution time. A linear speed-up is achieved when S_p is equal to p. Efficiency is another metric that estimates how well-utilized the processors are in solving the problem, compared to the cost of communication and synchronization. Efficiency is defined as $E_p = S_p / p$. For algorithms with linear speed-up the efficiency is 1, for algorithms with lower speed-up ratio it is between 0 and 1.

Figure 5 shows the runtime behavior for optimization strategy 1 with increasing number of Matlab workers. Runtimes are shown for the FSS optimization algorithm – however, all optimization algorithms have rather similar runtimes. Due to license limitations we only had Matlab's Parallel Computing Toolbox available which is limited to 8 workers (cf. Section 0). We measured runtimes and speed-up for up to 8 workers (average efficiency of about 0.95) and estimated the behavior of speed-up and runtime for a larger number of workers (based on this efficiency). Upgrading to Matlab's Distributed Computing Server is possible without any code-changes and thus only a license issue. When using eight workers, the NNDSVD initialization (the best NMF initialization strategy from the literature, Section 0) is a bit faster, but estimation shows that the proposed initialization strategy is faster when 12 or more workers are used. NNDSVD is already optimized and cannot be parallelized further in its current implementation.

Approximation quality: For evaluating the approximation results achieved by NMF using the factors W and H initialized by the optimization algorithms, we compare our results to random initialization as well as to NNDSVD. Figure 6 shows the approximation error on the y-axis (log scale) after a given number of NMF iterations for four NMF algorithms using different initialization methods (for DS-RAND). The initialization methods in the legend are ordered (top = worst, bottom = best). Since the MU algorithm (A) has low cost per iteration but converges slowly, the

first 100 iterations are shown (for all other algorithms the first 25 iterations are shown). For MU, all initialization variants achieve a smaller approximation error than random initialization. NNDSVD shows slightly better results than PSO and FWA, but GA, DE and especially FSS are able to achieve a smaller error per iteration than NNDSVD. For ALSPG (B), the new initialization strategy achieves better results than random initialization and also achieves a better approximation error than NNDSVD. This improvement is independent of the actual optimization algorithm. The same behavior can be seen for FastNMF (C) and BayesNMF (D). It has to be mentioned that FastNMF and BayesNMF were developed after the NNDSVD initialization. Surprisingly, when using FastNMF, NNDSVD achieves a lower approximation than random initialization. When comparing the different meta-heuristics, FSS achieves the best results amongst all optimization algorithms and achieves the closest approximation after 100 (MU) and 25 (ALSPG, FastNMF,

Figure 5. Runtime and speed-up measurement/estimation for DS-RAND using 1500 function evaluations per row/column for k= 5. As a reference, NNDSVD needs about 0.16 seconds for k=5. This indicates that if the number of workers is larger than 12, the proposed optimization strategy is faster than NNDSVD.

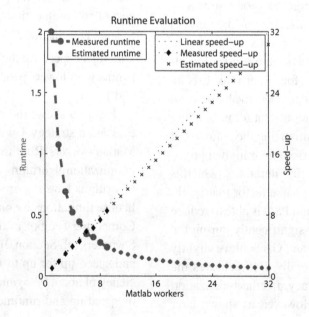

BayesNMF) iterations, respectively. DE and GA follow with a small gap since they are not as stable as FSS (i.e. they achieve good results for some, but not for all NMF algorithms.

Evaluation of Optimization Strategy 2

Figure 7 shows the convergence curves for the NMF approximation using optimization strategy 2 for different values of rank k (data set DS-RAND). Due to the relatively high computational cost of the meta-heuristics we applied our optimization procedure here only on the rows of W, while the columns in H remained unchanged.

Experiments showed that with this setting the loss in accuracy compared to optimizing both, W *and* H, is relatively small while the runtime can be increased significantly. m was set to 2 which indicates that the optimization is only applied in the first two iterations, and c was set to 20. As can be seen, the approximation error per iteration can be reduced when using optimization strategy 2. For small rank k (left side of Figure 7) the improvement is significant but decreases with increasing values of k (see right side of Figure 7). For larger k (larger than 10) the improvement over the basic MU is only marginal.

Figure 6. Approximation error archived by different NMF algorithms using different initialization variants (k=30, after 1500 fitness evaluations)

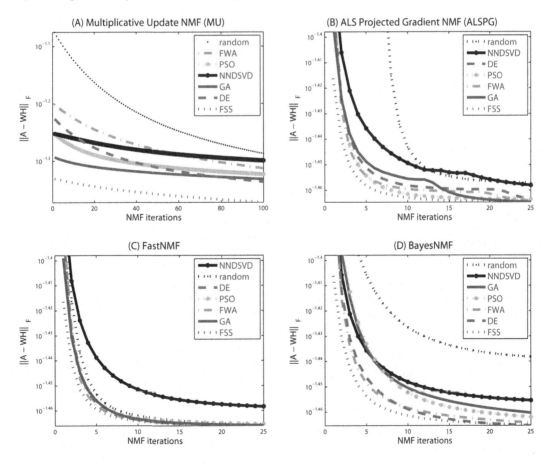

Figure 7. Accuracy per Iteration when updating only the row of W, m=2, c=20. Left: k=2, right: k=5

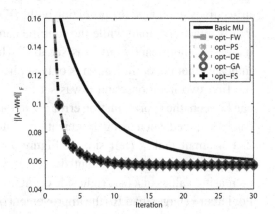 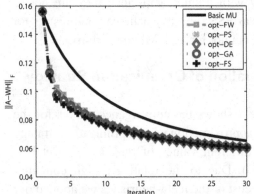

Runtime performance: Figure 8 shows the reduction in runtime for different rank *k* when the same accuracy as for basic MU should be achieved. Runtimes are shown for a parallel implementation using 32 Matlab workers. Basic MU sets the baseline (1 = 100%), the runtimes of the optimization strategy 2 (using different optimization algorithms) are given as $t_{opt-XX} / t_{Basic\,MU}$. For example, for small rank *k* the runtime can often be reduced by more than 50%. With increasing rank *k* the runtime savings get smaller and are only marginal for *k*=10. For rank *k* larger than 12 the basic MU algorithm is faster than optimization strategy 2.

Evaluation of the Classification Accuracy

Since optimization strategy 1 (initialization, Sections 0 and 0) achieves a faster, closer, and more stable approximation as optimization strategy 2 (iterative update, Sections 0 and 0) we evaluate the classification accuracy for this strategy. In the following, we measure the quality of optimization strategy 1 as pre-processing step for the two classification approaches mentioned in Section 0. Within the *static classification approach* any machine learning algorithm can be used for classification, but the approximation used for reducing

the dimensionality of the data set (SVD, PCA, NMF) needs to be applied on the complete data set. Contrary, the *dynamic classification approach* can be applied on the training data, the test data does not need to be available at the time of computing the approximation. However, this approach cannot be applied to all classification methods.

Static classification: We used three classification algorithms from the freely available WEKA toolkit (Witten and Frank 2005) to compare the classification accuracies achieved with the NMF factor *W* based on different NMF initializations: A support vector machine (SVM) based on the sequential minimal optimization (SOM) algorithm using a polynomial kernel with an exponent of 1; a k-nearest neighbor (*k*NN) classifier; and a J4.8 decision tree based on the C4.5 decision tree algorithm. Results were achieved using a 10-fold cross-validation, *i.e.* by randomly partitioning the data sets into 10 subsamples and then iteratively using one 9 subsamples as training data and 1 for testing.

Table 1 shows the overall classification results achieved with data set DS-SPAM1 using three different values of rank *k* and the three different classification methods mentioned above. The overall classification accuracy is computed as the number of correct classified email messages divided by the total number of messages. The

Figure 8. Proportional runtimes for achieving the same accuracy as basic MU after 30 iterations for different values of k when updating only the rows of W. (m=2, c=20)

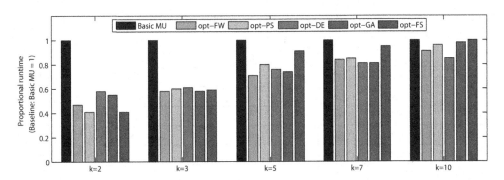

most-left column indicates the NMF algorithm and the second column the initialization strategy used for computing the NMF (RAND = random initialization). Note that the number of features is reduced to 30, 15 and 5, respectively, compared to 133. This reduction in the number of features significantly speeds up both, the process of building the classification model and the classification process itself. The best result for each NMF algorithm and each rank k is highlighted in bold letters. The proposed initialization strategies achieve better classification results as the state-of-the-art initialization method NNDSVD and significantly better results as random NMF initialization. Among the applied optimization algorithms there is not much difference, though FSS achieves a larger number of best results then the other algorithms. Results for J4.8 and kNN are very stable even for k=5 and are almost identical to the classification result achieved with all features. For SVM, the classification result tends to decrease with decreasing rank k. This behavior has been observed in another study (Janecek, Gansterer et al. 2008) where SVM has been applied on data sets from other dimensionality reduction methods (PCA). However, compared to NNDSVD and random initialization the proposed initialization methods achieve better results for all ranks of k. Comparing the different NMF algorithms it can be

seen the MU achieves lower classification accuracy compared to ALSPG, FastNMF and BayesNMF.

Table 2 shows the static classification results achieved with data set DS-SPAM2. Results are shown for the FastNMF, which achieved the most stable results of all NMF algorithms for this data set. Again, the proposed initialization strategy again achieves better results as NNDSVD and random initialization. Compared to DS-SPAM1, the results for this data set tend to decrease with decreasing rank k. This indicates that it is important to find a good trade-off between classification accuracy and computational cost.

Dynamic classification: Table 3 shows the classification results achieved with the dynamic classification approach described in Section 0 for DS-SPAM1. In general, the classification accuracies achieved for data set DS-SPAM2 using the dynamic classification approach are rather similar to the results for DS-SPAM1 shown in Table 3. The baseline to which the NMF-LSI variants are compared are given by a standard LSI classification using SVD as approximation algorithm (see Section 0). A basic vector space model achieves a classification accuracy of 0.911, while LSI achieves 0.911, 0.914 and 0.887, respectively, for rank k set to 30, 15 and 5. Similar to Table 2 (DS-SPAM2) the results are sensible with respect to the value of rank k. For very small values of k (5) the classification results generally tend

Table 1. Classification results (static classification) for DS-SPAM1

		J4.8			kNN(1)			SVM (SMO)		
		All Features: 0,973			All Features: 0,977			All Features: 0,976		
NMF Alg	Init	k = 30	k = 15	k = 5	k = 30	k = 15	k = 5	k = 30	k = 15	k = 5
ALSPG	DE	0,968	0,972	0,965	0,974	0,972	0,968	0,973	0,956	0,940
ALSPG	FSS	0,961	0,972	0,967	0,971	0,972	0,969	0,973	0,954	0,939
ALSPG	FWA	0,973	0,969	0,970	0,972	0,973	0,968	0,964	0,954	0,938
ALSPG	GA	0,970	0,968	0,969	0,973	0,970	0,968	0,973	0,957	0,947
ALSPG	PSO	0,971	0,972	0,969	0,977	0,971	0,968	0,972	0,954	0,937
ALSPG	NNDSVD	0,963	0,976	0,964	0,969	0,972	0,968	0,966	0,952	0,938
ALSPG	RAND	0,943	0,938	0,935	0,952	0,940	0,938	0,948	0,942	0,913
BAYES	DE	0,971	0,970	0,970	0,974	0,973	0,968	0,971	0,954	0,946
BAYES	FSS	0,966	0,973	0,971	0,976	0,971	0,969	0,975	0,953	0,947
BAYES	FWA	0,970	0,970	0,968	0,972	0,974	0,968	0,957	0,954	0,941
BAYES	GA	0,966	0,971	0,968	0,974	0,973	0,969	0,972	0,955	0,947
BAYES	PSO	0,968	0,967	0,969	0,970	0,971	0,970	0,966	0,957	0,937
BAYES	NNDSVD	0,968	0,972	0,968	0,970	0,973	0,969	0,966	0,952	0,947
BAYES	RAND	0,952	0,941	0,953	0,961	0,951	0,947	0,958	0,937	0,926
FAST	DE	0,966	0,969	0,969	0,977	0,973	0,968	0,970	0,955	0,946
FAST	FSS	0,967	0,971	0,970	0,976	0,971	0,969	0,975	0,953	0,947
FAST	FWA	0,968	0,970	0,969	0,971	0,974	0,968	0,957	0,954	0,941
FAST	GA	0,966	0,965	0,968	0,973	0,971	0,969	0,973	0,955	0,947
FAST	PSO	0,968	0,970	0,970	0,974	0,971	0,970	0,973	0,956	0,937
FAST	NNDSVD	0,966	0,973	0,970	0,970	0,973	0,968	0,966	0,952	0,939
FAST	RAND	0,954	0,949	0,937	0,958	0,951	0,941	0,957	0,935	0,917
MU	DE	0,955	0,952	0,965	0,966	0,959	0,968	0,962	0,953	0,940
MU	FSS	0,965	0,960	0,967	0,967	0,964	0,969	0,966	0,952	0,939
MU	FWA	0,949	0,956	0,970	0,964	0,966	0,968	0,959	0,955	0,938
MU	GA	0,954	0,961	0,969	0,966	0,966	0,968	0,961	0,944	0,947
MU	PSO	0,958	0,939	0,969	0,949	0,946	0,968	0,953	0,940	0,937
MU	NNDSVD	0,964	0,967	0,964	0,972	0,973	0,968	0,963	0,954	0,938
MU	RAND	0,941	0,937	0,947	0,948	0,941	0,951	0,951	0,930	0,927

to decrease. Overall, the initialization strategy based on meta-heuristics achieve much better classification accuracy as NNDSVD and random initialization, and also outperform basic LSI in many cases. The best results are again highlighted in bold letters. Especially GA and FWA achieve good classification results.

CONCLUSION

In this chapter we presented two new optimization strategies for improving the NMF using optimization algorithms based on swarm intelligence. While strategy one uses swarm intelligence algorithms to initialize the factors W and H *prior* to the factorization process of NMF, the second

Table 2. Classification results (static classification) for DS-SPAM2 (FastNMF)

		J4.8			kNN(1)			SVM (SMO)		
		All Features: 0,921			All Features: 0,907			All Features: 0,904		
NMF Alg	*Init*	*k = 30*	*k = 15*	*k = 5*	*k = 30*	*k = 15*	*k = 5*	*k = 30*	*k = 15*	*k = 5*
FAST	DE	0,918	0,893	0,863	*0,902*	0,880	0,821	*0,905*	0,865	0,798
FAST	FSS	0,920	*0,920*	0,773	0,895	0,889	0,826	0,894	0,880	0,773
FAST	FWA	0,916	0,916	0,864	0,887	*0,898*	0,797	0,893	0,885	0,757
FAST	GA	0,918	0,914	0,865	0,889	0,896	*0,827*	0,896	*0,891*	0,778
FAST	PSO	*0,921*	0,911	*0,878*	0,895	0,892	*0,850*	0,896	0,881	*0,827*
FAST	NNDSVD	0,919	0,911	0,811	0,895	0,894	0,816	0,894	0,882	0,766
FAST	RAND	*0,907*	*0,908*	*0,813*	*0,885*	*0,886*	*0,803*	*0,887*	*0,864*	*0,752*

strategy aims at iteratively improving the approximation quality of NMF *during* the first iterations of the factorization. Overall, five different optimization algorithms were used for improving NMF: Particle Swarm Optimization (PSO), Genetic Algorithms (GA), Fish School Search (FSS), Differential Evolution (DE), and Fireworks Algorithm (FWA).

Both optimization strategies allow for efficiently computing the optimization of single rows of W and/or single columns of H in parallel. The achieved results are evaluated in terms of accuracy per runtime and per iteration, final accuracy after a given number of NMF iterations, and in terms of the classification accuracy achieved with the reduced NMF factors when being applied for machine learning applications. Especially the

Table 3. Dynamic classification using DS-SPAM1. Basic vector space model (all features): 0,911.

Baseline	LSI	0,911	0,914	0,887		LSI	0,911	0,914	0,887
NMF Alg	**Init**	**k = 30**	**k = 15**	**k = 05**	**NMF Alg**	**Init**	**k = 30**	**k = 15**	**k = 05**
ALSPG	*DE*	*0,911*	*0,898*	*0,889*	*FAST*	*DE*	*0,912*	*0,895*	*0,888*
ALSPG	*FSS*	0,943	0,899	0,877	*FAST*	*FSS*	0,926	0,897	0,879
ALSPG	*FWA*	0,930	0,914	0,883	*FAST*	*FWA*	0,913	*0,912*	0,891
ALSPG	*GA*	0,927	*0,901*	0,896	*FAST*	*GA*	0,927	0,914	0,875
ALSPG	*PSO*	0,918	0,889	0,885	*FAST*	*PSO*	0,923	0,914	0,847
ALSPG	*NNDSVD*	*0,914*	*0,911*	0,840	*FAST*	*NNDSVD*	*0,911*	*0,913*	*0,846*
ALSPG	*RAND*	*0,901*	0,886	0,874	*FAST*	*RAND*	0,898	0,899	0,838
BAYES	*DE*	*0,911*	0,906	0,888	*MU*	*DE*	0,893	0,897	*0,834*
BAYES	*FSS*	0,926	0,897	0,879	*MU*	*FSS*	0,892	0,882	0,807
BAYES	*FWA*	*0,914*	*0,911*	0,891	*MU*	*FWA*	0,913	0,882	0,843
BAYES	*GA*	0,930	0,916	0,875	*MU*	*GA*	0,899	0,899	0,795
BAYES	*PSO*	0,922	*0,915*	0,848	*MU*	*PSO*	0,922	0,900	0,812
BAYES	*NNDSVD*	*0,904*	*0,913*	0,846	*MU*	*NNDSVD*	0,906	0,908	0,795
BAYES	*RAND*	*0,898*	*0,896*	*0,854*	*MU*	*RAND*	0,876	0,889	*0,817*

initialization strategy (optimization strategy 1) is able to significantly improve the approximation results of NMF compared to random initialization and state-of-the-art methods. Among the different optimization algorithms, the recently developed fish school search algorithm achieves slightly better results than the other heuristics. The iterative strategy (optimization strategy 2) can improve one of the basic NMF algorithms (the multiplicative update strategy) for very small rank k and can thus be used if a rough and very fast approximation method is needed. Moreover, the NMF subsets achieved with optimization strategy 1 have shown to clearly improve the classification accuracy of NMF compared to state-of-the-art initialization strategies, and also achieve better results as feature subsets computed with other low-approximation techniques.

Future work: Our investigations provide several important and interesting directions for future work. First of all, we will set the focus on developing optimization strategies that update the factor matrices W and H concurrently instead of applying an alternating update fashion where one factor is fixed and the other one is optimized. Moreover, we will apply the optimization strategies on NMF problems were sparseness constraints are enforced, i.e. the optimization strategies are enforced to compute solutions with a certain percentage of zero values. We also plan to use different NMF optimization functions (not based on the Frobenius norm) for our optimization methods and several recently developed NMF algorithms (HALS, multilayer NMF, etc.).

ACKNOWLEDGMENT

This work was supported by National Natural Science Foundation of China (NSFC), Grant No. 61375119, 61170057, and 60875080. Andreas wants to thank the *Erasmus Mundus External Coop. Window*, Lot 14 (2009-1650/001-001-ECW).

REFERENCES

Bastos Filho, C. J. A., Lima Neto, F. B., Sousa, M. F. C., Pontes, M. R., & Madeiro, S. S. (2009). On the influence of the swimming operators in the Fish School Search algorithm. In *Proceedings of Systems, Man and Cybernetics* (pp. 5012–5017). San Antonio, TX: IEEE.

Berry, M. W. (1992). Large Scale Singular Value Computations. *The International Journal of Supercomputer Applications*, 6(1), 13–49.

Berry, M. W., Browne, M., Langville, A. N., Pauca, P. V., & Plemmons, R. J. (2007). Algorithms and Applications for Approximate Nonnegative Matrix Factorization. *Computational Statistics & Data Analysis*, 52(1), 155–173. doi:10.1016/j.csda.2006.11.006

Berry, M. W., Drmac, Z., & Jessup, E. R. (1999). Matrices, Vector Spaces, and Information Retrieval. *SIAM Review*, 41(2), 335–362. doi:10.1137/S0036144598347035

Blackwell, T. (2007). Particle Swarm Optimization in Dynamic Environments. In Yang et al. (Eds.), *Evolutionary Computation in Dynamic and Uncertain Environments* (pp. 29–49). Berlin, Heidelberg: Springer. doi:10.1007/978-3-540-49774-5_2

Boutsidis, C., & Gallopoulos, E. (2008). SVD based Initialization: A Head Start for Nonnegative Matrix Factorization. *Pattern Recognition*, 41(4), 1350–1362. doi:10.1016/j.patcog.2007.09.010

Bratton, D., & Kennedy, J. (2007). Defining a standard for particle swarm optimization. In *Proceedings of Swarm Intelligence Symposium*, (pp. 120-127). Honolulu, HI: IEEE.

Chiong, R. (Ed.). (2009). *Nature-Inspired Algorithms for Optimisation*. Berlin: Springer. doi:10.1007/978-3-642-00267-0

Dai, H, & Wang, , Hu, & Wang, Y. (2013). Nonsmooth Nonnegative Matrix Factorization Algorithm Based on Particle Swarm Optimization. *Computer Engineering, 39*(1), 204–207.

Eberhart, R. C., Shi, Y., & Kennedy, J. (2001). *Swarm Intelligence*. San Francisco, CA: Morgan Kaufmann.

Goldberg, D. E. (1989). *Genetic Algorithms in Search, Optimization and Machine Learning*. Boston, MA: Addison-Wesley Longman.

Haupt, R. L., & Haupt, S. E. (2005). *Practical Genetic Algorithms* (2nd ed.). Hoboken, NJ: John Wiley & Sons, Inc.

Janecek, A. (2010). *Efficient feature reduction and classification methods: Applications in drug discovery and email categorization*. (PhD Thesis). University of Vienna, Vienna, Austria.

Janecek, A., & Gansterer, W. N. (2010). Utilizing nonnegative matrix factorization for e-mail classification problems. In M. W. Berry (Ed.), *Survey of text mining III: Application and theory* (pp. 57–80). Hoboken, NJ: John Wiley & Sons, Inc. doi:10.1002/9780470689646.ch4

Janecek, A., Gansterer, W. N., Demel, M., & Ecker, G. F. (2008). On the relationship between feature selection and classification accuracy. *JMLR: Workshop and Conference Proceedings, 4*(1), 90–105.

Janecek, A., Schulze-Grotthoff, S., & Gansterer, W. N. (2011). libNMF - A library for nonnegative matrix factorizatrion. *Computing and Informatics, 30*(2), 205–224.

Janecek, A., & Tan, Y. (2011). Iterative improvement of the multiplicative update NMF algorithm using nature-inspired optimization. In *Proceedings of the 7th International Conference on Natural Computation*, (pp. 1668-1672). Shanghai, China: IEEE.

Janecek, A., & Tan, Y. (2011). Using population based algorithms for initializing nonnegative matrix factorization. In *Proceedings of the 2nd International Conference on Swarm Intelligence (LNCS)* (vol. 67239, pp. 307-316). Berlin: Springer.

Jolliffe, I. T. (2002). *Principal component analysis*. New York: Springer.

Kennedy, J., & Eberhart, R. C. (1995). Particle swarm optimization. In *Proceedings of IEEE International Conference on Neural Networks*, (pp. 1942-1948). Perth, Australia: IEEE.

Kim, H., & Park, H. (2008). Nonnegative matrix factorization based on alternating nonnegativity constrained least squares and active set method. *SIAM Journal on Matrix Analysis and Applications, 30*(2), 713–730. doi:10.1137/07069239X

Kjellerstrand, H. (2011). *Hakanks hemsida*. Retrieved from http://hakank.org/weka

Langville, A. N., Meyer, C. D., & Albright, R. (2006). Initializations for the nonnegative matrix factorization. In *Proceedings of the 12th ACM Int. Conf. on Knowledge Discovery and Data Mining*, (pp. 1-18). Philadelphia, PA: ACM

Lee, D. D., & Seung, H. S. (2001). Algorithms for non-negative matrix factorization. *Advances in Neural Information Processing Systems, 13*(1), 556–562.

Li, H., Yang, J., & Hao, C. (2013). Non-negative matrix factorization of mixed speech signals based on quantum-behaved particle swarm optimization. *Journal of Computer Information Systems, 9*(2), 667–673.

Filho, C. J. A., Lima Neto, F. B., Lins, A. J. C., Nascimento, A. I. S., & Lima, M. P. (2009). Fish school search. In R. Chiong (Ed.), *Nature-inspired algorithms for optimisation* (pp. 261–277). Springer;

Lin, C.-J. (2007). Projected gradient methods for nonnegative matrix factorization. *Neural Computation, 19*(10), 2756–2779. doi:10.1162/neco.2007.19.10.2756 PMID:17716011

Paatero, P., & Tapper, U. (1994). Positive matrix factorization: A non-negative factor model with optimal utilization of error estimates of data values. *Environmetrics, 5*(2), 111–126. doi:10.1002/env.3170050203

Pedersen, M. E. H. (2010). *SwarmOps - Numeric & Heuristic Optimization Source-Code Library*. Retrieved from http://hvass-labs.org/projects/swarmops/cs/files/SwarmOpsCS1_0.pdf

Price, K. V., Storn, R. M., & Lampinen, J. A. (2005). *Differential evolution: A practical approach to global optimization*. Secaucus, NJ: Springer.

Raghavan, V. V., & Wong, S. K. M. (1986). A critical analysis of vector space model for information retrieval. *Journal of the American Society for Information Science American Society for Information Science, 37*(5), 279–287. doi:10.1002/(SICI)1097-4571(198609)37:5<279::AID-ASI1>3.0.CO;2-Q

Schmidt, M. N. and H. Laurberg (2008). Nonnegative matrix factorization with Gaussian process priors. *Comp. Intelligence and Neuroscience*, (1), 1-10.

Seung, H. S., & Lee, D. D. (1999). Learning parts of objects by non-negative matrix factorization. *Nature, 401*(6755), 788–791. doi:10.1038/44565 PMID:10548103

Snásel, V., Platos, J., & Krömer, P. (2008). Developing genetic algorithms for boolean matrix factorization. In *Proceedings of the Dateso 2008 Annual International Workshop on DAtabases, TExts, Specifications and Objects*, (pp. 1-10). Desna, Czech Republic: CEUR-WS.org.

Stadlthanner, K., Lutter, D., Theis, F., et al. (2007). Sparse nonnegative matrix factorization with genetic algorithms for microarray analysis. In *Proceedings of the International Joint Conference on Neural Networks*, (pp. 294-299). Orlando, FL: IEEE.

Storn, R., & Price, K. (1997). Differential evolution - A simple and efficient heuristic for global optimization over continuous spaces. *Journal of Global Optimization, 11*(4), 341–359. doi:10.1023/A:1008202821328

Tan, P.-N., Steinbach, M., & Kumar, V. (2005). *Introduction to data mining*. Boston, MA: Addison Wesley.

Tan, Y., & Zhu, Y. (2010). Fireworks algorithm for optimization. In Tan et al. (Eds.), *Advances in swarm intelligence* (pp. 355–364). Beijing, China: Springer. doi:10.1007/978-3-642-13495-1_44

Wild, S. M., Curry, J. H., & Dougherty, A. (2004). Improving non-negative matrix factorizations through structured initialization. *Patt. Recog, 37*(11), 2217–2232. doi:10.1016/j.patcog.2004.02.013

Witten, I. H., & Frank, E. (2005). *Data mining: Practical machine learning tools and techniques*. San Francisco, CA: Morgan Kaufmann.

Xue, Y., Tong, C. S., Chen, Y., & Chen, W. (2008). Clustering-based initialization for non-negative matrix factorization. *Applied Mathematics and Computation, 205*(2), 525–536. doi:10.1016/j.amc.2008.05.106

Zhang, Q., Berry, M. W., Lamb, B. T., & Samuel, T. (2009). A parallel nonnegative tensor factorization algorithm for mining global climate data. In *Proceedings of the 9th International Conference on Computational Science*, (pp. 405-415). Berlin: Springer.

KEY TERMS AND DEFINITIONS

Differential Evolution (DE): In DE, (Storn and Price 1997, Price, Storn et al. 2005) a particle is moved around in the search-space using simple mathematical formulation, if the new position is an improvement the particles' position is updated, otherwise the new position is discarded.

Fireworks Algorithm (FWA): FWA, (Tan and Zhu 2010) is a recently developed swarm intelligence algorithm that simulates the explosion process of fireworks. Two types of sparks are generated, based on uniform and Gaussian distribution, respectively.

Fish School Search (FSS): FSS, (Bastos Filho, Lima Neto et al. 2009, Bastos Filho, Lima Neto et al. 2009)is based on the behavior of fish schools. The main operators are *feeding* (fish can gain/lose weight, depending on the region they swim in) and *swimming* (which mimics the collective movement of all fish).

Genetic Algorithms (GA): GAs, (Goldberg 1989) are global search heuristics that operate on a population of solutions using techniques encouraged from evolutionary processes such as mutation, crossover, and selection.

Multiplicative Update (MU) NMF Algorithm: MU-NMF is one of the two original NMF algorithms presented in (Lee and Seung 1999) and still one of the fastest NMF algorithms per iteration. The update steps are based on the mean squared error objective function and consist of multiplying the current factors by a measure of the quality of the current approximation.

NMF Initialization: Algorithms for computing NMF are iterative and require initialization of the factors W and H since NMF unavoidably converges to local minima, probably different ones for different initialization. Contrary to random initialization, a proper non-random initialization can lead to faster error reduction and better overall error at convergence.

Non-Negative Matrix Factorization: The Non-negative Matrix Factorization (NMF, (Lee and Seung 1999)) leads to a low-rank approximation which satisfies non-negativity constraints by approximating a data matrix A by $A \approx WH$, where W and H are the *NMF factors*. NMF requires *all entries* in A, W and H to be zero or positive.

Particle Swarm Optimization (PSO): In PSO, (Kennedy and Eberhart 1995) each particle in the swarm adjusts its position in the search space based on the best position it has found so far as well as the position of the known best fit particle of the entire swarm.

Compilation of References

Aarts, E., & Korst, J. (1989). *Simulated annealing and Boltzmann machines: a stochastic approach to combinatorial optimization and neural computing*. New York, NY: John Wiley & Sons, Inc.

Adra, S. F., Dodd, T. J., Griffin, I. A., & Fleming, P. J. (2009). Convergence acceleration operator for multiobjective optimization. *IEEE Transactions on Evolutionary Computation*, *13*(4), 825–847. doi:10.1109/TEVC.2008.2011743

Adra, S. F., & Fleming, P. J. (2011). Diversity management in evolutionary many-objective optimization. *IEEE Transactions on Evolutionary Computation*, *15*(2), 183–195. doi:10.1109/TEVC.2010.2058117

Aeberhard, S., Coomans, D., & Vel, O. D. (1992). *Comparison of classifiers in high dimensional settings* (Tech. Rep. No. 92-02). North Queensland, Australia: James Cook University of North Queensland, Dept. of Computer Science and Dept. of Mathematics and Statistics.

Akyildiz, I. F., Su, W., Sankarasubramaniam, Y., & Cayirci, E. (2002). Wireless sensor networks: A survey. *Computer Networks*, *38*(4), 393–422. doi:10.1016/S1389-1286(01)00302-4

Al-Khayyal, B. (1991). Machine Parameter selection for turning with constraints: An analytical approach based on geometric programming. *International Journal of Production Research*, *29*(9), 1897–1908. doi:10.1080/00207549108948056

AlMurtadha, Y.M., Sulaiman, M.N.B., Mustapha, N., & Udzir, N.I. (2010). Mining web navigation profiles for recommendation system. *Information Technology Journal*, *9*, 790-796.

AlMurtadha, Y. M., Sulaiman, M. N. B., Mustapha, N., & Udzir, N. I. (2011). IPACT: Improved Web Page Recommendation System Using Profile Aggregation Based On Clustering of Transactions. *American Journal of Applied Sciences*, *8*(3), 277–283. doi:10.3844/ajassp.2011.277.283

Anderson, E. (1935). The irises of the gaspe peninsula. *Bulletin of the American Iris Society*, *59*, 2–5.

Andrey, P. (1999). Selectionist relaxation: Genetic algorithms applied to image segmentation. *Image and Vision Computing*, *17*(3-4), 175–187. doi:10.1016/S0262-8856(98)00095-X

Angeline, P. J. (1999). Using selection to improve particle swarm optimization. In *Proceedings of the IEEE International Joint Conference on Neural Networks* (pp. 84-89). IEEE.

Armarego, E. J. A., Smith, A. J. R., & Wang, J. (1993). Constrained optimization strategies and CAM software for single-pass peripheral milling. *International Journal of Production Research*, *31*(9), 2139–2160. doi:10.1080/00207549308956849

Audet, C., & Dennis, J. E. Jr. (2002). Analysis of generalized pattern searches. *SIAM Journal on Optimization*, *13*(3), 889–903. doi:10.1137/S1052623400378742

Bahceci, E., Soysal, O., & Sahin, E. (2003). Review: Pattern formation and adaptation in multi-robot systems. *CMU Tech. Report no. CMU-RI-TR-03-4*. Carnegie Mellon University.

Balasubramani, K., & Marcus, K. (n.d.). Artificial bee colony algorithm to improve brain MR image segmentation. *International Journal on Computer Science and Engineering*, *5*(1), 31-36.

Balch, T., & Arkin, R. (1998). Behavior-based formation control of multi-robot teams. *IEEE Transactions on Robotics and Automation*, *14*(6), 926–939. doi:10.1109/70.736776

Barahona, F., Grotschel, M., Junger, M., & Reinelt, G. (1988). An application of combinatorial optimization to statistical physics and circuit layout design. *Operations Research*, *36*(3), 493–513. doi:10.1287/opre.36.3.493

Bastos Filho, C. J. A., Lima Neto, F. B., Sousa, M. F. C., Pontes, M. R., & Madeiro, S. S. (2009). On the influence of the swimming operators in the Fish School Search algorithm. In *Proceedings of Systems, Man and Cybernetics* (pp. 5012–5017). San Antonio, TX: IEEE.

Bastos, F., Carmelo, J. A., Lima, N., & De Fernando, B. (2002). A novel search algorithm based on fish school behavior. In Proceedings of IEEE Int Conf on Systems, Man, and Cybernetics. Cingapura.

Bentley, P. J. (1999). *Evolutionary Design by Computers*. Morgan Kaufmann Publishers.

Berry, M. W. (1992). Large Scale Singular Value Computations. *The International Journal of Supercomputer Applications*, *6*(1), 13–49.

Berry, M. W., Browne, M., Langville, A. N., Pauca, P. V., & Plemmons, R. J. (2007). Algorithms and Applications for Approximate Nonnegative Matrix Factorization. *Computational Statistics & Data Analysis*, *52*(1), 155–173. doi:10.1016/j.csda.2006.11.006

Berry, M. W., Drmac, Z., & Jessup, E. R. (1999). Matrices, Vector Spaces, and Information Retrieval. *SIAM Review*, *41*(2), 335–362. doi:10.1137/S0036144598347035

Bezdek, J. C. (1981). *Patten Recognition with Fuzzy Objective Function Algorithm*. New York: Plenum Press. doi:10.1007/978-1-4757-0450-1

Bhandarkar, S. M., & Zhang, H. (1999). Image segmentation using evolutionary computation. *IEEE Transactions on Evolutionary Computation*, *3*(1), 1–21. doi:10.1109/4235.752917

Bhanu, Lee, S., & Ming, J. (1995). Adaptive image segmentation using a genetic algorithm. *IEEE Transactions on Systems, Man, and Cybernetics*, *25*(12), 1543–1567. doi:10.1109/21.478442

Binh, T., & Korn, U. (1997). *MOBES: A multiobjective evolution strategy for constrained optimization problems*. Paper presented at the 3rd International Conference on Genetic Algorithms. Brno, Czech Republic.

Blackwell, T. M., & Bentley, P. (2002). Don't push me! Collision-avoiding swarms. In *Proceedings of the Fourth Congress on Evolutionary Computation (CEC 2002)* (pp. 1691-1696). CEC.

Blackwell, T. (2007). Particle Swarm Optimization in Dynamic Environments. In Yang et al. (Eds.), *Evolutionary Computation in Dynamic and Uncertain Environments* (pp. 29–49). Berlin, Heidelberg: Springer. doi:10.1007/978-3-540-49774-5_2

Bloch, I., Milisavljevc, N., & Acheroy, M. (2007). Multisensor Data Fusion for Spaceborne and Airborne Reduction of Mine Suspected Areas. *International Journal of Advanced Robotic Systems*, *4*(2), 173–186.

Boccalatte, M., Brogi, F., Catalfamo, F., Maddaluno, S., Martino, M., & Mellano, V. et al. (2013). A Multi-UAS Cooperative Mission Over Non-Segregated Civil Areas. *Journal of Intelligent & Robotic Systems*, *70*(1-4), 275–291. doi:10.1007/s10846-012-9706-5

Bonabeau, E., Dorigo, M., & Theraulaz, G. (1999). *Swarm intelligence: From natural to artificial systems*. London, UK: Oxford University Press.

Bosman, P. A. N., & Thierens, D. (2003). The balance between proximity and diversity in multiobjective evolutionary algorithms. *IEEE Transactions on Evolutionary Computation*, *7*(2), 174–188. doi:10.1109/TEVC.2003.810761

Boutsidis, C., & Gallopoulos, E. (2008). SVD based Initialization: A Head Start for Nonnegative Matrix Factorization. *Pattern Recognition*, *41*(4), 1350–1362. doi:10.1016/j.patcog.2007.09.010

Bratton, D., & Kennedy, J. (2007). Defining a standard for particle swarm optimization. In *Proceedings of Swarm Intelligence Symposium*, (pp. 120-127). Honolulu, HI: IEEE.

Bratton, D., & Kennedy, J. (2007). Defining a standard for particle swarm optimization. In *Proceedings of the 2007 IEEE Swarm Intelligence Symposium* (pp. 120-127). IEEE.

Burer, S., Monteiro, R. D. C., & Zhang, Y. (2002). Rank-two relaxation heuristics for max-cut and other binary quadratic programs. *SIAM Journal on Optimization, 12*(2), 503–521. doi:10.1137/S1052623400382467

Burgard, W., Moors, M., Fox, D., Simmons, R., & Thrun, S. (2005). Collaborative multi-robot exploration. *IEEE Transactions on Robotics, 21*(3), 376–386. doi:10.1109/TRO.2004.839232

Buttyan, L., & Hubaux, J.-P. (2000). Enforcing service availability in mobile ad-hoc WANs. In Mobile and Ad Hoc Networking and Computing, (pp. 87-96). doi:10.1109/MOBHOC.2000.869216

Cagnina, L. C., Esquivel, S. C., & Coello, C. A. (2008). Solving engineering optimization problems with the simple constrained particle swarm optimizer. *Informatica, 32*(2), 319–326.

Cai, Z., & Wang, Y. (2006). A multiobjective optimization-based evolutionary algorithm for constrained optimization. *IEEE Transactions on Evolutionary Computation, 10*(6), 658–675. doi:10.1109/TEVC.2006.872344

Camilo, T., Carreto, C., Silva, J. S., & Boavida, F. (2006). An energy-efficient ant based routing algorithm for wireless sensor networks. In *Proceedings of 5th International Workshop on Ant Colony Optimization and Swarm Intelligence*, (pp. 49-59). Academic Press.

Campos, V., Glover, F., Laguna, M., & Martí, R. (2001). An experimental evaluation of a scatter search for the linear ordering problem. *Journal of Global Optimization, 21*(4), 397–414. doi:10.1023/A:1012793906010

Carmelo, J. A., Bastos-Filho, C.J.A., De Lima Neto, F.B., Anthony, J. C. C., Lins, A.J.C.C., Nascimento, A.I.S., & Lima, M.P. (2008). A novel search algorithm based on fish school behavior. In *Proceedings of IEEE International Conference on Systems, Man and Cybernetics* (pp. 2646-2651). IEEE.

Cassinis, R. (2000, June). *Multiple single sensor robots rather than a single multi-sensor platforms: a reasonable alternative*. Paper presented at the International Conference on Explosives and Drug Detection Techniques. Crete, Greece.

Castellano, G., Fanelli, A. M., & Torsello, M. A. (2011). NEWER: A system for NEuro-fuzzy WEb Recommendation. *Applied Soft Computing, 11*(1), 793–806. doi:10.1016/j.asoc.2009.12.040

Çelik, F., Zengin, A., & Tuncel, S. (2010). A survey on swarm intelligence based routing protocols in wireless sensor networks. *International Journal of the Physical Sciences, 5*(14), 2118–2126.

Chabrier, S., Emile, B., Rosenberger, C., & Laurent, H. (2006). Unsupervised Performance Evaluation of Image Segmentation. *EURASIP Journal on Applied Signal Processing*, 1–13. doi:10.1155/ASP/2006/96306

Chafekar, D., Xuan, J., & Rasheed, K. (2003). *Constrained multi-objective optimization using steady state genetic algorithms*. Paper presented at the Genetic and Evolutionary Computation Conference. Chicago, IL.

Chang, K. C., & Du, H. C. (1988). Layer assignment problem for three-layer routing. *IEEE Transactions on Computers, 37*(5), 625–632. doi:10.1109/12.4616

Charalampidis, D., & Kasparis, T. (2002). Wavelet-based rotational invariant roughness features for texture classification and segmentation. *IEEE Transactions on Image Processing, 11*(8), 825–837. doi:10.1109/TIP.2002.801117 PMID:18244677

Chelouah, R., & Siarry, P. (2000). Tabu search applied to global optimization. *European Journal of Operational Research, 123*(2), 256–270. doi:10.1016/S0377-2217(99)00255-6

Chelouah, R., & Siarry, P. (2005). A hybrid method combining continuous tabu search and Nelder–Mead simplex algorithms for the global optimization of multiminima functions. *European Journal of Operational Research, 161*(3), 636–654. doi:10.1016/j.ejor.2003.08.053

Chen, J. S, & Wei, G. (2002). A hybrid clustering algorithm incorporating fuzzy c-means into canonical genetic algorithm. *Journal of Electronics & Information Technology, 24*(2), 102-103.

Chen, Q., & Luh, J. (1994). Coordination and control of a group of small mobile robots. In *Proceedings of International Conference on Robotics and Automation* (pp. 2315-2320). Piscataway, NJ: IEEE Press.

Chen, S., & Montgomery, J. (2011). A simple strategy to maintain diversity and reduce crowding in particle swarm optimization. In *Proceedings of the 13th annual conference companion on Genetic and evolutionary computation (GECCO 2011)* (pp. 811-812). GECCO.

Cheng, K., & Dasgupta, P. (2007). Dynamic area coverage using faulty multi-agent swarms. In *Proceedings of IEEE/WIC/ACM International Conference on Intelligent Agent Technology* (pp. 17-24). Piscataway, NJ: IEEE Press.

Cheng, S. (2013). *Population diversity in particle swarm optimization: definition, observation, control, and application.* (Unpublished doctoral dissertation). University of Liverpool, Liverpool, UK.

Cheng, S., & Shi, Y. (2011a) Diversity control in particle swarm optimization. In *Proceedings of 2011 IEEE Symposium on Swarm Intelligence (SIS 2011)* (pp. 110-118). IEEE.

Cheng, S., & Shi, Y. (2011b). Normalized population diversity in particle swarm optimization. In *Proceedings of the 2nd International Conference on Swarm Intelligence* (LNCS) (vol. 6728, pp. 38-45). Berlin: Springer.

Cheng, S., Shi, Y., & Qin, Q. (2012a) Dynamical exploitation space reduction in particle swarm optimization for solving large scale problems. In *Proceedings of 2012 IEEE Congress on Evolutionary Computation, (CEC 2012),* (pp.3030-3037). Brisbane, Australia: IEEE.

Cheng, S., Shi, Y., & Qin, Q. (2012b). On the performance metrics of multiobjective optimization. In Y. Tan, Y. Shi, & Z. Ji (Eds.), Advances in Swarm Intelligence (LNCS) (vol. 7331, pp. 504-512). Berlin: Springer.

Cheng, S., Shi, Y., & Qin, Q. (2012c) Population diversity based study on search information propagation in particle swarm optimization. In *Proceedings of 2012 IEEE Congress on Evolutionary Computation, (CEC 2012)* (pp.1272-1279). Brisbane, Australia: IEEE.

Cheng, S., Shi, Y., Qin, Q., & Ting, T. O. (2012). Population diversity based inertia weight adaptation in particle swarm optimization. In *Proceedings of the Fifth International Conference on Advanced Computational Intelligence, (ICACI 2012)* (pp.395-403). ICACI.

Cheng, Y., & Church, G. M. (2000). Biclustering of Expression Data. In Proceeding of International Conference of Intelligent. System Molecular Biology, 8, 93-103.

Cheng, S., Shi, Y., & Qin, Q. (2011). Experimental study on boundary constraints handling in particle swarm optimization: From population diversity perspective. *International Journal of Swarm Intelligence Research,* 2(3), 43–69. doi:10.4018/jsir.2011070104

Chien, S., Sherwood, R., Tran, D., Cichy, B., Rabideau, G., & Castano, R. et al. (2005). Using Autonomy Flight Software to Improve Science Return on Earth Observing One. *Journal Of Aerospace Computing, Information, And Communication,* 2(4), 196–216. doi:10.2514/1.12923

Chiong, R. (Ed.). (2009). *Nature-Inspired Algorithms for Optimisation.* Berlin: Springer. doi:10.1007/978-3-642-00267-0

Choset, H. (2001). Coverage for robotics: A survey of recent results. *Annals of Math and AI, 31,* 113–126.

Clerc, M. (2008). Standard PSO 2007. Retrieved from http://www.particleswarm.info/Programs.html

Clerc, M., & Kennedy, J. (2002). The particle swarm - explosion, stability, and convergence in a multidimensional complex space. *IEEE Transactions on Evolutionary Computation,* 6(1), 58–73. doi:10.1109/4235.985692

Coello Coello, C.A., & Pulido, G.T. (2001). *Multiobjective optimization using a micro-genetic algorithm.* Paper presented at Genetic and Evolutionary Computation Conference. San Francisco, CA.

Coello Coello, C. A., & Christiansen, A. D.Coello Coello. (1999). MOSES: A multiobjective optimization tool for engineering design. *Engineering Optimization, 31*(3), 337–368. doi:10.1080/03052159908941377

Coello, C. A. C., Pulido, G. T., & Lechuga, M. S.Coello Coello. (2004). Handling multiple objectives with particle swarm optimization. *IEEE Transactions on Evolutionary Computation, 8*(3), 256–279. doi:10.1109/TEVC.2004.826067

Coleman, G. B., & Andrews, H. C. (1979). Image Segmentation by Clustering. *Proceedings of the Institute of Electrical and Electronics Engineers, 67,* 773–785. doi:10.1109/PROC.1979.11327

Conover, W. J. (1999). *Practical Nonparametric Statistics* (3rd ed.). New York: John Wiley & Sons.

Cooley, R., Mobasher, B., & Srivastava, J. (1997). Web Mining: Information and Pattern Discovery on the World Wide Web. In *Proceedings of Ninth IEEE International Conference on Tools with Artificial Intelligence* (pp. 558-567). IEEE.

Corriveau, G., Guilbault, R., Tahan, A., & Sabourin, R. (2012). Review and study of genotypic diversity measures for real-coded representations. *IEEE Transactions on Evolutionary Computation, 16*(5), 695–710. doi:10.1109/TEVC.2011.2170075

Cushman, D. L. (2007). *A particle swarm approach to constrained optimization informed by 'Global Worst.* University Park, PA: Pennsylvania State University.

Dai, H, & Wang, , Hu, & Wang, Y. (2013). Nonsmooth Nonnegative Matrix Factorization Algorithm Based on Particle Swarm Optimization. *Computer Engineering, 39*(1), 204–207.

Das, S., & Sila, S. (2010). Kernel-induced fuzzy clustering of image pixels with an improved differential evolution algorithm. Information Sciences, 180(8), 1237-1256.

de Castro, J. N., & Von Zuben, F. J. (1999). *Artificial immune systems: Part I -Basic theory and applications* (Tech. Rep. No. DCA-RT 01/99). Brazil, Campinas: School of Computing and Electrical Engineering, State University of Campinas.

De Jong, K. A. (1975). *An analysis of the behavior of a class of genetic adaptive systems.* (Unpublished doctoral dissertation). Department of Computer and Communication Sciences, University of Michigan, Ann Arbor, MI.

De Mot, J. (2005). *Optimal agent cooperation with local information.* (Doctoral Dissertation). Massachusetts Institute of Technology, Cambridge, MA.

Deb, K., & Goel, T. (2001). *Controlled elitist non-dominated sorting genetic algorithm for better convergence.* Paper presented at the 1st International Conference on Evolutionary Multi-Criterion Optimization. Zurich, Switzerland.

Deb, K., & Jain, S. (2002). *Running performance metrics for evolutionary multi-objective optimization* (Technical Report 2002004). Kanpur Genetic Algorithms Laboratory (KanGAL), Indian Institute of Technology Kanpur.

Deb, K., Pratap, A., & Meyarivan, T. (2001). *Constrained test problems for multi-objective evolutionary optimization.* Paper presented at the 1st International Conference of Evolutionary Multi-Criterion Optimization. Zurich, Switzerland.

Deb, K., Thiele, L., Laumanns, M., & Zitzler, E. (2005). Scalable test problems for evolutionary multi-objective optimization. In Evolutionary Multiobjective Optimization: Theoretical Advances and Applications. Springer.

Deb, K. (1991). Optimal design of a welded beam via genetic algorithms. *AIAA Journal, 29*(11), 2013–2015. doi:10.2514/3.10834

Deb, K. (2001). *Multi-Objective Optimization Using Evolutionary Algorithms.* New York, NY: John Wiley & Sons.

Deb, K., Pratap, A., Agarwal, A., & Meyarivan, T. (2002). A fast and elitist multiobjective genetic algorithm: NSGA-II. *IEEE Transactions on Evolutionary Computation, 6*(2), 182–197. doi:10.1109/4235.996017

Delande, D., & Zakrzewski, J. (2003). Experimentally attainable example of chaotic tunneling: The hydrogen atom in parallel static electric and magnetic fields. *Physical Review A., 68*(6), 062110. doi:10.1103/PhysRevA.68.062110

Domínguez, J. S. H., & Pulido, G. T. (2011). A comparison on the search of particle swarm optimization and differential evolution on multi-objective optimization. In *Proceedings of the 2011 Congress on Evolutionary Computation (CEC2011),* (pp. 1978-1985). Academic Press.

Dorigo, M., & Di Caro, G. (1998). AntNet: Distributed stigmergetic control for communications networks. *Journal of Artificial Intelligence Research, 9*, 317–365.

Dorigo, M., Di Caro, G., & Gambardella, L. M. (1999). Ant Algorithms for Discrete Optimization. *Artificial Life, 5*(2), 137–172. doi:10.1162/106454699568728 PMID:10633574

Dorigo, M., Maniezzo, V., & Colorni, A. (1996). The ant system: Optimization by a colony of cooperating agents. *IEEE Transactions. Systems, Man. Cybernetics B, 26*(1), 29–41. doi:10.1109/3477.484436

Dorronsoro, B., & Bouvry, P. (2011). Improving classical and decentralized differential evolution with new mutation operator and population topologies. *IEEE Transactions on Evolutionary Computation, 15*(1), 67–98. doi:10.1109/TEVC.2010.2081369

Duarte, A., Marti, R., & Glover, F. (2007). *Adaptive memory programming for global optimization. Research Report*. Valencia, Spain: University of Valencia.

Duarte, A., Marti, R., Glover, F., & Gortazar, F. (2011a). Hybrid scatter-tabu search for unconstrained global optimization. *Annals of Operations Research, 183*(1), 95–123. doi:10.1007/s10479-009-0596-2

Duarte, A., Marti, R., & Gortazar, F. (2011b). Path relinking for large scale global optimization. *Soft Computing, 15.*

Duarte, R., & Laguna, A. (2009). Advanced scatter search for the max-cut problem. *INFORMS Journal on Computing, 21*(1), 26–38. doi:10.1287/ijoc.1080.0275

Dudenhoefer, D., & Jones, M. (2000). A formation behavior for large-scale micro-robot force. In *Proceedings of 32nd Winter Simulation Conference* (pp. 972-982). Academic Press.

Dutta, R. K., Kiran, G., Paul, S., & Chattopadhyay, A. B. (2000). Assessment of machining features for tool condition monitoring in face milling using an artificial neural network. *Proceedings - Institution of Mechanical Engineers, 214*(7), 535–546. doi:10.1243/0954405001518233

Eberhart, E. C., & Shi, Y. (2000). Comparing inertia weights and constriction factors in particle swarm optimization. In *Proceedings of the Congress on Evolutionary Computation* (pp. 84–88). La Jolla, CA: IEEE Press.

Eberhart, R. C., & Shi, Y. (1998). Evolving artificial neural networks. In *Proceedings of International Conference on Neural Networks and Brain* (pp. 5-13). Academic Press.

Eberhart, R., & Kennedy, J. (1995). A new optimizer using particle swarm theory. In *Proceedings of the Sixth International Symposium on Micro Machine and Human Science* (pp. 39-43). Academic Press.

Eberhart, R., & Shi, Y. (2001). Particle swarm optimization: Developments, applications and resources. In *Proceedings of the 2001 Congress on Evolutionary Computation (CEC2001)* (pp. 81-86). CEC.

Eberhart, R. C., Dobbins, R. W., & Simpson, P. K. (1996). *Computational Intelligence PC Tools*. Academic Press Professional.

Eberhart, R. C., & Shi, Y. (2007). *Computational intelligence, concepts to implementation*. San Francisco, CA: Morgan Kaufmann.

Eirinaki, M., & Vazirgiannis, M. (2003). Web mining for web personalization. *ACM Transactions on Internet Technology, 3*(1), 1–27. doi:10.1145/643477.643478

EL-Melegy, M., Zanaty, E. A., Abd-Elhariez, W. M., & Farag, A. (2007). On cluster validity index in fuzzy and hard clustering algorithms for image segmentation. In *Proceedings of IEEE International Conference on Image Processing,* (vol. 6, pp. 5-8). IEEE.

El-Wardany, T. I., Gao, D., & Elbestawi, M. A. (1996). Tool condition monitoring in drilling using vibration signature analysis. *International Journal of Machine Tools & Manufacture, 36*(6), 687–711. doi:10.1016/0890-6955(95)00058-5

Englot, B., & Hover, F. (2012). Sampling-based coverage path planning for inspection of complex structures. In *Proceedings of International Conference on Automated Planning and Scheduling*. San Francisco, CA: AAAI Press.

Eusuff, M., Lansey, K., & Pasha, F. (2006). Shuffled frog-leaping algorithm: A memetic meta-heuristic for discrete optimization. *Engineering Optimization, 38*(2), 129–154. doi:10.1080/03052150500384759

Fang, X. D., & Jawahir, I. S. (1994). Predicting total machining performance in finish turning using integrated fuzzy-set models of the machinability parameters. *International Journal of Production Research, 32*(4), 833–849. doi:10.1080/00207549408956974

Fazli, P., Davoodi, A., & Mackworth, A. (2013). Multi-robot repeated area coverage. *Autonomous Robots, 34*(4), 251–276. doi:10.1007/s10514-012-9319-7

Felzenszwalb, P. F., & Huttenlocher, D. P. (2004). Efficient graph-based image segmentation. *International Journal of Computer Vision, 59*(2), 167–181. doi:10.1023/B:VISI.0000022288.19776.77

Feng, H. M., Chen, C. Y., & Ye, F. (2007). Evolutionary fuzzy particle swarm optimization vector quantization learning scheme in image compression. *Expert Systems with Applications, 32*(1), 213–222. doi:10.1016/j.eswa.2005.11.012

Ferranti, E., Trigoni, N., & Levene, M. (2009). Rapid exploration of unknown areas through dynamic deployment of mobile and stationary sensor nodes. *Autonomous Agents and Multi-Agent Systems, 19*(2), 210–243. doi:10.1007/s10458-008-9075-4

Festa, P., Pardalos, P. M., Resende, M. G. C., & Ribeiro, C. C. (2002). Randomized heuristics for the max-cut problem. *Optimization Methods and Software, 17*(6), 1033–1058. doi:10.1080/1055678021000090033

Filho, C. J. A., Lima Neto, F. B., Lins, A. J. C., Nascimento, A. I. S., & Lima, M. P. (2009). Fish school search. In R. Chiong (Ed.), *Nature-inspired algorithms for optimisation* (pp. 261–277). Springer;

Fine, B., & Shell, D. (2011). Flocking: Don't need no stinkin' robot recognition. In *Proceedings of International Conference on Intelligent Robots and Systems* (pp. 5001-5006). Piscataway, NJ: IEEE Press.

Fischer, F., Caprari, W., Siegwart, G., Moser, R., & Mondada, R. (2009). Magnebike: A magnetic wheeled robot with high mobility for inspecting complex-shaped structures. *Journal of Field Robotics, 26*(5), 453–476. doi:10.1002/rob.20296

Fister, J., Fister, I. Jr, Yang, X. S., & Brest, J. (2013). A comprehensive review of firefly algorithms. *Swarm and Evolutionary Computation, 13*(1), 34–46. doi:10.1016/j.swevo.2013.06.001

Fogel, L. J. (1962). Autonomous automata. *Industrial Research, 4,* 14–19.

Fonseca, C. M., & Fleming, P. J. (1998). Multiobjective optimization and multiple constraint handling with evolutionary algorithms, I: a unified formulation. *IEEE Transactions on Systems, Man, and Cybernetics, Part A:Cybernetics, 28*(1), 26–37.

Forsati, R., Meybodi, M. R., & Neiat, A. G. (2009). Web Page Personalization Based on Weighted Association Rules. In *Proceeding of International Conference on Electronic Computer Technology,* (pp. 130-135). Academic Press.

Fredslund, J., & Mataric, M. (2002). A general algorithm for robot formations using local sensing and minimal communication. *IEEE Transactions on Robotics and Automation, 18*(5), 837–846. doi:10.1109/TRA.2002.803458

Gabriely, Y., & Rimon, E. (2001). Spanning-tree based coverage of continuous areas by a mobile robot. *Annals of Math and AI, 31*(1-4), 77–98.

Galceran, E., & Carreras, M. (2013). Planning coverage paths on bathymetric maps for indetail inspection of the ocean floor. In *Proceedings of International Conference on Robotics and Automation* (pp. 4159-4164). Piscataway, NJ: IEEE Press.

Galceran, E., & Carreras, M. (2013). A Survey on Coverage Path Planning for Robotics. *Robotics and Autonomous Systems, 61*(12), 1258–1276. doi:10.1016/j.robot.2013.09.004

Gandomi, A. H., Yang, X. S., & Alavi, A. H. (2011). Mixed variable structural optimization using firefly algorithm. *Computers & Structures, 89*(23-24), 2325–2336. doi:10.1016/j.compstruc.2011.08.002

Gandomi, A. H., Yang, X. S., & Alavi, A. H. (2013a). Cuckoo search algorithm: A metaheuristic approach to solve structural optimization problems. *Engineering with Computers, 29*(1), 17–35. doi:10.1007/s00366-011-0241-y

Gandomi, A. H., Yang, X. S., Talatahari, S., & Alavi, A. H. (2013b). Firefly algorithm with chaos. *Communications in Nonlinear Science and Numerical Simulation, 18*(1), 89–98. doi:10.1016/j.cnsns.2012.06.009

Garrido, S., Moreno, L., & Lima, P. (2011). Robot Formation Motion Planning using Fast Marching. *Robotics and Autonomous Systems, 59*(9), 675–683. doi:10.1016/j.robot.2011.05.011

Geng, H., Zhang, M., Huang, L., & Wang, X. (2006). *Infeasible elitists and stochastic ranking selection in constrained evolutionary multi-objective optimization.* Paper presented at the 6th International Conference of Simulated Evolution and Learning. Hefei, China.

Ghaiebi, H., & Solimanpur, M. (2007). An ant algorithm for optimization of hole-making operations. *Computers & Industrial Engineering, 52*(2), 308–319. doi:10.1016/j.cie.2007.01.001

Glover, F. (1996a). Tabu search and adaptive memory programming - Advances, applications and challenges. In Interfaces in Computer Science and Operations Research. Dordrecht, The Netherlands: Kluwer Academic Publishers.

Glover, F. (1998). A template for scatter search and path relinking. In J. Hao, E. Lutton, E. Ronald, M. Schoenauer, & D. Snyers (Eds.), *Artificial Evolution: Proceedings of Third European Conference (AE '97)* (LNCS) (vol. 1363, pp. 13-54). Berlin: Springer.

Glover, F. (1986). Future paths for integer programming and links to artificial intelligence. *Computers & Operations Research, 13*(5), 533–549. doi:10.1016/0305-0548(86)90048-1

Glover, F. (1994). Tabu search for nonlinear and parametric optimization (with links to genetic algorithms). *Discrete Applied Mathematics, 49*(1-3), 231–255. doi:10.1016/0166-218X(94)90211-9

Glover, F. (1996b). Ejection chains, reference structures and alternating path methods for traveling salesman problems. *Discrete Applied Mathematics, 65*(1-3), 223–253. doi:10.1016/0166-218X(94)00037-E

Glover, F., & Laguna, M. (1997). *Tabu Search.* Boston: Kluwer Academic Publishers. doi:10.1007/978-1-4615-6089-0

Glover, F., Laguna, M., & Marti, R. (2000). Fundamentals of scatter search and path relinking. *Control and Cybernetics, 39*, 653–684.

Goemans, M. X., & Williamson, D. (1995). Improved approximation algorithms for maximum cut and satisfiability problems using semidefinite programming. *Journal of the ACM, 42*(6), 1115–1145. doi:10.1145/227683.227684

Gokce, F., & Sahin, E. (2009). To flock or not to flock: the pros and cons of flocking in long-range migration of mobile robot swarms. In *Proceedings of 8th International Conference on Autonomous Agents and MultiAgent Systems (AAMAS)* (pp. 65-72). AAMAS.

Goldberg, D. E. (1989). *Genetic Algorithms in Search, Optimization and Machine Learning.* Reading, MA: Addison-Wesley.

Goldberg, D. E. (1989). *Genetic algorithms in search, optimization, and machine learning.* Reading, MA: Addison-Wesley Pub. Co.

Gong, M. G., Jiao, L. C., Bo, L. F., Wang, L., & Zhang, X. G. (2008). Image texture classification using a manifold distance based evolutionary clustering method. *Optical Engineering (Redondo Beach, Calif.), 47*(7), 1–10. doi:10.1117/1.2955785

Gopal, A. V., & Rao, P. V. (2003). The optimisation of the grinding of silicon carbide with diamond wheels using genetic algorithms. *International Journal of Advanced Manufacturing Technology, 22*(7-8), 475–480. doi:10.1007/s00170-002-1494-9

Gunduz, S., & Ozsu, M. (2003). A user interest model for web page navigation. In *Proceedings of International Workshop on Data Mining for Actionable Knowledge (DMAK)*, (pp. 46-57). DMAK.

Gupta, A. K., Smith, K. G., & Shalley, C. E. (2006). The interplay between exploration and exploitation. *Academy of Management Journal, 49*(4), 693–706. doi:10.5465/AMJ.2006.22083026

Gutowski, M. (2001). Lévy flights as an underlying mechanism for global optimization algorithms. *ArXiv Mathematical Physics e-Prints.* Retrieved from http://arxiv.org/pdf/math-ph/0106003.pdf

Hadjukova, J. (2004). Coalition formation games: A survey. *International Game Theory Review, 8*, 613–641.

Hansen, N. (1997). Variable neighborhood search. *Computers & Operations Research, 24*(11), 1097–1100. doi:10.1016/S0305-0548(97)00031-2

Harada, K., Sakuma, J., Ono, I., & Kobayashi, S. (2007). *Constraint-handling method for multi-objective function optimization: Pareto descent repair operator*. Paper presented at the 4th International Conference of Evolutionary Multi-Criterion Optimization. Matsushima/Sendai, Japan.

Hartigan, J. A. (1972). Direct clustering of a data matrix. *Journal of the American Statistical Association, 67*(337), 123–129. doi:10.1080/01621459.1972.10481214

Haupt, R. L., & Haupt, S. E. (2005). *Practical Genetic Algorithms* (2nd ed.). Hoboken, NJ: John Wiley & Sons, Inc.

Hedar, A. R., & Fukushima, M. (2006). Derivative-free simulated annealing method for constrained continuous global optimization. *Journal of Global Optimization, 35*(4), 521–549. doi:10.1007/s10898-005-3693-z

Hedar, A., & Fukushima, M. (2006). Tabu search directed by direct search methods for nonlinear global optimization. *European Journal of Operational Research, 170*(2), 329–349. doi:10.1016/j.ejor.2004.05.033

Helmberg, C., & Rendl, F. (2000). A spectral bundle method for semidefinite programming. *SIAM Journal on Optimization, 10*(3), 673–696. doi:10.1137/S1052623497328987

Helwig, S., Branke, J., & Mostaghim, S. (2013). Experimental analysis of bound handling techniques in particle swarm optimization. *IEEE Transactions on Evolutionary Computation, 17*(2), 259–271. doi:10.1109/TEVC.2012.2189404

He, Q., & Wang, L. (2007). A hybrid particle swarm optimization with a feasibility-based rule for constrained optimization. *Applied Mathematics and Computation, 186*(2), 1407–1422. doi:10.1016/j.amc.2006.07.134

He, S., Prempain, E., & Wu, Q. H. (2004). An improved particle swarm optimizer for mechanical design optimization problems. *Engineering Optimization, 36*(5), 585–605. doi:10.1080/03052150410001704854

Heusse, S. G., Snyers, D., & Kuntz, P. (1998). *Adaptive Agent-driven Routing and Load Balancing. Communication Networks* (Technical Report RR-98001-IASC). Department Intelligence Artificielle et Sciences Cognitives, ENST Bretagne.

Hines, W. W., Montgomery, D. C., Goldman, D. H., & Borror, C. M. (2008). *Probability and statistics in engineering*. John Wiley & Sons.

Hingston, P., Barone, L., Huband, S., & While, L. (2006). Multi-level ranking for constrained multi-objective evolutionary optimization. In T. R. Runarsson (Ed.), Lecture notes in Computer Science (vol. 4193, pp. 563–572). Berlin: Springer.

Hirsch, M. J., Meneses, C. N., Pardalos, P. M., & Resende, M. G. C. (2007). Global optimization by continuous grasp. *Optimization Letters, 1*(2), 201–212. doi:10.1007/s11590-006-0021-6

Hojjatoleslami, S. A., & Kitter, J. (1998). Region growing: A new approach. IEEE Transactions on Image Processing, 7(7), 1079–1084. PubMed doi:10.1109/83.701170 PubMed

Holland, J. H. (1975). *Adaptation in natural and artificial systems*. Ann Arbor, MI: University of Michigan Press.

Holland, J. H. (2000). Building blocks, cohort genetic algorithms, and hyperplane-defined functions. *Evolutionary Computation, 8*(4), 373–391. doi:10.1162/106365600568220 PMID:11130921

Hölldobler, B., & Wilson, E. O. (1990). The Ant. Harvard University Press.

Ho, S. C., & Gendreau, M. (2006). Path relinking for the vehicle routing problem. *Journal of Heuristics, 12*(1-2), 55–72. doi:10.1007/s10732-006-4192-1

Hosseini, H. (2009). The intelligent water drops algorithm: A nature-inspired swarm-based optimization algorithm. *International Journal of Bio-inspired Computation, 1*(1/2), 71–79. doi:10.1504/IJBIC.2009.022775

Hsieh, M., Chiang, T., & Fu, L. (2011). *A hybrid constraint handling mechanism with differential evolution for constrained multiobjective optimization*. Paper presented at the 2011 IEEE Congress on Evolutionary Computation. New Orleans, LA.

Hu, X., Shi, Y., & Eberhart, R. (2004) Recent advances in particle swarm. In *Proceedings of the 2004 Congress on Evolutionary Computation (CEC2004)*, (pp. 90-97). CEC.

Huang, T., & Mohan, A. (2005). A hybrid boundary condition for robust particle swarm optimization. *IEEE Antennas and Wireless Propagation Letters, 4*(1), 112–117. doi:10.1109/LAWP.2005.846166

Hvattum, L. M., & Glover, F. (2009). Finding local optima of high-dimensional functions using direct search methods. *European Journal of Operational Research, 195*(1), 31–45. doi:10.1016/j.ejor.2008.01.039

Idoumghar, L., Melkemi, M., & Schott, R. (2009). A novel hybrid evolutionary algorithm for multi-modal function optimization and engineering applications. In *Proceeding of International Conference on Artificial Intelligence and Soft Computing*, (pp. 87-93). Academic Press.

Ishibuchi, H., Tsukamoto, N., & Nojima, Y. (2008). Evolutionary Many-Objective Optimization: A Short Review. In *Proceedings of the 2008 Congress on Evolutionary Computation (CEC2004)*, (pp. 2419-2426). CEC.

Ishibuchi, H., Tsukamoto, N., & Nojima, Y. (2010). Diversity improvement by non-geometric binary crossover in evolutionary multiobjective optimization. *IEEE Transactions on Evolutionary Computation, 14*(6), 985–998. doi:10.1109/TEVC.2010.2043365

Jain, A. K., Murty, M. N., & Flynn, P. J. (1999). Data clustering: a review. *ACM Computing Surveys, 31*(3), 264–323. doi:10.1145/331499.331504

James, T., Rego, C., & Glover, F. (2009). Multistart tabu search and diversification strategies for the quadratic assignment problem. *IEEE Transactions on Systems, Man, and Cybernetics. Part A, Systems and Humans, 39*(3), 579–596. doi:10.1109/TSMCA.2009.2014556

Janecek, A. (2010). *Efficient feature reduction and classification methods: Applications in drug discovery and email categorization.* (PhD Thesis). University of Vienna, Vienna, Austria.

Janecek, A., & Tan, Y. (2011). Iterative improvement of the multiplicative update NMF algorithm using nature-inspired optimization. In *Proceedings of the 7th International Conference on Natural Computation*, (pp. 1668-1672). Shanghai, China: IEEE.

Janecek, A., & Tan, Y. (2011). Using population based algorithms for initializing nonnegative matrix factorization. In *Proceedings of the 2nd International Conference on Swarm Intelligence* (LNCS) (vol. 67239, pp. 307-316). Berlin: Springer.

Janecek, A., Gansterer, W. N., Demel, M., & Ecker, G. F. (2008). On the relationship between feature selection and classification accuracy. *JMLR: Workshop and Conference Proceedings, 4*(1), 90–105.

Janecek, A., & Gansterer, W. N. (2010). Utilizing nonnegative matrix factorization for e-mail classification problems. In M. W. Berry (Ed.), *Survey of text mining III: Application and theory* (pp. 57–80). Hoboken, NJ: John Wiley & Sons, Inc. doi:10.1002/9780470689646.ch4

Janecek, A., Schulze-Grotthoff, S., & Gansterer, W. N. (2011). libNMF - A library for nonnegative matrix factorizatrion. *Computing and Informatics, 30*(2), 205–224.

Jan, M. A. (2010). *Zhang.* Colchester, UK: Computational Intelligence.

Jimenéz, F., Gomez-Skarmeta, A. F., Sanchez, G., & Deb, K. (2002). *An evolutionary algorithm for constrained multiobjective optimization.* Paper presented at the Congress on Evolutionary Computation. Honolulu, HI.

Jin, Y., & Sendhoff, B. (2009). A systems approach to evolutionary multiobjective structural optimization and beyond. *IEEE Computational Intelligence Magazine, 4*(3), 62–76. doi:10.1109/MCI.2009.933094

Jolliffe, I. T. (2002). *Principal component analysis.* New York: Springer.

Kahruman, S., Kolotoglu, E., Butenko, S., & Hicks, I. V. (2007). On greedy construction heuristics for the max-cut problem. *Int. J. Comput. Sci. Eng., 3*(3), 211–218.

Kaminka, G., Schechter, R., & Sadov, V. (2008). Using Sensor Morphology for Multirobot Formations. *IEEE Transactions on Robotics, 24*(2), 271–282. doi:10.1109/TRO.2008.918054

Karaboga, D. (2005). *An idea based on honey bee swarm for numerical opitmization* (Technical Report-TR06). Erciyesniversity, Engineering Faculty, Computer Engineering Deparment.

Karaboga, D., & Basturk, B. (2007). Artificial bee colony (ABC) optimization algorithm for solving constrained optimization problems. In *Proceedings of the 12th International Fuzzy Systems Association world congress on Foundations of Fuzzy Logic and Soft Computing* (IFSA '07). Berlin: Springer.

Karp, R. (1972). Reducibility among combinatorial problems. In R. Miller, & J. Thatcher (Eds.), *Complexity of Computer Computations* (pp. 85–103). Plenum Press. doi:10.1007/978-1-4684-2001-2_9

Kennedy, J. (1999). Small world and mega-minds: effects of neighbourhood topology on particle swarm performance. In *Proceedings of the Congress on Evolutionary Computation* (pp. 1931-1938). Washington, DC: Academic Press.

Kennedy, J. (2007). Some issues and practices for particle swarms. In *Proceedings of the 2007 IEEE Swarm Intelligence Symposium (SIS 2007)* (pp. 162-169). SIS.

Kennedy, J. N., & Eberhart, R. C. (1995). Particle swarm optimization. In *Proceedings of IEEE International Conference on Neural Networks*, (vol. 4, pp. 1942-1948). IEEE.

Kennedy, J., Eberhart, R., & Shi, Y. (2001). Swarm Intelligence. Morgan Kaufmann Publisher.

Kennedy, J., & Eberhart, R. (1995). *Particle swarm optimization*. Piscataway, NJ: IEEE Int Conf on Neural Networks.

Kennedy, J., Eberhart, R. C., & Shi, Y. (2001). *Swarm intelligence*. San Francisco: Morgan Kaufmann Publishers.

Kim, H., & Park, H. (2008). Nonnegative matrix factorization based on alternating nonnegativity constrained least squares and active set method. *SIAM Journal on Matrix Analysis and Applications*, *30*(2), 713–730. doi:10.1137/07069239X

Kirkpatrick, S., Gellat, C. D., & Vecchi, M. P. (1983). Optimization by simulated annealing. *Science*, *220*(4598), 671–680. doi:10.1126/science.220.4598.671 PMID:17813860

Kjellerstrand, H. (2011). *Hakanks hemsida*. Retrieved from http://hakank.org/weka

Koenig, S., Szymanski, B., & Liu, Y. (2001). Efficient and Inefficient Ant Coverage Methods. *Annals of Mathematics and Artificial Intelligence*, *31*(1/4), 41–76. doi:10.1023/A:1016665115585

Kohler, S., Utermann, R., Hagnni, R., & Dittrich, T. (1998). Coherent and incoherent chaotic tunneling near singlet-doublet crossings. *Physical Review E: Statistical Physics, Plasmas, Fluids, and Related Interdisciplinary Topics*, *58*(6), 7219–7230. doi:10.1103/PhysRevE.58.7219

Kohonen, T., & Honkela, T. (2007). Kohonen network. *Scholarpedia*, *2*(1), 1568. doi:10.4249/scholarpedia.1568

Koppen, M. X., Franke, M., & Vicente-Garcia, R. (2006). Tiny GAs for image processing applications. *IEEE Computational Intelligence Magazine*, *1*(2), 17–26. doi:10.1109/MCI.2006.1626491

Koza, J. R. (1992). *Genetic programming: On the programming of computers by means of natural selection*. Cambridge, MA: MIT Press.

Kundu, A. (1995). A new method to solve generalized multi-criteria optimization problems using the simple genetic algorithm. *Structural Optimization*, *10*(2), 94–99. doi:10.1007/BF01743536

Kurpati, A., Azarm, S., & Wu, J. (2002). Constraint handling improvements for multiobjective genetic algorithms. *Structure Multidisciplinary Optimization*, *23*(3), 204–213. doi:10.1007/s00158-002-0178-2

Laguna, M., & Marti, R. (2003). *Scatter Search: Methodology and Implementation in C*. London: Kluwer Academic Publishers. doi:10.1007/978-1-4615-0337-8

Laguna, M., & Marti, R. (2005). Experimental testing of advanced scatter search designs for global optimization of multimodal functions. *Journal of Global Optimization*, *33*(2), 235–255. doi:10.1007/s10898-004-1936-z

Langville, A. N., Meyer, C. D., & Albright, R. (2006). Initializations for the nonnegative matrix factorization. In *Proceedings of the 12th ACM Int. Conf. on Knowledge Discovery and Data Mining*, (pp. 1-18). Philadelphia, PA: ACM

Lawson, B. J., & Lewis, J. (2004). Representation emerges from coupled behavior. In *Self-Organization, Emergence, and Representation Workshop, Genetic and Evolutionary Computation Conference Proceedings*. Springer-Verlag.

Lee, B. Y., Liu, H. S., & Tarng, Y. S. (1998). Modeling and optimization of drilling process. *Journal of Materials Processing Technology*, *74*(1-3), 149–157. doi:10.1016/S0924-0136(97)00263-X

Lee, D. D., & Seung, H. S. (2001). Algorithms for non-negative matrix factorization. *Advances in Neural Information Processing Systems*, *13*(1), 556–562.

Lee, K. S., & Geem, Z. W. (2004). A new meta-heuristic algorithm for continues engineering optimization: harmony search theory and practice. *Computer Methods in Applied Mechanics and Engineering*, *194*(10), 3902–3933.

Lee, T. S., Ting, T. O., Lin, Y. J., & Than, H. (2007). A particle swarm approach for grinding process optimisation analysis. *International Journal of Advanced Manufacturing Technology*, *33*(11-12), 1128–1135. doi:10.1007/s00170-006-0538-y

Leong, W. F., & Yen, G. G. (2008). PSO-based multiobjective optimization with dynamic population size and adaptive local archives. *IEEE transactions on systems, man, and cybernetics. Part B, Cybernetics: a publication of the IEEE Systems, Man, and Cybernetics Society*, *38*(5), 1270–1293. doi:10.1109/TSMCB.2008.925757 PMID:18784011

Lepagnot, J., Nakib, A., Oulhadj, H., & Siarry, P. (2010). A new multiagent algorithm for dynamic continuous optimization. *International Journal of Applied Metaheuristic Computing*, *1*(1), 16–38. doi:10.4018/jamc.2010102602

Li, L. D., Li, X., & Yu, X. (2008). *A multi-objective constraint-handling method with PSO algorithm for constrained engineering optimization problems*. Paper presented at the IEEE Congress on Evolutionary Computation. Hong Kong, China.

Liang, J. J., & Suganthan, P. N. (2006). *Dynamic multi-swarm particle swarm optimizer with a novel constraint-handling mechanism*. Paper presented at the IEEE Congress on Evolutionary Computation. Vancouver, Canada.

Liang, J. J., Qin, A. K., Suganthan, P. N., & Baskar, S. (2006). Comprehensive learning particle swarm optimizer for global optimization of multimodal functions. *IEEE Transactions on Evolutionary Computation*, *10*(3), 281–295. doi:10.1109/TEVC.2005.857610

Li, H. (2009). Multiobjective Optimization Problems with Complicated Pareto Sets, MOEA/D and NSGA-II. *IEEE Transactions on Evolutionary Computation*, *13*(2), 284–302. doi:10.1109/TEVC.2008.925798

Li, H., Yang, J., & Hao, C. (2013). Non-negative matrix factorization of mixed speech signals based on quantum-behaved particle swarm optimization. *Journal of Computer Information Systems*, *9*(2), 667–673.

Li, K., Torres, C. E., Thomas, K., Rossi, L. F., & Shen, C.-C. (2011). Slime mold inspired routing protocols for wireless sensor networks. *Swarm Intelligence*, *5*(3-4), 183–223. doi:10.1007/s11721-011-0063-y

Lin, C.-J. (2007). Projected gradient methods for non-negative matrix factorization. *Neural Computation*, *19*(10), 2756–2779. doi:10.1162/neco.2007.19.10.2756 PMID:17716011

Li, P. G., & Wu, S. M. (1988). Monitoring drilling wear states by a fuzzy pattern recognition technique. *ASME Journal of Engineering for Industry*, *110*(3), 297–302. doi:10.1115/1.3187884

Liu, H., & Wang, D. (2013), *A Constrained Multiobjective Evolutionary Algorithm based Decomposition and Temporary Register*. Paper presented at the IEEE Congress on Evolutionary Computation. Cancún, México.

Liu, Z., Wang, C., & Li, J. (2008). Solving constrained optimization via a modified genetic particle swarm optimization. Paper presented at the International Workshop on Knowledge Discovery and Data Mining. Adelaide, Australia.

Liu, L. P., & Meng, Z. Q. (2004). An initial centrepoints selection method for k-means clustering. *Computer Engineering and Application*, *40*(8), 179–180.

Liu, T. I., & Wu, S. M. (1990). On-line detection on tool wear. *ASME Journal of Engineering for Industry*, *112*(3), 299–302. doi:10.1115/1.2899590

Li, X., & Tso, S. K. (1999). Drill wear monitoring based on current signals. *Wear*, *231*(2), 172–178. doi:10.1016/S0043-1648(99)00130-1

Lovbjerg, M., Rasmussen, T. K., & Krink, T. (2001). Hybrid particle swarm optimizer with breeding and subpopulations. In *Proceedings of the Genetic and Evolutionary Computation Conference*. Academic Press.

Luby, M., Sinclair, A., & Zuckerman, D. (1993). Optimal speedup of Las Vegas algorithms. *Information Processing Letters*, *47*(4), 173–180. doi:10.1016/0020-0190(93)90029-9

Lu, H., & Chen, W. (2006). Dynamic-objective particle swarm optimization for constrained optimization problems. *Journal of Combinatorial Optimization*, *2*(4), 409–419. doi:10.1007/s10878-006-9004-x

Luke, S. (2009). *Essentials of Metaheuristics*, Retrieved from http://cs.gmu.edu/~sean/book/metaheuristics

Luo, B., Zheng, J., Xie, J., & Wu, J. (2008). *Dynamic crowding distance-a new diversity maintenance strategy for MOEAs*. Paper presented at the 4th International Conference on Natural Computation. Jinan, China.

Lu, Z., Hao, J.-K., & Glover, F. (2010). Neighborhood analysis: A case study on curriculum-based course timetabling. *Journal of Heuristics*. DOI10.1007/s10732-010-9128-0

MacKenzie, A. B., & Wicker, S. B. (2001). Game theory in communications: motivation, explanation, and application to power control. In *Proceedings of GLOBECOM'01, IEEE Global Telecommunications Conference,* (vol. 2, pp. 821-826). IEEE.

MacQueen, J. (1967). Some methods for classification and analysis of multivariate observations. In *Proceedings of the 5th Berkeley Symposium on Mathematical Statistics and Probability* (pp. 281-297). Academic Press.

Madeira, S. C., & Oliveira, A. L. (2004). Biclustering Algorithms for Biological Data Analysis: A Survey. *IEEE/ACM transactions on computational biology and bioinformatics / IEEE, ACM*, *1*(1), 24–45. doi:10.1109/TCBB.2004.2 PMID:17048406

Mannadiar, R., & Rekleitis, I. (2010). Optimal coverage of a known arbitrary environment. In *Proceedings of International Conference on Robotics and Autonomous Systems* (pp. 5525-5530). Piscataway, NJ: IEEE Press.

March, J. G. (1991). Exploration and exploitation in organizational learning. *Organization Science*, *2*(1), 71–87. doi:10.1287/orsc.2.1.71

Mardia, K. V., & Hainsworth, T. J. (1988). A spatial thresholding method for image segmentation. *IEEE Transactions on Pattern Analysis and Machine Intelligence*, *10*(6), 919–927. doi:10.1109/34.9113

Marinakis, Y., Marinaki, M., Matsatsinis, N. F., & Zopounidis, C. (2011). Discrete Artificial Bee Colony Optimization Algorithm for Financial Classification Problems. *International Journal of Applied Metaheuristic Computing*, *2*(1), 1–17. doi:10.4018/jamc.2011010101

Mastellone, S., Stipanovic, D., Graunke, C., Intlekofer, K., & Spong, M. (2008). Formation control and collision avoidance for multi-agent non-holonomic systems: Theory and experiments. *The International Journal of Robotics Research*, *27*(1), 107–126. doi:10.1177/0278364907084441

Matthews, R. W., & Mattheus, J. R. (1942). *Insect Behavior*. New York: Wiley-Interscience.

Mauldin, M. L. (1984). Maintaining diversity in genetic search. In *Proceedings of the National Conference on Artificial Intelligence (AAAI 1984)* (pp. 247-250). AAAI.

Maulik, U. (2009). Medical image segmentation using genetic algorithms. *IEEE Transactions on Information Technology in Biomedicine*, *13*(2), 166–173. doi:10.1109/TITB.2008.2007301 PMID:19272859

Melkemi, K. E., Batouche, M., & Foufou, S. (2006). A multiagent system approach for image segmentation using genetic algorithms and extremal optimization heuristics. *Pattern Recognition Letters*, *27*(11), 1230–1238. doi:10.1016/j.patrec.2005.07.021

Mendes, R. (2004a). *Population Topologies and Their Influence in Particle Swarm Performance*. (Unpublished doctoral dissertation). University of Minho, Minho, Portugal.

Mendes, R., Kennedy, J., & Neves, J. (2003). Avoiding the pitfalls of local optima: How topologies can save the day. In *Proceedings of the 12th Conference Intelligent Systems Application to Power Systems (ISAP 2003)*. IEEE Computer Society.

Mendes, R., Kennedy, J., & Neves, J. (2004). The fully informed particle swarm: Simpler, maybe better. *IEEE Transactions on Evolutionary Computation*, *8*(3), 204–210. doi:10.1109/TEVC.2004.826074

Merloti, P. E. (2004). Optimization algorithms inspired by biological ants and swarm behavior. San Diego State University.

Mezura-Montes, E., & CoelloCoello, C.A. (2006). *A survey of constraint-handling techniques based on evolutionary multiobjective optimization* (Technical Report EVOCINV-04-2006). Mexico City, México: Academic Press.

Michalewicz, Z., & Schoenauer, M. (1996). Evolutionary algorithm for constrained parameter optimization problems. *Evolutionary Computation, 4*(1), 1–32. doi:10.1162/evco.1996.4.1.1

Michel, O. (2004). Webots: Professional mobile robot simulation. *International Journal of Advanced Robotic Systems, 1*(1), 39–42.

Miranda, V., Keko, H., & Jaramillo, A. (2007). EPSO: evolutionary particle swarms. In L. C. Jain, V. Palade, & D. Srinivasan (Eds.), *Advances in Evolutionary Computing for System Design* (pp. 139–167). Springer-Verlag Berlin Heidelberg. doi:10.1007/978-3-540-72377-6_6

Miyakawa, M., & Sato, H. (2012). *An evolutionary algorithm using two-stage non-dominated sorting and directed mating for constrained multi-objective optimization.* Paper presented at the Joint 6th International Conference on Soft Computing and Intelligent Systems (SCIS) and 13th International Symposium on Advanced Intelligent Systems. Kobe, Japan.

Mobasher, B., Dai, H., Luo, T., & Nakagawa, M. (2001). Improving the Effectiveness of Collaborative Filtering on Anonymous Web Usage Data. In *Proceedings of the IJCAI 2001 Workshop on Intelligent Techniques for Web Personalization* (ITWP01). Seattle, WA: IJCAI.

Mobasher, B. (2001). *WebPersonalizer: A Server-Side Recommender System Based on Web Usage Mining* (Technical Report). Telecommunications and Information Systems.

Mobasher, B., Cooley, R., & Srivastava, J. (2000). Automatic personalization based on Web usage mining. *Communications of the ACM, 43*(8), 142–151. doi:10.1145/345124.345169

Mobasher, B., Dai, H., Luo, T., & Nakagawa, M. (2002). Discovery and Evaluation of Aggregate Usage Profiles for Web Personalization. *Data Mining and Knowledge Discovery, 6*(1), 61–82. doi:10.1023/A:1013232803866

Nakano, S., Ishigame, A., & Yasuda, K. (2007). Particle swarm optimization based on the concept of tabu search. In *Proceedings of the IEEE Congress on Evolutionary Computation* (pp. 3258-3263). IEEE.

Narayanan, S., & Azarm, S. (1999). On improving multiobjective genetic algorithms for design optimization. *Structural Optimization, 18*(2-3), 146–155. doi:10.1007/BF01195989

Nie, S. D., Zhang, Y. L., & Chen, Z. X. (2008). Improved genetic fuzzy clustering algorithm and its application in segmentation of MR brain images. *Chinese Journal of Biomedical Engineering, 27*(6).

Nikhil, R. P., & Bezdek, J. C. (1995). On cluster validity for the fuzzy c-means model. *IEEE Transactions on Fuzzy Systems, 3*(3), 370–379. doi:10.1109/91.413225

Nock, R., & Nielsen, F. (2006). On weighting clustering. *IEEE Transactions on Pattern Analysis and Machine Intelligence, 28*(8), 1223–1235. doi:10.1109/TPAMI.2006.168 PMID:16886859

Olfati-Saber, R. (2006). Flocking for multi-agent dynamic systems: Algorithms and theory. *IEEE Transactions on Automatic Control, 51*(3), 401–420. doi:10.1109/TAC.2005.864190

Olorunda, O., & Engelbrecht, A. P. (2008) Measuring exploration/exploitation in particle swarms using swarm diversity. In *Proceedings of the 2008 Congress on Evolutionary Computation (CEC 2008)* (pp. 1128-1134). CEC.

Olugbemi, B. O. (2010). Influence of food on recruitment pattern in the termite, Microcerotermes fuscotibialis. *Journal of insect science (Online), 10*(154), 1–10. doi:10.1673/031.010.14114 PMID:20569122

Osborn, A. F. (1963). *Applied imagination: Principles and procedures of creative problem solving* (3rd ed.). New York, NY: Charles Scribner's Son.

Oyama, A., Shimoyama, K., & Fujii, K. (2007). New constraint-handling method for multi-objective and multi-constraint evolutionary optimization. *Transactions of the Japan Society for Aeronautical and Space Sciences, 50*(167), 56–62. doi:10.2322/tjsass.50.56

Paatero, P., & Tapper, U. (1994). Positive matrix factorization: A non-negative factor model with optimal utilization of error estimates of data values. *Environmetrics, 5*(2), 111–126. doi:10.1002/env.3170050203

Pal, N. R., & Pal, S. K. (1993). A review on image segmentation techniques. *Pattern Recognition, 26*(9), 1277–1294. doi:10.1016/0031-3203(93)90135-J

Palubeckis, G., & Krivickiene, V. (2004). Application of multistart tabu search to the max-cut problem. *Informaacines Technologijos Ir Valdymas, 2*(31), 29–35.

PARC. (2006). RMASE: Routing Modeling Application Simulation Environment. Available at http://webs.cs.berkeley.edu/related.html

Pardalos, P. M., Prokopyev, O. A., Shylo, O. V., & Shylo, V. P. (2008). Global equilibrium search applied to the unconstrained binary quadratic optimization problem. *Optimization Methods Software, 23*(1), 129–140. doi:10.1080/10556780701550083

Parsopoulus, K. E., & Vrahatis, M. N. (2002). Particle swarm optimization method for constrained optimization problems. In Technologies- Theory and Applications: New Trends in Intelligent Technologies, (pp. 214-220). Academic Press.

Passino, K. M. (2002). Biomimicry of bacterial foraging for distributed optimization and control. *Control Systems Magazine of the Institute of Electrical and Electronics Engineers, 22*(3), 52–67.

Passino, K. M. (2010). Bacterial foraging optimization. *International Journal of Swarm Intelligence Research, 1*(1), 1–16. doi:10.4018/jsir.2010010101

Pavlyukevich, I. (2007). Lévy flights, non-local search and simulated annealing. *Journal of Computational Physics, 226*(2), 1830–1844. doi:10.1016/j.jcp.2007.06.008

Pedersen, M. E. H. (2010). *SwarmOps - Numeric & Heuristic Optimization Source-Code Library*. Retrieved from http://hvass-labs.org/projects/swarmops/cs/files/SwarmOpsCS1_0.pdf

Perkins, C., & Royer, E. (1999). Ad-hoc on-demand distance vector routing. In *Proceedings of Second IEEE Workshop on Mobile Computing Systems and Applications* (pp. 90-100). IEEE. doi:10.1109/MCSA.1999.749281

Perona, P., & Malik, J. (1990). Scale-space and edge detection using anisotropic diffusion. *IEEE Transactions on Pattern Analysis and Machine Intelligence, 12*(7), 629–639. doi:10.1109/34.56205

Podolskiy, V. A., & Narmanov, E. E. (2003). Semiclassical description of chaos-assisted tunneling. *Physical Review Letters, 91*(26), 263601. doi:10.1103/PhysRevLett.91.263601 PMID:14754050

Premalatha, K., & Natarajan, A. M. (2010). Combined Heuristic Optimization Techniques for Global Minimization. *International Journal of Advance. Soft Computing Application, 2*, 85–99.

Price, K. V., Storn, R. M., & Lampinen, J. A. (2005). *Differential evolution: A practical approach to global optimization*. Secaucus, NJ: Springer.

Puig, D., Garcia, M., & Wu, L. (2011). A new global optimization strategy for coordinated multi-robot exploration. *Robotics and Autonomous Systems, 59*(9), 635–653. doi:10.1016/j.robot.2011.05.004

Pulido, G.T., & Coello Coello, C.A. (2004). *A constraint-handling mechanism for particle swarm optimization*. Paper presented at the IEEE Congress on Evolutionary Computation. Portland, OR.

Raghavan, V. V., & Wong, S. K. M. (1986). A critical analysis of vector space model for information retrieval. *Journal of the American Society for Information Science American Society for Information Science, 37*(5), 279–287. doi:10.1002/(SICI)1097-4571(198609)37:5<279::AID-ASI1>3.0.CO;2-Q

Ragsdell, K., & Phillips, D. (1976). Optimal design of a class of welded structures using geometric programming. *Journal of Engineering for Industry, 98*(3), 1021–1025. doi:10.1115/1.3438995

Ramos, V., & Almeida, F. (2000). Artificial ant colonies in digital image habitats – A mass behavior effect study on pattern recognition. In *Proceedings of ANTS'2000, 2nd International Workshop on Ant Algorithms,* (pp. 113-116). ANTS.

Rathipriya, R., & Thangavel, K. (2012). A Discrete Artificial Bees Colony Inspired Biclustering Algorithm. *International Journal of Swarm Intelligence Research*, *3*(1), 30–42. doi:10.4018/jsir.2012010102

Ray, T., & Won, K. S. (2005). *An evolutionary algorithm for constrained bi-objective optimization using radial slots*. Paper presented at the 9th International Conference of Knowledge-Based Intelligent Information and Engineering Systems. Melbourne, Australia.

Rechenberg, I. (1973). *Evolutions strategie: Optimierung technischer Systeme nach Prinzipien der biologischen Evolution*. Stuttgart, Germany: Frommann-Holzboog.

Rego, C., & Glover, F. (2009). Ejection chain and filter-and-fan methods in combinatorial optimization. In *Annals of Operations Research*. Springer Science+Business Media. DOI 10.1007/s10479-009-0656-7

Reinhard, J., & Kaib, M. (2001). Trail communication during foraging and recruitment in the subterranean termite Reticulitermes santonensis De Feytaud (Isoptera, Rhinotermitidae). *Journal of Insect Behavior*, *14*(2), 157–171. doi:10.1023/A:1007881510237

Rekleitis, I., New, A., Rankin, E., & Choset, H. (2008). Efficient boustrophedon multi-robot coverage: An algorithmic approach. *Annals of Mathematics and Artificial Intelligence*, *52*(2-4), 109–142. doi:10.1007/s10472-009-9120-2

Resnick, M. (1994). Learning About Life. *Artificial Life*, *1*(1-3), 229–242.

Resnick, M. (1997). *Turtles, termites, and traffic jams: Explorations in massively parallel microworlds*. Cambridge, MA: MIT Press.

Reynolds, A. M., & Rhodes, C. J. (2009). The Lévy fligth paradigm: Random search patterns and mechanisms. *Ecology*, *90*(4), 877–887. doi:10.1890/08-0153.1 PMID:19449680

Reynolds, C. (1987). Flocks, herds and schools: A distributed behavioral model. *Computer Graphics*, *21*(4), 25–34. doi:10.1145/37402.37406

Rocha, A. M. A. C., Fernandes, E. M. G. P., & Martins, T. F. M. C. (2011). Novel fish swarm heuristics forbound constrained global optimization problems, comp. In *Proceedings of Science and its App. -ICCSA 2011* (LNCS) (vol. *6784*, pp. 185–199). Berlin: Springer. doi:10.1007/978-3-642-21931-3_16

Roth, M., & Wicker, S. (2003). Termite: Ad-hoc networking with stigmergy. In *Proceedings of GLOBECOM '03, IEEE Global Telecommunications Conference* (vol. 5, pp. 2937-2941). IEEE.

Runarsson, T. P., & Yao, X. (2005). Search biases in constrained evolutionary optimization. *IEEE Transactions on System. Man, and Cybernetics, Part C: Applications and Reviews*, *35*(2), 233–243. doi:10.1109/TSMCC.2004.841906

Rutishauser, S., Correll, N., & Martinoli, A. (2009). Collaborative coverage using a swarm of networked miniature robots. *Robotics and Autonomous Systems*, *57*(5), 517–525. doi:10.1016/j.robot.2008.10.023

Sahin, T., & Zergeroglu, E. (2008). Mobile dynamically reformable formations for efficient flocking behavior in complex environments. In *Proceedings of IEEE International Conference on Robotics and Automation* (pp. 1910-1915). Piscataway, NJ: IEEE Press.

Saleem, M., & Farooq, M. (2005). Beesensor: A bee-inspired power aware routing algorithms. In Proceedings EvoCOMNET (LNCS) (vol. 3449, pp. 136-146). Berlin: Springer.

Saleem, M., Di Caro, G. A., & Farooq, M. (2011). Swarm intelligence based routing protocol for wireless sensor networks: Survey and future directions. *Information Sciences*, *181*(20), 4597–4624. doi:10.1016/j.ins.2010.07.005

Sankaradass, V., & Arputharaj, K. (2011). An Intelligent Recommendation System for Web User Personalization with Fuzzy Temporal Association Rules. *European Journal of Scientific Research*, *51*(1), 88–96.

Sathya, P. D., & Kayalvizhi, R. (2011). Modified bacterial foraging algorithm based multilevel thresholding for image segmentation. *Engineering Applications of Artificial Intelligence*, *24*, 595–615. doi:10.1016/j.engappai.2010.12.001

Sathya, P. D., & Kayalvizhi, R. (2011). Optimal segmentation of brain MRI based on adaptive bacterial foraging algorithm. *Neurocomputing, 74*, 2299–2313. doi:10.1016/j.neucom.2011.03.010

Schmidt, M. N. and H. Laurberg (2008). Non-negative matrix factorization with Gaussian process priors. *Comp. Intelligence and Neuroscience*, (1), 1-10.

Semet, Y., O'Reilly, U., & Durand, F. (2004). An interactive artificial ant approach to non-photorealistic rendering. In Proceedings of GECCO 2004, (LNCS) (vol. 3102, pp. 188-200). Berlin: Springer.

Seung, H. S., & Lee, D. D. (1999). Learning parts of objects by non-negative matrix factorization. *Nature, 401*(6755), 788–791. doi:10.1038/44565 PMID:10548103

Shao, Y., & Chen, H. N. (2009). Cooperative bacterial foraging optimization. In *Proceedings of International Conference on Future BioMedical Information Engineering* (pp. 486-488). Academic Press.

Shapiro, L. G., & Stockman, G. C. (2001). *Computer vision*. Prentice-Hall.

Shen, Q., Shi, W. M., & Kong, W. (2008). Hybrid particle swarm optimization and tabu search approach for selecting genes for tumor classification using gene expression data. *Computational Biology and Chemistry, 32*(1), 53–59. doi:10.1016/j.compbiolchem.2007.10.001 PMID:18093877

Shi, Y. (2011, June 11-15). Brain storm optimization algorithm. In Y. Tan, Y. Shi, Y. Chai, & G. Wang (Eds.), *Proceedings of the Second International Conference on Advances in Swarm Intelligence* (LNCS) (vol. 6728, pp. 303-309). Berlin: Springer.

Shi, Y., & Eberhart, R. (1998). A modified particle swarm optimizer. In *Proceedings of the 1998 Congress on Evolutionary Computation (CEC1998)* (pp. 69-73). CEC.

Shi, Y., & Eberhart, R. (1998). Parameter selection in particle swarm optimization. In Evolutionary Programming VII (LNCS) (vol. 1447, pp. 591-600). Springer.

Shi, Y., & Eberhart, R. (1999). Empirical study of particle swarm optimization. In *Proceedings of the 1999 Congress on Evolutionary Computation (CEC 1999)* (pp. 1945-1950). CEC.

Shi, Y., & Eberhart, R. (2001) Fuzzy adaptive particle swarm optimization. In *Proceedings of the 2001 Congress on Evolutionary Computation (CEC2001)*, (pp. 101-106). CEC.

Shi, Y., & Eberhart, R. (2008). Population diversity of particle swarms. In *Proceedings of the 2008 Congress on Evolutionary Computation (CEC 2008)* (pp. 1063-1067). CEC.

Shi, Y., & Eberhart, R. C. (1998) A modified particle swarm optimizer. In *Proceedings of the IEEE International Conference on Evolutionary Computation*. Anchorage, AK: IEEE.

Shi, Y., & Eberhart, R. C. (2008). Population diversity of particle swarm optimization. In *Proceedings of the Congress on Evolutionary Computation*. Hong Kong, China: Academic Press.

Shi, Y., & Eberhart, R. C. (2009). Monitoring of particle swarm optimization. *Frontiers of Computer Science in China, 3*(1), 31–37. doi:10.1007/s11704-009-0008-4

Shoham, Y., & Leyton-Brown, K. (2008). *Multi-agent systems*. MIT Press.

Shudo, A., & Ikeda, K. S. (1998). Chaotic tunneling: A remardable manifestion of complex classical dynamics in non-integrable quatumn phenomena. *Physica D. Nonlinear Phenomena, 115*(3-4), 234–292. doi:10.1016/S0167-2789(97)00239-X

Shudo, A., Ishii, Y., & Ikeda, K. S. (2009). Julia sets and chaotic tunneling: II. *Journal of Physics A. Mathematical and Theoretical, 42*(26), 265102. doi:10.1088/1751-8113/42/26/265102

Shylo, O. V., Prokopyev, O. A., & Shylo, V. P. (2008). Solving weighted max-sat via global equilibrium search. *Operations Research Letters, 36*(4), 434–438. doi:10.1016/j.orl.2007.11.007

Shylo, V. P., & Shylo, O. V. (2010). Solving the maxcut problem by the global equilibrium search. *Cybernetics and Systems Analysis, 46*(5), 744–754. doi:10.1007/s10559-010-9256-4

Shylo, V. P., Shylo, O. V., & Roschyn, V. A. (2012). Solving weighted max-cut problem by global equilibrium search. *Cybernetics and Systems Analysis, 48*(4), 563–567. doi:10.1007/s10559-012-9435-6

Sierra, M.R. & Coello Coello, C.A. (2005). *Improving PSO-based multi-objective optimization using crowding, mutation and ε–dominance*. Paper presented at the Evolutionary Multi-Criterion Optimization Conference. Guanajuato, Mexico.

Simon, D. (2008). Biogeography-based Optimization. *IEEE Transactions on Evolutionary Computation, 12*, 702–713. doi:10.1109/TEVC.2008.919004

Singh, A. K., Panda, S. S., Pal, S. K., & Chakraborty, D. (2006). Predicting drill wear using an artificial neural network. *International Journal of Advanced Manufacturing Technology, 28*(5-6), 456–462. doi:10.1007/s00170-004-2376-0

Smith, B., Egerstedt, M., & Howard, A. (2009). Automatic generation of persistent formations for multi-agent networks under range constraints. *Mobile Networks and Applications Journal, 14*(3), 322–335. doi:10.1007/s11036-009-0153-x

Smith, R. (2002). *The 7 levels of change* (2nd ed.). Arlington, VA: Tapeslry Press.

Snásel, V., Platos, J., & Krömer, P. (2008). Developing genetic algorithms for boolean matrix factorization. In *Proceedings of the Dateso 2008 Annual International Workshop on DAtabases, TExts, Specifications and Objects*, (pp. 1-10). Desna, Czech Republic: CEUR-WS.org.

Sorensen, K., & Glover, F. (2010). Metaheuristics. In Encyclopedia of Operations Research (3rd ed.). Springer Science+Business Media.

Sörensen, K., Sevaux, M., & Schittekat, P. (2008). Multiple neighbourhood search. In commercial VRP packages: evolving towards self-adaptive methods. Lecture Notes in Economics and Mathematical Systems, 136, 239–253.

Sowmya, B., & Sheela Rani, B. (2011). Colour image segmentation using fuzzy clustering techniques and competitive neural network. *Applied Soft Computing, 11*(3), 3170–3178. doi:10.1016/j.asoc.2010.12.019

Spears, D., Kerr, W., & Spears, W. (2006). Physics-based robot swarms for coverage problems. *International Journal of Intelligent Control and Systems, 11*(3), 124–140.

Srivastava, J., Cooley, R., Deshpande, M., & Tan, P. (2000). Web Usage Mining: Discovery and Applications of Usage Patterns from Web Data. *SIGKDD Explorations, 1*(2), 12–23. doi:10.1145/846183.846188

Stachniss, C., Mozos, O., & Burgard, W. (2008). Efficient exploration of unknown indoor environments using a team of mobile robots. *Annals of Math and AI, 52*(2-4), 205–227.

Stadlthanner, K., Lutter, D., Theis, F., et al. (2007). Sparse nonnegative matrix factorization with genetic algorithms for microarray analysis. In *Proceedings of the International Joint Conference on Neural Networks*, (pp. 294-299). Orlando, FL: IEEE.

Storn, R., & Price, K. (1997). Differential evolution - A simple and efficient heuristic for global optimization over continuous spaces. *Journal of Global Optimization, 11*(4), 341–359. doi:10.1023/A:1008202821328

Sundaram, R. K. (1996). *A First Course in Optimization Theory*. Cambridge University Press. doi:10.1017/CBO9780511804526

Symeonidis, P., Nanopoulos, A., Papadopoulos, A. N., & Manolopoulos, Y. (2008). Nearest-biclusters collaborative filtering based on constant and coherent values. *Information Retrieval, 11*(1), 51–75. doi:10.1007/s10791-007-9038-4

Sztipanovits, J. (2004). Probabilistic wireless network simulator (Prowler). Retrieved from http://www.isis.vanderbilt.edu/Projects/nest/prowler/

Takahama, T., & Sakai, S. (2006). *Constrained optimization by the ε constrained differential evolution with gradient-based mutation and feasible elites*. Paper presented at the IEEE Congress on Evolutionary Computation. Vancouver, Canada.

Takamu, S., Toshiku, G., & Yoshikazu, Y. (2003). A hybrid particle swarm optimization for distribution state estimation. *IEEE Transactions on Power Systems, 18*(1), 60–68. doi:10.1109/TPWRS.2002.807051

Talbi, E.-G. (2009). *Metaheuristics: From Design to Implementation*. New Jersey, NJ: John Wiley and Sons. doi:10.1002/9780470496916

Tanaka, M. (1995). *GA-based decision support system for multi-criteria optimization*. Paper presented at the International Conference on Evolutionary Multi-Criteria Optimization. Guanajuato, Mexico.

Tandon, V., El-Mounary, H., & Kishawy, H. (2002). NC end milling optimization using evolutionary computation. *International Journal of Machine Tools & Manufacture, 42*(5), 595–605. doi:10.1016/S0890-6955(01)00151-1

Tang, C., Zhang, L., Zhang, A., & Ramanathan, M. (2001). Interrelated Two-way Clustering: An Unsupervised Approach for Gene Expression Data Analysis. In *Proceedings in Second IEEE International Symposium. Bioinformatics and Bioeng.*, (vol. 14, pp. 41-48). IEEE.

Tan, P.-N., Steinbach, M., & Kumar, V. (2005). *Introduction to data mining*. Boston, MA: Addison Wesley.

Tan, Y., & Zhu, Y. (2010). Fireworks algorithm for optimization. In Tan et al. (Eds.), *Advances in swarm intelligence* (pp. 355–364). Beijing, China: Springer. doi:10.1007/978-3-642-13495-1_44

Tessema, B., & Yen, G. G. (2009). An adaptive penalty formulation for constrained evolutionary optimization. *IEEE Transactions on Systems, Man, and Cybernetics. Part A, Systems and Humans, 39*(3), 565–578. doi:10.1109/TSMCA.2009.2013333

Thangaraj, A., & Wright, P. K. (1988). Computer-assisted prediction of drill failure using in-process measurements of thrust force. *ASME Journal of Engineering Industry, 110*(2), 192–200. doi:10.1115/1.3187869

Theodoridis, S., & Koutroumbas, K. (2006). *Pattern recognition* (3rd ed.). New York, NY: Academic Press.

Tian, X. L., Jiao, L. C., & Gou, S. P. (2008). SAR image segmentation based on spatially constrained FCM optimized by particle swarm optimization. *Acta Electronica Sinica, 36*(3), 453–457.

Ting, T. O., Man, K. L., Guan, S.-U., Nayel, M., & Wan, K. Y. (2012). Weightless swarm algorithm (wsa) for dynamic optimization problems. In J. J. Park, A. Zomaya, S. Yeo, & S. Sahni (Eds.), *Network and Parallel Computing: Proceedings of 9th IFIP International Conference (NPC 2012)* (LNCS) (vol. 7513, pp. 508–515). IFIP.

Ting, T. O., & Lee, T. S. (2012). Drilling optimization via particle swarm optimization. *International Journal of Swarm Intelligence Research, 3*(1), 43–54. doi:10.4018/jsir.2012010103

Tomsovic, S., & Ullmo, D. (1994). Chao-assisted tunneling. *Physical Review E: Statistical Physics, Plasmas, Fluids, and Related Interdisciplinary Topics, 50*(1), 145–162. doi:10.1103/PhysRevE.50.145 PMID:9961952

Tovey, C. (2004). The honey bee algorithm: A biological inspired approach to internet server optimization. *Engineering Enterprise, the Alumni Magazine for ISyE at Georgia Institute of Technology*, 13-15.

Triki, E., Collette, Y., & Siarry, P. (2005). A theoretical study on the behavior of simulated annealing leading to a new cooling schedule. *European Journal of Operational Research, 166*(1), 77–92. doi:10.1016/j.ejor.2004.03.035

Tully, S., Kantor, G., & Choset, H. (2010). Leap-frog path design for multi-robot cooperative localization. *Field and Service Robotics. Springer Tracts in Advanced Robotics, 62*, 307–317. doi:10.1007/978-3-642-13408-1_28

Turgut, A., Celikkanat, H., Gokce, F., & Sahin, E. (2008). Self-organized flocking with a mobile robot swarm. In *Proceedings of International Conference on Autonomous Agents and MultiAgent Systems* (pp. 39-46). Academic Press.

Turner, J. S. (2011). Termites as models of swarm cognition. *Swarm Intelligence, 5*(1), 19–43. doi:10.1007/s11721-010-0049-1

Tzanov, V. (2006). *Distributed area search with a team of robots*. (Master's Thesis). Massachusetts Institute of Technology, Cambridge, MA.

Vaz, A. I. F., & Vicente, L. N. (2007). A particle swarm pattern search method for bound constrained global optimization. *Journal of Global Optimization, 39*(2), 197–219. doi:10.1007/s10898-007-9133-5

Veenman, C. J., Reinders, M. J. T., & Backer, E. (2003). A cellular coevolutionary algorithm for image segmentation. *IEEE Transactions on Image Processing, 12*(3), 304–316. doi:10.1109/TIP.2002.806256 PMID:18237910

Venkatraman, S., & Yen, G. G. (2005). A generic framework for constrained optimization using genetic algorithms. *IEEE Transactions on Evolutionary Computation*, *9*(4), 424–435. doi:10.1109/TEVC.2005.846817

Wagner, I., Altshuler, Y., Yanovski, V., & Bruckstein, A. (2008). Cooperative cleaners: A study in ant robotics. *The International Journal of Robotics Research*, *27*(1), 127–151. doi:10.1177/0278364907085789

Wang, P. (1989). Navigation strategies for multiple autonomous mobile robots. In *Proceedings of IEEE/RSJ International Workshop on Intelligent Robots & Systems* (pp. 486-493). Piscataway, NJ: IEEE Press.

Wang, X., & Li, J. (2004). Hybrid particle swarm optimization with simulated annealing. In *Proceedings of 2004 International Conference on Machine Learning and Cybernetics,* (Vol. 4, pp. 2402-2405). Academic Press.

Wang, Y. X., Zhao, Z. D., & Ren, R. (2007). Hybrid particle swarm optimizer with tabu strategy for global numerical optimization. In *Proceedings of IEEE Congress on Evolutionary Computation*, (pp. 2310-2316). IEEE.

Wang, J., Kuriyagawa, T., Wei, X. P., & Guo, D. M. (2002). Optimization of cutting conditions for single pass turning operations using a deterministic approach. *International Journal of Machine Tools & Manufacture*, *42*(9), 1023–1033. doi:10.1016/S0890-6955(02)00037-8

Wang, Y., Cai, Z., Guo, G., & Zhou, Y. (2007). Multiobjective optimization and hybrid evolutionary algorithm to solve constrained optimization problems. *IEEE Transactions on System, Man, and Cybernetics, Part B. Cybernetics*, *37*(3), 560–575. PMID:17550112

Wang, Y., Cai, Z., Zhou, Y., & Zeng, W. (2008). An adaptive trade-off model for constrained evolutionary optimization. *IEEE Transactions on Evolutionary Computation*, *12*(1), 80–92. doi:10.1109/TEVC.2007.902851

Wei, J., & Wang, Y. (2006). A novel multi-objective PSO algorithm for constrained optimization problems. In T. D. Wang, et al. (Eds.), Lecture notes in Computer Science (vol. 4247, pp. 174–180). Berlin: Springer. doi:10.1007/11903697_23

Weise, T., Zapf, M., Chiong, R., & Nebro, A. J. (2009). Why is optimization difficult? In Nature-Inspired Algorithms for Optimisation. Springer.

Wild, S. M., Curry, J. H., & Dougherty, A. (2004). Improving non-negative matrix factorizations through structured initialization. *Patt. Recog, 37*(11), 2217–2232. doi:10.1016/j.patcog.2004.02.013

Witten, I. H., & Frank, E. (2005). *Data mining: Practical machine learning tools and techniques.* San Francisco, CA: Morgan Kaufmann.

Wolberg, W. H., & Mangasarian, O. L. (1990). Multisurface method of pattern separation for medical diagnosis applied to breast cytology. *Proceedings of the National Academy of Sciences of the United States of America*, *87*(23), 9193–9196. doi:10.1073/pnas.87.23.9193 PMID:2251264

Woldesenbet, Y. G., Tessema, B. G., & Yen, G. G. (2009). Constraint handling in multiobjective evolutionary optimization. *IEEE Transactions on Evolutionary Computation*, *13*(2), 1–12.

Wolpert, D., & Macready, W. (1997). No free lunch theorems for optimization. *IEEE Transactions on Evolutionary Computation*, *1*(1), 67–82. doi:10.1109/4235.585893

Wu, K. L., & Yang, M. S. (2002). Alternative c-means clustering algorithms. *Pattern Recognition*, *35*(10), 2267–2278. doi:10.1016/S0031-3203(01)00197-2

Wurm, K., Stachniss, C., & Burgard, W. (2008). Coordinated multi-robot exploration using a segmentation of the environment. In *Proceedings of IEEE/RSJ International Conference on Intelligent Robots and Systems (IROS)*, (pp. 1160-1165). Piscataway, NJ: IEEE Press.

Xu, A., Virie, P., & Rekleitis, I. (2011). Optimal complete terrain coverage using an unmanned aerial vehicle. In *Proceedings of IEEE International Conference on Robotics & Automation* (pp. 2513-2519). Piscataway, NJ: IEEE Press.

Xu, L. (2011). *Graph planning for environmental coverage.* (Doctoral Dissertation). Carnegie Mellon University, Pittsburgh, PA.

Xue, Y., Tong, C. S., Chen, Y., & Chen, W. (2008). Clustering-based initialization for non-negative matrix factorization. *Applied Mathematics and Computation*, *205*(2), 525–536. doi:10.1016/j.amc.2008.05.106

Xu, R., & Wunsch, D. II. (2005). Survey of clustering algorithms. *IEEE Transactions on Neural Networks*, *16*(3), 645–678. doi:10.1109/TNN.2005.845141 PMID:15940994

Xu, S., & Rahmat-Samii, Y. (2007). Boundary conditions in particle swarm optimization revisited. *IEEE Transactions on Antennas and Propagation*, *55*(3), 760–765. doi:10.1109/TAP.2007.891562

Yang, B., Chen, Y., Zhao, Z., & Han, Q. (2006). *A master-slave particle swarm optimization algorithm for solving constrained optimization problems*. Paper presented at the 6th World Congress on Intelligent Control and Automation. Dalian, China.

Yang, X. C., Zhao, W. D, Chen, Y. F, & Fang, X. (2008). Image segmentation with a fuzzy clustering algorithm based on Ant-Tree. Signal Processing, *88*(10), 2453-2462.

Yang, X. S. (2014). Cuckoo Search and Firefly Algorithm: Theory and Applications. Heidelberg, Germany: Springer.

Yang, L. C., Zhao, L. N., & Wu, X. Q. (2007). Medical image segmentation of fuzzy C-means clustering based on the ant colony algorithm. *Journal of ShanDong University*, *37*(3).

Yang, L. J., & Chen, T. L. (2002). Applications of chaos in genetic algorithms. *Communications in Theoretical Physics*, *38*(1), 168–192.

Yang, X. (2008). *Nature-inspired metaheuristic algorithms*. Beckington, UK: Luniver Press.

Yang, X. S. (2008). *Nature-Inspired Metaheuristic Algorithms*. Bristol, UK: Luniver Press.

Yang, X. S. (2010a). *Engineering Optimization: An Introduction with Metaheuristic Applications*. Hoboken, NJ: John Wiley & Sons. doi:10.1002/9780470640425

Yang, X. S. (2010b). Firefly algorithm, stochastic test functions and design optimisation. *International Journal of Bio-inspired Computation*, *2*(2), 78–84. doi:10.1504/IJBIC.2010.032124

Yang, X. S. (2013). Multiobjective firefly algorithm for continuous optimization. *Engineering with Computers*, *29*(2), 175–184. doi:10.1007/s00366-012-0254-1

Yang, X. S., Cui, Z. H., Xiao, R. B., Gandomi, A. H., & Karamanoglu, M. (2013a). *Swarm Intelligence and Bio-Inspired Computation: Theory and Applications*. Waltham, UK: Elsevier. doi:10.1016/B978-0-12-405163-8.00001-6

Yang, X. S., & Deb, S. (2010). Engineering optimization by cuckoo search. *International Journal of Mathematical Modelling & Numerical Optimization*, *1*(4), 330–343. doi:10.1504/IJMMNO.2010.035430

Yang, X. S., Deb, S., Loomes, M., & Karamanoglu, M. (2013b). A framework for self-tuning optimziaton algorithms. *Neural Computing & Applications*, *23*(7-8), 2051–2057. doi:10.1007/s00521-013-1498-4

Yao, X., Liu, Y., & Lin, G. (1997). Evolutionary programming made faster. *IEEE Transactions on Evolutionary Computation*, *3*, 82–102.

Yao, Y., Li, X., & Yuan, Z. (1999). Tool wear detection with fuzzy classification and wavelet fuzzy neural network. *International Journal of Machine Tools & Manufacture*, *39*(10), 1525–1538. doi:10.1016/S0890-6955(99)00018-8

Yen, G. G., & Leong, W. F.Wen Fung Leong. (2009). Dynamic multiple swarms in multiobjective particle swarm optimization. *IEEE Transactions on Systems, Man, and Cybernetics. Part A, Systems and Humans*, *39*(4), 890–911. doi:10.1109/TSMCA.2009.2013915

Yin, P.Y., & Wu, H. (2013). Cyber-EDA: Estimation of Distribution Algorithms with Adaptive Memory Programming. In *Mathematical Problems in Engineering*. doi:10.1155/2013/132697

Ying, C., Shao, Z. B., Mi, H., & Wu, Q. H. (2008). An application of bacterial foraging algorithm in image compression. *Journal of ShenZhen University (Science & Engineering)*, *25* (2).

Yin, P. Y., & Chiang, Y. (2013). Cyber swarm algorithms for multi-objective nurse rostering problem. *International Journal of Innovative Computing, Information, & Control*, *9*(5), 2043–2063.

Yin, P. Y., Glover, F., Laguna, M., & Zhu, J. X. (2010). Cyber swarm algorithms – improving particle swarm optimization using adaptive memory strategies. *European Journal of Operational Research*, *201*(2), 377–389. doi:10.1016/j.ejor.2009.03.035

Yin, P. Y., & Su, E. (2011). Cyber swarm optimization for general keyboard arrangement problem. *International Journal of Industrial Ergonomics*, *41*(1), 43–52. doi:10.1016/j.ergon.2010.11.007

Yoshida, H., Kawata, K., Fukuyama, Y., & Nakanishi, Y. (1999). A particle swarm optimization for reactive power and voltage control considering voltage stability. In *Proceedings International Conference on Intelligent System Application to Power Systems* (pp. 117-121). Academic Press.

Yue, X. D., Miao, D. Q., & Zhong, C. M. (2010). Roughness Measure Approach to Color Image Segmentation. *Acta Automatica Sinica*, *36*(6), 807–816. doi:10.3724/SP.J.1004.2010.00807

Zeng, L., Wang, M. L., & Chen, H. F. (2008). Genetic Fuzzy C-Means Clustering Algorithm for Magnetic Resonance Images Segmentation. *Journal of University of Electronic Science and Technology of China*, *37*(4), 627–629.

Zhang, M., Geng, H., Luo, W., Huang, L., & Wang, X. (2006). A hybrid of differential evolution and genetic algorithm for constrained multiobjective optimization problems. In Simulated Evolution and Learning, (LNCS) (Vol. 4247, pp. 318-327). Berlin: Springer.

Zhang, Q., Berry, M. W., Lamb, B. T., & Samuel, T. (2009). A parallel nonnegative tensor factorization algorithm for mining global climate data. In *Proceedings of the 9th International Conference on Computational Science*, (pp. 405-415). Berlin: Springer.

Zhang, Q., Zhou, A., Zhao, S., Suganthan, P. N., Liu, W., & Tiwari, S. (2009). *Multiobjective optimization Test Instances for the CEC 2009 Special Session and Competition* (Technical Report CES-487). Essex, UK: University of Essex.

Zhang, W., Xie, X. F., & Bi, D. C. (2004). Handling boundary constraints for numerical optimization by particle swarm flying in periodic search space. In *Proceedings of the 2004 Congress on Evolutionary Computation (CEC 2004)* (pp. 2307-2311). CEC.

Zhang, Y. (2005). Routing Modeling Application Simulation Environment (RMASE). Available at https://docs.google.com/file/d/0B-29IhEITY3bbGY2VVo2SGxxR-FE/edit

Zhang, Y., Kuhn, L. D., & Fromherz, M. P. J. (2004). Improvements on ant routing for sensor networks. In M. Dorigo, et al. (Eds.), ANTS 2004, (LNCS) (vol. 3172, pp. 154–165). Berlin: Springer. doi:10.1007/978-3-540-28646-2_14

Zhang, Y., Simon, G., & Balogh, G. (2006). High-level sensor network simulations for routing performance evaluations. In *Proceedings of 3rd International Conference on Networked Sensing Systems*. Chicago: Academic Press.

Zhang, M., Luo, W., & Wang, X. (2008). Differential evolution with dynamic stochastic selection for constrained optimization. *Information Science*, *178*(15), 3043–3074. doi:10.1016/j.ins.2008.02.014

Zhang, Q., & Mühlenbein, H. (2004). On the convergence of a class of estimation of distribution algorithms. *IEEE Transactions on Evolutionary Computation*, *8*(2), 127–136. doi:10.1109/TEVC.2003.820663

Zhou, B., Hui, S. C., & Chang, K. (2004). An intelligent recommender system using sequential web access patterns. In *Proceedings of IEEE Conference on Cybernetics and Intelligent Systems*, (vol. 1, pp. 393-398). IEEE.

Zhou, A., Zhang, Q., & Jin, Y. (2009). Approximating the set of Pareto-optimal solutions in both the decision and objective spaces by an estimation of distribution algorithm. *IEEE Transactions on Evolutionary Computation*, *13*(5), 1167–1189. doi:10.1109/TEVC.2009.2021467

Zielinski, K., & Laur, R. (2006). *Constrained single-objective optimization using particle swarm optimization*. Paper presented at the IEEE Congress on Evolutionary Computation. Vancouver, Canada.

Zielinski, K., Weitkemper, P., Laur, R., & Kammeyer, K. D. (2009). Optimization of power allocation for interference cancellation with particle swarm optimization. *IEEE Transactions on Evolutionary Computation*, *13*(1), 128–150. doi:10.1109/TEVC.2008.920672

Zitzler, E. (1999). *Evolutionary Algorithms for Multiobjective Optimization: Methods and Applications*. (Ph.D. Dissertation). Swiss Federal Institute of Technology, Zurich, Switzerland.

Zitzler, E., Thiele, L., Laumanns, M., Fonseca, C. M., & Fonseca, V. G. (2003). Performance assessment of multiobjective optimizers: An analysis and review. *IEEE Transactions on Evolutionary Computation, 7*(2), 117–132. doi:10.1109/TEVC.2003.810758

Zungeru, A. M., Ang, L.-M., & Seng, K. P. (2012a). Performance of termite-hill routing algorithm on sink mobility in wireless sensor networks. In Advances in Swarm Intelligence, (LNCS) (vol. 7332, pp. 334-343). Berlin: Springer.

Zungeru, A. M., Ang, L.-M., & Seng, K. P. (2012b). Classical and swarm intelligence based routing protocols for wireless sensor networks. *Journal of Network and Computer Applications, 35*(5), 1508–1536. doi:10.1016/j. jnca.2012.03.004

About the Contributors

Yuhui Shi received a PhD degree in electronic engineering from Southeast University, Nanjing, China, in 1992. He is currently a Professor with the Department of Electrical and Electronic Engineering at Xi'an Jiaotong-Liverpool University, Suzhou, China. His current research interests include computational intelligence techniques (including swarm intelligence) and their applications. Dr. Shi is the Editor-in-Chief of the International Journal of Swarm Intelligence Research.

***

Li-Minn Ang received his PhD and Bachelor degrees from Edith Cowan University, Australia in 2001 and 1996 respectively. He was an associate professor at the University of Nottingham (Malaysia Campus) and is currently at the Centre for Communications Engineering Research, Edith Cowan University, Australia. His research interests are in the fields of wireless sensor systems, visual information processing, hardware architectures, and engineering education. He has published two books and over a hundred journal and conference papers in these areas. He has received research grants from the Malaysian government and industry for his research activities and has served as a reviewer for journals and conferences. Dr. Ang is a Senior Member of the IEEE and a Fellow of the Higher Education Academy (UK).

Shi Cheng received a BEng degree in Mechanical and Electrical Engineering from Xiamen University, Xiamen, China, an MEng degree in Software Engineering from Beihang University (BUAA), Beijing, China, and a PhD degree in Electrical Engineering and Electronics from the University of Liverpool, Liverpool, UK, in 2005, 2009, and 2013, respectively. Currently, he is a research fellow in the Division of Computer Science, University of Nottingham Ningbo, Ningbo, China. Dr. Cheng is an editorial board member of the *International Journal of Swarm Intelligence Research* (IJSIR). His current research interests include swarm intelligence, multiobjective optimization, data mining techniques, and their applications.

Prithviraj (Raj) Dasgupta is an associate professor of computer science at the University of Nebraska, Omaha and the founder-director of the C-MANTIC lab. His research interests are in multi-robot path and task planning, multi-agent decision making, and game theory. He has led multiple, large, federally-funded projects in the area of multi-robot/multi-agent systems and published more than 100 research papers in leading conferences and journals in his research area. He received his MS and PhD in Computer Engineering from the University of California, Santa Barbara and BTech in Computer Science and Engineering from Jadavpur University, India.

Mengjiao Geng was born in 10/20, 1987. She is a graduate student in the Automation College at Harbin Engineering University. Her research interests include nature inspired computing, image processing, magnetotactic bacteria optimization algorithm.

Fred Glover holds the title of Distinguished Professor, Emeritus, at the University of Colorado, Boulder, associated with the Leeds School of Business and the School of Engineering and Science, and is a cofounder and principal of Meta-Analytics, Inc.. He has authored or co-authored more than 400 published articles and eight books in the fields of mathematical optimization, computer science, and artificial intelligence. Fred Glover is an elected member of the U. S. National Academy of Engineering and is the recipient of the von Neumann Theory Prize, the highest honor of the INFORMS society. His numerous other awards and honorary fellowships include those from IEEE, AAAS, the NATO Division of Scientific Affairs, INFORMS, DSI, USDCA, ERI, AACSB, Alpha Iota Delta and the Miller Institute for Basic Research in Science.

Daryoush Habibi received his PhD and Bachelors degrees from the University of Tasmania, Australia in 1995 and 1990 respectively. He is currently the Head and Professor of Communications Engineering at Edith Cowan University and also serves as the Director for the Centre for Communications Engineering Research at Edith Cowan University, Australia. His research interests are in the fields of wireless sensor systems, QoS in communications engineering, smart energy systems, and engineering education. He has published over a hundred journal and conference papers in these areas. He has received research grants from the Australian government and industry for his research activities and has served as a reviewer for journals and conferences. Dr. Habibi is the editor-in-chief for the Australian Journal of Electrical and Electronics Engineering and also serves as President of the Australian Council of Engineering Deans.

Andreas Janecek received a PhD degree in Computer Science in 2010, and an MSc degree in Business Informatics in 2005, both from the University of Vienna, Austria. From 2010 to 2011 he worked as a post-doctoral researcher at Peking University, in Beijing, China, and in 2012 at the Universitade Politécnica de Pernambuco in Recife, Brazil. His main research activities are currently in the research areas of 1) data mining and machine learning algorithms, with a focus on high performance and distributed computing aspects of these techniques, and 2) computational intelligence, such as stochastic optimization, nature-inspired meta-heuristics, and swarm intelligence. Over the last years he has been very active in combining these two disciplines, which has resulted in several inter-disciplinary research activities. He has published more than 25 peer-reviewed publications, including several book-chapters, and he has won the best paper awards of IC-SI 2011 and 2013 (International Conference on Swarm Intelligence).

Manuel Laguna is the Director of Global Initiatives and the MediaOne Professor of Management Science at the Leeds School of Business at the University of Colorado Boulder. He started his academic career at the University of Colorado in 1990, after receiving his masters (1987) and doctoral (1990) degrees in Operations Research and Industrial Engineering from the University of Texas at Austin. He has done extensive research in the interface between computer science, artificial intelligence, and operations research resulting in over 100 publications, including four books. He has received research funding from private industry and government agencies such as the National Science Foundation, the Office of Naval Research, and the Environmental Protection Agency. He is co-founder of OptTek Systems, a

Boulder-based software and consulting company that provides optimization solutions. He is the editor-in- chief of the *Journal of Heuristics* and has been Division Chair, Senior Associate Dean, and Interim Dean at the Leeds School of Business.

Wen Fung Leong received her BS, MS and PhD degrees in electrical engineering in 2000, 2002, and 2008 respectively from Oklahoma State University, Stillwater. In 2009, she worked as a postdoctoral research associate for about 3.5 years at Boston College and was one of the participants in the 1000 Genomes Project Consortium. Currently, she is a postdoctoral research scientist in the Department of Electrical and Computer Engineering at Kansas State University. Her current areas of interest include computational intelligence, bioinformatics and crop modeling. She is a Member of the IEEE Computational Intelligence Society, American Society of Human Genetics, and American Society of Agronomy.

Hongwei Mo was born in 1973. He is a professor at Automation College of Harbin Engineering University. He received his PhD degree from the same university in 2005. He was a visiting Scholar of UCDavis,CA, USA from 2003-2004. His main research interests include natural computing, artificial immune system, data mining, intelligent system, and artificial intelligence. He had published 60 papers on artificial immune systems and nature inspired computing in international journals and conferences. He was the guest editor of a Special issue on Nature inspired computing and applications in the *Journal of Information Technology Research*. He was the author of 3 books in Chinese and he is the editor of the*Handbook of Artificial Immune Systems and Nature inspired computing:Applying Complex Adaptive Technologies*. He is a member of IEEE Computing Intelligence Society, IEEE Robotics and Automaton Society. He was also a program committee member at over 15 international conferences. He serves as the associate editor of the *International Journal of Computing Intelligence and Pattern Recognition*, a member of the editorial board for the *Journal of Information Technology Research* and International *Journal of immune computation, Journal of Man, Machine and Technolog*y and *Progress in Intelligent Computing and Applications*.

Quande Qin received a PhD degree in Management Science and Engineering from the School of Business Administration, South China University of Technology, Guangzhou, China. Currently, he is a lecturer in the College of Management, Shenzhen University, Shenzhen, China. His current research interests include swarm intelligence, evolutionary optimization and their applications in management and economics.

R. Rathipriya is working as an Assistant Professor in Periyar University, Salem, India. She received her Bachelors of Science and Masters of Science degrees in Computer Science from the Periyar University. Currently, she is pursuing her PhD in Bharathiyar University, India. Her research interests are in several areas of data mining, web mining, Optimization techniques (in particular, optimization of biclusters in web mining area), and Bio-Informatics.

Kah Phooi Seng received her PhD and Bachelors degrees from the University of Tasmania, Australia in 2001 and 1997 respectively. She was previously a professor of computer science and networked systems at Sunway University, Malaysia and is currently an adjunct professor at the Centre for Communications Engineering Research, Edith Cowan University, Australia. Her research interests are in the fields of intelligent systems, wireless sensor systems, and signal processing. She has published over a hundred journal and conference papers in these areas. Dr. Seng has received research grants from the Malaysian government and industry for her research activities and has served as a reviewer for journals and conferences.

Oleg V. Shylo is an Assistant Professor in the Department of Industrial and Systems Engineering at the University of Tennessee. He received a PhD in Industrial Engineering from the University of Florida in 2009. His research interests include discrete optimization, parallel computing and optimization in health care.

Volodymyr P. Shylo is a Leading Researcher at the Glushkov's Institute of Cybernetics and a professor. In 2003, he received a Doctor of Physical and Mathematical Sciences from the National Academy of Science of Ukraine. His research interests include probabilistic and local search methods for discrete optimization, algorithms, and software design for complex optimization problems.

Ying Tan is a professor at the Key Laboratory of Machine Perception (MOE) at Peking University, and at the Department of Machine Intelligence in the School of Electronics Engineering and Computer Science at Peking University, China. He is the director of the Computational Intelligence Laboratory of Peking University (CIL@PKU). He received his BS in 1985, tMS in 1988, and PhD in signal and information processing from Southeast University in 1997, respectively. Since then, he became a postdoctoral fellow then an associate professor at University of Science and Technology of China. He worked with the Chinese University of Hong Kong in 1999 and in 2004-2005. He served as Editor-in-Chief of the *International Journal of Computational Intelligence and Pattern Recognition*, Associate Editor of *IEEE Transactions on Cybernetics, International Journal of Artificial Intelligence, International Journal of Swarm Intelligence Research* (IJSIR), *International Journal of Intelligent Information Processing*, etc. He is a member of the Emergent Technologies Technical Committee (ETTC) and the Computational Intelligence Society of IEEE. He is or was the general chair of the International Conference on Swarm Intelligence (ICSI 2010-14) and one of the joint general chairs of BRICS CCI'2013, Program committee co-chair of IEEE WCCI 2014, and many other international conferences. He was honored with the Second-class Prize of National Natural Science Award of China in 2009. His primary research interests include computational intelligence, artificial immune system, swarm intelligence, intelligent information processing, and machine learning algorithms and their applications in computer security. He has published more than 200 papers in refereed journals and conferences in these areas, published several books and chapters in book, and received 3 patents.

K. Thangavel is presently the Prof. and Head of the Department of Computer Science at Periyar University, Salem. He completed his PhD at Gandhigram Rural University. His areas of interest are data mining, image processing, mobile computing and rough set theory and Optimization Techniques. He is reviewer of reputable journals. He received the Young Scientist Award 2009 from Tamilnadu State Council for Science and Technology.

T.O. Ting obtained a First-class honours degree in Electronic and Telecommunication Engineering from UNIMAS, Sarawak, Malaysia, MEng from Multimedia University, Malacca, Malaysia and a PhD in Electrical Engineering from The Hong Kong Polytechnic University (on a three years International Postgraduate Scholarship Award). He won the UNIMAS top award and Royal Educational Award during the congregation ceremony. One of his research articles won the IEEE SMC Best Student Paper Award at ICMLC 2006. He is currently a Lecturer with the Dept of Electrical and Electronic Engineering, Xian Jiaotong-Liverpool University. His main research is on the application of Computational Intelligence techniques in Engineering Optimization.

Yali Wu received a BS degree and an MS degree in automation from Taiyuan University of Science and Technology, Taiyuan, China, in 1997 and 2000 respectively. She earned a PhD degree in control science and engineering from the System Engineering Institute of Xi'an Jiaotong University, Xi'an, Shaanxi, China, in 2003. She is currently an Associate Professor in the School of Automation and Electronic Information at Xi'an University of Technology, Xi'an, Shaanxi, China. Her research interests include Swarm Intelligence Optimization and its application, Modeling, and Optimization of Complex Systems.

Lifang Xu was born on 12/28, 1973. She is a lecturer at the Automation College of Harbin Engineering University. She earned a Masters Degree and PhD degree in 2005 and 2008 at the same university, repectively. Her research interests include intelligence computing andintelligent control.

Xin-She Yang received his DPhil in Applied Mathematics from Oxford University. He worked at Cambridge University and then at the National Physical Laboratory as a Senior Research Scientist. He is now a Reader at Middlesex University, UK and an Adjunct Professor at Reykjavik University, Iceland. He is the inventor of a few metaheuristic algorithms including the bat algorithm, eagle strategy, firefly algorithm, cuckoo search, and virtual bee algorithm. He is the Editor-in-Chief of the *Int. J. Mathematical Modelling and Numerical Optimisation*, the IEEE CIS Task Force Chair on Business Intelligence, and the Director of the International Consortium for Optimization and Modelling in Science and Industry (iCOMSI).

Gary G. Yen received his PhD degree in electrical and computer engineering from the University of Notre Dame in 1992. He is currently a Professor in the School of Electrical and Computer Engineering at Oklahoma State University. His research interests include intelligent control, computational intelligence, and evolutionary multi-objective optimization. Gary was an associate editor of the *IEEE Transactions on Neural Networks and IEEE Control Systems Magazine* from 1994-1999, and of the *IEEE Transactions on Control Systems Technology* and *IEEE Transactions on Systems, Man* during 2000-2010. He is currently serving as an associate editor for the *IEEE Transactions on Evolutionary Computation* and *International Journal of Swarm Intelligence Research*. Gary served as Vice President for the Technical Activities of the IEEE Computational Intelligence Society in 2004-2005 and is the founding editor-in-chief of the *IEEE Computational Intelligence Magazine*, 2006-2009. He was the President of the IEEE Computational Intelligence Society in 2010-2011 and is elected as a Distinguished Lecturer for the term 2012-2014. He received Regents Distinguished Research Award from OSU in 2009, 2011 Andrew P Sage Best Transactions Paper award from IEEE Systems, Man and Cybernetics Society, and 2013 Meritorious Service award from IEEE Computational Intelligence Society. He is a Fellow of IEEE and IET.

Peng-Yeng Yin is a Professor inthe Department of Information Management at National Chi Nan University. From 1993 to 1994, he was a visiting scholar in the Department of Electrical Engineering at the University of Maryland, College Park. In 2000, he was a visiting Professor in the Department of Electrical Engineering at the University of California, Riverside. From 2006 to 2007, he was a visiting Professor at Leeds School of Business at the University of Colorado. Dr. Yin is a member of the Phi Tau Phi Scholastic Honor Society and listed in *Who's Who in the World*, *Who's Who in Science and Engineering*, and *Who's Who in Asia*. He is the Editor-in-Chief of the *International Journal of Applied Metaheuristic Computing*. He has also edited four books in the area of pattern recognition and metaheuristic computing. His current research interests include artificial intelligence, evolutionary computation, metaheuristics, pattern recognition, machine learning, and operations research.

Jia-Xian Zhu received his BS degree in Information Management at National Formosa University, Yunlin, Taiwan in 2006 and his MBA. degree in Information Management at National Chi Nan University, Nantou, Taiwan in 2008. He has published an article in the *European Journal of Operational Research*. His research interests include metaheuristics, machine learning, software engineering, and operations research.

Adamu Murtala Zungeru received his BEng Degree in Electrical and Computer Engineering from the Federal University of Technology (FUT) Minna, Nigeria, in 2004, MSc Degree in Electronic and Telecommunication Engineering from the Ahmadu Bello University (ABU) Zaria, Nigeria, in 2009, and PhD Degree from the University of Nottingham in February 2013. He is presently serving as a Senior Lecturer at the Federal University Oye-Ekiti, Nigeria. He is a registered Engineer with COREN and a Member of IEEE and ACM. He has served as Session Chair at the International Conference on Swarm Intelligence (ICSI), Shenzhen China, 2012. He has served as a technical Program Committee Member at IEEE-WCNC 2013, Shangai China, IEEE-WCNC 2014, Istanbul, Turey, ICCVE 2013, Las Vegas, USA, The 2nd Science One International Conference on Information Technology, Dubai, UAE, 2014, and CEIT'13, Sousse, Tunisia, 2013. He is an editorial board member of the *International Journal of Networking, IJICS, IJSET*, and *IJCSIT*. He has also served as an International reviewer to *JNCA ELSEVIER, Wireless Networks Springer, IET Networks, Simulation SAGE, International Journal of communication systems Wiley, Sensors MDPI*, and numerous others. His research interests are in the fields of automation, swarm intelligence, network routing, wireless sensor networks, energy harvesting, and energy management.

Index